MW01055489

THE SOUL OF TONE

CELEBRATING 60 YEARS OF FENDER AMPS

BY TOM WHEELER

ISBN-13: 978-0-634-05613-0
ISBN-10: 0-634-05613-1

Published by:
Hal Leonard Corporation
7777 W. Bluemound Road
P.O. Box 13819
Milwaukee, WI 53213

Library of Congress Cataloging-in-Publication Data

Wheeler, Tom (Thomas Hutchin)
The soul of tone : celebrating sixty years of Fender amps / by Tom Wheeler. – 1st ed.
p. cm.
Includes index.
ISBN 978-0-634-05613-0
1. Fender Musical Instruments–History. 2.Guitar amps–History. I.Title.
ML1015.G9W53 2007
787.87'1973–dc22
2007015680
Printed in China through Colorcraft Ltd, Hong Kong

First Edition

Visit Hal Leonard Online at **www.halleonard.com**

THE SOUL OF TONE

TABLE OF CONTENTS

Dedication **6**
Acknowledgements **8**

12 **Foreword** by Keith Richards
"Meet the wife!"

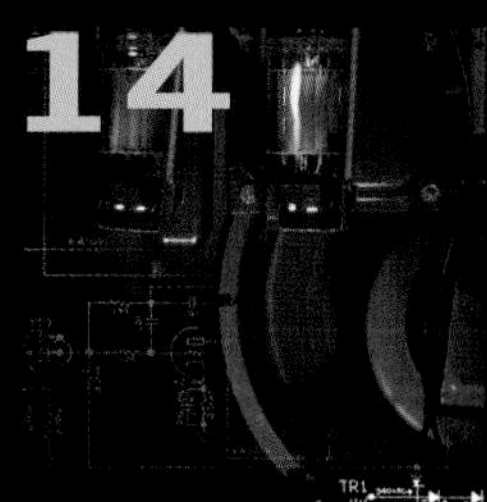
14 **Introduction**
Feel the Heat

22 **Chapter 1** The Other Legacy of Leo Fender
A Kind of Divine Perfection

36 **Chapter 2** Leo Fender: 20th Century Man

46 **Chapter 3** Electronic Journey
An Overview of Tube Amplification

64 **Chapter 4** Speakers, Baffles, and Cabs
The Basics

78 **Chapter 5** Tube Basics
Nomenclature
Functions
Types

88 **Chapter 6** Tube Performance
Bias, Single-Ended vs. Push/Pull, Class A vs. Class AB

98 **Chapter 7** Electrical Bloodlines
Classic Fender Amps: A Circuitous Approach

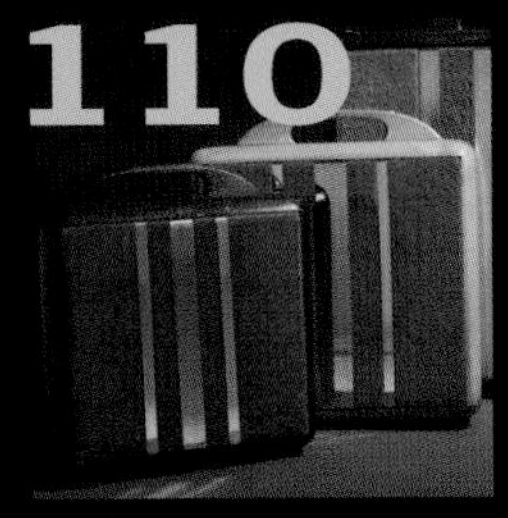
110 **Chapter 8**
In the Beginning
1940s: K&Fs, Woodies, and Early Tweeds

126 **Chapter 9**
The TV Fronts of 1948 to 1953
Pages From a Place Called Fullerton

144 **Chapter 10**
The Wide Panel Tweeds
1953 to 1955

156 **Chapter 11**
Fullerton High
The Class of '55

196 **Chapter 12**
From Tweed to Tolex
Leo Fender and the New Amps, Don Randall and the New Message

228 **Chapter 13**
Family Ties and Transitions
The Browns and Blondes Evolve

356 **Chapter 20** The Awakening
Rediscovering Good Tone

362 **Chapter 21** Into the 1990s
Push Buttons, Pro Tubes and New Tweeds

374 **Chapter 22** Forward into the Past
The Reissues

390 **Chapter 23** A Custom Shop of the Mind
Fender's Elite Hand-wired Amps

400 **Chapter 24** Watershed '95: The Arrival of Ritchie Fliegler

418 **Chapter 25** Tone Machines of the New Millennium

442 **Chapter 26** Going Digital, the Fender Way
Cyber Amps and G-DECs

456 **Chapter 27** FBA: Fender Bass Amplification
A Whole New Low-Down

468 **Chapter 28** The Tone Zone
Facts, Opinions, and Mythconceptions

478 **Chapter 29** The Great American Amp
If you had to pick just one, what is the Great American Amplifier, the tone machine *in excelsis*, the amp of amps?

496 **CD Listening Guides**
 = Vintage
 = Modern

Amp Collecting **488**

About the Author **495**

Photo Credits **500**

Index **502**

This book is packaged with two audio CDs containing over 100 tracks featuring both rare vintage and modern amps.

For Leo Fender, who started the company...

and Bill Schultz, who saved it.

ACKNOWLEDGEMENTS

I've always been fascinated by amplifiers, particularly Fenders, and how they allow our tiny-voiced, unamplified electric guitars to sing and roar. But I'm not really an amp guy, in the "Let me re-bias your Vibro-King for you" kind of way. I don't even own a soldering gun. In writing this book, I needed plenty of help, and I called on many people.

Ritchie Fliegler, Shane Nicholas, and their colleagues at Fender Musical Instruments are worthy heirs to the legacy of Leo Fender. Ritchie and Shane encouraged me to write this book, and I will be forever grateful to them for that, and for answering countless amp-related questions over a two-year period.

Authors gossip about how we are mistreated by publishers, but my fellow writers come away from these conversations green with envy when they hear about editor Brad Smith and art director Richard Slater at Hal Leonard. Thank you Brad and Richard for all of your wise counsel and hard work, for allowing this book to grow into something bigger and deeper than the one we initially envisioned, for making it look beautiful, and for your patience.

I have been an avid fan of the Rolling Stones and Keith Richards in particular ever since the boisterous opening riff to "Not Fade Away" burst out of the radio in my parents' Catalina in the spring of '64. Keith Richards is not only one of the greatest of all rockers but also a master of tone and an astute connoisseur of Fender tweed. I am honored to have him contribute the Foreword. Thanks and praises to Keith for his insights and good humor, and to his associates Jane Rose and Nicole Hegeman for their assistance.

Alan Hardtke and Perry Tate unlocked their treasure troves of collectible amps, providing access not only to every classic Fender but also to rare birds, prototypes, and unusual experimental models that somehow escaped Mr. Fender's lab four or five decades ago. Alan and Perry lugged around a lot of tweed and Tolex, thoughtfully considered which examples to photograph, and provided keen observations on the electronic and cosmetic evolution of these amps.

Greg Gagliano and Greg Huntington have studied Fender amps for many years and documented thousands of details. Having badgered them repeatedly and picked their brains, I am indebted to them for their willingness to share the information they have so painstakingly acquired. Both experts are quoted extensively here.

Special thanks to Greg Koch, who contributed enlightening demonstrations, jaw-dropping guitar pyrotechnics, and zany humor to the CD that accompanies this book. He approached the project with a combination of, in his words, "aplomb and savagery." Thanks also to Dave Rogers at Dave's Guitar Shop in La Crosse, Wisconsin, who provided the vintage Fender amps that you will hear

In Leo Fender's mind, the guitar and amplifier were inseparable components of the "instrument," so in the early days he sold them in matched sets. These are the first Fenders, the mid-'40s "woodies," front to back: Princeton guitar and amp set, Deluxe set, and a top of the line Pro amp with an Organ Button steel guitar.

teased, tickled, throttled, torched, and otherwise tested by the inimitable Mr. Koch.

My old pal Alan Rogan recounted many a tale about his work with devoted aficionados of Fender amps, including Pete Townshend, Eric Clapton, George Harrison, Keith Richards, and Joe Walsh. He also shared insights into his own impressive collection.

Aside from Ritchie Fliegler and Shane Nicholas, several current Fender amp designers, technicians, and marketing executives helped out with technical responses to my endless barrages of emails and with colorful, behind-the-scenes recollections. They are Keith Chapman, Dale Curtis, Bob Desiderio, Steve Grom, Bill Hughes, Mike Lewis, Richard McDonald, Jay Piccirillo, Dan Smith, and especially Matt Wilkens, who patiently explained various technical concepts until I finally grasped them. (Several of these key Fender employees are accomplished guitar players and are featured on one of the enclosed CDs, demoing amplifiers they helped conceive. You'll enjoy hearing their stories — and their hot licks.) Thanks also to Rich Siegle, Jason Farrell, and John Samora for all their help in researching Fender's archives and providing photographs.

I called on former Fender employees such as Bill Carson (anybody who uses "guinea pig" as a verb — as in, "Leo'd give me a prototype and I'd take it out to the club and guinea-pig it" — is OK in my book), Jody Carver, George Fullerton, PJ Geerlings, Lee Jackson, Bob Rissi, Paul Rivera, Bill Sterle, and especially Don Randall, a music industry giant in his own right.

In writing *The Soul of Tone* I was often reminded of acquaintances who have passed away, and I remain indebted to Leo Fender, Freddie Tavares, Forrest White, Bill Schultz, and Bob Perine. I remember them with fondness and admiration, and I hope this book does justice to their legacies.

The Pro Junior 60th Anniversary Woody, produced only in 2006, commemorates six decades of Fender's excellence in amplification. It features 1946 styling and a semi-transparent Honey Blonde finish over a solid ash cabinet.

In researching technical matters I exchanged scores if not hundreds of emails with amplifier designers, technicians, and company presidents outside the Fender organization. They were generous with their time and happy to provide their own insights into Fender's legacy of innovation and gold-standard tone. Mark Baier at Victoria Amp Co. and Steve Carr at Carr Amps provided comprehensive explanations of technical matters. Hartley Peavey, who was inspired to get into the electronics business by Leo Fender, sent more than a dozen letters and packages — 50-year-old magazine articles, circuit diagrams, books, old patents, and more. Blackie Pagano at Tubesville Thermionics offered helpful technical information and a provocative analysis of Mr. Fender's place in the history of 20th Century design and culture.

Thanks also to Eric Barbour at *Vacuum Tube Valley*, amp tech and columnist Terry Buddingh, Alexander Dumble, Andy Marshall at THD Electronics, Don Morris at ElectroPlex, Mike Soldano, and especially Randall Smith at Mesa/Boogie and Bruce Zinky at Zinky Electronics.

A big "thank you kindly" to my fellow authors for sharing information, suggestions, and in some cases photographs. They are Richard Smith, author of *Fender: The Sound Heard 'Round The World* (still one of the best books ever written about guitars) and guest curator of the Fender exhibit at the Fullerton Museum Center; John Sprung, coauthor of the authoritative *Fender Amps, The First Fifty Years* (referred to in these pages as Teagle & Sprung); Andy Babiuk, author of the terrific *Beatles Gear*; and Aspen Pittman, whose *The Tube Amp Book* could be sawn in half and still qualify as *the* tech reference source for guitar amps. All of these books remain invaluable storehouses of information, and all are cited in these pages. Mike Doyle, author of two books on Marshall, helped out as well. Also

Hear Greg Koch's Introduction to the Vintage Amps CD, Track 1.

recommended: *The Guitar Amp Handbook* and *Guitar Rigs: Classic Guitar & Amp Combinations*, both by Dave Hunter.

Thanks to my researchers, proofreaders, and transcribers: Bliss Bowen, Ally Burguieres, Celine Carillo, Molly Cooney-Mesker, Jordan Crucchiola, Linda Gampert, Katie Hale, Krystal Hilliker, Reese Lee, Margaret McGladrey, Tracy Miller, Robin Munro, Kathryn O'Shea-Evans, Laura Rausch, Joe Wheeler, Matt Wheeler, Paul Wurster, and especially Kera Abraham, Becky Taylor, Ellie Bayrd, and Sarah Gianelli. Thanks also to proofreader Mark Baker at Hal Leonard for his eagle eye and good suggestions.

I spent 14 wonderful years at *Guitar Player* magazine, and its articles are often quoted here. Thanks to all my pals there, especially Andy Ellis, Art Thompson, and Barry Cleveland.

Many thanks to Baron Wolman, Dick Waterman, Robert Knight, Lisa Seifert, Ebet Roberts, Neil Zlozower, Ken Settle, and the other photographers whose images enliven these pages, and also to our friends at the Michael Ochs Archives. Your compelling photos of artists capture the fun and exhilaration of live performance. The author and John Peden are grateful to Jeff Hirsch and the staff at New York's Foto Care Ltd. and to Clifford Hausner of the MAC Group for supplying a Leaf digital camera back that made a significant contribution to the studio photography done in New York.

Thanks also to Dave Belzer and Drew Berlin (Guitar Center's Burst Brothers), Rose Bishop, Mike Borer, Pattie Boyd, Cheryl Brewster, Matt Carr, Walter Carter, Larry Cragg at Vintage Instrument Rental, Dick Dale, Jol Dantzig at Hamer, Rick Davis, Deke Dickerson, Seymour Duncan, JD Dworkow, Nokie Edwards, Mike Eldred at the Fender Custom Shop, Reggie Felker, Peter Frampton, Harvey Gerst, Billy Gibbons, Bill Grey, Wallace Grover, George Gruhn at Gruhn Guitars, Jim Henke at the Rock and Roll Hall of Fame, Gregg Hopkins at Vintage-Amp Restoration, Mike Jones at the Conservatory of Recording Arts and Sciences, Nicole Julius, Henry Kaiser, Mary Kaye, Jennifer King, John Kinnemeyer at JK Lutherie, Rich Koerner at Time Electronics, Albert Lee, Seth Lichtenstein, Gernold Linke, Matt Marshall, Steve Melkisethian at Angela Instruments, Jackie Muth, Dan Neal, Mike Nemeth, Blaze Newman, Jas Obrecht, Les Paul, Taylor Peden, James Roy, Takashi Sato, Brian Shimkovitz, Paul Reed Smith, Steve Soest at Soest Guitar Repair, "Cactus Jim" Soldi, Karen Svoboda, Mark Tate, Larry Thomas at the Guitar Center Music Education Foundation, Travis Tingley and Jim Tracy at Triad Magnetics, Rick Turner at Renaissance Guitars, Doug West at Mesa/Boogie, and David Wilson at *The ToneQuest Report*.

Thanks to Anne, for her love and good cheer, and for inspiring the title that captures what I set out to accomplish in this book.

John Peden

When it comes to photographing musical instruments, John Peden is the best we have. His love of vintage amps and guitars, his taste, and his impressive technical skills have combined to provide us with scores of classic images over many years. His work has graced the pages of my own *The Guitar Book* (Japanese edition, 2000), *American Guitars*, and *The Stratocaster Chronicles*, Richard Smith's *Fender: The Sound Heard 'Round The World*, and several other books. His photos have also been spotlighted in *Guitar Player*'s Encore column and *Guitar World*'s Collector's Choice gatefolds.

John got wind of this project early on, climbed aboard with enthusiasm, and made thoughtful suggestions from the outset. *The Soul of Tone* is the biggest single repository of his work, and for that I am honored and grateful. It's a labor of love for both of us.

FOREWORD

A Message from Across the Way

I didn't start with Fender amps. I learned the hard way, which is why I know what I'm talking about.

In the early days, right about the time when we could afford pieces like nice electric guitars and amplifiers, there was a whole burst of new stuff coming out in England. You had Vox and Marshall and this incredible array, and in a way that made it a bit foggier for me, all the choices. I had a lot of experimentation, eventually having these beautiful guitars and never having the right amp to go with them, or very rarely. I knew they could sound better. Then one day I picked up my Fender guitar and went through a beautiful Fender Twin and … *Oh yeah! There it is! Meet the wife!*

When I heard that *sound*, suddenly I got this flash from Leo. It was like his message from across the way: It's all about the matched set, how the guitar and amp work together.

I never got a chance to meet Leo Fender, and I would have liked to, although I'm sure he would have been bored to death just to talk to one more guitar player. But if I could have spoken to him, I would have had this conversation: Guitar makers usually don't think to make amplifiers, and he was making amplifiers early on, hence his knowledge of impedance and all that, and I would have liked to have asked him how he got onto the idea of doing the integrated thing. Leo Fender took the whole guitar/amp thing the whole way. And it was such a perfect pair, like a nice pair of horses, I suppose, thoroughbreds, matched up with the right carriage in the olden days.

I have certain guitars that I seem to mate up to certain amps, but at the same time it's a lot of experimenting, especially in the studio. One day it's, *let's try the Champ — yeah, that'll do it.* Another time, *let's try the Twin with a couple of tubes missing.*

So I just take a bunch of amps and line them all up, and I plug into one, and I might say, no, not today. Sometimes you really want a big sound, but then it's a little Champ that gives you that big sound that day. Sometimes the big amps are just too big. You never know for sure until you try it that day, with that guitar. You know what you're looking for, but sometimes you wind up with a sound that's even better. For me, it's really a matter of, *line 'em up on parade!* Just give me a jack plug and a couple of minutes with each amp.

I don't work a lot with floor pedals — I need my feet to stand on! With Fender amps, I just don't need all that. We just got out of the studio, and I was using Fender amps pretty much all the time, as usual. It's been my way for a long time now. My Fender Twin gets a lot of work, let's put it that way.

For the upcoming tours the main arsenal will be Fenders. That goes without saying. The Twins are my favorites, not only in the studio but in the stadiums as well. I don't use any stacks or any of that. We just mike the Twins and shove it through. They're also very nice to stand in front of on the stage. They're not that loud, and they've got the sound.

I'm not particularly mechanically minded — guess what! — but you kind of pick it up by osmosis almost. I do get into tubes and transformers and all that, but then again when it comes to the "secret" of great tone, sometimes I think there's a bit of over-analyzing. I don't know whether you find a great tone, or if it finds you. It's a nebulous area. There's a certain point where one day, *that's it*. Suddenly the sound is there and you realize that you are there just to transmit it. Somehow, the tone lets you know —
Welcome home!

Suddenly the sound is there and you realize that you are there just to transmit it.

They're works of art, these amps and these guitars, but they're tools as well. They're dependable. You know you can always go back to your Fender amp. Without my Fender amps, I'd be lost, actually.

So thanks and praises to Leo for coming up with a great idea — so good that all people can do now is to try and copy it. That's how good it is. I've experimented a lot, tried all sorts of amps, but I don't change things 'round anymore. I found what I'm looking for.

Keith Richards

Somehow, the tone lets you know — Welcome home!

"TWIN REVERB-AMP AB763" SCHEMATIC NOTICE

THIS PRODUCT MANUFACTURED UNDER ONE OR MORE OF THE FOLLOWING U.S. PATENTS- #2817708, #2973681, 192859 & PATENTS PENDING.

C-FD

1 - VOLTAGES READ TO GROUND WITH ELECTRONIC V
VALUES SHOWN + OR - 20%
2 - ALL RESISTORS ½ WATT 10% TOLERANCE IF
3 - ALL CAPACITORS AT LEAST 400 VOLT RATING I

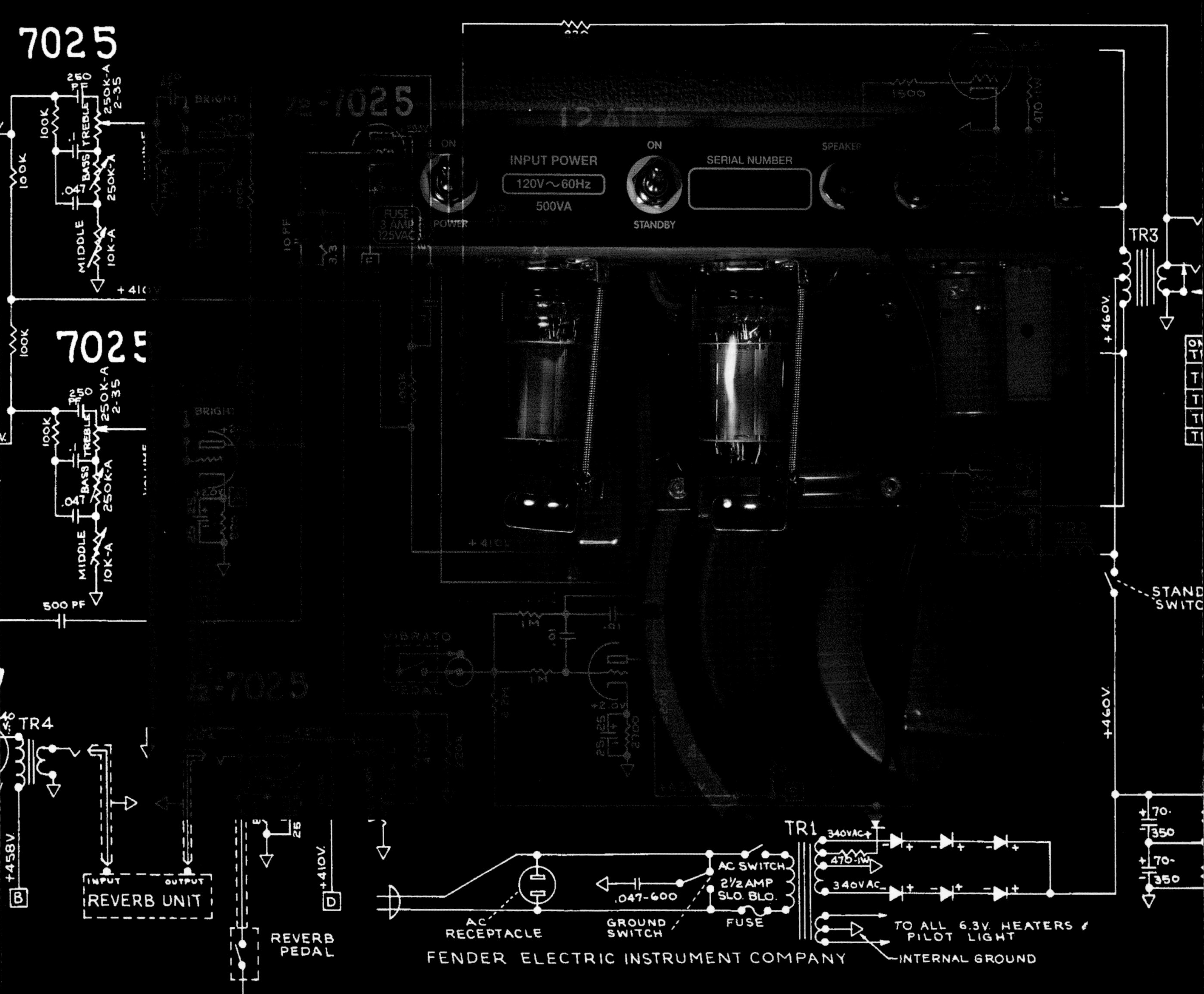

Feel the Heat

Is it any wonder that ancient cultures worshipped lightning? To this day we stand in awe before nature's big jolt, its power still fearsome, its mysteries still impenetrable. Throughout history, a few intrepid souls pondered those blinding, white hot veins flashing across the sky and dreamed of somehow harnessing electricity to the service of humankind. Some succeeded, transforming every aspect of our lives, including the way we play and hear music. A few recognized that, sure, musicians love our acoustic instruments, but sometimes we long for an experience more powerful, more thrilling, more … well, electrifying. One such dreamer was Leo Fender, who first put his lightning bolt logo on a guitar amplifier more than a half-century ago.

Leo Fender's first amps were little K&Fs built with his early partner, Doc Kauffman. Like the first Fenders, they bore a lightning bolt logo.

I discovered Jack Darr's *Electric Guitar Amplifier Handbook* before I discovered *Catcher In The Rye*. Back in my high school library it was the only title to turn up in the long oaken drawer of index cards under "electric guitar." The little manual with the drab cover was addressed to electronics experts who were already repairing PA systems and radios, and not to inquisitive teenage amateurs such as myself. Much of the text was over my head, and the schematic diagrams looked like modern-art hieroglyphics. Still, I was excited to unearth even a few clues as to how my elegant brown and gold Magnatone Mercury helped make my Jazzmaster twang so rich and righteous when I whammied out the lowdown guitar line to "Peter Gunn."

But well into the guitar boom of the '60s and for a decade or two thereafter, most of us didn't think too much about how our amplifiers worked their magic. Our admiration of these "accessories" was superficial, skin deep. We liked their Hi-Fi styling, their sporty suits of straw-colored tweed or blue-diamond Tolex or even turquoise Naugahyde tuck and roll. We liked how their grille cloths sparkled with colored threads and were bordered with gold or white piping. We liked how their leather suitcase handles felt to the grip, and how their jeweled pilot lights shined like little red beacons on a dark bandstand. Most of all we liked their electricity, their jolt, their juice.

Cool enough. But while we dug the looks and sounds of our Ampeg Reverbrockets and Supro Supers, we had no idea how they worked. Not that we weren't curious, it's just that while the top-panel knobs invited sonic experimentation, the rear panels were boarded up and emblazoned with ominous symbols; they warned of catastrophic damage and lethal voltages, giving our amplifiers' inner workings a Top Secret/Off Limits vibe.

Peering through the slots in the back we could glimpse a miniature metropolis in there, a skyline of canisters and transformers. We could see a metal chassis criss-crossed with colored wires connecting waxy little barrels and gumdrop discs, all stamped with coded stripes and arcane cryptograms. We could see utilitarian components that looked like they could have come out of a Red Army missile silo. Most intriguing of all, we could see the orange glow of warm glass tubes. We could feel the heat.

For years the Darr book and various tube manuals seemed to be the only literature on electric guitars and amps, other than the catalogs and price lists we scrounged from local music shops. Although early *Guitar Player* features occasionally addressed amplifiers, and my own *The Guitar Book* in 1974 covered a few basic concepts, it wasn't until the publication of Michael Doyle's *The Sound of Rock: A History of Marshall Valve Guitar Amplifiers* in 1982, Aspen Pittman's *The Tube Amp Book* in 1983, Don Brosnac's *The Amp Book* in 1983, Doyle's *The History of Marshall: The Illustrated Story of "The Sound of Rock"* in 1993, and Ritchie Fliegler's *Amps! The Other Half of Rock 'n' Roll* in 1993 that the amplifier finally began to get the attention it deserved. These authors were electronics experts or simply amp buffs who ignored the Keep Out signs on their Princetons and plexi's, ventured into the forbidden zone, mapped out the territory, and lived to tell the tale.

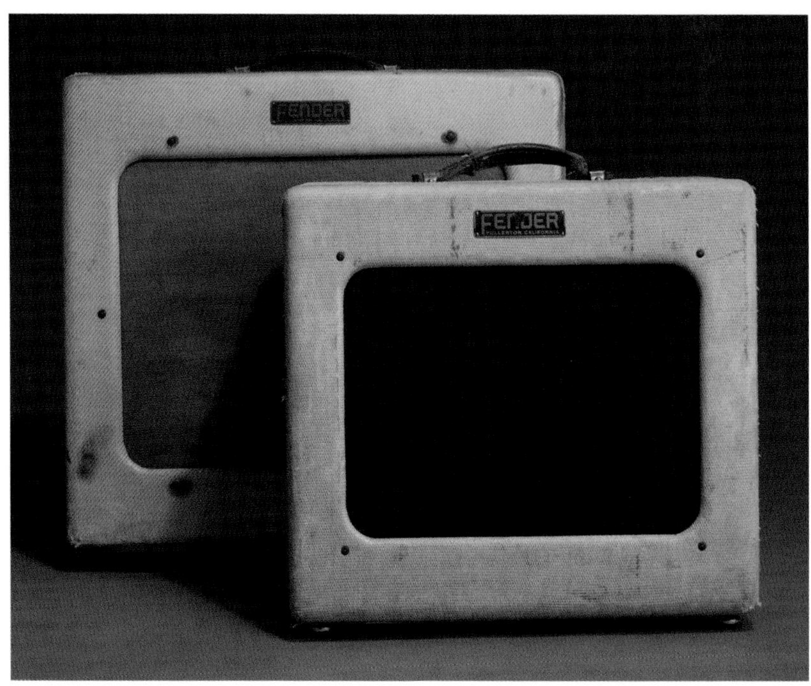

The grille's shape gave rise to the "TV front" nickname for Fenders made from 1948 to 1953. Here are a mid-line 1x12 Deluxe (in front) and top of the line 1x15 Pro.

Why on earth did it take so long for the rest of us to come to appreciate the significance of tube types, circuit designs, cabinet shapes, and speaker configurations? For one thing, great tone was for years something we could often take for granted, even if we were just getting started on guitar and didn't spend much money on gear. If your mom and dad sprang for one of the 4 watt, one-knob Fender Champs, chances are your Musicmaster would sound pure and sweet at low volumes; and if you stoked that little tweed lunchbox up to 12, just to see what happened, well, you launched yourself into a strange new realm where you might consider using different techniques or even creating another kind of music altogether. You were practically a different *person* with your Champ on 12 — Dr. Jekyll & Link Wray. (*Goodness, what's come over Tommy?*)

Another reason an appreciation of our amplifiers came late is simply that we were so deliriously intoxicated with our guitars. And who can blame us? Guitars are pretty and curvy. We embrace them, hold them close, use them to express our passions. We take them into the spotlight and present them to our audiences as extensions of ourselves: This is my guitar, this is who I am.

Amps are boxes. For years we stuck them on the stage behind us, down low where they were easy to overlook, in every sense. In a world of prom-queen guitars, could a wallflower speaker box with a luggage handle and a few radio knobs really proclaim to the world, "This is who I am"?

Oh, yeah. Belatedly, we came to recognize the obvious: Any signature electric guitar tone isn't even electric at all without an amplifier, and if we wanted to get serious about our sounds, we had better get serious about our amps — not just their cosmetics and external features, but their hard-wired nervous systems and mysterious orange-glowing hearts as well.

In our new quest for the holy harmonic grail, some of us relied on old methods — just plug in and listen — but now with more discriminating ears (*"I hear a little dip around 1k ..."*). Others journeyed deep into jungles of wires, schematics, and amp lore and emerged with fanatical preferences for Mullard 12AX7s or blue-frame alnico Jensen P12Ps.

It all starts with the controlled flow of subatomic particles inside glass tubes. These are Groove Tubes in a modern Fender amp, but they function like the tubes in classic Fenders from decades past.

This gradually increasing sophistication accelerated the evolution of a contemporary amplifier scene that aside from a time lag of several years paralleled the trends of the guitar market's last couple of decades: a rejection of "improved," corporate-manufactured products that didn't sound as good as their predecessors, the rise of new companies and boutique makers offering alternatives to familiar brands, the adoption of a new lingo with all the finger-poppin' swagger of guitarspeak (halfstack, piggyback, greenback, chickenhead), the emergence of a purist esthetic in which classic circuits, minimalist styling and superior components were favored over extraneous bells and whistles, the publication of specialized articles and books, stratospheric prices for certain anointed models, and a fixation on vintage minutiae. (*Which Fender combos used leftover piggyback Tilt-Back legs? When did Leo Fender remove the negative feedback loop from the narrow panel Pro — and when did he put it back?*)

As if making up for lost time, some of us went overboard. Having already fetishized the living daylights out of our guitars, we now laser-beamed our obsession upon the next logical targets. Suddenly we were in love with our amplifiers. It was as if the new object of our lust had been right there all along, underappreciated, like the Hollywood cliché of the plain Jane stenographer who slips off her glasses, lets down her hair, and transforms from schoolmarm to bombshell. A 24-year-old blonde Twin? *Va-va voom!*

In Leo Fender's day, the sounds of amps were described in plain English: not so good, pretty good, *damn* good. But now, guitar enthusiasts rhapsodizing about amplifier tones might as well be describing the rosy nudes of Rubens. Notes are not only colorful and sensuous, they are plump, they are round, they have girth. On the pages of guitar magazines, notes bloom and blossom like flowers, highs sparkle and shimmer and chime, lows rumble like thunder. Now we describe a note's progression across the arc of its lifespan the way a wine critic might guide us through a sip of Chateauneuf-du-Pape from bouquet to aftertaste. With every passing year we root out more facts and coin new terms. Our amps don't just have tubes and speakers and handles. They have black plates and blue bells and milk chocolate dogbones.

SPECIAL AMPLIFIER FEATURES

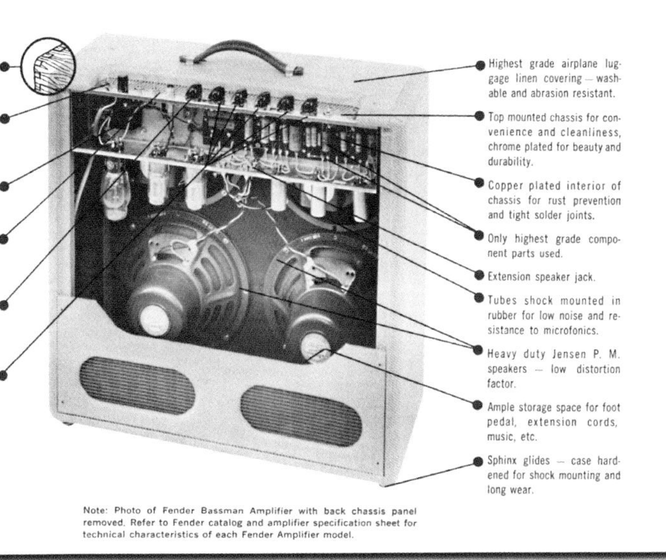

Mid-'50s Fender catalogs were jam-packed with specs.

You want to be heard when you're saying to your audience, "Thank yuh, well thank yuh veramuch." Early Fender amps were all-purpose workhorses used for guitar, bass, harmonica, vocals, accordion, you name it. Here the King of Rock and Roll speaks through a narrow panel Bandmaster to the hometown crowd at the County Fair in Tupelo, Mississippi, 1955. An armed policeman stands behind Elvis, perhaps to prevent some riotous outbreak.

We don't just listen to our amps, we psychoanalyze them. Some are like juvenile delinquents — aggressive, punchy, unruly. They have attitude. Some sound like dangerous pets. They growl and bite. Some amps sound sexy (they have tight bottoms, voluptuous middles), even vaguely kinky (they have spank). Some seem to be undergoing couples therapy — they are sensitive, responsive, *forgiving*, aggravating in some ways, yet so fulfilling in others!

In the face of all this, several large companies reappraised the worthiness of decades-old designs, embraced their storied pasts, reissued classics from bygone eras, and reinvigorated their commitment to quality control and innovation. Today we find ourselves in a new golden age of guitar amplification, with a dazzling array of products intended to satisfy every need, every taste, every budget. There is a whole forest of companies and products whose tangled roots for the most part reach back to a single place and time: Leo Fender's workbench in the 1950s.

Sharp tone, sharp looks: a sunburst Fender guitar and a blonde piggyback Fender amp. And thanks to Don Randall's genius for naming products, "Telecaster" and "Tremolux" sound as cool now as they did back in the day.

This book celebrates the life and times of the world's most influential guitar amplifiers. Some overlap with other books is unavoidable, but I have attempted to distinguish *The Soul of Tone* in several ways. First, it seeks to put one facet of Leo Fender's career — his amplifiers — in perspective, both in terms of musical equipment and also with respect to art, design, and popular culture. Then, on an introductory level it explains how tube amplifiers work. Chapters 3 and 4 provide an overview of amplification from pickups to speakers; Chapters 5 and 6 address tube types, biasing methods, output configurations, and classes of operation, emphasizing Fender's approach in each case. These chapters introduce terms you will encounter as the sounds and inner workings of Fender amps are explored throughout the book.

Second, while *The Soul of Tone* cites many technical details, it does not attempt to be a comprehensive, spec-heavy reference catalog or to document the feature-by-feature evolution of every Fender model. Many of the chapters contain information that would help determine the production period of this or that amp, but there is no comprehensive discussion of "Dating Fender Amps" per se. Over the past 20 years or so, any number of magazine articles and books have explored that topic in exhaustive detail, examining every external spec from the weave of the grille cloth and the punctuation of the fine print on control panels to the dimensions of output jack receptacles and the little white stripe around the aperture for the Bright switch. Much of this information is readily accessible on several websites, and I saw no reason to rehash it.

Instead, the general progression of the line is illustrated with representative samples of amps from different periods, and discussed in terms of how products and features reflected industry trends, shifts in musical tastes, commercial realities, and the philosophies of individual Fender marketers and designers. This book mentions only in passing the colors of Tolex, the types of knobs, the styles of cabinets and other details typically cited to distinguish one Fender from another. It focuses instead on the evolution of circuits and components, on how Leo Fender grouped these amplifiers into families, and on how his successors attempted to carry his legacy into the future.

Third, while I care about interleaved transformers, dual triodes, and coupling capacitors as much as most players, I've always been more interested in the sonic effects of all those components, and also in the people behind the design of Fender products — an impressive, idiosyncratic cast of characters indeed. I hope this book reveals at least a hint of their personalities, and how these men were themselves a product of their times, their place, and their industry. Fender history, already documented in other books, is re-explored here with an emphasis on the amps, and to a significant degree through oral histories from participants.

Fender products are more than wood, wire, and electronic components. Historically, they revealed a new vision of how youngsters and professionals alike might use guitars and amps to do a job, to have fun, to say something to the world about who they are. Accordingly, this book illustrates how Fender products were marketed in a body of literature that both reflected and influenced the popular culture of the time.

Where other useful books and websites reveal hundreds of details about specs and cosmetics, *The Soul of Tone* seeks to provide context. Where other resources provide the "what," this one seeks to explore the "why." Why did Leo Fender switch from octal 6 volt preamp tubes to miniature 12 volt tubes? Why would he feed 50 or 60 watts of power-tube output into a transformer that he knew would saturate at 28 watts? Why did he switch from one rectifier tube to two, and then to silicon diodes? Why did he adopt, and then abandon, cathode-follower tone stacks? Looking at the big picture, how did these and other developments reflect his evolving philosophies, and what effects did they have on the sound and feel of Fender amps? What effect did Fender amps have on musical styles? When a team of employees acquired the company from CBS, how would they face the challenges of a commercial environment Leo Fender scarcely could have imagined? How would they go about rescuing the Fender name?

Introduced in 2001, the Cyber amps combine solid state and digital technologies (and tubes, in the Cyber-Twin) to provide unprecedented versatility and programmability.

I've always been struck by the fact that Mr. Fender's commitment to no-nonsense function manifested itself not only in his amplifiers' ruggedness and practicality but also in their beauty. I hope you agree that a particularly American esthetic sensibility is depicted here, in photos of tweed and Tolex-covered cabinets but also in images of seemingly mundane details — an embossed nameplate, a stitched leather handle, the diamond-like facets of a pilot light.

The Soul of Tone also reflects on how Fender amplifiers not only captured good tone but came to define it, and became the standard by which other amps have been judged throughout the modern era of electric guitars. It's about the deep, elemental, and quirky relationships players have had with their Fender amps over the past six decades, and about the music these amplifiers were intended to accommodate and ultimately helped shape and revolutionize. *The Soul of Tone* is a tribute to Leo Fender and his descendants, makers of tools for modern day lightning worshippers who plug their guitars into nature's big jolt.

— **Tom Wheeler**, 2007

Do You Believe in Magic?

Anyone seeking to go into the deepest complexities of amplifier operation would need to bring to the table a couple of years of college trigonometry or at least a few years of workbench experience just to ante up for the discussion. Still, plenty of useful information is accessible to the non-technically inclined layperson, and this book attempts to sort it out. You will learn or be reminded of a few dozen specialized terms, explored here on a basic level. I hope *The Soul of Tone* is useful to knowledgeable *Fenderistas*, but it's also a book for those players who care about tone but might not know a triode from a transformer or think a phase inverter sounds like some doomsday weapon that 007 could have blown to smithereens in Dr. No's underground fortress. Accordingly, some of the more arcane formulas and concepts relevant to an amplifier's functions are ignored altogether. The point here is not to prepare you to convert your wide panel Deluxe into a mini-Marshall (please don't). Instead, *The Soul of Tone* attempts to help players understand a little better how our Fender amps work and why they sound the way they do. At several steps along the way, it reminds us that no amount of book learning can tell you what sounds good to you.

After all, it's easy to get so lost in the details of our gear that we forget why we play music in the first place. We took up the guitar because it spoke to us, because we wanted to be like our heroes, kick out the jams, make art, not because we always dreamed of *someday* running voltage through a long-tail phase inverter.

If I may amend a saying attributed to the 18th Century English satirist and poet Alexander Pope, a little knowledge can be a dangerous thing, but it can be a good thing, too, if kept in perspective. As my logic professor used to remind us back in law school, just because two things happen doesn't mean one causes the other. I may love the sound of my brown Deluxe with 6V6s in a push/pull output stage, but that doesn't mean the magic is in the 6V6s, or in the push/pull. Maybe it's the fixed biasing, or the GZ34/5AR4 tube rectifier. Maybe it's the way the output transformer has aged over time, or the way the speaker is coupled to the baffle board, or the distance from the open back to the wall in my living room.

Then again, maybe it's the spankin' fresh nickel-plated Power Slinkys on my 1961 Telecaster, or the thickness of the guitar's slab fingerboard, or the number of turns on the pickups. Maybe it's my right-hand fingernails. Maybe it's *all* of those things, and more, in an intensely complex web of interactions — electronic, mechanical, acoustical, and psychological. (Yes, psychological. I confess my perception of my Deluxe's undeniably great sound might be enhanced by its being one of the prettiest amps ever, or by its Leo-era mojo, or by its having been my tone buddy on a zillion gigs over three decades. Part of the reason my amp sounds good is that it's *my amp*. It's what I know. It's the standard for me.)

One mistake we make in obsessing about our gear is underestimating the artistry of the players whose tones and styles we grew up revering and now try to emulate. If you'll forgive the Yogi Berra syntax, Dick Dale is Dick Dale because he's Dick Dale, not because Leo Fender put a JBL in his Showman.

Some people may think they know how their amps work because they read a couple of magazine articles. I am not one of them. One of my favorite quotes about gear (it might have been from David Lindley) goes something like this: "If your amp sounds great, don't change anything. Don't even blow the dust off the tubes, because *you never know*." That's me. I'll never know. Experts comprehend this stuff in a profound, mind-twisting way, and some of them render amplifiers that help us attain fabulous sounds; we owe them a great deal. But in my experience, the most knowledgeable people are also the first to caution against ignoring the capricious subjectivity of taste. For most of us, no matter how deeply we get into the details of our gear, the emotional impact of great tone will always involve a little magic, maybe a lot of magic. Fine by me.

— TW

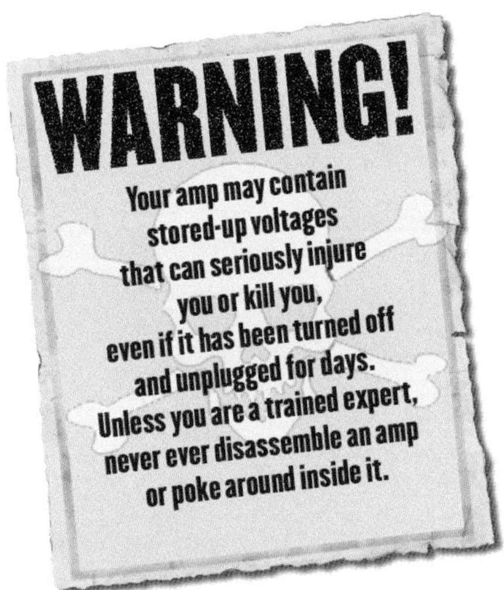

CHAPTER ONE

1

The Other Legacy of Leo Fender

A Kind of Divine Perfection

Suppose Leo Fender had never developed the Telecaster, the industry's first commercially viable solidbody and also its longest running success story. What if he had never designed the Stratocaster, the world's most exciting, popular, and influential electric guitar? Suppose he'd never invented the electric bass, which, as Quincy Jones said, "came along and gave music its real sound." Take away the Tele, take away the Strat, take away the Precision and Jazz Basses. Without these monumental achievements, what can we say then of the legacy of Leo Fender?

In his own way, the farm-born, self-taught genius from Orange County would remain the preeminent figure in the history of electric instruments because of the amplifiers that sprang from his restless mind and from his first and perhaps deepest love, electronics. More than any other person, it was Clarence Leonidas Fender who gave electric guitarists our electricity.

It just doesn't get much cooler than this: Gene Vincent and the Blue Caps giving a tweed Twin a boppin' workout in the studio.

The Amps Came First

Leo Fender built simple radios while still in grammar school and by the age of 13 was avidly pursuing electronics as a hobby. In the late 1930s he borrowed six hundred bucks and founded Fender Radio Service. For years before he ever put his name on amps or guitars, he designed, repaired, and rebuilt radios, record changers, and public address systems. And when he did start a musical instrument company of his own, he built lap steels and amplifiers, just as he had done at K&F, his brief mid-1940s collaboration with Doc Kauffman.

The Fender Electric Instrument Company (successor to the Fender Manufacturing Company) was already four years old by the time the Broadcaster appeared and began to turn conventional notions of electric guitars upside down. From a marketing standpoint, the electric guitar was the newcomer, an extension of an already established Fender product line. Collector/retailer George Gruhn: "Far more attention has been given by collectors to Fender guitars than Fender amps, but Leo's real genius was electrical and mechanical. While Rickenbacker, Gibson, Dobro, National, Kay and Harmony all had electric guitars even prior to World War II, the amplifiers of the day simply didn't kick butt. The Broadcaster didn't appear until 1950, but before that time Leo had made amps which even by *today's* standards are considered to be phenomenal sounding."

The amplifiers came first, not only at Fender but as an entire technology. No one invented an electric guitar and then said, "Now if we only had an amplifier to go with it." Fender's Ritchie Fliegler: "Before electric guitars there were all sorts of tube amplifiers — in radios, telephone switchboards, record players, transmitters, PAs, theater systems. Only after they had been around for years did people begin to think, 'Wow, if we could build guitars to go along with these things, they would be louder.' The guitar was really the 'afterthought,' the thing that was made to add on. The *amp* was the invention."

From the diminutive (but surprisingly loud) Champ to the mighty Showman, Leo Fender offered amps for every need. This tweed Champ is from the wide panel era of 1953 to 1955; this early-'60s blonde Tolex Showman has a single 15" speaker and oxblood grille cloth. Both amps are icons of their eras.

Today we think of classic Fender products as spectacularly visual objects: Lake Placid Blue Jaguars with matching headstocks, Fiesta Red P Basses with gold aluminum pickguards, butterscotch black-guard Teles and all the rest. The amps, too, were feasts for the eyes. We've all gazed with lust upon tweed Vibroluxes, blonde Twins, or blackface Deluxe Reverbs. We can see these guitars and amps everywhere, and imagine their evolution from drawing board to prototype to music-store display. We can feel them, too, as we snug that liquid-sculpture Strat body close to our own, and run our fingers over lacquered tweed or pebbled Tolex.

But some of Leo Fender's most enduring contributions are found in things we can't see and can't hold. He started with familiar tube manuals, widely available components, and standard circuits patented by Western Electric scientists at Bell Labs and licensed to Fender by AT&T/Western Electric. Then he re-imagined how the energy from runaway subatomic particles inside glass tubes might be harnessed to the service of a student guitarist, a seasoned pro, or an amateur who worked a day job at a filling station and played gigs in pool halls at night. Mr. Fender's vision was impaired (he lost an eye as a youth), and yet he could see electricity slamming into resistance. He could see a signal splitting in two, its fragments sent to separate tubes. He could see air molecules hammered by speaker cones.

Fender's Richard McDonald: "Those early circuits were widely available, but no one had built the kind of amps Leo Fender wanted to build, so he experimented with the position of the tone stacks, cabinets, components, filters. Remember, there were no guitar amp speakers, so he would build circuits and put existing PA or radio speakers in there and see them blow right up, so he went to people at Lansing and others: 'Hey, build a speaker that works in my product. I need excursion, and I can't get it unless you rethink your designs.' He wound up pushing the whole industry in a new direction."

Without the benefit of an engineering degree, Mr. Fender relied instead on his intuition and workbench know-how as he pondered the interaction of relatively high-wattage tubes and low-wattage output transformers, the coupling of low-efficiency speakers to resonant baffle boards, and how the "juice," as he called it, would be handled by a single 15 or a pair of 12s or a quartet of 10s. He had repaired other companies' amps, seeing what worked and what didn't. He had noted their shortcomings, learned from their mistakes. By the time his own amplifiers left the shop for the showroom floor, he had packed them with innovations and improvements.

George Gruhn: "In spite of all the modern advances electronically and technologically, there's nothing obsolete about early '50s Telecasters or mid '50s and early '60s Stratocasters or any of the Fender electric basses. The designs are timeless. It is, however, much more startling to realize how timeless Fender amps have proved to be. Tubes went out many years ago in virtually all other areas. You don't see wiring that looks anything remotely like a Fender amp on any new electronic gear. The Fender amp is remarkably unchanged over time. What other type of electronic equipment has stayed so steady over the years? When it comes down to how the electric guitar sounds to human ears, Fender got it right very early with their amps."

And the famously practical Mr. Fender did all this with typical production efficiency and thrift. He did it while making his products reliable and durable. Moreover, he designed them to accommodate the repair person, laying them out with a service-friendly elegance unmatched by his contemporaries. Mark Baier of Victoria Amps: "The guy who drew those schematics was the Michelangelo of electronic draftsmen."

Not a musician himself, Mr. Fender listened intently to suggestions from working professionals, trying a new speaker here, a new tube there, substituting transformers and capacitors and pots until he had it just right, just perfect, and then he fiddled with it some more, poking, tweaking, rearranging the jigsaw puzzle, probing for possible improvements in every component and haranguing his suppliers to improve their speakers and transformers. Ultimately he breathed a new kind of life into these amps, a sound as bracing and clear as glacier water, a sound that came to define good tone. Leo Fender's tweed and Tolex boxes were nothing less than the best musical instrument amplifiers the world had ever seen.

"I think the stroke of genius, really, was not his inventing the electric guitar, but inventing the amplifier to go with it."

Keith Richards,
inducting Leo Fender
into the Rock and Roll Hall of Fame,
January, 1992

Leo Fender, at the drafting table.

Fender's Mike Lewis: "Leo Fender was a pioneer in the whole concept of creating an entire line, especially with that kind of quality — one for the student, one for the serious amateur, all the way up to the professional. Someone would walk into a music store and say, 'I've got X amount of dollars,' and you could look up and down the whole line of Fenders and somewhere in there would be the perfect amp for that individual."

Although Mr. Fender solicited feedback from many sources, he ran the show and made all final decisions. Amp builder/repairman Blackie Pagano, of Tubesville Thermionics: "One of the things that makes Leo Fender's designs so enduring was that he really did them himself. He didn't go before a committee that was trying to make them cheaper. They were not cheap to buy. Those amps were priced like boutique amps are now."

The insights of Mr. Fender echo to this day, not only throughout the Fender line but across the entire industry. Hartley Peavey: "His circuits were 'cookbook' designs, AT&T/Western Electric circuits printed in tube manuals. He borrowed heavily. Nothing wrong with that. Hell, some of my designs were cookbook, too. Mr. Fender's brilliance was in the way he established the template for guitar amplifiers, and for 19 years he out-innovated the rest of this entire industry."

High style, rugged construction, bright tone and up-to-date features such as tremolo — it's all here in Fender's early-'60s top of the line combo, the Twin.

Author Aspen Pittman: "Were modern amps derived from late-'50s Fenders? From an implementation standpoint, yes. It's not really about what Leo Fender 'invented,' technically speaking. Almost everything in early Fender amps was in the RCA applications book they gave you when you purchased tubes. But Leo saw opportunities for improvement and innovation in transformer design and support hardware like caps and resistors, speakers, cabinets. He would take the basic building blocks and go to work. His genius was in the way he put it all together."

Shake It Up, Leo

If this all sounds familiar, it should. Mr. Fender didn't invent the solidbody guitar, either, and yet he can rightfully be called the father of that instrument because his Broadcaster/Telecaster's tone, durability, versatility, and production efficiency distinguished it from its relatively feeble predecessors and then went on to make it the first commercially significant guitar of its type. In other words, although he didn't invent the solidbody guitar, he invented the one that worked.

With the amplifiers, too, he took the same information and the same raw materials available to everyone else and put them together in new ways to create classic products. As Ritchie Fliegler told *ToneQuest Report*, "Good stuff and bad stuff are made out of the exact same thing. The parts list of the best amp you've ever heard and the parts list of the worst amp you've ever heard are practically identical. It's just a matter of shaking up the box right."

Leo Fender shook it up right. In fact, as with his guitars, it's remarkable how often the term "industry standard" comes up when discussing his amplifiers. A few of his concepts are so universal and so taken for granted we forget that someone had to come up with them in the first place. Fender popularized instrument amplifiers with multiple tone controls, for example. Some of Mr. Fender's own innovations and his adaptations of existing ideas — front panel knobs, top-mounted chassis, multiple speakers, piggyback cabs — were apparent, while others were hidden, heard but not seen.

Mark Baier: "If you go inside the guts of a modern day amp, chances are it'll have one of Leo's tone stacks in there, the phase inverter's going to be the same setup — pretty much every modern tube amplifier will be derivative in some way of what Leo was doing in the 1950s. Whether it was divine inspiration or he really knew what he was doing — and I think it was a bit of both — when he selected the kind of input amplifier circuits, his modifications to those circuits, the specific tone control stacks, the particular type of phase inverter, the choice of tubes, speakers, cabinets, and the way he put it all together, he created something that couldn't be bested. He'd done it!" Peter Frampton: "Fender amps fit every palate. You can't get out of a Twin what you can get out of a Deluxe Reverb, and vice-versa, but across the line they'll do it all."

The Common Denominator

For decades after World War II, guitarists across the country performed with a diverse array of electric guitars designed or manufactured by industry leaders such as Nathan Daniel, Ted McCarty, the Gretsch family, Semie Moseley, Alfred Dronge, F.C. Hall, and of course Leo Fender. Whether they played a Silvertone or an Epiphone, a Danelectro or a D'Angelico, whether they spoke with a Massachusetts twang or a Mississippi drawl, whether they wore silk suits in supper clubs or blue-stripe overalls in rural Grange halls, a common denominator for countless players of all styles was their Fender amplifier.

It came to be a standard not only for players but also for club owners and concert promoters. On a stage where a Detroit blues band might be followed the next night by laid-back jazzbos in silk socks and loafers, and the night after that by boisterous Oklahoma buckaroos decked out in lizard-skin boots and hubcap belt buckles, a house amp's versatility was mandatory. Its performance could mean the difference between an unforgettable concert and disaster. Clubs and arenas built their reputations among professionals on the reliability of their stage gear. With such high stakes, pro-

6G3 Deluxe schematic, from January 1961. Note 12AX7 and 7025 preamp tubes, 6V6GT power tubes, and GZ34 rectifier tube. Mark Baier: "The guy who drew those Fender schematics was the Michelangelo of electronic draftsmen."

These Princetons are photographed to scale, displaying the styles and evolution of amplifiers from Fender's first two decades.

woodie

TV front

wide panel tweed

narrow panel tweed

moters looked to the amplifiers coming not from the traditional music centers of Chicago and New York but rather from a town called Fullerton out there in the California orange groves. They installed Fender amps on stages from Texarkana to Timbuktu because musicians demanded nothing less. To this day, in many a venue, any house amp other than a Fender would raise eyebrows.

Recording studios are no different. Paul Reed Smith: "I've seen lots of studios without a Neve console. I've seen lots of studios without a Telefunken microphone. But I don't think I've ever seen a studio without a Fender amp, or *several* Fender amps."

The Man, the Sound

The former radio repairman who transformed the art and industry of popular music was a most unlikely revolutionary, a quiet man who loved his work. Leo Fender was never more at home than at his workbench, surrounded by Allied Electronics catalogs the size of phone books, spools of wire, stacks of schematics, and hand-labeled, open-front cardboard boxes of resistors and loose tubes piled on utilitarian metal shelves all the way to the ceiling.

The late photographer Bob Perine, whose images were essential to the success of Fender's early literature, said of his longtime associate Leo Fender, "Here was a man whose sole interest was making guitars and amps sound better, not worrying about the immeasurable whims of advertising. He was happiest hidden there in his Fullerton factory lab, soldering and tweaking and listening for results." As Perine told *Vintage Guitar* magazine, Leo brought his tube circuits to "a kind of divine perfection."

Historian Richard Smith has written: "Even in old age, after suffering several small strokes and progressive degeneration from Parkinson's disease, Leo Fender was dedicated to the point of obsession. He continued working every day he was able, sometimes seven days a week. Once asked in the 1980s why he did not retire and enjoy the fruits of his success, he replied, 'I owe it to musicians to make better instruments.' Leo Fender personified the American spirit of invention. He went to work the day before he died, Thursday, March 21, 1991."

For much of the pop music era, the sound of rock and roll was the sound of electric guitars through Fender amps. The Fender sound was not only a good tone, it was *the* tone, the gold standard. Although the Fender sound is constantly evoked and imitated, there's nothing like the real thing. As Joey Brasler of Bogner Amplification told a gathering of leading amp manufacturers (quoted in *Guitar Player*), "Nobody's 'Fender' sound is the same as Fender's."

Other domestic and overseas companies built worthy products over the years, as did dozens of independent builders. For certain musical styles, during some periods, some competitors could boast of beating Fender at its own game, particularly during the Dark Ages between Leo Fender's stewardship and the revitalization of the company by William Schultz and his associates. But over the long haul, across the spectrum from country, jazz, and blues to rock, soul, funk and beyond, no amplifier company has been as influential as Fender. Even its rivals owe much to their predecessor and competitor, and most of them freely acknowledge the debt. As Steve Carr of Carr Amps puts it, "What do we owe Leo Fender? Gosh, almost everything."

brown Tolex black Tolex (4 white knobs, '64 transition), black Tolex (black knobs), black Tolex with onboard reverb.

"Of all the things he did, I think Leo was most attached to the pickups and the circuits, the amplifiers."— George Fullerton

"I always thought Leo was more comfortable with the electronics, because when it came to the string instruments, he had to rely on practically everybody else, other than his own knowledge. So I think he favored the amplification. You should have seen that great big damn baffle he and Freddie built. It had something like 32 ten-inch speakers in it. It was on big casters, and he could roll it around the shop to test things. That thing was a monster."— Bill Carson

"I didn't call him 'Leo.' I always called him 'Mr. Fender,' out of respect. He was my inspiration for getting into the electronics business."— Hartley Peavey

"Leo Fender built amplifiers that were musical instruments."

— Rick Turner

"Leo Fender was really just an old radio repairman at heart. He created brilliant guitar designs, but the subtle brilliance of his amp designs is no less inspiring, and you can really feel his passion and soul when you contemplate an old Fender amp's exquisite simplicity, durability, and outstanding tone. I keep a photo of a grinning Leo in my shop. It inspires me and keeps me humble." — Terry Buddingh

"Leo hired me personally. I'll never forget it. I was like 20 years old but had already been doing electronics for years. I was nervous. Leo was very funny, with a dry sense of humor. He pumped me for about 10 or 15 minutes on what I knew about electronics. I said, 'I'm going to school and repairing TVs on the side.' He looked at me straight in the face and said, 'That must hurt — repairing TVs on your side [laughs].' And he said, 'Well, you sound good to me. You're hired.'

"Leo almost always wore slacks and a standard short-sleeve shirt, and he had a tool belt with screwdrivers and everything. He wore tinted glasses with big lenses. One time I was going through the factory with him and a guy approached him and didn't know who he was. He was asking him about cleaning up some stuff or doing some chores, and I realized, this guy doesn't know he's talking to the owner of the whole company. He thinks he's talking to the janitor."— Bob Rissi

"I knew Leo well. He was my boss. We worked together every day in the lab, and we lived five blocks away from each other. We went fishing. These designs were very dear to Leo. You know, he didn't have any kids. *These* were his kids."— Bill Sterle

"One time Leo pulled back a big run of amplifiers from the dealers because someone had inadvertently put in a potentiometer that was a quarter meg when it should have been a half meg. I doubt if anybody could have heard the difference, but that's how particular he was about the operation of his amplifier."

— Bill Carson

"Leo had a lot of yes men around him — *Oh yeah, Leo, this is a great amp!* I can understand that, but I wasn't like that. I would tell him, yes, it's good, and maybe it's just me, but I'm not getting the sound I need. And that's what interested Leo. Then he would start tearing the amp apart, tearing the guitar apart, the pickups. I had an appointment one time for a day, and he made me stay for four days, going back and forth and trying new things, and listening, always listening. He kept making modifications to the caps in the amp, other things, trying everything. Leo was always willing to make you happy, whatever it took, and I did get the sound I wanted."— Jody Carver

"He was, after all, the sound wizard, having trained his ear (and his eye, incidentally) to the finer points of musician preference. Though he had been fitted with a glass eye … when he was a boy, Leo was phenomenal at distinguishing between string gauges.

'That's a 065 D string,' he insisted to George Fullerton one day when stringing up a prototype Jazz Bass, while I was looking on.

'Sorry, Leo, it came out of the 070 bin,' Fullerton assured him.

'Well, it's not a 070. Go get the right size.'

'Come on, Leo, you can't tell the difference between 65 and 70 [thousandths of an inch] with your naked eye!'

'Of course I can. This is the wrong size.'

Fullerton trudged off grumbling but came back in a while with the correct string. 'Sorry, Leo, you were right,' he reported. 'It got put in the wrong bin.'"— Bob Perine, in *Vintage Guitar* magazine

the

"What do we owe Leo Fender? The same thing we owe Henry Ford — his creativity, his packaging, his market strategy, his thrift. Think of the bolt-on neck. That was a matter of economics. It was the same thing with his amps. In making them efficient to manufacture, he made them functional for the player. You know, Henry Ford specified that his gears were to be ordered in a special crate that he had designed himself. So he spec'd out not only the gears, but the packing crate. After the gears arrived at the plant and went to the production line, they'd disassemble the crate and use the boards as floorboards in the cars. Leo Fender was of that same spirit. He would always get the most out of his materials."

— Aspen Pittman

"What do we owe Leo Fender? That's a whole evening and a couple bottles of wine [laughs]. If it weren't for Leo Fender, this whole world of electric guitars would be very different. Who else produced a guitar amplifier in that era that sounds as good today? Nobody. People look back on the old Gibson amps with rose colored glasses, but those amps were dogs. Magnatone, kind of OK. Vox — good, but many were based on Fender circuits. The early Marshall? It's a 4x10 Bassman. [Marshall amp designer] Ken Bran even acknowledged they copied a 4x10 Bassman. Whether it was by accident, God's will, or whatever, Leo Fender made great sounding stuff. We still love the sound of those amps, and we still hold them up as the ultimate tone." — Paul Rivera

"As it turned out, every amp in the world ultimately is compared to a Fender."

— Kevin O'Connor, *The Ultimate Tone*

How many pieces of modern art do you see in this catalog photo from 1961?

C H A P T E R T W O

2

Leo Fender: 20th Century Man

Mr. Fender's amps and guitars changed the way musicians work with their tools. Most significant of all, they helped ignite whole new styles of music.

If amplifiers are Leo Fender's "other" legacy, there is a broader heritage as well, one that exceeds the boundaries of musical hardware altogether. Though his products may have benefited fewer people than did telephones or alarm clocks, he deserves a place in the annals of the 20th Century's great industrial designers, alongside figures such as Raymond Loewy, Henry Dreyfuss, and Charles Eames. Beyond their commercial success, their innovations changed how people live, interact, and see themselves and their place in the world.

Acknowledged as the father of streamlining, Raymond Loewy designed everything from logos for Shell, Lucky Strike, and Exxon to Frigidaire refrigerators, Air Force One's exterior graphics, even spacecraft. A few of his landmark designs or redesigns include the iconic Coke bottle of the mid-1950s, several ahead-of-their-time Studebakers, and the modern versions of the Greyhound bus and the steam locomotive.

The famously practical Henry Dreyfuss designed the spherical, take-me-to-your-leaderish Hoover Constellation vacuum cleaner (which floated on a cushion of its own exhaust), classic Westclox alarm clocks, John Deere tractors, Thermos bottles, washing machines, Eversharp's Skyliner fountain pen, the circular wall thermostat, a model city for the historic 1939 World's Fair, and one of the most widely used appliances of all time, Bell's Model 300 rotary telephone in basic black.

Charles Eames is best known for the Eames Lounge Chair, perhaps the foremost example of 20th Century modernist furniture. He and his wife Ray also pioneered designs and techniques for producing other types of furniture, as well as pre-fab houses and various products made with new techniques of wood molding.

Raymond Loewy described streamlining as "beauty through function and simplification." Henry Dreyfuss was chiefly concerned with practicality and what came to be called ergonomics. For Charles and Ray Eames, the essential condition for design was recognizing the need, and fulfilling that need through the latest in materials, components, and construction techniques. All of these concepts will sound familiar to anyone even remotely aware of the philosophy of Leo Fender.

You didn't have to buy an expensive model to tap into Leo Fender's sense of functional style. Good looks and purity of form were seen across the line, all the way down to student models such as the one-knob, "two-tone" Champ 600, built from 1949 to 1953. The variants shown here are labeled on their back panels *Fender CHAMPION "600"* (rear amp) and *Fender "600" Amp.*

Fender Follows Function

The design maxim most often associated with Mr. Fender is "form follows function." It was coined by American architect Louis Sullivan at the tail end of the 19th Century and adopted and refined by many of his successors, most notably Frank Lloyd Wright. In Wright's view, form and function are inseparable: function *is* form. Simply put, a product's design should derive from the manner in which it serves its purpose rather than considerations of mere ornamentation. Design a product that *works* better, and let its beauty flow from that.

It's hard to imagine a purer expression of that philosophy than Bill Carson's recollection of Mr. Fender's approach to design: "Leo used to say, if we've only got a hundred dollars to develop this item, it's got to be reliable, and it's a life or death matter for the musician for that thing to perform every time. We will spend as much of that hundred dollars as necessary to get that. If we've got four or five dollars left over, we'll work on the cosmetics." As Mr. Fender told this author: "Your best product, I think, always is first to work to the utility, and then try to make the utility have a pleasant appearance."

Of course, Leo Fender never intended to create one-off art objects. Like Loewy, Dreyfuss, and the Eameses, he designed practical items for everyday use. Blackie Pagano: "Leo wasn't trying to make these exalted icons of fetishistic obsession. You can tell everything about his philosophy just by looking at his amplifiers, because their form follows their function. This is part of the genius of Leo Fender, and why these designs have an enduring quality."

West Coast Cool

The influence of musicians' feedback on Mr. Fender's designs is a tale often told. Harder to pinpoint is the influence of the environment and events outside the Fullerton shop. But consider: Few developments in human history were as exciting or as technology-dependent as manned flight, and the aviation industry was headquartered in Leo Fender's back yard. A decade before he patented his first products, more than two dozen aviation manufacturers were already established in Southern California, home to 3,000 licensed pilots and site of a third of all airplane traffic in America.

The intertwined aerospace and defense industries

would keep Southern California on the cutting edge of technology. Over the years, plenty of Fender designers worked in aviation, automobiles, or aerospace as well as amps and guitars, from Leo's first partner, Doc Kauffman (Douglas Aircraft), and plant manager Forrest White (Goodyear Aircraft) to the technicians and execs from the auto and aerospace industries who joined Fender after its acquisition by CBS.

Southern California was also the center of a building boom in housing and an accompanying revolution in architecture. Although Mr. Fender may not have taken the inspiration for his amp cabinets directly from the squares and rectangles of suburban houses in the Western Ranch, American Ranch, and California Rambler styles, there's no question that those homes and Fender's amps were born of the same philosophy of putting function ahead of decoration.

Whitewall tires and woofers: Manning his mobile PA system, Leo Fender runs sound for the dedication of Fullerton's City Hall, 1941.

Christopher Hawthorne is the architecture critic for the *Los Angeles Times*. In language that could have been referring to narrow panel tweeds, he wrote, "But the residential designs [of Los Angeles] that have stood the test of time have not been those meant to impress the neighbors .... They have been nearer the opposite: ones featuring an honest and straightforward approach, a clarity about budget and materials, and an assertion of the Modernist ideal that great design shouldn't be reserved for the wealthy."

The post-War spirit of innovation wasn't confined to governments, corporations, or entire industries. It flourished in garages, workshops and tool sheds, too. The year the Fender Electric Instrument Company was established, 1946, also saw the founding of the So-Cal Speed Shop in Burbank; it's no surprise that Southern California gave birth to both the custom car and hot rod phenomena. Guitar makers and hot rodders have shared a great deal ever since, crafting precision-tuned machines with chrome parts on custom-colored bodies and emphasizing speed, performance, flash, sex appeal, and noisy fun.

Up the coast from Fender was America's original dream factory, Hollywood, making Southern California the center not only of the new industries and the new architecture but the new glamour as well. Southern California's vibrant post-War economy, its opportunities for self-reinvention, its magnetic pull on dreamers and mavericks, its spirit of can-do innovation, its tropical climate (which fostered any number of fun-centered trends — convertibles, surfing, backyard barbecues, suburban swimming pools), its new approach to everyday activities (drive-in restaurants, malt shops), and its ebullient, let's-go-to-the-moon confidence in technology all went hand in hand to stir up a heady atmosphere of new possibilities. Across the American cultural landscape, it was often heard: If it's cool, if it's exciting, it happens first on the West Coast.

For the designers of the post-War era, the effect of the new sensibility was not a rejection of style but rather the birth of a new style, one that stripped away traditional, tacked-on embellishments and allowed function to dictate bold new forms and shapes. There was something profoundly optimistic about it all. In jettisoning the past, the new designers embraced the future.

Loud, flashy, and roaring with attitude, electric instruments and fast cars have been associated with each other since the 1950s. These Hot Rod amps are among the most successful products in Fender's entire history.

Enter Leo Fender

It was in this environment that Leo Fender set about imagining the electric musical instruments of decades yet to come. Blackie Pagano: "Although I've been in audio for 30 years and have repaired hundreds of Fender amps, my primary interests are art, culture, and industrial design and how they interact. I consider Leo Fender to be one of the geniuses of the renaissance in design that occurred in America after World War II. It probably went back to the late '40s, with bebop and abstract expressionism. Then the '50s started an artistic shift, which ended up in the huge cultural shifts of the '60s. All these things are a continuum."

Despite revolutions in both music and electronics, Fender products have proved their staying power for more than half a century. When it comes to style, classic Fender amps still look as timeless and cool as one of Raymond Loewy's sleek Studebaker coupes. Durable? A properly maintained Fender will deliver the goods as reliably as it did during the Eisenhower administration.

And when it comes to tone, the Fender sound still dominates the market so thoroughly that even the highest-tech amplifiers of other manufacturers are routinely judged by their proximity to standards set decades ago in Fullerton. Fender's Mike Lewis: "Whenever anybody talks about their amp, they always refer to it in Fender terms. They all have a switch that says 'Tweed' or a knob that says 'Blackface.' If it's got a lot of headroom and a great clean sound, they'll say it's like a Twin. If it breaks up really sweetly, they'll say it's like a tweed Deluxe. Or, it's got that great Fender-sounding reverb."

The basics: Power switch, pilot light, tone and volume controls, input jack — even Fender's simplest amps provide a useful range of sounds for various applications.

Plugging into the Future

However impressive, the initial success and the continuing, pervasive influence of classic Fender musical tools are only part of the story. Those products had additional, transcendent qualities that provided pathways to unexplored territories, portals to the future itself. In the hands of creative musicians, these amps and guitars proved capable of sounds, techniques, and trends beyond Mr. Fender's expectations, even beyond his imagination. Examples abound, from high-wire trem-bar acrobatics to the glorious distortion of tube amps cranked far beyond their intended volume levels to "student" amps becoming treasured recording tools for famous guitar stars.

Aside from providing gear for stages, studios and rehearsal garages worldwide, Leo Fender facilitated the groundbreaking artistry of Dick Dale, Jimi Hendrix, Jeff Beck, Stevie Ray Vaughan and many others. In striving to build the best possible instruments for the players of his time, he built instruments for our time as well.

And yet the greatest of all testimonies to Mr. Fender's brilliance lies beyond his products' popularity, their timelessness, and even their suitability for radical new techniques and sounds. Leo Fender stands apart from contemporaries who succeeded merely in commercial terms because his amps and guitars helped change the way musicians work with their tools; most significant of all, they helped ignite whole new styles of music.

While he couldn't have foreseen the global music market's staggering variety of gear, today's multi-billion dollar industry rests on a shift in musicians' attitudes that owes much to Leo Fender. And while he couldn't have foreseen rock and roll, surf music, soul music, Motown, psychedelia, electric blues-rock, country-rock, funk, or other trends, it's almost impossible to imagine modern pop music without his instruments.

New Tools + New Attitudes = New Music

How did one man's inventive use of tubes, circuits, speakers, and features contribute to rearranging an entire musical landscape? The story goes back to the beginning, to two steel buildings on Santa Fe Avenue in Fullerton, where in 1946 Leo Fender first put his name on production guitar amplifiers. Over the next 19 years, he spoke often with electronics suppliers, remained well aware of

In 1960, Fender began covering its amplifiers in tough, fabric-backed vinyl Tolex. Collector Perry Tate: "The tag on the brown amp is the earliest Tolex tag I've seen; it says, 'as advertised in Holiday,' a popular magazine at the time. As it says on these tags, Tolex was manufactured by General Tire Corporation, which makes sense: This stuff wears like a tire."

advances in high-end audio, and incorporated some of those advances into his Deluxes and Pros and Twins. Blackie Pagano: "The history of electronic audio reproduction basically starts with radio and the earliest triodes used in simple, single-ended configurations. Later we see push/pull triodes and even push/pull transmitting triodes for audio, to achieve higher power levels and more headroom. [Note: "Headroom" refers to the amount of signal an amp can handle before clipping or distortion occurs — how loud it can go and remain clean.] Push/pull topologies existed long before pentodes were developed, but many of the earliest guitar amps were single-ended pentodes — the classic Champ setup. Push/pull pentodes were seen concurrently in higher powered, more expensive models.

"As a radio repairman, Leo probably fixed a lot of early triode circuits, but his guitar amp manufacture joined the party while the earliest pentodes were current — metal-bodied 6V6s and 6L6s. As successive versions of the pentodes were developed, he utilized them: 6L6Gs, 6L6GBs, 6L6GCs, et cetera. Each new version generally incorporated a significant increase in specs. More headroom became available to the designer and, more significantly, to the musician." (Note: The 6L6 is also described as a beam power tetrode; see 'Odes to Tone, Chap. 3.)

Fender continues to create variants on classic designs, such as the Custom Amp Shop's tweed Bass Breaker (a Bassman with two 12" speakers), and the Two-Tone, basically a 15W Blues Junior with one 10, one 12, and asymmetrical deco styling.

As Fender amps increased in available power and versatility, those attributes became industry-wide standards and selling points. These new technologies and products found their way into the hands of inventive musicians, with several results. Bands got louder. Distortion was added to the guitarist's sonic palette. Musicians sought to use these new tools in new ways. Ultimately, entire new forms of music emerged.

Blackie Pagano: "At the point where the tools changed, there was also a change in attitude. The people who adopted the new tools were thinking about their art a little differently than the people who were using the old tools. It was a huge break from tradition, and that blows open doors. You know, art changes culture; art is the cutting edge of culture. Today's high art is tomorrow's mainstream. Leo Fender managed to create new attitudes among musicians. It was true with his guitars, and also true with the amplifiers, absolutely.

"One example: The type of distortion people wanted to hear started to shift. It's an electronic fact that push/pull circuits cancel second harmonic distortion. Instead, odd-order distortion predominates — third, fifth, seventh, ninth — especially when you push them into clipping. And yet classic Fenders are by no means high-gain amplifiers. I'm talking about the *type* of distortion, not the quantity. I believe this contributed to a shift in taste. It seems now that people are always reaching for more distortion. Look at Marshall's evolution, from basically no distortion to insane levels of distortion. Music has become much noisier in general, and part of that cultural shift — punk and metal, for example — has to do with our becoming accustomed to those odd-order distortions, which in turn resulted from evolving circuit topology. We saw this beginning a little bit in the late tweed and then in the brown and especially the blackface eras.

"So the music is getting both louder and noisier because the evolution of amplifier technology permits it. I think those things are partially responsible for predicating a shift in music. I'm certain of it. Listen to the Sex Pistols' first album. When it came out, I listened to it *every day*, several times a day. And that thing sounded like such a snarling mess, so great. And now it kind of sounds tame. Why is that? It's because our perspective has shifted so hugely."

Leo Fender helped to stoke this evolution with his innovative guitars and amps. Even a special effect could influence an entire genre. As *Guitar Player*'s Barry Cleveland says, "Arguably, without the introduction of the [outboard] Fender Reverb, and the inclusion of spring reverb in Fender amps beginning with the Vibroverb in 1963, surf music would never have come into existence …. the wet quality of the Fender Reverb is the defining characteristic of the surf sound. Without that splash, the Ventures and Dick Dale would have been left high and dry."

New Interactions With Our Gear

Aside from triggering shifts in taste and styles, Fender's innovations also helped transform how musicians interact with their gear. Although we take for granted onboard effects and multiple tone controls, such features were unheard-of in the early days of amplified guitar. Leo Fender didn't invent tremolo, reverb or tone filters, but by putting tremolo and reverb in the world's most influential line of amplifiers, and by offering circuits with knobs for bass *and* midrange *and* treble, he accomplished much more than providing useful new sounds.

He encouraged, first, the very idea of the versatile amplifier and second, the concept that an amp's performance would be determined by its user, not just its designer. In the years BL (Before Leo), you pretty much took what you could get, made the best of it, and delivered whatever sound your guitar produced through that amp. But with Fenders, players became sculptors of their own sounds.

After all, if you hand a guitar player a piece of gear with knobs on it, he's going to twiddle them and see what happens. Guitarists' endless fascination with diverse sounds was sparked in part by Mr. Fender's simple yet flexible tone controls, presence knobs, Bright switches, inputs of different resistances, dual channels, and highly adjustable tremolo and reverb. Such features not only permitted sonic experimentation — they made it inevitable.

Blackie Pagano: "It's important to note that Leo Fender's designs reflected a cultural shift, but they also helped to *cause* that cultural shift. And this is why he is one of the great designers of the 20th Century. He rethought everything very creatively and came up with really good solutions, but the most important thing was not any single guitar or amplifier, or any detail about them. By developing these amps, he partially invented the sound of rock. Leo Fender wasn't a guy who just built guitars and amplifiers. He changed cultures."

Having sold more than 110 million albums worldwide, the Ventures are the best-selling instrumental rock band of all time. Lead guitarist Nokie Edwards (shown here on bass): "I had a brown Concert, and I also had a Bandmaster, the combo, with the three speakers, and I used that on the Ventures recordings way back. And then after that I got one of the blonde piggybacks — not the Showman, but I can't remember exactly which model it was. You use so many things over the years, sometimes it's hard to keep it all straight."

“If someone had asked Leo back then whether he was an artist, he surely would have said no. But it’s right in front of us. All we have to do is look.” — Reggie Felker

Leo Fender and the Whole One Hundred

Belgian amplifier collector Reggie Felker reflects on a famous quote about Leo Fender.

Bill Carson's comment about Leo's spending ninety-five bucks on utility and five bucks on cosmetics is a great quote. I've heard it before. But there's more to Leo Fender than his utilitarian philosophy, whether Leo knew it or not. It is not necessary for an artist to be self-aware in order to be an artist, and Leo's intentions had nothing to do with whether he created art. Artists are not necessarily the best people to judge their own work. Sometimes they are the worst people to judge it, and many lack an appreciation of it. They're too busy doing what they do to articulate it.

The Rolling Stones thought they were copying Muddy Waters and Elmore James. Eric Clapton thought he was copying Freddie King or whatever. Eddie Van Halen has said he was copying Eric Clapton. Well, when you hear Eddie Van Halen, do you hear someone copying Eric Clapton? Either he failed miserably in his attempt to copy, or he created original art. It doesn't matter whether he thought he was copying Eric Clapton. The art stands.

Leonardo da Vinci was doing a job. Mozart was doing a job. They would get a commission from the Pope or a patron and they did what they were hired to do. Countless other people were doing exactly the same thing, but only Leonardo came back with The Last Supper. Only Michelangelo came back with the Sistine Ceiling.

So, yes, Leo Fender was committed to utility, but everyone else confronted the same problems, and they all had the same tubes, the same ruler, the same drafting table, the same RCA manuals. Leo Fender was the only one to come back with a tweed Twin. He saw his amps as machines that did a job, but it's a disservice to his genius to leave it at that.

Leo's intention was to solve problems, so on his amplifiers he put the knobs on a raked-back panel in front, and chrome protectors on the corners, and he covered it in affordable Tolex, and gave it the script logo and that piercing red light, which could have been any color of the rainbow. It was all very utilitarian, but it just looks so freakin' cool! These were decisions that could have gone in any number of directions. If someone had asked Leo back then whether he was an artist, he surely would have said no. But it's right in front of us. All we have to do is look. Leo may have intended to spend ninety-five dollars on the utility and five dollars on the art, but you know what? He spent the whole one hundred on the art.

— Reggie Felker

"Rock and roll as we know it could not exist without Leo Fender."

— The Rock and Roll Hall of Fame

"His rare ability to rethink and solve musicians' problems shaped the sound of 20th Century music more than any single inventor."

— Richard Smith, *Fender: The Sound Heard 'Round The World*

"Thank God for Leo Fender, who makes these instruments for us to play."

— Keith Richards, upon his own induction into the Rock and Roll Hall of Fame

"Fender was a minimalist with an efficient mind who created simple and effective products. By nature, this made Fender amplifiers solid and reliable pieces of equipment — exactly the kind of thing that working musicians could rely upon. I think that in turn, this fact solidified Fender as a 'benchmark' sound. These trademark tones are burned into our consciousness and remain a reference point that guitarists use to this day."

— Jol Dantzig, Hamer Guitars

"Leo Fender is the father of the modern guitar amp. The whole concept of having a four-piece combo that could put out more sound than the big bands of the 1930s or even a western swing band of the late 1940s or early 1950s was first made possible by Leo's amps."

— George Gruhn

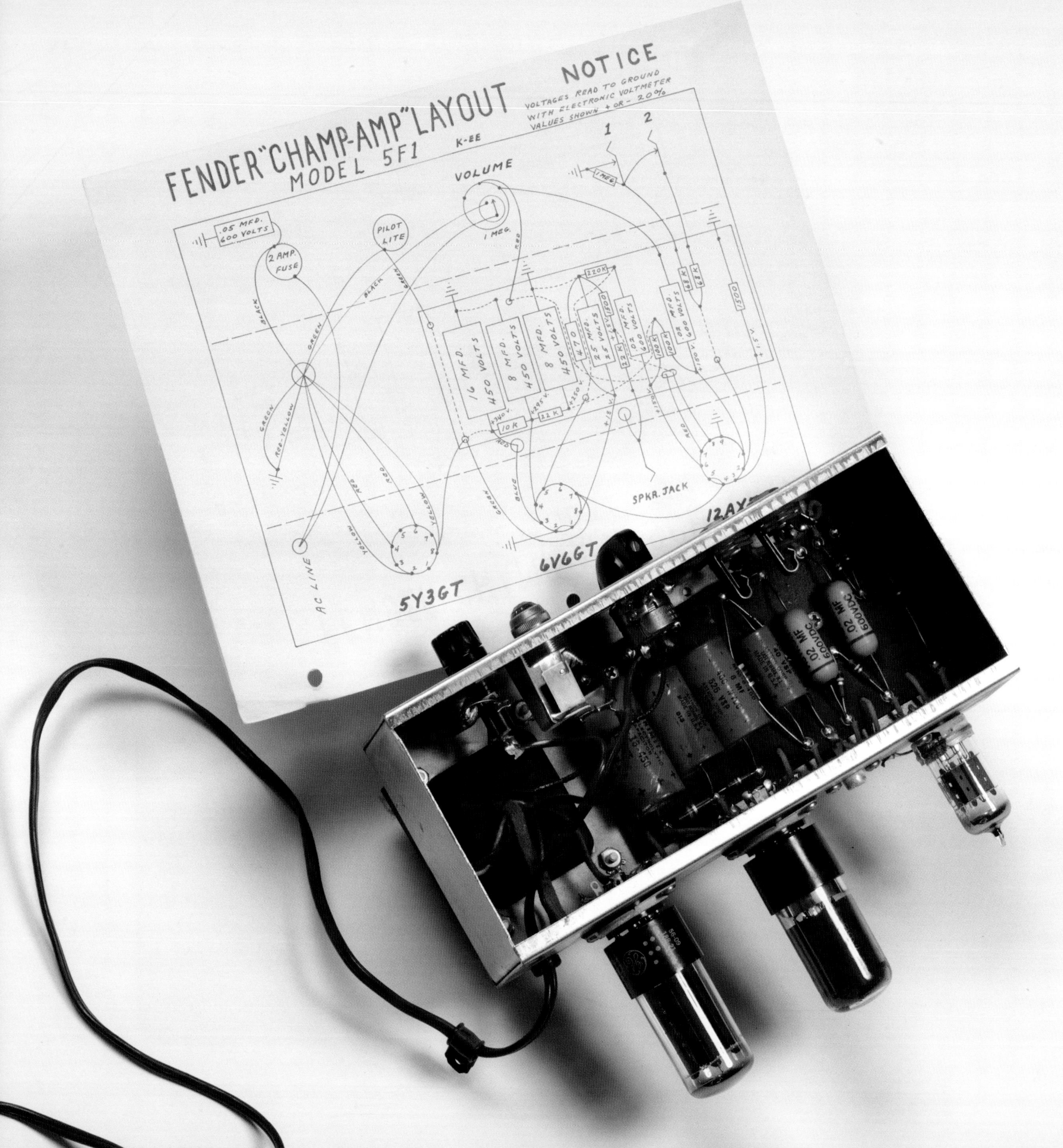

FENDER "CHAMP-AMP" LAYOUT
MODEL 5F1
K-EE
NOTICE
VOLTAGES READ TO GROUND
WITH ELECTRONIC VOLTMETER
VALUES SHOWN + OR - 20%
VOLUME
1 MEG.
.05 MFD.
600 VOLTS
2 AMP.
FUSE
PILOT
LITE
16 MFD.
450 VOLTS
8 MFD.
450 VOLTS
8 MFD.
450 VOLTS
220K
.02 MFD.
600 VOLTS
10 K
22 K
SPKR. JACK
AC LINE
5Y3GT
6V6GT

CHAPTER THREE

3

Electronic Journey

An Overview of Tube Amplification

Subatomic Buddies and Basic Terms

Let's get down, way down. If we really want to know why our Fender tube amps sound and perform the way they do, we need to start with the basic building blocks of the universe: subatomic particles. Notwithstanding those '50s-era cartoons depicting atoms as miniature solar systems with a couple of orbiters, an atom's positively charged nucleus is actually encircled by a whole swarm of negatively charged particles called *electrons*. They are tiny (even by subatomic standards), and they are our friends. Without electrons our toasters and Twin Reverbs wouldn't work. Without electrons we wouldn't have, well, electronics. Let's take a look at some of the terms you'll be seeing throughout *The Soul of Tone*. (Also see The Tone Zone: Facts, Opinions and Mythconceptions, Chap. 28.)

Electrical *current* refers to the quantity of electrons flowing over time through a medium capable of carrying them, called a *conductor*. Conductors range from the kind of copper wire used to connect the pickups in your guitar, to water, to the human body. In appliances and other devices, electrical conductors are often surrounded by *insulation*, which impedes the flow of electrons and keeps them from straying off course.

In an *alternating current*, or AC, the directional flow of electrons periodically reverses back and forth. When you plug your amp's power cord into a typical wall outlet in the U.S., you're tapping into a standard current of 120 reversals — that's 60 complete *cycles* — per second. Cycles per second is a quantity measured in Hertz, or Hz.

Direct current (DC), on the other hand, flows in one direction only. The wall outlet provides alternating current, but your amp requires direct current. As we'll see, amps employ a special component to rectify the situation.

The rate of movement of electrons through their conductor is measured in *Amperes*, or "amps." The energy that makes the current flow is measured in *Voltage* (V); this force is sometimes compared to the pressure of water flowing through a hose. *Wattage* (W) measures power, and is calculated by multiplying voltage times current.

Fuse, pilot light, volume knob and jacks on top, tubes on the bottom: Fender's late-'55 chassis layout for the 5F1 Champ reflects the functional purity of the amplifier.

Amp designers route the flow of current through pathways called *circuits*; for a half-century, the basic building block of any circuit was the audio tube. *Resistors* are components that diminish ("resist") the flow of current along those pathways. Resistance is measured in *Ohms* (Ω). Different types of resistors can let more or less current pass through, which provides one of many methods the designer can employ to fine tune the sound of an amplifier.

Putting several of these concepts together: When acting against a resistance of one Ohm, a force of one volt produces one amp of current (about 6.25 x 1,018 electrons per second, if you're counting).

A Chain of Many Links

Of course, providing adequate volume is just one of the amp's functions. We choose our amps because of their tone. Fender's Director of Technology Matt Wilkens: "I would not use a guitar amp as a hi-fi amp, or vice versa. A hi-fi amp *reproduces* sound. A guitar amp is a signal processor that just so happens to amplify, so it is a *producer* of sound. Leo Fender called his designs 'high fidelity,' and they were — compared to other guitar amps of the 1950s. But compared to hi-fi amplifiers of the day, Leo's amps had … let's call them 'significant deviations from fidelity.' Of course, those deviations from fidelity are what make a guitar amp a guitar amp."

Telecaster pickup: Its conversion of sound into current will be reversed at the opposite end of the signal chain with the help of another magnetized coil, the speaker's voice coil.

One of the themes of this book is that isolating the effect of a single element is often misleading, because any amplifier's performance results from a complex interplay of many factors. Ascribing an amp's great tone to a single component is sort of like attributing the success of a world-class bouillabaisse to the freshness of the saffron. While discriminating palates may indeed discern the subtle influence of a particular ingredient, any recipe depends on the blend of elements, sometimes dozens of them, and the cook's artistry in putting it all together. When it came to the recipe for great tone, Leo Fender was our master chef.

As we will explore in later chapters, your amp is like a pedalboard in one respect. Just as rearranging the order of a pedalboard's distortion, compression, and delay devices will affect its performance, your amplifier's sonic personality depends not only on the characteristics of each component but also on where each one is positioned within the circuit: before or after this or that tube, volume control, etc.

As far as Leo Fender was concerned, the guitar and its amplifier should be designed and built as a matched set. Author Richard Smith explained that Leo Fender viewed the amplifier almost like the bell of a saxophone, an inseparable part of the instrument. In fact, Mr. Fender's first K&F amplifiers could be purchased only with their partners, little crinkle-finish K&F lap steel guitars that were literally home-baked in Doc Kauffman's kitchen oven.

Somewhere along the way players and builders abandoned this concept (after all, a "mismatch" such as a Les Paul through a Deluxe or a Strat through a Marshall could produce compelling results). In any case, whether you're plugging a Squier Bullet into a Frontman 15 or a Custom Shop Strat into a Tone-Master stack, your own signature sound is all about the interaction of these two "halves" of your instrument. Tone begins in the hands of the player and ends in the perception of the listener, a chain of many links indeed.

The Journey Begins — Pickups, Pots, Cable

Conventional guitar pickups consist of a coil or coils of wire wrapped around a magnet or magnets. When we strum an E chord, the vibration of the ferro-magnetic metal strings disrupts the pickup's magnetic field, inducing a voltage in the coil and generating an alternating current whose electrical frequencies correspond to the musical frequencies of the chord. When we consider variables in pickup design, the number of wire turns in the coil, the composition, thickness and coating of the wire, the interaction of several complex magnetic properties, single-coils vs. humbuckers, the pickup's location along the string, and many others, it's apparent that this seemingly simple coil and magnet structure can be rendered in many configurations, each with its own tonal character.

From the pickup, the signal is typically routed to a volume potentiometer, or "pot" (a variable resistor that adjusts the signal's strength), and also to a tone potentiometer (another resistor that, along with a capacitor, acts as a high-frequency filter). As with other resistors, the resistance of pots is rated in Ohms (Ω); "k" means 1,000 Ohms, so 250k = 250,000Ω. Because lower-value pots can lend the perception of tonal breadth or "fatness," and their higher-value cousins can emphasize brightness, 250k pots (favored by Leo Fender) are often used with inherently bright single-coil pickups, while 500k pots are sometimes matched to humbuckers, as in late-'50s Les Pauls.

As you turn either a tone knob or a volume knob, the pot's influence on the signal may be uniform throughout its range. Such pots have a *linear taper*. For example, if the knob is rotated to the halfway mark, its influence on the signal or frequency is directly proportional, or 50% of its total effect. But because the human ear does not respond in a linear way to changes in tone or volume, guitar pots often have a *logarithmic taper*, also called an *audio taper*. Their influence is greater in some segments of their rotations than others; the effect may be subtle early in the rotation, and much more audible from, say, 7 to 10.

From the volume and tone pots it's on to the output jack, where our signal departs the guitar and travels toward the amplifier through a connecting cable that is shielded against extraneous noise and hum. Along this journey, the signal is influenced further by the cable's components, construction, and especially its ability to store a charge, called *capacitance*. Increased capacitance reduces high frequencies, so the quality of the cable may well make an audible difference in the tone and possibly the level of the signal.

Now, factor in even more variables at every step of the way — from the player's attack and the thickness of the guitar pick to the composition, tension, and gauge of the strings, the materials used for the guitar's components, solidbody vs. hollowbody, scale length, the length of the cable, and dozens more — and we can begin to understand how electric guitars can speak to us in such a multitude of voices, *before* their signals ever hit an amplifier.

Input Jacks

Finally (well, it's been only a fraction of a millisecond since we strummed that E chord), our signal arrives through the cable at our amplifier's port of entry, the input jack. Most Fenders have at least two inputs; input no. 2 often entails a resistor to "pad down," or reduce, the gain a bit.

On many two-channel Fenders (for example, a late-'50s tweed Bassman or a blackface Twin), each channel has two inputs; again, the second input in each case has a little lower gain than the first. Fender's Shane Nicholas: "I believe this design came about because it was so common for people to plug more than one device into their amplifier, and they needed a variety of patching options. The Fender Museum has a '50s Twin on display that we bought from an old accordion player. Inside the amp was an old photo of the guy playing a gig, and he's got his accordion and a vocal mike both plugged into his Twin."

Along its journey from guitar to amp, the signal is influenced by the cable's components, construction, and capacitance.

Inductance

In electrical terms, tone depends heavily on inductance (induction, inductivity), which is measured in Henrys and defined in science texts as an electrical phenomenon in which a change in the flow of current generates an "electromotive" force. In practical terms, inductance is a process of using a magnetic field to produce voltage (and in a complete circuit, a current). This should sound familiar — inductors include the pickups on your guitar.

Another description is particularly useful for guitar players learning about the electrical basis of tone: Induction refers to the efficiency of a coil in generating a current at a given frequency. The number of turns of wire in the coil, the shape of the coil, and the magnet's various properties are among the contributors to a pickup's inductance. A difference in inductance is essential to the differences in sound between, say, a relatively bright sounding, low-inductance single-coil pickup and a darker sounding, higher-inductance humbucker.

Like your pickups, your cable and your amplifier have several electrical properties. All of the properties of all of these components affect each other in complicated ways, which is one of the reasons why the same guitar works very differently with different amps. To simplify it, Fender's Ritchie Fliegler puts it this way: "The capacitance of the cable, the inductance of the pickup, and the input impedance of the amplifier all conspire to create a tone circuit. These things interact on many levels. For example, when you turn down the volume on the guitar, the tone changes as well. Why? It's because you've created this fabulous inductive tone control circuit as well as one that controls volume. The extent to which the high end disappears as you back off the volume control depends on the inductance of the pickups. Take a Gretsch Filter 'Tron pickup — very high inductance, even more than a Gibson humbucker, and the tone just vanishes instantly as soon as you back off that volume control.

"The game in amp design is to get the input impedance high, but not so high that it gets noisy. We don't think of an amplifier's impedance level as a 'tone control,' but it is, in a very real sense, because of the way all these things interact."

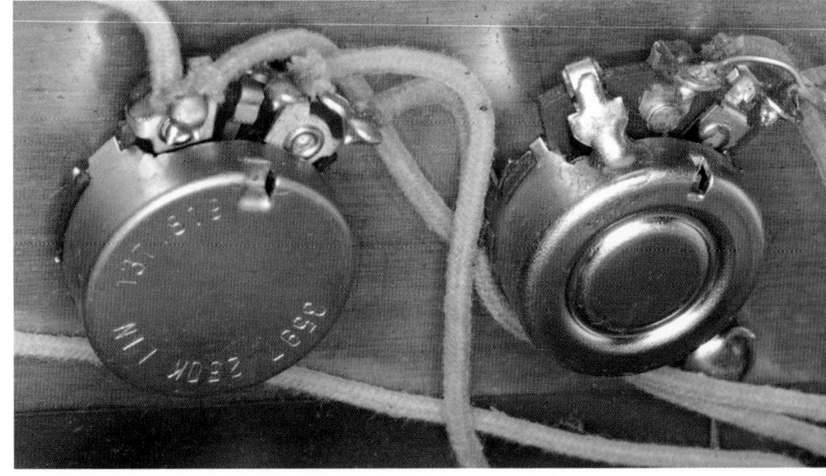

Fender amp chassis, detail. Front-panel knobs connect to interior potentiometers that control volume, tone, and effects such as reverb and tremolo.

Designed as multiple-function tools in an era when PA systems were less common, early Fender amps typically had inputs for both instruments and microphones.

Power Transformer, Rectifier, Caps, Choke

When you plug your tube amp into a wall outlet, you're tapping into relatively low-voltage, alternating current. However, your amp requires higher-voltage, direct current. The twin tasks of "stepping up" the voltage and converting the AC to DC are tackled by the *power transformer* and *rectifier*, respectively. Both are components of the power supply stage, and both can affect the touch responsiveness or "feel" of your amplifier.

The cord you plug into the wall is connected to the amp's power transformer, which converts electrical energy into magnetic energy, and then converts it back into electrical energy, all under controlled conditions. This provides a way to obtain different voltages for the power supply. To do this, transformers are constructed with two unequal lengths of wire (one for the input and one for the output) wrapped around a core. The number of windings in the input coil relative to the number of windings in the output coil determines whether the voltage is "stepped up" or "stepped down," and by how much.

Matt Wilkens: "Simply put, the transformer 'transforms' one voltage into another. Tube amp transformers provide several different voltages for different DC or AC supplies, including the tube plate supplies, the grid bias supply [more on plates and grids below], and typically 6.3V for the tube heater supply."

There are two types of rectifier, tube and solid state. Fender has used both types, including several kinds of tube devices, each with a distinctive influence on performance. See sidebar, next page: Rectifiers, Sag, Compression.

Sometimes described as a "reservoir of voltage," a *capacitor*, or cap, is a device that stores electrical charges. Power supply components include a set of filter capacitors. Their job is to smooth out the pulsations in the direct current coming from the power transformer. They maintain this constant level by storing energy when pulses are excessive (draining off the surplus, so to speak), and then discharging the right amount of energy when pulses diminish, to maintain the balance.

The choke (also "choke coil") is an element in the power supply used to suppress AC without affecting the flow of DC. Fender's Bill Hughes: "The word 'choke' is an old-school slang term to describe an inductor. Its impedance increases with frequency, and we use it in Fender amplifiers to remove the power line-related noise from the DC supply, so that the 6L6GC screen grids have a clean, quiet supply of voltage." Jim Tracy, Triad Magnetics: "Think of it as a single-winding transformer. It works in conjunction with capacitors to reduce ripple current."

Narrow-panel tweed Bassman, chassis detail showing various hand-soldered capacitors.

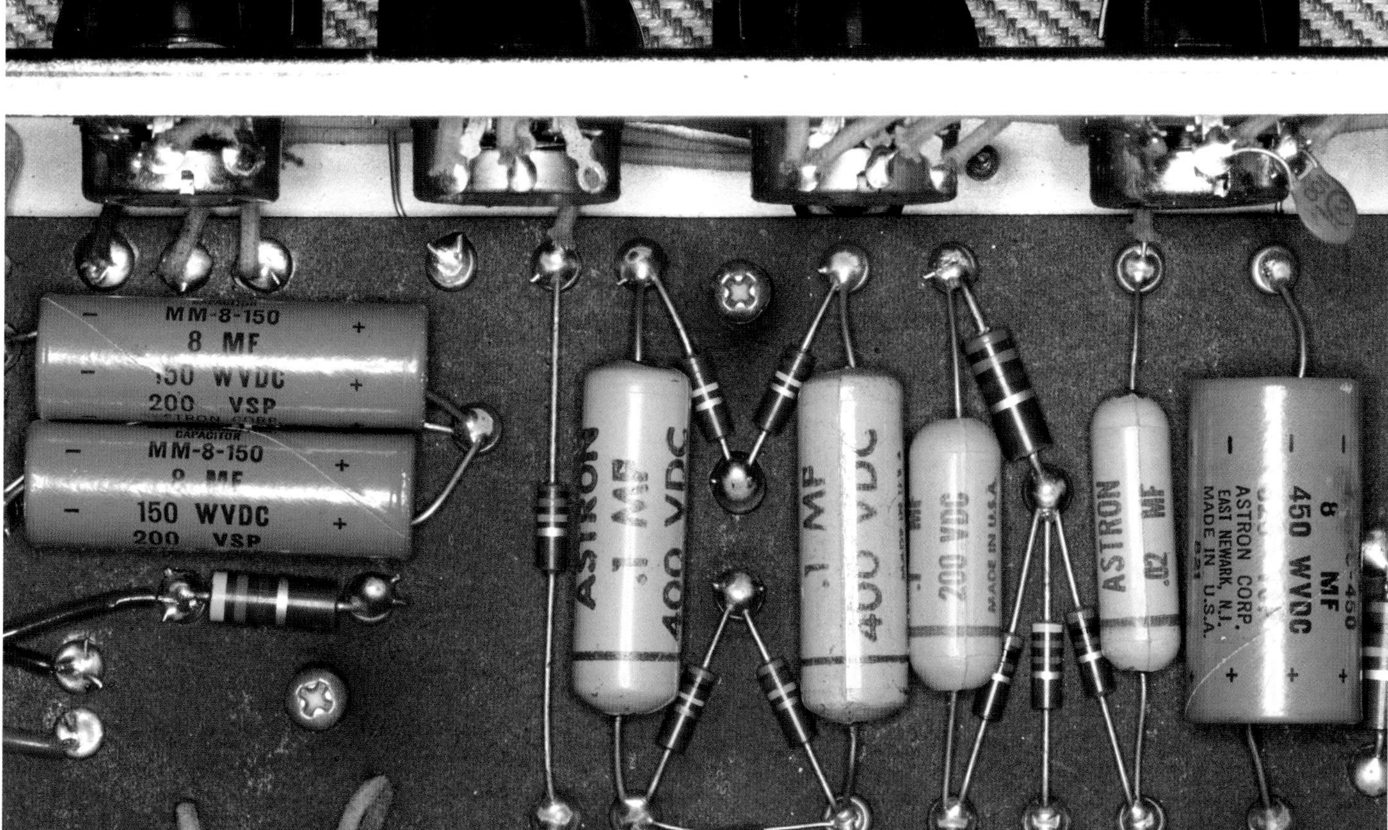

A tube rectifier imparts what technician/columnist Terry Buddingh called the "tactile bounce, resilient feel, and gradual attack envelope characteristic of a power supply that sags." This type (on the right), a 5Y3, was used in many Fenders, particularly the smaller models through the tweed era.

Rectifiers, Sag, Compression

An essential component of a tube amp's power supply stage is the rectifier, which takes the AC current from the wall outlet and converts ("rectifies") it to the DC current required by the tubes. You'll recall that in an alternating current, the directional flow of electrons periodically reverses back and forth. Rectifiers do their job by restricting the flow of current to one direction only. As Ritchie Fliegler writes in *Complete Guide*: "This newly rectified electricity is whisked away into a circuit to do some work, and that working flow of electrons is called plate current."

The guitar's signal does not pass through the rectifier, so theoretically that component has no effect on tone, yet we can often hear a difference between rectifiers because of the way they affect the amp's response to our touch, the way it feels.

Diodes are electronic devices with two electrodes or terminals. They come in tube and solid state types, and both are commonly used as rectifiers in guitar amps. Most contemporary amps (including tube models) use solid state rectifiers because they are more efficient, respond quicker, run a little cooler, cost less, and provide more headroom, a tighter feel, and a punchier low-end response. On the other hand, vintage buffs often prefer tube rectifiers, which react a bit more slowly and contribute to the easy breakup, "spongy" feel, and smooth distortion characteristic of several classic tweeds. Today, Fender uses solid state rectifiers in all models, except those reissues where authenticity calls for original-spec tube rectifiers.

Shane Nicholas: "In tweed amps and small to midsize blackface amps, rectification was accomplished with a tube. Some of the first guitar amps with solid state rectifiers would be the blackface Twin Reverb and Bassman head, and the Marshall Super Lead. Those amps were a little harder sounding, a little more efficient." (Later sections examine in some detail the rectifiers in tweed, brown or blonde Tolex, blackface, and other Fenders.)

The initial attack of a note is called its *transient*. This portion of the signal lasts only a few thousandths of a second and causes a brief burst of excess voltage or current, especially if the string is attacked vigorously.

Dynamic range describes the difference between the lowest and highest levels of an audio signal, or of a device that reproduces such signals. *Compression* refers to a reduction in dynamic range in which transient peaks are reduced while the softest parts are made relatively louder.

Shane Nicholas: "When you crank the amp up loud or play harder, a tube rectifier may not react quickly enough, so the amp is starved for power a little bit. This is known as 'power supply sag' or 'rectifier sag,' or 'rectifier compression.'"

Andy Marshall, THD Electronics: "The rectifier tube says, 'Wait a minute! I can't give you all that power at once.' So it drops a little bit, or sags, and then it comes back up." This slower initial response and ensuing "catch-up" causes a dip and swell effect in the output section. The overall result is a smoother sound with less bite and longer sustain.

The cumulative effects of various filters also contribute to an amp's feel. Highly filtered models tend to be tight and clear, with a sharper high-end definition, while underfiltered amps are sometimes characterized by a rounder sound. Matt Wilkens: "The rectifier tube causes a voltage drop in the power supply; the voltage drop increases with current demand. Because guitar amps are traditionally underfiltered, the sag is rather abrupt and propagates through the plate supplies for the tubes, causing what is called 'bias shift,' which reduces a tube's ability to amplify. All else being equal, a tube rectifier causes more sag than a solid state rectifier — thus, the 'magic' of the tube rectifier."

For many players, these differences are more than theoretical concepts; substituting rectifiers can noticeably alter the sound and feel of your amp. Most owners of a vintage Fender are well advised to maintain its value by keeping its components as original as possible. Otherwise, a solid state rectifier is often recommended if a tighter sound and increased power and headroom are more important than vintage-type sag. The design of many circuits allows their tube rectifiers to be replaced with plug-in solid state devices, but owners should consider such substitutions only after consulting a qualified technician.

Basic Tube Functions, Triodes

For the first two decades of Fender's existence, all of its amplifiers were powered by tubes, and to this day its most popular professional models are fueled by those beloved, quirky, glowing glass bottles.

The phrase "opposites attract" describes one of the fundamental laws of nature, in which those negative subatomic particles we talked about, or electrons, are attracted to positively charged ones. Unbound or stray electrons tend to flow toward a positive charge unless they run into opposing negative charges, filters, insulation, or other resistance of some sort.

Having undoubtedly fooled around with magnets, you've noticed that their opposite poles attract, while their matching poles repel. Electrons work the same way: In a battery, for example, they are attracted to the positive pole, and repelled by the negative pole. Many of the components in your guitar/amp/ speaker system are functions of this basic principle of electronics and magnetism: Opposites attract, likes repel.

A tube is an electronic amplification device consisting of an arrangement of specialized conductors called *electrodes*. As its name suggests, a *triode* is a tube with three electrodes — a negatively charged *cathode*, a positively charged *plate*, and a *grid*. The final piece is the heater. These elements operate in a vacuum and are sealed together in a glass bottle. The components are wired to pins on the tube's base, and those pins are mated to sockets that integrate the tube into the circuit.

As explained by *Vacuum Tube Valley*'s Senior Editor, Eric Barbour: "Cathodes in most familiar tubes, such as the 6L6 and 12AX7, are nickel sleeves coated with emitting oxides. Inside each sleeve, a small electric heater is inserted. By running current through this heater, the cathode is heated until it is orange-hot, whereupon it emits electrons.

"In some tubes, there is no separate cathode sleeve. The heater itself is also the cathode, a unit which is usually called a *filament*. The filament is heated by a current, and it emits electrons directly. This directly heated tube is the most primitive design for a vacuum tube. The original triodes invented by Lee De Forest in 1907 were made this way, and they dominated the electronics world until the 1930s. Directly heated tubes include antique radio triodes like the 300B and also large transmitting tubes used by radio and TV stations. Tubes in guitar preamps and power amps are typically indirectly heated, although some rectifier tubes such as the 5Y3 are directly heated."

When the heated-up cathode's negatively charged electrons "boil off," they head for their positively charged subatomic buddies on the plate, or anode (opposites attract). As you'll recall, this mad dash of electrons is electrical current. One way to think of it: The plate "collects" the current emitted by the cathode.

The amount of this current flow is regulated by the *control grid*, often a mesh, coil, or screen of plated wire positioned between the cathode and the plate. It stands in the way of those migrating electrons, and it works like this: Negative voltage is applied to the grid, so it opposes the flow of negatively charged electrons (negative repels negative). Increasing or decreasing the negative voltage increases or decreases opposition to current flow. So, *the amount of current permitted to flow from the cathode to the plate is determined by the amount of negative voltage applied to the grid.* The lower the control voltage (or blockage), the greater the current flow from cathode to plate. The greater the control voltage (or blockage), the lower the flow of current.

Functioning as a "valve" of sorts, the grid is sometimes compared to a water faucet or shut-off valve. In the UK, tubes are called "valves," as in, "Classic British valve amps include Marshalls, Voxes, and Hiwatts."

In short, the heater heats the cathode, which emits electrons, whose flow toward the plate is regulated by a voltage-controlled valve, or grid. In this manner, *we control current by applying voltage.* Amps amplify signals because small shifts in grid voltage trigger large changes in the flow of current to the plate. For more on tubes, see Chapters 5 and 6.

The tubes in this 5D8-A Twin, serial no. 0538, are specified on its chart. In the photo, from left: three 12AY7 preamp tubes, a 12AX7 phase inverter, two 6L6G power tubes, and two 5U4G rectifier tubes. Note the elegant simplicity of the hand-wired component layout.

'Odes to Tone

The two-electrode *diode* — "di" means two — is the simplest kind of vacuum tube and is used for rectification in many amplifiers. (Solid state rectifiers are sometimes called "diodes" for short, but technically, diodes can be either tube or solid state.)

As noted, a triode has three electrodes. A *dual triode* contains two separate tube structures in a single bottle, with a pair of each type of electrode, or six in all. (A tube's name often reveals the number of elements it has; Chap 5. The "7" in 12AX7, for example, denotes 7 elements: two cathodes, two grids, two plates, plus the heater.) The 12AX7 and 12AT7 dual triodes are used in many Fenders.

Developed in the mid 1920s, the *tetrode* adds a fourth element called a screen grid. Positioned between the control grid and the plate, this extra grid is a shielding device intended to increase stability and reduce stray capacitance and unwanted oscillations.

One drawback of early tetrodes was that some electrons could be knocked free from the plate when it was struck by stampeding electrons escaping from the hot cathode. These stray dogies, called "secondary emissions," could lower the plate current, waste energy, and introduce distortion. One approach to reducing such emissions and thus improving the tetrode's gain and overall performance was the *pentode*, a relatively high-efficiency tube that added yet another grid, called a suppressor, between the plate and the screen grid. Developed in the late 1920s, the pentode has five electrodes: three grids, a cathode, and a plate. (Note: Whether a tube has one, two, or three grids, they all serve to regulate current flowing from the cathode to the plate.) Pentodes are commonly used as power tubes in guitar amps, particularly from UK companies such as Marshall, Hiwatt, and Orange.

Another solution to the problem of secondary emissions was a sophisticated design called a *beam power tetrode*. In the mid 1930s, RCA engineers reconfigured the tetrode's control grid and screen grid, and they also replaced the suppressor grid with two "beam plates" in order to increase efficiency and reduce heat. The result was RCA's landmark 6L6 beam power tetrode.

The 6L6WGB, or 5881, is a variant of the 6L6, designed for rugged use in military and industrial applications. The 6V6 is another beam power tetrode. As we will see throughout *The Soul of Tone*, 6L6s, 5881s, and 6V6s are all widely used in the output stages of Fender amplifiers. Note: The 6L6 is described either as a tetrode or a modified or "virtual" pentode; some techs use the term "true pentode" to distinguish five-electrode tubes such as the EL34 and EL84 from beam tetrodes.

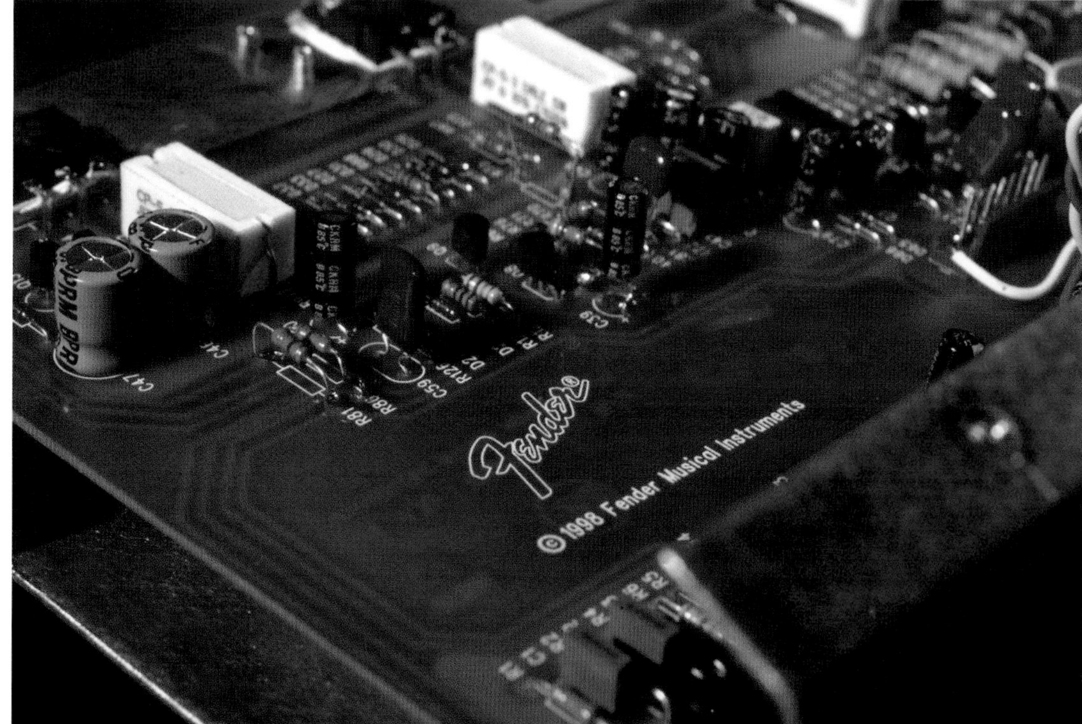

While durable solid state circuit boards like this one have replaced tube circuits in most amplifiers, Fender continues to offer both designs.

Preamp, Signal Processing, Effects

Fender amps are multi-stage amplifiers, containing a preamp and a power amp. The smallest Fenders use a single tube for each function, while high-powered models use several. The preamp is the first gain stage in the circuit and is charged with "preamplifying" the guitar's relatively weak output to a strength suitable for both signal processing and the massive, later-stage amplification required to drive the speakers. It's the primary tone shaping unit and an essential contributor to the amp's distortion characteristics.

Preamp tubes are usually dual triodes. As Myles Rose wrote in Aspen Pittman's *The Tube Amp Book*, "Unlike power tubes, where one tube is one tube, a preamp tube is two tubes in one bottle. There is an A side and a B side. They are independent units sharing only the heater. In one channel of a Fender blackface amp, as an example, the inputs use one side of the tube, then comes the tone stack; then the other side of that tube is used for the second gain stage."

Aside from their contributions to EQ and gain, preamp tubes typically power onboard effects such as reverb and tremolo. Fender's (and everyone else's) preamp tube of choice: the small-sized, big-sounding 12AX7 dual triode or its equivalent.

Signal processing entails routing the preamplified signal through tone controls (typically treble, bass, and perhaps mid), onboard effects such as reverb and tremolo, and sometimes an additional gain stage for further control over distortion.

Preamp tubes (as well as power amp tubes) are typically designated with a "V" for "valve," according to their order in the signal chain: V1, V2, etc. The designation dates back to J.A. Fleming's calling his 1904 diode device an "oscillation valve."

Tone Stacks

Tone controls typically entail pots and capacitors working together to regulate a signal's frequencies. Most tone controls in guitars and amps are passive filters that simply block frequencies in specified ranges, or *bands*, while allowing others to pass through to the next stage.

A typical treble knob is one such *band-pass filter*; when you turn it up, you're not actually adding treble or anything else; you're merely allowing more of the existing frequencies in the treble band to pass through. When you turn that treble knob down, you're filtering out, or "rolling off," high frequencies.

Tone filters are typically described in reference to the frequencies they cut or allow to pass (so "high-cut" is another term for "low-pass"). Aside from affecting their assigned frequencies, many tone controls also influence the level of the signal, which in turn may affect both the character of the distortion and the point at which it kicks in.

On amplifier schematics, tone control elements are often arrayed one on top of the other, giving rise to the term "tone stack." As we will see in later chapters, the sound and feel of Fender amps depend in part upon the design of their tone stacks and also their location within the circuit.

Channels

In the tweed, blackface, and silverface eras, Leo Fender's original designs provided not only two or more inputs (sometimes with varying degrees of gain, as mentioned earlier) but also separate channels in some cases, so that multiple instruments or even microphones could be plugged into the same amp. (The Fireballs helped pioneer instrumental rock in the late '50s and also scored hits with vocals; singer Chuck Tharp's microphone was often plugged into the same Tremolux used by guitarist George Tomsco.) Depending on the model, two-channel Fenders may also facilitate preset tones, different effects complements, and a choice between clean and distorted sounds. When the channels are footswitchable, selection can be made instantaneously.

Shane Nicholas: "Buck Owens told me that back in the '50s and '60s he and Don Rich used the same amp when they only had room for one in the trunk of the car! Old pictures of Bob Wills and others show the same thing. These kinds of Fenders have two individual preamp sections, with their own volume and sometimes tone controls. Those parallel channels then feed into the power amp. If you want to use one amp for multiple signals, two preamps work better than the clash of two guitars fighting for the same preamp.

"Hardly anyone uses more than one input on amps like the Super Reverb or '59 Bassman anymore. Though they work on the reissues like they did on the originals, the extra inputs are really there for historical accuracy. In modern channel-switching amps like the Hot Rod and Pro Tube Series, there are two or even three separate preamp sections to get different tones like clean vs. overdrive. They're not really for multiple instruments. In fact, most of those newer amps have a single input."

Power Amp, Phase Inverter

In Fender amps with push/pull power stages (Chap. 6), the first tube in the power amp is a *phase inverter*, also called a phase splitter. Often a 12AX7, 12AT7, or 7025 tube, the phase inverter splits the signal into halves which are sent to their own separate power tubes and later recombined.

The power amp does the heavy lifting, working with the output transformer to amplify the preamped and processed signal many times to a strength where it can drive the speakers. This stage usually entails two or four power amp tubes, also called output tubes. Compared to the little preamp tubes, they handle more wattage and produce more heat, and they may be the big honkers you see inside your amp (although some power amp tubes aren't much bigger than preamp tubes).

With extremely rare exceptions, the power tubes in vintage Fenders are either 6L6s or 6V6s of one variant or another. Except for the EL84-equipped Pro Junior and Blues Junior, and the 6V6-equipped Deluxe Reverb reissue, modern Fender tube guitar amps use 6L6s. (These things change. As we go to press, Fender has recently released the 6V6-equipped Princeton Recording model.)

The power amp makes its own, sometimes underrated contribution to your amp's tone, to how your amp responds to your touch, and also (when driven at higher volumes) its distortion characteristics; this latter effect is distinct from the distortion effects of preamp tubes, master volume circuits, or outboard devices.

Shane Nicholas: "A '50s tweed Deluxe is the perfect example of the rectifier sagging and the whole amp acting like a compressor. The effect is not precise, tight, or quick enough for most jazz or metal players, but it's great for blues and some rock styles." Bill Kirchen: "To my ears, the money rig is a Tele through a Deluxe. Someone loaned me a Deluxe back when we were recording the second Commander Cody album, *Hot Licks, Cold Steel & Truckers' Favorites*. We cut 'Semi Truck' with it, and I've loved that sound ever since."

John Fogerty, on his '58 tweed Deluxe: "I became a Leo Fender fan in my 40s. It took me that long to appreciate his genius. That tweed is absolutely perfect. It saturates just right, without getting too fuzztoney. It gives you that ultimate, awesome rock and roll sound."

While the 4x10 Bassman has inspired many an amplifier, the Deluxe has its share of descendants as well. David Lindley to Dan Forte, talking about his Dumble amps: "We went about getting the sound in those amps by taking an old Deluxe to Howard [now Alexander] Dumble and saying, 'We want this, but bigger and louder.'"

V *Hear the narrow panel tweed Deluxe, Tracks 2 - 12.*

 *Hear the 2007 '57 Deluxe, Tracks 24 - 29.*

Phase Inverters and Amp Performance

As described in this chapter, the phase inverter works in push/pull power stages to split the signal into two parts, which are sent to their own respective power tubes or sets of power tubes. Different types of inverters have distinct effects on both sound and responsiveness. (Note: Putting aside some hair-splitting technical details, experts interviewed for this book used "phase inverter" and "phase splitter" interchangeably.)

Paraphase: Push/pull Fenders of the late '40s and early '50s used a relatively inefficient paraphase inverter. Less common these days, it uses a pair of gain stages and therefore does entail some gain, which provides a grittier sound. Steve Carr, Carr Amps: "It has a harder time not distorting, which gives it kind of a gnarlier, raunchier sound. It's not so great as a phase inverter, but it does create a unique, funky low-fi distortion, which can be really neat, like in a lot of the tweed Fenders and some old Valcos — some pretty neat sounding amps."

Split-load: A relatively simple type of phase inverter is the split-load, also called the concertina or cathodyne inverter. Employed in the narrow panel Fenders of 1955 to 1960 (except the last of the tweed Twins and Bassmans), it uses only one triode, so one dual triode tube such as a 12AX7 or 12AT7 can handle two functions — driver and inverter. Although it has no gain, its grid can be driven into clipping, which provides another source of distortion. Mark Baier: "For example, when you turn up the treble control on a tweed Super, that control feeds the driver, and then that driver goes to the inverter. That clipping in the preamp stage is a different kind of effect than distortion in the power amp tubes. You get a creamier, compressed kind of thing rather than the grainy distortion you get with driving a power tube."

Many amps of the mid '50s, including Fender's E series, used this split-load inverter, a significant contributor to the sound of Fender in that era. Examples include the famous 5E3 Deluxe as well as several larger models. As Dave Hunter explains in *The Guitar Amp Handbook*: "The split-load PI is capable of producing a sharper signal with a little better fidelity than the earlier paraphase PI, but when pushed hard it still offers up some of its own distortion .... Its distortion is a little sweeter and richer than the paraphase, but it still doesn't give us full output-tube crunch and roar."

Steve Carr: "The concertina [split-load] is also what we use in our own Rambler, and we find that it has a sweet sound, but it can have a hard time driving the output tubes. To my ear those old Fender circuits with [split-load] inverters have a really pretty clean sound but don't always do distortion very well. They have a hard time pushing the power tubes."

Long-tail: A far more common, more complex, and more efficient type of phase inverter is the long-tail, as seen in many classic Fenders, notably the F series Bassmans and Twins. It does have some gain, and unlike the single-triode, split-load type, it uses two triodes, one feeding each side of the output section. Because it requires both sides of a dual triode tube, a triode from another tube is required to drive the inverter (so, designs featuring long-tail inverters have a higher parts count and are consequently somewhat more expensive to manufacture). Long-tail inverters are known for increasing the output section's accuracy and power, providing clean sound and headroom until driven hard, and then driving the tubes into distortion in a musical way. On amps with a feedback loop (Chap. 11), the signal is usually routed back to a long-tail phase inverter. Fender has used long-tails almost exclusively since 1960.

Comparisons: As Alexander Dumble explains, "The tone and distortion capabilities of the split-load phase splitters seem to be more applicable to some of the older tweed amplifiers, such as the 5E3 Deluxe and the Princetons, using the 6V6 tubes. However, to adequately stimulate more powerful output tubes such as 6L6s, the long-tail definitely has the advantage. It can easily develop the larger peak-to-peak signal drive levels needed to stimulate 6L6s. Leo Fender clearly succeeded in adapting the long-tail phase inverter to create amplifier classics such as the Bassmans and Twins. The tone and distortion characteristics of these amplifiers are of legend. The 'feel' of the split-load phase splitter is a bit stiffer than that of the long-tail. Also, it doesn't provide signal gain. It's basically a unity gain device. On the other hand, the long-tail phase inverter does have signal gain and therefore provides for a more dynamic tonal venue, with a more vibrant, responsive 'feel.'"

Mark Baier: "Comparing the two main types of inverters, you can drive the split-load into clipping, which might be what you want, but then again that restricts how much power you can get out of the amplifier. You get more power out of the long-tail, and if you're looking for headroom, it's an advantage that you don't drive it into clipping as readily. It's more balanced, and it's an effective way of making a louder amplifier. Leo Fender took the basic idea of the long-tail and changed the values a little bit, tweaked the circuit topology, and changed parameters and component values to suit his own vision. The long-tail, especially the way Leo used it, was a much more sophisticated design than the split-load inverter."

As Dave Hunter summarizes in *The Guitar Amp Handbook*: "Plenty of makers and players seeking an earlier breakup and a somewhat gnarlier distortion overall are still delighted with the split-load PI, while plummy, heavily compressed blues licks might still sound their best on the paraphase PI in a scruffy old 5C5 tweed Pro .... If you're trying to get a firm, powerful low-end with serious power-tube grunt when pushed hard, you're not going to achieve it to total satisfaction with a cathodyne PI, or at all with a paraphase. Or if you want that juicy sweet overdrive and easy compression that a mid-sized tweed amp provides at lower to medium volume levels, a long-tail pair PI might have trouble delivering. This isn't the sort of element you correct with modifications or add-ons, either; if your dream sound is the spongy, soft overdrive at low output levels, trade in that amp with the long-tailed PI for a Fender 5E3 Deluxe or one of its many clones."

Impedance, Output Transformer, Headroom

Compared to the scrawny voltage that hit the input jack a fraction of a millisecond ago, our newly power-amped signal is now brawny as a Viking. But it isn't ready to proceed from the power tube's plate to the speaker just yet, because the impedances of those two components are mismatched. *Impedance* (from "impede," to block) is a measurement of resistance in an AC circuit; it is measured in Ohms (Ω). It's like a crook in your garden hose that backs up the water pressure: The greater the impedance or blockage, the lower the flow of current.

This impedance mismatch between the tubes' plates and the speakers is huge. Plate impedance can be several thousand Ohms, while guitar amp speakers are typically rated at a relatively minuscule 2Ω, 4Ω, 8Ω, or 16Ω. Matching these impedances is the job of the *output transformer*, the last link in the signal chain prior to the speakers.

Otherwise similar amplifiers can vary in their output and performance if equipped with different transformers. One of the most fascinating things about original Fender amp designs is the way Mr. Fender matched transformers to different tube complements, outputs, and speakers. In *The Guitar Amp Handbook*, Dave Hunter compares a blackface Bandmaster and a Super Reverb and points out that although they have similar tubes and run at similar voltages, the Super Reverb, with its much sturdier output transformer, "puts out around 10W more power and has a noticeably bolder sound, with a firmer low end in particular .... The same applies for plenty of other amps carrying output tubes that could potentially give them similar wattage ratings, all else being equal, but output transformers that render them very different performers. The rule of thumb for output transformers goes: More iron equals more volume and better bass response."

Output transformers vary in design but generally feature two coils of windings with different amounts of turns. The primary coil is connected to the output tubes, the secondary coil to the speakers. The ratio of turns in the primary to the turns in the secondary determines the impedance parameters of the device, while the transformer's design and the quality of its materials affect its performance, particularly its frequency response.

GZ34/5AR4 rectifier tube, as used in classic Twins and Bassmans, among many other Fenders.

Fender used different types of transformers in the classic period. The tweed Super, for example, has a simple device called a *layer-wound* (or non-interleaved) transformer, with the primary winding around a bobbin and a secondary winding around *that*. The windings are separated by varnish-impregnated papers so they don't short out. An AC signal is inducted from the primary to the secondary coil, the amount of inductance depending on how far apart the coils are.

While other amplifier companies were content to use stock units, Leo Fender experimented relentlessly and demanded higher standards from his suppliers, including Triad, which built most of the transformers for Fender in the 1950s. The heavy-duty units in Fender's pro models had become industry standards by the end of that decade. This transformer sits in a classic 5F6-A Bassman.

In the more sophisticated *interleaved* transformer, the primary and secondary windings are leafed together — a few layers of primary, a few layers of secondary, more primary, and so on. The closer proximity of the windings makes for a better coupling, so the signal from the tubes is transmitted from the primary coil to the secondary coil with greater efficiency and higher fidelity. The sonic result is a flatter frequency response across the spectrum, particularly in the high end.

The "small iron" transformers found in, say, early-'60s Supers, Pros, and Bandmasters tend to saturate sooner and are quicker to distort. Interleaved "big iron" devices such as those found in early-'60s Concerts and Vibrasonics tend to produce more headroom, which in discussions of power amps refers to how much loudness an amp can produce before the onset of distortion. (Headroom is often discussed as a function of output, but while a Twin Reverb does indeed have a lot more headroom than a Champ, headroom depends on other factors as well, including speaker efficiency, output transformer efficiency, the number of gain stages, the type of rectifier, biasing, the level of the input signal — itself a function of the pickup's output — and more.)

Mark Baier, Victoria Amp Company: "What the output transformer transforms is energy. It takes the high voltage, low current energy created by the power tubes and transforms it to a low voltage, high current energy to drive the speakers."

Once its impedance is properly transformed, the signal heads for the speakers. Older amps and reissues often have only one output impedance setting, while more recent models may provide an impedance-selector switch that enables the user to add or substitute speaker arrays of different impedances. See sidebar: Output Transformers and Tone.

Output Transformers and Tone

Impedance matching is only one reason why the output transformer is important. As significant as any other tone filter in the chain, the output transformer can affect touch sensitivity, clarity and richness when the amplifier is played clean, how much note detail is preserved when the amp distorts, whether the amp can go from clean to distorted sounds without harshness, and how notes and chords sustain.

Alexander Dumble: "The specifications of an output transformer are dependent upon which output tubes are used, power level, and speaker loads. [Regarding] design, one must consider specific tonal requirements, especially when it comes to the frequency cutoff points. There are myriad design considerations that range from materials used to winding configurations. Tonal performance is totally dictated by the quality of steel core laminations, copper wire, dielectric strength, and competent coil winding and layering. The right output transformer is the final item in the signal chain of an amplifier, and will very much shape the tonal textures going to the speaker. If the output transformer is not right, then the amplifier's tone is going to be unlistenable."

Bruce Zinky, Zinky Electronics: "You want the voltages to be stable and not to waver, or sag under power. When you hit the strings hard, they should respond that way through the speaker. An amp that sags voltage doesn't have enough copper or iron in the transformer, both of which cost money (which is why most companies use such small ones). Old pawnshop amplifiers that drop a lot of voltage when you hit a cranked-up chord are cute for an effect or two, but not what you want when you are going for dynamic response at loud volumes. With an output transformer, you want extended bass response at maximum power, so that your tone and frequency response does not change when you turn your amplifier up at stage volume."

Replacing an output transformer that suffers from shoddy quality or has simply deteriorated with age can fundamentally alter an amp's tone. In fact, some designers go so far as to state that much of the credit for the warmth and character of tubes should actually go to their circuit partner, the output transformer. A similar claim: Substituting transformers can affect tone as much as substituting tubes, even more.

As always, the appropriateness of component types depends on the goals of the designer and your own taste as a player. (Some of the debates concerning transformers are addressed in The Tone Zone, Chap. 28.) If you want a clean sound with clarity and shimmer, you might prefer a higher quality, efficient output transformer. If you want great distortion, you might like a lower quality device that reproduces fewer frequencies, rolls off some highs, and softens the top end. Steve Carr: "Some of the transformers on those old plexi Marshalls aren't very good, technically, but that's a good thing, because when you crank them they're not showing you everything, and sonically you get a great result. The blackface Twin and Bassman have interleaved transformers, but in the Deluxe Reverb, for example, the transformer is non-interleaved, so there's some high-end roll off, and that's a significant part of its great sound."

Mark Baier: "Fenders like the late-'50s Twin and Bassman are the legendary examples of amps with interleaved transformers. Until that time, amplifiers were considered relatively lo-fi devices. Designers didn't worry too much whether they had expensive components like an interleaved transformer. The older layer-wound transformer is very inefficient, and yet those amps with older components are the ones some people look to today as the ultimate standard of tone."

The Guitar's Role in All This

The voltage applied to the tube's grid comes from two sources, internal and external. The negative voltage coming from the amp itself controls the electron flow when the tube is at rest, or "idling"; adjusting this control voltage is called *setting the bias*; see Chap. 6.

The other source of grid voltage is the signal from your guitar. When you bash out the opening riff to "Rebel Rebel," your guitar sends a small voltage to the grid. This operates the tube's "valve," altering the flow of current already set by biasing. The signal from your guitar kicks that idling tube into gear and puts it to work.

So, bias voltage is set at a predetermined level, and from there the voltage varies, becoming more or less negative depending on the signal coming from your guitar. As this voltage becomes more or less negative, it blocks more or less current. As Mesa/Boogie founder Randall Smith wrote in an article available on his company's website: "The bias conditions are what determine how much current flows through the big power tubes when you're not playing. And what drives your speakers is fluctuations in that current flow when you are playing."

You probably think of your guitar as a companion, a vehicle for artistic expression, a serious tool for making a living, perhaps an investment, even a work of art. You can also think of it as a variable frequency generator capable of unleashing torrents of subatomic energy.

Now you have a good idea of how your amplifier alters the signal from your guitar and prepares it for the next stage, the speakers. And yet while the effect of the amplifier, after all, is to amplify the sound of your instrument, it does not technically pump up your guitar's signal itself to a level sufficient to drive the speakers. That power comes from your amp's high-voltage power supply, not from your guitar.

The guitar's role is to influence *how* that power supply drives the speakers. As Randall Smith explains, we can think of the power supply as a jumbo DC battery of sorts: "What the amplifier does is to 'modulate' the power from that supply through the speakers in accordance with your guitar signal." Gerald Weber of Kendrick Amplifiers put it this way in *Vintage Guitar*: "It could be argued that a vacuum tube guitar amplifier is nothing more than a modulated power supply."

The DC at the front end of the transformer produces no current at the back end. This is essential: The signal that *does* make it through to the other side of the transformer is determined by what you play on your guitar.

Let's say you play an A note at 440 cycles per second (Hz). The signal you generate alternates between positive and negative voltage. You'll recall that when the tube is "idling," the steady-state current flowing through it is determined by the balance of opposing forces — the positive plate attracting electrons, and the negatively biased grid repelling them. (As always, opposites attract; likes repel.) Your guitar signal's *positive* voltage offsets the negative charge already set by biasing, reducing the obstacle to the flow of electrons; reducing the obstacle increases current. Your signal's *negative* voltage has the opposite effect, *adding* to the negative grid voltage set by biasing (increasing the obstacle, so to speak), which decreases current. So, when your signal hits the control grid, current both increases and decreases.

Through the functions of the power tubes, you are modulating, or fluctuating, by 440 times a second, the DC current at the front end of the transformer. The transformer blocks the current — *except* for those fluctuations. So, at the back end of the transformer, where the speakers are connected, *only the 440 Hz fluctuations appear*. Your speakers are driven by that 440 Hz signal, which you hear as an A-440 note.

Randall Smith: "Play a soft A-440 and the output valves in your amp let a little of that DC current flow from the supply through to the speaker, 440 times per second. (Now it's 440 Hz alternating current.) Play a *loud* A and the tubes allow a lot *more* current to flow, still at 440 Hz. Now that's basically how tube amplification occurs." Randall Smith's insightful dissertation, "Class 'A': Exposed & Explained," can be found at the Mesa/Boogie website and is quoted here with permission.

Wrap It Up

So there you have it, in a simplified overview. When you strike a note or chord on your Tele, Strat, or other 6-string variable frequency generator, you're converting sound into electricity; more specifically, you're generating a signal whose frequencies correspond to the frequencies of the music. That signal's tonal profile will be altered by many factors along its journey. It arrives at the tube's grid, where it modulates the biased current flowing from one electrode to another, which produces fluctuations in the current at the front end of the power transformer.

On the other side of the transformer, those fluctuations generate corresponding movements in the voice coil of an air-molecule pummeler, also known as a speaker (see Chap. 4). The coil moves the cone, which produces variations in air pressure whose frequencies, somewhat miraculously, correspond to the notes you played on your guitar. We call these pressure variations "sound." (A later section examines speakers, cabinets, and baffles in some detail.)

We have come full circle: The pickup's conversion of sound into signal has been reversed with the speaker's conversion of the amplified signal back into sound.

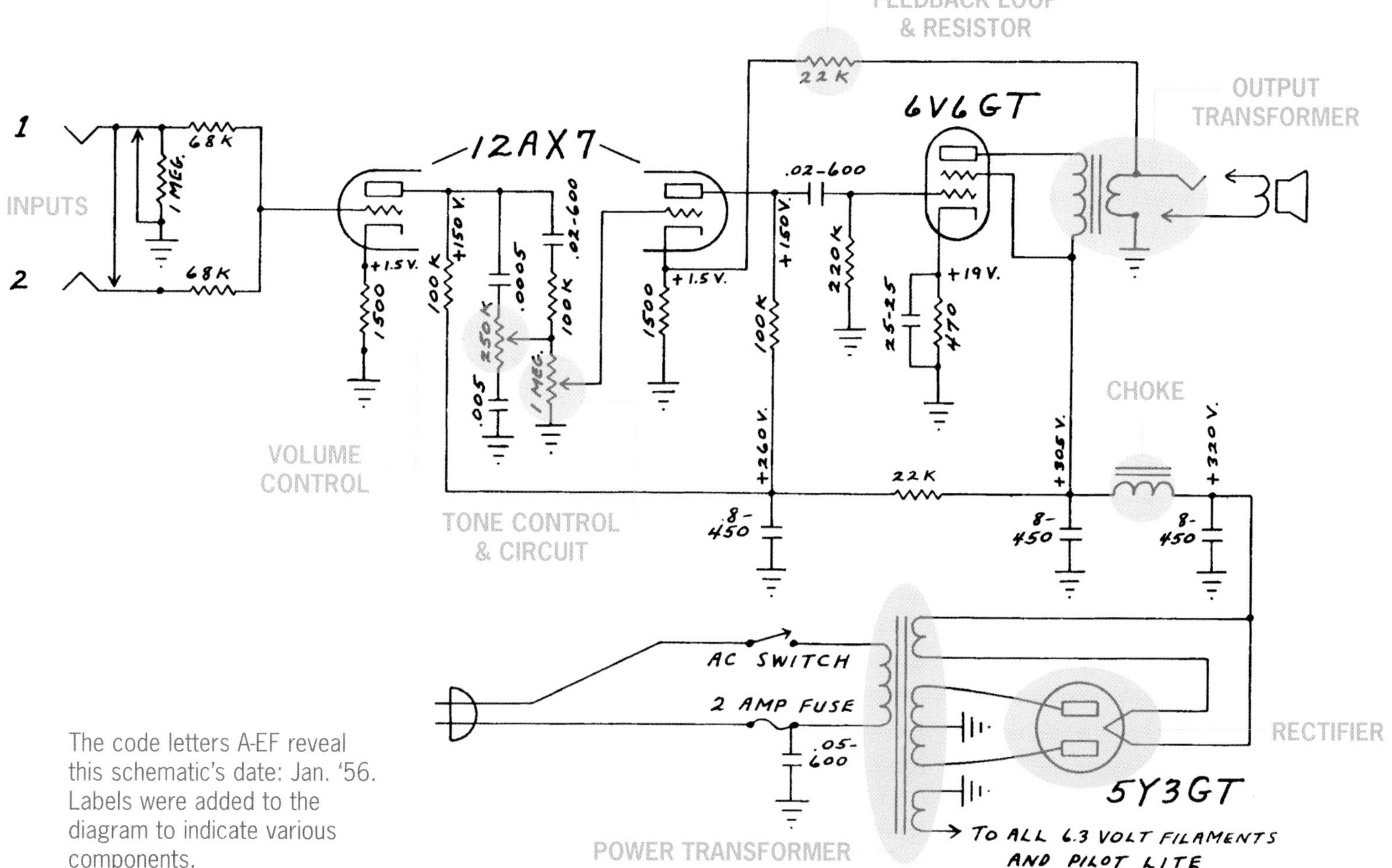

The code letters A-EF reveal this schematic's date: Jan. '56. Labels were added to the diagram to indicate various components.

CHAPTER FOUR

4

Speakers, Baffles, and Cabs

The Basics

Loudspeakers might be considered the vocal cords of your amplifier, and no discussion of Fender amps is complete without an examination of at least some of the important speakers Fender has used over the years. This and subsequent chapters include non-technical comments on various Jensens, Oxfords, Utahs, JBLs, Clevelands, and others. First, a quick look at how speakers work, and how they affect our sound.

Speaker Function

Your loudspeakers differ from those used in high-end audio in the same way your amp does: Rather than being designed to reproduce a sound efficiently and accurately (with "high fidelity"), they are designed for a very different reason: to color the sound. They are remarkably influential, an indispensable part of your instrument. In fact, compared to most of the elements in typical guitar amplifiers, speakers are among the most variable in terms of both sound and performance. Mark Baier: "There really is a big difference between a Jensen and a Celestion, for example. It's easy to discern, so I think it's legitimate to have a spirited debate about how they differ. It's a much more obvious thing than differences between tubes."

Transducers convert one kind of energy to another. Pickups, microphones and speakers are all transducers. Pickups and microphones convert sound into electrical energy, while speakers are electromechanical devices that convert that electrical energy back into sound. (Basic diagrams of conventional microphone and speaker elements look a little like mirror images of each other.)

A speaker's *voice coil* is a wire coil positioned within a magnetic field, the corollary to the pickup's magnetic coil at the front end of the signal chain. It is surrounded by a spider, a corrugated ring that acts like a spring. Its flexibility allows the suspended voice coil to move forward and back; those pulsations correspond to the incoming signal.

The spider is also attached to the smaller, inner ring (neck) of the speaker cone (driver, diaphragm), which typically is made of sturdy yet flexible paper and sometimes plastic or metal. The cone's outer ring is attached to the *surround* (or suspension), a flexible rim that supports the cone while allowing it to move. The whole assembly is held together by a metal frame, or *basket*.

Here's how it works: You'll recall that the motion of the guitar's strings disturbs the pickup's magnetic field, inducing a signal in the pickup's wire coil. Here the process is reversed. The signal — now massively amplified and impedance-matched — arrives at the speaker's voice coil, strikes its magnetic field, and pumps the coil in and out. This creates a corresponding piston-like motion in the suspended cone, which pummels surrounding air molecules and generates variations in air pressure. These fluctuations vibrate our eardrums and are perceived as sound. In other words, sound waves are variations in pressure sent through the medium of air. The faster the variation in air pressure, the higher the frequency of the wave. Higher-wave frequencies are interpreted by the brain as higher pitches.

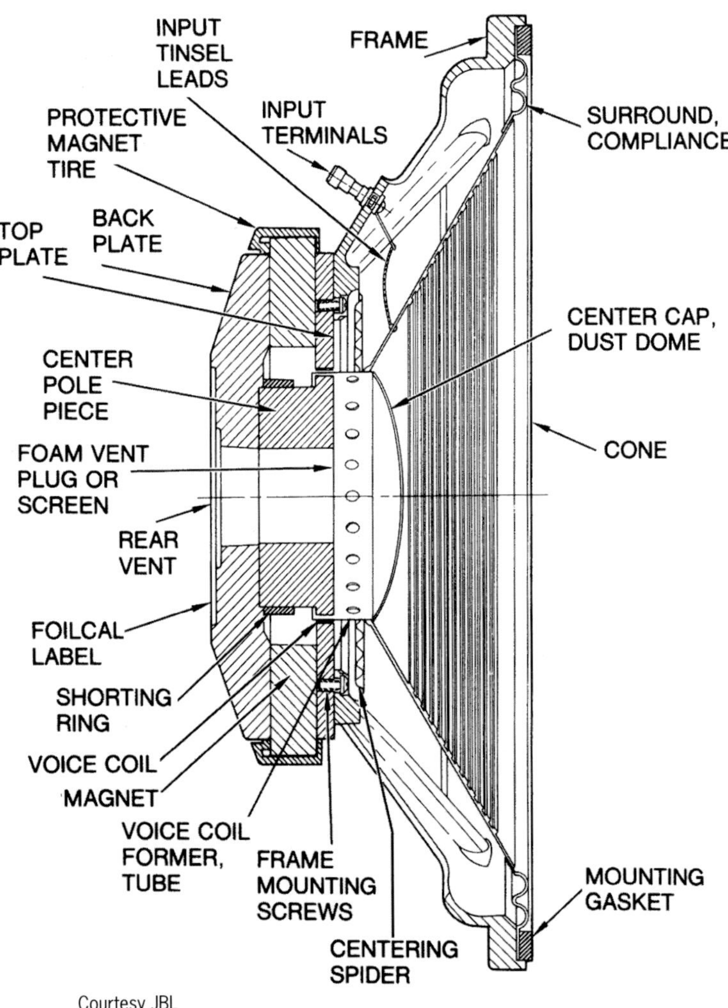

Courtesy JBL

Speaker Performance

Aside from its design, construction, power rating, and impedance, a speaker's sound is influenced by many of its performance characteristics, a few of which include:

its *transient response* (how quickly it reacts to a signal without blurring the sound),

its *damping factor* (how quickly it stops moving when the signal disappears),

its *efficiency* (how effectively it converts electrical signals into sound waves),

its *frequency response* (the range of frequencies it will produce; the range of human hearing is about 20 Hz to 20,000 Hz, although ultra-high frequencies above 20,000 Hz contain harmonics that can affect the way we perceive tone).

Speaker Size

Bigger cones move more air, which means more sound. This is not necessarily to say bigger cones mean *better* sound — that's a matter of taste and other subjective factors — but all other things being equal, an increase in cone area boosts the sound. In multi-speaker arrays, cone area is additive; a pair of 10s moves more air than a single 12, which moves more air than a single 10. However, loudness is not directly proportional to cone area. Two 12s are not literally twice as loud as a single 12, due to various factors, nor are they necessarily *perceived* to be exactly twice as loud, due to still other factors. Still, generally speaking, more cone area means an increase in perceived loudness.

Another factor is the amount of speaker travel forward and backward, or "throw." A longer-throw speaker can push a larger volume of air than a shorter-throw speaker of the same diameter.

Reproducing lower frequencies is a punishing task for a speaker, and it requires heavier-duty materials, an increase in the motion of the cone, and often a heavier magnet as well. Finally, it sometimes entails moving a relatively large volume of air. This may be accomplished with a longer throw, but more often it entails an increase in cone area, which translates to bigger speakers, or more of them, or both, as in a bass cabinet with eight 10s, four 12s, or a pair of 15s.

Large-cone speakers intended to handle mid to low frequencies are called *woofers*, while ultra-low frequencies are handled by even larger and/or beefier *sub-woofers*. While sub-woofers tend to be large, we should avoid overly broad generalizations such as "bass frequencies *always* require larger cones," or "big speakers can't produce highs." Given high-tech materials and recent advances in speaker design and cabinet design, it's possible to get good bass response from smaller speakers (even headphones can produce surprisingly low frequencies). And, some large speakers, even 15s, can sound crisp in the high end; a good example is the 15" Special Design Eminence speaker in the Vibroverb Custom. Sound and performance are further affected by how the speakers in a multiple-speaker array are connected to each other, and by cabinet design.

Multi-speaker Systems

Multiple speakers may be wired in series, in parallel, in series/parallel, or in parallel/series, depending on how their positive and negative terminals are connected to each other. One reason these connections are important is that they determine the total impedance, or "load," of the system.

In *series* connections, impedance is additive. For example, two 4 Ohm (Ω) speakers wired in series have a total load of 8Ω (4 + 4).

In a *parallel* array, impedance is reduced. Assuming the speakers are matched (all have the same impedance), the total impedance of the array equals the impedance of one speaker divided by the number of speakers. The classic late-'50s tweed Bassman, for example, has four 8Ω speakers wired in parallel, for a total load of 2Ω (8 ÷ 4 = 2).

A series/parallel system typically contains a pair of parallel-wired speakers and an additional pair of parallel-wired speakers, with one pair wired in series to the other pair. A parallel/series array is yet another method. The formulas for calculating total loads in such connections are somewhat complicated, but in any case it's essential that the impedance of the speaker or speakers matches that of the amplifier's output. A mismatch can result in poor performance or damage to the amplifier.

While the earliest Model 26s had Jensen G10RS field coil speakers, the majority had the 10" speaker shown here at lower left, a Jensen PM10C. The "PM" denoted "permanent magnet" and was later shortened to "P" on the blue bells. Perry Tate: "Invariably, those PM10C speakers [in Fenders] all have the same date codes, all within a week of each other. They're either 220631 or 220632, from the 31st and 32nd week of 1946. This lends credence to the often-repeated story that Leo got a great deal on a huge lot of them from Jensen; he supposedly got the idea for the [two-speaker] Dual Professional because he had so many 10 inch speakers to use up. This is one of them.

"The other two speakers here are both P10Rs, seen in any Fenders that used 10 inch speakers in the '50s, from Harvards and Vibroluxes to Supers and Bassmans. Somewhere in '57 or '58, Jensen changed from the gold foil label to the modern silver and blue label."

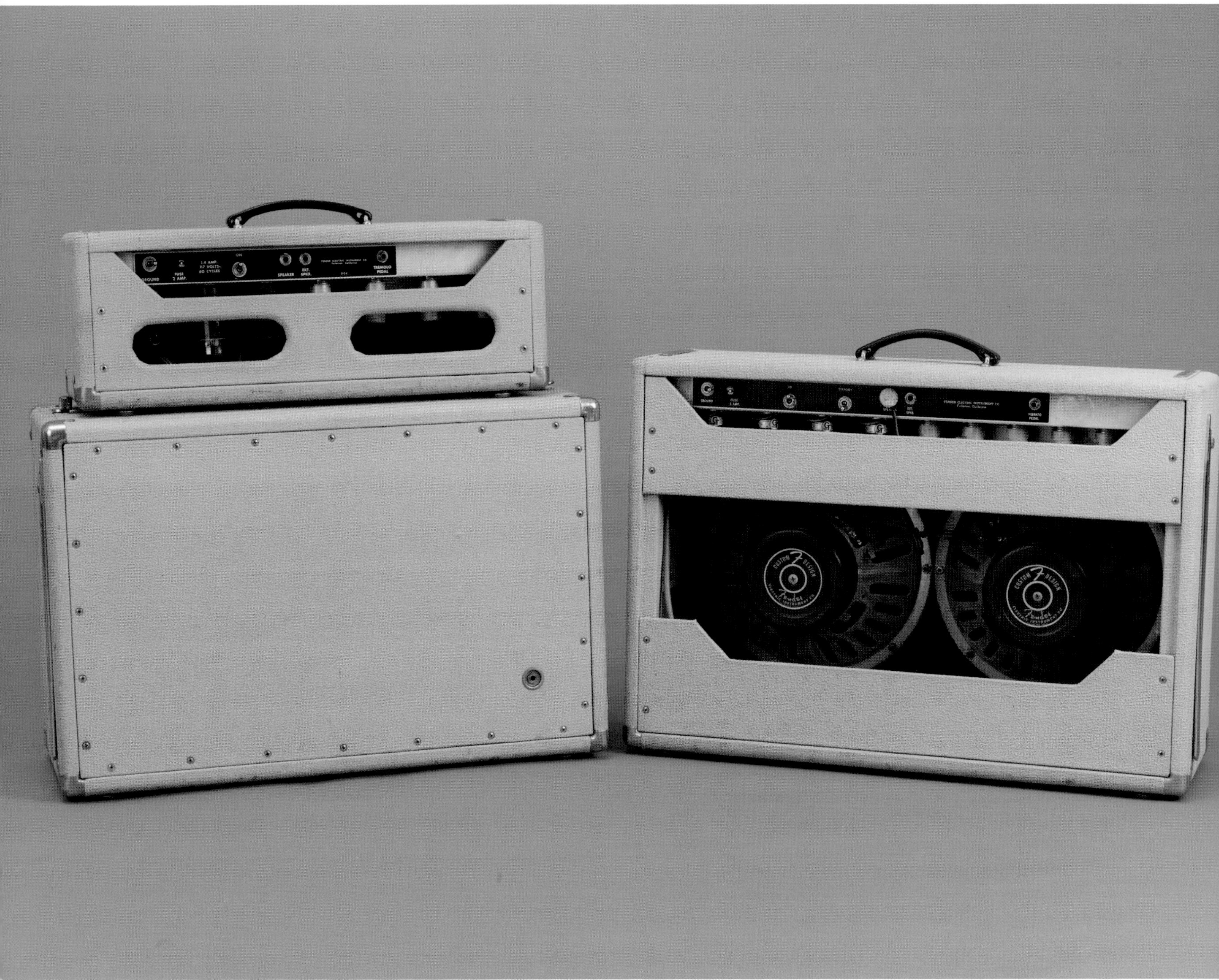

Fender has made many classic amps with both open and closed backs. Examples from the early '60s: a closed-back 1x10 Tremolux piggyback and an open-back 2x12 Twin combo.

Jensen's hefty P15N was used in tweed Pros and very early brown Pros.

The vaunted Jensen "blue bell" P12N. Perry Tate: "To many, this is the ultimate Jensen speaker. Offered only in the big box Twin, it always came with the large, round magnet cover, as shown here, and most sported the little red inspection sticker from the Los Angeles Building and Safety Department." Note the date code: 220903; 220 indicates Jensen, the 9 indicates 1959, and the 03 indicates the third week of that year.

Cabinet Design

Although its acoustical qualities are sometimes overlooked in favor of its cosmetics, an amplifier's cabinet is an essential contributor to its sound and performance. An amp and its speaker or speakers can be self-contained and enclosed in a single unit called a *combo*. Or, the speakers may be isolated from the amp and arrayed in a separate cabinet. Fender made only combo amps until the introduction of its first piggyback models at the outset of the Tolex era in 1960, and to this day it continues to make dozens of combo models, large and small. Recent examples of the two-piece design include the Custom Amp Shop Tone-Master of the mid-'90s.

A speaker cabinet can be either closed (sealed) or vented in some way. The mass of air trapped inside a sealed cab can dampen the speaker's movement, which affects speaker performance, for better or worse depending on your needs and tastes. Often found in stacks, sealed cabs generally handle more power and help focus the sound waves, dispersing the sound in a more directional fashion.

Vented cabs include the open-back combo amps made by Fender throughout its history. Remember that speakers move forward *and* backward, generating sound waves in both directions. (Recording engineers sometimes mike an amp in the back as well as the front.) Open-back cabs allow those rear-directed sound waves to make an easy escape. When reflected off surfaces behind the amp, these additional waves can contribute to a full, open, and pleasingly airy sound that helps fill a room. This is one reason why an open-back cabinet may sound less focused than sealed, more uni-directional cabs.

The Oxford 15M6 was used in the brown Pro from 1961 to 1963. It is similar to the 12M6 seen in Twins and Bassmans, and its evolution generally paralleled that of the 10K5s discussed in Chapter 13.

"When I came to the States, I got hooked up with Music Man and used one of their four-10 amps that was a lot like my old Bassman, only much louder. I used them for quite a few years. When I was with Eric Clapton, he was also using a Music Man. His had a big four-12 type cab, but he had just two 12s in there, set diagonally. He had the brilliant idea of opening up the back of the cabinet, cutting a hole in back. He would have them made for him with open backs, and I thought that was a cool idea. I know they're supposed to project more and be more efficient if the cabinet is enclosed, but I just like the overall sound with the open back, so I had some made up for me as well.

"I've recently come back to Fenders. My amp of choice at the moment is the Tone-Master 100 watt head with a big cabinet with four 12s. A friend of mine cut a slot in the back and it sounds great."

— Albert Lee

Fender at the juke joint: Jimmy "Duck" Holmes at the Club 2000, Clarksdale, Mississippi, 2006.

Other vented cabinets have holes in the front, or *ports*. Much more common in bass amps than guitar amps, ports typically redirect sound from the rear of the speaker to the front, where it is added to the sound generated by the cone's forward motion. Ports can be on the back or sides, too. Many bass cabs have rear ports, and a very few have side ports. One could argue that an open-backed cab acts like a port as well. At any rate, by designing ports that interact with the speakers and cabinet in specific ways, the frequency response of the system may be "tuned." (As we'll see, way back in 1952 and '53 Fender used a closed back with twin ports for the TV front Bassman.) An enclosure with ports tuned for enhanced bass response is called a *bass reflex* cabinet, a design dating back to the early 1930s. The terms "ported," "vented," and "bass reflex" are sometimes used interchangeably.

A *horn-loaded* cab entails a funnel-like component attached to the speaker. The horn makes the system louder by improving speaker efficiency, sometimes drastically. Fender generally avoids horn-loaded cabs, but one exception was the early-'70s, 435W 3-channel 400 PS bass amp, a real Goliath with an 18" speaker in a folded-horn (or "W bin") cab.

So which is better, sealed or open-back cabinets? It depends entirely on your needs, your tastes, your ears. There are many classic Fenders of both types.

Baffles, Phase Cancellation

Speakers are mounted to flat boards, or *baffles*, whose construction material, inherent resonance, and method of connecting to the speaker all affect the vibration and dispersion characteristics of the cabinet. Leo Fender's use of thin, resonant, and lightweight woods caused his speaker cabs to become another subtle yet important sound producer in the chain of amplification that begins with a disturbance in the magnetic field of the guitar's pickup and ends with pulsating speakers housed in a cabinet. Shane Nicholas: "Baffle boards are *very* important. On a late-'50s Bassman, for example, it's like the whole box is vibrating."

In an open-back cab, at some point the waves emitted from the front of the speaker meet with the waves emitted from the back; because these front and back waves are 180° out of phase, their interaction cancels certain frequencies. (Imagine a speaker mounted to a baffle of infinite size. The front waves would never "wrap around" the baffle — never meet the rear waves — so such cancellations would not occur. For this reason, sealed cabs are sometimes called "infinite baffle" enclosures.)

"I've got a '55 Pro that Sonny Curtis bought new. It's a very cool amp. He used it with Slim Whitman and with the Crickets, and he gave it to me quite a few years ago. It had the 15" Jensen, which I actually blew on a session, so I put a JBL in there. I've still got the Jensen, and I'll have it reconed. I've always loved Fender amps, but I often replace the speakers with something that will take a little more power. A lot of people like Fenders because of the way they break up, but I've never been one for a lot of distortion, so I prefer to use EV or JBL speakers so they can take more power and still be clean. The original speakers get a little flappy for me, a little soggy sounding. I like the tight sounds, especially getting the twang on the bottom strings."

— Albert Lee

Perry Tate: "This speaker looks as generic as can be, but it's a CTS, used in the blackface Vibroverbs and nonreverb Pros. People misidentify them all the time because they don't have prominent markings."

Although Fender occasionally used Utah speakers in Deluxe Reverbs, the standard speaker for those amps from 1964 to 1967 was this one, the Oxford 12K5.

Blackie Pagano, Tubesville Thermionics: "The frequency at which the front and back waves meet depends on the size of the baffle. Sound waves have a physical dimension. Lower-frequency waves are longer. The bigger the baffle, the longer the wavelength the speaker will reproduce before the wavelength reaches the edge of the baffle, goes around the edge, meets the back wave, and cancels. So, the bigger the baffle, the lower the frequency.

"We can think of a Fender with an open back as an 'open baffle' amplifier. It's not like a ported cabinet. Picture a speaker mounted in a door, just a plank of wood. Now fold the edges back into a box to make it portable. That's basically a Fender amplifier — an open baffle with folded edges. Then when you close the box, a number of things happen. The bottom line is, you get different low-end characteristics [in sealed cabs] than you do with open baffles because you don't have the same types of cancellations and roll-off characteristics."

Aside from these general categories (open back vs. sealed; combo vs. piggyback), cabinets are distinguished in many other ways: the composition and density of their materials, methods of joining corners, speaker mountings, hardware, coverings and speaker grilles, not to mention a whole array of acoustic factors influenced by their insulation, interior reflective properties, and size (in general, the larger the cab, the lower its frequency response).

Interactions

Your speaker/baffle/cabinet subsystem is like other parts of your amplifier in one respect: Designers take into account not only a long list of variables regarding each component but also the many complex ways in which the components interact.

While it can be useful to make "all other things being equal" comparisons, in fact all other things are not generally equal. To cite one example, substituting one speaker for another may entail different magnet structures, different power handling capabilities, or alterations to transformers or cabinet design, any one of which by itself can noticeably change an amp's sound. Another: While it is often said that a sealed cab produces more low end than an open back, remember that such generalizations may go out the window when we introduce other variables such as the dimensions of the baffle and the box; a big "open baffle" cab can produce more low end than a small sealed

A blackface Twin Reverb with factory JBLs. By 1973, Fender had gone to a slightly smaller cab for the Twin Reverb, so the speakers went back to a diagonal positioning. Mark Tate: "By this time JBL was painting their Fender speakers orange and black. This amp is an export model, as evidenced by the red voltage selector on the back panel."

box. Trade-offs are numerous. An increase in power output may entail a sacrifice of response in some frequencies, and so on.

The performance of the cab and indeed the amplifier itself is affected by its interaction with microphones, recording gear, and its environment — a room's size, shape, corners, absorptive and reverberant qualities, even the size and density of the audience. The perception of an amp's sound is also affected by its interaction with voices and other instruments in a band. A Tele lead pickup through a cranked 100W Tone-Master that sounds perfect cutting through a dense backdrop of sound may be painfully bright when played by itself in your living room.

Matching speakers to cabs offers another method of fine-tuning your tone. For example, Dave Gonzales of the Paladins reported that although he had previously found the sound of JBL 10s in open-back cabs to be harsh, when he put a pair of them in his closed-back Tremolux cabinet, they sounded full and warm while still maintaining their brightness.

Naming Jensens and Oxfords

Jensen speaker designations such as P10Q indicate the magnet type (P), speaker size (10″), and power handling capability (Q). Prefixes include PM or P (permanent magnet), C (ceramic magnet), and F (field coil magnet). The suffixes indicate a generally low power handling capacity in the R, S, and T types often found in Princetons and Champs, and medium capacity in the Q and P types. Greg Gagliano, in *20th Century Guitar*: "The Q and P suffixes … are especially good for multi-speaker amps up to 40 watts since multiple speakers divide the amp's total output power between them. For this reason, the P10Q is *the* speaker to have in the 5F6-A Bassman."

Collector Perry Tate: "With naming the Oxford speaker types, as you go forward in the alphabet you get bigger magnets and bigger voice coils. But with the Jensens, it's the opposite. As you go backwards through the alphabet — from the P10R to the P10Q, or from the P12R to the P12Q — you get the bigger magnet and voice coil."

"F" Stands for Fender: The JBL Connection

Heavy-duty JBL speakers were offered as premium options in Fender amps for years. Classic examples include the 16Ω D130 used in the early Vibrasonics. Perry Tate: "That was the first time a JBL was the stock speaker in a Fender, not just a special order, and it was their flagship model to boot. Of course, the D130F and D140F speakers that came in the Showman amps really put them on the map.

"Although JBLs cannot be dated by an EIA number, stock ones usually have either an ink stamp that matches the tube chart date code or a Fender factory stamp with the week and year [e.g., AA3563 = the 35th week of 1963]. You see these codes stamped sometimes on speakers, other times on the inside or outside of the chassis, and often on the inside of the cabinet. Some later '60s stock JBLs have a tiny Fender *F* punched into the foil JBL label; you have to look closely to find it. By 1968, Fender was apparently proud enough of JBLs to put special badges on the grilles of amps that came stock with them."

Shane Nicholas: "JBLs are not only rugged, but they also have a sound that many players prefer. They are bright, clean, and loud. If you had to take one combo amp to a rodeo gig and play it outdoors, unmiked, a Twin Reverb with JBLs is about as loud as it gets."

Among guitar players, the best known JBLs are the F series speakers in Fender amps. The man behind the F series is Harvey Gerst. He reports: "I was at JBL in the '50s and '60s, starting in shipping, then installation, Quality Control and Repair, and Customer Service. Later I started our Pro Department. I designed all four of the F series speakers — the D110F, D120F, D130F, and D140F. I was solely responsible for their proposal and development.

"When I was head of both the Quality Control and the Repair departments, we were getting higher than normal returns on the D131s and D130s in Fender amps. Repairing all those blown speakers was a pain. A few problems were obvious, such as rubbing from excess force and over-tightening at Fender during installation. Also, cones were cracking from outdoor use. I played guitar, and it seemed pretty simple to me that we needed some modifications to make these speakers more rugged. I wrote up a proposal to William Thomas, President of JBL, suggesting some inexpensive changes we could make to the 15" D130 and 12" D131. The modified D130 became the D130F, and the modified D131 became the D120F. I also suggested two new models that would give us a pretty complete line of MI

[Musical Instrument] speakers with a minimal investment, using parts from existing models. Those new speakers became the 10" D110F and the 15" D140F bass speaker.

"Regarding the D120F and D130F, there's some nonsense that we supposedly switched to 'rubberized surrounds,' and also went to heavier voice coils. Both claims are *totally* false. Instead, we used a high viscosity oil treatment on the surrounds to prevent them from drying out and cracking — and we had already been using this treatment on the D123, so it wasn't new. And we used standard voice coils, not heavier ones; I just opened up the gap a bit to prevent voice-coil rubbing from over-tightening.

"We completed the entire line, showed them to Fender and several other manufacturers, and they were an instant hit. Fender became our distributor for selling raw speakers to music stores, and we added Ampeg, Sunn, Standel, Mosrite, and Kustom as manufacturers who offered JBL options.

"The 'F' did stand for Fender — Fender was our biggest MI customer — but I didn't meet Leo Fender until after JBL, when I went to work with Harold Rhodes at Fender, also in the '60s. The F series speakers weren't designed because Fender complained, and they certainly weren't designed because any guitar players showed up at JBL with requests or suggestions. The two modified F series speakers were designed solely to make my life easier as head of the Repair department, and the two new F series speakers were thrown in as suggestions as to how we could increase MI sales without spending much money in R&D. That's the whole story."

It has often been reported that Dick Dale was in large measure responsible for the F series JBLs. Dale told *Guitar Player*: "At the Rendezvous, with 4,000 kids there, there was just no bottom. [Leo] couldn't understand what I was saying until I got him and Freddie [Tavares] to come down, and Leo said, 'I see what you mean.' We kept experimenting with the baffles and the speakers. We kept blowing those Lansing speakers, just ripping them. Finally we went to the Lansing Company and asked them how we could stop the speakers from coming apart ... they came up with the D130F."

Harvey Gerst is adamant that Dale's account is misleading. ("It took time for the surrounds to crack ... we had a *lot* of them, so [any one guitar player] would have been an insufficient sample to make that kind of change.") Still, Gerst's own detailed account does not preclude Dale's (perhaps indirect) influence. Leo Fender regularly received input from many musicians and dealers, either directly or filtered through Freddie Tavares, Bill Carson, Don Randall, salesmen, or other key associates. Dick Dale spoke to Leo Fender frequently (Dale told *Guitar Player* in 1981, "He'd call me every day. He'd call me at three in the morning and say, 'Dick, I've got something new!'"), and he visited the factory often. Richard Smith reports that as best he can recall, Mr. Fender himself backed up Dick Dale's version — that Fender and Dale visited JBL in person and requested tougher speakers. Perhaps they met with employees other than Gerst. (Dale himself reports in Chapter 13 that he met with executives rather than technicians; see page 237.)

Ralph Morris was at one time Director of Marketing for Tychobrahe, a pioneer in arena concert sound reinforcement. In 1960, he was assigned the task of upgrading the sound system at the Rendezvous Ballroom in Balboa, Dick Dale's "home" venue. On the Lansing Heritage website, he named his contacts in JBL Professional Sales, cited Dick Dale's thrashing of amps and speakers through ultra vigorous picking and high volumes, and reported that: "A couple of young sales engineers from JBL came down to Balboa, at the request of the Fender company, to see what they could do to improve the speakers for musical instruments. . . . The result of this effort was to design modifications to the D130 transducer, which was designated the 130F."

Harvey Gerst: "To the best of my recollection, *none* of the people he listed were even at JBL during the time the F series was created. We were on Casitas Avenue, and we didn't have any 'young sales engineers.' Hell, we didn't even have a 'professional division' until much later, and the first 'professional division' consisted of one person — me."

At any rate, the players blowing JBL speakers and the repair people stuck with fixing them all had the same goal. If JBL was aware that Fender amps and speakers were failing to meet the needs of a new generation of high-volume players, Leo Fender was certainly aware of it as well. Dick Dale and perhaps other players told Mr. Fender that for certain applications, his high-power amps needed sturdier, high-performance speakers. He found them at JBL.

Original Fender extension cabinets from the '50s and '60s.

Perry Tate: "These are neat because there were so few made they usually don't have a serial number, and when they do, it's often a very low number. The first one on the left has a Jensen P12R in a cab that would match a wide panel Deluxe. It actually has a 5C3 Deluxe tube chart, with a date code of CK — November '53 — and a handwritten serial number, 040. Next is a wide panel with a Jensen P15N, the only cab like this I've ever seen. Its code is CD — April of '53 — and the handwritten serial number is 0012. (See Date Codes on Tube Charts, Chapter 7.)

"The brown cabs seem to be the hardest to find. I know of one other, but this is the only one I've actually seen. It's a '61 with an Oxford 12K5, the same speaker as the Deluxe of that year. Interestingly, the black 12" cabinets came in two sizes. The first black one here matches a nonreverb Deluxe — perfect for the two or three guys who wouldn't cough up the extra dough for reverb but would spend it on a matching extension cabinet. The little brass badge on it is from a music store, H&H Music. The size of the next black cabinet matches a Deluxe Reverb. The last one on the right is the only 1x15 blackface extension cab I've come across. It has the same obscure CTS speaker seen in blackface Vibroverbs and nonreverb Pros.

"The tweed extension cabs came with a little wooden cleat inside for winding the cord. It had a hole drilled in it, presumably to stick the jack into after you wound up the cord; either that, or you'd run the cord through it to avoid accidentally yanking it off the speaker leads. It's in every tweed extension cab I've seen. The Tolex ones have a metal frame for winding the cord that looks like it came from the corner hardware store."

Fender uses Celestion speakers in a variety of models, including the Cyber-Twin SE, Princeton 650, Stage 1600, Stage 1000, the Super-Sonics, the Metalheads, and others.

Fender®

CHAPTER FIVE

5

Tube Basics

"What if Leo Fender had used 2A3s in his guitar amplifiers instead of 6L6s and 6V6s? Today's guitarists would likely have developed a very different idea of what a good guitar sound is."

— Eric Barbour, *Vacuum Tube Valley*, Fall 1995

Naming Tubes

Tubes used in American amplifiers typically have designations such as 12AX7 or 12AY7. The first digits approximate the required voltage of the heater: 12.6 volts in the examples here, but only when the tubes are connected in series. Preamps are typically wired in parallel, and in such cases these 12.6 volt tubes require half that voltage, or 6.3 volts.

Following the initial digit or digits are one or more letters, such as AX or AY. These mostly arbitrary codes differentiate electrical or mechanical details, and appear alphabetically to indicate a tube's design evolution; thus the 12AY7 followed the generally similar 12AX7.

The last digit typically indicates the number of elements in the tube. The 12AX7, for example, is a dual triode with two cathodes, two grids, two plates, and a heater — 7 elements in all. Finally, a letter may be appended to designate an updated version, such as 12AX7A. Unfortunately, this system is merely a generally agreed-upon scheme and is not airtight; plenty of tubes have arbitrary designations.

As the first "6" reveals, the 6L6GC power tube's heater requires about 6 volts — 6.3 to be exact, the same as the 12AX7 when wired in parallel. This matchup allows 12AX7 preamp tubes and 6L6GC power tubes (or other 6L6s, or their equivalents) to be connected to a single voltage source, as in many Fender amps.

Multiple Functions

Some tube types can serve multiple functions. The 12AT7, for example, was employed in Tolex-era preamps as a gain-stage tube, a phase inverter, and a reverb driver. Looking at it the other way, a single function can often be fulfilled by different but related tube types. For example, the 12AX7, 12AT7, 7025, 6SC7, 6SL7, and 6N7 all served as phase inverters in Fender amps.

Equivalency, Substitutions

"12AX7" does not identify only one tube. It classifies a whole family of similarly functioning tubes made in many varieties by several manufacturers in several countries over a period of decades. Many tube names are similar in this respect.

For half a century, tubes were widely used not only in consumer electronics but also in hundreds of industrial and military applications — everything from toaster-sized radios to room-sized computers. To meet these varying demands, a basic tube type was often modified to make it smaller, longer lasting, heavier duty, or whatever was required. These varieties carried their own names, as did European versions of familiar U.S. tubes. For example, members of the 12AX7A preamp tube family include the ECC83 (European nomenclature) and the 7025 (military or industrial nomenclature).

Although widely used in tube circles, "equivalent" is a slippery term. Tubes described as "equivalent" may differ in construction details, plate voltage, distortion characteristics, gain, and tone. In some reference sources, certain tube types described as being "the same" are indeed identical; in other cases they would be more precisely described as "equivalent but not identical."

The "transition style" blackface/blonde cab Bandmaster, shown here with a top of the line Jaguar guitar, was equipped with two 7025s, a 12AX7, a 12AT7, and a pair of 6L6GC power tubes that pumped out a loud 40W.

Tubes with similar or even nearly identical names may not be similar at all in construction, sound, or performance; they may be less "equivalent" than tubes with utterly different designations. The various 6L6s are good examples. Blackie Pagano: "First came the metal-enclosed 6L6, then the 6L6G, which was the glass-enclosed equivalent — the one in the ST shaped bottle, or 'Coke bottle.' The 6L6G's ratings are much different from the later 6L6GB, and also different from the 6L6GC. Except for the fact that these are all beam power amplifier tubes, they are very different from each other. Guitar amp designers cheated quite a bit on the ratings of these tubes, but there's only so much you can cheat. Just because two tubes say 6L6 in the prefix does not mean their parameters are anywhere nearly identical. They can be designed differently, sound completely different, and act differently in circuits."

These distinctions are essential to understanding tube equivalency. Blackie Pagano: "A 5881 (6L6WGB) is roughly the equivalent of the 6L6GB. It is *not* equivalent to the 6L6GCs that were used in, say, blackface Twin Reverbs. In a blackface Fender we typically see 450 volts, especially in an amp that's not cathode biased. That's 450 volts at the plate in a 6L6GC. That 6L6GC can handle 500 volts. But the maximum plate voltage for a 5881 is only 360. It's a very different tube. If you take a 5881 and throw it in a blackface Twin Reverb, it's going to blow up."

While we can generalize about the effects of this tube type vs. that one ("American" vs. "British" distortion, for example), it is also true that different manufacturers' versions of the "exact same" tube can perform differently. As Aspen Pittman points out, two 12AX7 preamp tubes can sound as different from each other as two guitars. Another example: He characterizes the performance of a particular 5751 as being such a departure from original specs as to render it "a 5751 in name only."

Replacements

If we are replacing original tubes simply because they have worn out and are no longer available, we might select substitutes intended to duplicate the performance of the originals. On the other hand, we may want something a little different — a bit more headroom, a tendency to distort sooner, a little more gain, etc. *The Tube Amp Book*, for example, reports that some of Groove Tubes' clients carry along several types of 12AX7s and select them according to the needs of particular gigs or even the acoustics of different rooms. (These are highly discriminating players, indeed.)

Keeping it in Perspective

Some guitarists obsess about the tonal qualities of one tube or another, often for good reason. But most major manufacturers and many boutique builders choose from only a few of the "same" or supposedly similar tubes, and yet their amps may sound and respond very differently from each other, either (1) because, as noted here, tubes that are supposedly "the same" may actually differ in important respects; or (2) because any amp's sound is affected not only by tubes but also by power output, circuit design, speakers, cabinets, other components, etc.

We wouldn't buy a guitar solely because of the weight of its tuners or the composition of its string nut. Then again, aware that such seemingly trivial factors can indeed affect tone, builders do consider them among the many ingredients in a successful recipe. Similarly, tube type is essential to an amp's performance, but it's only one factor among many.

Replacement tubes that work fine in some circuits may not work as substitutes for those same original tubes in other circuits, so play it safe. Never substitute tubes of different types or nomenclature without consulting a reliable amp tech.

JAN, Mil Spec

One common abbreviation is JAN, which stands for Joint Army Navy and indicates a tube designed for the U.S. military. As you would expect, tubes built to military specifications ("mil spec") are renowned for their durability, the assumption being, anything tough enough for the battlefield is tough enough for the bandstand. (The great Tung-Sol 5881/6L6WGB was used in many classic tweed Fenders. According to *The ToneQuest Report*, it could also be found in the circuitry of B-52 bombers.) The fact that high-tech military gear no longer uses tubes is one reason for a decades-long decline in quality control among manufacturers and the resulting decline in their tubes' consistency and reliability.

Mil spec tubes are indeed rugged, long lasting and mechanically stable — sometimes more so than their "civilian" counterparts, sometimes not. Increased ruggedness sometimes translates to less susceptibility to undesirable microphonics as well as greater power handling capability. Note that mil spec variants of some tubes may be constructed somewhat differently than their civilian counterparts and may sound different as well.

NOS

Another common abbreviation is NOS. This means New Old Stock, a paradoxical description that would be more precisely termed OBU: Old But Unused. The advent of transistor technology was so rapid that countless brand new tubes were suddenly deemed useless and relegated to dusty storerooms where they languished for decades. With the persistence of tube technology in guitar amplifiers and high-end audio (and given the near obsession with all things vintage), some of these old but unused tubes have acquired an unexpected usefulness, even a magical aura. They're a bit like that gleaming Mary Kaye Stratocaster that was stuck in an attic with its tags and strap and hasn't seen the light of day since Elvis got drafted. Today, the mere thought of an unclaimed set of RCA clear-tops sends tube aficionados rooting around flea markets like truffle hogs.

The lure of tubes that have been sitting there for eons — just *waiting* in The Warehouse That Time Forgot — is indeed compelling, but be careful. Some of these relics are mere rejects, tubes that years ago were judged inferior for sale but which are, technically, NOS. And, like any gear that's been lying around for a long time, the sonic value of NOS tubes depends not only on their initial quality but also on the conditions under which they have survived all these years.

New Old Stock items are often expensive. While some 12AX7s can run fifteen or twenty bucks, others can cost a hundred; a pair of particularly desirable 6L6GCs can cost more than twice that much.

NOS tubes may restore the authenticity of a vintage amp, and they may sound good in a new one, but be aware that responsible tube retailers spend tedious hours sorting the good ones from the bad, while others play fast and loose with tube designations. Some cads even resort to relabeling new tubes with vintage codes and counterfeiting the packaging. So purchase tubes with care from trustworthy sources. As always, listen. Trust your ears. Can you hear the difference? Is it worth the extra cost? (The debate about old vs. new tubes is addressed in The Tone Zone, Chap. 28.)

Made in the USA (and Mexico, and Singapore)

John Mark was a cryptographer and radio operator who went on to acquire vast experience in electronics engineering. He designed and developed tubes for RCA; other employers and clients included the U.S. Air Force, NASA, and the Atomic Energy Commission. In recent years he has been a consultant to Groove Tubes, a modern-day link to the glory days of tubes.

John Mark explained to Aspen Pittman that as a consequence of plummeting market demand, some prized NOS "American made" tubes from RCA, GE, and Sylvania were actually assembled elsewhere. Aspen Pittman: "It wasn't profitable to keep those factories going at five percent capacity, so while they continued to make a high percentage of the components in the U.S., some of the processing and assembly was done in places like Mexico and Singapore. Even that was not enough, and the primary U.S. manufacturers finally shut down."

12AX7

Although diminutive in appearance, the 12AX7 miniature dual triode is a giant among tubes, the most commonly used guitar preamp tube in history. Hundreds of variations have been manufactured in factories all over the world. Developed in the mid 1940s by RCA, it marked a leap forward in low-noise, high-gain applications. The 12 volt 12AX7 made early appearances in the 5C4 Super and 5C5 Pro as replacements for the 6 volt 6SC7s that were typical of the octal preamp tubes previously used throughout Fender's history.

Fender typically installed 12AX7s in the preamps of narrow panel models — usually in conjunction with 12AY7s — until the shift to 7025s in most of the early-'60s Tolex models (7025s are members of the 12AX7 family). All current tube Fender preamps use 12AX7/7025s.

12AX7 preamp tubes.

6V6

Designed in late 1937 by the RCA team that had developed the 6L6, the 6V6 was adopted by leading hi-fi companies and later by manufacturers of guitar amplifiers. It was used in many less expensive, low-power models, including several of Leo Fender's historic amps of the mid and late 1940s. Bright sounding at low volumes yet readily driven into a fat, warm distortion, it contributed to the signature tone of many classic electric blues guitar recordings.

A single metal-envelope 6V6 powered the Champion 800 of 1948 and 1949, as well as the "two-tone" Champion 600 of 1949 – 1953. The updated 6V6GT was used in later generations of the little dynamo, through the narrow panel models (which ran all the way to 1964, the last of the tweeds) and the blackface Champs of the mid 1960s.

A similar evolution is seen in the Champ's slightly bigger brother, the Princeton. Official schematics and layout diagrams show a single metal-envelope 6V6 in Princetons from 1948 to 1955, and a glass bottle 6V6GT in the 5F2 (early 1956 schematic) and 5F2-A (1957) versions; the GT was used throughout the Princeton's narrow panel phase. The power tube complement was doubled to two 6V6GTs for the brown Tolex and blackface Princetons, as well as their successor, the blackface Princeton Reverb of the mid '60s.

Everybody's favorite amp for mid-sized gigs, the Deluxe is another 6V6/6V6GT-powered classic. A pair of these sweet sounding bottles powered all tube Deluxes from the late '40s through the blackface Deluxe Reverb, the last Deluxe of the Leo Fender era. Fender continued to use 6V6s of one variation or another in silverface Deluxe Reverbs and early-'80s Deluxe Reverb II's, as well in the reissue '65 Deluxe Reverb.

Other Fenders powered by a pair of 6V6s (or 6V6GTs) included various tweeds — the Vibrolux, Tremolux, and some Supers. At the beginning of the Tolex era, these last three models switched to 6L6s, or 5881s, or in the case of rare, early Tremoluxes, 6BQ5s.

6L6

The 6L6 is the great American power tube, radiating a righteous glow in hundreds of models manufactured by dozens of companies. As opposed to the "British sounding" EL34 and EL84, the 6L6 and its variants are revered for their character, clarity, and warmth. To a significant degree, they are responsible for what has come to be called the classic American tube amp sound — or "Fender," for short.

The 6L6 was developed in the mid 1930s by RCA engineers who modified the grids on existing tubes in an effort to gain higher efficiency and lower distortion. Immediately successful, it found applications in the kinds of products Leo Fender worked on every day — table radios, record players, and PA systems. Manufactured by RCA, Philips/Sylvania, General Electric and others, early examples of the tube came in metal containers. Revised versions were housed in glass bottles and carried a G ("Glass") suffix. As is the case with the 12AX7 preamp tube, "6L6" came to classify a whole family of tubes: 6L6, 6L6G, 6L6GB, 6L6GC, etc.

A 6L6 can put out about 25W, or about 50W or more per pair, about 100W per quad; these outputs can vary signifi-

6V6 beam power tetrodes.

6L6 power tubes. Aspen Pittman, in *The Tube Amp Book*: "Many folks don't realize that Jimi Hendrix' classic guitar amp tone often came from a Fender blackface amp in the studio, and these always had the GE 6L6 clear top."

cantly among 6L6s produced by different manufacturers. Except for the relatively low-power models fitted with 6V6s, Fender amps from the mid 1950s through CBS generally were equipped with two or four 6L6s of one sort or another, or their equivalents. Mark Baier: "It made sense for Leo to use 6L6s. They were the most reliable tube on the market, and reliability was so important to him. He could have used EL34s, but those tubes are much more fragile. The 6L6s will take a lot of punishment, and when they do short out they generally don't take a lot of other stuff down with them, whereas when an EL34 goes south, all sorts of crazy stuff can happen.

"And the 6L6 is still in use to this day. There's an evolution to the construction and some modification, and it went from producing about 25 watts a pair to about 60 watts a pair today, but philosophically the concept is virtually unchanged for over half a century. Can you name one transistor that was being used even ten years ago that is still being used today? The 6L6 is still going strong, and the same can be said of the 12AX7. It's a real testament to how well those things were designed in the first place."

Aspen Pittman: "John Mark was the head of RCA, and he taught at Princeton and was on staff with Albert Einstein. He helped write the book on how to manufacture tubes, and he knew the guy personally who invented the 6L6. He thought the 6L6 was so popular with musicians because unlike a lot of tubes of the time, it had a big cathode — a big gas tank, so to speak. It's very dynamic. You could really get the pluck of a guitar, but in a lot of other tubes that pluck would become soft and squishy."

B.B. King lets the good times roll in a big way, accompanied by a Fender combo and a bevy of tassel-swingin' admirers.

7025

The popular, bright sounding 7025 was intended as a low-noise, military/industrial equivalent to the 12AX7, and was introduced into the Fender line in 1960's new Vibrasonic and Concert. The Champs continued to use 12AX7s, and the brown Deluxe and blackface Princeton Reverb used both 7025s and 12AX7s. Otherwise, the use of the 7025 preamp tube was virtually universal across the line for the last five years or so of the Leo Fender era and beyond, from the early brown and blonde Tolex amps through the blackface period (including the reverb models) and into the silverface amps of CBS.

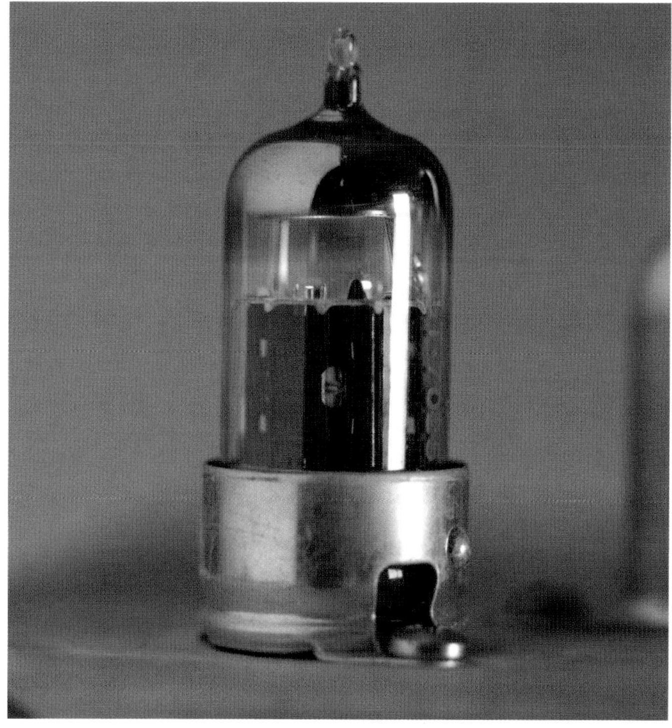

The classic 7025 is credited by *The Tube Amp Book* for "the characteristic sound of the Fender Tolex years."

5881

The stubby little 5881/6L6WGB is a beam power tube originated by Tung-Sol for use by the U.S. military. It was introduced in the September 1950 issue of *Radio & Television News*, in an article by Tung-Sol engineer C.E. Atkins. Mr. Atkins wrote: "For a long time there has been a growing demand for a tube with dynamic characteristics like the 6L6 but of a design that would cope more vigorously with the problems encountered in a heavy-duty audio output tube. The [5881] is short and stocky to ensure mechanical ruggedness. With shorter active electrodes, alignment is more readily maintained .... In the 5881, grid emission has been dealt a severe blow by the use of gold plated wire on this electrode .... the screen grid is painted with a special carbon suspension which is quite porous and, of course, very black. Its color, as any physics student knows, increases the radiation of heat away from it so that it can run cooler."

Fender used 5881s in several models in the '50s, including the 5B6 wide panel Bassman and F series Twins and Bassmans. But it was in the early 1960s when 5881s enjoyed their real Fender heyday. By late 1960, several brown Tolex models had switched from a pair of 6L6GCs to a pair of 5881s, including the Concert, Super, Vibrasonic, and Pro. Some went back to 6L6GCs as they evolved to blackface.

The 5881 is a beam power tube originally designed for rugged military use.

Rectifier Tubes in Pre-CBS Fenders

5Y3, 5Y3GT: Metal-envelope 5Y3 tube rectifiers were typically used in smaller, relatively low-power Fenders of the late '40s through about 1953.

5U4, 5U4G (GA, GB): From the late 1940s through the entire age of tweed, Mr. Fender often specified 5U4/5U4G (GA, GB) rectifier tubes in amps with a little more power.

GZ34/5AR4: While the vast majority of tweed Fenders were equipped with 5Y3s or 5U4s of one variety or another, exceptions included two of the most revered amps of all time, both tweeds: the 5F6-A Bassman and the high-power ("big box") 5F8-A Twin. Both appeared toward the end of the 1950s, and both were equipped with the rectifier tube of the future, the GZ34/5AR4. The GZ34/5AR4 rectified the current in most of the low-powered or mid-powered models in blonde and brown Tolex. It continued to be used in most tube-rectified blackface models from 1963 to 1965, and into the early CBS era.

Exceptions? Of Course

We should avoid unqualified generalizations such as "narrow panel Tremoluxes had 5U4s." That statement applies to only some of those models. From 1955 to 1960, narrow panel Tremoluxes were factory-equipped with at least three different rectifier tubes. Other outwardly identical Fenders also had different rectifiers.

The nomenclature of a tube reveals its evolution (the 5U4 was succeeded by the 5U4G, then the 5U4GA, etc.), but there were overlaps in Fender's use of "older" and "newer" rectifier tubes, as was the case with other components in many Fender products. A newer version of a particular amp may actually have a stock rectifier with an "older" designation.

The tale of the Pro provides another particularly anomalous cautionary tale. The brown Tolex version had the brand new solid state rectifier, while the mid-'60s blackface versions, including the Pro Reverb, went *back* to the GZ34/5AR4 tube, and the late-'60s silverface/CBS version went back further still, to the even "older" 5U4GB. Greg Gagliano: "I believe the switch back to 5U4GBs was one of simple economics. They were probably more abundant and cheaper. The 5U4GB does the same job as the GZ34 by supplying nearly the same milliamperage, but draws less filament current and has more 'sag' than the GZ34."

Solid State Rectifiers

Fender has used both tube and solid state rectifiers in its tube amps, often progressing from the former to the latter. Several models converted to solid state rectifiers when they transitioned from tweed to Tolex, while others made the switch in the middle of their blonde Tolex phase.

As noted, Fender uses solid state rectifiers in all models except those reissues where authenticity calls for original-spec tube units: The '59 Bassman LTD, '64 Vibroverb Custom (switchable to solid state for the César Diaz mod), '57 Twin, '65 Super Reverb, and '65 Deluxe Reverb.

Note: Subsequent chapters specify many details regarding tubes in various models.

Like ringin' a bell: Chuck Berry plays Carnegie Hall, June 1965.

This neighborhood dance party is like countless others in the mid-'60s, except for the house band — Frank Zappa and friends.

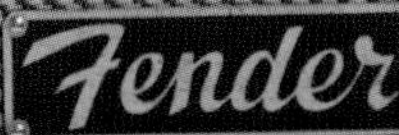
Fender
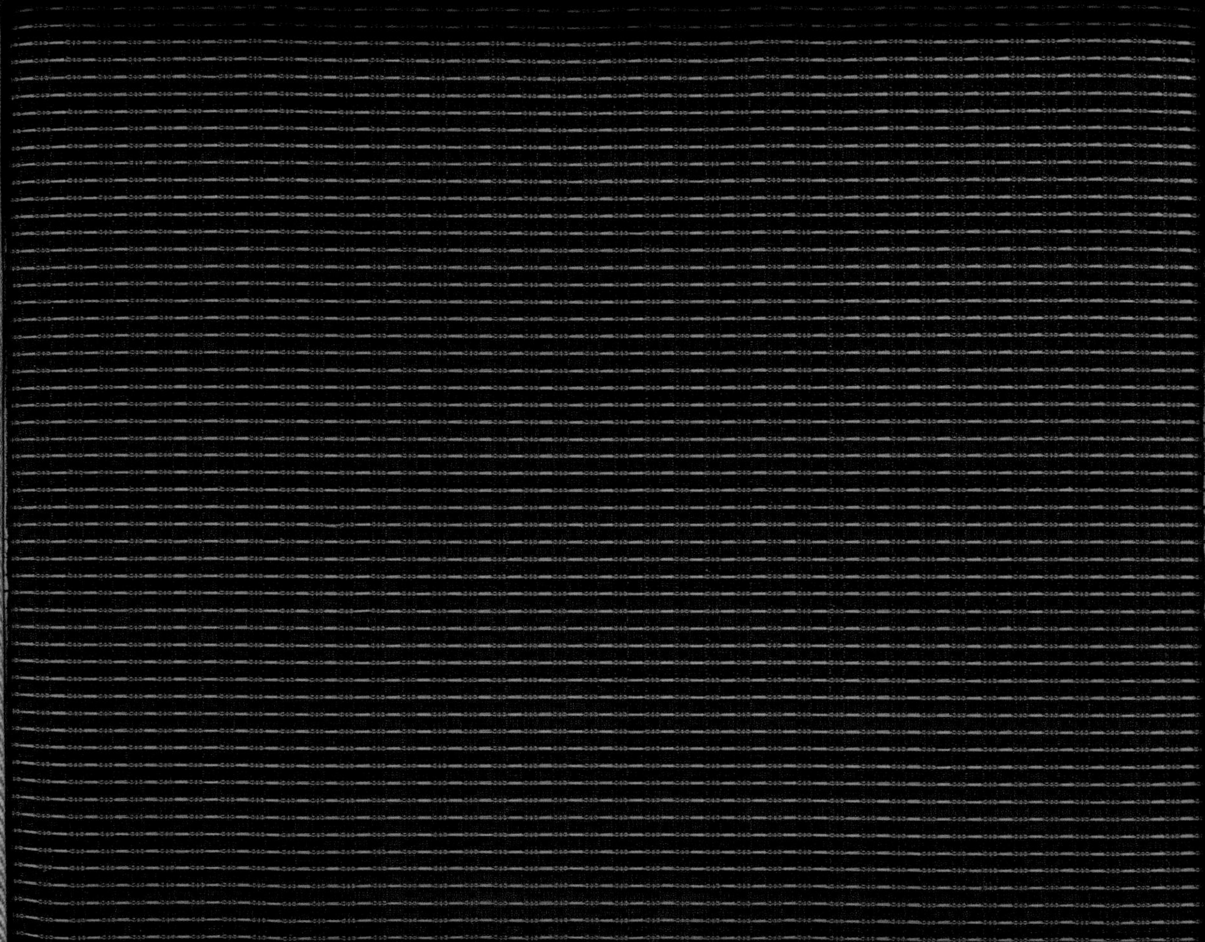

CHAPTER SIX

6

Tube Performance

Bias, Single-Ended vs. Push/Pull, Class A vs. Class AB

An Introduction to Bias

Think of how your car idles when you're sitting at a stop sign. Although you're not going anywhere, the ignition is on and the engine is running. If the car's idle is set too high, the engine will over-rev and waste fuel; too low, and it will underperform and may even stall.

When the amp is turned on, a vacuum tube "idles" when there is no signal present. Although it's not doing any work, electrons are flowing, and that flow is controlled by grid voltage. Adjusting this "control voltage" is called setting the *bias* — or in the words of author Ritchie Fliegler, "The Can of Worms in Pandora's Box." (It's a controversial topic.)

If tubes are biased in such a way that too much current flows, then they idle too high, too hot. They may perform fine. Then again, they may produce less power and more noise (the bad kind), even when you're not playing. If tubes are running hot enough, their plates may turn red, a warning of potential damage not only to the tubes but also to the amp itself.

On the other hand, if tubes are biased in such a way that too *little* current flows, then they are idling too low, running cold. The tone may sound weak and thin, with an unpleasant, "rattly" distortion even at low volumes. Tubes may last longer because they're not doing as much work, but they won't sound as good. They won't sound as loud, either.

In short, biasing affects tube function, tube life and general amp performance, including tone and distortion characteristics. Preamp tubes in modern amplifiers — in fact, in all Fenders after 1953 — are typically cathode biased (self biased) and need no adjustment, so discussions of biasing usually refer to power tubes (although exceptions are noted below). Let's examine general info about each biasing method and then Fender's various approaches over the years.

Like the Deluxe, the Princeton shown here kept its cathode biasing through the end of the tweed era. Teagle & Sprung speculate that retaining their cathode biasing might be "one possible reason for the popularity of the small amps in recording studios."

Biasing Methods

The classic *RCA Receiving Tube Manual* specifies three methods of biasing:

Fixed bias: Grid voltage is obtained from a fixed source such as a tap on the voltage divider of the *power supply*. By far the most common method of biasing power tubes, fixed biasing entails an independent supply of negative voltage connected to the tube's grid. It sets, or "fixes," the control voltage at a consistent level. Here, "fixed" means consistent; it does not necessarily mean permanent. A fixed bias may be adjusted, either by a potentiometer provided for that purpose or by substituting resistors of different values in the voltage supply. Many Fender amps have a small recessed screw on the rear or underside of the chassis, allowing easy bias adjustment.

Cathode bias: Grid voltage is obtained from the voltage drop across a resistor in the *cathode* circuit. This method of setting negative grid voltage is also called *self biasing* because it generates its own voltage rather than requiring a separate source for it.

Grid resistor bias: Grid voltage is obtained from the voltage drop across a resistor in the grid circuit. This now obsolete method was briefly used on preamp tubes in several early-'50s Fenders.

Fender's Matt Wilkens: "Here's the deal: The current flow is controlled by the grid voltage with respect to the cathode. For example, in most fixed bias amps, the output tube cathodes are attached to ground. The grid voltage is pulled below ground, making that voltage negative with respect to the cathode. The more negative (less positive) the grid voltage is with respect to the cathode, the less current flows. As the grid voltage becomes *less* negative (more positive), more current flows.

"In a self bias amplifier, a voltage develops across the grid resistor. The grid is usually referenced to ground. Since the cathode is of higher voltage than the grid, the grid voltage is again negative with respect to the cathode. Once the grid is at the same voltage as the cathode, the tube is in saturation [more on saturation in the following discussion of class of operation]."

Let's recap. Opposites attract; likes repel. Both principles are at work inside a tube. The negative electrons are attracted to the positive plate, but repelled to some extent by the grid's negative voltage. Setting the bias adjusts the balance between these opposing forces. As the RCA manual summarizes, "the object is to make the grid negative with respect to the cathode by the specified voltage" — regardless of biasing method.

Pre-CBS Power Tube Biasing

Most modern Fenders have push-pull output stages with a tube bias adjustment that enables varying the idling current in all the power tubes at once. In the vintage era, however, Leo Fender and his associates took several different approaches to biasing. Over the years, most of the pre-CBS line progressed from cathode biasing to fixed biasing. In the blackface era, the medium and larger amps were also fixed bias, but with a bias adjustment pot. Exceptions are noted below.

Late '40s to mid '50s: Cathode biased models included the Champion 800 and 600, the wood-body Professional ("woodie Pro"), the original Dual Professional, the TV front Bassman and Pro, the V-front Super, and all the wide panel tweeds.

Mid '50s through 1963: Fixed bias models included narrow panel versions of the mid-sized and larger amps, plus the entire brown and blonde Tolex lines. (See Exceptions, below.)

Generally 1963 through 1965: Fixed biasing (with adjustment pot) was used for almost the entire blackface line, including the new reverb models.

Exceptions

The low-wattage amps with 6V6 output stages retained their cathode biasing for years after their bigger, 6L6-powered tweed brothers adopted fixed biasing with the shift to narrow panel cabs in '55. For example, the Princeton and Deluxe stuck with cathode biasing through the end of the tweed era, then switched to fixed in the brown and blackface models. The Champ was unique in its use of cathode biasing all the way through to blackface.

The big picture: From the first of the narrow panels in the mid '50s through the brown and blonde Tolex era of the early '60s, almost all Fenders had fixed biasing. Exceptions: Champ, Princeton, Deluxe. When almost the entire line switched to blackface in '63 (the AA864 Bassman in '64), they went to fixed bias with an adjustment pot. Exceptions: Champ (still cathode biased) and Princeton (fixed, but without the adjustment pot).

Bias: Sound and Feel

Comparing the effects of biasing methods can be useful, so long as we remember that biasing is only one contributor to an amplifier's complex tonal character.

Cathode biasing is typically described as imparting a softer sound, "spongy," less stiff. It yields to your touch in a certain way, readily responds to your pick attack, and tends to round off the edges of your sound. When the amp is cranked, it tends to drive tubes into distortion a little sooner, and the sound is often described as a sweet musical sustain. On the other hand, fixed biasing has more headroom and delivers a bit more power. It's faster, more present.

Steve Carr: "Cathode bias has a little more of a midrange bloom and seems to have more clean sustain. Fixed bias tends to have a lot of bounce, a spanky sound, like if you snap your strings it'll track it really fast."

Mark Baier: "The cathode biased amp is a little more compressed. The harder you hit the strings, the more noticeably the tubes respond. It's more elastic, you might say, maybe more vocal. And you get a sense of feeling your own picking dynamic."

If this sounds familiar, it's because comparing biasing methods echoes the comparison of tube and solid state rectifiers, the former lending a more compressed sound and a dynamic feel, the latter delivering more power, more headroom, and a tighter response. These same aspects of sound and feel are raised again in the discussions of Class A vs. Class AB later in this chapter.

Perceived advantages of each biasing method depend on what you're looking for. One player might swear by cathode biasing's dynamic feel, while another might find it too mushy, too slow. One might prefer fixed biasing's quick response, while another might find it too clinical sounding. It's a matter of taste.

Generalizations aside, it's a mistake to think all cathode biased amplifiers or all fixed biased amplifiers sound and feel the same. They don't, any more than all foods prepared with pepper taste the same. Some amps do not fit

Lenny Kravitz, 1990.

these generalizations because of other aspects of their design or components. Steve Carr: "Designers can try to balance any of the negatives in other parts of the circuit, like when they pair a plump sounding preamp with a lean sounding output section, or they match an expensive transformer that reproduces a lot of high frequencies to other components that soften the sound a bit. It's the same with bias. Other parts of the circuit can complement some aspects of biasing and offset others."

Output Stage Configuration

Every amplifier may be categorized according to its *output stage configuration* and also its *class of operation*. Although these considerations are related (and sometimes confused), they are independent. Output stage configuration describes methods of arranging tubes in a circuit: single-ended, or push-pull.

Single-Ended

Single-ended is the one-lane highway of circuit designs. The signal voltage remains intact, and it runs along one path from tube to tube.

It's possible to have a single-ended amp with more than one power tube (Gibson's Gibsonette, for example), but all Fenders with single-ended output sections have only one power tube. Classic examples are the dirt simple, great sounding Champs (all the way through silverface, including the Vibro Champs), and pre-Tolex Princetons.

If we think of incoming alternating current as depicted by familiar sine waves, both the positive halves of the waves (the tops; above the 'x' axis) and negative halves (the bottoms) are amplified by a single power tube. Steve Carr: "In single-ended amps, the elements are all in a line, like three guys pulling on a rope. It's possible to get substantial power out of a single-ended design, but it gets expensive, so they're typically low power — say, 10 watts and under."

Push/Pull

The push/pull configuration is far more common. Instead of remaining intact, the incoming signal is split into halves that are amplified separately and later recombined. Again thinking of a succession of sine waves, a *phase inverter* tube (typically a dual triode such as a 12AT7, 12AX7, or 7025 in Fenders) splits the signal into diametrically opposed top (positive) halves and bottom (negative) halves. Over the years Fender has used several types of phase inverters, or phase splitters, all of which pass on the split wave components to separate power tubes.

One tube amplifies the tops of the waves, and another amplifies the bottoms. This is sometimes described as one tube "pushing" the signal while the other "pulls" it. In more powerful circuits, the wave tops get their own *pair* of tubes, as do the bottoms. So, push/pull designs always entail a phase inverter, and always use an even number of power tubes, usually two or four but sometimes more.

The majority of Fenders (generally, all of the mid-power amps) have two power tubes in a push/pull configuration. High-power tube Fenders (about 80W to 130W) typically have four power tubes in push/pull, including the late-'50s "big box" Twin and later Twins, the silverface Super Bassman, the various Showmans, and the Custom Amp Shop's Dual Professional.

At the output transformer, the amplified positive and negative halves are merged back together and sent to the speakers. As Jack Darr wrote back in '65, "The two tubes are fed signal voltages so that their grids are 180 degrees out of phase, or exactly opposite; one goes up while the other goes down. Because the plates follow the grids, plate current rises in one tube and falls in the other at the same time. By using a push/pull output circuit, *more than double* the output power of one tube is obtained [emphasis added]." Most output stages in Fenders as well as other brands employ the push/pull method because its increased efficiency means more power and less heat.

All Fenders with a single power tube are single-ended, and all Fenders with two or more power tubes are push/pull. Amp tech and columnist Terry Buddingh: "Single-ended amps are known for their rich lower-order harmonics. They just sound different from push/pull amps, which can be characterized as sounding more aggressive because of their stronger upper-harmonic emphasis."

In a single-ended Fender, that lone power tube can never rest. By contrast, in push/pull circuits, one side rests while the other works. This distinction will prove key in our next discussion, Class A vs. Class AB.

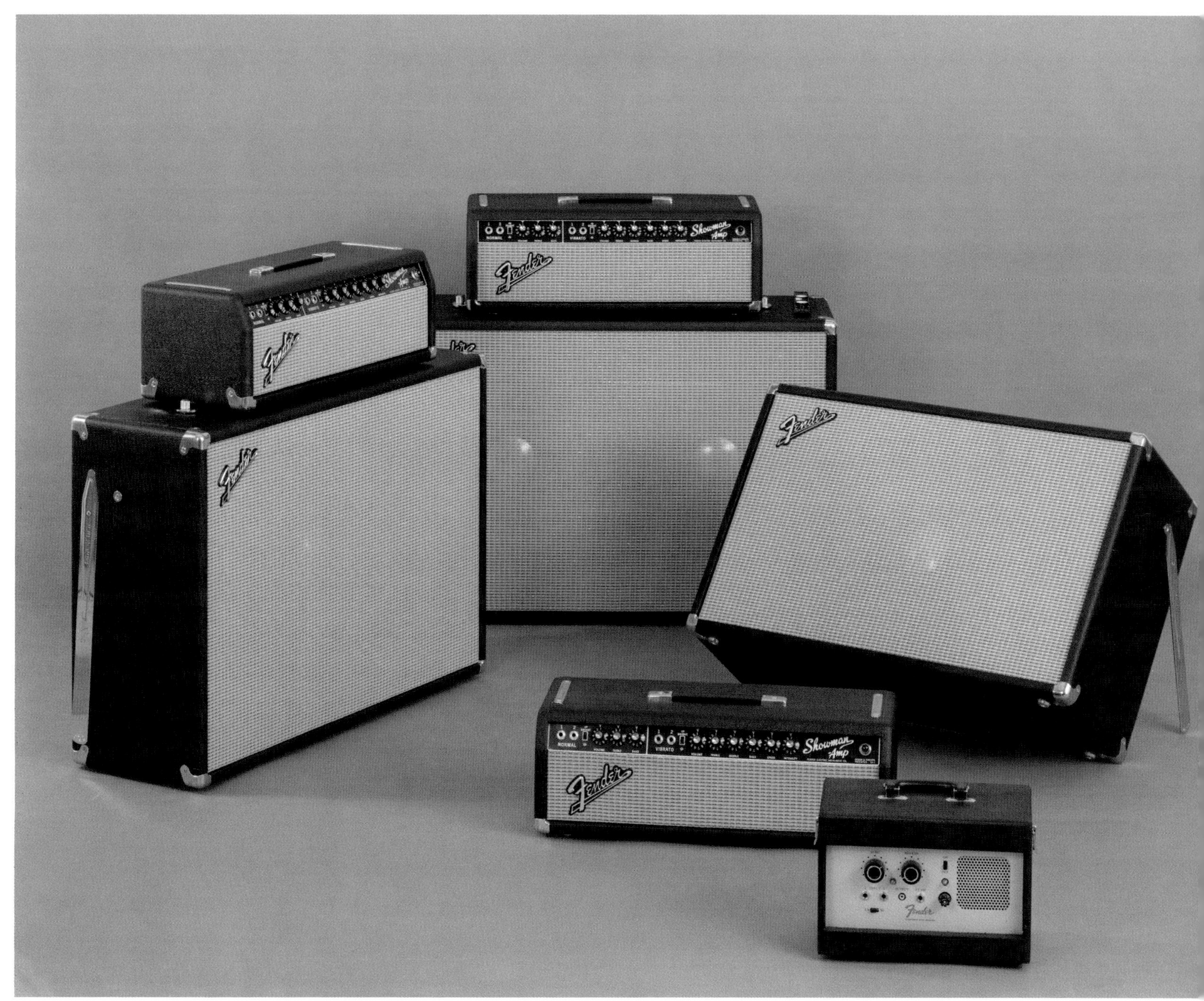

From the mid 1950s onward, most Fenders had fixed biasing. When most models evolved to blackface in '63, they added a bias adjustment pot. These fixed bias Showmans are pictured with Fender's Electronic Echo Chamber, a tape delay unit introduced in 1963.

Class of Operation, Cutoff and Saturation

You'll recall that in tubes such as a typical triode, the grid's negative voltage repels and thus regulates the electrons attempting to leap from the warmed-up cathode to the plate. In an idle tube, adjusting this negative voltage balances the electron flow and is called setting the bias.

The concept of "adding a negative" may seem odd at first glance, but "increasing the negative voltage" is just another way of saying "lowering the voltage." *Negative* grid voltage blocks current, so the lower the grid voltage, the lower the current. In fact, if the grid voltage is low enough, it will block the current altogether, a state called *cutoff.* Beyond cutoff, a further reduction in grid voltage has no effect, as the current is already reduced to zero, or cut off entirely.

At the other extreme, if grid voltage is increased to the point where current flow is at its peak, that state is called *saturation.* Further increases in grid voltage cause no increase in current flow, which is already maxed out.

The terms *Class A* and *Class AB* refer to biasing methods. As with the topic of bias itself, class of operation is controversial. (Terry Buddingh: "Writing about amplifier classes is like diving into the Everglades wearing a jacket made of raw meat.")

Regardless of the class of operation, basic grid functions remain the same: Power tubes are biased so that the grid is negative with respect to the cathode. Less grid voltage means less blockage of the current, so when the signal makes the grid voltage less negative, more current flows in the tube. When the signal makes the grid voltage more negative, less current flows.

Class A

According to the *RCA Receiving Tube Manual*, a Class A amplifier is one in which "the grid bias and alternating grid voltages are such that *plate current ... flows at all times.*"

Class A is the oldest method of running tubes and is universally employed for preamp stages and sometimes for modern power amps in models other than Fenders. In Class A, plate current flows for the entire 360 degrees of the incoming signal; in other words, the tube is "in conduction" (as opposed to cutting off) for 100% of the cycle. Because the valve never completely shuts off, outgoing plate current flows at all times. Even when the tube is idling (that is, with no incoming signal), there's always some movement of electrons through the grid, typically about 50% of the maximum possible current. To accomplish this, bias is set midway between saturation and cutoff, a method sometimes called "biasing in Class A." In Class A operation, tubes "idle" when no signal is present, but they never rest.

Class B

Fender's Class AB is a hybrid of Class A and Class B, so let's briefly consider the latter. You'll recall that Class A was biased midway between cutoff and saturation, and that the tube was in conduction (as opposed to cutting off) for 100% of the cycle. By contrast, Class B output stages are biased for much lower idle plate current — to the point or almost to the point where idle plate current is reduced to zero, or cut off; now the tube is in conduction for 50% of the cycle. At this state, current flow remains at zero until the arrival of input voltage from your guitar. The result is a vast increase in efficiency: At idle, no power is consumed, and no wasteful heat is produced.

Fender's Class Act: AB

According to the *RCA Receiving Tube Manual*, a Class AB amplifier is one in which "the grid bias and alternating grid voltages are such that *the plate current ... flows for appreciably more than half but less than the entire electrical cycle.*"

So, in Class A, grid bias is set midway between saturation and cutoff. In Class B it's set at cutoff, or close to it. In Class AB, as the name suggests, bias is set somewhere between these points — significantly closer to cutoff than in Class A, but not as close as in Class B. Some idle current is flowing, but nowhere near the maximum available. In Class AB, plate current flows for more than half (180 degrees) of the input cycle but significantly less than for the full 360 degree cycle. In other words, the tube is in conduction for more than 50% of the cycle but less than 100%. So, tubes are on at all times (whether signal is present or not), but not as "on" as they are in Class A.

For many decades now, almost all Fender amps have been Class AB. Leo Fender's intention was to reach an ideal compromise that secured the advantages of both Class A and Class B while avoiding their downsides. The modern Fender company remains committed to Class AB.

Premium
5881/6L6WGC
P/N 039214

Exceptions include vintage Class A Champs and Princetons with a single 6V6 power tube, making them departures from the Fender norm in both output configuration (single-ended rather than push/pull) and class of operation (Class A rather than AB). Shane Nicholas: "We did have a switch on the back of the Prosonic, introduced in the mid-'90s; it let you switch to a 'Class A' *sound*, but it wasn't true Class A, and I never felt it was a big advantage. Some people thought it would turn the amp into a Vox AC30, but of course the preamp, EQ, compression, speakers, etc. were all different." Matt Wilkens: "There is a misconception that an amp that has a cathode bias output stage is Class A by default. This is not true. An amp that has cathode bias can be Class A or AB. A tube amp with fixed bias can also be Class A or AB. The switch on the Prosonic made it 'more class A,' and made it cathode bias — *more* like a Vox AC30, but not a Vox AC30."

To Class AB's proponents, its high efficiency, increased power, cool running, longer tube life, headroom, and tonal properties make it the best of both worlds, and indeed, it's the most common operational class for medium to high powered guitar amps. Author, columnist, and manufacturer of Kendrick amplifiers Gerald Weber, in *Vintage Guitar*: "I prefer Class AB amplifiers. Everything we've ever heard by Jimi Hendrix, Stevie Ray Vaughan, Billy Gibbons, Eric Johnson, Robben Ford, etc. is Class AB." Matt Wilkens: "Class AB is the most common mode of operation because it gives the best power/performance value. At Fender, we currently do not make any Class A or single-ended tube amps."

Putting It All Together: Single-Ended, Push/Pull, and Class

In his very useful *The Guitar Amp Handbook*, Dave Hunter links output stage configuration and class of operation by reminding us that in true Class A, tubes are working the entire cycle of the waveform. They never rest, because there's no other tube to take up the slack. In a push/pull arrangement, however, one side shuts down during some part of the cycle while the other side amplifies. Such devices are Class AB amplifiers.

Dave Hunter: "By definition, one side of the [push/pull] tube pair of a Class AB amplifier rests for at least some portion of the cycle … in simple terms, that's really all there is to the definition of Class AB — or at least all you need to worry about." Regarding the single-ended amplifier, with its solitary power tube: "This single power tube can't rest for any portion of the waveform … so it instantly fits the definition of Class A." That is, because the single power tube never rests, plate current flows at all times.

This is only an introduction to the topics of class of operation and output stage configuration. It gets much deeper. Gerald Weber was asked about one of the most famous of all Class A amplifiers, the Vox AC30. He replied, in *Vintage Guitar*: "After much discussion … I'd say the class of operation is a design intention, whether or not the design is 100 percent valid by strict textbook definition." He went on to say that an amp can reach cutoff and saturation at the same time, that under certain circumstances a Vox AC30 could be driven into Class AB, and that "even a single-ended tweed Champ … can drive into Class AB if driven with a very hot pickup." All of these complexities are well beyond the scope of this book. In an interview with this author, THD's Andy Marshall began a sentence by saying, "One of the ways of interpreting Class A …. " Indeed, despite the clarity of the textbook definitions, several of these concepts, when applied in actual circuits, are subject to interpretation.

So how do you judge an amp if you don't have electronic experience or a physics degree? Just plug in and crank up. If you play more than one instrument, try the amp with a couple of guitars. Try it in different listening environments. Try it up close, and from across the room. Feel it. Listen to it. You'll know.

Class of Operation: Sound and Feel

Among some vintage amp connoisseurs, "pure Class A" has the sexy rep. Tubes are always fully operational, "on deck," ready to amplify an incoming signal instantaneously. This constant current can impart a smooth, compressed sound. Class A's emphasis on certain harmonics lends a musical richness and, according to its adherents, provides the ultimate in vintage tube warmth. Some players swear they can not only hear a difference but feel it as well; they sing the praises of Class A's dynamic, touch sensitive response.

But Class A has its drawbacks, too. Compared to AB, it is less efficient, runs hot, puts out less power, provides less headroom, and wears out tubes faster.

We're not concerned with Class A except as it contrasts to Fender's Class AB, but beware: Many amps that are marketed as "Class A" are actually cathode biased Class AB units. Terry Buddingh: "Many guitar players are obsessed with the 'Class A' buzz word. While there are many push/pull amps that have staked questionable claims to the Class A moniker, single-ended amps virtually guarantee true Class A operation."

Dave Hunter: "A lot of voodoo is talked about Class A … The main defining factors of 'that sound' we think we're seeking in a Class A amp have more to do with cathode biasing and a lack of negative feedback." (Negative feedback is explained in Chap. 11.)

Biasing, Class, and Transformers

In yet another example of the multi-layered interaction among an amplifier's components, one of the most important aspects of amplifier class involves the output transformer. The "duty cycle" of a transformer is full, or always "on," in Class A, but working only "part time" in AB. Ritchie Fliegler: "In Class A, the transformer is always 'lit up,' compared to Class B or AB. This requires transformers in Class A to be comparatively big and heavy. In AB, the transformer can be, say, 'half' the size because it's only doing half as much work at any given moment."

So, the class of operation affects not only an amplifier's tone, response, power, heat, tube life, and headroom but also the design of the transformer, which in turn affects its own, overlapping set of parameters — tonal warmth, efficiency, harmonic character, touch response, note detail, distortion characteristics, sustain, etc.

Summary

Biasing methods (fixed vs. cathode), output stage configuration (single-ended vs. push/pull), and class of operation (Class A vs. Class AB) are mostly independent of each other, although certain associations are common and others are unusual.

In practice, Class A is typically associated with single-ended output stages. To flip it around: Single-ended amps are almost always Class A.

Class AB is typically associated with push/pull outputs. To flip it around: Almost all push/pull amps are Class AB.

Single-ended amps are almost always cathode biased (and Class A). To flip it around: Most true Class A amps, and most amps that are *claimed* to be Class A, are cathode biased. Very few fixed bias amps are truly Class A.

Most fixed bias amps are Class AB, and most cathode biased amps are Class AB as well. Exceptions: the single-enders.

The larger, higher-powered Fenders changed from cathode bias to fixed bias in the mid 1950s.

Except for those with a single power tube, pre-CBS Fender output stages are push/pull, Class AB.

All current Fender output stages are push/pull and Class AB, with fixed bias.

That's a lot to remember, perhaps too much for most of us. Bottom line: Relationships among all these variables produce audible results as measured in frequency response, headroom, touch sensitivity, the amount and quality of distortion, actual loudness, perceived loudness, and more.

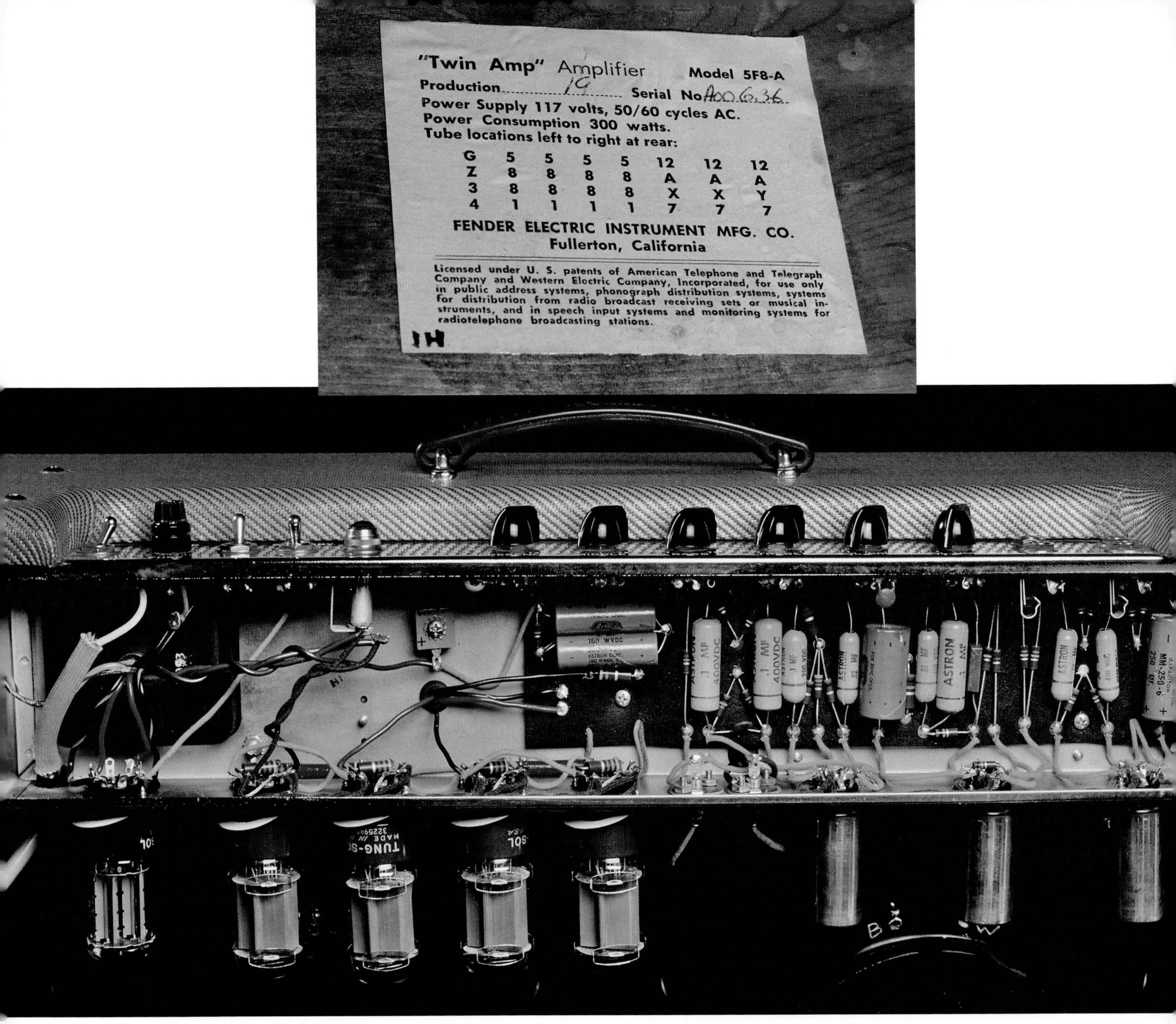

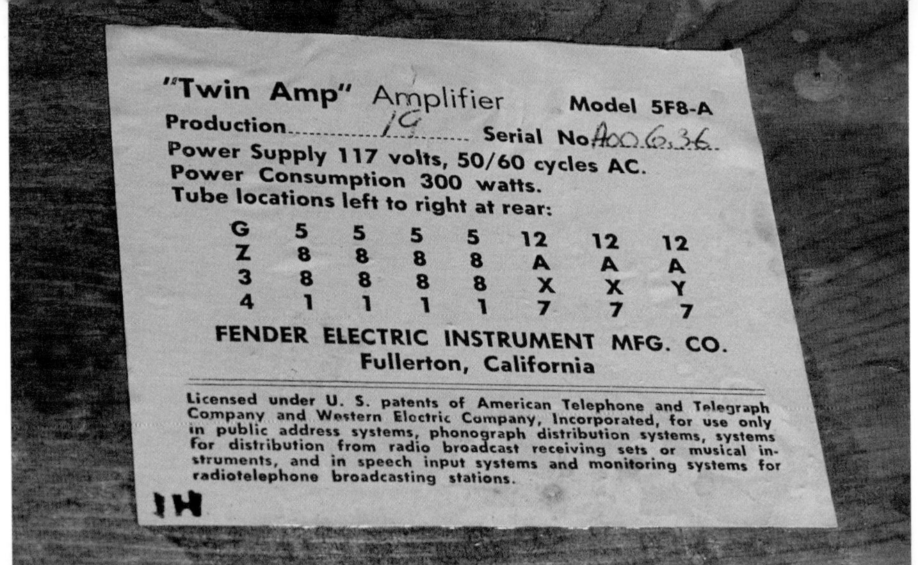

"Twin Amp" Amplifier Model 5F8-A

Production 19 Serial No A00636

Power Supply 117 volts, 50/60 cycles AC.

Power Consumption 300 watts.

Tube locations left to right at rear:

G	5	5	5	5	12	12	12
Z	8	8	8	8	A	A	A
3	8	8	8	8	X	X	Y
4	1	1	1	1	7	7	7

FENDER ELECTRIC INSTRUMENT MFG. CO.
Fullerton, California

Licensed under U. S. patents of American Telephone and Telegraph Company and Western Electric Company, Incorporated, for use only in public address systems, phonograph distribution systems, systems for distribution from radio broadcast receiving sets or musical instruments, and in speech input systems and monitoring systems for radiotelephone broadcasting stations.

IH

1959 "big box" Twin, serial no. A00636, and its tube chart. On the chart, "Model 5F8-A" identifies the decade of production (5 = '50s), the version or generation of the circuit (F), the model number (8, Twin), and a circuit update (A). Note that this particular amp comes from production run number 19. The date code at lower left is IH, or August '59 (although it looks like someone may have inked over the code by hand, the period is indeed correct for the 5F8-A). The tubes, from right: a 12AY7 at the front end, two 12AX7s, four 5881 output tubes, and a GZ34 rectifier tube.

CHAPTER SEVEN

7

Electrical Bloodlines

Classic Fender Amps: A Circuitous Approach

Grouping Fender amps is a bit like organizing all your relatives for a series of family reunion photos. You could put all the women in one photo, all the men in another, each spanning several generations. Or, group them by generation: kids in the front row, then parents, then grandparents. Or by family name: all the Schwartz cousins in one group, all the Williamses in another. Then start mixing categories: the Williams boys, the Schwartz girls, just the grandmoms, and so on. Fender's extended family of vintage tube amplifiers also may be categorized under several methods, all of which are useful and sensible: era of manufacture, power rating, speaker array, 6L6 vs. 6V6 power tubes, etc.

Two schemes prevail. The first addresses cosmetics and outward features such as cabinets, face plates, coverings, and knobs. After the somewhat miscellaneous styles and occasionally mystifying nomenclature of the Model 26s, Champions, and V-front amps, the line settled into a more cohesive look, generally progressing from the TV fronts to the wide panels, narrow panels, and finally the combos and piggybacks with front mounted controls — brownface, blackface, then the silverface look of the CBS era. Cabinets and coverings progressed from the historic woodies through various tweeds of the 1950s and Tolexes of the 1960s and thereafter.

The other common method of grouping Fender amps is by model name. Like the cosmetic approach, it's useful. Any Champ is smaller and simpler than any Deluxe of the same vintage, which is smaller and simpler than any Twin of the same vintage.

Such methods are effective for dating the approximate era of an amp or family of amps — for any given model, the narrow panel followed the wide panel, Tolex followed tweed, black followed blonde, and so on. But as anyone familiar with vintage Fender amps can tell you, these generalizations have many exceptions. Several periods within the vintage era (the mid 1940s through the mid 1960s) saw overlaps of older and newer styles in cabinets, face plates, coverings, or all three.

Sometimes these overlaps occurred by design. The lifespan of the original tweed Champ, for example, extended through the blonde and brown Tolex period and even into the blackface era. Other times, Fender was simply using up a batch of components before installing their replacements. (Students of Fender history will see parallels to the guitars.

A "newer" Stratocaster might feature leftover parts, such as an "older" decal, pickguard, or fingerboard.)

Why all the inconsistencies? Simple: Leo Fender and his associates were designing a line of products to be sold *right now* in a highly competitive marketplace that was subject to shifts in popular tastes, general economic trends, and advances in technology. Everyday production was further affected by shortages of some parts, excesses of others, updates in tooling, and so on. In the early days, even a couple of workers calling in sick for a week or two could result in products going out the door with minor inconsistencies.

Another factor was Mr. Fender's almost relentless pursuit of perfection. Little concerned with the internal uniformity of every wide panel Pro or every blonde Bandmaster, he constantly strove to improve his products, sometimes changing a spec in the middle of a production run. Designing scores of products that would appear to evolve with consistency over a 60-year company history was hardly a priority at Fender or any other manufacturer.

Under the Hood

The amplifiers' appearances, features, and model names were based to a significant extent upon marketing considerations. Internally, however, we find in some groups of amps strong family ties; in others we find fundamental distinctions that are not suggested either by cosmetics or by model names. In fact, when trying to get a handle on what makes these amps tick, cosmetics and model names can actually lead us astray. For example, consider the blackface Pro and the "transition" Bandmaster (blonde cabs, black control panel) from the mid '60s. Their appearances and model names suggest they are very different amps: One is a black combo with a 15" speaker, the other a blonde piggyback with two 12s. In fact, their circuits are nearly identical.

It works both ways: Fenders with different looks or model names can have similar specs. At the same time, amps with nearly identical looks or model names can have utterly different specs. One might assume from its name that the Vibrosonic Reverb was more or less a Vibrasonic plus reverb. In the words of John Belushi: *but nooohh*. The slight alteration in spelling — "Vibro" vs. "Vibra" — was the least of their differences. In fact, these two amps shared little beyond their single 15" speakers and Fender badges.

The Vibrasonic was a pre-CBS, 40W brown Tolex amp with two 6L6s, while the Vibrosonic Reverb was a CBS silverface model with more than double the power, four 6L6s, tilt-back legs, a master volume circuit, and (on later models) a distortion switch. It didn't even appear until almost a decade after the Vibrasonic was dropped. It wasn't a Vibrasonic of any kind. (It was basically a silverface Twin Reverb with a 15.) Despite their similar model names, the Vibrasonic and Vibrosonic Reverb were far more *dissimilar* than, say, a Super and a Pro, or a Concert and a Bandmaster from the same era.

Yet another wrinkle was the occasional misuse of a technical term, a shortcoming hardly confined to Fender. For example, see the discussion of tremolo vs. vibrato, Chap. 14.

In *The Soul of Tone* we certainly pay attention to the usual methods of organizing these amps, but if we want to see them the way Leo Fender did — from the inside — merely charting the cosmetics and model names won't suffice. The sound and performance of these musical instruments depend on their internal designs and their tubes, speakers, caps, transformers, and other components, rather than the color of their Tolex or the shapes of their knobs. While their exteriors and model names are important, their true bloodlines are electrical currents running through circuits.

As mentioned in the Introduction to this book, the intent here is not to provide a database detailing the particulars of every variety of every Fender amp (there are more than 100 combinations of models, cabinets, and circuit variations — and that's only the ones made before 1965). However, by looking at representative samples of amplifier subfamilies (the 40W brown combos, the mid-power blackface reverbs, etc.), we can grasp the general evolution of the line, and also gain insights into how Mr. Fender himself saw the big picture.

First, some notes about circuit labels and codes.

Circuit Codes: Tweed, Brown, and Blonde

Starting in the early '50s, a three-character code appearing on tube charts affixed to the amps' interior side panels revealed the decade of manufacture, then a circuit variation, and finally the model. In 5A5, for example, the first 5 denotes the 1950s; A is the earliest circuit (it would be fol-

When matching name plates and cabinet styles to circuits, there were no doubt occasional overlaps or exceptions, so the following statements are generalizations. At top: The block style name plate appeared on the TV front amps, which employed the A circuits in 1950 and 1951. It continued to be used during the transition from the TV fronts to the wide panel tweeds (1952 and 1953, B circuits), on the early wide panels of '53 and '54 (C circuits), and the later wide panels of '54 and '55 (D circuits).

The E and F circuits appeared in the narrow panel era, during which at least three types of script name plates were used: a simple *Fender*, *Fender* with the model name, and *Fender* with the model name plus *-Amp*. Generally, smaller amps such as the Champ and Princeton had the one-word plates, while the larger amps sported model names; however, script plates on several narrow panels (for example, Deluxe, Pro, and Super) appeared with and without model names, the model-name versions generally on later editions.

When the cabinets of the top-end Fenders were redesigned in 1960, the small, flat rectangular tags were replaced by hefty stand-alone Fender logos rendered in script and mounted on the grilles. The flat-plate version shown here appeared on brown and blonde Tolex amps of the early 1960s (G circuits). The G circuits extended into some of the earliest black Tolex amps. The example at bottom is one of several raised-script logos typical of the blackface and silverface periods of the 1960s and 1970s.

lowed by version B, then C); and the second 5 indicates the model, in this case the Pro.

Model numbers from the vintage era include:

1 Champion or Champ

2 Princeton

3 Deluxe

4 Super

5 Pro

6 Bassman

7 Bandmaster

8 Twin

9 Tremolux

10 Harvard

11 Vibrolux

In some cases, identical letters reveal identical circuits. For example, the 5B5 TV front Pro circuit is the same as the 5B4 V-front Super, while the 5C5 Pro is identical to the 5C4 Super (i.e., the two 5B's are the same, and the two 5C's are the same). The wide panel "D" circuits work the same way: 5D5 Pro = 5D4 Super. Greg Gagliano: "I consider these pairs of circuits to be identical, though there were some minor cap value differences between the 5B4 Super and 5B5 Pro circuits. Also, there was a short-lived early 5C5 Pro circuit that used a 6SN7 phase inverter instead of a 6SC7. Except for this tube, the circuit is still identical to the 5C4 Super."

Such Fenders with otherwise identical or nearly identical circuits are distinguished by their speaker complements, cab dimensions, model names, and sometimes their transformers as well. For example, the Pros and Supers cited here are easily differentiated despite their electrical similarities.

In other cases, circuits with the same letter designation bear only a remote familial resemblance to each other, such as the bottom of the line 5C1 Champ and top of the line 5C8 Twin, both early wide panel tweeds. So, while later sections of this book explain common threads among the various circuit families, there's no such thing as a universal Fender A, B, or C circuit. Instead, the letters are most useful in distinguishing variations of the same model: Champ (circuits 5C1, 5D1, 5E1, etc.), Deluxe (5A3, 5B3, 5C3, etc.), and so on.

This system extended through the early years of the next decade, with the first 6 denoting the 1960s. The original model numbers from the 1950s continued to be used. Examples: 6G2 Princeton, 6G9 Tremolux, and 6G11 Vibrolux. As Fender added models to the line, the Tolex-covered newcomers received their own code numbers:

12 Concert

13 Vibrasonic

14 Showman

16 Vibroverb

Model 15 was the outboard reverb unit of the pre-CBS period.

Theoretically, a letter appended to one of these codes indicates a relatively minor update. In the case of the various narrow panel Bassmans, for example, 5E6-A followed 5E6. A more substantial redesign was designated 5F6, which was followed by its own modification, 5F6-A. Sometimes, though, the shift from one circuit to the next A or B version was significant. For example, the narrow panel 5E5 Pro has a single tone knob, while the 5E5-A has knobs for presence, bass, and treble, among other differences. The early-1960 brown Tolex 6G5 Pro has five preamp tubes, while the late-1960 6G5-A has six preamp tubes and a different arrangement of the bass, treble, and volume knobs (B, T, V in the earlier circuit; V, T, B in the later one), among other differences. (See the discussion in Chap. 11 comparing the 5F6 and 5F6-A Bassmans.)

This system spanned the transition from tweed to Tolex. Examples include all the tweed Princetons through 1960 (5A2, 5B2, 5C2, 5D2, 5E2, 5F2, and 5F2-A), as well as the brown Tolex Princeton of 1961 to 1963 (6G2). In these Princeton designations, note that the first digit designates the 1950s, then the 1960s; the letters change to reflect a progression of circuit revisions; and the model number, 2, stays the same.

The following is a rough guideline and is offered with a disclaimer: There are overlaps, gaps, and other exceptions, most notably the 5F1 Champ, which was made through 1964 (that is, a tweed amp continuing into the Tolex period — even the *blackface* Tolex period). Greg Gagliano: "Some of the circuits bridge different cosmetics. For example, the TV front and wide panel Super can be found with the 5B4, 5C4, and even the 5D4 circuits, depending on the year." Very generally, however, the letter codes on most pre-blackface charts do correspond to particular periods and cabinet types:

A = 1950 – 51, TV front

B = 1952 – 53, TV front, wide panel

C = 1953 – 54, wide panel

D = 1954 – 55, wide panel

E = 1955 – 61, narrow panel

F = 1956 – 61, narrow panel

G = 1960 – 64, brown, blonde and early black Tolex

Circuit Codes: Blackface and Silverface

Fender employed a different system starting with the shift to blackface in 1963. The new method — two letters, three numbers — tells us more about the date, but unlike the previous system it does not reveal the model. Without knowing whether it's a Vibrolux or a Twin, the designation is useless. Once we know the model, however, the two letters tell us the order of the circuit relative to other circuits for that particular amp, and the three letters correspond to the month and year the *original* circuit was designed.

Example: The AA in circuit AA763 tells us it's the original version, while the 763 indicates the date the circuit was devised: 7/63, or July 1963. The B in AB763 tells us it's the next version, but the 763 in AB763 still refers back to the original AA circuit, not to the date of the AB revision. So, the code does not reveal the date when AA evolved to AB.

There is no such thing as, say, a universal AA763 circuit. The AA763 designation was applied to several models in the 1963 line, from the Princeton and Deluxe up to the Super Reverb and Showman. Another example: Several AB763 circuits appear in various models (Super Reverb, Twin Reverb, Bandmaster, Deluxe Reverb, etc.), and no

Big Jack Johnson playing his Stratocaster through a Hot Rod DeVille 410 at Red's Lounge in Clarksdale, Mississippi, April 2006. Photographer Dick Waterman speculates that Big Jack is "probably the biggest name on the northern Mississippi juke joint circuit."

two are alike. In fact, some are very different from each other.

Once again, the system is most useful when comparing different versions of the same model, such as the AB763 blackface Twin Reverb and its AC568, AA769, and AA270 successors in silverface.

Examples of the AA circuits overlapped the blackface and silverface periods. AA circuits included the blackface AA763 Super Reverb and blackface AA864 Bassman, as well as the silverface AA1069 Pro Reverb and AA270 Super Reverb. Some AB circuits also overlapped the blackface and silverface periods. The AB's included many blackface Fenders, as well as silverfaces such as the AB568 Super Reverb and AB668 Pro Reverb. As you can see, the last three digits in all these examples do indicate references to the blackface (7/63, 8/64) and silverface (10/69, 2/70, 5/68, 6/68) periods.

Date Codes on Tube Charts

On many Fenders from the '50s and '60s, the month and year of manufacture are revealed in two-letter date codes stamped on the tube charts. The first letter designates the year, based on A = 1951, B = 1952, etc. The second letter indicates the month: A = January, B = February, etc., through L (December). Perry Tate: "Theoretically, the system starts in '51, but I've never seen an A or a B. We start seeing them in '53, with the C stamp, then D for '54 and so on. They used the system through 1967, ending with Q.

"A lot of people wonder about serial numbers. They're roughly chronological, but you can figure out the date of manufacture a lot more accurately by dating the components and looking at the tube chart and any ink stampings on the chassis. If the tube chart is September '63, then the components better be dated no later than that; otherwise it's quite likely that something has been changed."

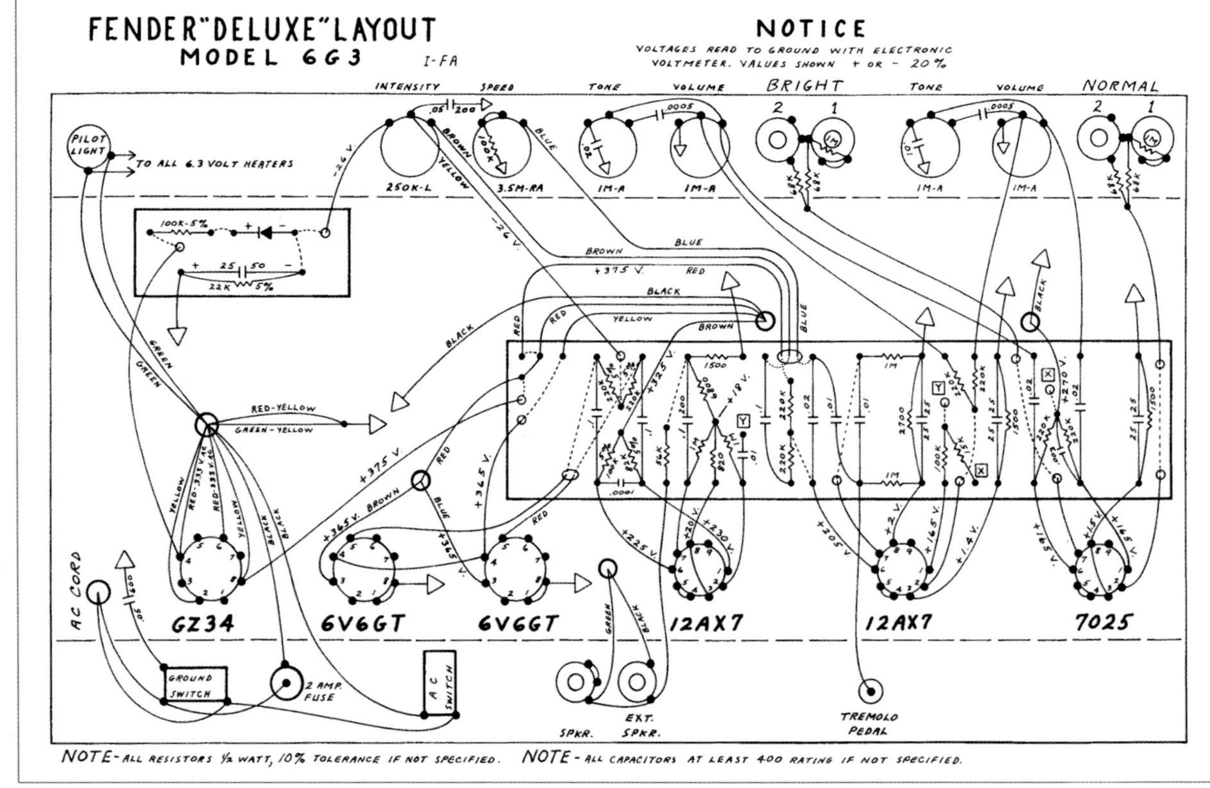

Fender 6G3 Deluxe chassis layout, dated I-FA (Sept. '61), from a flipped-over, workbench perspective. The front panel's inputs, knobs and pilot light are on top. Just below them is the pan, with capacitors and other components. The tubes, from right: preamp tubes, 12AX7 phase inverter, two 6V6GT power tubes, and a GZ34 rectifier. At bottom, the rear panel's jacks, switches, and fuse.

Component Codes

Speakers, transformers, pots and other components are often dated with an Electronic Industries Association (EIA) code number. The first digits indicate the manufacturer (220 is Jensen, 465 is Oxford, 606 is Schumacher, 830 is Triad, etc.). The remaining digits indicate the year, and then the week of manufacture. The last two digits are the week (01 to 52). Prior to those two digits is the year code, either one digit (6, 7, etc.) or two digits (56, 57, etc.). If it's a one-digit year code — 7, say — then you need to know the decade, which should be easy given the many differences between amps of different decades.

Example: A speaker stamped 220634 is a Jensen (220) manufactured in the 34th week of 1946, 1956, or 1966; their speakers were quite different from decade to decade, so dating them is easy. Transformer codes also often have six digits. Pot codes typically list the last two digits of the year instead of just the last one, so they often have seven rather than six digits in all.

This Jensen 12" speaker from the 1950s bears the code 220932, which reveals the date of manufacture: the 32nd week of 1959.

Production Numbers

Tube charts often display the word *Production* followed by a handwritten number. Perry Tate: "My best guess is that 'Production 1' means the amp is from the first production run of that particular *version* of that model. In my experience, when they made a change to the model, they started the production number sequence over again. So, for example, changing from a Concert 6G12, of which there were at least 36 production runs and probably many more, to a Concert AA763, you would end up with a new 'Production 1' again, and then run number 2 of AA763, then number 3, and so on, until they changed the circuit again. I've paid close attention to all of the Production 1 amps I've seen, and they follow a pattern, however unintentional. They often have no metal corners on the cabinet, and many times there is no Fender logo on the grille. The first run also frequently has a different type of speaker than what you would normally see in subsequent runs."

Circuits and Sounds

Sometimes the change from one circuit to its next iteration would be so minor that we couldn't hear a difference, while in other cases the shift could reflect a substantial redesign with audible results, more power, additional controls, etc.

Remember also that sonic differences between amps with different circuits *may* be due to circuitry but also could result from any number of other factors — cabs, speakers, transformers, one amplifier's individual quirks, the aging of components, etc. To look at it from the other side: If you were to spend a zillion dollars on five 5F6-A Bassmans in original condition, there is no guarantee that any two would sound exactly alike. After all, while we may like the sound of an old amp because of its design and components, we may also like the sound of an old amp because it's *old*. Over time, resistors or other components can "drift" from original specs, tubes can "burn in," speakers can lose a little high end, and so on. Ritchie Fliegler: "Amps are like people. We all get a bit saggy, mellow, and tend to drift as time marches on."

Steve Carr: "Like anything that is used, an amp becomes a better tool. It wears in and is more musical. Guitars do the same thing; they seem to settle in over time. The wonder of tube design is it can operate safely over a wide range of component variance, so you have this organic melding and life. Sometimes it goes in a nonmusical direction, but usually things that are used a lot seem to become better and better at their function."

Multiple Codes

If the exterior cosmetics or the model name won't specify precisely what's under the hood, then surely the circuit designations will do so, right? Up to a point, yes, but early Fender amp circuits were actually classified in three ways.

First, any individual circuit is defined by its physical components and actual topography, or layout.

Second, it bears the circuit code as it appears on the tube chart — 5B5, AA763, etc.

Third, in 1954 Fender started using date codes on schematics. Although it refers to a particular circuit, this three-letter code reveals the month and (after the hyphen) the year the schematic was drawn, and not necessarily the date when the circuit was actually modified. Each letter corresponds to a number. In a schematic marked I-FC, for example, I, the ninth letter of the alphabet, indicates the ninth month; F = 6, and C = 3. So, schematic I-FC was drawn in September '63.

Overlaps, Gaps, and Other Mismatches

Ideally, the circuit itself, circuit code and schematic code would correspond in every detail. However, mismatches sometimes occurred because a leftover tube chart with an older circuit designation was stuck inside an amp whose circuit had been modified. For example, a tweed-era chart might be affixed to the interior wall of a Tolex amp. (The famously frugal Leo Fender wasn't about to throw away a stack of tube charts, even if they were somewhat outdated.)

An amp might be designed, prototyped, and displayed (perhaps at a trade show) months before the commencement of actual production. Another wrinkle: Schematics were often drawn up months after the circuit was laid out. For example, the initial Vibrasonic is a '50s circuit according to its 5G13 circuit code, and yet its schematic is dated January '60. During these various interims, the ever restless Mr. Fender may have tweaked the circuit. The result is that even if a circuit and its tube chart code do match, the schematic may reflect a later, tweaked version of the "same" circuit.

Finally, Fender also published official "layout" diagrams showing the actual location of components and the

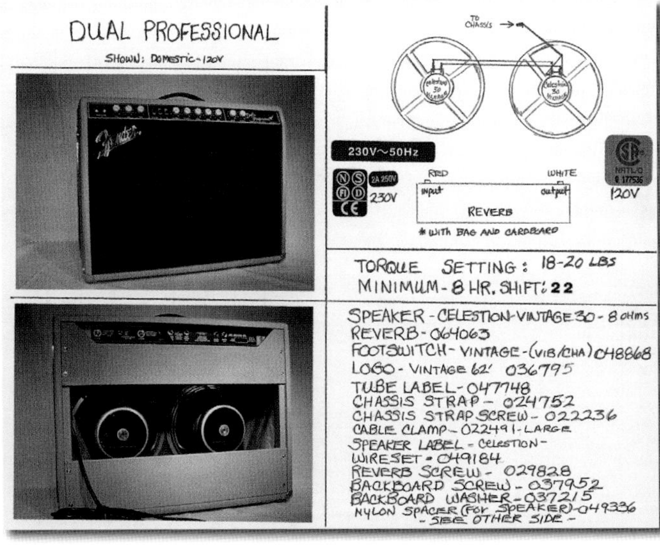

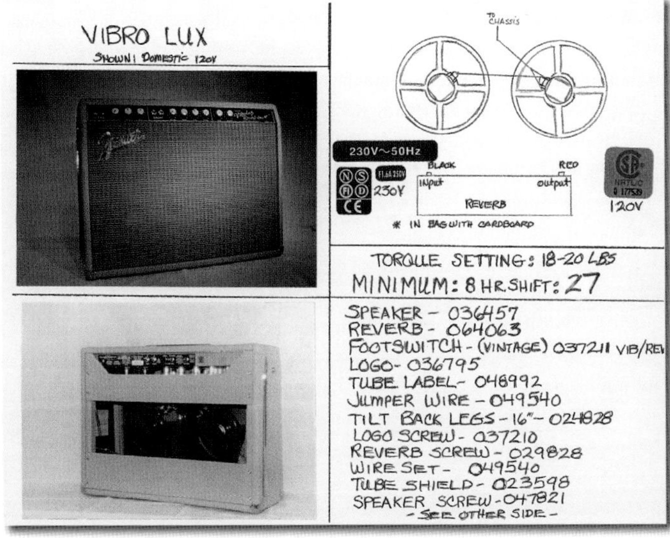

These sheets are samples of in-house documents prepared by Fender's QA (Quality Assurance) or Engineering department as reference guides for factory technicians, inspectors, and sound testers.

various wired connections for a given circuit. Once in a while, a layout differs from the equally official schematic. One example is the 5C1 Champ, which specifies a 6V6 power tube on the schematic but an updated 6V6GT on the layout. Another is the 5E9-A Tremolux; its layout specifies a 5U4GA rectifier, while the schematic for the "same" circuit specifies a 5Y3GT.

So, given occasional leftover tube charts, sporadic mid-production-run updates to circuits, and various time lags (not to mention the occasional typo, such as an official schematic that designates the Deluxe with a 4 instead of the proper 3), it's possible that an amplifier's tube chart *and* its schematic *and* its layout diagram might all vary from the actual circuit — and perhaps from each other.

Such irregularities appear throughout the entire period when Fender used these codes and systems. Back in the 1950s, a tube chart dating to the earlier wide panel era might be affixed to a narrow panel amp. After Mr. Fender sold his company, occasional mismatches continued, as when a blackface chart showed up in a silverface amp.

Nevertheless, we can generalize about Fender circuits, so long as we allow for variations. Blackie Pagano: "I have fixed many hundreds of Fender amps, but I take each one individually. Even though they are production built devices, really they are all different to me. Leo spec'd these amplifiers to plus or minus 20 percent in terms of voltages. That's a range of 40 percent, a huge leeway. In practice I've found the spread to be much smaller; nevertheless, each one is different, and I think that's part of the reason why they have become iconic objects. I still get excited fixing these amps today. Part of the charm is when I open up a tweed Champ and there's a little piece of tape in there and written on the tape is *Lupe* — the legendary Lupe [Lopez], one of Leo Fender's original employees, a housewife who sat there wiring Fender amplifiers. You don't have to pay a specialist to do point to point on the scale Fender was doing it. It was the most practical way to go at that time, just as, I suppose, circuit boards are the most practical way of doing it now.

"When I open up a Fender amplifier, although I'm very familiar with everything in there, it becomes an intuitive process. It goes beyond components and schematics. There's a huge variety, even among amps of the same model and same era. Many small variations can add up to noticeable differences in sound. Even though they are mass-produced items, they are quite individual because these differences can give each amp its own character which musicians are quite attuned to, and also because yesterday's mass-production construction values are today's 'boutique' construction values."

"There's a huge variety, even among amps of the same model and same era."

— Blackie Pagano

"I've been chronicling the several Leo Fender technical breakthroughs and elevations for these past many years, with special attention to the 5C though 5F circuits, the 6G, and the AA to AB series. They still sound wonderful and sometimes make modern amplifiers sound dull by comparison. Mr. Fender's genius lives on. The influences of these amplifiers have been paramount on several amplifier manufacturers right to the present time. I'm sure you are aware that the basic Marshall amplifier is still a Fender amplifier modeled on the 5F6-A Bassman and 5F8-A Twin."

— Alexander Dumble

Circuits, Codes, and Schematics

Greg Gagliano is an environmental toxicologist with deep experience in compiling and managing databases. He has examined hundreds of Fender amps and documented thousands of details, particularly regarding circuits. Some of his research has appeared in 20th Century Guitar *magazine. Here he contributes several insights, from interviews with the author.*

The first Fenders I've seen with any kind of circuit designation were around 1950 or 1951. That was the 5 series, such as the 5A3, the 5A6, etc. They start showing up in the midst of the TV front period [1948 to 1953]. The system was not used consistently. That's the problem. You see it only on a few amps. The 5A5 Pro really stands out. That's one of the earliest codes I've seen.

Some charts have inaccurate circuit codes. For example, a Pro from 1960 might say 5G5, even though that first 5 is supposed to mean '50s, not '60s. Technically, it's a 6G5. The G was correct — the next iteration of the circuit — but they had jumped the gun and printed up too many charts with the 5, before production actually started in early 1960. So you have a later amp with the older, mismatched tube chart.

The schematic came later still, after production began, so even though you can find a tube chart that says 5G5 Pro, you won't find a 5G5 schematic. There's no 5G5 circuit. It's a nonexistent amp. Another way to look at it: A 5G5 tube chart code and a 6G5 schematic code might actually refer to the same 6G5 circuit.

There were other examples. You might see a 5F6 on a Tweed Vibrolux. There was no 5F6 Vibrolux. It was a 5F11. [5F6 was a Bassman.] There were also some Deluxes that had what we call "mistake" labels. They didn't want to slow down production, so they just used up the labels they had until the next batch came in. They were pretty frugal.

Also, some modifications were never documented, such as transitional hybrids of various 6G circuits [including 6G4 and 6G5] and their A successors in the brown amps of 1960: 6G4-A and 6G5-A.

The shift to the new system [e.g., AA763] was concurrent with the shift to blackface in 1963. After CBS took over in 1965, they continued the nomenclature until about 1972. They also continued the problems. Neglecting to update the circuit codes until they got around to drawing up the schematic was especially widespread in the CBS years. By now it's almost common knowledge that this happened, so people know you can't always go by the tube label. You really have to pull the chassis and take a look at it. After the early '70s they went with a completely different system that, as far as I can tell, doesn't have any rhyme or reason to it.

Sometimes a circuit might bridge the shift from one cabinet style to the next one, so different generations of one model may have identical circuits. Most of the time, though, an across-the-line shift in cabinet style did correspond to an across-the-line shift in circuits. Examples include the evolution from the wide panel to the narrow panel tweeds, and especially the narrow panels to the Tolex amps.

My database has thousands of entries, and it's helpful in researching production trends and the evolution of circuits. One of the things I'm looking at is the total production per model, and what the production numbers on the tube charts mean. They didn't start using those numbers until the late '50s, and they stopped at the end of the blackface era. It appears that these are basically batch numbers, but they are often misinterpreted. It's not necessarily chronological. So a production number 1 on a Super Reverb tube chart from 1966 doesn't mean that's when Super Reverb production started. All it means is that's when they started a new run of the numbers. So, I'm working on things like how many units per batch were made, and that's where the database really comes in handy.

John Mayer and his Rory Gallagher Tribute Strat, onstage with a collection of Fender amps, 2005.

The first Fender amplifiers: 1x8 Princeton (also called the Student model), 1x10 Deluxe (also called Model 26), and 1x15 Professional. These three "woodies" feature all-original cabs, finishes, trim, and mohair-type grille coverings. Two of the three original grille colors are seen here; the third is a yellow/gold.

CHAPTER EIGHT

8

In the Beginning

1940s: K&Fs, Woodies, and Early Tweeds

Leo Fender had no interest in building "vintage" products. The quality, styling, and gold-standard tones of old Fender amps — all enhanced by time and nostalgia — may have imbued them with a vintage radiance and rendered them icons of a bygone era, but to Leo Fender it was all about the new. He kept his eye on current trends in audio and pushed his suppliers to upgrade their standards to meet his own. He strove to use improved components and the latest circuitries in order to provide players with ever more sophisticated tools.

He succeeded. The first two decades of Fender amplifiers were marked by continuous advances in tubes, speakers, and other components, not to mention *more* of pretty much everything — more models, features, power, volume, and headroom.

Doc Kauffman, K&F Manufacturing

Leo Fender's first amplifiers were built in association with his early partner, the late Clayton Orr "Doc" Kauffman. As this author wrote in *American Guitars*, Doc and Leo were two of a kind, relentless experimenters: "Kauffman fashioned steam engines from five-gallon milk cans when he was a kid, and built farm machinery, sanders, tools, radios, police transmitters, and a motorcycle. He also claimed to be the first man to install amplifier components in the top of the cabinet — the way it's done on virtually all amps today — simply to avoid the trouble of having to bend over to make adjustments." (This author recalls being given a ride by Doc one time. On the front seat of his car he kept what looked like a backscratcher he had modified so that he could reach over and unlock the passenger side door without having to shift in his seat.) He was a kind, gentle man, loved and admired by all who knew him. He died on June 26, 1990.

Back in '22, Doc had moved to California from his family's farm in Kansas. He played in various bands around Orange County and in the 1930s was a chief designer of electric guitars for Rickenbacker. He struck up a friendship with kindred spirit Leo Fender. Doc Kauffman told this author: "Leo came in one day, and he said, 'Hey, you've been building guitars around here — do you want to build some together?' And I said, 'Well, sure. Sounds okay to me.'" The two friends called their short-lived company the K&F Manufacturing Corporation, an impos-

Matched set, 1945:
This K&F lap steel and amp have matching gray crinkle paint jobs.

ing moniker for their tiny outfit. They taught themselves to weld, made many of their own tools, and in 1945 went to work building amps and lap steel guitars, often laboring until midnight. The finishes on the earliest K&Fs were baked on, in the Kauffman family's kitchen oven.

Doc and Leo soon relocated to the K&F "factory," a shed behind Leo's radio shop in Fullerton. While Leo and Doc built a few amps during World War II, perhaps only a half-dozen, most K&Fs were completed after the war, from November 1945 through mid 1946. They didn't look like the foundations of an electronics empire, but that's what they were, these simple boxes with their leather handles, their lightning bolt logos, and their workbench/science fair vibe.

Doc and Leo parted ways in 1946 but remained lifelong friends. Doc Kauffman told this author: "I got scared of the business. I had been saving money through the war, and I wanted to get a home and pay for it. My dad was a credit boy all his life — owed money on the farm and everything — so I told myself I'd never go into debt for anything. Leo was different. He'd go into debt on an investment like a house afire! He didn't care. Besides, he was smart. He's a pursuer, boy, day and night. That's what put the guitar where it is.

"Anyway, I didn't have much faith in guitars, and I asked Leo to buy out my half of the business. He kept making those little ol' K&Fs for a while after I left him, until all the nameplates were used up. Then he went on his own. You know, he never talked about the future. One day he told me — I'll never forget — I asked him, 'Leo, what in the world would you be doing if you and I had never met?' He said, 'Well, I'd probably have two or three radio stores or TV repair shops.'"

Exposed wood is seen where this K&F was held in a clamp or bracket during the spraying of the finish. The few surviving K&Fs were basically handmade and feature an inconsistent mix of inputs and knobs. This one has two inputs (one for your guitar buddy or music teacher) and no knobs at all. Why build an amp with no tone or volume controls? That's what the knobs on your guitar were for. Remember, Leo Fender saw the amp as an integral part of the guitar. In his mind, the "instrument" was guitar, cord, and amp.

Old friends looking back: Doc Kauffman, left, and Leo Fender, with some of the K&F gear they built many years before this photo was taken.

Ray Massie

Another important contributor to Fender's early amp designs was Ray Massie, a repairman at Fender Radio Service. Mr. Fender had received no formal training in electronics or engineering of any kind, relying instead on his intuition and his experience repairing radios, PAs, turntables, and other devices. He also drew upon the skills of early associates such as Kauffman and Massie.

Don Randall (see Chap. 12): "I think Ray had a lot to do with the early circuits because he was in that business to begin with. Leo was coming to it out of his repair business and his work with public address systems and so on. Ray knew a lot about circuitry, and Leo didn't know that much about it at the very beginning. Of course, he learned everything eventually. But Ray really knew that stuff. I think he knew more about circuits than Leo did when they started. I wouldn't say that he was actually designing products, but I think he had a big hand in helping with some of the technical details and so forth."

Forerunners: K&F Amps

The early K&F amps were essentially handmade, featuring bent steel chassis, mesh grilles of flat metal, durable leather handles, rear-facing (as opposed to top-mounted) control panels, and field coil speakers, which according to Teagle & Sprung's *Fender Amps, The First Fifty Years* "required an electric current to create the necessary magnetic field." Most were finished in a gray crinkle paint, and the grilles were typically sprayed with flock, a powdered "cloth." The amps' sturdy cabinets reveal that Leo Fender's passion for durability went back to his earliest products.

There were no model names on these primitive amps, no circuit boards, and no labels for the control knobs. Several variations can be found in surviving amplifiers, and indeed, there was no K&F "line" at all, as the term is used today. Still, certain amps did share several features. Author/collector John Sprung: "I have had in my possession three different sized K&Fs, all with a crinkle finish: a 1x8 (no controls, just an input jack — what more do you really need?), a 1x10 (two inputs; tone and volume controls), and a 1x15. My belief is that by the end of Doc and Leo's partnership, they had three established models. They do correspond to the [later Fender] 1x8 Princeton, 1x10 Deluxe, and 1x15 Pro."

The large K&Fs were early manifestations of Mr. Fender's affinity for 15s. They are exceedingly rare, and it's likely that only a very few were built, on custom order. John Sprung wrote in *20th Century Guitar* (July 1997): "After years of scouring the planet for even a rumor of a Deluxe K&F, one has finally surfaced. Until now the only evidence of the existence of such an animal were photos of bands such as Bob Wills and His Texas Playboys (see page 46 of Richard Smith's book, *Fender: The Sound Heard 'Round the World*). It's not like the 8 and 10 inch models are common. I know of only three Student and three Standard models." This particular 1x15 K&F had a tube complement that would look familiar to any student of early Fenders: two 6L6s, a 6N7, a 6SL7, a 6SN7, a 6SC7, and a 5U4 rectifier.

Doc and Leo's amplifiers featured tubes that hung vertically from their top-mounted chassis, a detail that would characterize later Fender amps and virtually all modern guitar amps as well. Don Randall told *Guitar Player*: "It's best to put [tubes] in the bottom of the cabinet, to put the weight down at the bottom and make the unit sit on the floor and not be top-heavy. But musicians have a habit of throwing everything they have in the back of the amp. As a consequence they started having broken tubes, broken connections and all kinds of things, and they collected all the dirt in the world. So the next move was to put the tubes on the top where the controls were available, and musicians could still throw their foot pedals, their cords, and their sack lunches or whatever in the bottom and not disturb anything."

Cluttered bench and bare walls: A long list of classic designs came from Leo Fender's spartan work area, pictured here in 1950. As author Richard Smith noted, this photo shows a circuit diagram drawn by hand on an upright piece of cardboard, which Mr. Fender presumably consulted while working on this prototype amp.

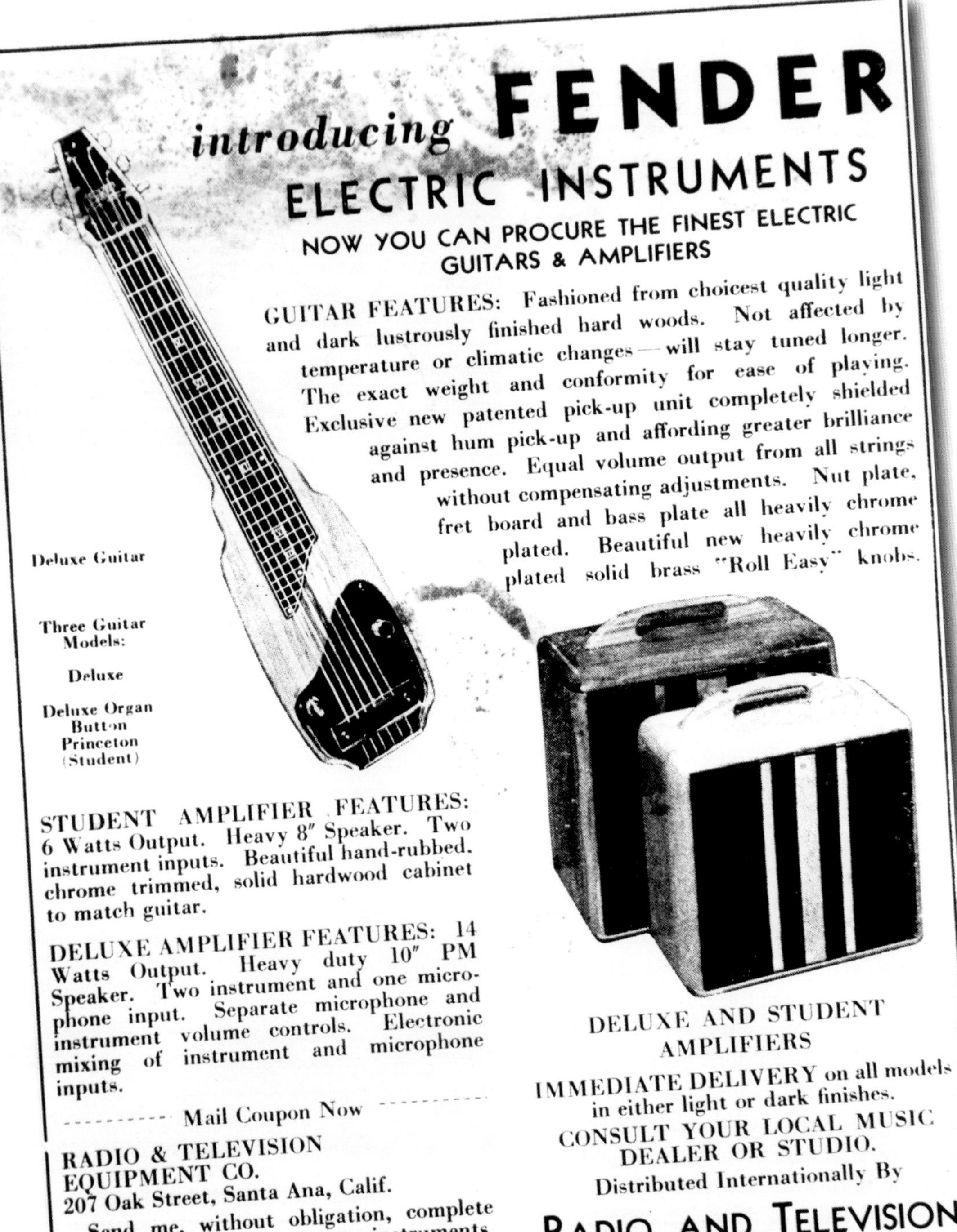

introducing FENDER
ELECTRIC INSTRUMENTS
NOW YOU CAN PROCURE THE FINEST ELECTRIC GUITARS & AMPLIFIERS

GUITAR FEATURES: Fashioned from choicest quality light and dark lustrously finished hard woods. Not affected by temperature or climatic changes—will stay tuned longer. The exact weight and conformity for ease of playing. Exclusive new patented pick-up unit completely shielded against hum pick-up and affording greater brilliance and presence. Equal volume output from all strings without compensating adjustments. Nut plate, fret board and bass plate all heavily chrome plated. Beautiful new heavily chrome plated solid brass "Roll Easy" knobs.

Deluxe Guitar

Three Guitar Models:
Deluxe
Deluxe Organ Button
Princeton (Student)

STUDENT AMPLIFIER FEATURES: 6 Watts Output. Heavy 8" Speaker. Two instrument inputs. Beautiful hand-rubbed, chrome trimmed, solid hardwood cabinet to match guitar.

DELUXE AMPLIFIER FEATURES: 14 Watts Output. Heavy duty 10" PM Speaker. Two instrument and one microphone input. Separate microphone and instrument volume controls. Electronic mixing of instrument and microphone inputs.

DELUXE AND STUDENT AMPLIFIERS

IMMEDIATE DELIVERY on all models in either light or dark finishes.
CONSULT YOUR LOCAL MUSIC DEALER OR STUDIO.
Distributed Internationally By
RADIO AND TELEVISION EQUIPMENT CO.
207 Oak St., Santa Ana, Calif.

Mail Coupon Now

RADIO & TELEVISION EQUIPMENT CO.
207 Oak Street, Santa Ana, Calif.
Send me, without obligation, complete descriptive literature on your instruments.
NAME ....
ADDRESS ....
CITY .... STATE ....
DEALER ☐ STUDIO ☐ STUDENT ☐

Dating to 1947, this may be the first magazine ad for Fender instruments. It announces the two-member line of amplifiers: the 1x8 Student model and the 1x10 Deluxe. (The 1x15 Pro was likely available only on special order.)

In front, two 1x10 Model 26s; note variations in decorative chrome strips and shades of grille color. Perry Tate: "The one on the left is a very early one with two chrome strips instead of three, one of only two I've seen. It is serial number 219; I've heard of only one woodie with a lower number, so I doubt they started with 001. At right is number 712.

"The two 1x10 amps in the middle are true transition models. They look like Fender woodies, but they have K&F chassis, so they predate the Model 26s. The amp on the left even has the K&F logo at the lower right on the back panel. They're primitive, with components just soldered to each other — no turret boards — and the control panels are plain, without writing or labels. These 'woodie K&Fs' both have Jensen G10RS field coil speakers. It seems they tried different layouts and parts, like the three inputs in a triangle, and if something worked, they stuck with it. The earliest Model 26s have an almost burlap type cloth, which you can see here on these transition amps. Behind them are two 1x15 woodie Pros."

INST. VOL.
FENDER
ELECTRIC
INSTRUMENT CO.
Fullerton California
SERIAL NO.
MODEL
MIC. VOL.
MICROPHONE
INSTRUMENTS
TONE
OFF
ON
FUSE
Jensen
electro-dynamic
SEE PATENT NOTICE
MADE IN U.S.A.
Concert Speaker
MODEL
A-15
JENSEN RADIO MFG. CO. CHICAGO, U.S.A.

Among the most distinctive characteristics of the K&Fs were their field coil Jensen speakers. John Sprung: "Jensen used three speaker designations. The P, as in P12N, P10R, etc., stood for Permanent magnet — in this case, an alnico. The C, as in C12N, C10R, etc., stood for Ceramic magnet. Into the 1940s, magnet technology still wasn't up to producing a permanent magnet strong enough and small enough to work on a speaker. Lots of experimentation took place. The earliest permanent magnet speakers actually used a horseshoe magnet.

"The F, as in F15N or F12N, stood for Field Coil magnet. Electromagnets were the only type of magnet strong enough, small enough, and able to be shaped properly for use on a speaker. It is quite easy to distinguish a permanent magnet from a field coil. Permanents have only two wires attached to the output transformer. Field coils have at least a couple of extra wires, necessary to produce the high voltage needed to power up the magnet. I learned about field coil magnets the hard way. Unlike permanent magnet speakers, the field coils pack quite a wallop! Stick your fingers in the wrong place, and it's kind of like the toaster in the bathtub trick. So all you do-it-yourselfers, beware and remember: two wires OK, four wires, you pay!" (See Chap. 4 and also The Tweed 4x10 Bassman: The Ultimate Guitar Amp? in Chap. 11 for more on Jensen speaker designations.)

The K&Fs were forerunners of the first Fender brand amplifiers. For example, John Sprung reported that the 1x15 K&F he encountered was strikingly similar to the 1946 to 1947 Fender Pro: "The cabinet designs were nearly the same .... Richard Smith speculates that Leo Fender and Ray Massie would have built this amp together and that Doc Kauffman played through it to test for desirable tone .... The speaker is a Jensen A15 field coil, like the one found on the wood Pro." Other extremely rare amps have surfaced on occasion, and they appear to be missing links, what Sprung has called K&F/Fender "in-betweeners." One example was an amp with a Fender Model 26 type exterior but a grille cloth that was coarser than the materials used on standard Fenders.

In the shift from K&Fs to the first Fenders (the "woodies"), the model names moved around a bit. The 1x15 K&F may have been considered the "Deluxe," but in the Fender line, the Deluxe was the 1x10 mid-line amp. The 1x8 K&F and the 1x8 Fender Princeton were "student" models, a position that was soon reassigned to the smaller Fender Champion 800 of 1948. Putting aside the shifting model names, and remembering that there were variations among the basically handmade K&Fs, we can still discern clear lineages between the K&Fs and the woodies, as revealed by their general dimensions and shared speaker arrays: 1x8, 1x10, and 1x15.

1x15 woodie Pro, serial no. 501. Like most or all woodie Fenders, it's from 1946. (This is the actual amp that Fender reverse-engineered when designing the 50th Anniversary woodie Pro reissue; Chap. 23.) Woodie Pros were typically equipped with a Jensen Electro-Dynamic A15 field coil speaker. Perry Tate: "Instead of a permanent magnet, it has a very high impedance coil, and it's only magnetized when current passes through it. As late as 1951, Pros occasionally still came with an F15N field coil Jensen, which was really an oddity by then."

The First Fenders: The Woodies

After Doc Kauffman's departure in 1946, Mr. Fender established the Fender Manufacturing Company, which in December 1947 was reorganized as the Fender Electric Instrument Company. By then, the earliest Fender brand amplifiers were circulating among local musicians. Unfortunately, many of them suffered from manufacturing defects such as noisy speakers, failing tubes, and even exploding capacitors. Mr. Fender worked long and hard to learn from his mistakes, constantly experimenting with new designs and new procedures. Within two or three years, Fender began to acquire a reputation for high quality. Thanks to Mr. Fender's uncanny ability to meet the needs of musicians, Don Randall's innovative promotional literature, and the efforts of Randall's capable sales and marketing team, that reputation would blossom in the 1950s into a national and then an international renown.

The first Fender brand amps are nicknamed "woodies" because of their hardwood cabinets and matching handles. According to Richard Smith, Leo Fender received a shipment of hardwood intended for steel guitar bodies in 1946, but the one-inch thick pieces were too thin for their intended use. "As it sat in an empty lot, Leo designed the first line of Fender amps in order to use it before termites could eat it."

Woodie Professional, detail. The earliest Fender logo picked up the lightning-bolt theme of the K&F amps.

The three models were the Princeton, Deluxe, and Professional. Just as the K&Fs had served as forerunners to the woodies, the woodies would evolve into the more familiar Fender amps of the 1950s. The 1x8 woodie was a small, 6W, two-input model; Fender advertised it as the "Princeton (Student)" model. The 14W, three-input, 1x10 woodie Deluxe of 1946, also called Model 26, had controls for tone and volume. It was a direct descendant of 1945's 1x10 K&F, and would evolve into the tweed Deluxe in about April of 1948. The six-tube, 1x15 Professional had descended from the biggest of the K&Fs and would evolve into the tweed Pro. Princetons, Deluxes, and Pros would be cornerstones of the line for much of the next 60 years.

These amps appeared in several different natural wood grain finishes: "gleaming blonde maple, black walnut, and dark mahogany," sometimes specified as simply "light or dark finishes." They featured rear-facing control panels, and grille cloths of various colors, generally red, blue, or a yellow/gold. What was perhaps the earliest magazine advertisement for Fender products dates to 1947 and specifies two of the woodies, the 1x8 Student model and the 1x10 Deluxe.

The woodies were gussied up with three protective metal strips mounted vertically over the speaker openings, a detail that would "add flash and brilliance to their already sparkling appearance." The new Fender logo carried over the K&F lightning bolt and bore the words "Fender Electric Instrument Co., Fullerton, California." How rare are woodie Fenders? Perry Tate: "There seem to be a lot more Model 26s than other woodies. My earliest one is serial number 219, and the latest is 1279. I used to speculate that Leo might have skipped a bunch of numbers, but I do have two sequentially numbered Model 26s, 393 and 394. If you assume they didn't skip numbers, there could theoretically be a thousand or more of them out there. The woodie Princetons are seen far less frequently, and they didn't have serial numbers, so it's hard to even guess how many were made. Woodie Pros are quite rare and were likely available only on special order."

This eye-poppin' rig from 1946 proves that Leo Fender was thinking big from the beginning. Perhaps a one of a kind setup, it's a 1x15 woodie Pro with a 12" extension speaker in a matching cab (by 1946 standards, it's practically a Marshall stack). The extension speaker's stamp dates it to the 28th week of 1946. The set is owned by the Burst Brothers. Brother Dave Belzer: "Left to right on the amp's panel, there's the microphone input and its volume control, the instrument input and its volume control, then two more inputs stacked on top of each other and their volume control, which is unlabeled, then a master tone control. The last input is for the extension cab; the switch next to it selects both cabs together or the extension cab alone. All the inputs work and sound good. The volume gradually goes down as you move from the microphone input, to the instrument input, to the unmarked inputs."

Primal tweed: The Dual Professional, so rare that it seems to have been excluded from early Fender literature, and yet profoundly significant for the long list of features it introduced. Why two speakers? Apparently Mr. Fender got a super deal on a big batch of 10″ Jensen PM10Cs and needed to use them up (Chap. 4).

Early Tweed: Dual Professional, V-Front Super

What was the first "modern" Fender? The Tremolux, with Fender's first onboard effect? The Vibrasonic, which introduced front-panel knobs? The Vibroverb, which first combined tremolo and reverb? Consider the Dual Professional, which dates to late 1946 or early 1947 and was built for only a year, at most. Although short-lived, this milestone has few rivals when it comes to premiering a long list of major innovations, features that would be seen on countless Fenders to follow.

The Dual Professional introduced a new cabinet style that in various incarnations (TV front, wide panel, narrow panel) would distinguish Fender amps all the way through the 1950s. It introduced to the line the now familiar family of "tweed" luggage linen coverings, as well as another Fender hallmark, the top-facing, chrome-plated control panel. It was Fender's first model with twin speakers. Furthermore, this forerunner to the V-front Super (late 1947 to 1952) introduced to Fender amps the on/off switch, finger-joined cab construction, the pilot light, and the use of circuit boards. Few amps, by any manufacturer, ever boasted innovations so numerous or ultimately so influential.

Featuring a distinctive vertical metal strip that held the baffle boards together, the Dual Professional was produced concurrently with the woodies. According to Richard Smith, it never appeared on a price list or in a catalog and was intended to use up an oversupply of 10″ speakers Leo had purchased on the cheap. Curiously, the Dual Professional and V-front Super seem to have been excluded from the early ads.

The V-front Super of late '47 to '52 was the successor to the similar 2x10 V-front Dual Professional. It had a pair of 10″ Jensen P10Rs on slightly canted baffles for extra sound dispersion. Compared to its TV front stablemates, it may have seemed like a throwback to the late-'40s look of its forebear, but aside from its slanted speakers and chrome center strip it actually foreshadowed the next-generation "wide panel" cabinets of 1953 to 1955. The tubes in both the Dual Professional and the earliest Supers were typical of the day — a 5U4 or 5U4G rectifier, two octal preamp tubes, two metal-envelope 6L6s, and a paraphase inverter.

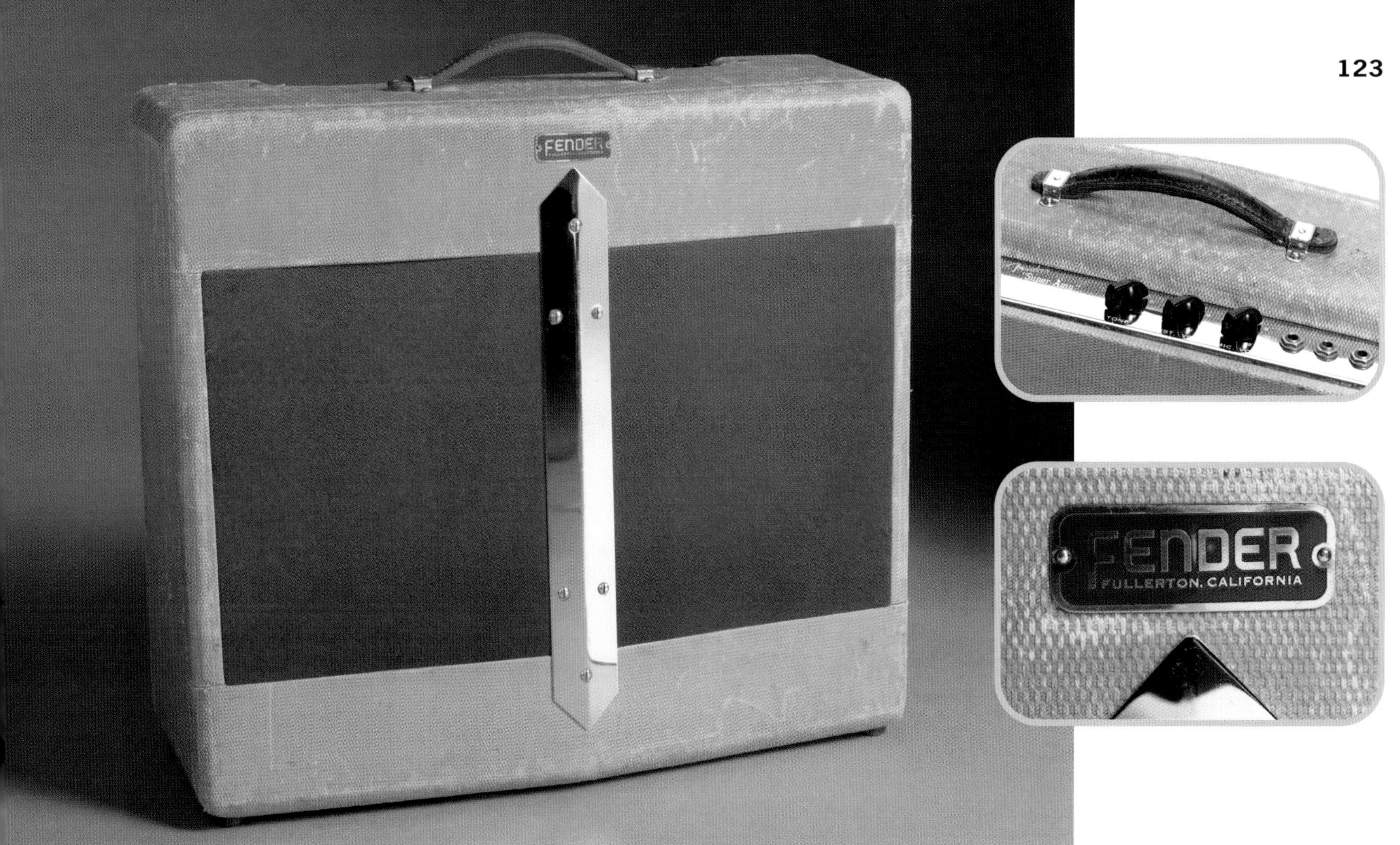

V-front Super, successor to the Dual Pro.

A sturdy cabinet with linen covering, a stitched leather handle, and chickenhead knobs on a durable, mirror-finish panel: This would be the Fender look of the 1950s.

Owner Alan Hardtke: "John Sprung christened this covering 'vertical tweed,' in that it doesn't have a diagonal pattern. The earlier Dual Professional had the same pattern of tweed, but it's more of a white color, not so yellow. So, first there's white vertical tweed, then the more yellow vertical tweed seen here, then diagonal tweed without a contrasting thread, and finally the common diagonal tweed with the contrasting thread that we see on the wide panel and narrow panel amps of the mid and later 1950s."

Tweed Patterns

Gregg Hopkins of Vintage-Amp Restoration, St. Louis, has examined and reconditioned hundreds of tweed Fenders, perhaps more than a thousand. He details the evolution of the various patterns: "You have to be careful because of some overlaps between older and newer patterns of tweed, but we can generalize. On the earliest tweeds, like the Dual Professional, there's a linen fabric with what's called vertical tweed, or a dot tweed, rather than a solid diagonal stripe. I think the only model I've seen it on is the Dual Pro. I've seen stock Dual Pros with linen covering that has no discernible dot or line pattern at all, just a near-white, almost canvasy material. The undotted or unlined fabric may have been first, then the dotted or vertical pattern.

"What came next was a light diagonal tweed, with less contrast between the stripes and the straw colored background than people normally think of. We see this lighter, low-contrast diagonal tweed on the TV front amps, and it extends into some of the early wide panels. The familiar tweed with the more contrasting stripe starts to come in with some of the wide panels, so there's an overlap, and it extends through the narrow panels to the end of the tweed era.

"Any kind of mass produced fabric is going to differ from one production run to the next. Another factor that makes these things look unique is that some of the amps that have spent their lives under covers or in dark rooms are considerably lighter than amps that have been out there in the world and in smoky bars and so on for 50 years. The unprotected amps tend to darken up."

Billy Gibbons

Billy Gibbons in *Guitar Player*, on the Dual Professional that he used to record ZZ Top's *Antenna*: "It looks like it lived at the bottom of the Mississippi for about a year, was pulled out, and then put back down. It's absolutely the best sounding thing, thank God, because it looks atrocious. It's absolutely raunchy. It's torn and scratched. They used a peculiar kind of airline luggage linen. They call it a tweed, but it's minus stripes [the square weave pattern]. It's really cool. It was Fender's first amp with two speakers. They're quite rare. Later they continued the production under the name of Super."

Billy Gibbons, from an interview with the author: "These low-wattage amps escaped the attention of a lot of folks because when we grew up the thing to have was a badass Marshall stack of 100 watts. We all wanted to be like Jimi Hendrix and Queen and Jeff Beck and the rest of them, and it wasn't until much later when we realized that sometimes you don't need all that. As these vintage pieces started to become collectible, one thing was to have a nice topic of conversation in your living room. They also started showing value in the studio when you could get monstrous sounds out of this tiny little thing.

"My very first amp when I was a kid was a Champ. I've still got it. Steve Cropper gave me his Fender Harvard, which he cut a lot of those early Stax recordings on. Back in the day we described a setup we nicknamed The Amp Cabin, and basically that was just our nickname for this stack of amps that we built in a box with a microphone in the middle. We took every little crazy thing and balanced them all and made this little tiny house inside the studio. It was built out of just whatever amps we could find. We'd run one, and then we'd run two or three. We played with different combinations, enjoying the variety. We had an omni-directional mike in the center of this madness, and we were intrigued by it all. Some of the combinations were productive, some were dismissible, and then some combinations were significantly different than others so we mapped out a chart of which ones were desirable, and which ones might be usable for a special effect now and again.

"We had a couple of Champs. One was a little two-tone. They called it the Champ 600. We've still got all of this stuff in the warehouse. We've got the Harvard. We had a single-15 Pro with that kind of pinkish-brown Tolex, a '60, '61. We had an early blonde piggyback Tremolux with the maroon grille cloth. I believe it was two 10s. We spent a lot of time matching up amps to guitars. Like on 'Blue Jean Blues,' that was a Stratocaster, and we tried using a Marshall, but it was just too dirty. 'Blue Jean' was better suited for a lot cleaner tone. Go back and play it, man; I mean, it was crystal clear. I'm inclined to think it was a little brown Tolex Fender Deluxe, single 12, because it only had volume and tone on the faceplate, and I remember cranking that tone knob all the way up and keeping the volume low to maintain a real clear signal."

We Are the Champions: 800 and 600

Small in stature but mighty in influence, the Champion 800 of 1948 and 1949 was the ancestor to a long line of Champs. It sported a unique greenish linen covering and a control panel "finished in a very attractive gray-green hammerloid finish with white marking." By about the summer of '49, it was replaced with the identically circuited "two-tone" Champion, or Champion 600.

Coming Up

Also appearing in the late 1940s was the new "TV front" cabinet style. George Gruhn: "By then, the tweed Fenders could crank out more power, to the point of totally eclipsing *anything* that the prewar amps could do." Details of the TV fronts and the Champion 600 are discussed in Chapter 9.

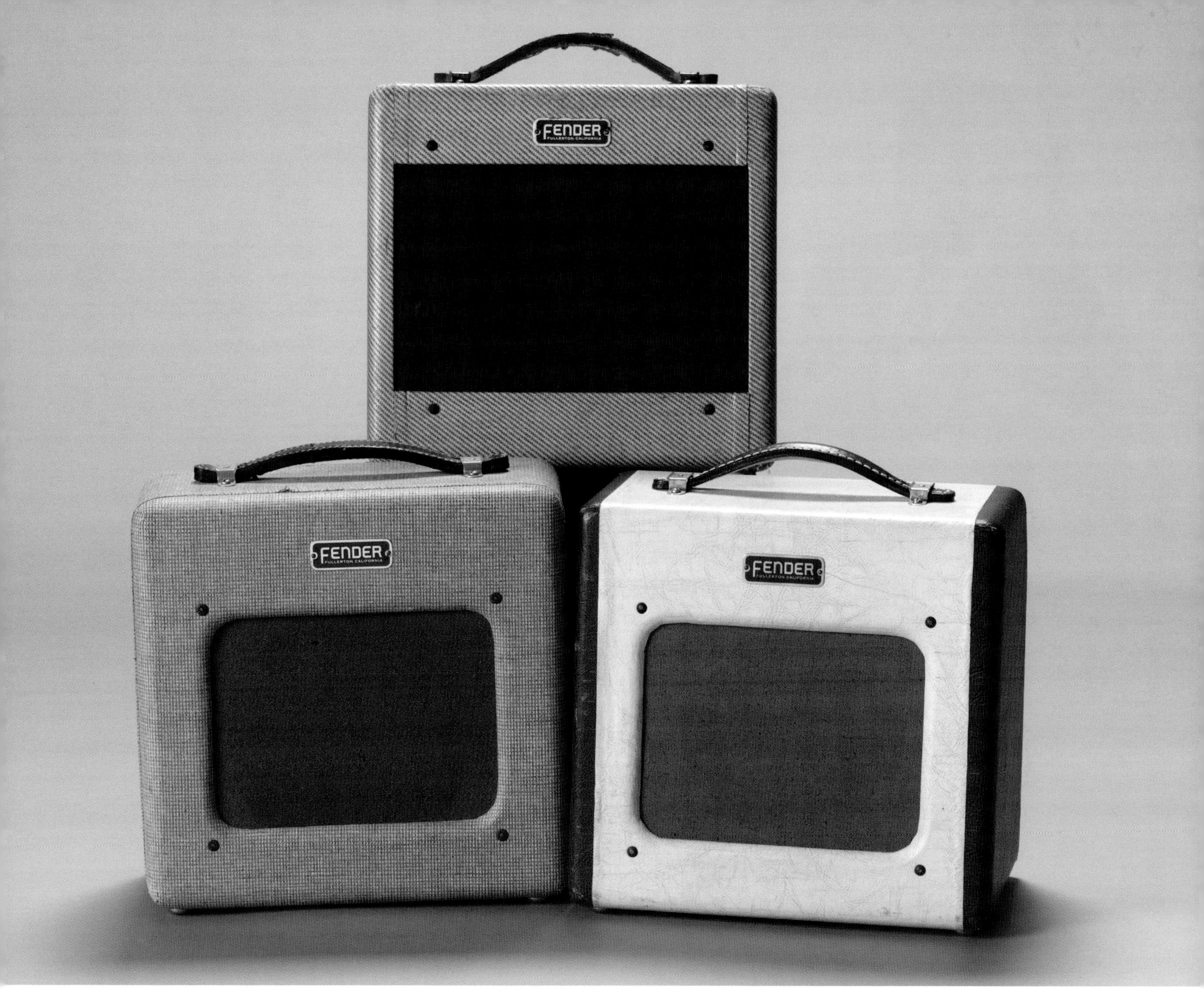

The first three generations of the Champ: The earliest is the exceedingly rare Champion 800 in the gray-green linen covering (left). It was followed by the "two-tone" leatherette Champion 600 (right; also see Chap. 9). On both amps, the chassis is made of an angled piece of copper-plated sheet metal, which slides into slots and is fastened to the back of the wooden cabinet with screws. The 800 has an 8″ speaker, and the two-tone has a 6″ speaker. The two-tone 600 was succeeded by the wide panel tweed Champ [top], with a 6″ speaker.

Hear the Champ 600, Tracks 54 - 55.

WDIA
WDIA
BEE-BEE KING
STAR OF WDIA
MEMPHIS TENN.

CHAPTER NINE

9

The TV Fronts of 1948 to 1953

Pages From a Place Called Fullerton, California

As we saw in the previous section, the Fender amps of the mid and late 1940s included the three woodies (Princeton, Deluxe/Model 26, and Professional), plus the two Champion/Champs (models 800 and 600), as well as the Dual Professional and its successor, the V-front Super. That same decade saw substantial updates of the Princeton, Deluxe, and Pro; these were the first of the "TV front" models.

A Note About Dates and the Big Picture

A document of the evolution of Fender amplifiers could entail a series of parallel columns of text, each addressing one aspect: actual circuits, dated schematics, dated wiring diagrams, pot codes, speaker codes, circuit codes, model names, the details printed in catalogs, price lists, ads and brochures, and finally, outward features such as cabinets, coverings, name plates, and so on.

Young man blues: The once and forever King of the Blues, B.B. King, at WDIA in Memphis, the first radio station in America programmed by black professionals for black audiences. B.B. King used Fender amps as soon as he could afford them, graduating to his favorite, the Twin.

Here's the thing: No two of these columns would line up with precision. As explained in this and other chapters, generalizations about Fender amps typically have so many exceptions, and so many different *kinds* of exceptions, that the only way to know with certainty what's inside a vintage Fender is to open it up and look. So, while the dates presented here result from much research, remember that they are generalizations. The goal here is to chart the big-picture evolution of these amplifiers as reflections of advancing technologies, players' tastes and needs, and Mr. Fender's personal vision.

Bass-Mans, Band Masters, and Twin-Amps

Throughout its history Fender has sometimes spelled the name of a product a few different ways, as seen particularly when comparing amplifier control panels or schematics to catalog text (in some early-'50s literature the Telecaster appears as the Tele-caster). Despite the typically hyphenated model names on amp control panels, here we will use the far more common unhyphenated spellings — Twin, as opposed to Twin-Amp — as seen in the vast majority of Fender catalogs and guitar literature in general.

FENDER

"Tweed" and "blackface," like "silverface," were nicknames for a couple of decades. In this book they are lowercased most of the time (e.g., tweed Princeton), yet capitalized when the terms, now legally protected, are part of a proper name (the Tweed Series of the early '90s).

A Place Called Fullerton

For most guitar companies, literature such as advertisements, brochures, price lists, and catalogs provide at best only the most general information regarding product specs. Often they are simply inaccurate, such as when old catalog blurbs are reprinted despite a product's updating, or when photos and text don't match, or when illustrations picture prototypes rather than production models.

Fender is no exception. In fact, it must have racked up some sort of record when it comes to such mismatches. Some early amplifiers were never pictured in the literature, and some of the illustrations did not precisely depict actual production models. A particularly Leo-esque complication was that he improved his products so frequently that no series of catalogs could be expected to keep up. Accordingly, throughout *The Soul of Tone*, production dates often come from sources other than company literature.

But Fender's publications are useful for other reasons. They reveal much about the company's philosophy, its perceptions of its customers, as well as the general evolution of amps and instruments from one era to the next. If we read between the lines a bit, we can also discern Fender's take on how its products related to each other and to those of its competitors.

Throughout the classic period from Fender's founding to its sale to CBS almost twenty years later, its literature brims with a confidence in the gear and an exuberance about players making music, whether practicing at home, participating in studio-sponsored classes, or stepping into the spotlight with their livelihoods on the line.

Mr. Fender's name was never mentioned in these publications. The notion that a softspoken former radio repairman would someday be revered as a titan of his industry and even romanticized as a fabled, legendary figure would have seemed as alien to Mr. Fender as the New York Dolls. Forrest White's first encounter with the Fender name was typical. As he recalled in his book *Fender, The Inside Story*, he attended a Cowboy Copas concert and thought the steel guitar on stage produced "the most beautiful, clear sound I had ever heard." He met the musician and asked to see the guitar. "I found out the name was Fender. I asked him why it was called that, and he said that was the name of the man who made it, in a place called Fullerton, California, not far from Los Angeles."

Leo Fender's famous dedication to serviceability fairly drips from the pages of these catalogs, and in places he speaks as much to his fellow repairmen as to players. Manufacturers typically give some sort of obligatory lip service to the ruggedness of their products, but how many guitar companies of the early 1950s — or any time — would go so far as to specify in their general catalogs anything like this:

> "The Fender line of amplifiers is so constructed that every part is accessible by simply removing the back plate. When this plate is removed, it exposes the entire component parts assembly of the amplifier with the one exception of the power transformer." [It goes on to explain how the power transformer is removed.] "Upon inspection, it will be noted that all of the component parts such as resistors, condensers, etc. within the chassis are substantially mounted on terminal boards, and these boards in turn are held in place by machine screws, making it impossible for parts to vibrate and shake loose …."

Here is the kind of commercial literature that almost disappeared in the era between Fender's first golden age and the rise of boutique amps decades later, a publication reflecting not only the strategy of the marketing department but a voice from behind the drawing board as well.

It's impossible to read these catalogs and brochures without absorbing Fender's commitment to providing high-quality amps and guitars to eager youngsters, discriminating professionals, and everyone in between. And it wasn't just the expensive amplifiers that Leo Fender took seriously; across the product line, his message was as straightforward as a Princeton circuit, as loud and clear as a Pro with a JBL: *This gear sounds good, and it's tough as nails.*

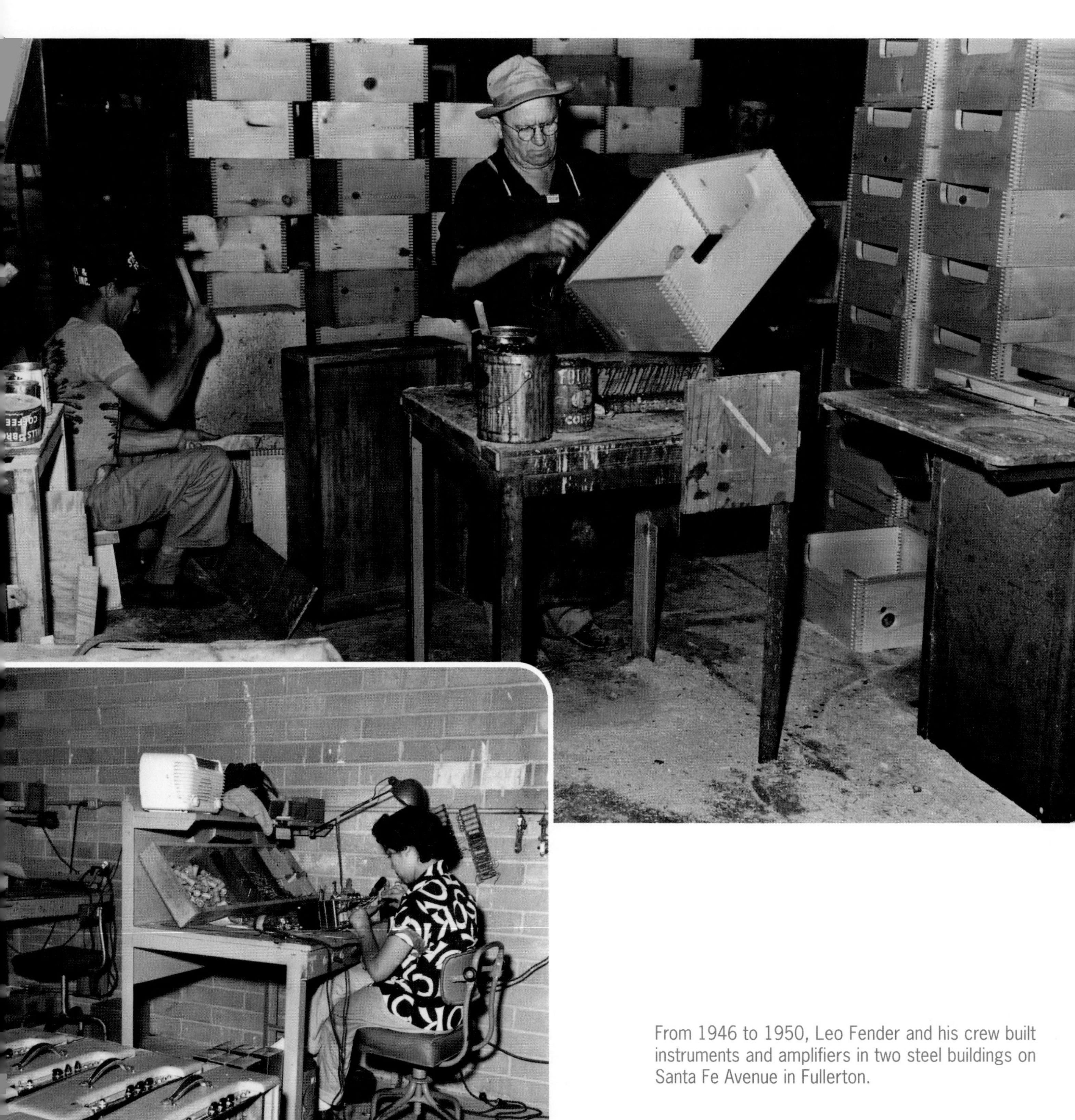

From 1946 to 1950, Leo Fender and his crew built instruments and amplifiers in two steel buildings on Santa Fe Avenue in Fullerton.

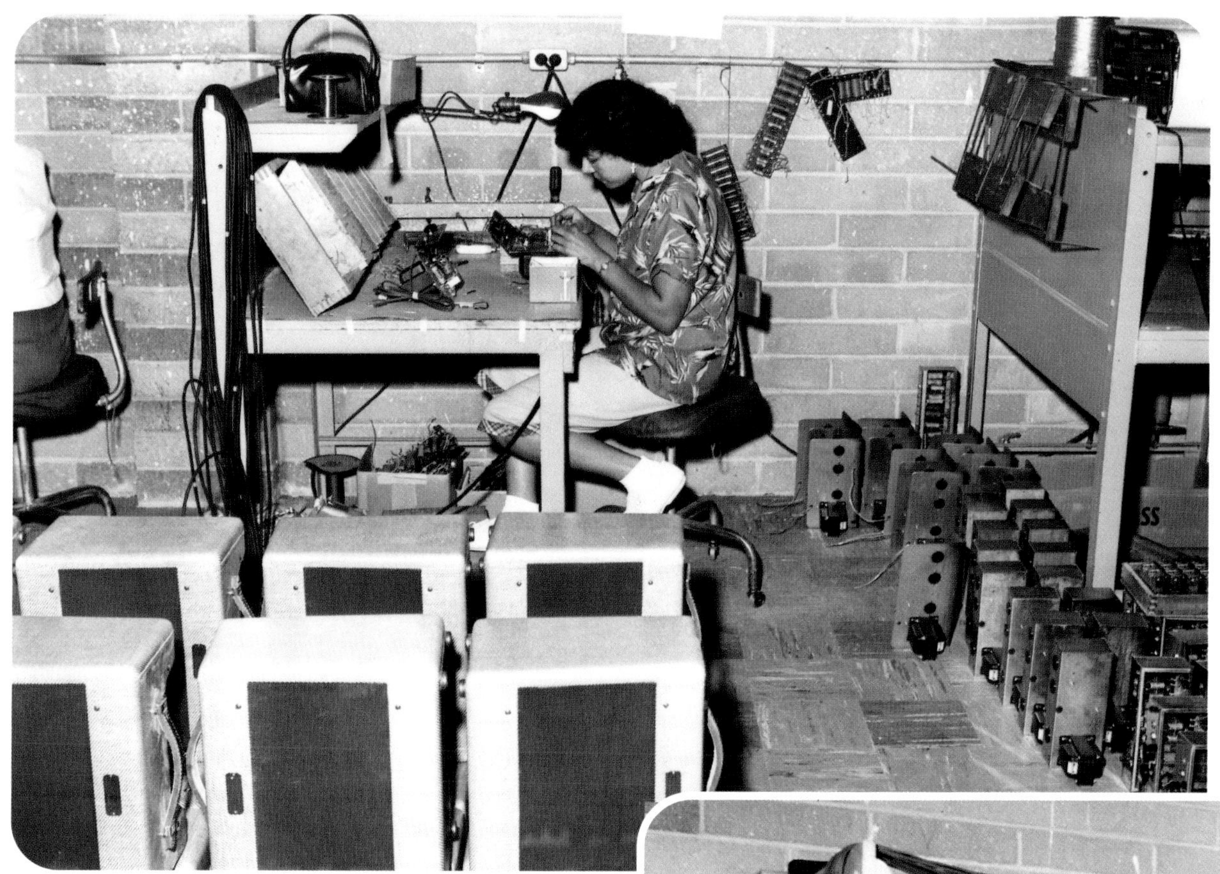

Mr. Fender expanded his shop with a cinder-block building in the summer of 1950. These workers are assembling amplifiers in the Santa Fe Avenue facility, early '50s.

Bill Carson: Leo always leaned toward the unit being very serviceable. Along with the TV thing that was going on at the time [a marketable concept of user serviceability], a big thing with Leo was to get that chassis out in just a couple minutes and get a good look at it where you could see what was wrong and test it. He leaned toward ninety-nine percent serviceability and only one percent cosmetics.

Tom Wheeler: And yet the amplifiers looked great.

Bill Carson: [Laughs.] Yeah, they did.

"Much of the success of those early amps has to do with their build quality. As a repairman Leo would see other amplifiers' shortcomings and know what not to do. I can imagine him saying, 'Well, they could have done this better, and they could have done that better.' First and foremost he was building amps that could withstand the rigors of the road. And if something did go wrong, they were simple to service. The way the parts are laid out on that component board was so clean, rather than having them flying all over the place, with resistors soldered right to a tube socket or an input jack or whatever. Leo put everything on that fiber eyelet board, and everything was laid out neatly. Reliability and serviceability made his amps landmarks. If you were a pro, you used a Fender."

— Mark Baier, Victoria Amp Co.

"Fine Electric Instruments"

The "Fender Fine Electric Instruments" catalog of 1950 showcased several steel guitars and introduced the revolutionary new Esquire electric "Spanish" guitar, one of the most important instruments of the 20th Century and a forerunner of the Broadcaster, "Nocaster," Telecaster, and every other successful solidbody guitar. Most players are familiar with the terms "pedal steel," "Hawaiian guitar," and "lap steel," but in early Fender literature such instruments were often called simply "guitars." It was the ground-breaking Esquire that needed the "electric Spanish" description to distinguish it from the "regular" lap-style instruments Leo Fender had been building since World War II.

The amp line numbered just five models, all of them by now familiar names to the Fender faithful. Except for the uniquely styled V-front Super, they represented the "TV front" cabinet style, now two to three years old, depending on the model. (The sixth member of the TV front era was a bass amp, called simply "Amplifier" in 1951, "Bassman" in 1952 and thereafter.)

Each amp featured the black "chickenhead" pointer knobs common to the radio market. They were arrayed on a top-mounted, chromed control panel, a detail introduced on the Dual Professional. Except for the Champion, the TV front cabinets were covered in "the highest grade of airplane luggage type linen." Fender didn't call it "tweed," but that's the name enthusiasts came up with years later to describe the striped cloth that covered these amps until the onset of the Tolex era in 1960. (There were several tweed patterns, some more common than others.) Emphasizing its cardinal virtue of durability, Fender assured prospective customers that the linen covering was "ideal for long and faithful use under the most trying conditions." The speaker baffles were covered in a brown fabric similar to mohair.

The three amps in the upper tier were the TV front 1x12 Deluxe ($89.50), the V-front 2x10 Super ($169.50), and the TV front 1x15 Pro ($199.50). Each had three knobs: separate volume controls for one or more instruments or microphones, and a single tone knob. At the time, accommodating more than one input device was a priority, while a single knob was deemed adequate for tonal flexibility.

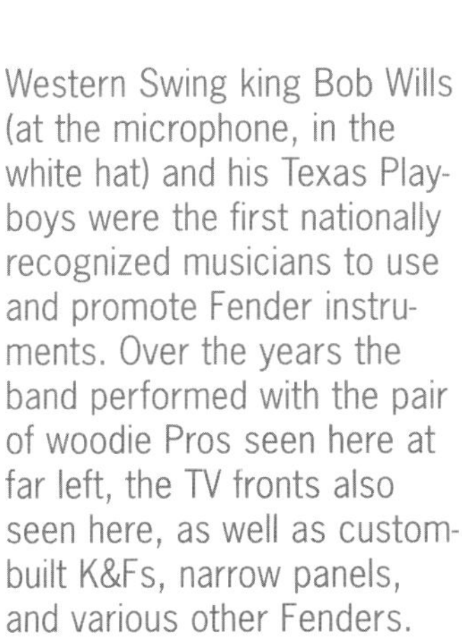

Western Swing king Bob Wills (at the microphone, in the white hat) and his Texas Playboys were the first nationally recognized musicians to use and promote Fender instruments. Over the years the band performed with the pair of woodie Pros seen here at far left, the TV fronts also seen here, as well as custom-built K&Fs, narrow panels, and various other Fenders.

Down a step from the 1x12 Deluxe was the $64.50 1x8 Princeton, which looked like the other tweeds, only smaller, and sported two knobs instead of three — one volume (abbreviated here as V) and one tone (T). Note: The woodie 1x10 Deluxe having evolved to a tweed 1x12, there were no 1x10 models in the 1950 catalog.

At the bottom of the line was the Champion, a little one-knob amplifier not much bigger than a lunchbox. Also called Champion 600, this $49.95 model appeared alongside the entry-level Champion steel guitar; together they were billed as nothing less than "one of the finest low-priced combinations in musical history." (Sixty years later, the description still stands.)

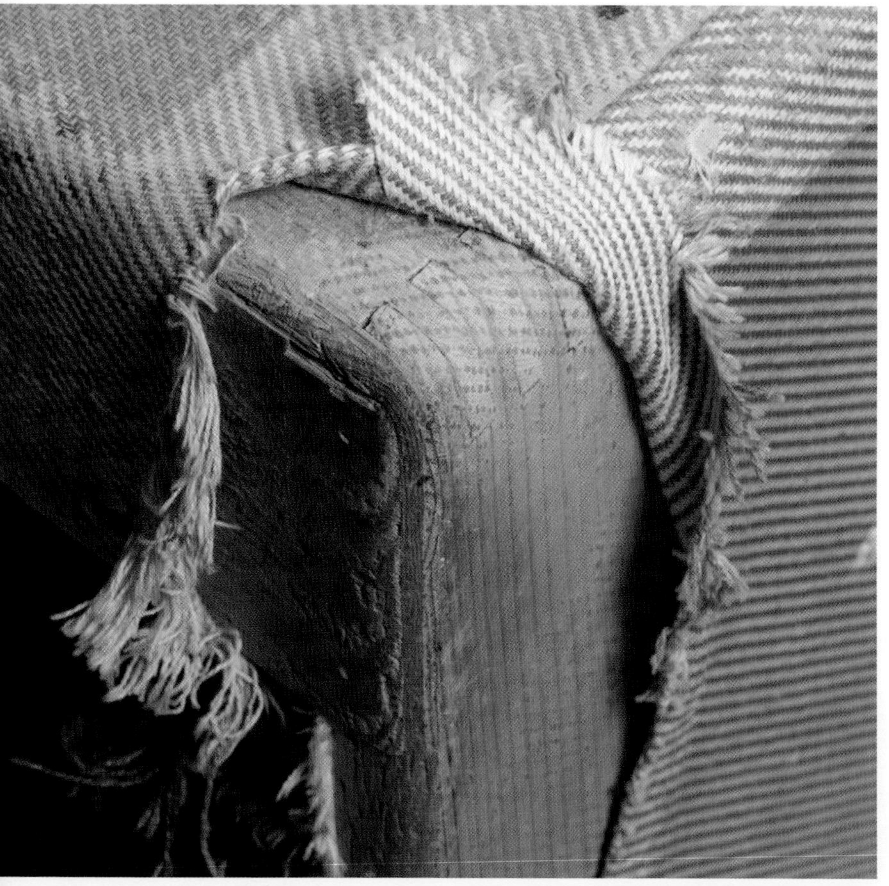

When Leo Fender promised that his amps were rugged, he wasn't fooling around. Lock jointed corners, as seen on this zillion-gig tweed tone warrior, helped keep Fender amps in working order long after many competitors had succumbed to the rigors of the road.

The Pro and the Super had four input jacks, the Deluxe three. The Princeton had two, as did the Champion, revealing Mr. Fender's opinion that even a "student" amp should accommodate not only your guitar but also your microphone, or a rhythm guitarist, or your teacher's guitar. (If you bought one of the larger Fenders, your whole band could play through the thing, and some did.)

The 1950 catalog's Introduction concluded with this: "The Fender people hope to always be close to the feelings of those who buy, sell, and play electric instruments, because that is the greatest source of information for the development and improvement of the instruments." Fender's wish came true. For years to come, a continuous stream of feedback from players and dealers would result in countless improvements to the guitars and amps and sometimes in entirely new models.

Two-Tone Champ

Although it had a little 6" speaker, was short on features, and was marketed as a student model, Fender's least expensive amp bore a feisty name — Champion — and came from the same sturdy stock as its bigger brothers: "ruggedly constructed of 3/4" solid wood, lock jointed at the corners." This "fine, low-cost unit" had its own look, with an angled, rear-facing panel instead of the top-mounted chrome plate found on its tweed siblings, and a slightly different cabinet shape; rather than tweed, it was covered in brown and cream leatherette, giving rise to its "two-tone" nickname. For a small product it had many names: Champion in the catalog, Champion 600 on its interior paper label, and "600" Amp stenciled on the control panel. The two-tone would run until 1953.

TV Front Deluxe

Successor to the hardwood-cab Model 26, the TV front Deluxe premiered in 1948 with the musical combo of an octal preamp tube, two 6V6 output tubes, cathode biasing, a small output transformer, a single alnico-magnet Jensen P12R 12" speaker, and a modest output of about 12 to 15W. It was the first tweed version of a long-running dynasty of beloved club-gig amplifiers. (Who *hasn't* played a gig with a Deluxe of one vintage or another?) In its day, the TV front

Left to right: songwriters Dub Williams and Eddie Miller, Lydia Sanchez (who assembled and signed many a tweed Fender) and Leo Fender, winter '50 - '51. Note the 3-knob, 1x15 top of the line Pros in front, and the stack of two-tone Champ 600s behind Mr. Fender.

Deluxe cost $99.50 and was Fender's most popular amplifier. According to Richard Smith, Leo Fender's records revealed that 1,539 Deluxes were shipped in 1951, nearly fifty percent more than any other model. Famed for its rectifier sag at higher volumes, smooth compression, and eagerness to lapse into creamy distortion, the Deluxe would become the most revered 1x12 combo of all time, a cornerstone of the Fender line and an indispensable tool for countless players at all levels. Author Dave Hunter: "It flatters the traditional electric blues soloist like few other amps out there."

An early Fender amp was a thing of beauty from the inside as well as the outside. Its logical layout and neat hand-wiring made it not only functional but also easy to service.

TV Front Pro

Like the Deluxe, the TV front 1x15 Pro was a successor to a charter member of the Fender line, the hardwood-cab Professional. In the 1950 catalog, four of the five descriptions of amplifiers used the word "rugged," while in the case of the Pro, Fender went so far as to specify "a cabinet which is especially constructed to withstand the added weight and the abuse to which professional instruments are sometimes subjected." Fender backed up the claim with cabinets of solid pine, finger joined at the corners for extra strength.

TV Front Bassman

In 1952, Fender unveiled its 1x15 Bassman amp, although before Don Randall conceived the name, the literature had called it simply "Amplifier." It was a two-knob, two-input companion to the just-introduced Precision Bass, yet another milestone from the mind of Leo Fender. Although Mr. Fender hoped acoustic bassists would convert to his radical invention, he also designed the Telecaster-like P Bass for guitarists who could double on the new instrument.

With respect to the amplifier, however, Fender acknowledged the technical challenges of reproducing low frequencies by billing the Bassman as a "bass only" device. Consequently, it featured a "specially designed" Jensen P15N speaker as well as a short-lived experiment in cabinet design: Unique among Fender amps, the early Bassman had a closed back with two large circular ports. An April 1952 press release quoted Don Randall's description of the Precision Bass and its tweed companion: "Everything has been considered to make this a most foolproof amplifier. This is one of the most revolutionary combinations ever offered." George Gruhn: "Not only did Leo Fender make the first good, powerful guitar amps, but he also made the first amp that was worth calling a bass amp. He didn't invent the fretted bass — Audiovox had done that — but the Fender Precision was the first commercially successful fretted electric bass. Audiovox had an amp, too, but it wasn't very good. Leo had the bass — *and* the amp to go with it."

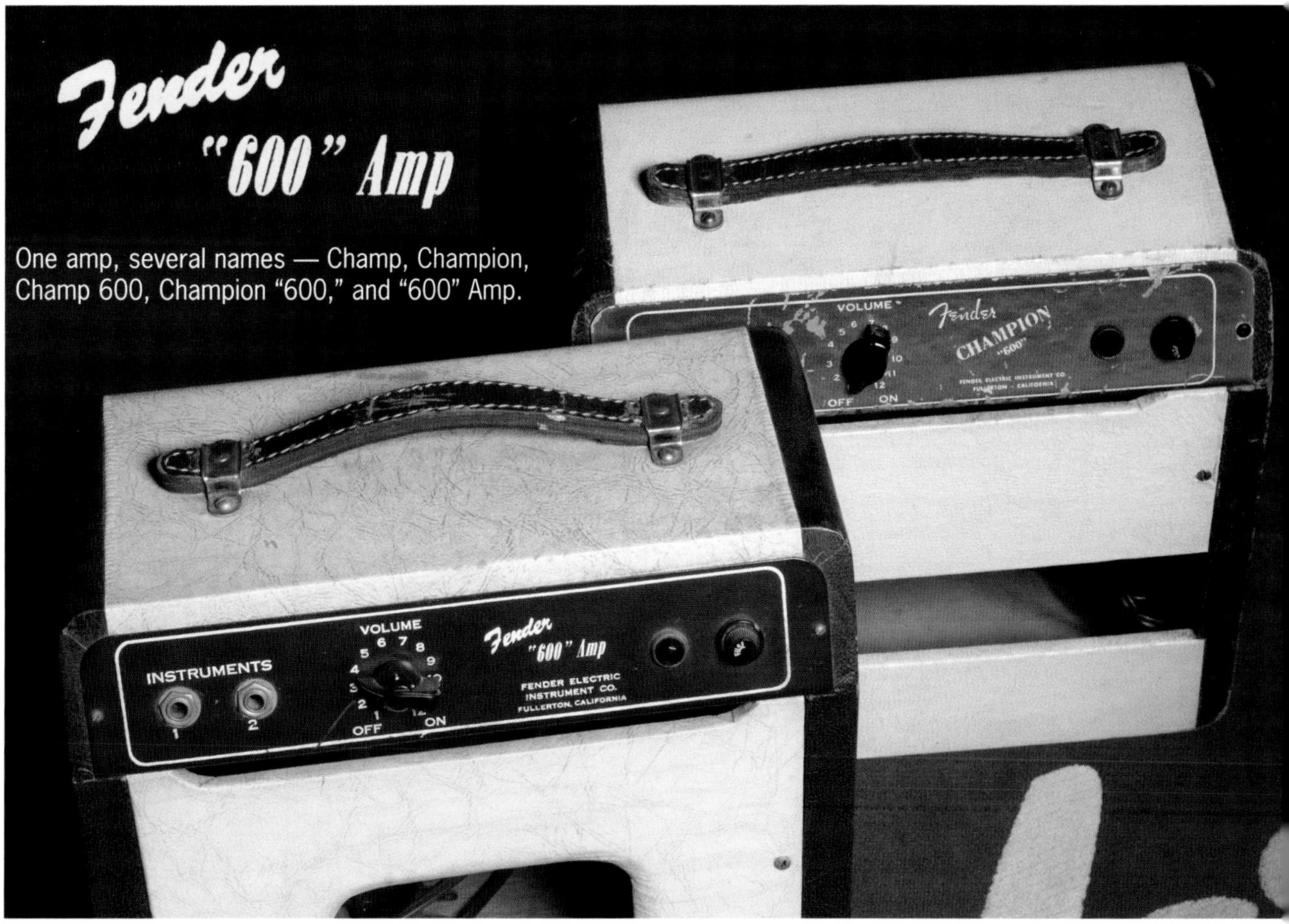

Two versions of the two-tone: the "600" Amp (the quote marks are part of the name), and the Champion "600." Perry Tate: "The lighter colored one is serial no. 143, from 1949. The one with the slightly marbleized coloring is no. 3392, from 1952. These are examples of Fender using something other than a Jensen speaker on occasion. Both have Cleveland Electronics 6 inch speakers. All of the Clevelands I've seen have kind of a light blue anodized finish. For example, I have a 1950 Princeton and a 1950 V-front Super with Cletrons, from Cleveland Electronics. The EIA code, 433, tells you it's a Cleveland speaker. I've seen them only in '49 and '50."

Fender "600" Amp

One amp, several names — Champ, Champion, Champ 600, Champion "600," and "600" Amp.

Circuits in Woodies and TV Fronts

Before Mr. Fender settled into the nearly exclusive use of 9-pin 12AX7s and 12AY7s in the mid 1950s, he employed in his hardwood-cab and TV front models a variety of larger, octal-base (8-pin) preamp tubes: the 6SN7, 6SC7, and 6SL7 (all dual triodes), as well as the 6SJ7 pentode. Power tubes were 6V6s in the smaller amps and 6L6s in the larger ones, setting the general pattern that the tube amps would follow throughout Fender's history. Phase inverters were of the early paraphase type, and rectifiers were 5U4s or 5Y3s.

These were low-power amplifiers (certainly by the standards of later decades), with simple circuits, a single channel, and no effects. The top of the line Pro, for example, had one tone knob, one speaker, and an output of about 20W to 25W. It did the job, and it sounded great.

TV front Deluxe, chassis detail picturing a pair of octal 6SC7 tubes.

Two-tone Champion 600 [right] and TV front Princeton. The woodie Princeton had appeared in 1946 and two years later evolved to the TV front version shown here. Ever sensitive to the rigors of hard playing, Leo Fender did not design these amps to be coddled. Even the modestly appointed 1x8 Princeton would "withstand a terrific amount of abuse."

Built only a month or so apart, these TV front Deluxes illustrate a problem and the solution. Players used the cabinet's rear cavity to store guitar cords, sheet music, a pack of Luckys, a couple of bottles of Schlitz Black Label or whatever, and sometimes tubes were damaged when stuff got moved around. The later cab on the left shows Mr. Fender's solution, an extended upper panel that provides access while protecting the tubes. According to Richard Smith, the alteration occurred in the summer of 1951.

Hear the "Deluxes Gone Wild" Jam, featuring narrow panel, blackface, brown, and TV front Deluxes, Tracks 22 - 23.

Les Remembers Leo

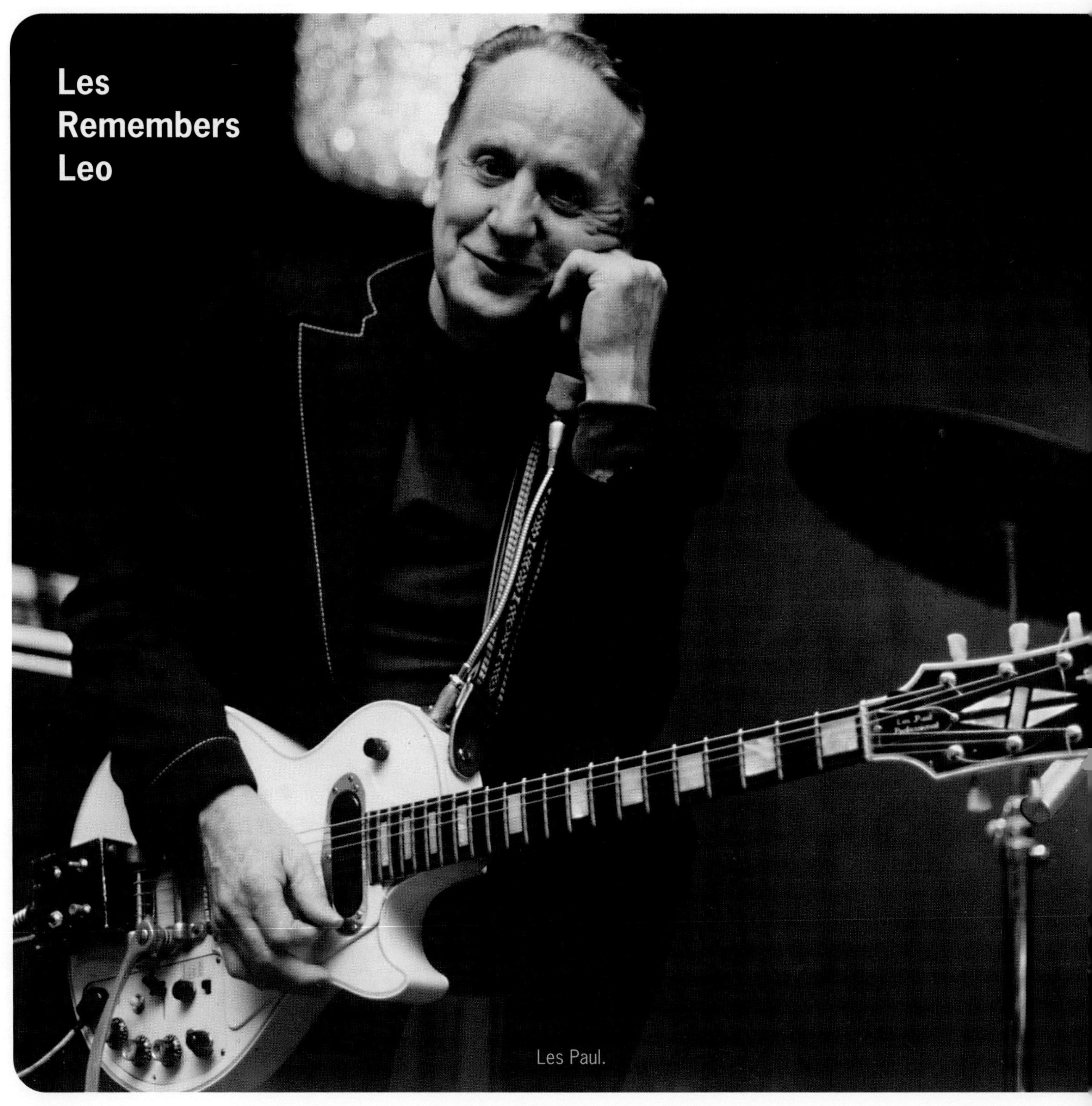

Les Paul.

Richard Smith has written, "All electric guitar pickups had what Leo Fender called 'performance deficiencies,' peaks and valleys in the audio spectrum. Leo realized that a good guitar amplifier should compensate." Les Paul agreed (from an interview with the author):

"Off and on I've used Fender amps my whole life, especially if it was in a country western band. Back when Leo was just starting, he would come over to the studio in the back yard of my house in Los Angeles, and he would want to get comments on his amp. I did a lot of recording for other people in my back yard. It wasn't to make money but just for me to learn how to record. I was teaching myself how to record a French horn, how to mike a piano, whatever it might be, and Leo would come over when he knew a date was coming in and he was furnishing them with a guitar and an amplifier. He would ask questions, lots of questions, and we would discuss what was good and what wasn't good.

"It was a very interesting time. There were so many problems to be solved. The electric guitar in general was anything but correct. The pickups were just under the string wherever you chose to put them, and there had to be a lot of equalizing, or something done, so the wrong move at the guitar could be corrected at the amplifier. By wrong move, I mean the way the pickup is made. I'm just talking about electric guitars in general. There was nobody out there building [electric] guitars up until that time who had really gone to school, studied it, and really understood all the problems. So, consequently there was a lot of hoodoo.

"But Fender was willing to listen, and they made alterations all the time to better a condition that wasn't right to begin with. Leo talked to musicians all the time, but most of them weren't actually building instruments and designing as well as playing them, so he and I really did have a lot to talk about. We spent hours talking about it.

"With the high impedance [pickups], every foot of cable you put in there — oh my God, it's just endless, the problems. I could write nine books on all the things that would be desirable to do differently, but we've gone down this long road [of high impedance systems] for so long. Trying to build the amplifier, there were just so many problems, and they seemed insurmountable. If you box up the cabinet, you've got a resonance that's going to interfere with the bottom end, and if you open-back it, you've lost so much energy. But of the bunch, the Fender amplifier has stood head-high through it all, and in Leo's time, and still today, it's because Fender listened to the customer.

"With the guitars, Leo went his way and I ended up going down a different road to get the sounds I wanted, which were preferable from the Gibson side of things. I was with Gibson, and I stayed loyal to them. They were number one, and Fender hadn't really started. But Leo and I agreed that it was a compromise between the guitar and the amplifier. Electric guitars were never perfect, and the amps were never perfect, but they were designed to be kind of a matched set so they would work together for you.

"Leo Fender never felt he had come near completing his wish to get the sound he wanted to hear, and I didn't do any better than he did."

— Les Paul

TV front versions of the mid-line Deluxe (right) and top-of-the-line Pro.

"A Telecaster never sounds more like a Telecaster than when it's plugged into a Fender amp. Like we say around here:

Scientific proof! Your Fender guitar sounds like itself through a Fender amp!"

— Richard McDonald

George Fullerton recalls meeting country superpicker Jimmy Bryant: "We finally got that Broadcaster out on the market. One night Leo and I took one up to a ballroom called Riverside Rancho in L.A. A young fellow came over, about my age, I guess, and he wanted to know what we had, and we said, we have a guitar here, and he said, can I try it, and we said sure, that's why we have it here.

"When the band took a break, this player asked the bandleader if he could plug it into one of their Fender amps up on the stage. I'm not sure which model of amp it was. Bandleader says sure, go ahead. So he just sat on the stage with his feet hanging over the side and started playing that guitar through that amp. It was an amazing thing. The band never went back to playing that night, and the dancers never went back to dancing. He must have sat there an hour and a half, maybe even two hours, playing that guitar all by himself. That was Jimmy Bryant. That was the night we met him. Everybody just crowded around this young man playing that Fender guitar through that Fender amp."

Capitol
RECORDS
Jimmy Bryant

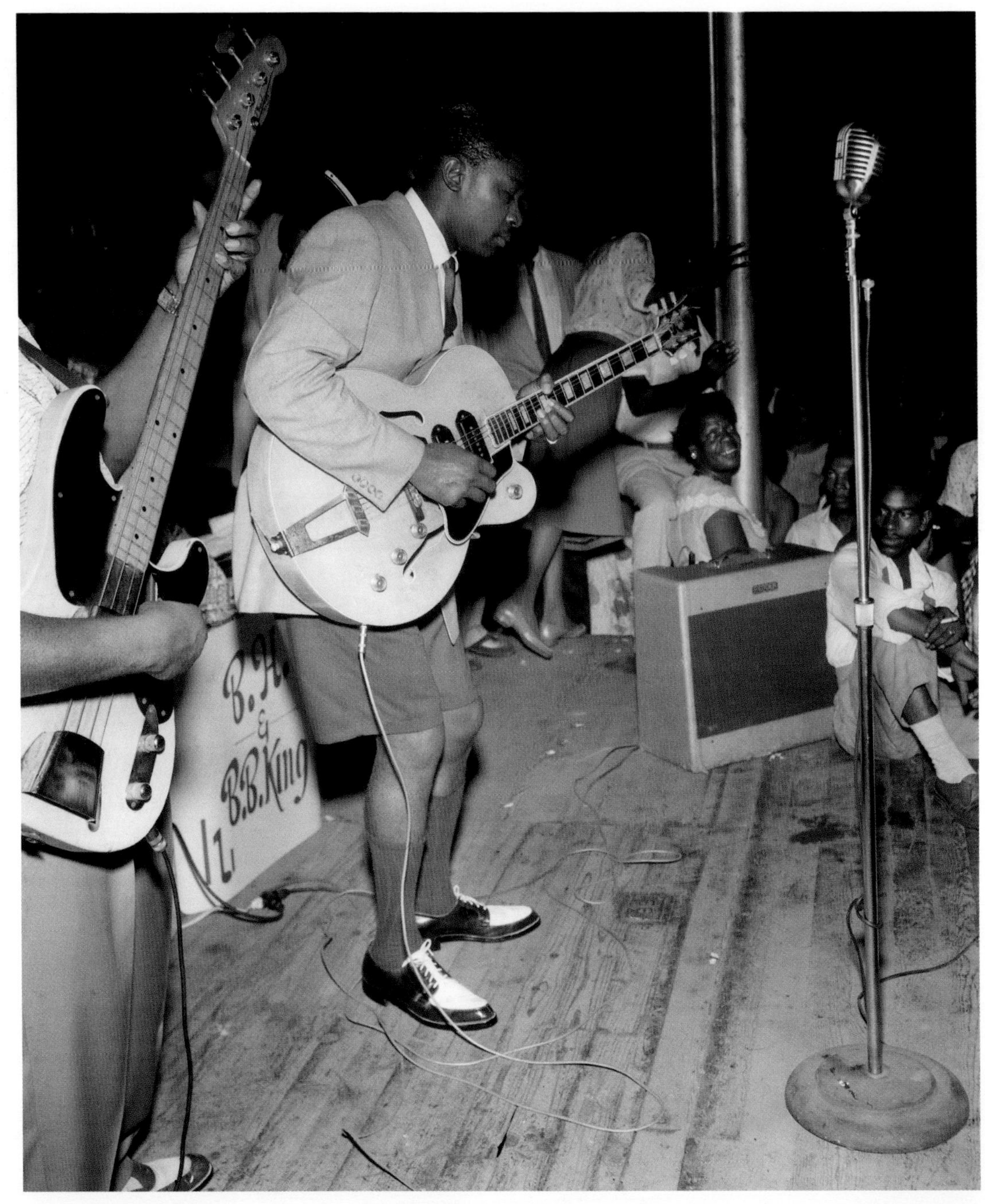

Three P-90s through a wide panel tweed Fender — in the hands of B.B. King? Have mercy! The up-close crowd, the stylin' suit, and the Bermuda shorts are merely additional reminders that we can be cool, but we can never be *this* cool. In the book *The B.B. King Companion*, B.B. cited a quote from his cousin Bukka White in reference to this photo. It alludes to the racism King encountered as well as to his lifelong mission to use music to bring the races together: "I used to think that look was kind of hot stuff. If you come up and you're not dressed nice, you look like you're a beggar. But dressed up, the white people see you, and you're like a preacher or something like that, so you get by a little bit easier." The amp is either a Pro or a Bandmaster (they shared the same 20x22" wide panel cab).

C H A P T E R T E N

10

The Wide Panel Tweeds

1953 to 1955

The big news in 1954's catalog was the announcement of the astonishing Stratocaster guitar, profiled alongside an expanded amplifier line with redesigned cabinets later nicknamed the wide panels. These cabs featured broad, tweed-covered panels above and below the speaker opening, and dark brown linen grille cloth in place of the mohair type fabric of the early TV front period. The wide panel era actually spanned from early 1953 to 1955, and most of the "new" developments in 1954's catalog were a year old; the "new" Bassman was *two* years old and had already evolved from its initial TV front cab to the new wide panel.

Now numbering eight models, the amp line included updates of the Pro, Super, Deluxe, Princeton, Bassman, and "student" model (Champion), as well as the newest members of Fender's expanding family, both from '53 — the 2x12 Twin and the 1x15 Bandmaster (or Band Master, as it was called in some literature for its first couple of years).

Today we think of a 1x15 amp as being something of a specialty item, but Mr. Fender — committed to sturdy construction and ever in search of clean headroom — was particularly fond of 15s. After the arrival of the Bassman and Bandmaster, the 1x15 cab was Fender's most common arrangement. In the 1954 line, for example, each amp had a unique speaker complement all to itself: 1x6, 1x8, 2x10, etc. The exceptions were the 1x15 models, and there were three of them: Bassman, Bandmaster, and Pro. Each was fitted with Jensen's P15N loudspeaker.

Wide Panel Cabs and C Circuits

As with the earlier woodies and TV fronts, most of the C circuit amplifiers of the wide panel era specified octal preamp tubes such as the 6SC7, 6J5, and 6SJ7. However, the schematics for the 5C4 Super and the identically circuited 5C5 Pro specified "6SC7 (12AY7)" and "6SC7 (12AX7)" tubes, marking the transition from older, 6V octal tubes to the miniature, 9-pin 12V devices that have powered Fender tube preamps ever since. Early 5C4 Supers and 5C5 Pros used the octal 6V tubes, while later versions of the same C circuits used the mini 12V tubes. Greg Gagliano estimates the switch occurred in mid 1954. Aspen Pittman: "The schematics specify both tube types to cover anyone who might have bought one of those amps during the transition period. The circuits are the same,

Wide panel Deluxe (left) and Princeton.

although the tubes do not sound the same."

Fender continued to employ its standard tube types in the output sections: 6V6/6V6GTs in the Champ, Princeton, and Deluxe, and 6L6s or 6L6Gs in the more powerful models; the brand new, top of the line 5C8 Twin specified either 6L6s or the tubes that would power famous Fenders in years to come, small-bottle 5881s. Rectifier tubes in C circuit amps were 5Y3/5Y3GTs or 5U4Gs.

In the TV front era even the top of the line Pro had featured only a single tone control, but we see in the wide panels the first glimmer of a new approach to versatility that would characterize the evolution of Fender amps for decades to come: the addition of separate bass and treble controls in amps such as the 5C7 Bandmaster and 5C8 Twin.

Champ

The wide panel Champ Amp of 1953 to 1955 entailed both the 5C1 and the 5D1 circuits and was the successor to the two-tone leatherette Champion 600. For a year or two, however, it seemed Fender couldn't figure out what to call it. Like both earlier and later versions, this model appeared by itself and also as a member of Fender's steel guitar/amp set, but in both instances the '54 catalog called it the "student" amplifier (the "S" was sometimes capitalized, as if Student Amplifier were the official name); confusingly, there was no Champion in that catalog's copy, and no Champ, even though Fender was making these amplifiers under one name or the other — or both.

So, like its two-tone predecessor, early versions of the wide panel Champ had three names, but they were slightly different this time around: Student Amplifier in the catalog, Champ Amp on the paper label, and "600" Amp on the control panel (later wide panel Champs added yet another variation and were labeled *Champ Amp* on the control panel). All this merely reveals that Fender Sales, Inc., only a year old in 1954, and the factory were working out their communication as well as various wrinkles in the marketing.

Greg Gagliano: "This is why early catalogs cause so much confusion. The model names were on the Champ tube charts as early as 1948. These were the Champion 600, which was common, and [the earlier] Champion 800, which was very rare. A lot of the 600s actually have 800 tube charts with the '800' marked out and '600' marked in. The name change from Champion 600 to Champ occurred around October 1953, but it took a while — as it often did — for the catalog to catch up. There are even tweed 'Champion 600' 5C1 tube charts and tweed 'Champ' 5C1 tube charts, but [despite the slightly different names] both amps are the same. By the way, the only Fender 'Student model' I've heard of (in real life, not a catalog) is a woodie."

This fuzzy nomenclature seemed to parallel the amp's unique styling, which, while attractive, nevertheless set it apart from the other models up the line. Unlike its one-of-a-kind, leatherette covered predecessor, from the front the wide panel version did indeed look like the rest of its contemporaries, only smaller. From the back, however, it was once again unique, with a slightly canted, rear-facing panel.

At any rate, the surprisingly loud little amp reflected Fender's conviction that today's buyer of a student model is tomorrow's professional customer. It was touted as being "well suited to the player who does not require the high power of a larger amplifier, or for the student who necessarily must carry his amplifier and guitar to and from class." Indeed, with your Harmony Stratotone strapped across your back and your Champ in the basket of your Schwinn Black Phantom, you were geared up and ready to roll.

Deluxe and Princeton

"Tops in style and beauty" (and who can argue?), the wide panel 2x6V6GT Deluxe was a favorite of Scotty Moore, who reportedly used one on some of the most important recordings in the history of popular music: Elvis Presley's early sides for the Sun record label in Memphis. It had three knobs (V, V, T) and three jacks (two for instruments, one for a microphone). Typical of Fenders of the era, all the chickenheads went to 12. Circuits 5B3, 5C3, and 5D3 varied with respect to tubes, feedback loop, and other particulars, although each was mated to a Jensen 12" P12R Concert Series speaker.

The wide panel Princeton had two jacks and two knobs (V, T), and it put out about 4½W. Circuits 5B2, 5C2, and 5D2 of this cathode-biased 1x8 amp varied with respect to preamp tubes, power tubes, and rectifier, evolving in each case from metal-encased tubes to modern glass bottles.

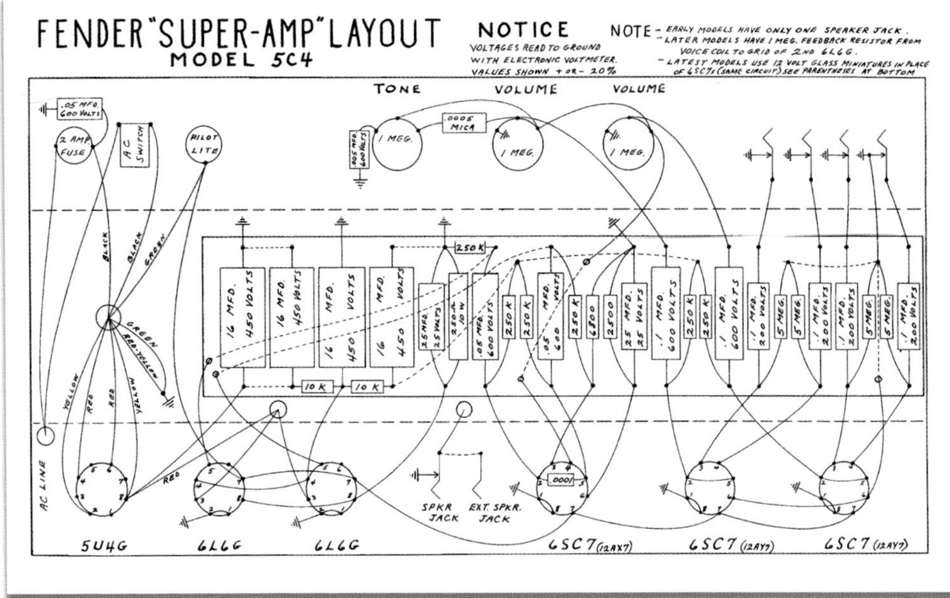

Chassis layout, 5C4 Super. The preamp tubes are specified to be "6SC7 (12AY7)," marking the transition from 6V octal tubes to the 9-pin 12V devices seen in later Fender tube amps. Mark Baier: "Those schematics were just so beautiful, man. It's all right there. And those Fender layout drawings that show where all the components go — had it not been for them, I probably would have never built my first amplifier."

Super

In a step toward cosmetic consistency across the line, the wide panel 2x10 Super dropped the angled baffles and chrome center strip that had distinguished both the earlier V-front Super and the Dual Professional. It had a pair of Jensen P10Rs, four jacks, and a single tone knob. Decades before rock guitarists discovered the glories of even-harmonic distortion in these amps, Fender promised the Super and others would deliver "excellent distortionless power."

The 1x15s: Pro, Bassman, Bandmaster

The 2x6L6G wide panel Pro featured the line's new "modern styling," which included not only the new cabinet design but also a new brown linen baffle covering. Its four input jacks and two volume controls reflected Fender's continued emphasis on accommodating multiple instruments or microphones, but its single "full range" tone control now seemed a bit limited for an upscale model, at least when compared to the increased versatility of its newer stablemates, the Bandmaster and Twin.

The marketing of the wide panel 5B6 Bassman represented one tactic in Fender's somewhat uneven commercial strategy. Powered by a pair of 5881s and featuring a heavy-duty Jensen P15N, it boasted a "unique speaker housing for bass emphasis," and was billed as "a new high in bass amplification." The catalog went so far as to assert: "It is not a hashed-over guitar amplifier, but an instrument that has been designed for the reproduction of bass and bass only." This made sense and was no doubt Leo Fender's original intent, but when marketing later versions, the company would soften its approach and

Wide panel Champ Amp.

Hank Thompson and his Brazos Valley Boys, ready to swing in late '53 with a trio of new wide panels and a TV front. Second from right: the very accomplished guitarist and longtime Fender employee Bill Carson. Front and center: Carson's Telecaster.

"I did the same sort of thing with the amplifiers that I did with the guitars — take them out on the bandstand, try them out and get back to Leo and Freddie [Tavares] and let them know how things were working, and what changes I might suggest.

"I worked on the early Twin. Everybody wanted clean volume. They didn't want the distortion in those days. I was working with PeeWee Whitewing in Hank Thompson's band. I was with that band in '52 and '53. PeeWee played steel guitar, and he and I were using Fender Pro amps, but there was a Standel that had a big speaker — it might have been a 15 inch James B. Lansing. The Standel was so loud and real clean, and that's what we wanted, but it just didn't have any color to it. It wasn't warm at all. Leo shipped us some prototypes he was working on, and that was right at the start of the Twin project. I liked the sound quite a bit, so I ended up using one of the brand new Fender Twins.

"Then in 1954 I was working locally in Orange County and South L.A. doing nightclub things, and Leo would bring an amp out to the bandstand, and I started going back and forth to the company quite a bit. I might go out with a prototype with an unplated chassis and no markings, no way to indicate the control settings, no numbers, just a piece of tape stuck on there where you could mark it with a ballpoint pen if you wanted to, just a raw breadboard model. And I would not only give Leo my comments, but I would collect comments from other players, too, about how we perceived the unit. And then Leo would go to work on it to try to meet those specs."

— Bill Carson

acknowledge what players were quick to discover — the new model was suitable for instruments other than bass, particularly guitar and harmonica. As noted in Chapter 9, the wide panel Bassman seen in this chapter has a ported back, a bottom-mounted chassis, and top-mounted control panel, all features it shared with its predecessor, the TV front Bassman.

The 1x15, 2x6L6G Bandmaster of 1953 did not appear in some literature of the wide panel era, but it was big news in the '54 catalog. (Teagle & Sprung report: "Prototype Bandmasters with the old TV front cabinets are rumored to exist but were never catalogued.") Like the 2x6L6 1x15 Pro, the 2x6L6 1x15 Bandmaster had volume controls for both instrument and microphone, but unlike the Pro it had separate knobs for treble and bass, and this extra tonal flexibility was its distinguishing characteristic. Like the Bassman, its speaker was Jensen's P15N.

Twin

Although it was officially re-announced in the '54 catalog, the 5C8 Twin had already been on the market for a year or so, originally billed as the Twin 12 Amplifier and also the Twin 12 Artist Model's Amp. From the literature, the new 25W, 2x6L6/5881 model seemed like any other wide panel Fender (although with two 12" Jensens and an extra tone knob), but in fact it was a milestone. It joined the Super as the second two-speaker Fender, this time with a combined cone diameter of 24", biggest in the line. Fender accurately termed its separate controls for bass and treble "the latest in electronic advances." Like the other new model, the Bandmaster, the Twin had four knobs — bass, treble, and two volumes. The 5D8 version of the wide panel era would feature yet another important advance, the presence control for even more tonal versatility. Circuits 5C8 and 5D8 (its schematic dating to June '54) differed with respect to several tubes: preamp, phase inverter, and rectifiers.

Fender's wide panel 1x15s: a Pro in front, a road-worn Bassman at left, and a Bandmaster on top (note the block letter nameplates, typical of wide panels). Alan Hardtke: "This single 15 Bandmaster is scary clean. It got to live its life under a cover. It's shiny, it's frightening. It's like in *Spinal Tap* — don't touch this amp! Don't even look at it!"

FENDER
FENDER
FENDER

> "It might come as a surprise to some people that the earliest input I had, whenever I was in Leo's shop, was oriented toward amplifiers instead of instruments. He was basically an electronics builder, so while he didn't know too much about guitars and intonation, he was very relentless when it came to sound reproduction. Phrases and terms such as 'does it put hair on your chest?', 'fat,' 'does it thin like skim milk?' and 'has it got muscle?' may sound old fashioned nowadays, but such was the dialect of many musicians back then, and it was uncanny how Leo Fender could take such requests and get the sound of his amplifiers to conform to what players wanted."
>
> — Bill Carson
>
> from his book *My Life and Times with Fender Musical Instruments*

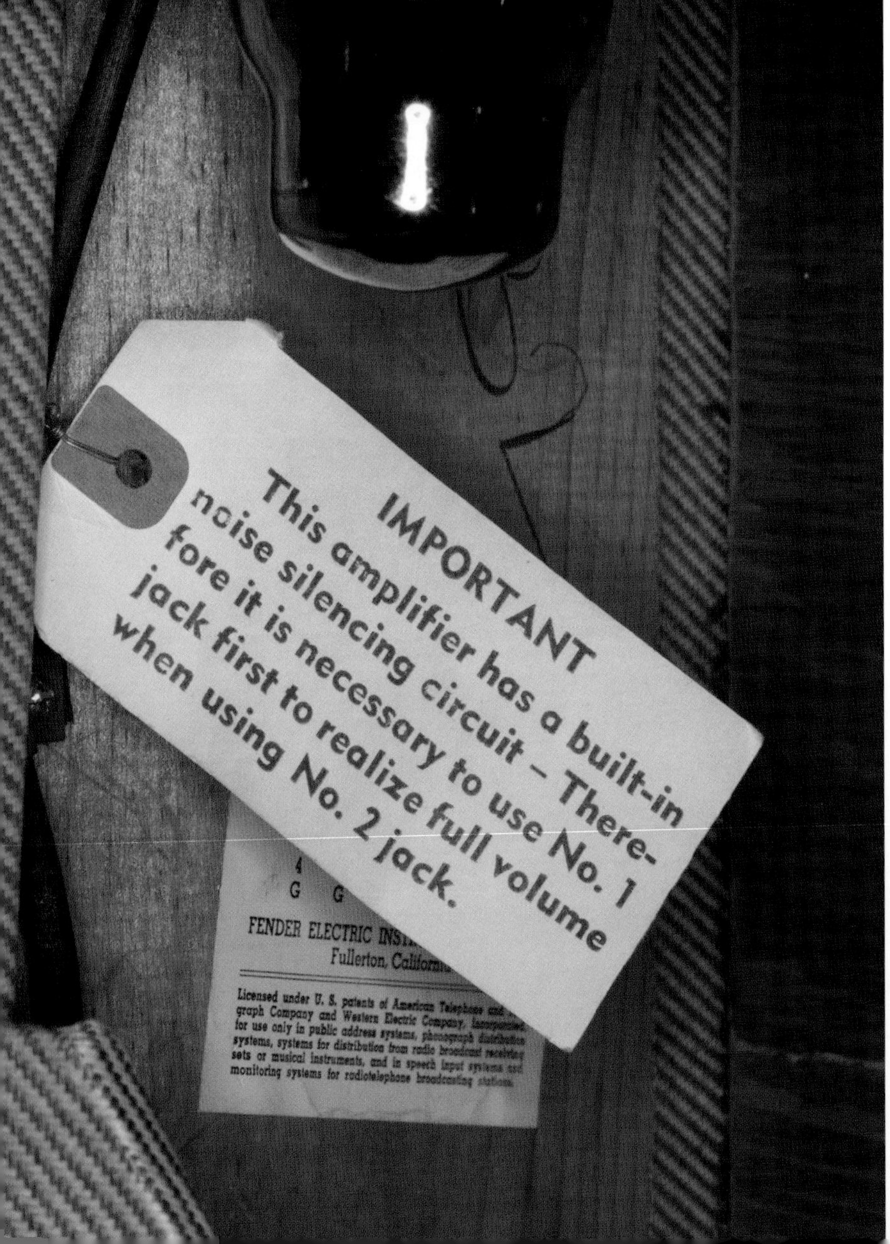

The D Circuit Preamps

Smaller 9-pin tubes such as 12AX7s and 12AY7s gradually replaced octal units in almost all commercial tube gear, and Fender's D circuit preamps of the later wide panel period reflected the trend. Following the lead of the 5C4 Super and 5C5 Pro, the D circuit preamps featured 12AX7s and 12AY7s across the entire line. The power tubes (6V6GTs, 6L6s) and rectifiers (5Y3GTs, 5U4Gs) were generally similar to those in the C circuits, with updates in some cases.

On the Road with Jody Carver

Former Fender road rep Jody Carver is a highly regarded steel guitarist and a member of the Steel Guitar Hall of Fame. Jody Carver: "I started with Fender about the end of '53. Gretsch had a little bit of the market, Gibson to some extent. The big competitor was Ampeg, especially for bass amps. They had the B-15, and for guitarists they had the Reverbrocket. Ampeg was a local outfit in Jersey, and with Fender way out in Fullerton, the freight charges were an issue.

"Those other companies started to see Fender gaining ground, so they responded with some strategies like bigger discounts and free delivery, and I was a sitting duck. It was all a response to Fender's potential. Our amps had a little too much bite for some of the jazz

Wide panel Bandmaster, detail. Alan Hardtke: "This is my scary clean Bandmaster. I've never seen this tag before, but apparently it's factory-stock."

players. They were playing Premiere amps and other things. It took a while for these Fenders to go over at first, and a lot of the dealers wouldn't stock a wide variety of inventory. But it slowly started to gather some steam.

"I learned one thing years ago. I didn't just walk into a store and announce, *Hey, I've got an amp that's going to blow you away!* Instead, I would hand the guitar to someone who could play better than me, and let the *player* come up with the conclusion — *Wow, this Fender is a great amp!* That was a lot more convincing than hearing it from the salesman's mouth.

"And another thing: We didn't make the dealers buy a whole lot of amps. There was no minimum order. If they wanted to try one or two, that was fine. 'Try it out, see what you think of it. If you like it, you can buy it; if you don't, I'll be happy to take it back.' From a salesman's point of view, this left a lot to be desired because I was taking a risk, but people liked the amps. The products were strong, extremely reliable, and I never had to take one back."

Rugged Individuals

"Leo Fender was terrific to work for, but he was absolutely fanatical when it came to quality. Everything he built was overbuilt. His house was overbuilt. His amps were overbuilt. On his boat, he had parts that didn't need replacing at all, but he replaced them anyway — with heavier-duty parts. I've seen an amp fall off a truck. It might bash in a corner, but the cabinet would still hold together, and the amp would still work.

"Leo was the kind of guy who would give you the shirt off his back, but if he ever took it back, he'd take it back one stitch at a time [laughs]. What I mean is, he was fanatical about quality, and if you were doing something, no matter how small it was, if it wasn't right he would have you do it over again. And over. And over. Everything had to be right for that musician. Everything was as rugged as it could be."

— Bill Sterle

Wide panel Super (rear) and an especially noteworthy Twin, serial no. 001. Alan Hardtke: "The Twin is a married piece, meaning the chassis left the factory in a different example of this same cabinet style and then was installed in this particular cab at a later time. The serial number appears in the usual place, in the bottom of the chassis, next to the speaker input jack."

Wide panel amps await inspection and shipping at Fender's new factory at 500 South Raymond Avenue in Fullerton, circa 1953.

"Leo's favorite band was always Bob Wills and His Texas Playboys. Eldon Shamblin came by one time. The bus door came open and two amplifiers fell out of the damn thing and crashed on the ground. Eldon came in with an amp and parked the chassis on a chair and the speaker cabinet somewhere else, and it still worked for the rest of the tour [laughs]. Leo had a real big time showing everyone how built-up a Fender amplifier was."

— Bill Carson

"One of the beautiful things about these Fender circuits is their simplicity. In my experience as a designer, we prototype all sorts of elaborate ideas, and they sound okay, but you find as you take things away the sound almost always gets better and better."

— Steve Carr

"I remember having a conversation with Leo Fender a number of years ago and getting a chuckle out of him as he told me how amazed he was that so much scrutiny was being given to how things were done in the early days of Fender. He said that they had taken what they were doing in the '50s and '60s so matter of fact back then. They were hardly thinking at the time that they were building future classics. They were trying to make an affordable, good-sounding, quality amplifier while still trying to make a buck. Leo also mentioned that for reasons of cash flow and/or inventory problems, they would resort to using alternate vendors from time to time. They kept a careful eye on the cost of materials and their supply, rather than hand-picking components with alleged magical tonal qualities."

— Sergio Hamernik
of Mercury Magnetics,
in *ToneQuest Report*, January 2002

Jody Carver: "When Fender came in, they really rocked the world."

CHAPTER ELEVEN

11

Fullerton High

The Class of '55

From 1950 to 1954, Leo Fender spearheaded the most potent creative surge in the history of electrical instrument manufacturing. He designed the first commercially successful solidbody guitar, invented the modern electric bass, and introduced what would become the most influential of all electric guitars, the Stratocaster. By '54, his Esquire and Telecaster were well established as the Broadcaster's descendants. The Precision Bass was gaining acceptance and would soon transform popular music. The Stratocaster, destined for dominance, bided its time.

But after introducing these groundbreaking instruments over a short four-year period, Mr. Fender would wait another four years before unveiling his next top of the line guitar, the Jazzmaster of 1958. By all accounts a tireless workaholic, he now focused his prodigious energy on an already comprehensive line of amplifiers ranging from a little 4W student model to the mighty Twin.

Elvis Presley makes history, and Fender was there. The King sometimes used a tweed Bandmaster for his microphone, and bassist Bill Black often used tweed Bassmans for both acoustic and (after the summer of '57) electric bass.

The Narrow Panel Tweeds

Although the wide panels had scarcely been around for a couple of years, it was time for new models, new features, and a new look across the line. With more speaker grille and less wood in front, the fresh cab design — which also sported a more modern grille cloth — acquired the "narrow panel" nickname. Some narrow panel tweeds appeared as early as the fall of '54, but generally speaking, they were designed for the 1955 model year. They would characterize the entire line for five years (or up to nine years, depending on the model), longer than the woodie, wide panel, brown/blonde Tolex, or pre-CBS blackface eras.

Aside from their new cabs, the Class of '55 may have appeared to be similar to their wide panel predecessors, but under the hood Leo Fender continued to advance the art of the amplifier with significant refinements. Featuring some of the most acclaimed models in the history of instrument amplification — such as the 5E3 Deluxe, the 5F6 and 5F6-A 4x10 Bassmans, and the E and F series Twins — the narrow panel Fenders offered technological advancements, signature tones, handsome appearance, ruggedness, and a something-for-every-player variety that would

A match made in Fullerton: This 1954 Stratocaster positively sings through this tweed 5F6-A Bassman.

Kid in a candy store, no doubt daydreaming about which of these Fenders he'd love to take home. This is the cover of the '58/'59 catalog. By the summer of '58, Fender offered 11 narrow panel amplifiers, from the $59.50 Champ to the $399.50 Twin.

take Fender to the pinnacle of amplifier manufacturing.

Highlights among the narrow panel tweeds:

Whereas cathode biasing had been used in the wide panel amps, the mid-sized and larger Fenders now converted to fixed bias.

The unveiling of the 5E9 Tremolux in 1955 was historic, marking the first time Fender had installed an onboard effect of any kind on an amplifier. In time, the repercussions of this move and Fender's later installation of tremolo and reverb on various models would resound throughout the industry. The Tremolux preceded the trem-equipped Vibrolux by about a year, and Fender's first reverb-equipped amp, the Vibroverb, by about eight years.

The Bassman was rendered in its 4x10 cabinet for the first time. Over the next five years it would appear in five different electronic versions, culminating in what many players consider to be the finest *guitar* amp of all time, the 5F6-A Bassman of 1958 to 1960.

Within a year or so of the debut of the narrow panels, all of the models above the Tremolux (Super, Bassman, Pro, Bandmaster, and Twin) would feature the new presence circuit.

The relatively new Bandmaster evolved to its 5E7 circuit (the catalog was still calling it Band Master some of the time). Instead of its single Jensen P15N, the May 1955 schematic specified three speakers, all 10s. The Bandmaster would keep this arrangement all the way through its

Narrow panel Tremolux (front) and 3x10 Bandmaster. The Tremolux is equipped with an unusual but factory-stock tremolo footswitch made of wood, seen in front. On this Bandmaster, note the plastic "dog bone" handle, which generally followed the stitched leather type seen here on the Tremolux.

rare, brownface Tolex combo version of 1960.

Five of the new narrow panels featured 6V6 power tubes (Champ, Princeton, Deluxe, Tremolux, and also the 5F10 Harvard) — or six amps if we count the Super, which in its narrow panel form was fitted with both 6V6GTs (5E4-A, July '55 schematic) and 6L6Gs (5F4, March '57).

As if Fender had finally decided to admit it to the club, the mighty little amp at the bottom of the line finally received the top-mounted, chrome control panel. Although it would continue to be referred to as the "student amplifier" in photos of the steel guitar/amp set (and as the Champ "600" Amp on price lists as late as Dec. 1960), the Champ Amp had otherwise finally acquired a single name, applied consistently in the catalog copy and on the amp's label as well. With the redesign of the Champ's cabinet, Fender amps had a uniform cosmetic look all the way across the line.

Several of the models would reflect updates in power tubes, rectifiers, and tone stacks.

A Twin's Tale

One particular Fender amp linked Eric Clapton, B.B. King, and George Harrison.

"I have a high-power Twin with the four 5881s. Eric used to rent it as a spare for his own. This was the same amp that I let George use on the Carl Perkins television special that was done over here in the UK with Eric, Ringo, and others [*Carl Perkins & Friends: A Rockabilly Session*, 1986]. When John Porter produced the *Deuces Wild* duets album by B.B. King, with Eric and others, he asked me to bring 'round a couple of amps. B.B. plugged into this same Twin. He looked at me and went, 'That's the best amp I've plugged into in 35 years.' I'm thinking, what's he talking about? To me it just sounded like B.B. King — you know, perfect! But when he heard it [laughs], boy, did he know. He used it on that album."

— Alan Rogan

Eager students must have felt exhilarated carrying around an amplifier with an unmistakable family resemblance to Fender's hefty pro models. Narrow panel Champs were made with both an 8" speaker, left, and a 6" speaker, right. Cesar Rosas told Dave Rubin: "Eric Clapton told me he used tweed Champs throughout all the [Layla] sessions, and that even Duane Allman used a Champ to play slide with. He talked about the Layla sessions as having his best tone."

Keith Richards on the Main Ingredients

Tom Wheeler: *Your sound has a lot of distortion, and yet you can still pick out the individual notes of a chord. Any tips on how to do that?*

I don't know. I always wished that somebody could have told me that years and years ago, and I'm actually still working on that. It's really finding the right guitar with the right amp.

More than the boxes?

More than the boxes, yeah. If you've got a good sound, you can always add a bit of this or that and fiddle around with it, but it's got to be there. The main ingredients are the right amp with the right guitar."

— from *Guitar Player*, Dec. '89

1956 "small box" narrow panel 5E8 Twin, serial no. 00392.

Meet the New Boss

A mighty roar of exhilarating music, the epic *Who's Next* was released in the summer of 1971. It's invariably listed among the greatest albums of the entire rock era, and it electrifies new generations of listeners to this day. Alan Rogan: "We still have the same setup that Pete used on *Who's Next*: the orange Gretsch 6120 that Joe [Walsh] gave to Pete, a tweed Bandmaster with three 10s, and the powered Goldrich volume pedal — Goldrich being Manny Goldrich, from Manny's in New York. You can hear two distinct guitar sounds on *Who's Next*. One is the Gretsch, and the other is Pete's SG. He also had a Twin and a Bassman — I'm guessing it was a blonde, early '60s — and he used the Gretsch guitar with the Twin *and* the Bassman on 'Won't Get Fooled Again.'"

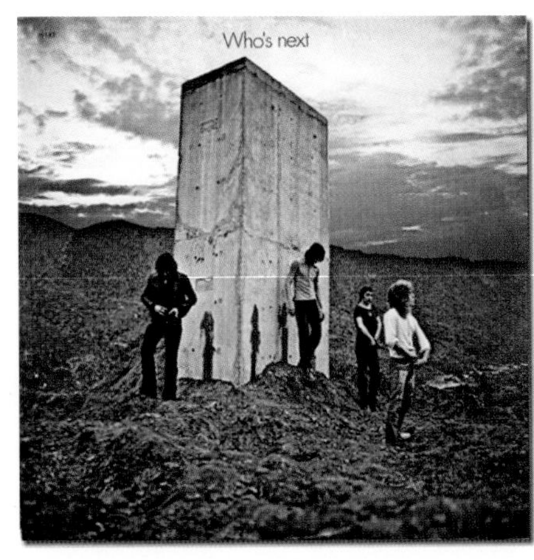

Boss tweed: The mighty tweed Twin ruled the Fender line back in the 1950s and is today one of the most collectible amplifiers on the planet. Twenty thousand dollar price tags are not unheard-of for "big box," four output tube Twins like this one.

 *Hear the high-powered tweed Twin, Tracks 44 - 46.*

The Tweed 4x10 Bassman: The Ultimate Guitar Amp?

First built in the fall of 1954 for the 1955 model year, the original narrow panel 4x10 Bassman is sometimes called the best guitar amp ever. At the very least it is one of the two or three most collectible amplifiers from Fender — or any other maker. But why? What is it about the tweed 40W Bassman with four Jensen 10s that elevates it to such an exalted status?

For starters, it's powerful, it's loud, and it's sensitive to the player's touch. It sounds great, responding beautifully across the frequency spectrum. It exhibits a sparkling, harmonically rich tone at low and moderate volumes. At louder volumes it thickens with a sweet distortion that only seems to get creamier the more it's cranked. It is particularly well matched to certain popular guitars, especially the Stratocaster. Its last incarnation, the 5F6-A, spawned many a boutique amp, not to mention the prototypical Marshalls.

Andy Marshall founded THD Electronics, makers of the first commercially available 4x10 Bassman-style "clones." Andy Marshall: "Those Fender Bassmans became successful for many reasons. Let's say it's 1959, and you buy yourself a Les Paul Standard and a Bassman to go with it. If you turn the volume on that amp above 3 or so, you are going to get kicked off the bandstand, because nobody wants to hear that type of distortion. *Nobody*. Turn it up to 10 and you'd get a monstrous overdrive sound — an early ZZ Top, Rory Gallagher type of overdrive, not quite Van Halen or Metallica. Back in '59, that kind of sound would probably get you sent to the priest for an exorcism, but people gradually began to notice that the overdrive in its own way was very pleasant. It was very even, without a lot of peaks in the frequency response. You could get a whole range of notes to sustain well, and that's one reason for the Bassman's popularity."

The 4x10's immediate predecessor was the wide panel 1x15 5B6 Bassman of 1953 to 1955. Players had complained that it couldn't adequately amplify low frequencies, particularly the notes on the low E string. Tired of those fuzzed-out, honky tones, bassists complained to dealers, and word got back to Fullerton. A related problem was that the 15" speakers weren't just underperforming — sometimes they couldn't handle the power and blew. John Peden picked up the story from an early Fender warranty repair person in New York: "The most common repair in the area in the early days was replacing the single 15 in Bassmans. If you blew your one speaker, you couldn't finish the gig. You were dead in the water. Players' opinions were getting back to Leo and Don Randall — *these amps are driving us crazy*. But with four speakers, you could yank the wire from one speaker if it malfunctioned and keep playing. You might not even know of the malfunction. The other speakers would keep you going."

The 4x10's success as a guitar amp is invariably described as ironic, given its original intended function as a bass amp. But while forebears such as the 5B6 were indeed marketed as "bass only" products, by the mid 1950s Fender was well aware of the Bassman's greater potential. George Fullerton: "Guitar players were picking up on it right away. I consider it the best Fender amplifier ever built."

Although the late Freddie Tavares was quick to deflect attempts to credit him for any of Fender's guitars or amplifiers, he was instrumental in the development of the historic narrow panel Bassman, according to his colleague and longtime Fender veteran Bill Carson: "The 4x10 Bassman was essentially Freddie's entire design. Leo was working on something else at the time. Freddie put this thing together. The attempt was to make kind of a two-edged-sword bass amp that guitar players could use, too, so it could fulfill two roles and make it more acceptable to the buying public. It was also the choice of harmonica players for a long time. I think it was toward the end, when it was ready to go into production, before Leo had anything to do with it at all. Freddie just kind of ran it by him and got his OK to go ahead and do it."

In terms of circuitry, there were actually several tweed 4x10s, starting with the 5D6 in late 1954, 5D6-A (1955), and the 5E6 (1956). The most highly regarded versions are the last two, 5F6 and 5F6-A, both powered by a pair of 5881s rather than 6L6Gs. The 5F6 of 1956 added a midrange control, substituted a long-tail phase inverter for the split-load inverter of the 5E6, and sported extra jacks — high and low gain inputs for each of the two channels, Normal and Bright.

The 5F6-A was the last of the line, and it's the most revered Bassman of all, perhaps the most revered *amplifier*

Ⓥ *Hear the tweed 4x10 Bassman, Tracks 73 - 81.*

of all. Like the 5F6, it's a 4-input amp with a mid control, a 12AY7 at the front end of the preamp, and a pair of 5881s in the output stage. The 5F6/5F6-A has been thoroughly picked and prodded for clues as to why it works so well, and it seems to combine the perfect array of preamp components, output tubes, power, negative feedback loop, passive tone controls, cab, baffle, and speakers. As Dave Hunter explains in *Guitar Rigs*, the positioning of the cathode-follower tone stack (see discussion later in this chapter) helps to make the 5F6/5F6-A particularly touch-sensitive, while the presence control facilitates a sharp, top-end edge without undue harshness.

With its emphasis on high frequencies, the new presence circuit may have seemed like an odd addition to the Bassman, an amplifier previously described by Fender as "designed for the reproduction of bass and bass only." But the new feature went hand in hand with a new marketing approach, a departure from the earlier, narrower strategy. As explained in the '55 catalog, the Bassman (then in its 5E6-A incarnation) was for bass, yes, but it was also "an excellent amplifier for use with other musical instruments. It is truly a most flexible unit." Fender would continue this tactic all the way to the end of the amp's narrow panel incarnation. In 1960, for example, Fender explained that the Bassman "may be used with other instruments due to its wide tone response and circuit design."

Dave Hunter wrote: "Tube rectification adds a further degree of touch and tactile 'squash' to the Bassman's playability when the amp is driven hard, yet three other ingredients — a quality choke [filtering coil], a hefty output transformer, and a negative feedback loop — serve to keep this slightly compressed-feeling amp firm in the lows, snappy in the mids, and crackling in the highs."

There are significant differences between the 5F6 and the 5F6-A, although whether they account for audible differences between one particular half-century-old 5F6 and one particular half-century-old 5F6-A would have to be addressed on an individual basis, given other variables. Blackie Pagano: "Remember that besides the differences in the circuits, one would also have the natural differences in specs — plus or minus 20 percent — not to mention however much the ancient parts had drifted from tolerance, which can be very considerable. There are too many variables to make a general assessment.

"The biggest difference is the rectifier tube, an 83 mercury vapor rectifier in the 5F6 versus the 5AR4 [GZ34] in the later 5F6-A. I have done considerable experimentation with mercury vapor tubes for hi-fi, and they certainly impart a different sound.

"The second huge difference is in the operation of the negative feedback loop, which affects not only the way the presence control operates but also the overall gain of the preamp and how the amplifier interacts with or damps the speakers. Negative feedback alone is a very deep subject.

"Third, the resistor commonly called a 'grid stopper' was removed in the later version. This is a 1500Ω resistor in series with the signal input [grids] of the power tubes. The purpose is to dampen ultrasonic oscillations which may occur."

When researching THD's tweed 4x10 amp project, Andy Marshall examined scores of original Fender Bassmans. He adds: "Both the 5F6 and the 5F6-A had a filter choke in the power supply. 'Choke' is another term for an inductor. [There are several types but] basically it is a coil of wire of some sort. An inductor or choke will pass lower frequencies better than higher frequencies. If it's placed in series in the circuit, it becomes a high frequency filter, whereas a capacitor will pass higher frequencies better than lower frequencies, so it blocks lower frequencies. The power supply choke was a way of reducing the hum without having a ton of filter capacitors, and it did contribute to the sound. If you take it out and replace it with a resistor of the same value, the amp will have a lot more hum and will sound different."

One of the best output transformers ever installed in a guitar amp, Triad's heavy-duty, large-core, interleaved unit was another important factor, especially with respect to the Bassman's powerful low end. Andy Marshall: "The output transformer really has to be viewed not just as an impedance matcher but as a serious tonal component, and the 4x10 Bassman had a bigger interleaved unit. It was designed to deliver bottom end and power. It did a good job, and it produced a nice, sweet, even sound. Was there super magic in it? No, but if you take a nice 5F6-A with a good condition original transformer and replace it with a brand new high quality unit, if you can't tell the difference, you should probably have your hearing checked. Will the new one be better? Maybe, maybe not. That's up to what you like. But it will make a difference."

Jensen
LOUDSPEAKER
SPECIAL
DESIGN
Jensen
LOUDSPEAKER
SPECIAL
DESIGN

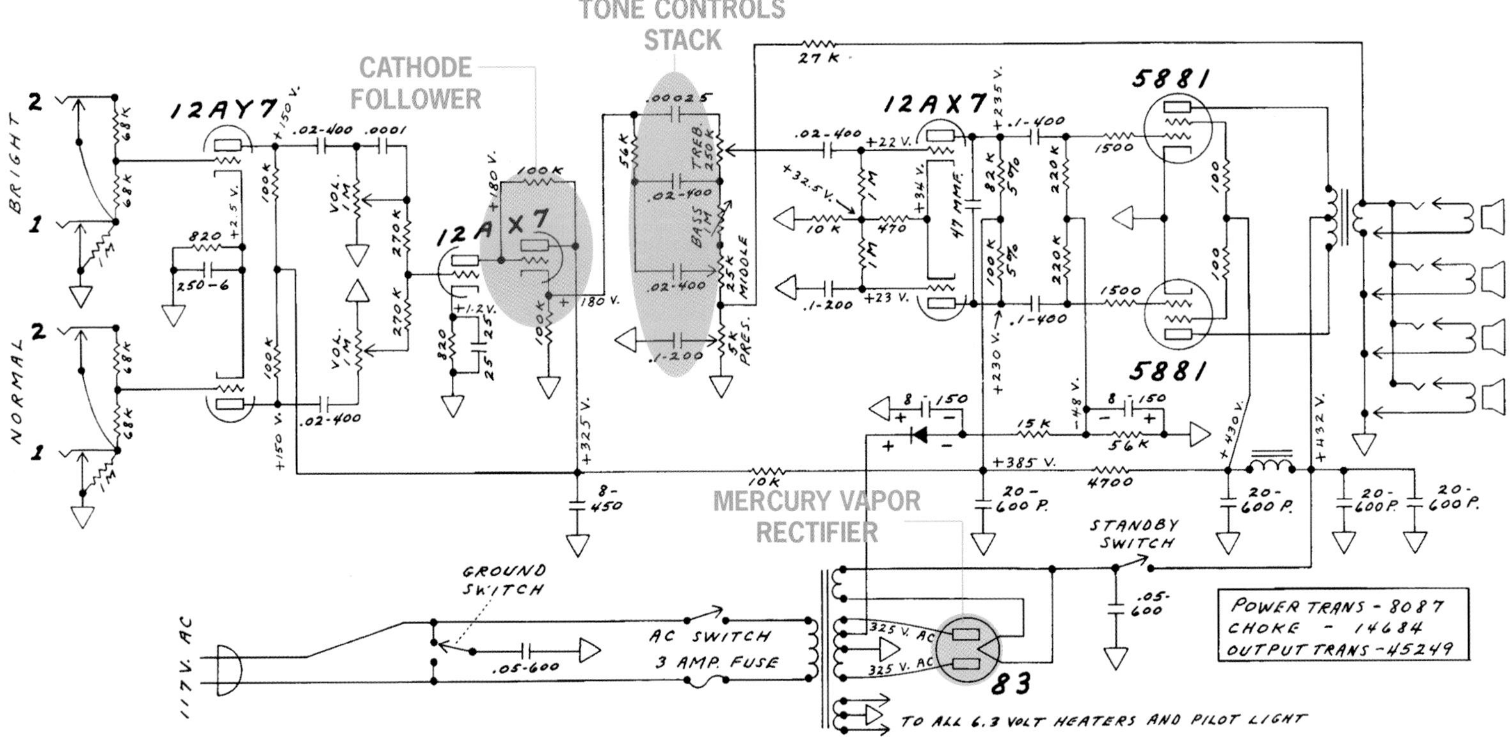

The circuits and components weren't the only features to evolve during the lifetime of the 4x10 Bassman. As Greg Gagliano has written, the Bassmans of 1959 and 1960 were often equipped with Jensen P10Q speakers instead of the typical P10Rs: "The P10Qs were a welcome upgrade and provided the Bassman with even better bass response and headroom."

The 5F6-A was built through 1960 and was discontinued when the Bassman and much of the rest of the line converted from tweed to Tolex. It was succeeded by the 6G6 Bassman of 1960, a blonde Tolex 1x12 piggyback powered by four 7025s and two 5881s.

The legend of the tweed Bassman arose from its power and tone. One of the countless Bassman tales was told by Buddy Guy in *Guitar Player*: "I went up on stage with this long guitar cord and did what I had to do, and I had this little Fender Bassman amplifier, which was blowing the big ones off the stage because it was in good shape. The next night the other group came over and said, 'Man, don't ever send us on after you.'" It gained a reputation for dependability, too. Shane Nicholas: "Ronnie Hawkins said the Hawks had nothing but Bassmans on stage — two for the piano, two for the bass, two for the guitar, two for the voice. Can you imagine a Telecaster through two Bassmans [laughs]? But they just thought it was the best amp you could get."

There are other fine amplifiers with legions of devotees, but for many players, Fender's big, square tweed box with the uncluttered control panel is the ultimate tone machine. Billy Gibbons: "When all is said and done, I go back to the house and plug into a 4x10 Bassman and just turn it up."

"That old Bassman, I remember I loaned it to Otis Redding and he had it in his trunk when he totaled his Cadillac. When he brought the amp back to me, I plugged it in and it was fine."
— Buddy Guy

Photographer Bob Perine placed himself in this promo photo, circa 1958. Using his flat-plug cord, he connected his metal-guard Jazzmaster to a 4x10 Bassman and a new, tweed covered EccoFonic, a tape-echo device marketed for a time by Fender.

Hear the "Rockin' Bassman" Jam, featuring the tweed 4x10 Bassman, Tracks 82 - 83.

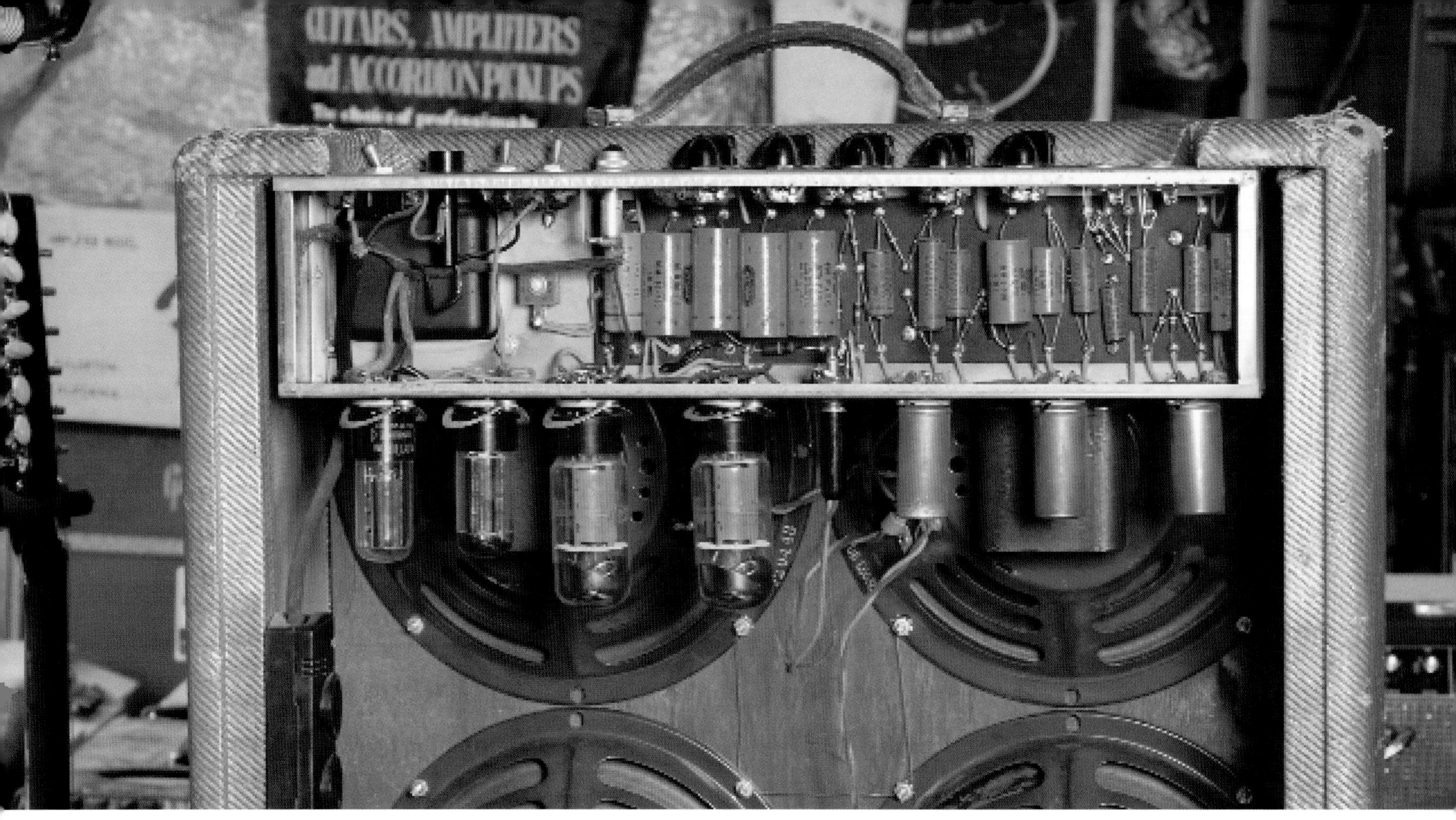

The appearance of the 4x10 Bassman is almost invariably dated to 1955, but on this 5D6, the tube chart is stamped DL, which indicates December '54. Perry Tate: "This one is serial number 0077. The 5D6 had dual 5Y3 rectifier tubes and was very short lived. I do know of one more of these, and it's dated November '54."

Ham and Eggs and a Hell of a Sound — Strats and Bassmans

Bill Carson: "With Leo, the main thing about the guitar and the amp was this: He recognized that one was no good without the other. He used to call them 'ham and eggs,' and they both had to be right."

Mike Lewis: "When I started playing my Stratocaster through tweed amps, it dawned on me: These are the amps that were built at the same time the Stratocaster was designed. This is what it's supposed to sound like. Some people find the Strat's bridge pickup overly bright, but just plug it into a tweed Fender and it's awesome and rich. It's all about the way the amp and the guitar work together, because that's how Leo Fender saw it." Shane Nicholas: "I think a Strat sounds particularly good through a Bassman. I always liked a Telecaster through a Deluxe, and a Strat through a Bassman. Maybe the Bassman gives the Strat a little more authority in the bottom end, which the Strat benefits from."

Otis Rush to *Guitar Player*'s Dan Forte: "I watched Earl Hooker …. He had a Strat, so I bought one. He had an old Fender Bassman, so I got that, put them together, and developed a hell of a sound. I used to sing and play through that amp. It takes a lot of punishment."

Jeff Beck (to Paul Freeman, Entertainment News Service): "The best adventure is the Fender Stratocaster and the amplifier that went with it. That could keep me out of trouble on an island for the rest of my life."

Pete Townshend, in *Guitar Player* magazine: "Guitar players have always known. You get the right Strat. You get the right guitar cable. You plug it into the right old Fender amp, and you get the sound."

Sincerest Flattery: The Fender/Marshall Connection

Elsewhere in this book, Alexander Dumble, Mike Soldano, Peter Frampton, Paul Rivera, Paul Reed Smith and author Dave Hunter all refer to Marshall's basing its prototype amps on Fender's 4x10 Bassman. (The tweed Bassman also served as the inspiration for the first Mesa/Boogie circuit, which was housed in a Princeton cab.) Aspen Pittman: "Marshall copied Fender's basic circuit — virtually no difference at all. They even lined up the jacks the same way, and the on/off switch, the standby switch. I think the whole motivation for those early Marshall amps was to copy the more expensive Fenders so blokes on a pension in England could afford to buy one for their kids." Zakk Wilde put it this way, in *Guitar Player*: "Amp-wise, you've got Fender and Marshall. Fender was first, and the original Marshall was basically a dupe of a Fender Bassman. You can't reinvent the wheel." Pete Anderson, in *Guitar Player*: "My Fender 4x10 Bassman is perfect! There are really only two types of amps worth considering. One is a Bassman; the other is a Twin or Deluxe."

Historian Michael Doyle wrote two books on Marshall. In *The History of Marshall: The Illustrated Story of "The Sound of Rock,"* he explained that in 1962, Ken Bran was hired by Jim Marshall to be the service engineer at Marshall's musical instrument shop in London. Marshall instructed Bran to design an amplifier. In *The History of Marshall*, Jim Marshall recalled: "Obviously we looked at the Fender amps, because they were my favorite amplifier, and the Bassman seemed to be nearer the sound that people were talking about ... so we were influenced by it, but after all, there is nothing new in valve technology; it's all been done before."

Despite the "nothing new" comment, Jim Marshall went on to put his name on hugely successful amplifiers that did have their own look and certainly their own distinctive sound. As he told Michael Doyle: "When I started selling amplification, I listened to many amplifiers, and my favorite then was the Fender without any doubt at all. It had a nice sound, but it's not the sound that we have." Thanks to a tip from Albert Lee, this author was able to track down the owner of the very amp that Ken Bran

An early Marshall head and a Fender 5F6-A Bassman. Ritchie Fliegler: "I've examined the prototype on display at Marshall. Its circuit is not 'similar' to a Bassman, it's not 'derived from' a Bassman — it *is* a Bassman, even in the quirky layout of the controls."

These immaculate Champs facilitate comparisons between grille cloths and cabs of the narrow (left) and earlier wide panel styles. These little dynamos may be a half-century old, but they're in new condition — right out of their boxes, their cords still coiled and wrapped in the original factory tape. Note the "600" label and the early example of Fender's script logo on the wide panel's box. Amps courtesy Norman's Rare Guitars.

examined while prototyping the first Marshall. His name is Mike Borer, and he recently retired from his position as a rep for Peavey after a long career in musical instruments.

Mike Borer remembers: "I was manager at Jim Marshall's music store when he began building his amps. Before then, I worked in a music store in London called the Lew Davies Shop, which was owned by Selmer. Albert was a customer there and that's when we met. I also met Jim Marshall while I was working there, in '57 or '58. He was a drum teacher then, and he used to bring in his drum pupils.

"One day, a US serviceman stationed over here brought the Bassman in question into the Lew Davies store. The shop purchased it, as he was returning to the States, and we put it into stock. It had a transformer screwed into the bottom of the cabinet to drop the voltage, as it was a 120 volt version. Soon after, I sold it to the bass player with Adam Faith & the Roulettes. They were a chart-topping '60s band, pre-Beatles. I bumped into that bass player a few years later and found they had a deal with Vox, and they all had AC30s. He still had the Bassman locked away in a cupboard at a school where they used to rehearse. He said if I wanted it, he would sell it to me. I met him at the school that weekend and paid him £60 for it. I wish I'd hung on to it. It was a great amp.

"I had been with Cliff Bennett & the Rebel Rousers from about 1958 to 1961, and in '61 I joined Jim Marshall's retail store. The following year, after initially making speaker cabinets, it was decided to build guitar amps. The Bassman was such a great-sounding amp that Jim asked to borrow it. I brought it in to work. Ken Bran drew up the [Marshall] schematic from it across the street in the old, smaller original store, and the rest, as they say, is history."

Keith Richards, on recording *Steel Wheels*: "There's plenty of using very small amps, little Champs."

"I love the clarity of Fender amps, and the warmth of the tubes."
— Albert Lee

Ivy Leaguers: Are Some Harvards Actually Princetons?

The Harvard appeared only in the narrow panel cab but with two circuits, 5F10 and 6G10. The June '56 schematic for the 5F10 specifies a most unusual preamp tube, the 6AT6, as well as a pair of 6V6GT output tubes. The 6G10 schematic of April '62 specifies modern 12AX7s but only a single 6V6GT output tube.

What would explain Fender's dropping the Harvard's output section from two tubes to one tube? Some vintage buffs who track thousands of Fender amplifiers speculate that the later, one-tube Harvards are nothing more than re-badged Princetons. Sticking Princeton circuits in Harvard boxes would have allowed Fender to use up leftover tweed-era components while avoiding having two different Princetons on the market at the same time. We're speculating here, but Fender's thinking might have been: Who would buy an old 1x6V6 tweed Princeton when the new 2x6V6 brown Tolex version was on the showroom floor? On the other hand, what are we going to do with all of these leftover Princeton chassis and all of this leftover tweed?

The theory that later 6G10 Harvards were actually re-badged Princetons would help explain the extreme rarity of such Harvards, and also the fact that they seem to have Princeton-type serial numbers. Greg Huntington: "The 6G10 Harvard circuit shown on the April '62 schematic is *identical* to the late-'50s/early-'60s tweed Princeton circuit; both use only one 6V6, in contrast to the 'real,' two-6V6 5F10 Harvard, and also in contrast to the two-6V6 brown Princeton. By sticking a few late-'61/early-'62 Princeton amps into Harvard boxes, Fender could kill two birds with one stone — help get rid of tweed Princeton amps, and fill the last few Harvard orders."

At any rate, the Harvard was unveiled in 1955, but not in time for the catalog of that year. Except among collectors and students of vintage Fenders, it is generally overlooked, perhaps because other than the Vibrasonic it was the only pre-CBS Fender to appear in a single external version (in this case a narrow panel tweed). Although it shared basic design details common to other Fenders, and although the name was revived years later for a solid state amp, the tweed Harvard effectively had no ancestors, no descendants.

Narrow panel Harvard (top) and Vibrolux. The $129 Vibrolux appeared in 1956, built into the same cabinet used by the Deluxe of the time. It was Fender's second amp with tremolo, employing the variable fixed bias type (Chap. 14). It was succeeded by the brown Tolex Vibrolux in 1961. Shown here is the common, cone type foot switch.

Play it, Steve! The profoundly influential Steve Cropper used his Esquire or a Tele though a Harvard on dozens of hits from the Stax/Volt era, including the classic instrumental "Green Onions." Billy Gibbons spoke about the ZZ Top song "Goin' So Good" to *Vintage Guitar* magazine: "I was attempting to call attention to the inspiration provided by so many of the great works of Steve Cropper's guitar technique. His sound, which has become so identifiable, emanated from his use of the Fender Telecaster with a Fender tweed Harvard amp. To this day, that is a stunning combination when used either with a single rear pickup or even switching to the middle position, igniting both pickups. It seems the Harvard is just right for a close-miked studio setup that can provide some real grit when you bear down with it. It's a tough combo to beat... very, very soulful!"

But the Harvard did hold an important place during the entire narrow panel era. At the time of its introduction in '55, there were no 1x10 Fenders, and the newcomer filled that niche. With two knobs, three inputs, and about 10W, the 1x10 Harvard fit nicely between two of its 6V6-powered siblings: the 4½W, 1x8 Princeton and the 15W, 1x12 Deluxe. In most respects the 5F10 Harvard can also be thought of as a tweed Vibrolux without tremolo.

Triad and Schumacher Transformers

In the 1950s, many of Fender's output transformers, power transformers, and chokes were made by Triad Magnetics in nearby Venice Beach. Triad's Travis Tingley: "Venice Beach was only a hop, skip, and a jump from the factory in Fullerton, so it was convenient for people from Fender to visit here and discuss the components. I think you have to remember that a lot of the great sounds coming out of Fender amps were probably the result of happy accidents. I've read that Leo Fender never intended his amps to be turned all the way up, for example.

"On a lot of the output transformers that we were making for Fender, we used M19 steel, a lower grade than the M6 steel you would see in hi-fi audio transformers. The M6 was 'grain-oriented,' meaning it was rolled out under a magnetized roller, but the M19 was non-grain oriented. On some of the transformers [in Fenders] you see higher and lower grades of steel alternating in the laminations, and all of these details contributed to the sound. Around the end of the tweed era, Mr. Fender moved almost everything over to Schumacher transformers."

Jim Tracy went to work at Triad in January 1959 and remembers meeting Mr. Fender. Fender was a big company by then, and the fact that the founder would personally visit Triad to discuss the specs and performance of their transformers says a lot about his approach to his job. Jim Tracy: "He wasn't a three-piece suit kind of guy at all. He was totally hands-on, and even though he was a big executive type of person, he knew his stuff — the specs and the details."

Perry Tate: "In the early years, especially in the smaller Fenders, you would see oddball transformers like Pepco, for example, which is in all three of my woodie Princetons, or Dongan, Thermador, and ECCO. But by the narrow panels of the mid '50s and through the end of that decade, Triad was the order of the day, making both power transformers and output transformers. You start seeing Schumachers in 1960, and by '61 Fender was done with Triads. Almost all Fender transformers in the '60s were Schumachers, with minor exceptions, like some Showmans in the late '60s with transformers from Better Coil and Transformer Co."

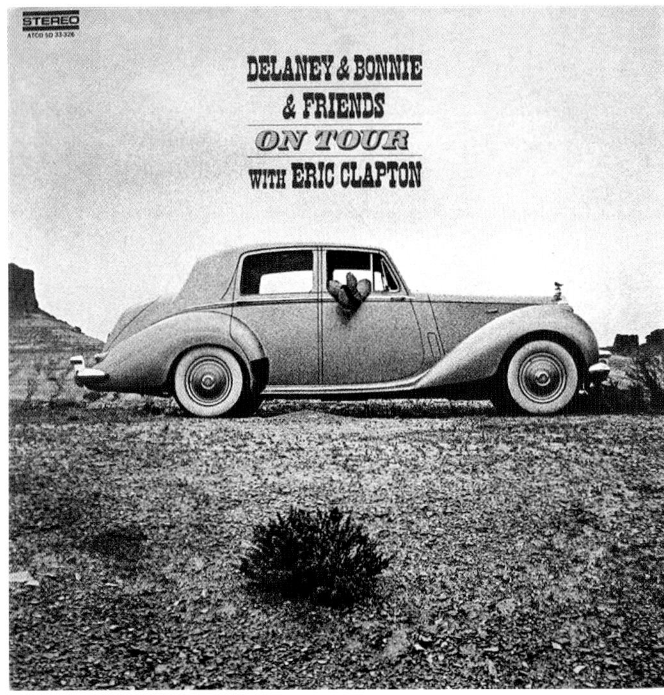

Delaney Bramlett on Eric Clapton, George Harrison, Jimmy Page, and the amplifier used on "Coming Home," in *Guitar Player*: "It was this Fender Champ that I had souped up with this Lansing instead of the little ol' Champ speaker, and I had big tubes put in it. It still had that Champ sound, but with more power. Eric fell in love with the damn thing, and George did, too. I gave one to Eric, one to George, and one to Jimmy Page, 'cause they all loved 'em. That whole recording [*Delaney & Bonnie & Friends On Tour With Eric Clapton*] and Eric's album [*Eric Clapton*, featuring "Let It Rain," "Blues Power," and "After Midnight"] was done with Champs. We even figured out a way to use them onstage, as preamps on top of big amps. We blew a few of 'em up before we found out how to do it. I can still hear Eric using it in the studio. I can recognize the sound."

Mark Baier on Transformers, Wattage, and Speakers

In the vintage period, Fender used both 28W transformers and 40W interleaved transformers. As Mark Baier explains here, the way wattage, transformers, and speakers interacted was essential to Fender's tone.

The mid-'50s tweed Pro, Bandmaster, and Super, and later the Vibrolux Reverb and Pro Reverb, all used the same 28W transformer, and to this day the same basic type is still being used. Those amps all had two 6L6s, which are capable of producing 60 watts of power if you really drive them, and yet you've got this small transformer that can't process that much energy. Why would Leo Fender do that? He could've produced more volume with the 40W transformer, with its larger, heavier mass of steel and more laminates.

My theory is, look at the speakers they were using in that era. Those Jensens were rated at 9 watts! Anytime Leo needed a 10" speaker in the tweed amps he would use P10Rs. In about 1960 he started using P10Qs, which had a little more power dissipation, but for the most part all the '50s amps with 10s had that P10R, a 9 watt speaker. If Leo had fitted those amps with the larger transformer and passed along all that extra power, he would have blown speakers left and right. I believe he was trying to reduce the speaker failure rate, and reduce the amount of service.

The maximum the smaller transformer is going to present to the speakers is 28W. After that point it saturates and starts to get hot, and the effect is a different kind of compression than what you get with power tubes clipping. A transformer starts to saturate on the low frequencies first, the lows being the hardest ones for that transformer to swallow. So, the Fenders using that smaller unit tend to have a reduced low-end response once that 28W saturation is reached, because fewer lows are passed on to the speaker.

I speculate that the reason we see so few tweed Bandmasters, Supers, and Pros still working is that a lot of them did get blown out. Even with that 28W transformer, the two 6L6s put some stress on that speaker, and you could have a cascade type of failure. The speakers blow, which causes the output transformer to short out, and then the tubes don't know what to do with their energy, so they blow up, and you can have a catastrophic failure throughout the output section. This all depends on how many speakers you have, because the strain of the wattage lessens when you dissipate it among, say, the four 10s in a 5F6 Bassman.

When Mr. Fender changed wattages and speakers, he could change the transformer, too. From about 1955 to 1957, the 5E8/5E8-A [small box] Twin had an enormous piece of steel on there, even bigger than Leo's typical 40W transformers. That Twin also had a pair of Jensen P12Qs, and those speakers are a big reason for the vibe of that circuit. They are very dynamic and "bouncy," very sensitive to pick attack. They were probably rated for about 16 watts instead of only 9, so Leo might have felt he could use a bigger transformer on there, perhaps in an effort to get more low end. On the 5F8/5F8-A [big box] Twin of the late 1950s — with Jensen P12Ns, four 5881s instead of two 6L6Gs, and a whole lot more output — it's basically two Bassman transformers stuck together, exactly twice the size of the Bassman unit.

Detail, 5F6-A Bassman panel with the new presence control. Leo Fender: "We felt the guitar player should have the option of giving that treble a little extra boost."

Mr. Fender in His Own Words

Here are excerpts from an interview with the author, May, 1978; the full interview appeared in *Guitar Player*.

When did you become involved with amplifier work?

Leo Fender: I used to do all sorts of amplifier and PA work back in the '30s. I built equipment for musicians or rented it to them. One job I particularly remember — back in '32 or so, when Franklin Roosevelt was elected — they had what they called the March of Dimes, a benefit organization to help handicapped kids. They had this huge event, a ball to raise money, and I was contracted to do the PA work for it. And then there were the annual Halloween parades in Anaheim; I did those, too. Mainly, though, it was working with musicians.

You were selling amps before you began to build guitars; is that right?

For a while there, yes. One successful amplifier was the first Super. You know, Fender's had the Super amplifier in one form or another for, what—thirty years now? More than that, I guess. The first one was unique. It had twin speakers — pretty unusual in those days, although you might not think so now. And we had them arranged so that if you looked at the amplifier from the top, the front of it had a V shape; the speakers were angled to give you wide dispersion.

What inspired you to come up with the piggyback design?

As bass amplifiers got more powerful, we thought that it would be better to isolate the speakers from the vibration of the amp chassis — put the speakers in their own enclosure. We [first considered] it on bass amplifiers, and then we extended the idea to several of the guitar amplifier models.

The presence control was a unique and much-discussed feature. What did it do?

That was a real popular thing. Really, what it did was, it took the place of the Bright switch that we used later. You know, most amplifiers don't have such a good response in the higher frequency ranges, and we felt the guitar player should have the option of giving that treble a little extra boost.

"Giving That Treble a Little Extra Boost" Negative Feedback, Presence Control

A negative feedback loop is a circuit in which some of the output transformer's voltage is injected back into the preamp, out of phase, typically at the phase inverter in Fenders. The feedback loop's purpose is to reduce distortion in the output section. It also helps to keep the speaker from over-excursion at low frequencies, to keep it from "bottoming out." Given Mr. Fender's goal of higher fidelity, it's no surprise that most Fender amps from the classic period (and later) have feedback loops.

Steve Carr: "The feedback loop increases the damping factor, so the amp has more control over the speaker, almost as if the amp can sense how the speaker is moving; generally this means a tighter bass with more snap. You can also get the inherent sound of your amp to come through a greater variety of speaker configurations, as if the speaker's influence is taken out of the equation a bit. A downside of negative feedback is that it can cause its own type of distortion [especially when the amp is overdriven], which can be nonmusical, and it can remove some high-end speed and naturalness, creating sort of an opaque 'blanket' over the top end."

On some Fenders with negative feedback loops, the effect is fixed across the frequency range; one example is the Deluxe Reverb. On other models the negative feedback can be varied with the *presence* knob, an often imitated circuit introduced by Leo Fender on some of the high-end tweeds. Negative feedback lowers the gain of the output section, but the presence control can reduce that gain-lowering effect in the high frequencies, letting more highs come through. In short, turning up the presence knob *increases* high-frequency gain in the output section. Matt Wilkens: "In the '59 Bassman, for example, even with the presence all the way up, the low end is still under control. Still, it's good to turn the bass down if the amp is played really loud!"

Steve Carr: "Negative feedback reduces distortion, so using the presence control, which diminishes that effect, can cause an increase in high-end distortion." Whether any such distortion is perceived, and whether it's considered unmusical, and whether any such disadvantage outweighs the increased control over high frequencies, is a matter of individual taste.

The three 6V6 amps at the bottom of the narrow panel line: Champ, Deluxe (in the middle), and Princeton.

 *Hear the narrow panel tweed Deluxe, Tracks 2 - 12.*

Shane Nicholas: "I run my '59 Bassman with the presence all the way up, meaning little or no negative feedback, so I get the sizzle; then I set the treble fairly low to compensate. I am guessing that Leo preferred more negative feedback, and more speaker control, and less harmonic chaos — therefore 'higher fidelity.'"

The presence control first appeared on the two-rectifier 5D8 Twin of mid 1954, the second and last version of the wide panel model. It continued to be featured on the Twin, and over the course of the next year or so it was added to the first-edition narrow panel 5E7 Bandmaster (May '55 schematic). It was also added to later editions of other narrow panel tweeds: the 5E4-A Super, 5E5-A Pro, and 5E6-A Bassman; so, the very earliest narrow panel versions of those three amps did not have the control, but later narrow panel versions did.

The presence control continued to be a distinctive feature through the shift from the tweeds to the brown/blonde Tolex amps of the early '60s. When the line converted to blackface (in 1963 for most models), the presence knob was dropped and generally replaced with the Bright switch (Chap. 14).

To summarize, negative feedback provides headroom, affects the speaker's response to the amp, reduces one kind of distortion and in the process reduces gain. To some listeners, a feedback loop makes the sound a little less aggressive, perhaps a bit less midrangey, but with a tighter feel and more of an abrupt shift into distortion. The presence control *offsets* some of these effects in the high frequencies, which may add a bit of high-frequency distortion when the amp is overdriven but also imparts a desirable brightness distinct from that of a conventional tone control. As Fender literature put it, the circuit provided "a brilliance and realistic quality heretofore unobtainable in any other amplifier."

Aside from the models with feedback loops and presence controls, Fender amps also include models with no feedback loops at all (such as the first-edition narrow panel Pro, the 5E5 of 1955), and feedback loops but no presence control (for example, the 5E2 Princeton).

Almost all modern Fenders have feedback loops, although exceptions include the Vibro-King and the Custom Vibrolux Reverb. Shane Nicholas: "I personally like this type of amp, because I want to control the dynamics with my picking hand. Our current amps without negative feedback have a distinct dynamic response. I have compared an original 1965 Vibrolux to the new one, for example. To my ear, it's like the speaker can be more easily driven when you play harder, and there is a little more high-frequency harmonic 'sizzle' and 'crack.'"

The E Circuits, More Tone Control

The E circuits of the narrow panel era continued Fender's same general applications of 12AX7 and 12AY7 preamp tubes, 6V6GT and 6L6/6L6G output tubes, and 5Y3GT and 5U4G/5U4GA rectifiers (but see the section below regarding rectifiers in Bassmans and Twins).

The trend toward increased control of tone continued with the addition of presence controls and, to some of the amps that didn't already have them, separate bass and treble controls. A couple of the models had acquired all three in their D circuits, but in any case, by their later E circuits (such as the Pro's 5E5-A), controls for presence, bass, *and* treble were offered on the Bandmaster, Bassman, Pro, Super, and Twin.

Interactive Controls, Channels

Any guitarist examining the front panel of a typical Fender would likely assume that each tone knob affects only its designated frequencies: bass, mid, or treble. Not quite. While this assumption is a useful starting point, the knob adjustments for each frequency range may affect the performance of other tone knobs as well. So, turning up the treble knob will likely affect the way the bass control works, turning down the mid control may affect the function of the treble knob, and so on.

This is not a bad thing. The various interactions can be complicated, but the guitarist willing to explore them will learn to play his or her amplifier with more subtlety, just as an organist might use the drawbars on a Hammond B-3. As a matter of fact, the interactivity of controls was part of Leo Fender's plan from the very beginning. Remember, he expected his amps to be used not only by instrumentalists but by vocalists, too, often together.

Richard Smith writes in *Fender, The Sound Heard 'Round The World*: "With a voice and an instrument coming from the same speaker, Leo wanted to avoid the mix sounding like mush. He felt that the guitar channel needed deep bass

Narrow panel Super and Pro. Earlier versions had only a single tone knob, but during their narrow panel phase, the 5E4-A Super (July '55 schematic) and 5E5-A Pro (Oct. '55 schematic) went from three to five knobs: vol, vol, treble, bass, and presence.

and high treble, notes above and below a voice's midrange. So the tone control was really a mush control on his first amps; it worked on both channels simultaneously to separate voice frequencies from the guitar frequencies. Turning it up added highs to the instrument channel and *cut highs in the microphone channel*. Thus, an amplifier's use prescribed the way Leo engineered it; he wanted to make instruments more than loud, and *considered the human voice in designing his tone circuits for guitar* [emphasis added]."

Tone knobs not only affect each other but the volume control as well. On most Fenders, setting the tone controls to zero shuts off the sound entirely, regardless of the volume knob's setting. On amps where the tone controls affect the volume to this drastic extent, their effects on each other are also more likely to be apparent. The 4x10 Bassman, however, is an exception in both respects: It will still amplify your signal with its tone controls at zero, and the tone controls' effects on each other are usually somewhat less noticeable.

It's difficult to generalize about how each knob affects every other knob because interactions vary from model to model. Matt Wilkens: "For a given setting on a '59 Bassman, turning the treble control up or down will indeed increase or decrease treble, but it will also move and vary the depth of the mid notch somewhat. The effect is not so noticeable that the player is likely to say, hey, the treble control is messing with the mids — and the bass, too. On the other hand, if you're listening for it, you'll hear it.

"In some designs, however, the effects are *really* noticeable. Some tone stacks are loaded in such a way that turning down the treble control actually turns up the bass. Our '57 Twin Amp reissue works just like the original. Turning up the bass and treble controls produces a clearly audible mid notch that isn't there at all with those controls on 5." These effects are hardly confined to Fenders. Most tube amps — Marshalls, Voxes, etc. — are similarly interactive.

Aside from the interactive effects of controls in a single channel, some players swear they can hear the effects of one channel's controls on the other channel. When the Vibrasonic appeared in 1959, the way its 7025 preamp tubes were configured made the two channels' volume controls truly independent, marking a new direction for Fender.

Detail, 5D8 Twin: The first two tubes are the output tubes; at right are the big honkin' dual rectifiers.

Another misleading assumption: Except for the designated effect, a Reverb or Vibrato channel sounds exactly like the other channel. But a reverb circuit, for example, affects overall tone even when the reverb is turned off. In a typical blackface circuit, a big resistor between the first two 12AX7s shunts some of the signal to a 12AT7 and then to a transformer that drives the reverb tank. The reverbed signal is mixed back in with the unreverbed signal, and an extra gain stage restores the volume lost when the signal passes through the big resistor. The signal then goes to the phase inverter at the end of the preamp stage.

Steve Carr: "This is subjective opinion, but adding that reverb circuit is a huge thing. Essentially you can think of it as a parallel effects loop. It changes the tone of the whole amp, rolling off the top in a pleasant way. There's still plenty of treble, but it's just different, with a musical warmth. You can hear all this readily. In my experience, most people use the Reverb channel even if they're not going to use the reverb. With its extra gain stage, it's almost like it has a bit more of a compelling sound."

In summary, the implications of the control panel's labels are accurate up to a point, but the deeper view is that settings affect not only their designated functions but also each other. To get the most out of your amp (particularly if it's a tweed Fender or a reissue of one), assume that almost everything is connected to almost everything else. A practical approach: Try both channels. Pick the one that sounds better, even if it has an effect you're not planning to use. Adjust its tone and volume controls with an ear to their interactions; then, as an experiment, see if the *other* channel's settings have any effect. As always, the "right" setting is what sounds best to you.

Evolving Rectifiers in Bassmans and Twins

When it comes to warm, harmonic distortion produced at moderate volumes in a cranked tube amp, Leo Fender may have already built the ultimate tone machines by, say, '53 or '54. But he never intended for his amps to be played consistently at full volume, and despite his idiosyncrasies and departures from convention, in one respect he was like other amp designers of his time: For him, distortion was the enemy, headroom the goal.

Examine the following info regarding components in Bassmans and Twins. These circuits date to the mid and

This amplifier doesn't exist, at least officially. Built in 1955 at the dawn of the narrow panel era and once owned by George Fullerton, it's a one of a kind, entirely original Twin with two 10s instead of two 12s. The cab was scaled down to the size of a narrow panel Super, and it bears an anomalous block style nameplate rather than a script tag typical of narrow panel Fenders.

late '50s (the last of the tweeds) and the early '60s (the first of the Tolexes). For each amp we see the circuit code, the date from an official layout or schematic, output tube complement, and rectifier(s).

The Bassmans
5E6-A: Jan. '55, 2x6L6, two 5U4GA rectifiers
5F6: June '57, 2x5881, type 83 rectifier
5F6-A: Sept. '57, 2x5881, GZ34 (5AR4) rectifier
6G6: Feb. '61, 2x5881, GZ34
6G6-A: Jan. '62, 2x5881, solid state ("diode") rectifier

The Twins
5D8: June '54, 2x6L6, two 5Y3GT rectifiers
5E8-A: Jan. '55, 2x6L6G, two 5U4Gs (or GAs)
5F8: June '57, 4x5881, type 83 rectifier
5F8-A: Sept. '57, 4x5881, GZ34
6G8: June '60, 4x6L6GC, solid state ("diode") rectifier

Among the conclusions we can draw: Mr. Fender's quest to improve his amplifiers entailed much experimentation with rectifiers; he was well aware of evolving technologies in tube amplification outside the guitar business and strove to incorporate new developments to improve his own products; and finally, any rectifier arrangement that would enable the amp to deliver more clean volume was the way to go. (This last goal was also reflected in the doubling of output tubes in the 5F8 and later Twins.)

Previous Fenders had used either a single 5Y3 or 5U4 rectifier, and most F series amps used an updated 5Y3, the 5Y3GT. But as Mr. Fender increased the power and volume of select high-end models, he faced a challenge: A single tube rectifier can supply only so much current before it fails. The solution was to double up on the old tube rectifiers, or to try new ones, or, when the technology became available, to convert from tube to solid state.* He tried all three.

Mark Baier: "The use of two rectifiers in the power supply illustrates the extent Leo Fender was willing to go to in achieving headroom. Before 1960, having more than one rectifier tube was routine in powerful amplifiers, whether large industrial amps or audio types. Western Electric, Altec, McIntosh, Grommes, Bogen, et al all had designs that utilized two (or more) rectifiers — but in a *guitar amp*? Unheard of! Leo Fender's desire to make the ultimate professional musical instrument amplifier, one without peer, is limned in this dual 5U4 power supply.

"Disadvantages to using two 5U4s include requiring twice as much current to heat them up, which in turn entails a larger, more expensive power transformer and contributes to the amp operating hotter. There is also the added expense of buying one more socket and tube.

"But there are three big practical advantages, one being the ability to deliver more electrons! Second, we can also double power supply *capacitance* (50 mu's vs. 100 mu's), ensuring that those electrons are readily available for use. The third advantage is the reduction, by half, of the internal resistance of the rectifier arrangement. This is what accounts for the most commonly cited attribute of the multi-5U4 setup: less voltage drop across the tubes. Less internal resistance equals less voltage drop across the rectifier, which equals less 'sag.' This configuration therefore supplies a 'faster,' higher voltage to the power supply, which in turn increases the available power and headroom of the amplifier."

Shane Nicholas: "If you take something like a tweed Deluxe and turn it all the way up and hit your low E string, that power supply just cannot keep up. You get that rectifier sag, so the two rectifiers working in tandem was an effort to get less of that compression when you play hard and loud."

When replacing the mid-'50s dual-5U4 arrangement, Mr. Fender first used a type 83 mercury vapor rectifier in both the Bassmans and Twins. This tube performed very well but was expensive, somewhat less available, and potentially dangerous in case of breakage. As noted in the table above, Mr. Fender then switched to the 5AR4/GZ34 tube, an appreciable improvement over the venerable 5U4 and the tube of choice in the next generation of tube-rectified Fenders.

*"Solid state" has negative connotations among some players because some amps with solid state *circuits* sound inferior to some tube amps, a distinction that has little to do with our discussion here. We are talking about tube amps that happen to have solid state *rectifiers*. These are bona fide tube amps. They include some of Fender's most desirable vintage models and should not be confused with "solid state" amps — some of which sound fine, by the way, but that's a tale for a later chapter.

Matt Wilkens cites one more good reason to try something other than a single rectifier in high-power Fenders: "Amps with four 5881s just *ate* 5AR4/GZ34s, so having just one of those in such amps would be particularly hard on the rectifier." He adds that a short run of tweed Twins featured a *pair* of 5AR4/GZ34s.

These changes provide insight into Mr. Fender's thinking in the mid and late '50s. Mark Baier: "Both the 83 and the 5AR4 have much less voltage drop (internal resistance) than the 5U4, making it apparent that decreasing voltage drop across the rectifier was the main reason for employing two 5U4s in the first place. My opinion is that, later, Leo was well aware of the availability of the GZ34 but waited a while to see if it held up in the real world before using it in his own amps."

Narrow Panel Cabs and F Circuits

The narrow panel Fenders included many examples of both E and F series circuits. While the D and E circuits had featured major updates in preamp tubes, the F circuits saw few changes in that department. The rare and unusual 5F10 Harvard of the mid 1950s combined a 12AX7 and a 6AT6. Otherwise, the narrow panel tweeds of 1955 and thereafter (including the 6G10 Harvard) all used 12AX7s, 12AY7s, or a combination of the two types.

Throughout various points in Fender's history, models at or near the top of the line were the first to be fitted with features or components that would eventually characterize other models down the line. As we've seen, the E and F series saw significant advances in rectifiers. The F series was marked by additional developments in power tubes and tone stacks in, once again, the last of the narrow panel Bassmans and Twins. The 5F6 and 5F6-A Bassmans and the 5F8 and 5F8-A Twins of the late 1950s all had output sections powered by 5881s — two in the Bassmans, four in the high-powered Twins. (Output sections in other models generally used Fender's standard 6V6GTs or 6L6Gs.)

These later narrow panel Bassmans and Twins were also noteworthy with respect to their control panels. The 5F6 and 5F8 acquired mid knobs, continuing the amps' incremental expansion of tonal flexibility. With their new control panels — presence, mid, bass, treble, plus separate volume knobs and two inputs for each channel — the 5F6/5F6-A Bassmans and 5F8/5F8-A Twins were the most versatile one-channel Fenders from the vintage period.

By the way, these models are called both one and two-channel amps, depending on how the terms are defined. Ritchie Fliegler: "I would call them two-channel amps, but this is really about nomenclature, not electronics. A blackface Twin has clearly defined, different channels, Normal and Vibrato. It's a two-channel amp by any definition. However, an amp like one of the Hot Rod models is considered to have three channels by almost everyone, but it's really a one-channel amp with three modes. The tweed Bassmans and Twins are somewhere in between — separate volume controls, but shared tone controls, very much like the PA mixers of the time."

1956 "small box" Twin. Note the diagonal mounting of the original Jensen P12Qs. Perry Tate: "The earliest Twins had P12Rs, and those lasted about five minutes [laughs], and then they went to the P12Qs. These small box Twins are rare. In all my years of collecting, I've come across twice as many big box Twins."

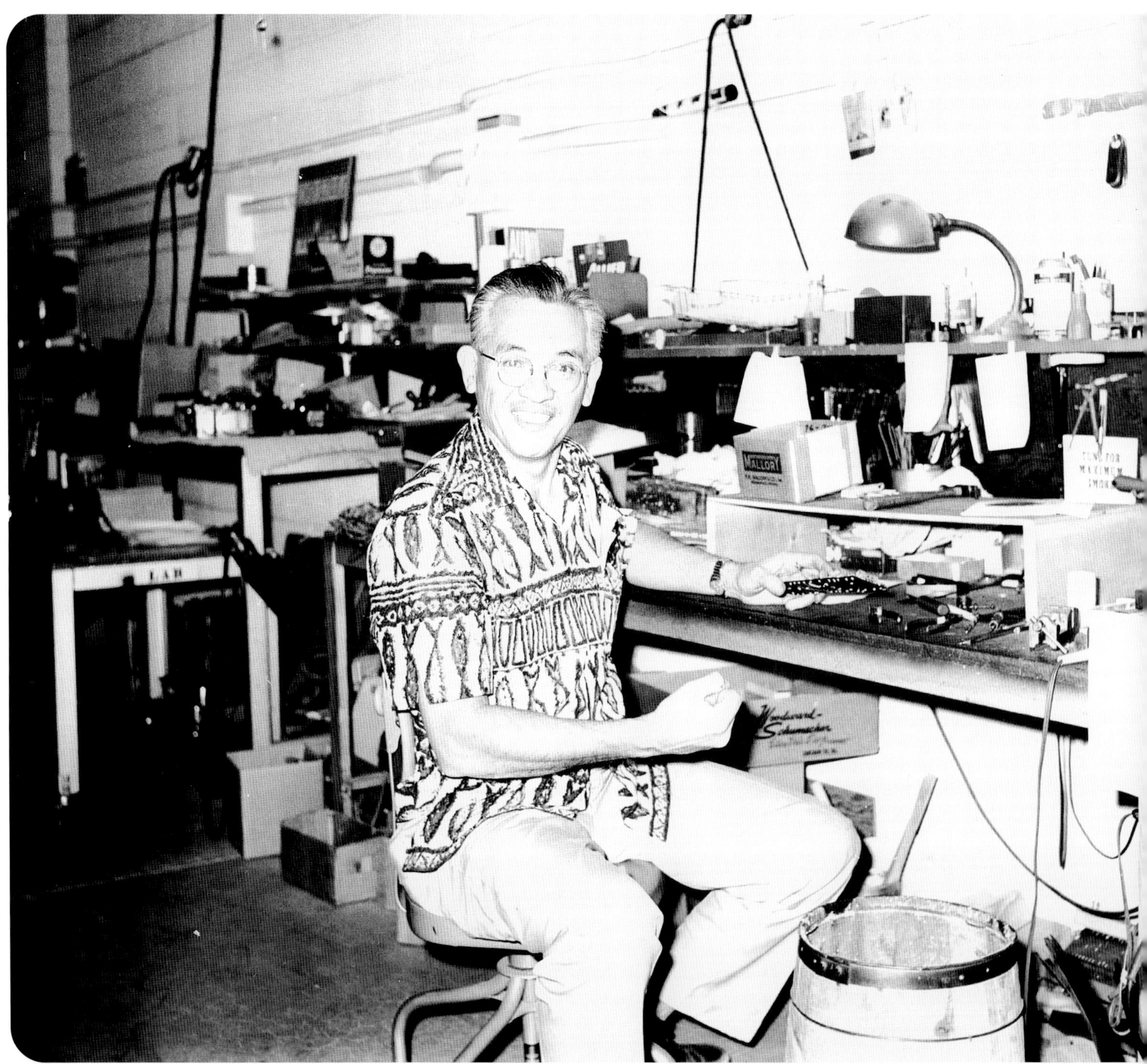

Freddie Tavares at his workbench in the Fender lab, 1960s. Leo Fender didn't play guitar. Lucky for him, Freddie Tavares did. During the 1950s and 1960s, Freddie's skills and musical taste were essential to the success of Fender amps and guitars. Dick Dale called him Leo Fender's "number one man."

Freddie Tavares

Hawaiian-born Freddie Tavares arrived at Fender in March of 1953 and made key contributions to the Stratocaster's design, several other instruments, and many of the classic Fender amplifiers of the '50s and '60s. He was perhaps the most admired and loved Fender employee in the vintage era. Bill Carson, who credits Mr. Tavares with much of the design work on the iconic 4x10 Bassman, said of him, "In my opinion he was the greatest man in both musical talent and personal integrity that I worked with at Fender." (Also see PJ Geerlings' recollections, Chap. 17.) Mr. Tavares died in 1990.

"Freddie was the guy who played guitar for Leo Fender. Leo wasn't a player. Leo was very good at talking to musicians and interpreting what they had to say, but he really depended on Freddie, who was always there and really had a big influence on the performance of the amplifiers and the quality of the sound — speakers, enclosures, reverb, and so on. Freddie was doing all the schematics and was very, very instrumental in terms of what Fender considered good sound.

"Freddie was absolutely wonderful, very pleasant and funny, had a joke every day. I must have learned 800 or 900 jokes during the years I was there. He almost always wore a Hawaiian type shirt with the flowers, and he loosened up the mood for everyone, so you could get the job done and enjoy yourself, too. He had the best input of anybody. All the musicians who came in to try the gear really liked him."

— Bob Rissi

"Freddie Tavares — oh man, what a human. He was still in R&D when I worked at Fender in the early '80s. He was the tie to the ancient past. I'm sure he's up in heaven now with a saint's hat on, because he really was a saint of a person. He was friends with the girls who wound the pickups and soldered up the amplifiers and everybody on the assembly line. He used to write birthday songs for people in R&D and when their birthday came along he'd sing it to them."

— Paul Rivera

"Freddie was loyal to the movie and recording industry along with Fender. He did a lot of work in those industries. I've seen Leo follow Freddie to the gate — 'Freddie! Come back, we've got to finish this project!' But Freddie would say, 'Well, I've got a recording session.' So sometimes Leo couldn't get quite as much Freddie as he wanted. But Leo put up with it because Freddie was so good. He got more done than anybody else. He got as much done in two hours as most people did in two days. He would go at a fast pace from one building to another; that's how he got his exercise. He did everything very detailed, very methodically, and he just harbored no wasted time for anything.

"There was a new amplifier company. I can't remember their name. They were trying to get it off the ground in Los Angeles. They came to me and had an amplifier and wanted to know what I thought about it. They asked me to keep it and play it. I took it out to the lab, and Freddie and Leo tore the damn thing all apart [laughs], to see what they had going there. I don't think they ever found a great deal that surprised them in other products, one way or the other."

— Bill Carson

Cathode Follower Tone Stacks

Several high-end Fenders of the narrow panel and early Tolex eras owe part of their legendary tone and response to their "cathode follower" tone stacks. "Cathode follower" refers not to any particular component but rather to the order in which components are connected. Just as your effects pedalboard will sound different if you rearrange the order in which the stompboxes are connected, the same elements of an amplifier may work together in very different ways depending on the order in which they are wired into the circuit. The location of a tone stack, for example, can affect an amp's performance well beyond the knobs' labels of "Treble," "Mid," and "Bass."

You'll recall from Chap. 3 that a 12AX7 is a dual triode — two tubes in one, so to speak. In each self-contained side, current flows from a cathode to a plate, and is regulated along the way by voltage applied to one or more grids. Sometimes thought of as a collector of electrons, the plate is the destination, the final stop on the journey of electrons inside the triode. From there, "plate current" is directed to the next element of the circuit — another preamp tube, a tone stack, a phase inverter, etc.

1959 5F8-A "big-box" Twin. Note the side by side speaker mounting of the great sounding Jensen P12Ns. According to Perry Tate, the larger cabinets date as early as mid 1957.

But in a cathode follower arrangement, the output is taken straight from the cathode, rather than the plate. As spelled out in the *RCA Receiving Tube Manual*: "In this application, the load has been transferred from the plate circuit to the cathode circuit of the tube. ... The output impedance is quite low, and very low distortion may be obtained." In *The Guitar Amp Handbook*, author Dave Hunter explains that the tone controls in certain Fenders are positioned between the cathode of a second gain stage (consisting of two triodes in a single 12AX7) and the input of the phase inverter. In other words, the cathode, not the plate, drives the tone stack.

What's so special about a cathode follower? For one thing, it operates as an impedance matcher, making the tone controls theoretically more effective, more precise, and less interactive. Steve Carr: "Cathode followers have high input impedance, which means they are easy to drive, and low output impedance, which means they can drive the thing *after* them with authority. That is why they can interact with tone circuits differently than a regular gain stage."

Many players feel a cathode follower affords a noticeable increase of touch sensitivity, making the amp especially dynamic and responsive. Play lightly and the amp remains clear and bright; dig into the strings and the amp bites back. Paul Rivera reports that a cathode follower — as used in the late '50s Bassman, for example — adds a compression effect and also "changes the harmonics, adding more even order [harmonics] to the distortion." Amp tech and columnist Terry Buddingh: "Like any bit of tube amp lore, the cathode follower's merits can be debated. Some claim it enhances the tone control's effectiveness while providing a broader range of dynamically responsive textures and colors." Don Morris, of ElectroPlex amps, adds: "With a cathode follower, the amp can drive the tone circuit without losing most of the signal level, regardless of the tone settings. A cathode follower gives the amp a more 'aggressive' attack, and helps maintain a healthy amount of low-end thump. Players can experience this effect especially when overdriving the amp."

Schematics for the 5F6 and 5F6-A Bassmans and the 5F8 and 5F8-A Twins all date to mid or late 1957; these same circuits were used in those amps through the end of the tweed era. But while the F series Bassmans and Twins were Fender's most highly acclaimed cathode follower amps, Mr. Fender actually employed cathode follower circuits in several models starting in 1955, at the outset of the narrow panel period. These amps used various drivers (12AX7s, 7025s, 12AY7s) and included the 5E7 Bandmaster, 5E6 and 5E6-A Bassmans, 5E5-A Pro, 5E4-A and 5F4 Supers, 5D8 and 5E8 Twins (all tweeds), as well as the blonde Tolex 6G6, 6G6-A, and 6G6-B piggyback Bassmans (bass channel only).

Neil Young onstage in 1993 with his Les Paul, Old Black, accompanied by Steve Cropper and bassist Duck Dunn. Above the "Fender Deluxe" sign we can see the Whizzer atop Neil's trusty tweed Fender. Young told writer Jas Obrecht: "My amplifier is an interesting world unto itself. The Whizzer sits on top of my Fender Deluxe, which is the brain of the whole thing. The whole thing is very deep." For more on the Whizzer, turn the page.

Neil Young's Whizzer

Neil Young bought his tweed Deluxe at Sol Betnun's "music store," actually a funky old house on Larchmont Boulevard in Hollywood that was so crammed with used gear you could hardly walk around in there. He paid $50 for it in 1967. Neil told *Guitar Player*, "I took it home, plugged in this Gretsch guitar and immediately the entire room started to vibrate ... If you have it up on 12 then it just saturates completely and opens up after the attack. But if you back it down it will catch the attack. I use that sound a lot."

Young's tattered tweed tone tool is controlled via an ingenious contraption nicknamed the Whizzer; blending '50s circuitry and high technology, this Deluxe is like nothing else on earth. Veteran audio and video technician/engineer Rick Davis redesigned the Whizzers (there are two of them) and built several other custom electronic systems for Young. He explains, "The original analog Whizzer was designed and built by Sal Trentino for the Rust Never Sleeps tour [1978 - 1979]. It controlled the volume knob and was limited to two settings. Neil used Sal's machine for years before asking me to redesign it. My systems are digital three-knob controllers, with multiple presets. The first is a copper version I designed in 1991 using all discrete TTL [Transistor-Transistor Logic] CMOS [Complementary Metal-Oxide Semiconductor] logic, and the backup is a brass version from 1992 using a Motorola MC 6811FC1 microcontroller.

"Once the Whizzer is in place on top of the amp and powered up, Neil uses the three black knobs to find the sound settings he wants. The knobs are coupled through the electronics to servo motors, which in turn rotate the Deluxe's Tone, Inst. Vol, and Mic Vol knobs in real time. Once Neil finds the sounds he likes, he can store the settings in memory and assign them to the four pushbutton switches on the Whizzer's top panel. As a result he has four stored presets, with each knob having a unique setting, and he can call them up at his vocal microphone from his red footswitch. Each preset calls up one of the stored presets from memory, which tells the servos where to spin to set the knobs to the desired position. The stored settings are non-volatile, meaning Neil doesn't lose them when the power is turned off. He can, however, over-write the memory anytime he wants.

"The whole reason for this elaborate way of dealing with Neil's amp controls is that he absolutely will not allow anything to be put in the signal path between his guitars and the amp, and for good reason. Otherwise I could have done it in a much easier way."

Neil Young's longtime friend, equipment tech, and sometime band member Larry Cragg (http://www.vintageinstrumentrental.com) adds: "The digital readout goes up to 12, just like the knobs on a tweed Deluxe. We set the volume presets at 1.9, 6, and 10, which is the most distorted, and then at 12 it compresses a lot, which is part of Neil's thing. He has a Fender reverb unit before the amplifier, and when the Whizzer gets up into those higher numbers, it overloads the power stage because we have the knobs turned up so high. We're into output tube saturation here. That's where the 'bloom' is — 'bloom' is what happens after you pick the note. You get the most complex wave form in the output tubes. I hate that concept of the totally distorted preamp with a very clean power amp. It sounds buzzy.

"I run 6L6s in Neil's Deluxe, not 6V6s, and I saved a huge stash just for that amp. I change tubes often. The idle current is rated very high on them, so not only does the amp use 6L6s, but they are particularly hot 6L6s. We have two high-powered fans blowing in the back to keep the transformer from frying, and to keep it from sagging after 20 minutes of performance or so.

"For the 12AX7s, I go through a lot of tubes and actually listen to them in the amp. You can't really tell how it's going to sound until you put it in the amplifier. I catalog the characteristics of each tube, because they're all different. We prefer the old Chinese 12AX7s. They're not like what you get now. Neil likes them because it's the most in-your-face tone.

"Another thing — most people don't realize how much they're losing just going through the volume and tone controls on the guitar. Even when your volume is all the way up, you're losing a shocking amount of tone to ground. So recently I modified Neil's Les Paul, Old Black. There used to be a phase switch in there. I put a little switch in that same hole, and it bypasses the volume and tone control on the bridge pickup and connects the pickup directly to the [output] jack. You're normally getting 85 percent of the sound, but Neil can get 100 percent, and it's amazing how much difference it makes. On Neil's guitar, it's always bypassed. It kicks butt. In conjunction with the Whizzer, it's overwhelming."

On Thrasher's Wheat, an archival website devoted to Neil Young, an observer described a film of Young's induction into the Rock and Roll Hall of Fame on January 13, 1995: "Young joined Led Zeppelin onstage for an all-out guitar duel with Jimmy Page .... At one point, after seemingly endless jamming and soloing between the two legends, a clearly exhausted Page drops his hands from his guitar as if to concede defeat ... one can see Page patting Neil's amplifier as if to say, 'You've got a hell of a sound from your equipment.'"

Larry Cragg: "Neil uses the Whizzer and that tweed Deluxe all the time, no matter how big the concert hall is. We just put it through the P.A. It's been rated at 19 watts, but no one believes it. It's really loud. We're about to go out with Crosby, Stills, and Nash. Those guys all have really powerful amplifiers, but this thing just kills them."

Baggy pants, the hippest shoes in Hollywood, and overwhelming talent: Little Richard rips it up on the set of 1956's *The Girl Can't Help It*. Nathaniel Douglas must've sounded mighty and righteous with his Esquire plugged into this tweed Bassman.

Clockwise That Chickenhead to the Max, and Let the Good Times Roll

Consider the year 1956. Although rock and roll had already had its first number one hit the previous year with Bill Haley's "Rock Around the Clock," the charts were mostly dominated through the first few months of '56 by the likes of Dean Martin, Tennessee Ernie Ford, and the Four Lads. By summer, however, Elvis Presley, Frankie Lymon, Little Richard, Carl Perkins, Fats Domino, and Gene Vincent had all bopped and shimmied and slammed their way into the Top 20. The rock and roll rebellion was in full tilt, and America saw the ascension of a boisterous new youth culture. In the age of flat-top cats and dungaree dolls, Chuck Berry captured the mood: *My temperature's rising, the juke box blowin' a fuse.*

Out in Fullerton, however, there might not have been a whole lotta shakin' goin' on. Leo Fender was tappin' his toe to infectious instrumentals like "Steel Guitar Rag" and bar-stool heartbreakers like "Bubbles in My Beer" and was likely oblivious to the impending rock and roll storm. He might not have known what to make of, say, Screamin' Jay Hawkins, and leather-clad rockers like Gene Vincent must have been the furthest thing from his mind as he erased and redrew the details of his schematics and fussed over his prototypes.

Nevertheless, in a most harmonic convergence of events, rock and roll arrived right on the heels of Fender's refining its comprehensive line of high-quality amplifiers. With the new narrow panel look, the Bassman in its impressive 4x10 configuration, new models such as the Tremolux of 1955 and the Vibrolux of 1956, the revamped king-of-the-hill Twin, and an array of products appealing to everyone from first-timers to headliners, Fender was poised to set the amp world on fire.

Decked out in tweed luggage linen and sporting a mirror-finish chrome panel and a stitched leather handle, any one of these amps would look killer in the back seat of your hot rod Lincoln (or mom and dad's Chevy Nomad wagon). It would spiff up the bandstand, too, and would make a too-happenin' centerpiece for your band's black & white promo photo. When it came to volume, all you had to do was clockwise that chickenhead to the max. You'd likely be the loudest cat in any ballroom, roadhouse, or high school gym. Most important of all, your tweed Fender amp would make your guitar ring out like God's own Telecaster.

Despite all that, the impact of rock and roll on Fender amp sales was gradual rather than sudden, more slow burn than wildfire. Don Randall: "The arrival of rock and roll made a difference in the whole music business, but I can't say it meant a whole lot just to Fender, not at first. At first we were practically all country, but we had to change along with the styles. Rock and roll opened up new markets for us, but it was only part of the picture. As we grew and became more expansive we were able to accommodate musicians from more styles. It took time, and we all had to work just night and day to make it happen."

"On that night the tone wasn't right, and I said, 'Well, if you want a '50s sound, I've got to play this Fender through a Fender amp,' and there happened to be a Champ there. I said, 'That's the one.'"

—Waddy Wachtel, on recording the solo on Linda Rondstadt's "It's So Easy."

Rockabilly Hall of Famer Paul Burlison on recording with the Rock 'N' Roll Trio: "We recorded a lot of our stuff in the '50s at Owen Bradley's Studio in Nashville, in the same room where they recorded all the Grand Ole Opry stuff. Back then, we just sat in a circle out in the open and looked at each other and nodded. There was no drummer's booth or singer's booth. I had a little old Fender Deluxe amp sitting up on a stool close to me with a mike in front of it."

Burlison is credited with being one of the very earliest players to achieve a fuzztone sound on record. He used it, for example, on "The Train Kept A-Rollin'" in May of '56. "We were playing in Cleveland, Ohio, and just before the show started, the leather strap on my Fender amp broke and the amp fell to the floor. When I plugged the guitar in, it had a real fuzzy sound. I looked in the back of the amp and one of the tubes was barely sticking in the prongs. It was acting as a rheostat. The guitar sounded pretty good, so I left the tube the way it was. And so from then on, whenever I wanted to get that sound I'd just reach back there and loosen the tube. You could tell when you were getting it — it sounded real funky."

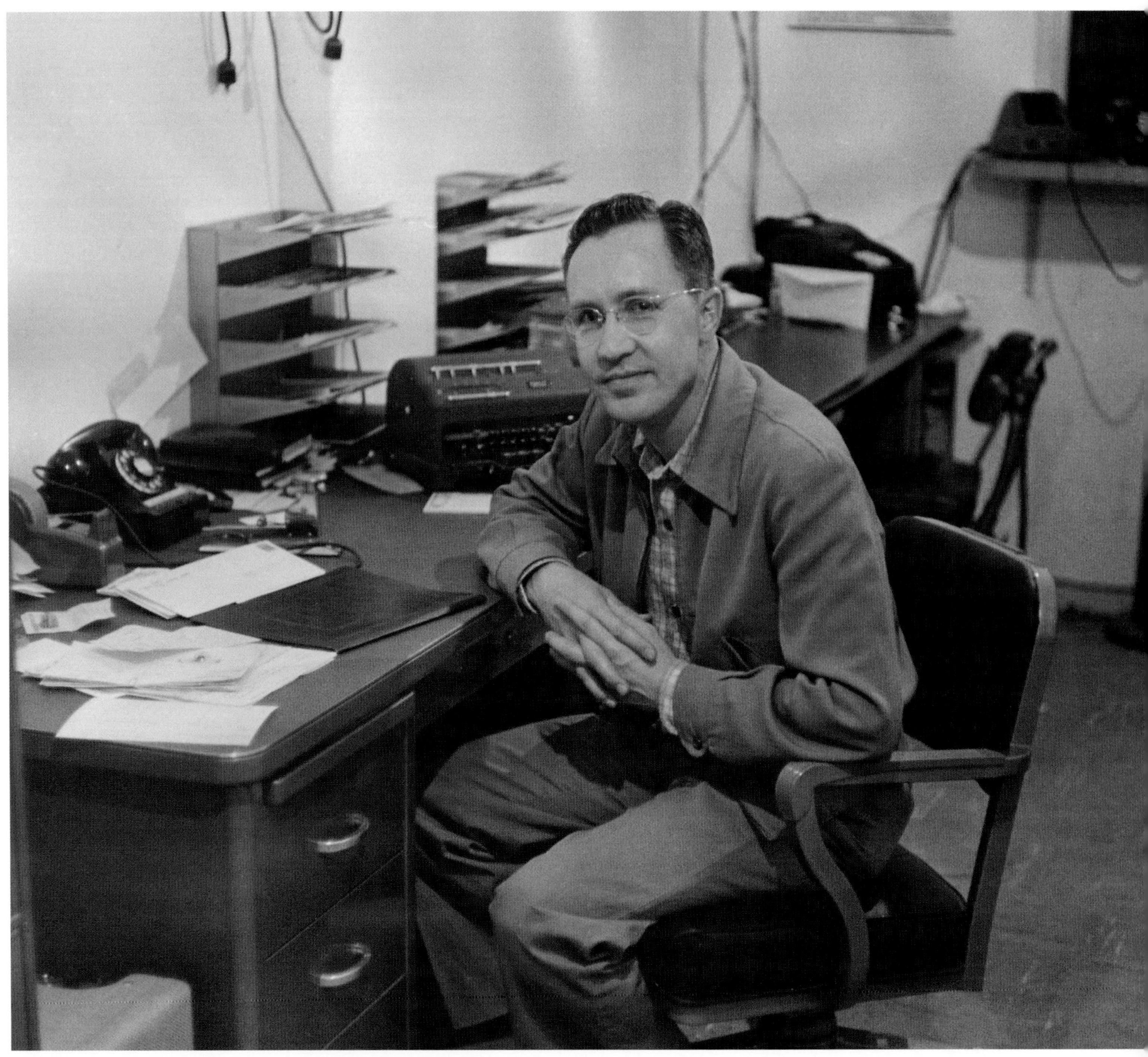

Plant Manager Forrest White. A CBS exec instructed him to sign off on the new solid state amps. Mr. White told this author, "There was no way in heck I was gonna okay those things. I couldn't have looked Leo in the eye if I had ever approved products that were not worthy of the Fender name." When CBS pressed him to go along, he walked away from the job he loved.

The White Amps

By the mid-'50s Fender was a substantial company, and yet Leo ran it much as he had run his repair shop — by the seat of his pants. Lucky for Leo, Forrest White entered his life on May 20, 1954 and worked for him and his successors until December '66. Forrest brought crucial skills to Fender. He became its Plant Manager, and then Vice President and General Manager, shepherding the factory through phenomenal growth in the '60s. He significantly modernized and increased the efficiency of the growing facility. A true keeper of the Fender flame, he was in his later years a caretaker to a collection of mementos and catalogs that he readily displayed with pride. His tales of the old days often took on a parable-like quality, illuminating attributes of his colleagues' characters or the superiority of Fender products.

In 1955 Leo established a second brand name to complement the Fender line, possibly to increase the distribution of steel guitars and student amps into music stores and especially teaching studios without ruffling the feathers of official Fender dealers. Leo was never effusive with praise or recognition, but he named the new line of bluish gray amps and student steels after Forrest. As Richard Smith recounted in *Guitar Player*, "One day Forrest was in the wood shop and a stockroom employee asked him where to put the White labels. Forrest questioned what he meant, and the man said, 'You know, the White labels.' Forrest replied, 'Well, if they're *white*, send them back.' The employee persisted, 'No, you don't understand,' and showed Forrest the new tag. Leo had named the new studio line after Forrest without telling him."

As is clear to anyone who read Forrest's book, *Fender: The Inside Story*, Forrest White idolized Leo Fender. It's hard to imagine any employee in the entire history of the company who would have been more deeply moved by the gesture. Not many of the Princeton-like White amps were made, but Forrest never forgot the honor.

Ascribing an almost totemic significance to the first amp off the line, Forrest wrote in his book: "I have the first White amplifier. It is still in the original carton and has never been opened." The box was sealed with tape and a note that bore the words "Save for Forrest, AS00001," perhaps in Leo Fender's own hand. The seal was finally broken, and the amp is pictured on page 194. Owner Perry Tate: "It was in Aspen Pittman's collection, and after it left his hands and before I got it, someone who didn't know any better took it out of the box. Instead of taking it out from the bottom, they broke the seal on top. It's only been out of the box about three times."

On December 6, 1966, a CBS Fender exec asked Forrest to sign off on the new solid state amplifiers, later reviled as the lamest of the post-Leo CBS fiascos. "I can't," he told the man, "because they are not worthy of Leo Fender's name." Rather than contribute to diminishing the Fender reputation he had worked so hard to establish, Forrest White walked away from it all. He was always proud to recount this story and in retrospect may have viewed it as his finest hour.

He died in 1994. This author wrote in *Guitar Player*: "A few days before Forrest White died on November 22, I called to say goodbye. Although his voice was weak, his spirit was strong. He talked without hesitation about the cancer that had come upon him suddenly and spread quickly. There was no talk of last minute cures or other miracles, but plenty of reflection upon his career at ground level zero of a guitar explosion that rocked the world: the Fender factory."

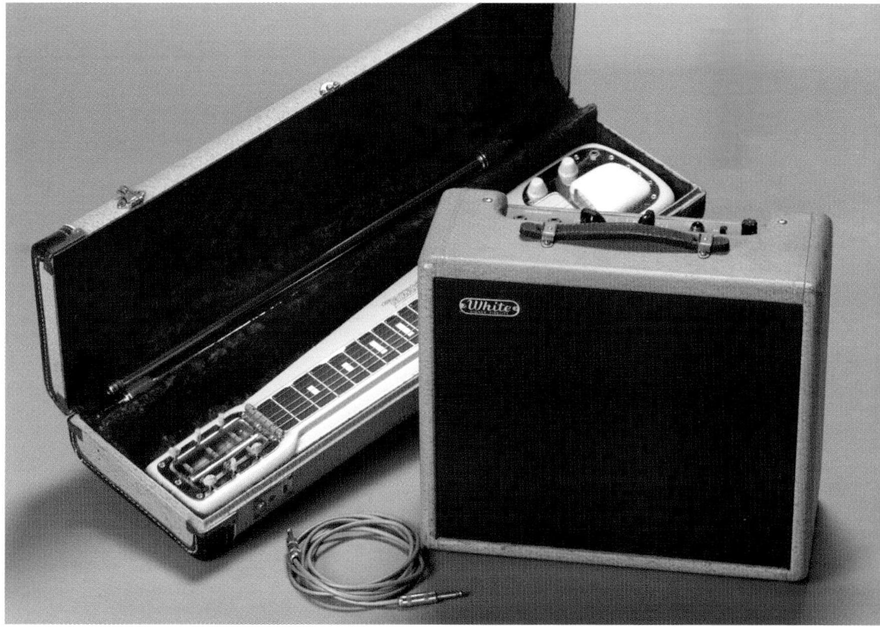

A beautiful, all-original White set; note the nonpedal steel guitar's legs stowed in the original plush-lined case. The grille mounted tag reads *White Higher Fidelity*.

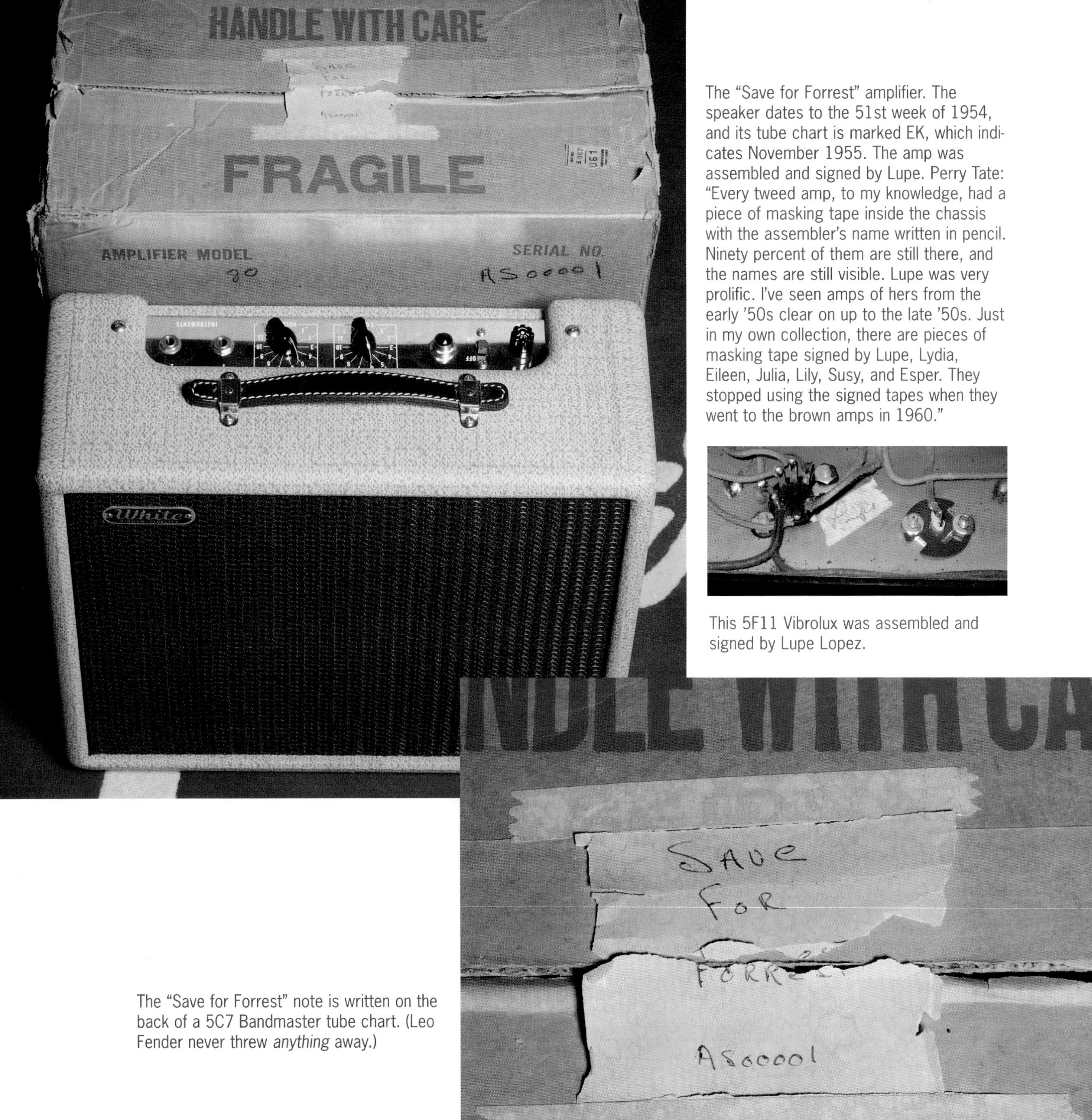

The "Save for Forrest" amplifier. The speaker dates to the 51st week of 1954, and its tube chart is marked EK, which indicates November 1955. The amp was assembled and signed by Lupe. Perry Tate: "Every tweed amp, to my knowledge, had a piece of masking tape inside the chassis with the assembler's name written in pencil. Ninety percent of them are still there, and the names are still visible. Lupe was very prolific. I've seen amps of hers from the early '50s clear on up to the late '50s. Just in my own collection, there are pieces of masking tape signed by Lupe, Lydia, Eileen, Julia, Lily, Susy, and Esper. They stopped using the signed tapes when they went to the brown amps in 1960."

This 5F11 Vibrolux was assembled and signed by Lupe Lopez.

The "Save for Forrest" note is written on the back of a 5C7 Bandmaster tube chart. (Leo Fender never threw *anything* away.)

"I have a couple of White amps from the '50s, Fender student models that commemorate Forrest White. They have a single 8 inch speaker and a transformer unlike any other Fender. To me, a Champ or a White turned up to 12 sounds infinitely better than any distortion pedal."

—Dan Vickrey
of Counting Crows

A half-century old, and brand spankin' new: the very first White amp. The wrap around the cord is original. The cord has never been uncoiled. The amp has never been played. It's never even been plugged in.

The most influential guitarist of rock and roll's first generation (and some would say the greatest of all rockers, period), Chuck Berry has been a regular user of Fender amps for his entire career. He told this author, "When we went up to Chicago, I had one of the little Fenders with the flat control panel carved out of the back, and the whole thing was covered with a leatherish, funkyish, tableclothish material [laughs]. On the first records, like 'Maybellene,' we didn't have reverb, but later when I used Fender amps, I would just use the reverb right on the amp." One particularly reverby example is the too-cool-for-words solo on 1958's "Sweet Little Rock and Roller."

CHAPTER TWELVE

12

From Tweed to Tolex

Leo Fender and the New Amps, Don Randall and the New Message

In the late 1950s, factory modifications to E and F series amps had generally been circuit-based, with updated rectifiers, tone stacks, power tubes, and so on, all appearing in similar narrow panel cabinets. But in the early 1960s, Fender stunned the music world with an entirely new line of products that boasted new models, new features, and a whole new look to boot.

Although the new design was on display at the summer 1959 NAMM show (reportedly, some early exhibits displayed dummy cabs with no electronics), company records suggest that full production did not begin until later in the year, or possibly January 1960. These new products would define the modern guitar amplifier for years — at least, until the next generation of Fenders. While most of the model names were familiar, almost everything else was spankin' new, including dual channels, cabinets with slant-back, front-mounted controls, and extra-rugged, fabric-backed, vinyl Tolex covering (tweed would soon be on its way out). Several early-'60s models sported a whole new cab design for Fender: the piggyback.

Another departure from convention was the grouping of the newly redesigned models into the Professional Amplifiers, a line within the line (also see Chap. 13). Having a series of amps that looked and functioned differently from their stablemates, and were set apart and given an elite status, presaged the multi-series Fender amp catalogs of decades to come.

Generally, the earliest examples had a light brown or tan color with a somewhat pinkish hue. In less than a year, they changed to a darker, slightly more chocolaty cab color and a darker, oxblood grille cloth; after another year and a half, they acquired a light, wheat colored grille cloth. (Some cosmetic details appear in subsequent sections here, but for a thorough listing and illustrations of the various tweeds, Tolexes, grille cloths, handles, knobs, nameplates, etc., see Teagle & Sprung's *Fender Amps, The First Fifty Years*.)

Aside from cosmetic changes — flat, grille-mounted *Fender* logos, round knobs instead of chickenheads, "dogbone" handles, etc. — the evolution of Fender amps during this period may be charted in three categories, with typical overlaps: the expansion of the line, the evolution of cabinets and control panels, and a new approach to circuits, the G series.

Three beauties with the rough Tolex and the maroon/oxblood grille of the early blonde period. Ry Cooder told *Guitar Player*: "My amp is just an old blonde Fender Bassman top that sounds good. It has the simplest circuitry so that it isn't coloring the sound too much, yet it has that warm, fat tube sound." Eddie Van Halen to Jas Obrecht, 1980: "When I'm at home, I use a little old white Fender Bandmaster. You get a tube distortion and it sounds real good … I'll tell you, the best sound I ever get is sitting home alone playing through that little Bandmaster cranked on 10."

Hear the blonde Tolex Showman, Tracks 58 - 59.

New Fenders for the New Decade

In scarcely more than a year, the line increased from 11 to 14 amps, one new model at a time. The July 30, 1958 price sheet listed the Twin, Bassman, Bandmaster, Pro, Super, Tremolux, Vibrolux, Deluxe, Harvard, Princeton, and Champ. All 11 were familiar model names, some a couple of years old, others dating all the way back to the days of the woodies and TV fronts. By late 1959, Fender was touting its brand new 1x15 Vibrasonic, at the very top of the line, along with the 4x10 Concert. The Showman would follow by the late fall of 1960.

The 14 amps in the line of late 1960 and 1961 ranged from the Champ (still called Champ "600" in the price list) up to the piggyback Showman. They weren't cheap. For the price of a Showman you could outfit your rhythm section with a brand new Precision Bass and a Telecaster Custom (the one with the binding and the sunburst finish), and still have enough left over for a practice-room Princeton.

Sample list prices from December 1960 are shown here converted to approximate contemporary dollar values: Princeton ($82.50, $550), Super ($244.50, $1,600), Twin ($429.50, $2,800), and Showman ($550, $3,600). So in terms of expense, buying a top of the line Fender was the equivalent of acquiring a Fender Custom Amp Shop model in the mid '90s, or buying a full-featured boutique amp today. (Current price tags on vintage classics such as tweed Bassmans and tweed Twins seem astonishing, but in the case of other highly desirable vintage Fenders, their current prices are nearly the same as their original costs, when adjusted.)

Leo Fender's new amplifiers were not only exceptional performers; the influence of their exterior design has never been exceeded by any manufacturer's amps. They weren't just good looking. They were so ultra-cool that bands would sometimes buy Fender amps that matched their other Fender amps, or their guitars — even their clothes.

The Astronauts and their mind-boggling display of Fender blondes, 1964. Note the cool trick of hanging the guitars on the amps, their necks aligned just so.

Very early, supremely scarce brown Pro, built no later than the spring of 1960. The earliest brown combos (some of them, anyway) had metal knobs with indented dot markers. Fender amp collector and researcher Greg Huntington: "I used to own Super amp serial number 00001, and it had those knobs. They were also likely on the Vibrasonic on display at NAMM in 1959. These amps are so early and so rare that we might consider them prototypes." This example has the early, unusual Bass, Treble, Volume knob array.

Seymour Duncan: "When I saw the Yardbirds with Jimmy Page, they were all using matching Dual Showmans. Way back, I saw the Fendermen live. They had a big hit with 'Muleskinner Blues,' and up on the stage they all had matching blonde piggyback Showmans tilted back and blonde reverb units. They were playing blonde Jazzmasters and a blonde Precision Bass. They had matching jackets. It was just so great. I remember it like it was yesterday."

Vanguards: Vibrasonic and Concert

While all Fenders would eventually convert to Tolex cabs, the vanguards of the new order were the all-new combos, the Vibrasonic and the Concert. (The Vibrasonic is often considered the slightly earlier amp, but note that the factory numbers were: 12 Concert, 13 Vibrasonic.) Richard Smith has some of the personal records of former plant manager Forrest White. These "Balance of Orders" entries were used to keep track of production requirements. Certain entries reveal when orders for the Vibrasonic were sent by Fender Sales to the factory, and they include notations that seem to indicate some of the requests were unfilled for a period of months.

Nevertheless, examining all of the entries, Richard concludes: "At least 101 Vibrasonics were delivered to Fender Sales in 1959, or at least before January 4, 1960. However, it's clear that the records are incomplete for the period, so additional orders could have been made and filled. Remember, they filled orders as needed and didn't stock up on items that would sit and wait for orders. They made products in batches or production runs that made economic sense, and it seems that Fender Sales held on to orders until they had enough for a full production run — say, 50 units for the popular items. It's my impression they made almost one model at a time until the order was done. So, if you went out to the line one week they would have Twin chassis, and the next week it might be Concerts."

Greg Gagliano communicates with other Fender amp buffs and maintains a database detailing information on about 17,000 Fender amps built from 1946 to 1984. He reports that they have never seen a single 1959 Vibrasonic, so they believe it is extremely unlikely that any Vibrasonics were shipped before 1960. Their view is not necessarily contradicted by the records archived by Richard Smith, which indicate that the first Vibrasonics may have shipped as late as the first week of January 1960.

The Professional Amplifiers of 1960 sported brown Tolex coverings, front-mounted control panels, flat, grille-mounted *Fender* logos, round knobs instead of chickenheads, "dogbone" handles, and the most versatile Fender circuits yet. (Also see Chap. 13.)

Small amps, big tones: Fabulous Thunderbirds Kim Wilson and Jimmie Vaughan get the joint jumpin' with a pair of brown Princetons.

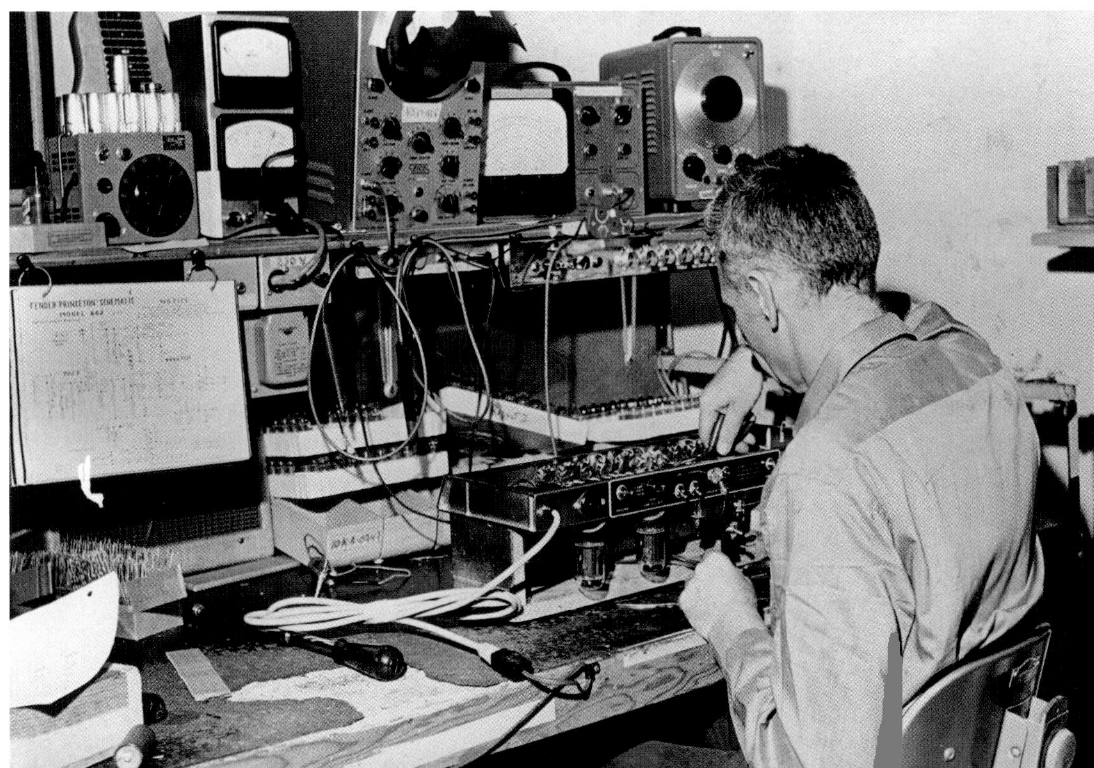

Amp technician Bob Standen at the factory, working on a Princeton chassis (the schematic is dated August 1961).

Vibrasonics in 1959? This photo reportedly bears that date, and pictures Johnny Cash's guitarist, Luther Perkins, playing a futuristic, all-gold Jazzmaster through a Vibrasonic at the Fullerton plant as employee Bob Hines looks on. The amp is supposedly a prototype, but it sure looks ready for the showroom. (Historic note: Cash recorded "I Walk the Line" at the Sun studio in Memphis on April 2, 1956; Perkins' inimitable guitar riff was rendered with his 1955 Esquire and a tweed Champ.)

In promoting the new design, Fender concentrated in particular on the new flagship. One catalog featured the Vibrasonic on its cover, then again in a prominent full-page photo surrounded by Stratocasters and top of the line Jazzmasters, and yet again alongside the steel guitars with which its power and hefty JBL were particularly well matched. Mr. Fender's continuing pursuit of headroom is revealed in the Vibrasonic's initial catalog copy: "Not only does it produce tremendous, distortion-free power, but it also offers exceptionally clean amplification through the use of the Lansing D130 15 inch high fidelity speaker."

In the early '60s the electric bass was fully a decade old, but Fender continued to face the formidable challenges of amplifying the new instrument, particularly in rock and roll performances where volumes were on the rise. The earliest 4x10 Tolex Concert was advertised alongside the last of the 4x10 tweed Bassmans. One surprising detail reveals a gap between Fender's intentions for the Concert and its eventual use by musicians: The catalog promised that it was "suitable for use with all amplified instruments including the Precision Bass and Fender Jazz Bass." But the 4x10 Concert would be less successful as a bass amp than its 4x10 tweed predecessor; of course, both were fine guitar amps.

At any rate, like other Fenders, the Concert was touted as providing "tremendous power free from distortion," and like most of the other brown Tolex combos it featured a solid state rectifier, "which eliminates the heating problem encountered with glass tube rectifiers."

"Freddie [Tavares] and I played a two-man job one time, and Freddie said, 'I'm going to bring a prototype amp over to the job and see what you think about it.' It had a big, honkin' JBL speaker. It had a lot of volume, and it overshadowed the Standels that I had heard earlier. I'm not positive, but I'm pretty sure that was the amplifier that became the Vibrasonic, and Freddie did have a lot to do with the design of that one."

— Bill Carson

The Vibrasonic debuted at the top of the line in 1960. In keeping with its lofty status, it was equipped with a stock J. B. Lansing speaker. It also featured tremolo, which for years had been offered on the mid-level Tremolux and Vibrolux but, oddly, never on a top-tier model. All of the guitars in this 1960 catalog photo are beautiful, although the Jazzmaster at far left is particularly stunning and unusual. Unlike most companies, Fender pictured its guitars and amps together, reinforcing Leo Fender's sense of their inseparability and also spotlighting the modernity of all Fender products.

Fender Firsts

Distinctive Fender hallmarks of the vintage era included multiple tone knobs, front-mounted control panels, heavy-duty components, piggyback cabs, and other innovations often touted in the catalogs as "Fender Firsts." Rival inventors and companies sometimes disputed these claims. The Standel company, for example, was at one time considered a significant competitor to Fender in Southern California music circles. Its endorsers included the likes of guitar superstars Chet Atkins and Merle Travis. *Vintage Guitar* magazine and other authorities have credited Standel's founder, the late Bob Crooks, with introducing several innovations soon adopted by Fender and others, including separate bass and treble controls, open-weave grille cloth, and the use of JBL speakers in production guitar amps.

An adequate discussion of Crooks' claim that Standel was the first to put JBLs in a guitar amp would distinguish earlier field coil speakers and later cast-frame speakers; more important, it would acknowledge that the JBLs in Fender amps were reportedly designed specifically to meet Leo Fender's own specifications. Crooks' claim to have originated the piggyback design should be qualified by noting Gibson's much older amps with separate heads and speaker cabs, by acknowledging Mr. Fender's tweed piggyback (a June '57 one-off built *three years* before the appearance of the Tolex production models, Chap. 13), and finally by detailing the differences between Standel's piggybacks and the vastly more popular Fenders.

The Bandmaster on top is typical of several of the earliest brown Tolex models from the first six months or so of 1960. It features the unusual B, T, V control array, the so-called "burlap" textured, slightly pink Tolex color, and the cabinet's sharp edge, or "shelf," above the control panel. The slightly later brown Super is different and more common in all respects, with a conventional knob array, the smoother, somewhat more chocolaty Tolex color, and a rounded edge above the panel. The older, tweed style grille on the Bandmaster was seen on some but not all of the early brown Fenders. The Super's grille is much more typical of the brown Fenders.

Alan Hardtke: "By the way, you see that circle around the handle attachment on the Bandmaster? You see this kind of pattern from time to time. We all assumed that people put a beer can or a coffee cup on top of the amp. But then we began to notice marks appearing on the *side* of the amp, so it had to be something else. The beverage theory also wouldn't explain this one, because you couldn't set a can or a glass in that spot. Somebody figured out that the brown stains are from knots in the pine underneath."

Fender's early piggybacks featured a speaker "Projector Ring" intended to eliminate the cancellation of front and rear soundwaves. Hartley Peavey provided data and illustrations of a system sold in the late 1950s by Lafayette Radio, a New York based supplier of electronics parts. Hartley Peavey: "These folks produced a 'ducted port' Eliptoflex enclosure that was apparently copied first by Ampeg and later by Fender and ended up being the basis for Fender's early piggyback designs. The 1x12 Bassman and 1x12 Showman [like the Eliptoflex] used a spun metal ring mounted to a baffle board wherein the port was around the edge of the speaker."

Researching Crooks' assertion that Standel was the first to use closed-back cabs would entail investigating the history of Ampeg and perhaps others. Although Fender's Professional Amplifiers of 1960 bore little resemblance to the Standels of the late 1950s, some of those Standel models did have front-mounted knobs.

Standel's legacy is noteworthy, to be sure, and Bob Crooks' amplifiers were indeed innovative. Still, assessing the true novelty of their individual features would require researching the history of at least half a dozen manufacturers, a project well outside the scope of this book. Guitarist, collector, and columnist Deke Dickerson interviewed Mr. Crooks several times in the mid 1990s. Deke Dickerson: "He was a very nice guy, but he did have some bitter feelings about coming up with these innovations and having Fender usurp them to greater success. It was a lot like the Paul Bigsby headstock versus the Leo Fender Strat headstock situation, in that he definitely still held a grudge after all those years. [Paul Bigsby crafted a headstock similar to the Stratocaster's several years before the Strat's debut in 1954. Bigsby's influence on Leo Fender was a source of friction between the two men and has often been debated.]

"One thing for sure about those Standel cabinets — they were highly advanced for their time. They were ported and baffled with a closed back like a hi-fi cabinet, and I don't think any other guitar amp manufacturers were making anything like that at the time. Bob also claimed to be the first to offer separate bass and treble controls, but I don't think that's the case. I've never been sure about that claim.

"Bob Crooks had the unfortunate timing to make the best clean sounding amp ever made precisely at the time

The earlier cab on top has a dogbone handle, rough Tolex, and oxblood grille; the other has the flat handle, smoother Tolex, and wheat grille of the later blonde period. Fender often mixed older and newer features, but these groups of details are generally associated with each other.

This well-worn Deluxe, its handle fortified with tape, is accompanied by George Harrison's legendary rosewood Telecaster. Custom built for George by Fender employee Phil Kubicki, the guitar was used on "The Long and Winding Road," among others, and is seen in the film *Let It Be* and in footage of the Beatles' swan song performance on the Apple Records rooftop in London. George gave the guitar to his close friend Delaney Bramlett. It was later sold at auction for $370,000.

that musical tastes changed and distorted tones became in vogue — for which a cranked-up Fender was the perfect choice."

Don Randall: "Bob Crooks was a pleasant guy, and I worked with him for years at Randall after I left Fender. I don't recall ever looking at his products particularly closely at Fender. We were generally aware of other products, but we just had so much work to do we didn't spend that much time looking at other companies' amps. I don't think his Standel amplifiers were that applicable or influential as far as what we were doing over at Fender."

This author sees it this way: Inventors of commercial products are aware of existing designs and use them as starting points for their own attempts at improvements or redesigns. Bob Crooks was one such inventor who was no doubt aware of, say, early Gibson amps with separate heads and cabs. Leo Fender was another; he surely knew of Ampeg's Reverbrocket, a reverb-equipped combo that preceded his own Vibroverb (in fact, as many as a dozen manufacturers were producing amps with onboard reverb prior to the Vibroverb). As noted in Chap. 1, Mr. Fender didn't invent the solidbody electric guitar, but he invented the one that mattered, the one musicians accepted, and he can rightfully be called the father of that instrument. While the Telecaster's predecessors have been forgotten by everyone except knowledgeable guitar history buffs, the Telecaster remains an industry staple after nearly six decades.

Many of Mr. Fender's other products also incorporated existing concepts that he put together in new ways. His use of the latest technologies and sturdier components raised the bar for his entire industry. He added his own improvements, which were usually substantial and occasionally radical (as with the Stratocaster, for example). Then he reorganized the elements in more durable, more effective, and more attractive packages. Typically, the resulting Fenders decisively outperformed, outsold and outlasted their competitors. So, whether a particular "Fender First" was a never-before-seen departure from convention or a substantial improvement to previous designs, Fender's descriptions of these advances as "innovations" were well justified. Hartley Peavey: "Leo's real genius was in collecting information, combining it with his experience, and blending that into a workable product that was not only fair in price but very reliable."

Phasing in the New Amps

The conversion from tweed to Tolex was gradual, evolving in two general phases. Along with the Concert and Vibrasonic, the 1960 literature pictured brown Tolex versions of the other Professional Amplifiers — Bandmaster, Pro, Super, and Twin (more on the Twin below) — alongside familiar tweeds: Bassman, Tremolux, Vibrolux, Deluxe, Harvard, Princeton, and Champ. All were combos.

Phase two (as revealed, for example, in the December 1960 price list) saw three major developments. Fender had yet another all-new, top of the line model, the Showman. Along with that amp, the Tremolux, Bassman, and Bandmaster had all converted to the new piggyback design in which the amplifier and speakers were housed in separate cabs. Finally, the piggybacks also sported white knobs, maroon grille cloth, and a new Tolex color: off-white, or "blonde," in what has come to be called the "rough" texture.

Several of these developments are sometimes dated to 1961, despite their appearance in the literature from late 1960; indeed, some of the piggybacks may have been advertised for the first time as late as mid 1961 or even later in the case of the Showman.

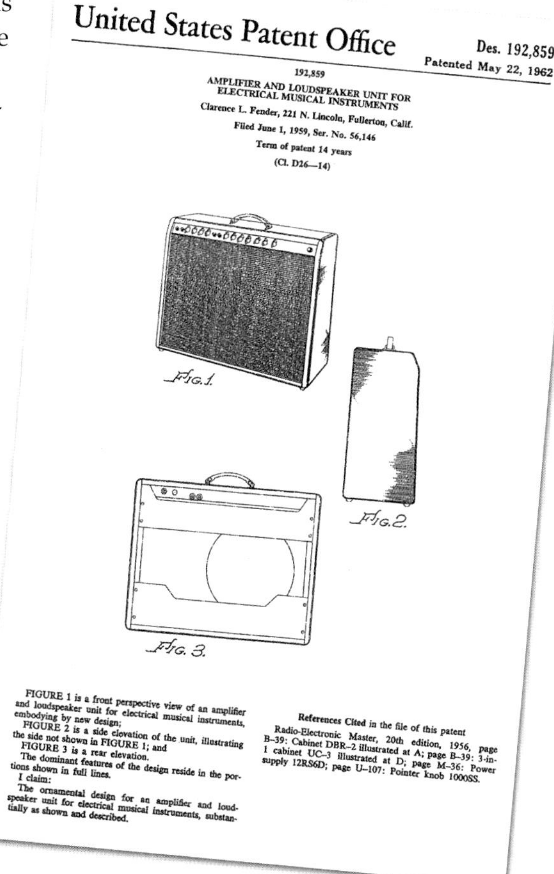

United States Patent Office

Des. 192,859
Patented May 22, 1962

192,859
AMPLIFIER AND LOUDSPEAKER UNIT FOR ELECTRICAL MUSICAL INSTRUMENTS
Clarence L. Fender, 221 N. Lincoln, Fullerton, Calif.
Filed June 1, 1959, Ser. No. 56,146
Term of patent 14 years
(Cl. D26—14)

FIGURE 1 is a front perspective view of an amplifier and loudspeaker unit for electrical musical instruments, embodying by new design;

FIGURE 2 is a side elovation of the unit, illustrating the side not shown in FIGURE 1; and

FIGURE 3 is a rear elevation.

The dominant features of the design reside in the portions shown in full lines.

I claim:

The ornamental design for an amplifier and loudspeaker unit for electrical musical instruments, substantially as shown and described.

References Cited in the file of this patent

Radio-Electronic Master, 20th edition, 1956, page B–39: Cabinet DBR–2 illustrated at A; page B–39: 3-in-1 cabinet UC–3 illustrated at D; page M–36: Power supply 12RS6D; page U–107: Pointer knob 1000SS.

Fender's design patent for an instrument amp with its controls mounted on a slant-back front panel was filed on June 1, 1959 and granted on May 22, 1962.

So while early-1960 literature pictured a mix of brown Tolex combos and tweed combos, the late-1960 and 1961 literature portrayed an even more diverse mix of tweed combos, brown combos, blonde piggybacks, and one blonde combo — the Twin.

By this time, almost all Fenders were covered in Tolex of one color or the other. Only a few of the low-end amps retained their tweed cabs and top-mounted control panels — now a decidedly old-school look among the newly slicked-up, Tolex-attired Fenders. As noted elsewhere, the Champ was made with an F series circuit, tweed cab, and top-mounted control panel all the way through 1964, long after the rest of the line had evolved to G circuits, Tolex cabs, and front-mounted controls (apparently overlooked for years, it skipped the brown Tolex phase altogether and went straight from tweed to black).

Both the blonde color and piggyback cabs were generally associated with high-end Fenders such as the new Showman and the revamped Bassman and Bandmaster. But there were exceptions, too: a top-tier model that was blonde but not a piggyback (the Twin), top-tier models that were neither blonde nor piggybacks (the Concert and Vibrasonic), and a blonde piggyback that was not a top-tier amp at all (the mid-level, redesigned Tremolux, which at $229 listed for less than half the price of the $479 Vibrasonic).

Muddy Waters at Carnegie Hall, 1965. Although pictured here with a Gibson SG and a blonde Bassman, he is much better remembered for playing a Telecaster through a Super Reverb. "A lot of the sound is the amp," he explained. "I'd rather always use my own amplifier. It's the Fender with the four 10 inch speakers, the Super. Even if I'd forgotten my own guitar and had to borrow one, I could make the sound come out of that amplifier."

Control Panels and Features

A whole new approach to circuitry is revealed with a mere glance at the control panels of the new Professional combos of early 1960 and the piggybacks that soon followed. Each of the initial combos had two channels: Normal, with (left to right) bass, treble, and volume controls; and Vibrato, with bass, treble, volume, speed, and depth controls. Note the unconventional order of the bass, treble, and volume knobs: B, T, V. These "center volume" layouts distinguish the very earliest of the brown amps (as do metal knobs, which may have appeared only in catalogs or on prototypes), and were succeeded before mid 1960 by the now conventional arrangement: volume, treble, bass.

Each had a presence control that functioned in both channels. The mid tone knob was dropped from the blonde Bassman and Twin (it would reappear three years later on the Twin, in the blackface reverb era).

The trend in a nutshell: more features in '60 and '61. The brand new models — Concert, Showman, and Vibrasonic — all premiered with presence controls, tremolo, and dual, separately adjustable channels. As noted, the Tolex updates of the Twin, Bandmaster, Pro, and Super also shared those same features. As other redesigned models were phased in, they generally acquired new features as well. For example, the tweed Vibrolux and Tremolux already had tremolo; in their early-'60s Tolex versions, both featured dual channels (Normal and Bright) with separate banks of controls. Compared to their predecessors, the brown Princeton added tremolo, the blonde Bassman added dual channels, and the brown Deluxe added both tremolo and dual channels.

Missing link: the Spotlites Concert. This 4x10 Concert is so early it predates the discontinuation of the 4x10 tweed Bassman by several months. Externally, it's a '60s style Tolex Fender with a tube chart dated JC, or March 1960. Internally, it's mostly tweed. In fact, it's labeled as a '50s amp — 5G12, rather than 6G12. The Jensen P10Rs are dated from the 42nd, 43rd, and 44th week of 1959.

Mark Tate: "The power and output transformers are the tweed-era type, without date codes. The power transformer is a Triad 8087, the choke is a 1959 Schumacher 125C1A, and the output transformer is a Triad 45249 — these are exactly the same ones used in the 5F6-A tweed Bassman. The only components not from 1959 are pots dated 137-6008 (8th week of 1960). Most of the 1960 Bassmans, which were still tweed, had P10Qs, so to see P10Rs in a brown amp is unusual. These early Concerts had only five preamp tubes, as opposed to later 6G12 models with six. This one has a 5U4 rectifier tube, but later stock-spec Concerts had solid state ones. By the end of 1960, Concerts had different transformers and the standard P10Qs rather than P10Rs, and they were labeled as 6G12 models. The original owner stenciled his band's name on the grille, and rather than trying to restore it and risk damaging the material, I left it. It's cool."

While the Spotlites Concert is something of a missing link revealing Leo Fender's evolving the tweed Bassman into the Tolex Concert, it is labeled "production run no. 2," suggesting that there were even earlier examples — brown Tolex Concerts that under the hood were perhaps even more tweedy.

Fender in the House

"I was working with the entertainment manager at the Golden Nugget in Las Vegas, and he and I came up with an idea to do away with having everyone bring all their gear in and out all the time. Instead, Fender would provide everything and just leave it onstage, a full set of equipment so musicians wouldn't have to haul everything in. This was about '62 or '63 — the beginning of 'house amps,' as we call them today."

— George Fullerton

"Leo Fender's genius is that everything he did was efficient and simple. His pure and straightforward approach has allowed his products to withstand both the winds of change and the brutal knocks of time and touring. As a traveling musician who often relies upon rental gear, I can count on Fender's designs to be a solid foundation for my sound wherever I go. For this we all owe a debt of gratitude."

— Jol Dantzig, Hamer Guitars

Perhaps the most recorded guitarist in history, the late Tommy Tedesco, center, played on thousands of sessions with everyone from Ella Fitzgerald to Elvis Presley, Frank Sinatra to Frank Zappa. He can also be heard on scores of TV soundtracks (Bonanza, M*A*S*H, Batman) and movie soundtracks (*The Godfather*, *Jaws*, *The Deer Hunter*). He is fondly remembered by all who knew him for his wiseguy sense of humor and pranks, his no-nonsense advice, and his willingness to take promising newcomers under his wing. His monthly "Studio Log" in *Guitar Player* ran for many years and was one of the most popular columns in the entire history of the magazine. Tommy is shown here on a session with Howard Roberts (left) and Ray Pohlman.

Tone Stacks Move Upstream

As noted previously, several tweeds (and the Bass channels in some piggyback Bassmans) employed cathode follower tone stacks, most notably the F series Bassmans and Twins; see Chap. 11. In those amps, the tone stacks were "downstream" — late in the signal chain, immediately preceding the phase inverter and output stage.

Except for the Bassmans, however, this approach was abandoned in the new G series circuits at the outset of the Tolex era. Dave Hunter, in *The Guitar Amp Handbook*: "Fender only stuck with its cathode follower tone stack for around five years — and its climactic three-knob version [mid, bass, treble] for about three — before changing it completely in the quest for a cleaner preamp signal and more headroom in the brownface amps of 1960 and the blackface amps that followed. But because Marshall lifted its circuit wholly from a 5F6-A Bassman in 1962, this tone stage was passed on."

In the new models, tone stacks were moved "upstream," closer to the inputs, between the two triode sections of the first preamp tube. Techs sometimes refer to a "left" or "right" orientation of components because of the way amp schematics are typically laid out, with the inputs at left, speakers at right; Fender schematics are prominent examples. So, compared to the earlier cathode follower circuits, the Tolex amps moved the tone stacks to the left.

Apparently, this was yet another example of Mr. Fender's pursuit of a cleaner signal and more headroom, and the new arrangement would be carried over from the brown/blonde era to the blackface amps of 1963 and thereafter.

Tone stacks are sometimes cited as examples of "lossy" circuits or components, meaning they cause a loss of energy. Referring to the older, cathode follower amps, Matt Wilkens explains: "Having the lossy, passive tone controls just before the power amp allows the previous gain stages to produce a larger signal to drive the power amp. The larger signal produces more distortion — not necessarily clipping — and therefore, more tube 'magic.'" In the new arrangement, however, Mr. Fender got what he wanted: Moving the tone circuit upstream provided more headroom for the subsequent gain stage.

The downstream/upstream debate typically has the tweed proponents swearing by the cathode follower's contribution to enhanced dynamics and response, as well as its readiness to lapse into creamy, musical distortion. Mike Soldano: "Placing the tone controls later in the circuit makes for much better tone when dealing with distorted

'63 style all-tube reverb unit reissue. David Grissom, in *Guitar Player*: "The [effect] I use most is the Fender Reverb unit, which actually seems to enhance the sound of the guitar. More cloth wire, more tubes to go through — it's a 'warm box,' if nothing else. ... If I take that Fender spring reverb, I can make almost any amp sound good."

signals. The tone is warmer and fuller, and the bass doesn't 'fart out' like the newer amps, when pushed, are prone to do." Terry Buddingh: "Nothing like the dynamic response of a great tweed Fender; that's why I dig them so much."

On the other hand, as Dave Hunter writes in *The Guitar Amp Handbook*: "It's undeniable that many of the good brown-, black-, and silverface Fender amps using this [newer] tone stack still have bags of touch and dynamics."

New Tubes

Along with their Jensen Concert series speakers (a JBL in the Vibrasonic), reconfigured tone stacks, and a gradual shift from Triad to Schumacher transformers, Fender's new amps sported new preamp tubes and power amp tubes. The early '60s was the age of the 7025 tube, which was used across the entire line in the G circuit preamps, either exclusively or in combination with 12AX7s.

Pete Townshend's Generation

"Pete has used Fender amps off and on for 40 years. The Who's first album was recently re-released in a deluxe edition. In America it was called *The Who Sings My Generation.* [Aside from the title cut, the album also includes 'The Kids Are Alright.'] I said, 'Oh, Pete, it sounds fantastic,' and he told me exactly what he used on it: two Rickenbackers — a 6-string and a 12-string — and a blonde Bassman head with a Marshall 4x12 cab. That was the sound on that album, from 1965."

— Alan Rogan

Dick Dale, a giant in instrumental rock and pioneer of reverb. Note the reverb kit, suspended in midair to avoid jostling its springs with unwanted knocks. Dick Dale: "I used to wrack my brain trying everything I could think of — foam, pillows, blankets, everything. Believe it or not, setting it on foam made it even worse, but I've found that if I could hang it from a ceiling that was solid, with no vibration, then I would get the pure sound coming out of it. All of these things matter. Everything makes a difference. I've spent my whole life, 51 years of it [laughs], trying to do all these thing to get the right sound."

Fender had installed 5881 output tubes in the late-'50s Bassmans (5F6, 5F6-A) and Twins (5F8, 5F8-A). As in other cases, these innovations in top-tier amps would soon be adopted in other top-tier models and also filter down to several mid-level amps.

The major shift occurred in 1960. While the initial G circuits of the Bandmaster, Super, Concert, Vibrasonic, and Pro all date to January 1960 and specify 6L6GC output tubes, schematics for the "A" circuits of all those amps date to November of the same year and reveal a shift to 5881s.

The Bassman continued to use 5881s in its early Tolex phase. Output tubes in the Twin went back and forth: 5881s in the late-'50s tweeds; 6L6GCs in the 6G8 circuit dated June '60; 5881s again in the 6G8-A of Nov. '60; and 6L6GCs again in the AB763 blackface Twin Reverb, Mar. '64.

Although significant, the age of the 5881s was short lived. Except for some of the 6V6GT amps (e.g., Princeton, Princeton Reverb, Deluxe, Deluxe Reverb), the AA and AB circuits in the blackface non-reverb and reverb models would either premiere with 6L6GCs or, like the Twin/Twin Reverb, shift from 5881s back to 6L6GCs.

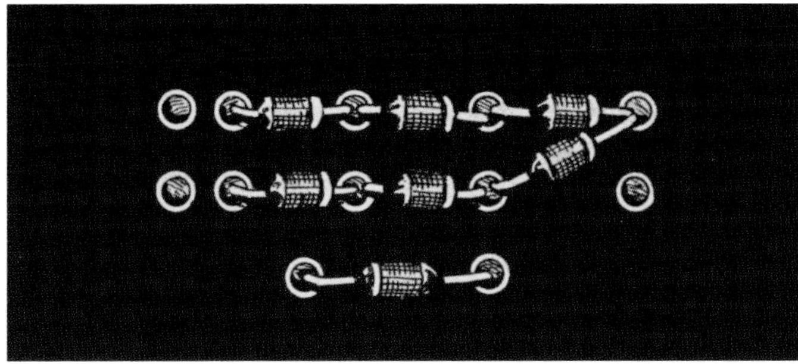

Who else but Fender would display in its catalog an artist's rendering of silicon rectifiers?

"If I want to just play at home and get the sweetest, most beautiful tone, it's still the old Strats or Les Pauls through anything old that's Fender. The amps they had with the separate reverbs — that stuff is the best."

— Carlos Santana

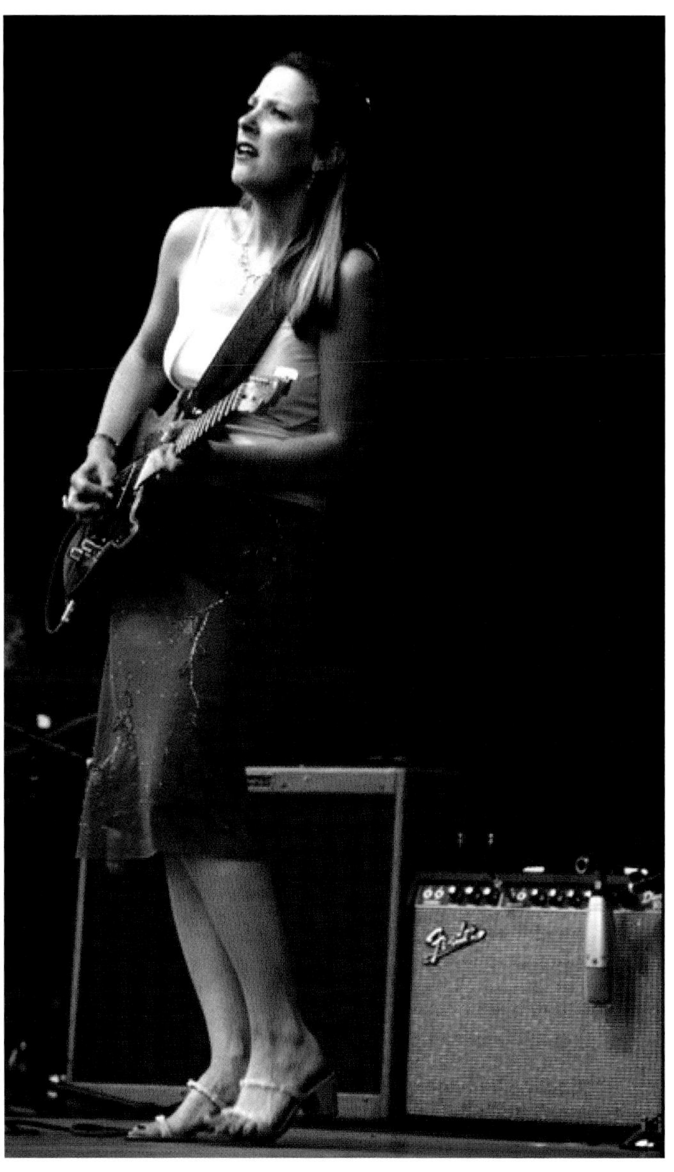

Susan Tedeschi, in *Guitar Player*: "When I fly to gigs, the venue furnishes my amp. I ask for a blackface Fender — a Super Reverb, Vibrolux Reverb, or Deluxe Reverb."

These much beloved 6V6-fueled Fenders helped countless players sound great on small and medium-sized gigs, appeared on thousands of recordings, and packed more bang for the buck than just about any amp from any maker. The great session player Louie Shelton remembered the studio scene of the 1960s and 1970s: "Fender Princetons ruled … An awful lot of big records were cut with just a Tele or a 335, a Princeton or a Deluxe, and one or two pedals." Ry Cooder, in 1980: "I use a small Princeton [in the studio] with the controls set at about mid treble and mid bass. I used it for just about everything on *Bop Till You Drop*, with a few exceptions. If you run slide through a small, powerful amp with a small speaker, and crank it up, it begins to sound pretty good."

Gregg Allman, on brother Duane: "He changed his recording methods a lot, like down at Muscle Shoals, he'd take a Fender Princeton and turn it on to full blast and cover it with baffles." Bill Harkleroad (also known as Zoot Horn Rollo), a veteran of Captain Beefheart's Magic Band: "Back then we used to think bigger equaled better; now I wish I'd used little, funky Fenders." Keith Richards, in *Guitar Player*: "Probably the biggest mistake inexperienced players make is thinking that to have a lot of volume in a studio you need a huge amp. It's probably the opposite. The smaller the amp, the bigger it's going to sound, because it's already going to sound like it's pushed to its limit."

Rectifiers and Redundancy

While the vast majority of tweed Fenders had been equipped with a 5Y3 or 5U4 rectifier tube of one variety or another, exceptions included two of the most revered amps of all time: the 5F6-A Bassman, and the high-power ("big box") 5F8-A Twin. The schematics for both amps date to Sept. 1957; as we saw in a previous section, both were equipped with the rectifier tube of the future, the GZ34/5AR4.

Now, in the brown/blonde Tolex era, the 5Y3GT and 5U4GB tubes were being phased out. Most mid-powered Fenders were equipped with a GZ34/5AR4 tube, including the Tremolux, Deluxe, Vibrolux, Super, Vibroverb, and some Bassmans.

In the early '60s, solid state silicon diodes were deemed sufficiently reliable for use in high voltage power supplies, and Mr. Fender adopted them in most of the new Tolex amps (see Chap. 11 for a discussion of evolving *tube* rectifier technology in the tweed amps). An exception was the GZ34-equipped Super.

In its first blonde piggyback version, the 6G6 (Feb. '61 schematic), the Bassman kept its GZ34 tube; in the 6G6-A (Jan. '62), however, it joined most of the other Tolex amps and converted to the solid state devices. (Reminder: Schematics were often drawn up months after the amps appeared on the market.)

The rationale behind the change in rectifiers was likely a continuation of Mr. Fender's unvarying pursuit: increased volume without distortion. Mark Baier: "In 1960, silicon rectifiers were state of the art [but] with absolutely no real-world track record in consumer goods. So I don't think Leo was ready to bet the bank on these new rectifiers. He ended up using three per side, effectively tripling the redundancy in case of field failures! Using six diodes in an amp where two would have worked says a lot about Leo Fender, the man. A Fender amp was always a professional tool first, with reliability and utility being paramount."

Recapping the progression of rectifiers during the evolution from tweed to Tolex: During the late '50s, Mr. Fender's goal of more clean volume had entailed in some models either doubling up the old 5Y3s or 5U4s, or adopting the more efficient 5AR4/GZ34. The quest continued in the early '60s with his implementation of solid state diode

ToneQuest Report said of the brown Deluxe, "The overdrive is deceptively huge. Here is the one if you like overdrive! The tone is fat and creamy, fatter sounding than a tweed Deluxe and nastier than the blackface, just right … you won't find a better amp in its class." *TQR* also pointed out that the brown Vibrolux, with its two 6L6s and a 1x12 combo cab, filled a "supremely attractive and practical" niche in the early-'60s line. *TQR*: "The less powerful brown amps running 6V6s offered limited distortion-free headroom, and the 1x15 Pro, Vibrasonic, and the 4x10 Concert are louder, cleaner, and they don't always produce much overdriven grease and grind without modification. … Chalk it up to a happy accident or Leo Fender's clairvoyant ability to plumb the full potential of an amplifier design, but the brown Vibrolux has revealed a very distinct type of magic that we had not experienced before."

The best-known example of a Strat through a brown Vibrolux is likely Mark Knopfler's classic work on "Sultans of Swing," from Dire Straits' debut LP of 1978. Mark told longtime Fender Germany employee Gernold Linke that the "Sultans" amp was a '61 Vibrolux that belonged to Dire Straits bassist John Illsey at the time. Mark had replaced its broken Oxford speaker with a Fane from a Sound City amp.

rectifiers in most of the Professional Amplifiers. (The rest of the line continued to use tube rectifiers throughout the blackface era and into the CBS/silverface period.)

Ritchie Fliegler: "Back in the day, two tube rectifiers were needed to handle the current of these high-powered Fenders. Readily available single tubes were simply too small. It was really the invention of cheap, solid state diodes that allowed amps to get big. The rest of the stuff was already there."

Today, Fender uses solid state rectifiers in all models except those reissues where authenticity calls for original-spec tube rectifiers: The '59 Bassman LTD, '64 Vibroverb Custom (switchable to solid state for the César Diaz mod), '57 Twin, '65 Super Reverb, and '65 Deluxe Reverb.

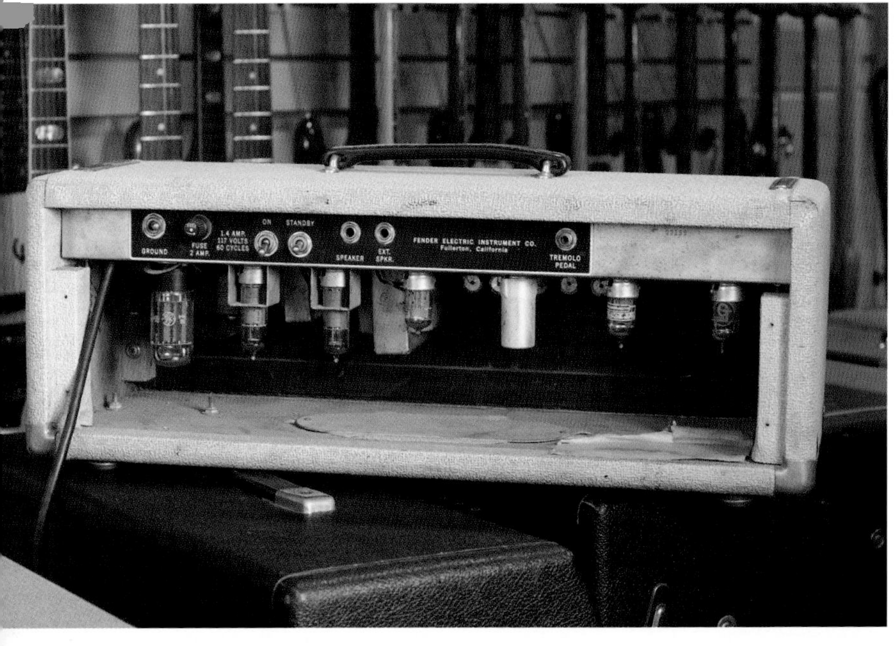

The 6G9 Tremolux (April '61 schematic) had a particularly anomalous output tube complement, with a pair of the small 6BQ5/EL84 beam power pentodes often used in Beatles-era Vox amps; these tubes were promptly replaced in the 6G9-A and 6G9-B with conventional 6L6GCs. Perry Tate: "These are super rare. I've only seen three of them in my life. You can see those neat little brackets they used to hold on the 6BQ5s."

Don Randall and Bob Perine

Leo Fender's uncanny knack for solving musicians' problems was only one factor in his company's success. He had plenty of help, sometimes from people whose talents and personalities were very different from his own. For example, when it came to takin' care of business, Leo Fender turned to Don Randall. The dynamic, even dashing World War II veteran shared with Mr. Fender a background in electronics and a tireless commitment to their work. Otherwise, the two men couldn't have been more different.

The history of the music industry has no shortage of good ideas that were insufficient to guarantee success by themselves. Products must not only work; they must be packaged, advertised, marketed, sold. Don Randall was personable and engaging. He had a zest for getting out among the public. In other words, he was the perfect complement to the introverted, lab-bound, almost reclusive Leo Fender.

Randall worked for the Radio & Television Equipment Company, or Radio-Tel, distributor of products by Fender and other manufacturers. He played a significant role in the success of Fender's revolutionary Broadcaster/Telecaster of 1950 (for details, see Richard Smith's authoritative and engaging *Fender: The Sound Heard 'Round the World*). In 1953, a new organization was established to distribute Fender amps and guitars exclusively. Called Fender Sales, it was located in Santa Ana and headed by Don Randall. By then Mr. Fender was developing his next masterpiece, the Stratocaster, and once again Mr. Randall was instrumental in bringing the new guitar to the marketplace.

While Mr. Fender was apparently content to evolve the early version of the "Fender guitar" (the Telecaster) into its next incarnation (the Strat), Mr. Randall insisted on having an entire line of guitars and amps, another incalculable contribution to the company's success. In fact, it's hard to overstate Don Randall's influence. In *Fender: The Sound Heard 'Round The World*, Richard Smith addressed the unique 2x10 tweed Twin amplifier (Chap. 11) and observed, "It shows how Leo experimented with different configurations. Randall decided which ones to sell." At the end of the Leo Fender era, Mr. Randall negotiated the sale of the company to CBS, netting a figure several times in excess of what Mr. Fender had expected. After leaving Fender, he founded Randall Instruments.

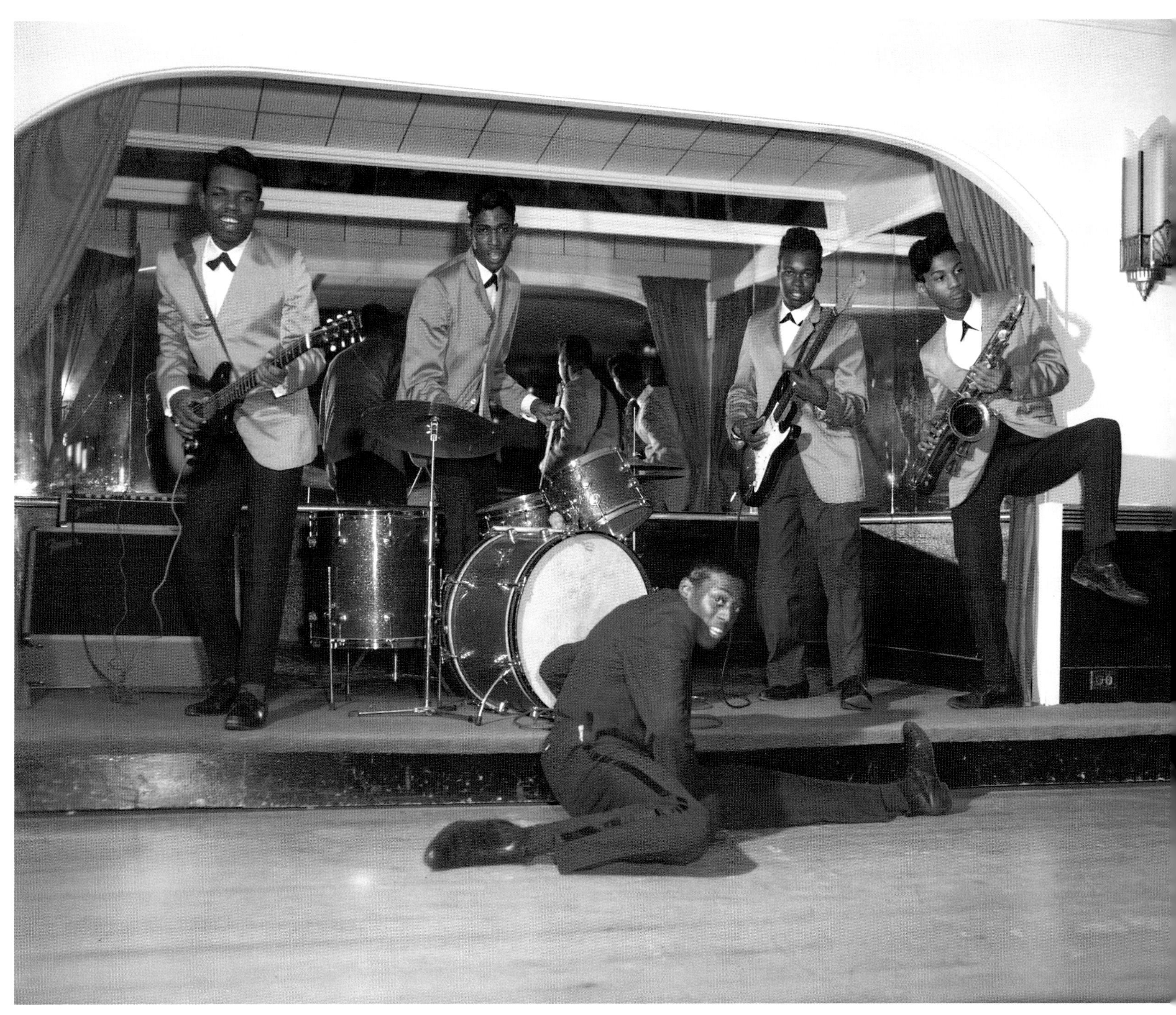

David Ruffin, later of the Temptations, and his band strike a pose at the Club Pony Tail in Harbor Springs, Michigan, 1962. Both hard workin' guitarists are plugged into an equally hard workin' piggyback Bassman. During performances, Ruffin's microphone was plugged into it, too.

The New Look

By the early '60s, Fender literature surged with vitality, youth, and splashy colors. A couple of the brochures from 1960 and 1961 feature different cover photos of four people posing with their Fender gear. They seem to embody the ideal nuclear family celebrated across American culture and commerce. Two of the four are female, which in itself sets these brochures apart from virtually the entire body of professional-level guitar literature up to that point. With occasional exceptions (Mary Osborne, Mary Kaye), women were portrayed in other high-end catalogs as props, if at all. On these Fender covers, however, the most prominent person is a girl who looks about 11 years old. This bold departure revealed another aspect of the new message: Fender amps and guitars are for serious professionals, sure, but they're also for anyone excited about making music with stringed instruments — families, amateurs, even youngsters.

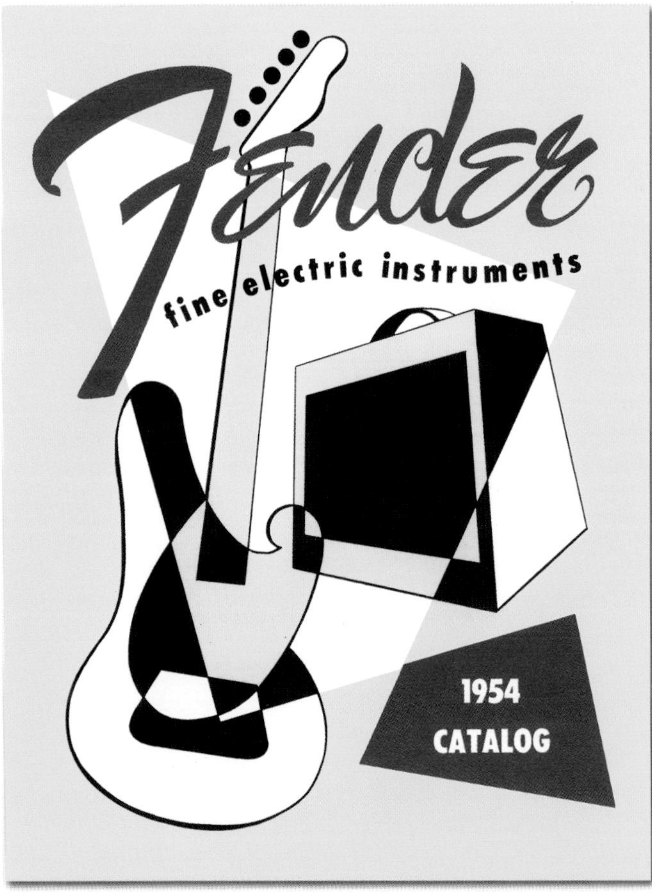

Don Randall's Fender catalogs of the 1950s sometimes featured images of guitars or amps rendered as jazzy abstractions. The subliminal slogan seemed to be: *Come to Fender, and plug into the new.*

The late Robert Perine was another essential contributor, one who lived in Southern California and dug electric guitars but otherwise was far removed from Mr. Fender's circle of radio buffs, electronics engineers, and western music aficionados. He was an artist whose watercolors are displayed in more than 200 collections worldwide, as well as in several museums. He was also a graphic designer, art teacher, and author. One of his books details the history of his alma mater, the prestigious Chouinard Art Institute. By the early 1930s Chouinard was acclaimed as one of the nation's most progressive art schools, and as a student and instructor there, Bob Perine rubbed shoulders with cutting-edge critics, painters, and designers, several of whom gained international acclaim as leading influences on the development of Modernism.

Yet another of Perine's talents was photography. Although he apparently considered his work with a camera almost as a sideline (some of his published bios don't even mention it), his photos were indispensable to Fender's public image. Bob enlisted his three daughters, who recruited some of their fellow students from Laguna Beach High School to participate in catalog photo shoots. He posed the teenagers in board shorts and bikinis on nearby beaches, put guitars in their hands, and used surfboards and his own '57 Thunderbird convertible as props. These images helped inject Fender squarely into the mythos of Southern California as America's Shangri-La, an earthly paradise evoked by surf music, beach movies, palm-tree postcards, and sports car culture.

Just as remarkable as Perine's oceanside tableaux were his studio photos, which reflected his lifelong background in fine arts. In Fender catalogs of the early '60s, guitars were posed like paintings on artists' easels or alongside ornate picture frames and sleek designer chairs of molded plastic. Through Perine's lens, Jazzmasters and Showman amps seemed perfectly at home among beatnik sculptures, paint brushes, tubes of oil paint and semi-abstract portraits reminiscent of LeRoy Neiman. Suspending some of the

A typical scene at the factory, early 1953. The always dapper Don Randall is looking sharp and ready to call on dealers or to chair a sales meeting, but here he consults with two legendary musicians on Fender products under development. From left: Randall, steel guitarist Leon McAuliffe, unidentified man, steel guitarist Noel Boggs, and Freddie Tavares.

guitars in midair added a dreamy, gravity-defying element to the art-gallery ambiance. Compared to the stuffy bowtie and brown wingtip vibe of other companies' brochures, the image of a blonde piggyback tilted skyward on skinny chrome legs looked like a Salvador Dali.

A whole generation of players got the message: These Fenders are not only works of art, but works of *modern* art. In some of the most significant literature of the entire electric guitar era, Randall and Perine rendered layouts that were fun, imaginative, and compelling. Have any electric instruments ever looked so good?

Don Randall: "Putting these things together was a dual activity, you might say. I worked closely with Bob and supervised him, but only up to a point. He did good work on his own. Fender and the other companies probably all looked at each other's ads and brochures from time to time, but I just didn't see much that impressed me. The whole point of those set-ups with the paintings and the art was to attract attention to the amps and the guitars, to do something different that set us apart. Bob always had those props — the sculptures and so on — because he had his hand in all sorts of art things.

"We were doing something different with our amplifiers and our guitars, and we wanted those catalogs to reflect that."
— Don Randall

Fender fun for the whole family: The 1960 catalog cover.

"For most of the players, if it just worked all right and sounded good, that was fine with them."

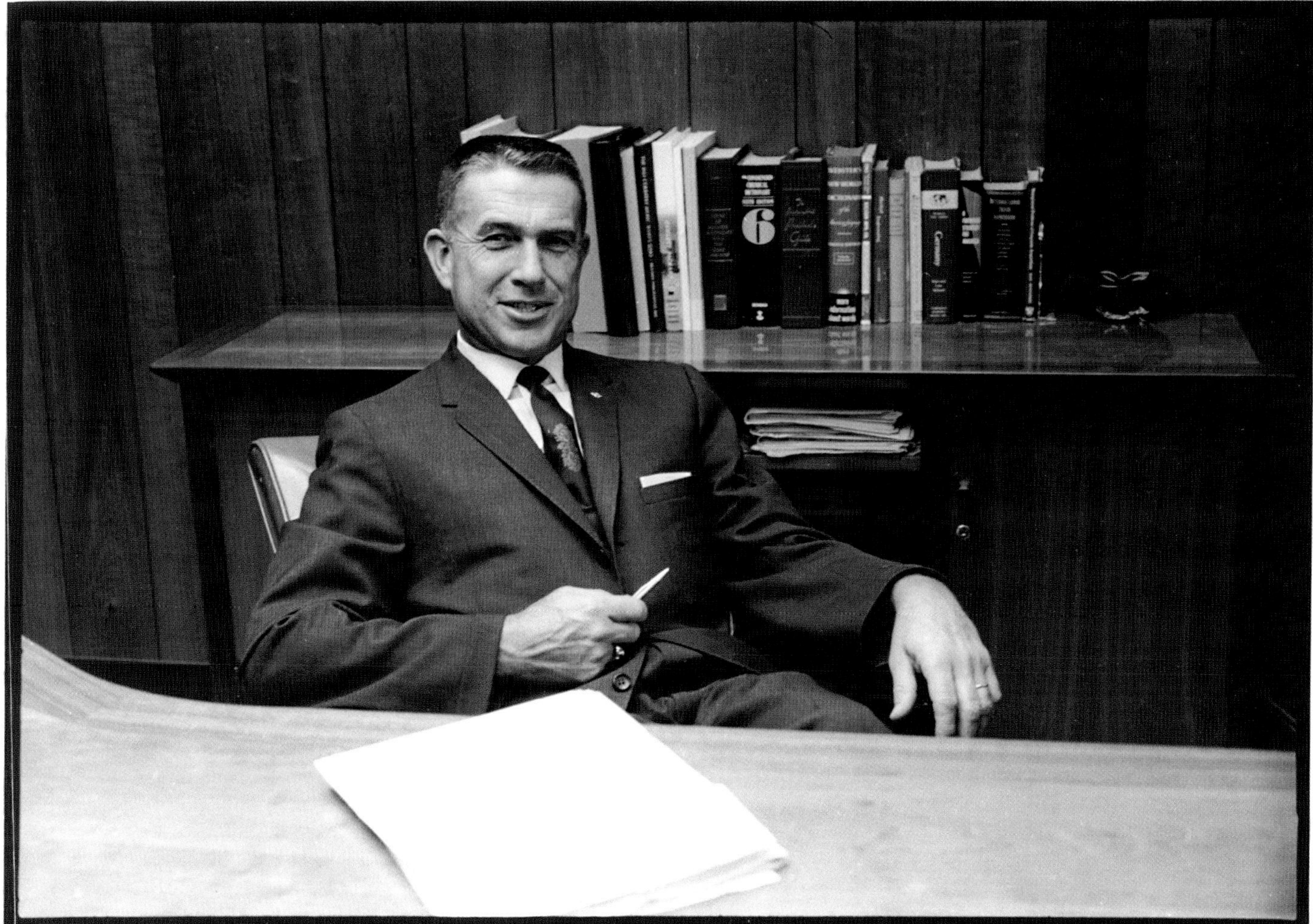

Don Randall in his office at Fender Sales, October, 1966. Aside from assembling what Leo Fender's former partner Doc Kauffman called "a sales distributorship like nobody had ever seen in the world," Don Randall also helped revolutionize the way guitars are marketed, even the way they are perceived by the general public. This author once wrote that as a music industry marketing genius, Don Randall had no equal.

Getting the Job Done
A Conversation with Don Randall

Don Randall's brilliance in marketing Fender guitars and amps through innovative ads and catalogs is documented here and elsewhere. It turns out he also contributed to the design of Fender amplifiers.

When you set up Fender Sales in 1953, what was your approach to the marketplace?

There really wasn't much going on with respect to the amplifiers, or the guitars for that matter. It was just getting started. My role and the role of the people I worked with in sales was the same with respect to the amplifiers as with the guitars, although it worked a little different in practice. We were always very interested in getting all the information we could, and we had quite a bit of discussion about the amplifiers, trying to get feedback from the field.

Would musicians request certain components, speakers, and those sorts of details?

Not so much. I was out in the field a great deal in the early days, and we didn't get all that much feedback. The people we were dealing with were knowledgeable about music, of course, but not very knowledgeable about electronics. So my job was to listen carefully to everything they had to say and then convert it to the electronics end of things.

Compared to the old-school ads of competitors, Randall's "you won't part with yours either" images were practically surreal.

Did you get a different kind of feedback regarding the amps vs. the guitars?

Yes. Some of the musicians were pretty smart guys, with useful ideas, but they didn't get into the actual design, as much as they might with the guitars. With guitars, we would send a prototype out with a musician, and he might say, well, I'd like to have the volume control moved a bit, and the guitar would go back out with someone else, and we'd do this six times or ten times or whatever it might be, and some of these ideas were very specific. It wasn't like that with the amplifiers. For most of the players, if it just worked all right and sounded good, that was fine with them.

How did you document the feedback you were getting?

Leo and I were working very closely together, so we just met and talked very frequently — every day, practically. There were a lot of little things that needed to be corrected, and Leo wasn't too fast to move sometimes. We were using some tubes that had to be eliminated because they had so many microphonics they just couldn't handle it, and it took Leo a while to realize that and to change over. Normally, we would make corrections every day.

Why did you switch to 12AX7s?

We'd been using those larger [octal] preamp tubes, and we started developing circuits with the smaller ones. The older, larger ones were noisier and just plain troublesome. We got down to the 12AX7s, and they were much more compact and not as likely to have those microphonic problems.

Some of your early circuits were AT&T/Western Electric designs available in tube manuals. What distinguished the Fender designs?

We did develop our own tone control system, and that was very important. Most of the other tone control systems at that time were pretty linear in their response. Our system was unlinear, and the response was more apparent around 300 or 400 cycles. That boost in there was a key part of the Fender sound.

Who were your primary competitors?

We felt we didn't have any. When we first started, the other string instruments out there were mostly Mickey Mouse, and most of the companies in the amplifier business didn't really know what they were doing. The other products out there in my opinion were what I would call drugstore type amplifiers. And they all had about the same type of tone response. If you took one of our amplifiers and set it next to these others, the difference in tone was very noticeable. Other companies just weren't selling enough amplifiers or doing a good enough job in merchandising them.

What was their problem?

They weren't really technically qualified to merchandise them, but at Fender we were pretty well qualified because our background was electronics, radio, sound, and that sort of thing.

Aside from collecting feedback from musicians, what was your role at Fender, specifically regarding amplifiers?

It was all pretty mixed up, and I had my hands in almost everything that was going on — circuits, cabinets, their appearance, marketing — and we worked on all these things at the same time. I was doing a fair amount of design work.

Circuits? Actual amplifier design?

Oh, yes, absolutely.

I don't think I've seen a single account of your contributing to the electronic design of Fender amplifiers.

[Laughs.] I've just never made an effort to become known that way. But my original background was circuit design and electronics, and I continued to do that at Fender, working on circuits. See, I had been in the radio and broadcast business prior to getting into the music business, and that carried over to my work at Fender. I was actually stronger in that field because of my background in electronics.

Do you remember which models you worked on?

I can't say exactly which ones, because the amps from the smallest to the largest were pretty much the same sorts of things. We would vary the voltages and get bigger cabinets and speakers and more power as you moved up the line, and more features, but all those early amplifiers are pretty much the same when it comes right down to it. We used the same general types of tubes and circuits, the same basic design.

And did you help out with that basic design?

Oh, yes, but only to a limited extent.

Did you work at the factory?

Not in the lab with Leo and Freddie Tavares. We had a separate place in Santa Ana, at Fender Sales. I did electronic design work from that office, and also from my home, where I had a little lab with testing equipment and so on. Leo was the head guru, and I was helping him get the job done. I can't say I stood there at the bench and worked on it that way, but I had countless meetings with Leo, and we often discussed electronic details. But Leo didn't require too much help that way. I gave him feedback on electronics only to a certain extent. He was pretty clever himself. I would just try to corner that cleverness and channel it into the music business and get things done that I thought were serviceable for musicians to use.

Custom color visions and blonde Tolex dreams, 1961: posed like artworks, Fender's ogle-worthy amps and guitars inspired boundless gear lust.

Did you continue to help out with circuits as the line progressed from the tweed era into the Tolex era?

Not as much. As we got bigger, I didn't have a whole lot of time to work on that sort of thing.

In the late '40s and early '50s, Fender amps had several different styles. Right about the time you started Fender Sales, the line acquired a consistent look, with most models having the same type of cabinet and overall appearance. Did you have anything to do with that evolution?

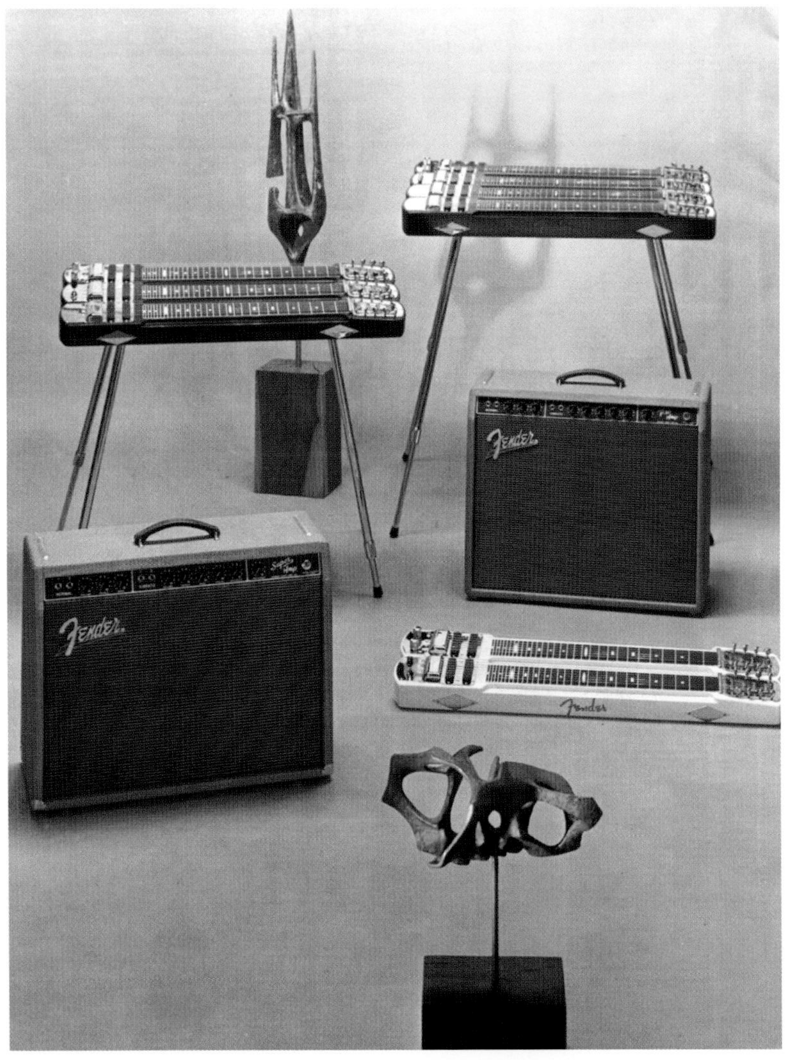

Powerful pro-quality instruments, bright colors, arty props: the look of Fender literature in the early 1960s.

Well, I hate to say it, but I think I had a lot to do with it [laughs]. I pretty well developed that idea, a line that had a recognizable look throughout the whole spectrum. I felt it was important that you could see an amplifier on a stage somewhere and know right away it was one of ours.

The line changed again after a few years, from the tweed cabinets with top-mounted controls in back to Tolex cabs with front-panel knobs.

I was probably the main factor in making that change as well. It was important to modernize. The Tolex worked well, and the black color worked especially well. I was taken with the black as being more professional looking. I was directly involved in that transition from the older amps to the newer ones with the controls in front. But we're talking about a time when Fender still wasn't a very big operation. It wasn't something that took all of my time. I was still working directly in the electronics field in addition to my work at Fender, so I spoke to working musicians [in both capacities] all the time and found out what they needed to get the job done. When a company is young and small, it just doesn't require as much planning. You're always trying to do new things, and just trying to make the company go.

Your catalogs and ads were much different than those from your competitors. What was your strategy?

Simply to figure out a way of merchandising that was better than what we were seeing from other companies. We did have an emphasis on youth. Of course, our company was new. We were pretty young ourselves, and that probably had something to do with it.

Did your products "sell themselves"?

It was a tough racket, even back then. The problem was not the competition, or our own products. Our amplifiers were excellent. The problem was getting the word out. People hadn't heard of us. They were used to the other companies that had been around a long time, and used to their products. That's what made it tough to get our stuff sold. I would go out, sometimes for six weeks at a time, contacting dealers, just trying to get the word out, but it took time to get the merchandise recognized and accepted. We were new and different, and people weren't used to the name.

Did you name any of the amplifiers?

I named every one of them. I named all of the string instruments, too, with one exception, and that was the Precision Bass. Leo had 'Precision Bass' in his mind. He wanted that, so that's what we called it. Otherwise, Telecaster, Stratocaster, Princeton, Champ, Vibrolux, Twin — I came up with all of them.

Was there a particular amplifier that marked a turning point and helped establish Fender in the market?

It wasn't so much that there was any particular product or development that was a turning point. The growth of Fender was a long, slow, gradual thing. You know, when we started out, we only had one or two amplifiers to sell — same with the guitars — and we just kept expanding it until ultimately we had a fairly wide line, but it didn't happen overnight.

What's in a Name? Lux, Sonic, Vibro . . .

In *Guitar Player* magazine's "What's in a Name" column of July 1978, Mr. Randall explained his method for concocting Fender model names: "I usually write down all kinds of names, jillions of them, trying to keep within a family of some kind. Then I start sorting and culling them out, seeing which ones have the best sound when they are said aloud, that leave a feeling of what the item is supposed to be. I also try to stay away from things like 'student' or 'beginner,' because nobody wants to be a student or beginner. Our first beginner's amp became 'Champ,' again on the principle that nobody wants to be a beginner. After you have a few, why, the names just kind of fall in line."

"I had lots and lots of knock-down, drag-outs with Leo on design. And he was pretty hard headed at times, and amenable at other times, to what you were trying to do. He would go along with [marketing] suggestions — if he wanted to. My way with him was to let it come around as just an idea, nothing too astounding or blunt. I'd say something like, 'You know, Leo, we were talking about this the other day, and your idea was pretty good [laughs].' And he'd say, 'Yeah, we ought to try that.' So we'd dance around on that kind of deal for a long time, and things would go ahead and change."

— Don Randall

Sam Hutton

One of the many colorful characters who worked at Fender during the Leo years and thereafter was Sam Hutton. Drew Berlin, one of Guitar Center's "Burst Brothers," knew him well. Here's his remembrance: "Sam and I were friends for a long time, and I was with him in the hospital the day before he died. He worked at Fender in the '60s and into the '70s. He was in charge of Tolexing everything. He was an inspector toward the end of the line, and he signed everything he inspected in pencil with an 'S' with two lines through it to make the 'H,' so it looked sort of like a dollar sign. From the early '60s to the late '60s, he'd mark the inside of the cabinet, usually on the bottom but sometimes on the side. He was ensuring that the Tolex was done correctly.

"He had a nice, rather large house in a residential section of Fullerton, and every room was dedicated to amplifier parts. One room was speaker chassis, one room was amplifier chassis, one room was cabinets, and he slept on a small cot in the living room. His house was just overwhelmed with everything, and then he had a glue machine out in the garage, and according to his doctor that's what killed him, the fumes from the hide glue. He just worked in too close a proximity for too many years.

"Sam liked to find amps that needed recovering, and then he would refurbish them, and he and I partnered up on a lot of projects. He thought that if he recovered something it would be worth more, because he was the guy from the factory who had originally done it, and I really had to explain to him that that was not the case with vintage amps. He did the most incredible job and he was the guy, but of course it was not worth as much because it was not original. I introduced him to a lot of people, and he ended up doing Keith Richards' cabinets, for example.

"Even though Sam didn't play, amps were his passion and he became quite a serious collector and amp enthusiast. He was a very quiet man and looked a little bit like Santa Claus, a real salt-of-the-earth kind of guy. I used to stay with him all day sometimes and listen to his stories about the old days at Fender."

The late Michael Bloomfield, shown here with singer Nick Gravenites, was one of the most important American guitarists of the entire electric guitar era. His searing yet sweet melodies inspired countless blues-rock players, and his use of Telecasters, gold-top Les Pauls and sunburst Les Pauls helped spark the mania for vintage versions of all three instruments. He favored Super Reverbs and Twins, and also affectionately recalled to this author "an ancient tweed Fender Deluxe that's been souped up to sound like a Mesa/Boogie ... another amp I have is a '60s model Fender Pro Reverb, which I like to use in clubs when I play with a band." Michael is shown here in concert at San Francisco's Old Waldorf in late 1976 or 1977. The Bassman's wheat grille dates it to circa 1963. Photo courtesy Norman Dayron, Mike's long-time producer and friend.

Things to Come: The 6G16 brown Vibroverb appeared in 1963 at the tail end of the brown/blonde Tolex period. It was a milestone, Fender's first amplifier with onboard reverb. Author Richard Smith called it "the high point of self-contained combo amp design" (see Chap. 29). With the addition of reverb to Fender's standard setup of two independently adjustable channels and tremolo, the 6G16 set the stage for the new age in Fender amps: the blackface era. Note that although it does have tremolo ("Vibrato"), the channels are configured as Normal and Bright rather than Normal and Vibrato.

Rockabilly/swing master Brian Setzer tears it up in 1999, running his Gretsch hollow-body through a pair of blonde Bassmans. He told *Guitar Player*: "I try to get a sound that's right on the edge, just before it breaks up too much. I tend to adjust the volume a lot as I play, though it's usually between about 4 and 5 1/2. It's real loud. I've had no problem playing huge outdoor settings .... The combination of a closed-back cabinet and a solid state rectifier makes for a tighter sound, which the Gretsch needs.

"Guys who use solidbodies tend to prefer older Fenders because they're mushier. But hollowbody guitars *breathe* — the sound comes out of the speaker and goes back through the guitar. That's why I need the punchier sound of a Bassman with a 2x12 cabinet ... I take them to Billy Zoom, who replaces the filter caps and biases them properly. He also rewires the speaker cabinet with this really thick cable that can carry more current. The whole idea is to get the amps back to sounding the way they did originally. We also install 30 watt Celestions. I like the way they sound, and they can take more punishment than the original Jensens .... I've [also] got quite a few of the vintage Bassmans, where I won't touch the speakers because the amps sound so nice." Even in the studio, Brian often records with two Bassmans.

CHAPTER THIRTEEN

13

Family Ties and Transitions

The Browns and Blondes Evolve

The Tolex Fenders of 1960 to 1963 have often been overlooked, their sonic qualities downplayed. After all, their tweed forebears and blackface successors were dominant in their respective eras, remain benchmarks of tone and performance, and virtually define "vintage American amp." The typical view is that the browns sound great but are less bright and powerful than the blackfaces, yet not as warm and crunchy as the tweeds. But another way of saying the same thing is to call them a blend of tweed and blackface, and do we have a problem with that?

Mike Letts, in *ToneQuest Report*, quoted the common "midway between tweed and blackface" description and wrote, "There is some truth there, but they really are unique. They will have some of the mid emphasis of the tweeds, but they do not have the scooped mids, sparkly clean tone and high trebles of the blackface amps. They will not break up as much or as quickly as the tweeds. What they do have is a round, thick tone, very fat and warm, and very old-school, of course. A classic tone … Think nice, solid mids, treble voiced a bit lower than the blackface amps, and huge lows second to none … They do want to stay clean until pushed hard, then they growl like a big fat bear, with an authority not heard in the more popular blackface amps … the rewards are some of the nicest Fender tones ever."

> "Brown Fender amps are generally cleaner sounding than tweeds at comparable volume settings, and they possess a more subtle attack with less high frequency emphasis and power than the blackface amps … A few knowledgeable cyber-surfing amp gurus have even begun to call them the best sounding amps Fender ever made."
>
> – *ToneQuest Report*

Tremolux, Vibrolux, Vibroverb: similar engines under the hood.

Blonde Tremolux, Brown Vibrolux, Brown Vibroverb

Although seemingly a "normal" blonde piggyback, the early-'60s Tremolux was one of Fender's most idiosyncratic amplifiers. Atypical of Fender, it used 6BQ5 power amp tubes in its earliest, short-lived version, the 6G9. Its blonde Tolex covering was intended to give it an elite status among top-line models such as the Showman and Twin, while its piggyback construction might suggest a heavy-duty speaker array.

But the Tremolux of 1961 to 1963 (6G9, 6G9-A, 6G9-B) not only had far less power than the Showman or Twin, it actually had a little less power than the 40W combos (about 35W), because its smaller transformer delivered slightly lower voltages. And despite the separate speaker cab, the various speaker arrays of the piggyback Tremolux (1x10, 2x10, some 1x12) actually offered less cone area than any of the 40W combos; the one exception was the biggest Tremolux, the 2x10, which matched the 2x10 Super.

The blonde piggyback, top of the line look might also imply top of the line features, but while the nine-knob, brown 40 watters all had a presence circuit, the eight-knob Tremolux did not. One final difference: The Tremolux (and the electrically similar 6G16 brown Vibroverb) used a bias modulation tremolo, while the brown and blonde 40s used a multi-tube, split-signal tremolo. (See Tremolo Evolves, Chap. 14.)

The blonde 6G9-A and 6G9-B Tremolux is closely related to the brown 1x12 6G11 and 6G11-A Vibrolux and brown 2x10 6G16 Vibroverb of the same period. The Vibrolux and Tremolux are electronically identical except for the output transformer, and except for the Vibroverb's reverb knob, all three have nearly identical control panel layouts.

The blonde piggyback may seem very different from the two brown combos shown here, but all three designs share a 35W output, two 7025s, two 6L6GCs, fixed bias, a GZ34 tube rectifier, a long-tail phase inverter, and a variable-bias trem circuit powered by a 12AX7. Greg Gagliano: "The brown Vibroverb is clearly based on the Vibrolux/Tremolux topology as the first gain stage, phase inverter, and power sections are the same among the three models. The Vibroverb circuit differs mainly because of the added reverb circuitry, but it also has some additional power supply filtering."

While the Tremolux's mix of top of the line appearance and modest specs may seem incongruous, it was just one more example of Leo Fender, Don Randall, and their associates juggling the puzzle pieces to make sure every guitarist could find just the right blend of performance, appearance, and price within the Fender line.

The 40W Brown Combos: One Basic Circuit, Five Great Amps

A quintet of Fender's best loved, best looking, and best sounding amps all shared the same basic circuit: the brown Tolex versions of the Pro (shown elsewhere in this section), Bandmaster, Concert, Super, and Vibrasonic. Called the Professional Amplifiers, they made their debuts together.

Although in some respects a clear successor to the 4x10 tweed Bassman, the loud, sweet sounding brown Tolex 4x10 Concert was a new model (and in one way a forerunner of the Super Reverb). Like the new Vibrasonic, it had been advertised in 1959, and samples were circulated in that year, but for all intents and purposes it was a "new for 1960" production model.

Also in 1960, the long-familiar Super, Bandmaster, and Pro were given the new brown Tolex duds and front-panel cabs. The Bandmaster would promptly evolve to its blonde piggyback edition within a year, while the Super, Concert, and Pro would remain as brown Tolex combos until they went to blackface in '63 (the Super as the new 4x10 Super Reverb). The Vibrasonic would be made only through 1963 and would remain in its brown combo incarnation during its entire, brief lifespan. (As noted elsewhere the Vibrosonic Reverb of the 1970s had little in common with the Vibrasonic.)

Aside from their combo cabs and brown-on-brown cosmetics (brown Tolex, handles, faceplates, and knobs), all five of these early-'60s siblings shared the following specs: 40W, two 7025 preamp tubes, two 6L6 or 5881 power tubes, a revised tremolo circuit, a negative feedback loop with presence knob, fixed bias, and a 7025 long-tail phase inverter. The Bandmaster, Vibrasonic, Concert, and Pro had solid state rectifiers, while the Super had a GZ34 tube.

The 40W brown combos evolved more or less together in several respects, changing from the "center Volume" control panels to the "Volume, Treble, Bass" panels in the spring of 1960; from the pinkish Tolex to the darker brown Tolex late

40W Brown Combos.

Hear the "What Can Brown Do For You?" Jam, featuring the brown Tolex Vibrasonic, Vibroverb, and Princeton, Tracks 52 - 53.

in the summer of 1960; and from the tweed style brown grille cloth to the oxblood cloth in about August of 1960. By the fall of that year, the only new Fenders with tweed-era grille cloth were the ones still in tweed cabs. In about the spring of 1962, the oxblood cloth on these amps started to be replaced by the wheat colored cloth, with substantial overlaps typical of Fender at that time. (Smaller brown combos had already acquired the wheat colored cloth.)

Where the 40W browns differed was in their cabinet shape, output transformers, and speaker configuration: two 10s in the Super (this would be the last of the historic 2x10 Supers, one of the greatest amps of all time), three 10s in the Bandmaster (a speaker array we would not see again until the Vibro-King), four 10s in the Concert, and one 15 in both the Pro and the Vibrasonic. Despite the similar circuits, each amp had its own sonic personality due to differences in cabs, transformers, and speakers.

Interestingly, there were no 12″ speakers in the original Professional series amps of early 1960, although the smaller Deluxe had one, as did the top of the line Showman 12 of late 1960. The mighty Twin, of course, had two. (The brown Vibrolux would appear in 1961; only slightly less powerful than the 40W combos, it nicely filled the 1x12, mid-power combo niche. From 1961 through CBS, 12″ speakers were featured in singles or doubles in several models, both combos and piggybacks: Deluxe, Vibrolux, Bandmaster, Bassman, some Showmans, a few rare Tremoluxes, and the Twin.)

The Brown 1x15 Combos: Vibrasonic vs. Pro

Comparing the early-'60s brown versions of the Vibrasonic and Pro reveals just how precisely Leo Fender was tuning these amplifiers to particular needs and tastes. (This pair is also discussed in the section on 40W combos.) The Vibrasonic is about two inches wider; otherwise they seem on paper to be virtually identical. Both are 40W non-reverb amps with tremolo. They have the same cosmetics, including their evolution from the pinkish brown to the darker brown Tolex, and the same shift in grille cloth from brown to maroon/oxblood to wheat.

Each has two channels, nine brown knobs, a presence circuit, two 7025 preamp tubes, two 6L6GC/5881 power tubes, a solid state rectifier, and a 7025 long-tail phase inverter. Their handles and nameplates are the same style.

Brown 1x15 Combos.

Each has a single 15, although the Vibrasonic's speaker is a JBL D130F. According to the *Fender Amp Field Guide*, later versions of both amps used 12AX7s in the tremolo circuit, leaving one-half of a 12AX7 unused. Both amps were discontinued in 1963.

The Vibrasonic's extra width is explained by its use of the same chassis found in the single-speaker blonde 6G14 Showman. But other than a difference in cabinet size and an upgrade in the speaker, what could possibly distinguish the Vibrasonic from the Pro? Greg Gagliano: "The Vibrasonic has a *huge* output transformer that's very similar to the one used in the blonde Showman. This tranny doesn't saturate readily, and that was the whole idea. Plus, that JBL was heavy-duty. The Vibrasonic's sound was meant to be super clean, since it was intended to be used for steel guitar." Greg Huntington adds: "Because the Vibrasonic used the same iron [both the power transformer and output transformer] as the Showman, it really produces closer to 50 watts. The Vibrasonic is effectively a Showman with only two power tubes and a 1x15 combo cabinet."

Phantom Browns and Phantom Blacks Tales of Twins and Piggybacks

The new Professional Amplifiers of 1960 supposedly numbered six models, including the new brown Tolex Twin. One problem: Evidence that such an amp was ever manufactured ranges from sketchy to squat.

Many players first heard about the new amps during the first half of 1960, in articles and ads in publications such as *Musical Merchandise Review* and *Music Trades*. One early article addressed the new line but listed only five amps — no Twin. The brown Twin did appear in advertisements, Fender flyers, and also in a Fender-prepared insert bound into a summer 1960 issue of *Down Beat* magazine, but that *Down Beat* entry is clouded by oddities.

For one, the new Twin is specified as having been scaled down, with only two 6L6GCs; it had already evolved from the 2x6L6G E series to the 4x5881 F series. Granted, maybe the F series Twins blew speakers once in a while, but how likely is it that Leo Fender would solve that or *any* problem by enfeebling his mighty Twin, historically the flagship of the line?

There's a problem with the insert's photo, too. To some observers, the model name on the Twin's control panel looks fishier than a bucket of chum, and the cab doesn't look quite big enough for a 2x12. Looks OK for a 2x10, though ... like, say, a brown Super. According to *ToneQuest Report*, it *is* a brown Super — the same amp from the brochure's facing page, with its face plate apparently hand-painted with a wrong-looking "Twin Amp." Paul Linden, in *TQR*: "Clearly, as of approximately April 1960, when these images were submitted to Fender Marketing for proof and publication, there was not only no brown Tolex, small box Twin amp, but there was no faceplate to put on one-offs or prototypes. With the first high-powered 6G8 Twins [in the familiar blonde] rolling off the lines in June, the window for even a one-off is terribly narrow." Elsewhere he concluded, "It is very likely that no such amp was ever made."

No argument here. But true believers would remind us that a doctored face plate doesn't *prove* the amp never existed. Maybe the brown Twin was in the works, not quite ready for the catalog's photo shoot, and Leo Fender or Don Randall insisted on its inclusion in the brochure, believing that it would soon go into production. (If you were Fender or Randall, would you want announcements of your groundbreaking Professional series to exclude the *Twin*, of all amps?)

Let's address the two-tube/four-tube issue. An authentic production version (even a limited-production version) of a low-power brown Twin would prove that the new model did indeed revert back to a smaller chassis, smaller cab, and a 2x6L6GC output section, at least for a time. That's news. We've seen transitional, mixed-feature Fenders before. What makes the low-power brown Twin a compelling legend is the model's exalted status; plus the idea that Leo Fender would in a sense take a step backwards in reducing its chassis, tubes, and cabinet; and finally the fact that unlike various prototypes or one-offs, it was prominently pictured in official literature — several times.

On the other hand, a four-tube brown Twin — such as the one pictured in Teagle & Sprung, p. 191 — could be merely another transitional anomaly, perhaps an otherwise stock 4x6L6GC 6G8 that the ever-frugal Fender happened to cover with the remaining stockpile of brown Tolex before busting open the stash of the new blonde vinyl. Teagle & Sprung, in reference to the full-power version: "Needless to say, the transitional brown Tolex Twins are very rare amps, but they do exist!"

(continued on page 239)

Surf bands were often four or five-piece groups. Not Dick Dale's Del-Tones. With three guitars, three horns, bass, drums, and keys, this slammin' rock and roll juggernaut routinely blew the roof off the joint at gigs around Southern California's beach communities. As for Dick Dale himself (here bearing down on his lefty Strat), he was blowing speakers and frying his Fender amplifiers — dozens of them. He hammered his friends Leo Fender and Freddie Tavares with his needs for bigger, louder, and tougher gear. Fender responded with a beefed-up, JBL-equipped Showman.

The Showman: Dick Dale

The King of The Surf Guitar Reflects on
Leo Fender, Freddie Tavares, the Showman Amp, and JBL

Dick Dale is best known as King of The Surf Guitar, but that honor, although justified, is too narrow to embrace the diversity of this self-taught, eclectic musician. Although the title The Father of Loud has been applied to amp manufacturer Jim Marshall, it was Dick Dale who first recognized high volume's emotional power and artistic potential. While most guitarists were inspired by other guitar players, the young Dick Dale was enthralled by the primal, pelvis-tilting rhythms of drummer Gene Krupa, captivated by the howls and bellows of jungle cats, and invigorated by his daily regimen of surfing along the California coast. He simply refused to accept the equipment that was available to him and implored Leo Fender to build amplifiers and effects that could help him to produce the mighty roar of sound he imagined. One result was Fender's top of the line amplifier of the 1960s, the JBL-equipped Showman (see photos, Chaps. 1 and 12).

The following first-person account is taken from an interview with the author in December 2006. Dick Dale talks like he plays guitar — fast. So buckle up.

In the '50s, they had no idea of what loud was. Nobody played loud. That's why they call me the father of it all. That's why Forrest White said if it weren't for Dick Dale, you wouldn't be playing the guitars and amps that you're playing today, because there was nobody before me. Nobody had power. Other people say, "Well, I was playing at the same time," and I say, "Yeah, well, what amps were you playing through, pal?" I was the guy who was blowing up the amplifiers, setting 'em on fire. The reason they call me the father of heavy metal is that we created the first powerful transformers and then the first 15" D130F speakers, and that's how the Fender Showman amp came to be. They called it the Showman because that's what Leo Fender called me: the Showman.

I was raised with every style of music there was, from big band to holy roller to — country was my favorite. I loved Hank Williams. That's always been my love. I'm a romantic. I don't consider myself one of these musicians. I'm just a manipulator of an instrument. I play by ear and I can play every instrument there is and get sounds out of it and get passion, pleasure, pain, whatever. I don't even call myself a guitar player. I don't know the first thing about an augmented ninth or a thirteenth chord and I don't give a shit. My favorite instrument is piano, and whatever I play — tenor sax, harmonica, trumpet, accordion, drums — I just have many windows in life and I'm always going forward. I always wanted my guitar to sound like Gene Krupa's drums, so I used heavy strings and played a certain way that nobody else played.

Before I was with Leo, I was with the Town Hall Party in Compton, California, a country music television show. This was in 1955. That's when I had a little teeny Gibson amplifier with about a 6" speaker. At that time, no one had created an output transformer with the wattage I needed. I had won this Elvis imitation contest. Elvis used to take me screaming up and down Hollywood Boulevard in his Stutz Bearcat, but that's another story.

Anyway, my father took me down to meet Leo. I said, "I'm Dick Dale. I'm a surfer. I don't have any money. Can you help me out?" Leo just looked at me and he said, "Here, try this guitar. I just made this guitar." It was the brand new Stratocaster. Leo wanted me to beat it to death. He would laugh and say to Freddie Tavares, "Freddie, when it can withstand the barrage of punishment of Dick Dale, then it is fit for human consumption."

Leo would call me up and we would sit in his living room in the wee hours listening to Marty Robbins over one of these little amps that he had. Leo hated stereo. He hated anything that changed the sound. I was his number one personal guinea pig. Anything that came out of his brain, like the 6-string bass, I was the one who pioneered it. Even the Fender Rhodes piano — I pioneered that at the Hollywood Bowl.

The Three Musketeers

Freddie and Leo and I used to be the Three Musketeers. It all came out of Leo's head. Leo was like an Einstein. And Freddie — nobody could ever play a guitar as knowledgeably as Freddie. He could do a song like [sings], "Look at me, I'm as helpless as a kitten up a tree … " and he would do full six-string passing chords for every goddamn note. What gets me pissed off is that all these people, including the guys who had been working [at Fender] all those years, have all this so-called knowledge about what was going on with the amplifiers. They don't know *shit*, because they weren't sitting in the room when it was just me, Leo, and Freddie. And there was just one other person who would stick his head in that little teeny room, and that was Forrest White — "Hi Dick, how you doing?"

Reverb

I was the guy that made Leo reach out and do other things. I made him create reverb, echo, all these extra things because I was trying to make my voice sound like a singer's voice. Leo came up with the idea for a reverb because I stole the idea out of a Hammond organ. Now, surf music came before reverb. My first album with "Miserlou" on it, which has become like a national anthem — on the Olympics, the football, the baseball, every damn thing you see, and it created the movie *Pulp Fiction*, it was the inspiration for that movie, Quentin Tarentino told me — that song was played without any reverb on that first album. That album was called *Surfer's Choice*. We did over 88,000 copies, which is like four million today. "Miserlou" was played with 60 gauge strings to get that heavy percussion sound, and I had to record it 98 times, but that's another story.

Anyway, Leo was not working on reverb before I came to him. I took the idea to him. It was my idea for him to make it because I wanted the reverb for my voice. I didn't know I wanted the reverb. All I knew was, I wanted that sustaining sound. Piano was my favorite, and when I put my foot down on the pedal, the note would sustain and not sound dry.

So the reverb had nothing to do with the guitar, at first. It was about us trying to find how to make my voice sustain. Once we had reverb on the voice, it was my idea to try reverb on the guitar. I had a little old Hammond organ and I saw this switch that said "reverb," so I hit it and it sustained the note and I go "Wow!" So I took the back off. I used to take everything apart. There was a can in there with springs inside it, and I took it to Leo and Leo built a version with tubes. I took my Shure dynamic "birdcage" microphone, like the one Frank Sinatra used to sing through. He carried that with him everywhere he went so that his voice would sound really nice. See, Frank wanted to manage me, but that's a whole other story.

Anyway, so that's where I got the microphone idea. I plugged that mic into that reverb and plugged that reverb into a Bogen 100W tube amplifier. Then we had the [JBL] D130 speakers — not the D130F, that came later — and I put a D130 in a cabinet and stuffed it with fiberglass and that was my vocal system. It was something that I built at home.

Fried Jensens and a New Transformer

I kept telling Leo that the guitar speakers were not strong enough. In those days, we didn't use microphones [for guitar], so the amps had to fill the hall. With a hundred people it was okay, but with a thousand people, their bodies would soak up the bass response. I had been using a little Gibson and then a Standel. I kept trying Leo's amps, but they would catch on fire. I burned up 40 or 50 amps. Before Leo came up with [the Showman], the Fenders I was using weren't Deluxes or Bassmans or anything like that. They were just prototypes that Leo built for me, and I'd keep frying them.

Leo had a bunch of speakers on this rolling thing he made. They were all Jensens. I would fry those pieces of crap like you wouldn't believe. Now, I could not play the guitar like Freddie. I would just be banging on the string, making chords and singing Hank Williams songs, and I would do a drum beat on the guitar. Leo kept asking me, "Why do you have to play so loud?", and it was Freddie who said, "You know what? We have to go see Dick Dale in person." Freddie was the one who dragged Leo down and stood in the middle of four thousand people at the Rendezvous. Freddie told me this story. He said to me: "Leo looked at me and he said, 'Now I know what Dick is trying to tell me.' Back to the drawing board."

So Leo went back and he worked on this and he called me up at 1:00 in the morning or whatever it was, and he says, "Dick! I got it, I got it, I got it, I got it! Come down and try it!" So I went down and he had created the first 85W output transformer that peaked at 100W. For my amp, the secret is that output transformer. Most output transformers only favor highs, or mids, or lows — they don't favor them all. And Leo was the only man who ever did the winding on that transformer to favor all three. They tried to copy it. People took it apart and analyzed it, but no one could copy it. And that's why they call it the Dick Dale output transformer, and that output transformer has never been matched by anybody. Not by Marshall, not by anybody.

We would try to put it through a Jensen speaker and it just didn't do shit, so Freddie, Leo and myself — there were none of the so-called technicians from Fender, no one but me, Freddie, Leo and my father — we went to JBL.

The Showman, the JBL D130F

I can't remember the names of the people that we spoke to at JBL — [laughs] I don't even remember 30 seconds ago — but they weren't technicians. They were executives, the guys who pulled the strings. Leo told the JBL guys that he wanted a very heavy magnet, something like a 12 pound magnet, and they looked at him like he was crazy. They laughed at him. They said, "What are you gonna do? Put it on a tugboat?" And Leo just very quietly looked at them — and I'll never forget this — he said, "If you want my business, you make it," and that was it.

One thing I really wanted to hear was the click of the pick, and it was my idea to put the aluminum dust cover on the front. To me, I felt it was giving that metallic click sound when you pick with a pick, and I used a heavy gauge pick on those 60 gauge strings. I start with a .016 unwound, an .018 unwound, a .020 unwound, a .039 wound, a .049 wound, and a 60 wound. They used to call them bridge cables. The theory is, the thicker the string, the fatter the sound.

We plugged that 85W transformer into the head. We didn't really have a wrapping for the amplifier head, but I needed to use it that night and the only thing he had was that cream [Tolex], and Leo says, "Oh my God, don't let anybody see it because they are going to want it 'cause you're playing on it, but it's gonna stain with coffee and cigarette butts." He says, "It's very impractical," but I said, "Oh, I love it, I love it, I love it!" This was the first [blonde] amp.

So the next week he calls me and says, "Come on in. I gotta show you a surprise." And I went down there. He had the amp. He said, "This is you. You are the Showman. This is your amp." And I saw these workers working on all these heads and they were all in the cream-colored covering and that's the Dick Dale amplifier.

So my connection with Freddie and with Leo, my heavy gauge strings, that Gene Krupa drumming style that I played on the guitar, and then beating up on the Stratocaster and burning up all those speakers and coming up with heavy JBLs — all those things came together in that Showman. That amp was created for me. That amp is the Dick Dale amplifier.

So this was all fine, but the problem was I wanted it to be even bigger. I took six of those [Showman] heads and six cabinets just to be funny and I wired them all together in San Bernardino one night, at the big San Bernardino auditorium, and when I plugged in and hit it, my feet went off the ground! You couldn't control it. I went back to my normal single, but I still wanted it to be bigger, so I went back to Leo and said, "I want to put two speakers in the same cabinet." Leo goes, "What? Now I gotta change the output transformer again."

So he went back to the drawing board, and the result was the Dual Showman, with two speakers. That first 85W transformer, which peaked at 100W, made Dick Dale the father of heavy metal. No one had that kind of sound. Now, this second transformer was 100W, peaking at 180W and favoring highs, mids, and lows so that when it came out of that speaker, it was so fat. It was just what I wanted, just like Gene Krupa's drums coming through my 60 gauge strings. See, Dick Dale plays the guitar like drums, which is my first instrument. Playing like I do with that drumming style — *dicka-dicka-dicka-dicka-DAH!* — that would confuse the speaker, and that's why we had gone back to JBL. My style was so hard and so fast that it would confuse the speaker. With the speaker pulsing in and out, it would blow. Freddie Tavares would hold this speaker in his hands and put his thumb and fingers on both sides and start pushing it up and down and he'd go, "Dick, how are you doing this?" You could hear it grinding inside because it was not moving evenly all the way around. It was dancing all over the place, out of control.

So JBL fixed that speaker so the surround would have more flexibility, more movement, and not blow. [Dick is asked if it's possible that there were other players who were also giving feedback to JBL.] No, we are the ones who created that goddamn speaker! I don't remember [Harvey Gerst or] any names [from JBL]. All I know is, we had to build that speaker for that amplifier. They called it the D130F, F for Fender. After that, I never blew a single speaker, except when a cone finally rotted. Leo was bolting those heads down to the speaker cabinets, and I found that those 5881 tubes were being destroyed because of the heavy pulsations. So in performance, I no longer put the head on top of the speakers.

After we did the Dual Showman, I didn't continue to work on the amplifiers because the Dual Showman was the ultimate of the ultimate of the ultimate. It has never been duplicated. I still use it. I'm using one right now.

Leo just really appreciated that I was clean, never used a drug in my life, I don't smoke, I've never put alcohol in my body, and that's why right now at the age of 69 I'm doing 38 concerts in 42 days. I have had one guitar in my career — the Stratocaster that Leo Fender gave me — and I still use the Showman amplifier he created for me.

HOW TO ENJOY YOUR NEW FENDER CUSTOM-ENGINEERED AMPLIFIER

Do we really care why the young woman on the floor is listening to *The Ventures Walk Don't Run* and other albums in the middle of a recording session? Heck, no. What matters is — look at all these cool amps (and dig that jazzy painting). On guitar is photographer Bob Perine, who obviously knows how to enjoy his new Fender custom-engineered amplifier.

The blonde 6G8/6G8-A Twin of the early 1960s. Fender's top of the combo line had great looks, a whopping ten tubes, plenty of power, tilt-back legs, gobs of kingpin mojo, and one of the best tremolos of all time.

Hear the blonde Tolex Twin, Tracks 49 - 51.

The *Down Beat* brochure provides specifications, but in this case they don't add up. As *ToneQuest Report* pointed out, the specified two-tube output section suggests a small box, and yet the cited cab dimensions are those of the big box version. Given the Twin's admitted tendency to blow speakers on occasion, *TQR* conjectured: "It stands to reason that Leo Fender needed time to verify the capacity of whatever speakers would eventually be used in the Twin amp, and it seems likely that this situation gave rise to both a temporary suspension of production of the Twin, and the opportunity to introduce a new flagship, the Vibrasonic. From this perspective, it seems possible that the low-powered brown Twin amp is merely a mirage."

For Greg Huntington, the myth is not a possibility; it's a certainty. He is a musician, electrical engineer (now retired after a quarter-century career with Hewlett-Packard), and for many years a researcher with a specialty in Fender amps. He was also a consultant to the authors of the *ToneQuest Report* articles on the brown Twin. Regarding that project, he says: "I want to emphasize the conclusion that the small box brown Twin is a myth. When comparing [the *Down Beat*] photos of the brown Twin and the brown Super, high resolution analysis shows all the knobs in exactly the same rotations, and all the nuts (on the four jacks) in exactly the same rotational orientation, and the logo meeting all threads identically at all edges of the logo, and all threads of the grille cloth meeting the edges of the baffle identically in all places on all four edges.

"High-res analysis shows the supposed Twin in the photo has a 24 inch wide cabinet, like the Super. But there *is* no small box brown Twin, because a 2x12 wouldn't fit into that narrower cab unless it were as tall as a Bandmaster or a Concert. Now, I have maintained for years that Fender *could* have built a two-tube, 2x12 Twin in the same box they used for the two-tube, 1x15 Vibrasonic, but that has a 26 1/4 inch width, not what I assume most people mean when they refer to a 'small box.' In other words, I would not be flabbergasted to see a somewhat smaller Twin that was basically a 2x12 Vibrasonic, but so far no one has ever produced a single example."

But one believer is Steve Soest, a longtime vintage expert and Fender specialist: "I'm sure these amps exist, the small ones. There's a photo of one in an ad. The front panels are shorter than a blonde Twin, so I've always suspected they went back to two power tubes for this model. Also, I believe the small box Tolex Twin would have a center volume knob, and the knobs would be nickel instead of plastic. It would probably have the sharper edge on the top of the cabinet, and the 'pinker' rough brown Tolex, too, like the early Vibrasonic."

Maybe the idea of a low-power brown Twin isn't so incongruous after all. Leo Fender changed specs all the time, but would he really downgrade his top of the line amp? Well, the Twin was no longer at the top. In fact, with the Vibrasonic in the stores and the Showman in the works, the Twin by 1960 had been relegated to the number-three spot. And don't forget, the Vibrasonic had two power tubes, not four. Mr. Fender may have found it illogical to continue marketing a number-three amp that was significantly more powerful than his new number one. (Rumors have circulated that Peter Frampton once owned a brown Twin, but Frampton, himself an astute amp collector, remembers no such amp.)

This author finds no evidence of the low-power brown Twin, but whether or not Fender ever produced one or perhaps a handful of such prototypes, what *is* revealing is the sheer number of inconsistencies in the literature. Much more significant than the occasional catalog glitch, they likely reflect various uncertainties about the Twin, as well as the hectic pace of innovation at Fender at the dawn of the 1960s.

Specifically, this author finds additional support for the "temporary suspension of production" theory in a Fender flyer that pictures the Twin. It's a different photo than the one in the *Down Beat* insert. The "Twin-Amp" script on the panel looks somewhat more authentic, but once again the photo and the text are inconsistent in several respects. First, like the *Down Beat* Twin, this one supposedly has a low-power output section with two tubes, and yet the width is specified to be a full 27 1/2", seemingly better suited to the high-power, four-tube chassis. Second, there are two listings of speaker specs, and they are contradictory. In one, the copy is partially blacked out; this correction was done in the printing process and not by hand. Parts of the digits are still visible, and they specify two 10s rather than two 12s. The other listing specifies the correct two 12s. Third, a speaker dust cover is visible through the grille cloth, and the "Twin" in this particular photo appears to have *neither* the two 10s *nor* the two 12s — it appears to have a single, offset 15, and may in fact be a Vibrasonic with an altered name plate.

(continued on page 245)

The Supremes headline a traveling revue in the early '60s, backed up by "Motor Town" (later "Motown") mainstay Robert White on Jazzmaster.

Fender

SEE! The biggest amps in the history of the world! HEAR! The loudest amps on earth! It's King Kong, it's Ben-Hur, it's — it's Neil Young and Crazy Horse on the Weld tour, February 1991, with just about the coolest stage props ever: gigantic blonde piggy-back Fenders (with working pilot lights, no less).

Fender didn't make piggyback Vibrasonics, or blonde Vibrasonics, or brown Bassmans, and yet here they are. As mind-boggling as they are beautiful, these lab experiments were either specially ordered by favored customers or simply the products of Leo Fender's ever-restless mind. Perry Tate: "The Vibrasonic has only one channel wired up, and the unused holes on the panel are filled with steel plugs. The gentleman I bought it from ran into Forrest White at a Dallas guitar show and showed it to him. Forrest remembered this amp, and also recalled a second piggyback Vibrasonic, which had both channels wired up, so there's one more of these out there somewhere. This one has matching gold frame Oxford 12M6 speakers in a standard 2x12 cab of the era. There's no hardware for attaching the head, either on the head or the cabinet; it just sits on top. It was a prototype or experiment, so apparently they didn't bother with those details. The components' dates range from 1960 to 1962 and are obviously unaltered, so this amp almost certainly left the factory in '62, possibly with an employee."

The Bassman at first glance appears to be remarkable mainly for the color of its Tolex, brown instead of the standard blonde. Remarkable indeed; it may be one of a kind. But perhaps even more significant is its date of manufacture. This Tolex Bassman piggyback was built during the era of the tweed Bassman combo. Perry Tate: "Like the Vibrasonic, it's very clean. Note the color of the so-called 'dogbone' handle. There were two colors: the early light brown, or 'milk chocolate,' as seen here, and the later 'dark chocolate,' used from late 1960 until the flat strap handles appeared in 1963. They actually started using the milk chocolate dogbones on large *tweed* amps in late '59. Except for the early pink/brown Tolex, this amp is very similar to the early production Bassmans, with the tube rectifier. They ran the first production 6G6s this way for a short time before they went to the solid state rectifiers. The tube chart is actually a 5F6-A chart, stamped JB, which is February 1960. This is many months before the end of tweed Bassman production, and a full year before the piggyback Bassman was mentioned in a price list."

Front row: Tweed-era amps covered in factory-stock Tolex rather than tweed. These are ultra-rare transitional experiments, '50s style cabs sporting the fabric of the future. From left: a black Tremolux atop a black 1x15 extension cab; a brown Tolex 4x10 Bassman atop a 1x15 extension cab in rough brown Tolex; and a blonde 3x10 Bandmaster atop a cream/blonde Tolex 1x15 extension cab. Owner Alan Rogan suggests: "These are certainly rare, but I've seen a few others with the odd covering. I couldn't have ended up with as many unusual ones as I've had unless Leo was churning them out once in a while just to try new things." Photograph by Pattie Boyd.

Okay, so there's a blacked-out typo and a few incongruities in a Fender catalog. So what? True, we've seen inconsistencies before, but there's no denying the fact that official, contradictory references to the brown Twin are far more numerous than usual. Perhaps for a short time Mr. Fender did have a 2x10 Twin on the drawing board, if not on the production line. (He built one back in '55, as we saw in Chap. 11.) Like the announced reduction in output tubes, the planned decrease in speaker size could have reflected an eventually abandoned strategy of scaling down the Twin so as to reposition it relative to the newer, two-tube Vibrasonic.

Yet another wrinkle with respect to the Twin's evolving speakers may have provided additional reasons both for production delays and for inconsistencies in the literature. Greg Huntington: "Fender needed to keep the idea of the 'flagship' Twin alive, even though they were desperately stalling until JBL developed the D120F speakers that could handle a full-power, 4x6L6 Twin. They needed to keep the Twin name alive — even in a period when no Twins were built — because they *did* have the blonde Twin almost ready to go."

Another inconsistency: Although the new Tolex Twin was announced in early 1960, the price lists in January, June, and July of that year all specified "linen" (tweed) covering. While an inaccurate price sheet might not be unique, it does seem odd that this kind of mistake would be repeated over such a long period, given that dealers used the price sheets for ordering purposes. If dealers were ordering tweed Twins but receiving Tolex Twins instead, surely they would have let their Fender road reps know about the discrepancy. To look at it from the factory's point of view, given Fender's justifiable pride in the new Tolex Twin, would they fail to correct the repeated publication of outdated specs? Perhaps it was no mistake. No matter what the catalogs and ads said, Fender was making tweed Twins at least through March of 1960 and perhaps later. It's not until the price sheet of September of that year that we finally see the new price, a heavier weight, and the Tolex covering — and these were certainly *blonde* Twins.

Uncertainties regarding the Twin may also have been linked to uncertainties regarding its replacement: Despite the Vibrasonic's being advertised all through the last half of 1959, records suggest that it didn't ship until late in the year or even January of 1960, as noted earlier.

And then there's the Fender catalog from the period, a much longer and more heavily illustrated document than the flyers, price sheets, or the *Down Beat* insert. Whereas in the insert the Twin photo was likely faked, in the catalog it's nonexistent. The omission of a photo of the famous Fender Twin in an official, in-depth catalog is too conspicuous to be chalked up to typos or deadlines. Something's up.

The text addresses the Twin, but the section is about half the length of those of the other Professional amps. Where blurbs for the Bandmaster, Concert, etc. conduct a knob-by-knob, jack-by-jack tour of the control panels in true Fender fashion, the sketchy Twin copy offers only vague assertions ("tremendous distortionless power with wide tone range characteristics," etc.) and makes no reference either to the Twin's old complement of tone controls or the new two-channel arrangement with Vibrato and no mid knob.

This author suggests that the copy writers shortchanged the Twin simply because they didn't know what to say, and that the catalog, the *Down Beat* insert, the flyer, and some of the ads were all produced while details of the new Twin were up in the air, perhaps due to a planned (but scrapped) downsizing relative to the Vibrasonic. Still, Fender easily could have put together a couple of different Twin variants in brown before settling on a unique distinction for the once and future king of the single-cab line: The early-'60s Twin — its mighty four-tube output section intact — would be Fender's only blonde combo.

Brown Piggybacks?

If a brown Twin is rare, how about a stock brown piggyback? Do they exist? Conventional wisdom has it that the brown Tolex combos of early and mid 1960 were joined later that year and in 1961 by the piggybacks in blonde. The conventional wisdom is accurate, and perhaps we should leave well enough alone and move on with our lives.

But there's one more oddity in the 1960 *Down Beat* insert that's hard to ignore. Like most Fender catalogs of the time, this one displays photos of endorsers. As is typical, most of them — the Mulcays, Nappy Lamare — would have been best known to fans of pop and country music. But the brochure also includes a photo of the Champs, of "Tequila" fame, a rippin', honkin', chart-toppin' sax and guitar-driven combo that any rock and roller would be quick to recognize. They are outfitted with a trio of Profes-

This almost certainly one of a kind tweed piggyback Bassman was made for bassist Cecil Johnson in the late 1950s. It was purchased by "Cactus" Soldi, of Valley Music in El Cajon, California. His son, guitarist "Cactus Jim" Soldi, tells the tale: "Cecil Johnson was a rep for a music wholesaler and an upright bass player. He was only five-two or five-three, and the burden of carrying all his gear to these upstairs ballrooms like they used to have was pretty daunting. So he asked Leo about it, and Leo said, 'Would you be willing to carry two packages if they were lighter?' As far as I know, this was the first Fender piggyback, and Cecil said the same thing — it was the first one, basically a combo amp split into two pieces for carrying convenience. It was never a production thing, and I've never heard of any others in tweed. My dad acquired it from Cecil, and we had it here in the store on Main Street in El Cajon for many years. It was part of a collection sitting in the back. We finally sold it."

In a 1989 letter to John Sprung, the purchaser, Steve Kinkel, reported that a stamped code, GF, revealed a manufacturing date of June 1957. So, Leo Fender was experimenting with piggyback designs three years before introducing the familiar blonde piggyback amps of 1960 and 1961. Photo courtesy John Sprung.

sional series Fenders, one of which is — drum roll — a piggyback. It's the only piggyback in the brochure. It looks like it might be light brown rather than the blonde of first-generation production piggybacks. (Richard Smith: "It's hard to state for certain. I believe it's brown." Teagle & Sprung also refer to it as a brown amp.)

Were there stock brown piggybacks, other than the brown Bassman shown here? Richard Smith: "Dick Dale swears his first one was brown, or at least he did in the 1980s." Come to think of it, if Dick Dale or the Champs got very early piggybacks with Tolex coverings, they would have to be brown because the blonde Tolex hadn't been delivered to Fender yet. At any rate, if piggybacks existed (in whatever color), why weren't they featured in the brochure? If Fender was willing to go to the trouble to paint "Twin Amp" on a brown Super to promote the supposedly upcoming brown Twin, wouldn't they have found a way to include among the new models the same new piggyback the Champs are posing with?

Let's relax. These are Fender catalogs, not history books. We are expecting too much consistency and logic here. A simple explanation: The piggyback design was

On the set of the 1965 Disney film *The Monkey's Uncle*, the Beach Boys brought along a blonde Fender piggyback to go with their matching instruments and sport jackets. Beach movie queen and former Mouseketeer Annette Funicello fills in on tambourine.

being field tested; it was almost ready for public announcement but not quite. Fender's attitude may have been: *The Champs are popular, they play this new "rock and roll" music the kids like, let's run the photo for PR purposes and not worry about showing an amp in the background we're not yet marketing. What's the big deal?* Perhaps a more likely possibility: No one even noticed. Certainly no one at Fender in early 1960 could have foreseen the rise of the vintage market, let alone the buzz among collectors that inconsistent catalog details might ignite.

"Don't Exists"

Although there is no evidence of any significant production of brown piggybacks or brown Twins — small box *or* big box — Leo Fender built prototypes of all sorts of stuff, and custom amps for influential artists like Dick Dale. Richard Smith: "And don't forget, bands went for matching amps onstage, so if you're playing on the Tomorrowland Terrace at Disneyland and all the other guys have brown Concerts, shouldn't the new Twin you're ordering be brown, too?"

Leo experimented feverishly with new designs — putting some into production, some on the back burner, scrapping others. There were surely several one-off (or "ten-off" or whatever) amps. These are the legendary minotaurs and chimeras of Fender lore, mythological creatures with gills and feathers, wings and hooves. How about a *piggyback* Concert? Or a *brown* Showman? Steve Soest: "Back in the 1970s there was a brown Tolex Concert *head* with a 2x10 bottom at Stanton Music [Stanton, CA] in the teaching room for years. Kinda looked like a Tremolux with a larger head. It had a tube chart and the whole enchilada. I tried to buy it several times, but when they went out of business it disappeared.

"Also, I've seen two original Showman 12 amps in *brown*: serial #PB00005 and #PB00003. Strangely enough, they had Vibrasonic output transformers (16 ohm) and an RCA speaker jack (only one) on the back panel. The brown faceplates appeared to have been painted everywhere except where the lettering and numbers were, leaving them an aluminum color rather than white, and the lettering was a different size. They had brown knobs, the cabinets had deeper jack cups, the thumbscrew lockdowns were different, and the speaker cabinets were shallower. I have also seen two Showman 15 cabinets in *brown* in the shallower configuration as well. All these were odd, but they were factory stock."

Another platypus: Teagle & Sprung reported that they examined a *brown* 4x10 Bassman and were convinced it was original. Yet another: Greg Gagliano reported an original *tweed* Concert: "It's unknown if the tweed covering was a mistake — 'Oops, I thought this was a 4x10 Bassman cabinet' — or intentional, perhaps a special order."

Alan Rogan is a renowned guitar tech whose clients over the years have included George Harrison, Eric Clapton, Keith Richards, Mick Jagger, Pete Townshend, John Entwistle, and Joe Walsh. He recalls: "In the mid '80s I was working with Keith Richards. When we went from Paris to New York, I went over to S.I.R. [Studio Instrument Rentals] and found a Twin, the high-powered kind. It was a tweed *style*, with the controls in back, on top, but it was covered in brown Tolex. Totally original, never recovered. I also found at least three other Fenders with tweed-era controls on top in the back, but Tolex coverings: a 4x10 Bassman in brown, a 1x12 Tremolux in black [officially, the Tremolux didn't convert to black until '63, after it had been reconfigured as a piggyback], and a three-10 Bandmaster combo in the rough white Tolex. All these amps would have been from 1959 through '61 or so.

"The high-power [big box] Twin I found for Keith at S.I.R. had already been heavily modified. I got it for next to nothing — 300 dollars, plus 200 for the flight case [laughs]. It was just great, with a fiery sound, but it was running too hot. It was frying, and it finally killed itself. John Peden introduced us to his friend César Diaz, and César came up to New York. He brought a chassis with him and stayed there all night while we were working. He turned that amp into a perfect '59 or '60 tweed-style Twin, just fantastic. Keith used it on *Dirty Work*, and I presume he may use it to this day." [Note: *Guitar Player* reported that Keith Richards used the brown Twin, serial no. A00003, on the *Steel Wheels* album and tour in 1989 and 1990. His guitar tech explained, "Keith hesitated to subject it to the rigors of the road, but we treat it gingerly, and it sounds great."]

Greg Huntington reports the existence of special-order *blonde* Concerts: "In fact, Sam Hutton [Chap. 12] did a lot of specials in the early '60s for Leo's friends or associates. They were one-offs, but made with existing materials and supplies, just mixed and matched differently with (at most) a bit of special woodworking. These sorts of special orders are fun and interesting, but they're no big deal. They are fundamentally different from something like the small box brown Twin, which is a myth concerning a *production* amp that never existed."

Perspectives

So what are we to conclude from evidence of amps that officially don't exist? For those of us who love this stuff, let's rejoice in the uniqueness of the too-cool one-off that surfaces on occasion, while reminding ourselves that rare birds may say little about the evolution of the species. As recently as a couple of decades ago, many of us assumed that back in the vintage era major guitar companies made decisions based on logic and consistency. Therefore, a product with an unusual mix of features must be significant, some sort of missing link. Now we know better. While most guitars and amps were indeed the result of long-term planning and coherent marketing strategies, others were experiments that were never intended for broad public distribution, one-offs made for personal use by employees, special orders, limited-production models made for a single retailer or chain, or products intended to use up leftover parts.

Any human, even Leo Fender, can concentrate on only so many things at once. Consider what was happening at Fender in 1959. Company growth was explosive. The new top of the line Jazzmaster guitar was just a year old. Guitars and basses were converting to rosewood fingerboards, along with dozens of other developments. An entire new line of amps was in the works, including a new top dog, the Vibrasonic; yet another new kingpin, the Showman, would follow right on its heels. Is it any wonder that the Twin — now relegated to the number three spot — found itself in limbo for a few months?

If the Champs photo was taken in early 1959, as some researchers have suggested, then Fender would have had functioning piggyback amps for more than a full year prior to their official debut, which should come as no surprise. In fact, Cecil Johnson's tweed piggyback reveals that Leo Fender was experimenting with the piggyback concept even earlier.

Eric Clapton tries out his iconic 335 through a Fender blackface/blonde cab piggyback. The photo was likely taken on the same day in mid 1969 as the photo shoot for the "alternative" cover of Blind Faith's sole album.

Settling on final details of the new Tolex line may have involved any number of experiments, prototypes, and mutants of different colors, some of which escaped the lab. Consider Alan Rogan's stock, "tweed-style" Tremolux, which proves that Leo's earliest experiments in black Tolex not only predated the black production Fenders of 1963 but actually coincided with or predated the blonde Tremolux of 1961.

Whew. For a book that supposedly cares more about the grand sweep, the big picture, we've spent a lot of time on tiny details here. Do we really care whether a catalog photo from four or five decades ago was altered, or whether Fender made this or that oddball amp? Well, sure. But the deeper value of these examples is that they provide insights into Fender's history, production practices, and literature.

Magazines and printers have deadlines. There comes a point when they say to the marketing guys, *Hey, we're going to press, so send us whatever you have — now.* At Fender, sometimes what was available for the photo shoot didn't match projections for the upcoming line (in one case, a new amp was planned but unavailable for the photo, so Fender positioned a mandolin headstock to cover up the name on the older version's outdated front panel). Any pre-CBS literature was basically Fender's best guess as to how it was all going to play out in the months to come.

Surely Mr. Fender would have been surprised and perhaps amused at all the fuss created by his transitional models, prototypes, and experiments. Such oddballs were inevitable. Was there ever a period in Fender's first twenty years when the company was *not* "in transition," with a mix of outdated products gathering dust somewhere, hot-selling contemporary amps and guitars in the stores, promising newcomers in catalogs and ads, prototypes in various stages of completion out in the field for testing, others on the workbench, others on the drawing board, and still others only a twinkle in the old man's eye?

Early '60s Oxford Speakers

In *Fender, The Sound Heard 'Round The World*, Richard Smith reported that Leo Fender discontinued his use of Jensen speakers and switched to Oxfords because he believed they would have a better frequency response and a more durable construction. He added, "Oxford would make speakers to Leo's specifications when Jensen would not. About 1963 Jensen capitulated and Leo renewed his relationship with the company. (Players generally agree that the Jensen blue caps sound crisper and more resonant than later, more durable Oxfords and Jensens made to Leo's specs.)"

Shown here is a collection of Oxford 10K5 10" speakers from Fender amps. Perry Tate: "For years I've heard dealers say, 'This early-'60s Fender has original Jensens.' They're actually Oxfords, but most of them don't say 'Oxford' on them anywhere. There were some Oxfords in Champs and a few other amps before 1960, but generally throughout the '50s, most of the speakers were Jensens. After the blue bell Jensen era, starting in 1961, Fender began using Oxford speakers almost exclusively. These came in the brown and blonde amps, and early blackfaces, too.

"At the upper left is a silver frame Oxford 10K5 with a tall metal cover, a Fender 'spaghetti logo' label, and the date code stamped on the alnico magnet; these came in Concerts and Supers during most of 1961. Middle, top: Alnico got expensive so they went to ceramic magnets. This 10K5 is the same as the first speaker but with a ceramic magnet and a shallower metal cap, seen from late '61 into early '62. Date codes were now stamped on the frames. Beginning in early 1962, we see the upper right version — gold frame, with the same metal cap and logo, probably the most common version of this speaker.

"Lower left: Same speaker, but with a glossy brown *plastic* cap with a Fender logo molded into it. This is the only original speaker I've ever seen in the famous brown Vibroverbs, and it was used from late '62 through mid '63. Lower center: A few of the blackfaces continued to have the gold frame speakers but quickly switched to 10K5s in black, often painted over the gold finish. Leftover brown

plastic caps were used on a small number of these, so you see brown caps on black speakers for a brief transitional period. Lower right — black speaker, black cap, molded Fender logo. These are quite rare, and are the last speakers that would use a magnet cover in a Fender amp. I haven't seen any of these past August of '63.

"These different frame and cover combinations were also seen on the Oxford 12" and 15" speakers of the time."

Speaker basics, see Chapter 4.

NORMAL
VIBRATO
Twin
Reverb-Amp

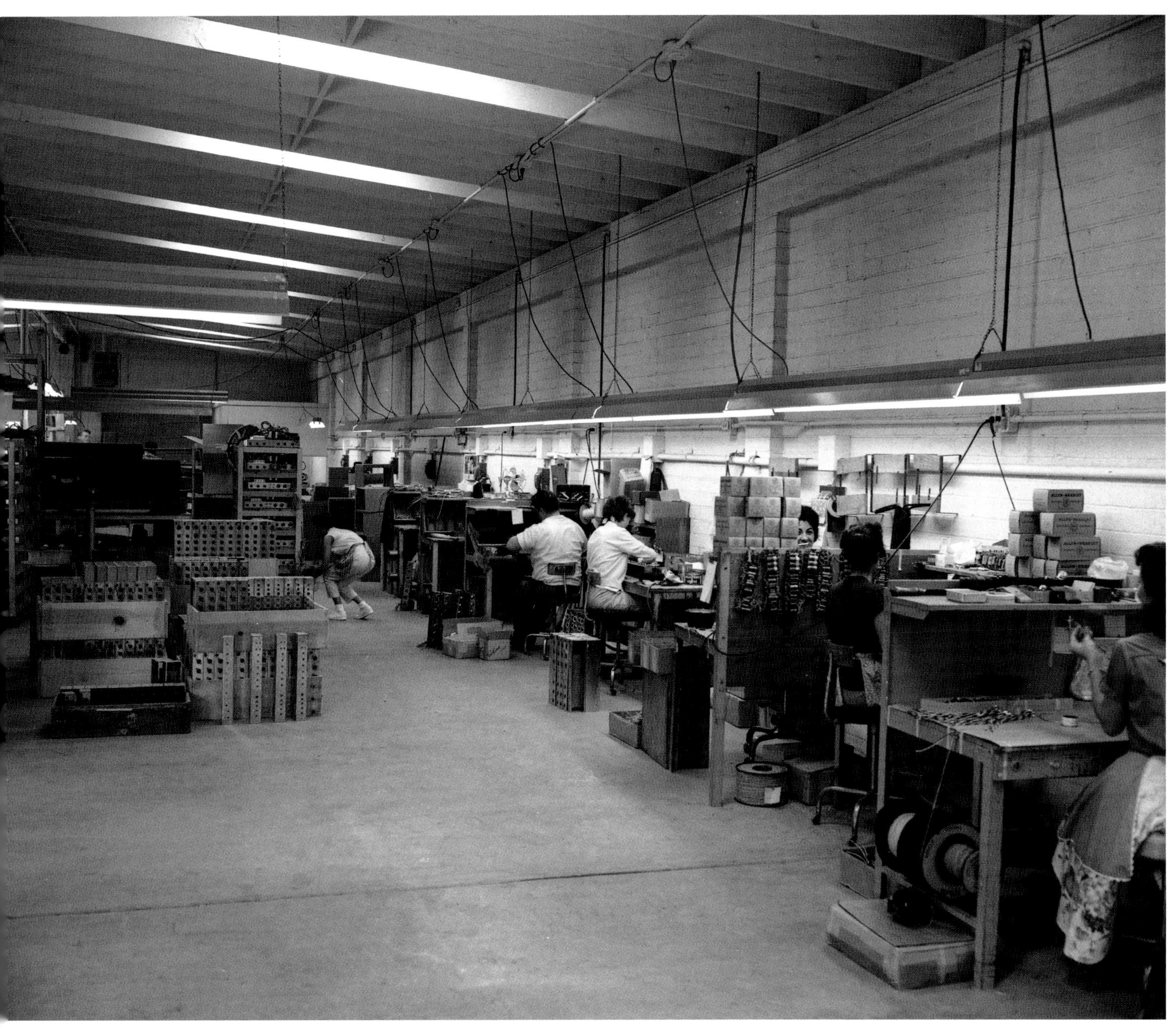

This page and facing page: Wiring, assembling, and testing amps, circa 1963.

Buddy Guy at Cambridge Commons, Cambridge, Massachusetts, 1968. At the 20th Annual Rock and Roll Hall of Fame Induction Ceremony, Eric Clapton spoke about Buddy Guy, who first played in London in 1965 at the Marquee Club. Writer Hugh Ochoa quoted Clapton's remarks: "In the flesh, he was earth shattering. His style, on every level, was fantastic, doing all the things we would later come to associate with Jimi Hendrix. Playing with his teeth, his feet, and behind his head, he brought the house crashing down.

"But beyond all that, it was his actual playing that got through to me. With only a drummer and a bass player behind him, he gave a thundering performance, delivering the blues with finesse and passion in a way I'd never heard before. All in all, everything about that night was deeply profound for me. The blues was clearly alive and well. And it looked good, too. For as well as being the real thing, musically, Buddy was a star. His suit, his hair, his moves, his sunburst Strat, everything was sharp and perfect. He was for me what Elvis was for most other people. My course was set, and he was my pilot."

CHAPTER FOURTEEN

14

Into the Black

The Landmark Amps of 1963

The year 1963 marked the debut of the blackface amplifier line, a watershed in Fender history. In fact, it's no exaggeration to say the debut of the blackface Fenders was a landmark in the history of electric instruments. Structurally, their cabinets were similar to the browns and blondes. The "face" in "blackface" refers to the front control panels ("face plates"), which on almost all models went from brown to black in '63. These new panels were fitted with black skirted knobs with silver centers and white numbers (exceptions included a few early blackface Princetons and Bassmans with round, unnumbered white knobs). The previous method of displaying the numbers for the knobs was to put them on the panels; each unskirted knob had a pointer. Now, however, numbers were displayed on the skirts of the new knobs. (Some amps have the new numbered knobs placed on old numbered panels, at least in some of the photos for the 1963/1964 literature picturing the new Bassman and Tremolux; it's unlikely any such amps were distributed.)

While "blackface" technically refers to the color of the face plates, for many guitarists the term simply means "black Fender." Some early models have black face plates and blonde cabs (discussed below), but most blackface amps are indeed covered in black Tolex, the new color having replaced the blondes and browns of the early 1960s. The black cabs were beautifully set off with silver sparkle grille cloth and new black handles.

Bill Sterle and the First Black Fenders

Former Fender employee Bill Sterle is a gunslinger — literally — a fast draw artist who performs in western shows under the name Marshall Knight. (He owns Paladin's holster, the one seen in the opening shot of TV's classic *Have Gun Will Travel*.) In the 1960s, he designed Fender's 12-string guitar, with Freddie Tavares' guidance, although as Bill recalls, "Naturally, Leo had to put his finishing touches on it." Bill claims that the black Tolex was his brainchild. That may well be true, but this may also be an example of an idea having multiple fathers, an event not uncommon in Fender history (remember that Mr. Fender was experimenting with black Tolex by the tail end of the tweed era or, at the latest, the brown/blonde period). In any case, the decision would have been taken only with Don Randall's input and approval.

Leo Fender's amps came with protective covers from the very beginning. Starting from the right we see a K&F, then a Princeton (no flap for the handle, just an oval opening); this second cover was often seen with TV fronts and wide panels. The next cover is a fairly common type from the narrow panel era, and it's followed by a cover often seen with the later narrow panels of the late 1950s and the brown amps of the early 1960s; owner Alan Hardtke: "It has more of a marbleized or flecked texture to the fabric, and it's a little more patterned." The last one is the standard black cover from the blackface era and later periods. Alan Hardtke: "It was available in different black materials, with or without the name of the amp on the cover. These covers are associated with general periods, but I'm sure that if Fender was loose about using capacitors and transformers depending on what they had in stock, you can bet they were loose about covers."

Bill recalls: "I went to work for Leo in 1960. I believe it was June. My job was designing the amplifiers. I had been a broadcast engineer when I met Leo, and I had a background in design. I worked on the production line for about a year to get familiar with all the equipment. I was a test engineer in manufacturing, and I helped design a few changes that implemented a faster production. Leo liked that, and he pulled me off the line and put me into the lab with him.

"He had been designing the amplifiers, but then he dropped that ball in my lap a little bit. So I helped design the black, pre-CBS amplifiers. When I came to work for him, he still had a couple of the hound's-tooth [tweed] cabinets on the student models, and the others had the brown or the buff [blonde] Tolex. The buff was pretty, but don't get any dirt on it! It was quite porous, and the dirt would stick to it like glue. You had to scrub it to keep it decent looking.

"Leo and I went around and around on the colors and I said, hey, you need to do something different on those amps with the covering. The black was my idea. I asked him what color covering he had inside his Cadillac, and he says black, and I says, what color luggage you got, and he says black, and I says, why not put black on the amps? Black is luxurious. Take a black Cadillac — stands out like a neon sign. Matter of fact, I got one in my garage right now. Look at luggage — the black has more luxury. I thought, well, wait a minute, this equipment is professional, why don't we make it in black? Let's look a little classier than plain old brown and buff.

"Leo introduced it on a few sample pieces, and people started standing in line, wanting to know when they could get them in black. And then he ordered material and put them into production. It was a hit, almost overnight. They went over like gangbusters. Once we had the black cabinets, we tried some gold grille cloth and figured, nope, that's not going to cut it. But then we tried the silver grey, and that went over like gangbusters, and from there it just literally snowballed."

Transition '63, Mixing Names

The year 1963 saw overlaps between old and new models, but not merely between amps with similar names (Super vs. Super Reverb, brown Vibroverb vs. blackface Vibroverb, etc.). It was much more complicated than that, a mix-and-match-o-rama where features, colors, specs, and model names seemed to be jumbled every which way.

For example, can you name a 40W combo from that year with four 10s? It could be a Concert near the end of its brown Tolex lifespan, or a late-'63 black Concert, but it could also be a new blackface Super Reverb.

Or how about a 40W combo with one 15? In '63 that could have been a brown Pro, or a late-'63 blackface Pro, but also a blackface Vibroverb.

Or how about a 40 watter with two 12s? A blonde Bandmaster piggyback would fit that description, but so would a blackface Pro Reverb combo.

This period was not the only time Fender mixed features in amps or guitars, but being the transition between the familiar brown and blonde amps and the blackface newcomers, 1963 saw more than its share of confusing mismatches among model names, specs, and features. A good example: Fender made an amp very similar to the Super, with added reverb, but instead of calling it the Super Reverb they called it the Vibroverb. They also made an amp similar to the Concert, with added reverb. Did they call it a Concert Reverb? No, that's the one they called Super Reverb. Teagle & Sprung: "Things would make more sense, and amps would have more direct ties to their past, if Fender would have called the brown Vibroverb the Super Reverb. Then we'd have a 4x10 Concert Reverb instead of a Super Reverb; a 1x15 Pro Reverb instead of the black Vibroverb; a new improved Vibrolux Reverb with an extra 12 instead of the Pro Reverb; and a 2x10 Super Reverb instead of the Vibrolux Reverb."

Aspen Pittman: "There was a lot of planning and thought that went into these designs, but sometimes a particular detail might have come from Leo just using up whatever he had, so you see a brown era component in a black era amp sometimes, that sort of thing, forever confounding collectors. That stuff went on all the time. Leo was constantly playing with the components, trying new parts, rearranging, always tinkering, always trying to make it better. The sales department — he probably drove them nuts. We owe him a huge debt for his tenacity, for staying in business and, above all, for putting the musician first."

The Rolling Stones at the Hollywood Bowl, 1967, with Keith Richards on a Les Paul (that's a poster of a young Keith on the wall).

When is a Tweed Black? When is a Blackface Blonde?

You'll recall that when Fender adopted Tolex cab coverings for some models during 1960 and 1961, the Twin went from tweed to blonde, the piggybacks were also blonde, and all the other amps were brown Tolex or tweed. The tweed holdouts would gradually convert to brown Tolex, with the exception of the Champ. The year 1963 saw the adoption of new Tolex textures and new Tolex colors. On many of the blackface Bandmasters, Tremoluxes, and Bassmans that were shipped in the last half of 1963 and early or mid '64, the blonde Tolex had a new, smoother texture (see Chap. 12). There was also a shift to a smoother texture in the brown Tolex on a few reverb units.

The smooth-blonde/smooth-brown Tolex phase was transitional. Generally, the year 1963 saw the gradual replacement of the various blondes and browns with another new Tolex covering across the line — smooth and black, instead of either brown *or* blonde. For most of the amps, the shift to black cabs went hand in hand with the shift to black control panels. So, "blackface" means a black Fender with a black control panel.

Except when it doesn't. At the outset of the blackface era, piggyback Bandmasters, Tremoluxes, and Showmans did indeed have black control panels and black knobs, but some of them kept their blonde cabs for a year, maybe a year and a half. Such mismatches are inevitable, given the inherent flaw of the whole blonde vs. blackface lingo: One term refers to the color of the cabinet, the other to the color of the control panel.

But if the amp has both a black control panel *and* a black cab, then it's a blackface for sure, right? Not necessarily. For some enthusiasts, the true criteria are circuits, not colors. Consider the 6G6-B Bassman. This blonde piggyback received the new black control panel in mid-'63 but retained — in some cases — its smooth blonde Tolex covering; both blonde and black versions were shipped. By

Airborne over blackface: Cheap Trick's Rick Nielsen at the Paradise in Boston, June 1978.

“Blackface” means a black amp with a black control panel. Except when it doesn’t.

Most blackface Fenders have black skirted knobs, but there are exceptions. The “’64 transition” white-knob Bassman shown here was made until August 1964 and appeared in the 1964/65 catalog (printed in ’64). Note that despite the black panel, it has the older, 6G6/A/B “blonde” type of control array — a presence knob but no Bright switch. The Princeton is from the same general period. The white-knob reverb unit was made until 1966, when the tube-driven box was replaced with Fender’s solid state reverb unit.

the middle of 1964, the blonde Tolex was replaced with black, but the 6G6-B circuitry was not updated with the "true" blackface AA864 circuit until August 1964. Thus in the space of only 14 months or so, the piggyback Bassmans comprised several different versions that mixed panels, cab coverings, and circuits — not including the white-knob version made until August 1964 and appearing in the 1964/65 catalog, and not including blackface circuit revisions in 1965. So, to nitpick, a "blackface Bassman" is not an amp; it's a family of amps.

The Champ is another example of an amp acquiring the black Tolex and black face plate at different times. In the case of the blackface Bassmans, some were still made in blonde cabs before all of them converted to black cabs. With the Champ, however, the black Tolex came first. In fact, the new cabinet color preceded pretty much everything — new cabinet shape, new blackface panel, new circuit. So, the Champ's switch from tweed to blackface occurred in 1963 if we're looking at the color of the Tolex, but 1964 if "blackface" refers to circuitry.

To look at it another way: The first of the black Champs had older tweed-style boxes and chrome control panels. According to Greg Gagliano: "The 'tweed' 5F1 Champ was in production until August 1964. From December 1963 to August 1964 that amp was covered in black Tolex instead of tweed. The true blackface AA764 Champ went into production in November 1964."

If a black tweed Champ sounds like an odd description, how about a blonde circuit? Greg Gagliano: "Unlike the Champ, which took a production hiatus for a few months between the last [black-covered] 'tweed' circuit and the true blackface circuit, the production of Bassmans overlapped during August of 1964. They all had black cabs by then, but Fender made some with the old style 'blonde' 6G6-B circuit and some with the new 'true blackface' AA864." Ritchie Fliegler: "It would have been easier and would have taken less time to make them all the same, but throwing away parts was anathema to Leo Fender, so these sorts of mismatches are most likely explained by having stockpiles of leftover parts."

So, some mixed-feature, factory stock Fenders have (1) a newer color but an older cabinet shape, control panel, and circuit; (2) a newer control panel but an older color and circuit; (3) a newer color and control panel but an older circuit. Whew.

Through the Looking Glass

Once we begin to examine all the exceptions to the familiar Fender amp jargon, we find ourselves down the rabbit hole and through the looking glass, where sometimes a "tweed" amp is black (or brown), or a "blackface" amp is blonde, or an amp with a black face isn't a "true blackface." (Trick question: True or false — blonde Bandmasters have a Bright switch but no presence control. Answer: It depends on the era. Earlier *rough* blonde Bandmasters have a presence control but no Bright switch, while later *smooth* blonde Bandmasters have a Bright switch but no presence control.)

Such mismatches were common among Fender products, although in the case of the mixed-feature amps the inconsistencies were sometimes apparent even to the untrained eye; they characterized some of Fender's most important, top-line products; and they lasted for a significant period, unlike, say, the occasional one-off factory stock guitar with this or that leftover part.

On the other hand, looking at the big picture — all of the late-'50s tweeds vs. the early-'60s brown and blonde amps vs. the post-'63 blackface amps vs. the CBS silverface amps — the exceptions, although numerous, may seem relatively short-lived or otherwise minor. Although far from precise, "tweed," "blonde," "brown," "blackface," and "silverface" are routinely used to describe general eras, and to that extent they are useful. Also, despite inconsistencies, gaps, and overlaps, we can still generalize in helpful ways about the tubes, biasing, tone stacks, tremolos, and other aspects of Fender amps in this or that era.

By the way, some experts find it more convenient to categorize Fender amps by face plates rather than cab colors. Greg Huntington: "Since the blonde and brown amps were almost concurrent, guys I know think in terms of *four* eras, not five: tweed, brownface, blackface, and silverface. This avoids the confusion over the types of blonde (and even brown) cabinet coverings, and tends to suggest a useful and accurate circuit differentiation between tweed and blackface."

So, what *do* we call a blonde amp with a black control panel? Some Fender enthusiasts stick to the original meaning of "blackface" and apply it to any Fender with a black panel, regardless of cab color. Others might ask about the circuitry before answering. Many others, however, would call a blonde amp blonde, regardless of

These three amps are often referred to as “transition” models, although all were manufactured for a year or more and were the standard versions of their day: a rear-panel Champ in black rather than tweed; a blackface, white-knob version of the brown Princeton; and a Bassman with a blackface panel, blonde Tolex, a “blonde” type control array, and white knobs. Note that the grilles on the Champ and Princeton may appear to be wheat, but both are typical silver-thread grilles in which the silver has yellowed.

panel color or circuit. Smooth blonde Tolex amps with black panels were offered for more than a year, so they may be considered standard Fenders. In cases where a few models left the factory with mixes of newer and older features, we will call them "transition" models, which certainly sounds more dignified than "using up the leftover scraps" models.

Whether it was because Leo Fender and Don Randall had changed their minds on the look of the new Fender line or simply because the racks of blonde Tolex and bins of white knobs had finally been emptied, by the end of 1964 the whole line of guitar amplifiers had converted to black cabs, blackface panels, and black knobs, with handsome silver sparkle grille cloth. For the first time since the tail end of the tweeds, Fender amplifiers had a uniform look.

Continuum: From Tweeds to Blackface

We can view the blackface era as a mix of brand new concepts, plus relatively recent ideas from the brown/blonde phase, and still others going back to tweed. Matt Wilkens joined Fender in September 1989 and serves as Director of Technology as we go to press. He explains: "There's a real continuum in the circuits from tweed through blackface, and in some cases the changes were not nearly as drastic as the evolution of cabinet styles, colors, and other details might suggest."

As always, Leo Fender continued to experiment with components, substituting a 12AT7 phase inverter for the 7025 in this or that amp, or trying out a new rectifier arrangement. He replaced the tone knobs on some amps with separate bass and treble controls, and he added mid knobs to one channel of some amps (and to both channels on the new Twin Reverb).

Greg Huntington: "It's also worth noting that with the change from the tweed circuits to the browns and blondes and then the blackfaces, there was an appreciable increase in power-supply voltages, resulting in a more powerful, brighter, stronger, and fuller sound with greater punch and frequency response. This went hand in hand with the wider-band speakers that were becoming available at the same time.

"Another general trend: Over time, Leo tended to increase the amount of feedback in his amps [not to be confused with the overdrive kind of feedback; see Negative

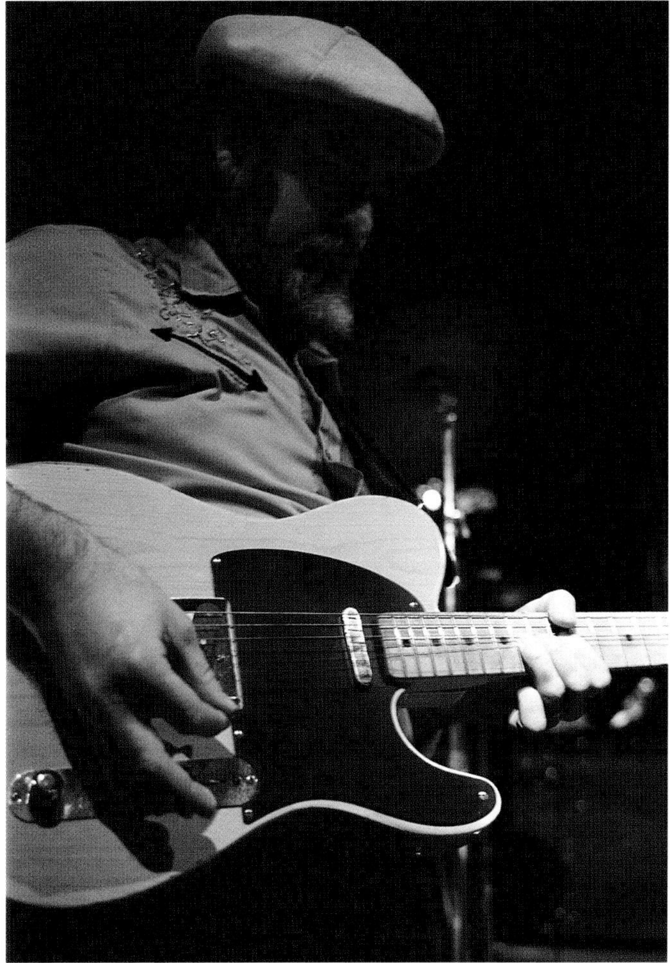

The late Roy Buchanan, whose searing Telecaster style remains unforgettable to all who saw him. Seymour Duncan recalled: "Roy Buchanan would use a blackface Vibrolux Reverb all the time, and it broke up really nice for him. He would turn it around on a chair and mike it from the back because, he told me once, it was a little too harsh on his ears to mike it from the front, and he just liked the tone of it coming from the back. From the front, it was so bright, you had to EQ it down, but from the back it softened the sound a little bit, and you didn't have to do all that EQing. It avoided overloading the microphone, so he just thought it gave him a fuller sound. He also avoided having any feedback problems by not having it face him directly." Buchanan told *Guitar Player*: "I use a Fender Vibrolux amp. The reverb is on 2, which gives it a little more ring and sustain. The volume and tone controls are full out, but the volume is not always wide open on the guitar. It's just there in case I need it."

Hear the "Mark 'n' Roy" Jam, featuring the Vibrolux Reverb, Tracks 42 - 43.

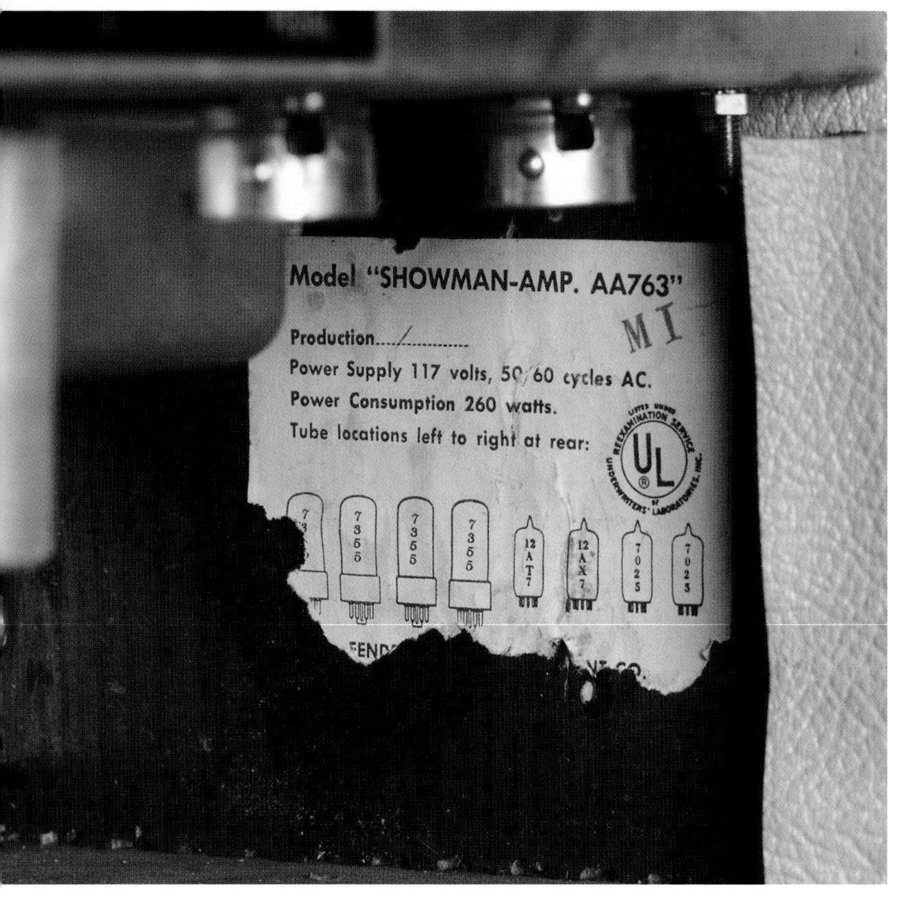

This is the tube chart in a very rare and highly prized blackface/blonde cab Showman. Its AA763 circuit appeared in the early fall of 1963, while the cabs were still covered in smooth blonde Tolex. For a couple of months the output section used four 7355s, as shown here, instead of 6L6GCs. Greg Gagliano, in *20th Century Guitar*: "Though we don't know why 7355s were used, perhaps Leo got a good deal from RCA on a boatload of these tubes, so he tried them out in the Dual Showman and Twin Reverb. So why did he switch back to 6L6GCs? Probably because the 7355s aren't rated to operate at the higher voltages that the Dual Showman and Twin Reverb could dish out. They are a smaller tube, similar to a 5881/6L6GB and hence can get hotter than a tube with a larger envelope." Note the "Production 1" designation. The "MI" reveals the month (I = September) and year (M = 1963) of manufacture.

Hear the "Twin Geeks" Jam, featuring the blackface Twin Reverb, Tracks 87 - 90.

Feedback, Chap. 11] — no feedback on some of the tweeds, moderate amounts on the brown amps, and slightly more on the blackface and silverface amps. This decreased distortion and increased bandwidth, for more of a 'hi-fi' sound in the post-tweed Fenders compared to the grungy, roots-blues 'dirt' you hear in most tweed amps at higher volumes."

The extent to which we can generalize about circuit differences between tweed, brown/blonde, and blackface Fenders depends in part on which level of the Fender line we're talking about. Let's separate the low-end models from the rest of the line. Greg Huntington: "Looking at the mid-size and larger brownface amps — some in blonde, some in brown — those circuits are virtually *identical*, whether they are in a rough blonde Tolex piggyback Bandmaster or, say, the equivalent brown amp, the Super. While they are very similar to each other, they are collectively *different* from the tweeds or blackface amps that might seem similar or carry the same model name." However, the same cannot be said for the smaller amps, where the same circuit might be found in both tweed and brown models, or in both brown and blackface models. Greg Huntington: "A brown Princeton, for example, is virtually identical to a tweed Vibrolux. A brown 6G2 Princeton is identical to the blackface, black Tolex 6G2 Princeton."

The other major changes that distinguished the blackface period occurred in the Bright switch, tone stacks, treble controls, tremolo, and of course the most significant innovation in years, the addition of onboard reverb.

Bright Switch

The Bright switch is found in both channels on many Fender guitar amps (we're excluding the two-channel Bassmans here, which had a "Deep" switch on one channel). It was introduced on most of the high-end models at the start of the blackface era in 1963. Leo Fender told this author that he saw the Bright switch as performing the same function as that of the earlier presence control (Chap. 11), and indeed, both are used to increase perceived brightness, although with different methods. Many players prefer the extra range of control provided by the variable presence knob vs. the newer two-position Bright switch.

Pre-blackface amps with presence controls included the Super, Bandmaster, Bassman, Concert, Pro, Showman, and Twin; all dropped the presence knob and were fitted with Bright switches when they went to their blackface versions.

(The blonde Tremolux did not have a presence circuit, but it did add Bright switches in blackface.) Fender continues to use Bright switches on amps such as the Hot Rod Deluxe, Hot Rod DeVille, and the 100W Twin Amp, as well as on the reissues where authenticity calls for it, such as the '65 Super Reverb.

Amp tech and columnist Terry Buddingh: "A Bright switch is simple. All it does is add a small capacitor across the volume pot. Being tied to the volume pot, its effect is stronger at lower volume settings. In that regard, it functions more like one of those Loudness switches you see on hi-fi's, to compensate for our non-linear hearing. If the Bright switch sounds a little harsh at low volumes, you can change the 120pF capacitor across the pot to a lower value, about half.

"The Bright switch's origin goes back to a small capacitor in some of the tweed 5E and 5F series amps built in the mid to late '50s [namely the "pro" models such as the Super, Pro, and Twin; on the other hand, the Champ, Princeton, Harvard, Deluxe, Tremolux, and Vibrolux did not have this feature]. The Bright channel had the capacitor — usually 100pF — which shunted highs around the volume control, just like the later amps' Bright switch. Back in the tweed days, you plugged into the Bright channel to access the cap, instead of flicking a switch."

Clean-cut and fully loaded: With all this blackface firepower, these lads could blow the punch bowl across the rec room. Let's hope the volumes are below 2 as they rip through "Penetration" and "Wipe Out." Typical of Fender imagery in the mid 1960s, this photo appears in the *Fender Electric Guitar Course, Book Two.*

Plate-Driven Tone Stacks

As noted previously, Mr. Fender used cathode-follower tone stacks in certain Fenders dating back to the 1950s, including some tweed Bandmasters and the legendary 5F6/5F6-A Bassmans and 5F8/5F8-A Twins.

Fender Strat, serial no. 6704, with the Vibrolux Reverb that belonged to the late Clarence White, a member of the Kentucky Colonels and later the Byrds, co-inventor of the B-Bender, and a profoundly influential musician in both electric and acoustic guitar circles.

This concept carried over into the brown/blonde era, where we see cathode followers in the Bass channels of the blonde Tolex 6G6, 6G6-A, and 6G6-B piggyback Bassmans. Fender's Matt Wilkens: "In the brown/blonde era, it was a mix of cathode-follower tone stacks on the Bassmans and, in the other models, tone stacks driven off the plate. It was the plate-driven arrangement that carried over into blackface almost exclusively. Plate-driven tone stacks are important features of blackface Fenders."

New Tone Controls and Scooped Mids

Many tone stacks in brown and blonde Fenders had a tapped treble control. When you turned it down, it would actually cut the treble response. But in the blackface era, the tone controls — speaking very generally here — worked a different way. If you turned the treble all the way down, it pretty much provided a *flat* treble response, rather than an actual cut. Matt Wilkens: "I think somebody decided that being able to cut the treble was actually *too* dark, so they abandoned that in the blackface era. And I think it's fair to say this change is one of the reasons we hear the term 'scooped,' or 'scooped mids' when people describe the tone of the blackface amps compared to earlier Fenders. The browns do indeed have a midrange emphasis, whereas the blackfaces have a lot of bass, a lot of treble, and a dip in the midrange. That change in the treble control definitely contributed to that." On a frequency response curve, the characteristic midrange scoop of the blackface sound would look a little like a smiley face: high in the basses and trebles, low in the mids.

Headroom and Distortion

One of the strongest threads running through Mr. Fender's career was the quest for cleaner sounds at higher volumes, or more headroom. This pursuit found its ultimate expression in the blackface amps. The browns and blondes were generally cleaner than the tweeds, for several reasons — the evolution of tubes, for one; the markedly higher power supply voltages for another. But Fender's idea with the blackface amps was to strive for an even cleaner sound, and the tone stacks and feedback circuitries were adjusted with that goal in mind. In the case of an amp like the Twin, for example, the idea was simple: *really clean, and really loud.*

Matt Wilkens: "The new tone stacks not only changed the way the frequencies shifted when adjusted, but they also made the amps a little more forgiving when they did distort. You could drive the amplifier into distortion, but the frequency content did not *sound* as distorted. In other words, it faked it better; it stayed cleaner and held on to some of the high frequencies even in distortion, and that too would be in keeping with Leo Fender's apparently never-ending quest for more volume and cleaner headroom."

With Speed and Intensity: Tremolo Evolves

Tremolo is a change in *amplitude*, which is the strength or level of a signal. For our purposes, we can think of amplitude as volume. You can approximate a tremolo effect with the volume knob on your guitar or amp. The amount of fluctuation in amplitude is typically called "intensity" or "depth," and the tempo of the shift is called "speed" or "rate."

Early Vibro-Champ from 1964, basically an AA764 Champ with tremolo.

The somewhat similar *vibrato* effect is a change in pitch, which is why a Stratocaster's whammy bar is technically a hand vibrato. So, wavering your guitar's volume up and down in a rhythmic fashion (with a knob) and wavering its pitch up and down in a rhythmic fashion (with a whammy bar, or your fretting finger) produces somewhat similar yet distinguishable tremolo and vibrato effects, respectively.

Just as Leo Fender called his Stratocaster's vibrato a tremolo, he also called his tremolo circuit a vibrato (except when he called it a tremolo). Fender guitars and amps are so influential that their technically incorrect use of these terms over half a century has contributed to the interchangeability of "vibrato" and "tremolo" among many players and much of the industry. Even experts sometimes use the terms interchangeably, not because they don't know any better but simply because the practice is so common. This book often uses "vibrato" in reference to a channel, because that's what it says on the face plate, and the more accurate "tremolo" in reference to the circuit. In any case, both tremolo and vibrato allow for variations in effect from slow, woozy undulations to staccato hummingbird heartbeats. Fender amps employed several methods of achieving tremolo over the years. Although they all entailed tube oscillators, they produced noticeably different results.

Power Tube Grid Bias Tremolo

In the early days, Fender achieved the tremolo effect by modulating an amplifier's power tube grid bias. Various authorities refer to this method as "grid bias" or "bias modulation" tremolo. The first Fender with trem was the historic cathode-biased Tremolux of 1955, and it tapped the phase inverter tube's cathode. According to Teagle & Sprung: "… as the signal from the oscillator 'collided' with the bias voltage, the tube would be shut down and turned back on in synch with the oscillator." Potentiometers connected to the amp's Depth and Speed knobs regulated the effect.

A variation appeared in later amps with fixed biasing, including some of the Tremoluxes and several of the browns (Vibrolux, Vibroverb, Deluxe). They used a 7025 or 12AX7 oscillator tube to modulate the bias of the power tubes.

Multi-Tube, Split-Signal Tremolo

The brown Tolex Vibrasonic, its companions in the Professional Amplifiers of the early '60s — Bandmaster, Pro, Super, Concert, Twin — and also the Showman all featured what Fender called "Harmonic Vibrato," a new and more complex sounding circuit. Where the earlier method had employed a single dual triode (or in some cases half of a dual triode) and had worked in the output section, the new arrangement used at least two tubes (and sometimes three)

Although James Burton is best known for his work with Ricky Nelson, Elvis Presley, and Emmylou Harris, and Glen Campbell is a country music star, both also have distinguished histories as session players. Here they work together in the 1960s, Glen with a custom Mosrite and James with his signature Telecaster. James Burton told Steve Fishell: "My main guitar was always the '53 Tele, and I used it on all the records. I had a Fender Deluxe and a Twin at that time, but I was using a Fender Vibrasonic with a 15 inch Lansing speaker quite a bit on the early sessions with Ricky. I also used a Fender Concert a lot. I liked a lot of presence and clear notes. I didn't really like that fuzzy or thin sound." With Elvis, James often used a Twin Reverb onstage and a Deluxe in the studio.

and worked on the preamp signal. The signal was split into high and low-frequency components that were set against each other to create a particularly lush tremolo effect.

Mark Baier: "I think many people consider the trem like we see in the brown Concert to be the mother of all tremolos. It was a unique way of achieving the effect, a pretty radical approach. Leo must have been feeling especially creative. A high/low pass filter network divides the frequencies — some above a certain point, and some below that point — and they go through an oscillator, which turns them on and off; then they are flipped 180 degrees out of phase and are recombined. When the high frequencies are going down, the low frequencies are coming up, and vice-versa. The effect is, the highs and the lows swirl around each other."

Matt Wilkens: "This scheme modulated the bias of a tube that was used as a dedicated gain element. In the 6G12 Concert, to pick an example, the high-frequency side and the low-frequency side switch back and forth in a smooth, sinusoidal fashion. The phase difference between the two halves is what makes it such a nice effect in the more expensive brown amps. Remember, other bias schemes were used in the more economical amps during that same time. Grid bias (bias modulation) tremolo was used in some tweeds (5F11 Vibrolux, 5G9 Tremolux) and some browns (Vibroverb, Tremolux, Vibrolux). The tweed 5E9-A Tremolux modulated the bias of the phase splitter."

Fender's patent for this tremolo (2,973,681) was filed on June 8, 1959 and granted on March 7, 1961. U.S. Patent Office documents specify that, "The out-of-phase relationship should be such that the higher-frequency components are at peak amplitude while the lower-frequency components are at minimum amplitude, and vice-versa .... The illustrated circuit generates and makes use of two equal and opposite tremolo waves .... The end product is *neither a conventional tremolo nor a conventional vibrato*, but is instead a tremolo in which predetermined bands of frequencies in each note are alternately suppressed and enhanced in a certain manner [emphasis added]."

Hartley Peavey speculates that an article written by Richard H. Dorf in the April 1954 edition of *Radio Television News* might have inspired the new Fender circuit. Mr. Peavey has analyzed the schematic and concluded that "the net result is a rather effective tube type tremolo with some accompanying phase shift." He adds, "The first edition of Fender's variant came out in the [Vibrasonic] and was extended to the first Concert. Fender later added another tube and made its circuit even more like Dorf's article ... this required six 12AX7/7025s along with the output tubes, and I believe this was done in '60 or '61 [as seen in the 6G8 Twin's schematic, for example]. This in no way diminishes what Leo and his team accomplished but simply points out that they adapted technology as much as they innovated ... most of the tube amps today (including our own) can trace their lineage back to those units presented to the marketplace in the late '50s and early '60s by Leo and company."

Princeton Reverb. Seymour Duncan: "I went to Trans-Maximus Studios in Memphis with Steve Cropper. Jeff Beck recorded some of his best stuff there. They had a little Princeton Reverb up on a table, and it had an old Shure microphone stuck in front of it, and all the knobs were cranked all the way up. Jeff was using a Stratocaster back then, and you can really hear the sound of that amp."

Hear the Princeton Reverb, Tracks 56 - 57.

Riding with the King: In another one of those "doesn't get much cooler than this" moments, B.B. King, Eric Clapton and Elvin Bishop put a trio of blackface Fenders to good use during an impromptu jam session. B.B. told *Guitar Player* magazine: "When they first made the Twin, I used it all the time because I never found another amp that satisfied me like it did." Albert Garcia of Fender: "The Twins that B.B. didn't like were ['70s] models where they added things like a master volume, a gain control, a more powerful output and power supply that upped the power from 85 watts to 100, and finally to 135 watts. But now we have the '65 Twin reissue." B.B. King: "I still use the Twin because they returned to the old way of making them, and I again started to find the sound that I used to hear."

These amps are bookends of a classic Fender model, generally representing the beginning and end of the non-reverb blackface Deluxes. The one on the left is a production no. 1 amp, dated MI, or September '63. The other one is virtually unused, with all the extras — cover, footswitch, warranty card, schematic, and brochure. It's dated OL, or December '65.

Blackface Photocell Tremolo

The multi-tube approach of the early 1960s was "partsy" and expensive, and this consideration became even more acute when Fender added reverb to many of the blackface amps. Matt Wilkens: "That's when they went to a less parts-intensive tremolo that allowed them to fit a reverb section in there. I think they really wanted to stick with a small tube tray — they just wanted to keep the six small tubes across the back. This is conjecture on my part, but with those multi-tube tremolos, I think they took a look and said, 'If we're gonna get a reverb in there, something's gotta go.' Look at the 6G8 Twin. It has *three* 7025s, just for the tremolo. Expensive, yet effective! You couldn't fit a reverb in there, which is why the blonde one was a Twin and not a Twin Reverb."

Mark Baier: "That tremolo with multiple tubes does have an incredibly high parts count, and they might have been looking for something more economical. They might also have discontinued it because they thought the high/low pass filter network stepped on the tone a little bit."

Fender's records reveal that the "official" introduction of the new trem was January 1964, but they had been shipping blackface amps with the new circuit since July of '63, in the high-end AA763 amps with trem. The new circuit employed a photocell/neon bulb arrangement. Matt Wilkens: "This is a light-dependent resistor, or LDR. When you turn the Speed knob, you're turning a variable, low-speed oscillator, and that flashes the neon bulb at the rate of your choosing, which turns on the LDR, which shunts signal to ground [like a level control], which causes an attenuation. Basically it just takes a signal and cuts it out at

Hotel room jam '83: Keith Richards and Ronnie Wood double up on a blackface Deluxe Reverb.

Hear the blackface Deluxe Reverb, Tracks 13 - 21.

a selected speed, and that's what tremolo is, as opposed to warbling the pitch in a true vibrato. Almost all blackfaces have a photocell tremolo." Exceptions include the Princeton, Princeton Reverb, and Vibro Champs, which kept the power tube grid bias trem.

Comparing Fender Trems

The original grid bias tremolo of the tweed era is smooth and pleasing. The highly acclaimed, multi-tube type of the early 1960s is also smooth, with a bit of perceived phase shifting for an especially lush effect. The photocell trem of the blackface era is a little more abrupt, a bit choppier than either of the two earlier types. All three general tremolo types are highly regarded, and each has its fans.

The complex tremolo of the blonde and brown Fenders is one reason why those amps are so highly esteemed among many players. Mark Baier: "I like the brown Concert type of tremolo because of that a little bit of pitch shifting going on, and it doesn't cut out completely like the effect you can get with the photocell tremolo."

Pitch shifting? It's often been said that Fender never produced an amp with true vibrato, but Matt Wilkens offers this qualification: "When you're talking about perception, I think the brown-era, multiple tube 'Vibrato' channel *did* in fact have a true vibrato. The phase shift caused a pitch shift, which is the definition of vibrato, so despite the conventional wisdom, I would call that circuit a phase-shift vibrato. Some of the [early '60s] Fenders used three tubes instead of two, and there were variations in the circuits, but the end result was a phase shift in each case."

Mark Baier: "Because of the way that circuit was designed, you do get some additive and subtractive phase elements. People sometimes call it a pitch shifting device. Technically, it's not, but the highs and lows do beat against each other, and you can perceive a little bit of that swirling effect."

Matt Wilkens: "I somewhat agree with Mark about the phase shift vibrato, in that it did not change pitch, but when the high-pass and low-pass sections are summed together, the frequencies that are affected by both the high-pass and low-pass sections (in the crossover region) do shift. Alternately, the high-pass phase 'lead' network dominates; then the low-pass phase 'lag' network dominates. As the output of the circuit goes from phase-lead (high frequency) dominant to phase-lag (low frequency) dominant, the pitch goes down. From lag to lead dominant, the pitch goes up."

We're deep into semantics. As is often the case with audio, there's a difference here between technical specs and perceptions. Greg Huntington: "As an electrical engineer, I can tell you there is no phase shifting going on, and no pitch shift. However, as a guitarist, I agree that the interplay between the volume-modulation of the highs and the volume-modulation of the lows running 180 degrees out of phase with each other creates a perception of pitch shifting, and sure enough, it sounds sort of like vibrato."

The Real Thing: Fender Reverb

Whether we're talking about onboard circuits or separate, stand-alone units, Leo Fender's reverb set standards for the entire industry. As Bedrock's Jay Abend told a group of his fellow amp manufacturers in *Guitar Player*, "If you put spring reverb in a tube amp, you've got to live up to the Fender reverb legacy."

The reverb effect is achieved by splitting the preamplified signal and routing part of it through a series of springs of differing lengths whose coils delay the sound. The delayed sound is then combined with the original signal. More specifically, as Ritchie Fliegler explains, "the reverb effect is achieved by splitting the preamplified signal and then boosting the 'to be reverbed' part a good bit. Then that boosted energy is sent through transducers that convert the electrical energy into mechanical energy in a fashion similar to what happens in a speaker — only this time a spring is being driven instead of a paper cone. As one set of springs vibrates in tune with the original signal, the other set feels the sympathetic vibrations in much the same way a loud electric guitar in a music store sets off the acoustic guitars in the same room.

"That delayed mechanical energy and the continuing decaying vibration is picked up by another set of transducers to be turned back into an electrical signal. The delayed sound is then combined with the original signal, and the blend of the two can be adjusted with various controls."

On Fender's classic outboard device (and on the modern Fender amps that integrate the same circuit — Dual Professional and Vibro-King), the Dwell control adjusts the amount of signal sent to the reverb "tank," or

pan, and the Mixer knob adjusts the balance between the "dry" (unreverbed) and "wet" (reverbed) signals. The Tone knob affects only the reverbed portion of the signal.

Mr. Fender's development of his reverberation circuit was similar to many of his contributions, in that he drew upon existing concepts and adapted them in new ways to create products that not only met the requirements of the musicians of the day but also inspired new sounds and techniques. The Hammond Organ Company had already created a multiple-spring reverb circuit for its popular home keyboard systems (basing it in part upon still earlier inventions by Bell Labs), and Mr. Fender licensed Hammond's basic Type 4 reverb design for his own products.

When we think of heavy reverb, we often think of surf music and Fender-fueled records by the Surfaris, the Ventures, and of course surf guitar king Dick Dale. But as this author wrote in *The Stratocaster Chronicles*, "Popular stereotypes to the contrary, surf music was rooted not in some romanticized vision of a sandy, palm-tree paradise but rather in gritty late-'50s and early-'60s R&B, as well as the raucous guitar and sax instrumentals of Duane Eddy, Link Wray, the Fireballs, Johnny & the Hurricanes, and local hero Dick Dale."

Dick Dale told *Guitar Player*'s John Blair: "The wet, splashy sound of Fender reverb had nothing to do with creating the 'surf sound.' It was only later that reverb and surf music became synonymous. The reverb came about after I explained to Leo Fender and Freddie Tavares, his number one man, that I didn't have a natural vibrato in my voice, and that my live show was ninety-five percent singing, and my guitar played the lead while I sang. I wanted to sustain my voice like a piano sustain pedal. I told Leo I had a Hammond organ at home, and it had a button that gave you a reverb sound. Leo built a device that had a Hammond Organ Company spring tank mounted inside, and when I plugged a Shure Dynamic 'birdcage' microphone into it, I was able to sing and sound like Elvis. That was the birth of the Fender reverb. Later, when I plugged my Stratocaster into the reverb and played some of my instrumentals, it was icing on the cake. Only then did my Fender reverb sound become associated with surf music."

Once surf music evolved to its familiar reverb-drenched incarnation, the splashy, bottom-of-the-well sound became inseparable from the style. As Dan Dugmore told writer Dan Forte: "It was surf music time. I had a Bandmaster with the separate Fender reverb unit, too. That was so important. I said, 'This is what makes these guys sound so good.' My parents said, 'Dan, you don't need that little box, too, do you?' 'Yes! This is the whole reason it sounds that way.'"

As noted elsewhere in this book, it's an oversimplification to think of the brown Vibroverb and the reverb-equipped blackfaces as being otherwise identical to their non-reverb predecessors. Fender's Matt Wilkens: "The addition of reverb was a significant change, not only because it added this lush, very desirable effect, but also because it rearranged some of the amplifiers' internal architecture. This is one of several reasons why we hear differences in the sounds of the blackface reverb amps compared to the nonreverb tweeds, browns, blondes, and blackfaces."

Fender's reverb remains the gold standard for the worldwide guitar amp industry. As Barry Cleveland explained in a *Guitar Player* review of Fender's brown Tolex 1963 reissue reverb kit, "Though you commonly find spring reverb patches in modeling units and digital reverbs, they never totally nail the luscious sounding ambience of the real thing."

"When I started at Fender, the amps didn't have reverb. We added reverb, but reverb was a problem because you couldn't jar the amp at all. I got to thinking. I had a neighbor that had a plastics house, and I got to talking to him. What we wound up doing, we put the reverb springs in a vinyl bag, so it would 'float' inside that cabinet. It was suspended; it had some give. It was a little crude, but it helped. If you hit the cabinet directly, naturally it would get upset, but if the entertainer just stomped his foot on the bandstand, it wasn't going to shake up that reverb spring."

—Bill Sterle

Introduced in 1963, the Electronic Echo Chamber combined a transistorized circuit with a tape-type delay variable to 400 milliseconds.

The Non-Reverb, Mid-Power Blackfaces

The non-reverb blackface Bandmaster, Concert, Pro, Tremolux, and Vibrolux (see photo, page 276) all appeared with AA763 circuits in the late summer or fall of 1963, except for the AA763 Vibrolux (early 1964). All five had outputs in the 35W to 40W range, and all shared a pair of 7025s in the preamp, a pair of 6L6GC/5881s in the power amp, fixed bias (with an adjustment pot), a 12AX7 photoresistor trem, and a 12AT7 long-tail phase inverter.

It seems sensible at first glance to subdivide these amps by cabinetry: two piggybacks and three combos. But internally some of their similarities and differences are unrelated to cab design. For example, the piggyback Bandmaster and combo Concert had solid state rectifiers; the other three had GZ34 tubes.

As we have seen in other families, these somewhat similarly circuited Fenders also differed in speaker complement: Vibrolux (one 12), Pro (one 15), Tremolux (now with two 10s, with rare 1x12 exceptions), Bandmaster (two 12s), and Concert (four 10s). Within this five-amp group, subgroups also differed in their transformers and output impedances.

All five had Normal and Vibrato channels, although the Vibrolux's Vibrato channel was mislabeled "Normal" (at least on some models), seemingly providing a baffling choice between "Normal" and "Normal." All five had black control panels with black knobs. However, the Bandmaster and Tremolux had smooth blonde Tolex cabs and gold sparkle grille cloth from November 1963 to June 1964. Cosmetically, these "transitional" piggybacks are in the blonde group, but in terms of their circuits, they are full-fledged blackface amps.

In their non-reverb blackface incarnations, the Vibrolux would last only three months (from January through

The AA763 non-reverb, mid-power blackfaces shared similar outputs, preamp tubes, power tubes, a fixed bias, a 12AT7 phase inverter, and a photoresistor tremolo.

Jeff Beck. Equipment tech Andy Roberts told *Guitar* magazine: "When we go into the studio, we'll take a selection of guitars and amps, but nine times out of ten he'll use a Jeff Beck Signature model and a Fender Twin Reverb." Co-producer and engineer Leif Mases, on Beck's 1993 *Crazy Legs* album, in *Guitar Player*: "We used four amps simultaneously for the solos. We ran a Tremolux … and a Bassman in parallel, miking them with Shure SM-57s and tube Neumann U47s. Both amps were in a dry-sounding wood room. A Fender Concert amp with a 2x12 cab was placed in a stone room for ambience. We put a Twin in an echo chamber we discovered under the stone room, and fed a signal from the Concert to the Twin's speakers." Producer Stuart Colman added: "The Concert's cabinet was set on its back, facing upwards, and we placed a mike at the ceiling. That gave us a thick, wide sound."

March of 1964), the Concert and Pro until 1965, the Tremolux until '66, and the Bandmaster until '67. After their one to four-year lifespans, these original blackfaces would meet different fates.

The Vibrolux was succeeded by the Vibrolux Reverb ('64 to '67); both versions were offered for a period in 1964. Similarly, the Pro was succeeded by the Pro Reverb ('65 to '67), which overlapped it during 1965. The blackface Bandmaster was followed in 1968 by both reverb and nonreverb Bandmasters with new circuits and silverface cosmetics.

Although the Concert model name was revived in later decades for higher-powered models, the original 40W Concert was not succeeded by a reverb model or even a silverface nonreverb version. After gracing the Fender catalogs for 11 years, it was the end of the line for the Tremolux; it was quietly dropped from production after September 1966.

The Mid-Power Blackface Reverbs

The mid-'60s, mid-power blackface reverbs included the Super Reverb ('63 to '67), the short-lived Vibroverb ('63 to '64), the Pro Reverb ('65 to '67), and the Vibrolux Reverb ('64 to '67). They shared many features beyond their typical blackface cosmetics — black skirted knobs, silver sparkle grilles, etc. Each had a 7025 in the Normal channel, and a second 7025 as well as one-half of a third 7025 in the Vibrato channel. Each had two 6L6GC power tubes, a 12AT7 long tail phase inverter, fixed adjustable bias, a GZ34 rectifier tube, a 12AX7 photoresistor tremolo circuit, and a reverb circuit with a 12AT7 driver and one-half of a 7025 for recovery.

Each had nine knobs except for the ten-knob Super Reverb, which had an added mid control in the Vibrato channel. Rather than presence controls, all had Bright switches for both channels. All were 40W amps except for the Vibrolux Reverb, which put out about 35W due to its smaller, lower-voltage transformer.

These amps arrived at their blackface reverb incarnations through different routes. In some cases, performance features were added to the amps' predecessors to result in new models; in other cases, features remained generally the same while exterior cosmetics were changed. The Vibrolux Reverb and Pro Reverb added the reverb effect to nonreverb blackface versions. On the other hand, the all-new blackface Vibroverb succeeded the already reverb-equipped brown Vibroverb. The Super was altered in both respects, evolving from the brown nonreverb version to the blackface Super Reverb.

Most bewildering of all, the speaker complement of every one of these amps differed from that of its immediate predecessor. The Pro went from one 15 to two 12s in the Pro Reverb, the Super from two 10s to four 10s in the Super Reverb, the Vibrolux from one 12 to two 10s in the Vibrolux Reverb, and the brown Vibroverb from two 10s to one 15 in the black Vibroverb. As noted elsewhere, the blackface Super Reverb's closest ancestor wasn't the Super at all, but rather the 4x10 brown Concert, and before that the 4x10 tweed Bassman. There are many such examples, all revealing how Fender model names often failed to reflect the evolution of circuits or features.

Pete Townshend: "I had a Fender Pro and a Fender Vibrasonic and a Fender Bassman top, and I used to drive Marshall 4x12s with those amplifiers, and when I heard Hiwatt I was over the moon, because they sounded to me much more like a really good, top line, mid-'60s Fender amp."

from *Guitarist Magazine*, Feb. 2005

"The people whose tone I like still are B.B. King and Otis Rush, because they are back to playing with Twin Reverbs, just naked. The emotion creates all the things that you are supposed to create, not the gadgets."

— Carlos Santana

The mid-power blackface reverbs.

 *Hear the blackface Super Reverb, Tracks 60 - 70.*

 *Hear the blackface Vibrolux Reverb, Tracks 32 - 41.*

Super Reverb-Amp
FENDER ELECT. INST. CO.
Fender
Vibroverb Amp
FENDER ELECT. INST. CO.
Fender
Pro Reverb Amp
FENDER MUSICAL INSTRUMENTS
Fender
Vibrolux Reverb-Amp
FENDER ELECTRIC INSTRUMENT CO.

The incomparable Danny Gatton used a variety of Fender amps throughout his too-brief life: late-'50s Twins, a Super Reverb, Bassman reissues, modified Vibroverb reissues, Vibro-Kings, and others.

Eric Johnson's stage rig employs a pair of blackface Deluxe Reverbs.

Robbie Krieger on recording his solo in the Doors' "Light my Fire": "I got the tone simply by plugging my Melody Maker into a Fender Twin Reverb and cranking the amp up to 10."

"All the great [bouzouki] players play Fender Twins with everything but the bass on 10, including the reverb. It's brain-splitting treble … There's incredible music from around Lake Toba in Sumatra, Indonesia, called Batak, which they play on little guitars called Kecapi. They're traditional musicians, but … if they had access to a Fender Twin, they'd certainly use it."

— Ben Mandelson, head of GlobeStyle Records, a world-music label based in London, in *Guitar Player*

Derek Trucks on his '64 Super Reverb: "I found it in a pawn shop and got it for a steal. I haven't found any amps that have matched it. I've definitely looked, but I haven't found any that have a truer tone."

Postcard from the edge: "TV tray" Fender amps lounging at lakeside, 1968.

Left: When we think of the words "Fender Bassman," this is not the image that pops to mind. The longest lived of the first-round transistor Fenders, the 105W 3x12 Bassman with the "TV tray" control panel was made from 1966 to 1971, and it cost $595 — about 55 bucks more than a 2x15 tube Bassman (see the next chapter for details on the transistor models).

CHAPTER FIFTEEN

15

CBS and the Takeover of '65

Changing of the Guard

Many scientists believe a giant asteroid hit the earth about 65 million years ago, causing massive disruptions and aftershocks, a poisoning of the atmosphere with noxious gasses and smoke, and a long period of darkness that led to the decline and ultimately the mass extinctions of once-dominant species. Sounds like Fender after CBS.

Fender's own nuclear winter began with a painful irony. Mr. Fender not only sold his company to corporate execs who all but squandered his legacy, but he did so at the first light of an incandescent age in popular music. The new era was characterized by several phenomena that all stoked the boom in guitar manufacturing: an emphasis on virtuoso instrumental prowess, a revolution in songwriting, the rise of bands who wrote their own music over scripted, prefab teen idols, and eventually the ascent of the guitar hero as an icon of pop culture.

Fender changed hands the first week of 1965. Of that year's top twenty singles, eleven would be recorded by the Beatles, the Rolling Stones, or the Byrds. That same year, Bob Dylan released both *Highway 61 Revisited* and *Bringing It All Back Home*, and the Yardbirds released *Having a Rave Up*. The following year alone would see the release of the Beatles' *Revolver*, the Beach Boys' *Pet Sounds*, Dylan's *Blonde on Blonde*, the Rolling Stones' *Aftermath*, and other profoundly influential albums. If 1965 and 1966 were remarkable, 1967 was astonishing. *The Doors* was released in January. *Are You Experienced?* hit the record racks on May 12. Twenty days later: *Sgt. Pepper's Lonely Hearts Club Band*.

But as the sun rose on a new age in music, and on relatively young companies like Marshall and Vox, it would soon appear to have set on Fender, at least in terms of quality (in terms of dollar sales, Fender was doing just fine). By the time of the Woodstock festival in 1969, Fender amps were two years into the silverface era, and three years into the age of solid state. As we will see, the silverface tube amps were generally similar to the blackface models, at least for the first couple of years. But the first and second generation transistor amps, some of the later silverface models, and many of the Fender guitars of the 1970s didn't measure up to the amps and instruments of the 1950s and 1960s, and the prestige of the entire line suffered as a result.

At the time of the CBS acquisition, Fender occupied the nine rectangular buildings at the right of the photo. The huge CBS addition is at left.

What went wrong? Paul Rivera: "Ed Jahns and Freddie Tavares told me that the muckey-mucks at CBS felt like — We've got these country bumpkins in Fullerton. They don't know what they're doing. Let's hire some guys from Ford — they know how to mass produce stuff. So they got some auto people in there, and they changed everything, even the way they paid workers. Instead of paying them by the hour, they paid them on a per-piece basis, which fostered a different mindset. They changed inspection methods, too. These auto guys said — We don't inspect the way you guys do; we just let our dealers fix the problems. So quality control was not 'job one' at CBS back then."

Another problem was that well into the '70s, Fender's profits were supposed to make up for substantial losses in other CBS music firms. The Gulbransen organ company, for example, was founded in 1904 and acquired by CBS in 1973. According to employees during the mid '70s, Gulbransen's declining profits were offset with CBS' "creative" accounting, which left Fender unable to reap the rewards of its own successes. (According to William Schultz, the problems caused by using Fender's revenues to make up for other companies' losses persisted right up until CBS sold Fender in 1985.)

In terms of amp design, one of the biggest problems was CBS' restructuring of the relationship between R&D, marketing, and the factory. In the early days, communication had been informal but effective — basically, "Let's go to the coffee shop for ham sandwiches and iced tea, doodle a few ideas on the napkins, and talk about stuff." Such informality couldn't work in a big company, but even when Fender reorganized its production under the supervision of Forrest White in the mid 1950s and then grew substantially in the early '60s, communication among Leo Fender, Freddie Tavares, Don Randall, Forrest White, and other principals was continuous and productive.

But like many large corporations, CBS was rigidly compartmentalized and top-heavy with execs who knew more about theories of management than details of their products. Paul Rivera: "In the early CBS period, R&D was never guided by anyone in marketing who knew what the hell they were talking about. No one gave them any guidance on what path to follow to get a proper sound in an amplifier. The marketing people in CBS Fender at that time could not speak electronics, so there was a huge gap between what R&D was thinking and what marketing was requesting. CBS Fender was this big-ass country club — a lot of employees sitting around producing few products and few ideas. They had so many dumb products. I mean, the Starcaster — give me a break. If you looked at their PA systems you'd wonder, *are they even aware of what's coming out of Mississippi?* Fender was far removed from reality, and people blame those products, but it wasn't R&D's fault. It was marketing's fault, a failure of leadership."

Paul Rivera's recollections are confirmed by those of Bill Carson, already a veteran employee by the time of the CBS acquisition: "When CBS took over there was the usual fear of what a big, complex company might do to little Fender. They sent teams that didn't even know each other down there to do a variety of reports based on how the company was operating. They would talk to individuals in a nearby motel room they had rented up the street. It didn't do a whole lot for morale.

"There was a big influx of people who didn't know what the hell they were doing. Some of them had backgrounds in auto parts and all sorts of things, and they just didn't understand the music business. CBS was draining Fender to meet some numbers, because we were supporting all these sister companies that weren't making a profit like Fender was. This all trickled down to the foremen and the supervisors, and the order was: Push the product out the door. Then by the '70s, it was just miserable. Seeing this stuff go out the door that just wasn't right — guitars and amplifiers both — I almost quit a half-dozen times. We did lose a lot of very good people, just through the frustration of it.

"The new guy running amplifiers for CBS was Paul Spranger. He was an electronics guy from the aircraft industry. At first they left the circuits pretty much alone, maybe just some modest tweaking here and there, for about two or three years before Spranger started to get really wild ideas. He put out that god-awful Zodiac series. There wasn't a good amp in the bunch, I don't think. That was his baby. They also put out a bunch of god-awful little PA systems. Then there was the Contempo organ. Laughingly we called it the Contemptuous. Boy, it was a mess, a pile of junk, but thankfully people didn't buy the damn thing, so it didn't last too long. But those amps — that really hurt us."

"This all trickled down to the foremen and the supervisors, and the order was: Push the product out the door."

— Bill Carson

The 11-tube, 95 pound, 2x12 Super Twin of the mid '70s. From left, knobs 6 through 10 are EQ controls, and the last two are for distortion and output level.

CBS and Blackface Fenders: Credit Where Credit's Due

For the first several decades of Fender history, the very best of the amplifiers were built while Leo Fender ran the company. The first-generation solid state amps and many of the later silverface tube models were less stellar than the Leo-era amps, and some were downright substandard. This has led some people to assume that all CBS-era amps are inferior to all pre-CBS amps. Not true. While the deterioration in quality resulted in large measure from the cost-cutting and production compromises imposed by CBS, the decline didn't kick in until a few years after the takeover. In most significant respects, CBS Fender tube amps made from January 1965 through late 1967 are very similar in sound and performance to their pre-CBS ancestors. As we will see in discussions of silverface amps (Chap. 17), the cumulative effects of a long list of factors didn't begin to add up to noticeable problems until 1968 or later, and even then only in certain models.

CBS promptly changed the name of the company from Fender Electric Instruments to Fender Musical Instruments. On the pre-CBS amps with front control panels, the company name was printed in one of several variations: *Fender Electric Instruments*, *Fender Electric Inst.*, *Fender Elect. Inst.*, etc. CBS used up stockpiles of pre-CBS panels through the late summer or fall of '65, months after the acquisition, leading some people to wrongly conclude that their CBS Fenders are pre-CBS. The older labeling identifies pre-CBS blackfaces and some of the earliest CBS blackfaces, while the newer *Fender Musical Instruments* identifies a CBS product for sure.

Early CBS blackfaces are fine amps, practically identical to their predecessors in some cases. For example, the circuits in the 2x12 blackface Pro Reverb and the pre-CBS 1x15 blackface Pro are very similar. Teagle & Sprung went so far as to assert: "One only has to play through a blackface Pro Reverb to realize it would be a few years after CBS' takeover before a noticeable difference in quality of sound occurred. If you happen to use a Fender guitar, or other brand with single-coil pickups, the author recommends these amps as the best all-around amp ever made — by anyone."

Super Twin

The silverfaces, the first-generation solid state Fenders, and the models of the early 1980s accounted for the vast majority of amplifiers manufactured by CBS Fender; all are covered in later chapters. One exception was the mid-'70s, 12-knob Super Twin. Built for only two years, it was a complicated, 180W 2x12 screamer with several features that were most unusual for Fender, including a whopping six 6L6s and a 5-band active EQ. Covered in black Tolex, with a black grille bordered in white, it was a striking departure from the silverface look. It sported onboard distortion and other features typical of the period. Renowned for its loudness and ultra-clean sound (if not for the quality of its distortion), it was succeeded by the 180W Super Twin Reverb of the late 1970s.

Viking of volume Ted Nugent, for whom a Twin Reverb is a practice amp. Excerpts from a 1979 *Guitar Player* interview with this author:

I'm using strictly Fender Twins now. I crave Fenders. I've always used them. I've tried everything, and I've had amps built to my own specs. Nothing makes a guitar sound more like a guitar than Fender amps.

The way your band is spread out onstage, do you ever have trouble hearing yourself?
People in the next *county* don't have trouble hearing me. I use six Fender Super Twins and six Fender bottoms with two 18 inch speakers in each cabinet. Only two amps are miked for the sound system. The rest are just blasting stage volume.

CBS and the Transistor Amps

A Designer's Perspective

Bob Rissi started working for Leo Fender on August 7, 1961, doing light engineering, quality control, and electronic testing of all the amplifiers. He left in February 1963 after receiving an offer from Rickenbacker but was hired back by Fender's Forrest White in 1964, during negotiations with CBS. He reported to Paul Spranger until Bob left Fender for good on March 10, 1967. He returned to Rickenbacker and went on to design the highly regarded Transonic amplifiers used by the Jeff Beck Group, Led Zeppelin, and others. He later founded his own amp company, Risson. Here is Bob Rissi's eyewitness account of Fender's adoption of solid state amplifier design at the beginning of the CBS era.

Bob Rissi, right: "This was 1967. I'm training a new tech at the workbench. We're testing a solid state power amp, checking the percentage of distortion on the scope at different frequencies."

When CBS took over and Paul Spranger was put in charge of R&D, I accepted a position as a project engineer in the design lab. They needed someone who knew tube amplifiers inside and out, as well as someone who had studied some solid state.

I respected Paul Spranger tremendously. He was one of the most intelligent and most advanced people I've ever known, as far as solid state was concerned. He also understood tube amplification, but he wasn't reared in it the way I was.

When everything started to go bad, they put the blame on Paul, and that's not accurate. Some bad things are written about him that I don't agree with. He had education, ingenuity, and ability, but he hadn't worked in the amplifier field. He didn't really know what players wanted and hadn't worked in the practical end of it. He had been involved in military designs — the Sparrow missile or something like that for the Navy, guidance systems and so forth. If he had been used right and if CBS had worked with everybody properly, they could have worked it out.

When they put Paul in the job, they didn't give him the Freddie Tavares-type guidance that Leo had received all those years. Leo was still around for a few years after CBS came in. He was supposed to be a consultant, but it always seemed to me they sort of pushed his opinions out of the way. He didn't have much say. They didn't pay much attention. I think if they had had Leo and Freddie guiding the *sound* of the things, with Paul Spranger doing the engineering, they could have come up with a good product. The solid state product Paul designed could have been everyone's violin amp, or everyone's acoustic guitar amp, but they thought they could go after the rock guitar market with it, and then later, when they messed up production of the amps, they killed the possibility of finding *any* market for them.

I was the project engineer on almost all of Paul Spranger's solid state amplifiers. People don't realize those amplifiers were pretty doggone good quality, but there were problems. Back when Leo was running everything, the idea was, "What does the musician want?" Send it out, see if it plays in the field the way the musician wants it — lots of testing, lots of feedback. A lot of people were brought in to listen and give their opinions, and Leo designed around that. I learned from him that that's the best way to design. Design what the market wants, and the market was guitar players who had been playing through tube amps for years. But CBS had a new way of looking at it. The attitude changed. Now it was, "Fender is so big and so good, if we made something, then *we* would set the sound, the trend."

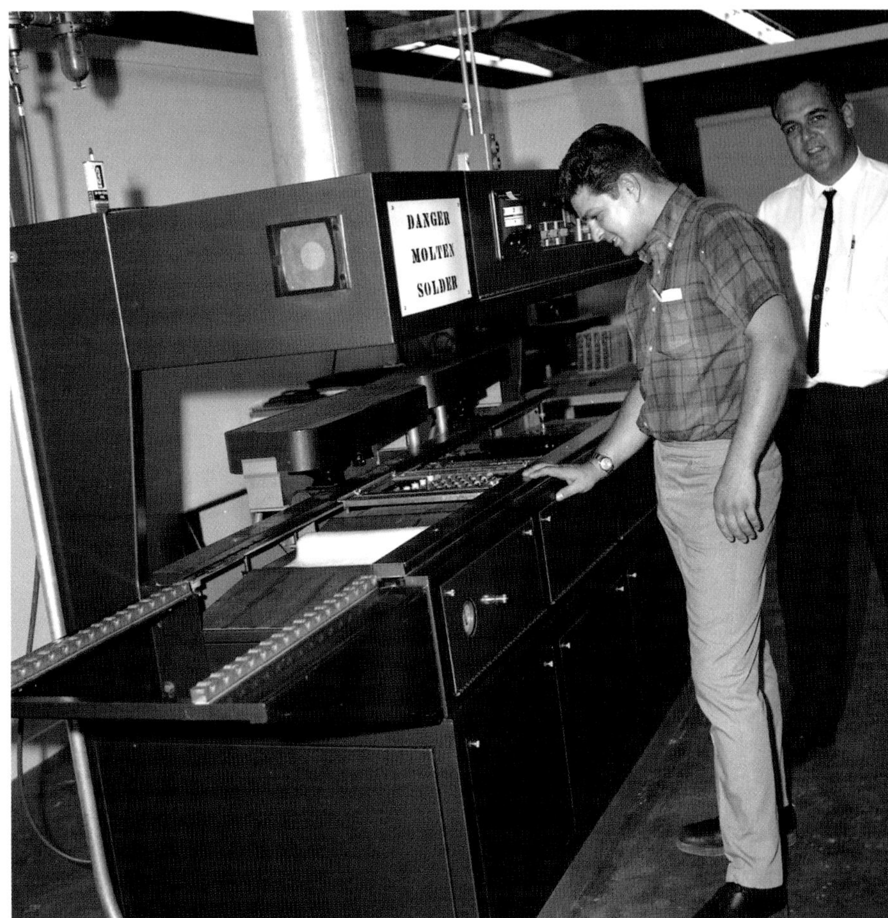

Wave solder machine, used for soldering printed circuit board assemblies at the Fender factory, mid 1960s.

The goal was to make a pure amplifier, something awesome that didn't distort. This was Paul's doing, but don't misunderstand — he was doing what I'm sure he was directed to do. No one was there to shoot that down, to tell him to do something else. You don't blame Paul for that.

On the other hand, I didn't agree with that concept, because the amplification of the guitar was always a tube thing, and you always had overtones in the sound. I noticed right away that when we started building these new amps, the PA's had an awesome clean sound, and the bass amps were good, too; they got rid of a lot of distortion. A lot of people even today like solid state bass amps. Acoustic players who were playing through a PA loved the sound. Violinists loved it. Some of the country players who wanted that bright twangy sound liked it, but the rock players noticed the lack of warmth, overtones, and the natural overdrive. They went right back to tubes.

Direct-coupling was another problem. I felt the solid state had to emulate the tube sound, but I was just a project engineer. I put my opinions out, but they weren't necessarily agreed with. In a tube amp, the voltages vary so

CBS Fender tube amps made from January 1965 through late 1967 are similar in sound and performance to their pre-CBS ancestors. They were sold alongside the new solid state models.

much between one tube and the next in the different stages that you can't just run the plate from one tube into the grid of the next one. You have to have resistors and capacitors in between them, and that changes the phase and is one of the factors that creates overtones. That was always what the guitar had sounded like through an amp.

With transistors you could take the collector of one transistor and run it right into the base of the next one. And that's what Fender did with their early solid state amps. Fender direct-coupled most everything, and the amps sounded sterile, musically. In my own solid state amps for Rickenbacker, like the Transonic, I used capacitive coupling, more like you'd have in a tube amp. It sounded really good, but Fender did nothing like that. In some versions of the amps, they did have some capacitor circuits in them to enhance tones, and Fender experimented with different transistors, but the amps didn't ever sound like a tube amp. They just sounded a little less sterile than their other ones.

When they went into production, there was considerable resistance from factory workers against shifting from old-time methods to the more cutting-edge printed circuit manufacturing. They really liked building rugged tube amps the way they had always done it. They weren't familiar with printed circuit boards or solid state equipment, and they weren't real anxious to change. It was a simple design to build, but they had some component problems, and they didn't put them together right.

When they chose the material for the printed circuit boards, that's when I decided to quit. I knew that large boards had to be made out of G10/FR4 military type Fiberglass [a laminated composite impregnated with an epoxy resin]. It didn't twist or warp under heat. At the last minute they went with Cinclad, a lower quality, less rigid material. It worked fine in Citizens' Band radios, where the boards were 2x2″ or 4x4″, but it warped in 13″ or 14″ boards like you'd see in a Twin or a Deluxe Reverb. They used flow solder machines, with the board on a little track, and it would hang and be pulled on a conveyor through a fountain of solder; it would solder beautifully on the G10/FR4 boards in the prototypes, but in production, with the lighter Cinclad boards, they warped.

I think Paul Spranger could see I wasn't going to take the blame for what I knew was about to happen. Later on they changed the process, but that's how they did it at first, and that's why I left. I went in and said, "Look, I'm not going to sign off on this. It's not going to work, and I don't want to do it." I *wanted* to build solid state amps that sounded like tubes, but I totally rejected the quality of that board. I was only 26 when I left.

Another thing: With those solid state amps, the production versions were different than the ones we had prototyped in the lab. They had procedures for how to test the products after assembly, but they really weren't testing components prior to assembly. No one in the lab — and we were the ones designing the stuff — was involved at all in assembly. I requested that they make me liaison between the lab and the factory, or at least get someone to do it, but I found out later that after I left, nobody went over there to the factory to direct them on how to build these amps.

I gave my two weeks' notice and left Fender to take a position as head of R&D at Rickenbacker before real production started at Fender. I was told that Paul was leaving Fender before my two weeks were up. When I received my letter of recommendation it was signed by Dick Evans, who took over Paul's job title.

I heard about the problems at Fender and felt many of them could have been avoided with good direction and choices. A major avoidable problem was that they had these little sockets where the transistors went in, and when they put them together they sometimes turned them around and the transistors went in backwards. It didn't show up in testing, and it didn't short, but in the field, with the wear and tear, the anodizing wore through on the heat sinks and it shorted out. The amps started blowing up. There was really nothing wrong with the design, but with the backwards transistors shorting out, that really hurt Fender.

In the first few runs, they had a high failure rate because of those Cinclad boards and having those backwards transistors in there. They were able to fix them easily — turn the transistors around and fix whatever had burned up — but it was too late. The players didn't want them fixed. By then, they didn't want them at all.

*Tom Wheeler: **Fender tube amps set standards for the world industry. Why switch to solid state with CBS? Was that your idea?***

Leo Fender: No, but I think that it was a good step for them to do, except that the item had problems in it the way they went about it.

Transistor amps are good, if you do them right.

— *Guitar Player*, May 1978

"Mr. Fender sold out in 1965, and ironically that's the year I started. There was talk of CBS putting a lot of money in and building an R&D center, and I thought, 'They're gonna roll right over me.' As it turned out, it was the best thing that happened to me. The [early] Fender gear didn't have a lot of fancy things on it — just basic, straight ahead, working man's stuff. But CBS took everything that had been done and redid it and screwed it up."

— Hartley Peavey

"I learned from Leo to design what the market wants, and the market was guitar players who had been playing through tube amps for years. Well, CBS had a new way of looking at it.

"When they chose the material for the printed circuit boards, that's when I decided to quit."

— Bob Rissi

Fender amps look right at home with artists of every style. Hank Thompson's Brazos Valley Boys continued their association with Fender, sporting new blackface amps in the mid 1960s.

According to the 1969 catalog, these paisley-clad singers and their boss band are “dazzling the world with a solid state rock-in!” First-generation transistor Fenders with “TV tray” control panels included (left to right): Deluxe Reverb, Pro Reverb, Super Reverb, Bassman (in rear), Twin Reverb, and Vibrolux Reverb.

CHAPTER SIXTEEN

16

Trial and Error

The Solid State Experiment

At the time of the CBS acquisition, no other company on earth could match Fender's amplifier line. It was the largest in Fender's 19-year history, with 18 tube-based blackface models. These included updates of familiar amplifiers such as the Pro, Deluxe, Princeton, Champ, Bassman, Bandmaster, and Tremolux; plus blackface versions of amps that had appeared for the first time in brown or blonde cabs from 1960 to 1963 (Concert, Showman 12, Showman 15, Double Showman, Vibroverb); plus the Super Reverb, which had replaced the brown 2x10 Super; the Twin Reverb, which had replaced the blonde Twin; the new Vibro Champ; as well as the reverb-equipped updates of recent blackface models: Deluxe Reverb, Princeton Reverb, and Vibrolux Reverb.

The new parent corporation soon changed the name of the Fender Electric Instrument Company to Fender Musical Instruments. For the next 15 years, the amp line would evolve on two general fronts. First, from 1966 to 1971, Fender would embrace and then temporarily abandon solid state amplifier technology. Second, the styling and circuits of the tube models would evolve from blackface to silverface.

The Gamble

In the mid 1960s, Leo Fender, his immediate successors, and pretty much everybody else in electronics and audio thought that transistorized (solid state) circuits would generally replace tube-based technologies. They were right. The vast majority of tube-based devices, including many guitar amps, would one day be replaced by solid state units. But back then, the promising new transistors remained untested in musical gear, and many of the more subtle aspects of tube performance did not translate to the newfangled solid state circuits. It would take years of development and a pile of substandard products before transistor amps would be refined to the point where discriminating musicians would accept them.

Fender faced the same challenges as other companies bold enough to invest in transistorized products in the early days. The distinctions between the operation of tubes and transistors in guitar amps are numerous and complex, but among the most significant are differences in the transient response (how the amp reacts to a note's attack) and the reproduction of harmonics, particularly when the amp is clipping. Compared to their warm sounding, tube-based

Bob Rissi: "I felt as though solid state was doomed from the start at Fender, if only by the lack of cooperation and bad attitude between those who designed the line and those who were to produce and sell it." See his account in the previous chapter.

counterparts, the first-generation transistor Fenders and other early solid state amps were routinely described as sterile or clinical sounding at low to moderate volumes. When pushed into distortion, solid state amps were criticized as sounding harsh, strident, or unmusical compared to the "fatness" or "crunch" of tube amps pushed toward their limits. According to internal documents intended only for circulation among Fender technicians and marketers, CBS engineers — who were designing both tube and solid state products at the time — announced that in their view, "no solid state amp will ever duplicate the sound of a tube amp."

Another key distinction: When tubes fail, they often do so gradually. Performance suffers, but an amp with tired tubes may still get you through a gig, and the problem is often fixed with a simple tube replacement. By contrast, when solid state components fail, they sometimes take down other components with them. The consequences can include total amp failure and substantial repair bills.

Fender's fizzled experiment started in the summer of 1966 and lasted until 1971. Not every at-bat results in a home run, and musicians can forgive the occasional strikeout, but in retrospect the early solid state Fenders seemed to thumb their little transistorized noses at everything Leo Fender stood for. Not only did they sound tinny, but (a gasp of disbelief is appropriate here) they were also unreliable. These were the amps that fried their components, the ones Bill Carson hated, the ones that compelled Forrest White to walk away from his job in disgust.

Solid State, Round One

One of the more unfortunate aspects of the early solid state debacle is that CBS squandered a good measure of its most precious resource — Fender's reputation for quality — by attaching the model names of long-revered tube amps to several of the doomed transistorized newcomers. In 1966 and 1967, CBS introduced the 105W, 3x12 piggyback Bassman, the 105W, 2x12 Twin Reverb (its speakers were mounted vertically rather than side by side), the 56W, 2x12 Pro Reverb, the 56W, 4x10 Super Reverb, the 42W, 2x10 Vibrolux Reverb, the 2x15 Dual Showman, and the 32W, 1x12 Deluxe Reverb. All but the Bassman had dual channels, Bright switches, and "Vibrato."

The styling — "assures a modern look for years to come" — was unlike anything Fender had ever done, or would ever do again. Alongside a couple of conventional amps onstage, one of these transistor Fenders would stand out like a hickey on prom night. The vented, slant-top control panels seemed as big as TV trays and were rendered in silver colored metal with oversized, flat-top knobs that looked like aluminum checkerboard pieces. But the starship control pod styling was the least of their problems. They were prone to failure and sterile sounding. A few of these models were so decisively rejected by guitar players that they remained in the line for only a year or two. The solid state Bassman would hang on until 1971.

Just Don't Plug Into Them

"CBS brought in a bunch of guys from aerospace, and they had all been building solid state. We had already tried solid state. In fact, I was instrumental in going out to Motorola in Arizona, getting solid state devices to try in our amps. I told their engineer, 'Look, we need something that can take a hundred watts, more like 175 when you look at the surges.' Now, that's a lot of heat that you've got to get rid of. Motorola gave me some samples of [components], but they just wouldn't cut the mustard.

"So these CBS guys who came out of aerospace, they said, well, we can build a solid state amp. I tried to tell them, a guitar is brutal on a circuit, and it would just *cremate* those early solid state things. They told me to mind my own business. They're in charge, so okay.

"This was in the very earliest days of CBS. They built a bunch of solid state amps, took them to the music trade show. We had four at the show and something like eight in backup, back in Fullerton. The first day out, three amps died at the show. We had to fly out four more. They received them. Two hours later, we get another phone call. Those were dying. We kept sending them amps, but it got to where we couldn't do anything more, so when people at the show said, 'Can I try the amp?', they just told them, 'No, these are for display purposes only.' They wrote orders just on the appearance of them, and they built thousands. You wouldn't believe how many of those amps came back."

—Bill Sterle

The Super Showman XFLs

A couple of years after the appearance of the earliest transistorized Fenders, CBS added a pair of giant piggyback Super Showmans to the line, the XFL-1000 and XFL-2000. The circuit design was novel, even radical: The heads were preamps, and the speaker cabs contained the power amps. The styling, while still a departure for Fender, was much cleaner than the TV tray/control pod motif. It looks fresh and modern to this day.

Each of these behemoths had two 70W power amps (140W total). The XFL-1000 had four 12s; the XFL-2000 had eight 10s. The whole idea was a mix-and-match approach. Fender offered a stock rig for $1,495 featuring the Super Showman preamp/head and two powered 4x12 cabs for a total output of 280W; you could add or subtract speakers and power depending on your needs.

The XFLs were products of their time, back when amps typically were not miked in concert and were expected to fill the hall by themselves. Power was status, and volume was king. Accordingly, the titanic new Fenders were built and priced on a scale scarcely imaginable back in Leo Fender's day, or today for that matter. The top of the line Super Showman XFL-2000 had a mind-boggling 16 JBL speakers (although you could add even more if you really wanted to) and listed for an equally mind-boggling $2,443 in 1969 — more than $12,000 in today's currency.

To look at it another way, instead of buying the XFL-2000 rig, you could stick with tubes and for the same budget buy a brand new Twin Reverb with JBLs, a piggyback Bassman, a piggyback Bandmaster Reverb, and a Super Reverb, and still have enough dough left over for a few weekends in a cheap motel. It seems unlikely that any guitarist in his or her right mind would pay for a rig that, price wise, made today's top of the line boutique models look like practice amps, but Fender reasoned: *If you can plug your whole band into it, it's not such a bad deal.*

These sophisticated, powerful amplifiers were conceived by Seth Lover, best known for his design of Gibson's humbucking PAF, the most storied pickup of all time. Fender had lured him away from Kalamazoo with a hefty pay raise a couple of years after the CBS acquisition. Mr. Lover told *Vintage Guitar*'s Stephen Patt: "The idea was, Fender wanted a three-channel guitar amp, one for the bass player, one for the accompaniment, and the last for the lead guitar. There'd be reverb and tremolo on the third channel only. The accompaniment would have the oil-can vibrato [Fender's Dimension IV Sound Expander, a chorus/vibrato effect], and [another channel] had a fuzz. But anybody who had an amplifier didn't *want* anybody else plugging in to his amp! It's just human nature. But Fender thought they were building this for trios, and people would lap 'em up. *Look, here's an E-tuner built into the head!* I wanted a switch added so the lead guitar could access any effect he wanted, in case some fella decided to use this all by himself. But instead, they came up with jumper cords, to bridge the channels. Nobody liked it, though."

Feelin' Groovy: The Zodiac line

Fender catalogs from the 1950s and early 1960s had featured some of the hottest players in country music — Jimmy Bryant, Noel Boggs, Leon McAuliffe — plus an occasional jazz star such as Monk Montgomery. When it came to rock and roll, however, Fender literature was blissfully unhip. Buddy Holly, Scotty Moore (who in the early days favored a 1952 Deluxe, among others), and Ritchie Valens were nowhere to be seen. After all, Leo Fender probably didn't know Little Richard from Liberace. He liked the West Coast Ramblers and Lawrence Welk.

But the late 1960s was the dawning of the Age of Aquarius. Leo was out, the suits were in, and the new attitude was: *Forget about the West Coast freakin' Ramblers. We're talkin' Strawberry Alarm Clock, the 13th Floor Elevators, the Peanut Butter Conspiracy.* CBS was determined to hop aboard the magic bus, to listen to the flower people, to float downstream on whiffs of incense and peppermints (the color of time). According to the new order, Fender acoustic guitars would appear in "a kaleidoscope of wild natural colors." Electric guitars and basses would be available not only in insufficiently freaky finishes like sunburst but also in blow-your-mind pink paisley and love-is-all-around blue flower.

Now, when it came to amps, how would Fender outgroovy the competition? How would it appeal to shaggy-haired, bell-bottomed guitar dudes in scarves and ruby-colored granny glasses trippin' through covers of "Green Tambourine" and "Pictures of Matchstick Men"? By offering products that "make the happenings happen!" By "dazzling the world with a solid state 'rock-in!'" With can-you-dig-it transistor amplifiers named after signs of the Zodiac! Cue Austin Powers: *Groovy, baby! Yeah!*

Intended as premium-quality products, the Zodiacs all came with stock JBLs, faux gator-hide coverings, and price tags that would pop out your eyeballs like a lust-crazed cartoon tomcat. The 42W, 2x10 Taurus was a relatively small combo at the bottom of the line. It cost $550, more than a piggyback Bandmaster Reverb. Other models included the 56W, 2x12 Scorpio, the 105W, 3x12 Capricorn, and the 105W, 4x12 Libra, which at $899 cost more than a tube Pro Reverb and a tube Bandmaster put together.

Bob Rissi: "In my opinion that Zodiac series was another mistake. They just used pretty much the same circuit boards they used in the earlier solid state amps and stuck them in a different chassis — maybe with a couple of little changes — and put them back out on the market, *looking* more like tube amps, but when you took them apart they were pretty much the same boards. It wasn't worth it. They should've thrown those boards away and come up with a new design. Those Zodiac amps didn't go anywhere."

This Is the End

The bummer-dude price tags alone likely would have doomed the Zodiacs and XFLs to oblivion, but if one more coffin nail were needed, it came in the form of a disconcerting tendency to blow up. Paul Rivera and Lee Jackson would arrive at Fender in the 1980s, both having had experiences with Fender solid state amps of the late 1960s and early 1970s. Paul Rivera: "Fender had a trainwreck history in solid state. The Libra, the Capricorn, the XFL powered-speaker amps, those late-'60s solid state Deluxe Reverbs and Twins — just the worst sounding amps, dogs, and they blew up, so when we arrived we basically had to wipe out that history."

Lee Jackson: "Those XFLs were an absolute disaster. They caught on fire, literally. I had one, and one time it shorted out and blew all four cones at me, just toasted them with some incredible amount of voltage. It was like the scene in *Back To The Future* where the kid plugs in and *boom* — he's blown across the room."

Seth Lover, in *Vintage Guitar*: "Two things were always a problem. One, they wouldn't tighten the screws down enough to hold the power transistors to the heat shields, and they'd blow. Also, the soldering machine was never cleaned, and consequently there were always bad connections. Things just didn't work. Why, I built test equipment for our production runs, and 40 of the 50 would fail! Always the same problems, so they just abandoned that venture. I did speak up about what the source of the failures was, but they didn't want to listen."

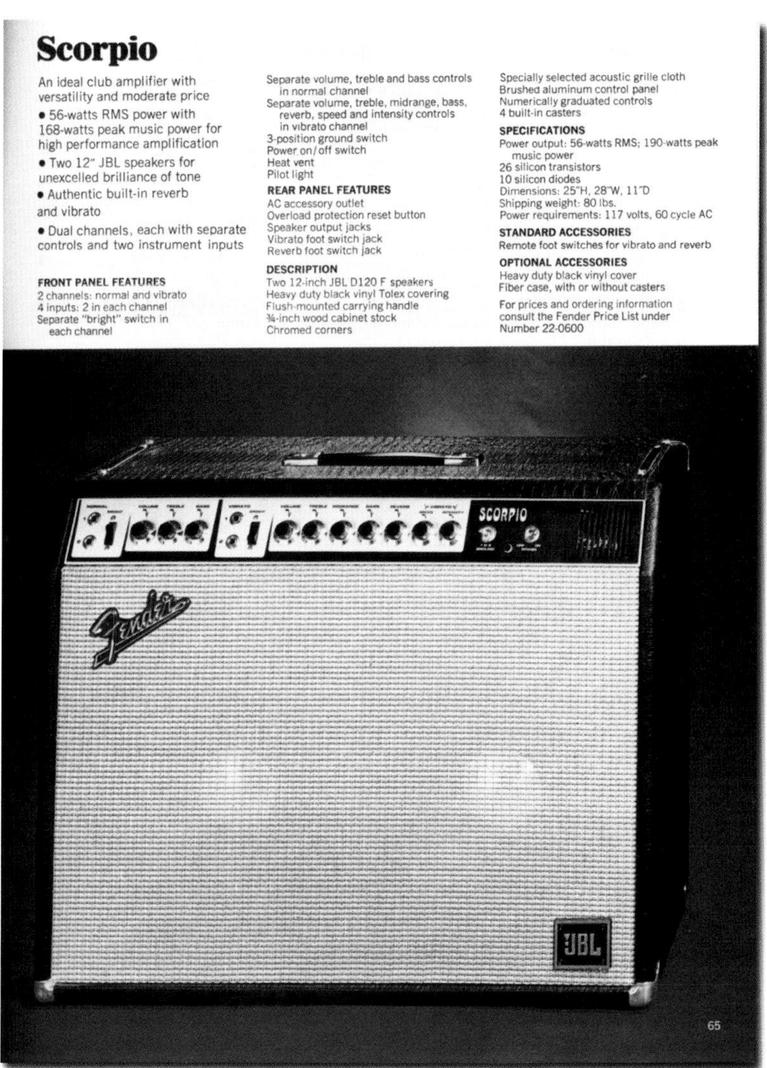

The 56W Scorpio was powered by 26 silicon transistors and boasted a pair of JBL D120F speakers. The literature called it "an ideal club amplifier with versatility and modern price."

Super Showman

Fender's top of the line in
all-transistor amplification

- All-transistor pre-amp with three channels to provide Fuzz, Reverb, Dimension IV and Vibrato
- Separate bright switch, volume, treble, bass and midrange controls for each channel
- Two XFL-1000 or XFL-2000 speaker modules give 280-watts RMS power with 616-watts peak music power to provide incomparable wall-to-wall sound
- XFL-1000 consists of one Super Showman pre-amp and two XFL 1000 power speakers
- XFL-2000 consists of one Super Showman pre-amp and two XFL 2000 power speakers
- JBL speakers optional

SUPER SHOWMAN PREAMPLIFIER

FRONT PANEL FEATURES
3 channels; normal, sound expander, vibrato & reverb
6 inputs: 2 in each channel
Separate "bright" switch in each channel
Fuzz control
Dimension IV control
Reverberation control
Vibrato speed and intensity controls
Master volume control
"E" tuner on/off switch
3-position ground selector switch
Power on/off switch, pilot light

REAR PANEL FEATURES
AC accessory outlet
Output jack (to power speaker)
Separate accent controls for reverb, sound expander and fuzz
Remote foot switch pedal jacks for vibrato/reverb, sound expander and fuzz
Ground post

SUPER SHOWMAN POWER SPEAKERS

Power output for each power speaker: 140-watts RMS; 308-watts peak music power
Four heavy-duty 12-inch speakers in XFL 1000. (JBL D-120F speakers optional)
Eight heavy-duty 10" speakers in XFL-2000 (JBL D-110F speakers optional)
Input jack, level control
Output jack, ground post
Sound switch for solid state or tube sound
Power on/off switch, overload reset button
AC accessory outlet

DESCRIPTION
Heavy duty black vinyl Tolex covering
Flush-mounted carrying handles
¾-inch wood cabinet stock
Chromed corners
Specially selected acoustic grille cloth
Brushed aluminum control panel
Numerically graduated controls
Pilot light

SPECIFICATIONS
49 silicon transistors, 19 silicon diodes
Solid state rectifier circuit
Dimensions: preamp—11¼"H, 28"W, 9¼"D; XFL-1000—30½"H, 28"W, 12¼"D XFL-2000—48"H, 28"W, 12¼"D
Shipping weight: XFL-1000, 229 lbs.; XFL-2000, 265 lbs.
Power requirements: 117 volts, 60 cycle AC

STANDARD ACCESSORIES
Foot switches for special effects

OPTIONAL ACCESSORIES
Heavy duty black vinyl covers
Fiber cases, with or without casters

For prices and ordering information consult the Fender Price List under Numbers 22-0200 thru 22-0205 for Super Showman XFL-1000, 22-0300 thru 22-0306 for Super Showman XFL-2000.

Super Showman XFL 2000 Shown

62

Project Overkill: The 3-channel, 6-input, top of the line Super Showman XFL, 1970. The catalog copy promised "incomparable wall-to-wall sound."

CBS' strategy was so inept during the psychedelic era their motto could have been: *Turn on, tune in, screw up.* Fender execs were ridiculed for the transistor amps, and they deserved it. (Teagle & Sprung on the Zodiacs: "Fender's moon must have been in the nut house when they designed this series.") Fender paid a price, too, with a new and unfamiliar reputation for poor quality. The stigma lasted for years after the solid state models were dropped in 1971. Remember, back then there was nothing like the amount of detailed information we have at our fingertips today. Players made few distinctions between this or that technology. Information traveled by word of mouth, and the word was: Twin Reverbs don't sound so good any more. Super Reverbs are unreliable. *I bought a Deluxe Reverb, man, and it blew up on a gig.*

Fender Senior VP Richard McDonald makes a valid point: "One element that people don't consider when discussing some of the early attempts at solid state amplification is how little was really known about this new technology. The early solid state development was controlled by the military. It wasn't like Fender or anyone else had a bevy of engineers at their disposal who were experienced at getting good guitar tone from these new things called transistors. Much like the aviation industry's early days, a lot of evolution was yet to come."

Fender would stay away from solid state amplifiers for an entire decade, and indeed, the technology evolved considerably during the interim. Solid state amps would reenter the line in the early 1980s. Widely embraced, they proved essential to Fender's success in the years to come.

Dead Transistor Blues

Fender's first solid state amps were atrociously bad. See, in the old days, when you went to design a tube amp, you went to the tube manuals, which had all the specs. That's what Mr. Fender did. There's nothing wrong with that. Hell, I get a lot of my ideas out of a book, too. If you knew what you were doing and you followed the parameters in the book, the thing would generally operate and for the most part was fairly reliable.

Leo Fender had a long tradition of driving his tubes pretty hard by routinely applying more voltage than the tube manuals specified. If it said 300 volts, they'd put in 350 or 400 or whatever. They would push the limit, and as long as you were reading factual material and working with componentry that is conservatively rated, you can get by with that. That worked pretty well back in the old days, because the tubes were made in the United States, the manuals were accurate, and the tubes were conservatively rated. Remember, the 6L6 and 6V6 had been around for decades, so we knew how to write specs to accommodate those tubes.

When transistors came along, you could get them from a lot of sources — Motorola, RCA, Bendix, etc. Myself, Kustom, Shure, Crown, Acoustic — practically everybody used RCA single-diffused silicon transistors, because they were far less prone to destruction than the germanium devices that people were using before that time.

The stuff printed in the old tube manuals had been pretty much "right on," so apparently Fender (like the rest of us) also took at face value the information printed in the early transistor manuals. But a lot of those transistor manuals were inaccurate. I made the same mistake, until I figured out that the transistor manuals were generally bullshit and could not be relied on. One problem was, early transistors were extremely sensitive to heat. They would enter a failure mode called "thermal runaway" in a heartbeat. After Leo left, Fender took the same approach to transistors that they took to tubes — "over-voltaging" them — with disastrous results. People built them and put them out in the field, and guess what? They blew up.

— Hartley Peavey

Jimi Hendrix, shattering barriers in 1968 with what appear to be early trim-ring silverface Fenders, probably Dual Showmans. Although better known for his use of Marshalls, Hendrix often performed and recorded with Fenders. Former Kiss session guitarist Bob Kulick to *Guitar Player*'s Art Thompson, on Jimi's early days in Greenwich Village: "I only saw Jimi using Fender Dual Showmans, Twin Reverbs, and Bassmans .... He was always after more volume and sustain. Sometimes he'd hook two amps together, and he had a small, two-knob fuzzbox."

In 1965 and 1966, Jimi's mainstay was a Twin Reverb. Aspen Pittman: "There's a real misconception about what he was using in the studio simply because everyone saw him onstage all the time with Marshalls. Studios just weren't ready for the kind of volume we were seeing on stages in the late '60s. These were efficiently built rooms designed to take a standup bass and a few other instruments. The microphones and all the gear were designed around certain ideas about maximum volume. So you come in there with a stack of Marshalls — or Sunns, which Hendrix also used — and even though they sounded great onstage, in the studio it was the opposite. They couldn't get a sound. I'm pretty sure there was a Twin Reverb in most studios in those days. The cleaner type of Hendrix stuff must have been Fender amps. Those records are very Twin sounding, very thick in the midrange, very 6L6, not like a Marshall, and according to people who were there at the time, that's what he was using. 'Wind Cries Mary' — that's a Twin Reverb, man, no question about it."

In 1969, the Jimi Hendrix Experience began taking their gear to West Coast Organ & Amp Repair in Hollywood. West Coast Amp tech David Weyer reported: "We kept most of his Fender Showmans stock. I modded some with 6550 tubes, but that required building heavier-duty power supplies. We usually just tuned the Fender stuff to sound as good as possible. Jimi had some 2x15 bottoms that would come in all torn up with the speaker grilles kicked in. We'd recover them, replace the broken speakers, and send them back out."

CHAPTER SEVENTEEN

17

The Silverface Era

Post-Leo Tube Amps, Round 1

Among Fender amp fans, few words raise more eyebrows than "silverface," a term generally used to describe most of the CBS-era tube models from the late 1960s through the early 1980s. Compared to other Fender amp families, silverfaces have a poor reputation. That reputation may be deserved, but only with respect to certain models with particular circuits, features, and construction details. As with other Fender families, generalizations about silverface amps have asterisks attached.

Depending on your taste, some of the amps may not sound very good, particularly when overdriven. On the other hand, many perfectly fine examples have been neglected, undervalued, or unfairly disparaged because the stigma against silverface amps is imprecise and overly broad. Part of that ill repute may actually derive from the inferiority of Fender's other late-'60s amps, the doomed, first-generation transistor models. Those tinny sounding, failure-prone turkeys fostered a "Fender is on the decline" reputation that, however unreasonably, probably tainted the tube models of the same era, even some of the better ones.

In any case, perhaps because the range of their quality is so great — from substandard (for Fender, anyway) to stellar — generalizations about silverfaces entail even more qualifications than usual. What we can say is that, sure, our chances of finding a great Fender are higher among the vintage blackfaces; or, to look at it the other way, the odds of encountering an amp with poor sound and relatively shoddy construction are higher among the silverfaces, at least the later examples of certain models. Second, original-spec blackface amps are worth more than their silverface counterparts in similar condition.

But when it comes to unqualified generalizations, that's about it. After all, we're talking about three dozen models whose components in some cases were evolving constantly for more than a decade. As we've seen, Fender models from any era can vary in sound. Given the relatively wide range of component values and variations in production, two blackface versions of the same amp from the same year can sound noticeably different; two silverfaces can sound noticeably different; and a blackface and a silverface can sound more similar than two blackfaces or two silverfaces.

When we take into account the fact that old amps have components with varying degrees of wear, or components

Silverface selection: Note the blue block lettering (red on the Bronco). Trim rings around the grilles of both combos and heads (the Vibro Champ, top right, for example) were used in 1968 and early 1969, indicating earlier amps than silverfaces without the rings.

On the **left**, from top: '72 Champ, late 1967 Bassman (yes, a silverface with all 1967 parts), '68 Super Reverb, '68 Bandmaster, '69 Deluxe Reverb, and (in front) a '74 Bronco.

Right, from top: '68 Vibro Champ, '68 Twin Reverb with factory JBLs (note JBL badge), '70 Dual Showman Reverb head, and '75 Princeton Reverb.

that have been replaced, or speakers that have been reconed, the variations are even more numerous, the generalizations even less useful. So as we examine the evolution of the silverface group, remember that if you're shopping for gear you plan on actually using (as opposed to collecting or reselling), observations about the history of the entire line are far less important than how a particular amp sounds to you.

Subgroups

"Silverface" is often equated with "CBS," but while all silverface Fenders are indeed CBS amps, not all CBS amps are silverfaces. As we saw in Chapter 15, CBS made blackface amps for a good two and a half years, longer and in greater numbers than Leo Fender did.

There's no such thing as a universal, one-size-fits-all silverface circuit. To get a handle on the tube amps of the first 15 years under CBS, it's useful to subdivide them into rough categories based on circuitries. As usual, these groupings are not discrete; overlaps and exceptions are typical. Putting aside for a moment non-silverface tube Fenders such as the Super Twin, the groups are:

Category 1: The CBS blackface amps, '65 through the late summer of '67.

Category 2: Amps with new silverface cosmetics but the old blackface circuits, generally August '67 through mid '68.

Category 3: CBS amps with "true silverface" circuits but without master volume controls, generally '68 or '69 through the early '70s.

Category 4: Silverface amps with master volume circuits, or pull boosts or other pull switches, or ultralinear transformers. The master volumes appeared in 1972 (on the Twin Reverb, for example), the pull boosts by 1976, the ultralinear transformers in 1977. Some amps had pull-switch volume knobs; others had pull-switch masters. By the middle of the decade, most or all of the larger reverb amps had masters *and* boosts of one type or another — the Dual Showman Reverb, Quad Reverb, Super Six Reverb, Vibrosonic Reverb, Bandmaster Reverb, Super Reverb, Pro Reverb, and Twin Reverb. This trend would continue. In the amps of 1981 and early 1982, all Fender guitar amps except the Champ and Vibro Champ featured gain boosts of some sort.

Author/collector/retailer John Sprung: "Those late-'70s master volume silverfaces with the pull-switches were horrible. When I was selling amps, that was one feature you did not want to see. You pull that switch and you turn your amp into the most horrible sounding piece of junk. But the early silverfaces were fine amplifiers, good Fenders."

To "blackface forever" purists, amps in Category 4 may well sound inferior to those in 1 or 2. In fact, the later you go, the worse it gets. That is, the "best" silverfaces are the early ones of the late '60s, while the "worst" ones date to the late '70s or early '80s, at least according to conventional wisdom. But again, these generalizations must be qualified; for example, some of the dubious circuit alterations of mid 1968 were reversed in mid and late 1969.

The most maligned silverfaces are some of those in Category 4, but remember that Categories 3 and 4 cover many models and more than a decade of gradual shifts in components, features, and construction, so beware of assertions that amps in any of the categories all sound the same. They don't.

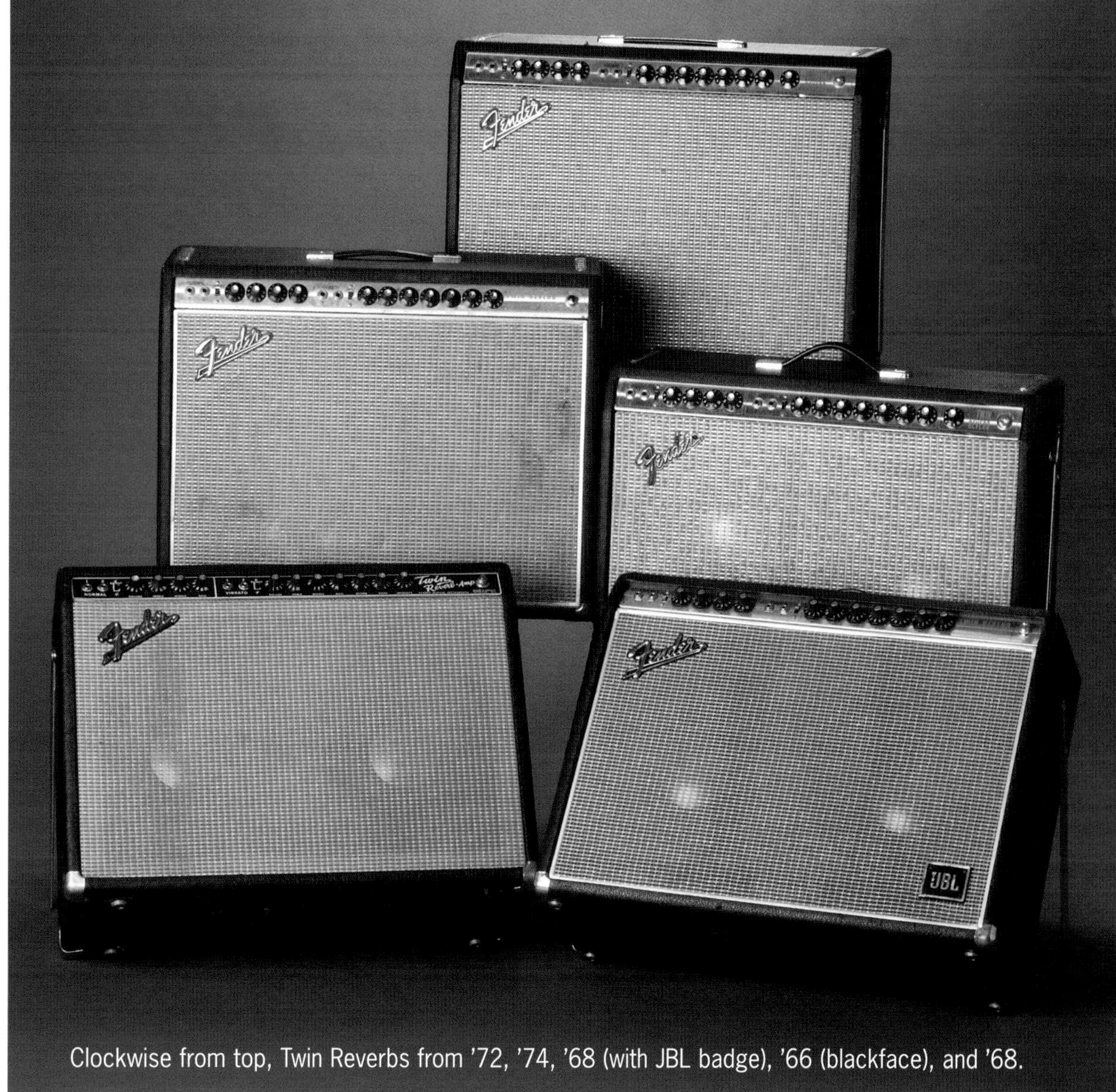

Clockwise from top, Twin Reverbs from '72, '74, '68 (with JBL badge), '66 (blackface), and '68.

Cosmetics

"Silverface," like "blackface" and "brownface," refers to the color of the front control panel. The new panels had a brushed aluminum look with the model names in blue block lettering (the Bronco had spiffy red lettering; it was a re-badged Vibro Champ and part of the Bronco guitar/amp set targeted to students). Suddenly, the old white script on blackface panels looked a little quaint, perhaps a bit country-westernish (now, of course, it looks classic). Early silverfaces bore black vertical lines that subdivided the control panels into sections, and an aluminum-looking border strip, or "trim ring" around the edge of the sparkly, silver-blue grille. The silverface look appeared as early as April of 1967 on a few scattered examples and was adopted across the line by the fall of that year.

After about a year of production, the front panel's black lines were dropped from some models (exceptions included the Bassman, which kept its black-line panel into the fall of 1969), and the bluish grille cloth was changed to the more familiar and more metallic looking silver version. The strip around the grille was dropped in late 1969 or perhaps early 1970, depending on the model. One anomaly — there's a typo on the back panels of some Fenders from late 1965 and early 1966. The "C" in "CBS" stands for "Columbia." On these amps, however, it's spelled "Colombia," like the country.

Bean Counters in the Driver's Seat

Why mess with a good thing? CBS was a successful corporation presumably managed by bright, talented people. Shortly after their acquisition of Fender, the new owners built a massive, 175,000 square foot manufacturing facility for amps and guitars, clear evidence of their willingness to invest in the company and their intent to take it to new levels of production and profitability. But if blackface Fenders dominated the market, why would CBS alter their cosmetics, circuits, features, and construction methods?

For one thing, Leo Fender never stood still, so updating and evolving the products was a time-honored Fender tradition. However, CBS had zero experience in manufacturing guitars and amps and wrongly assumed that its standard corporate practices would improve Fender products. Its sheer size was also significant. A vast corporation, it was not immune to the mentality that infused much of American business in the 1960s. Greg Huntington: "I worked at Hewlett-Packard for many years, and I can tell you that all across American industry in recent decades there have been lots of pressures to lower costs in the bigger companies, and CBS was a big company. Hardly anybody on a major scale was building products the same way they built them just a few years before. It was the 1960s, the space age. New products were modern and flashy and silvery. It was all about change. A lot of this was cost-cutting, too. The bean counters were in the driver's seat."

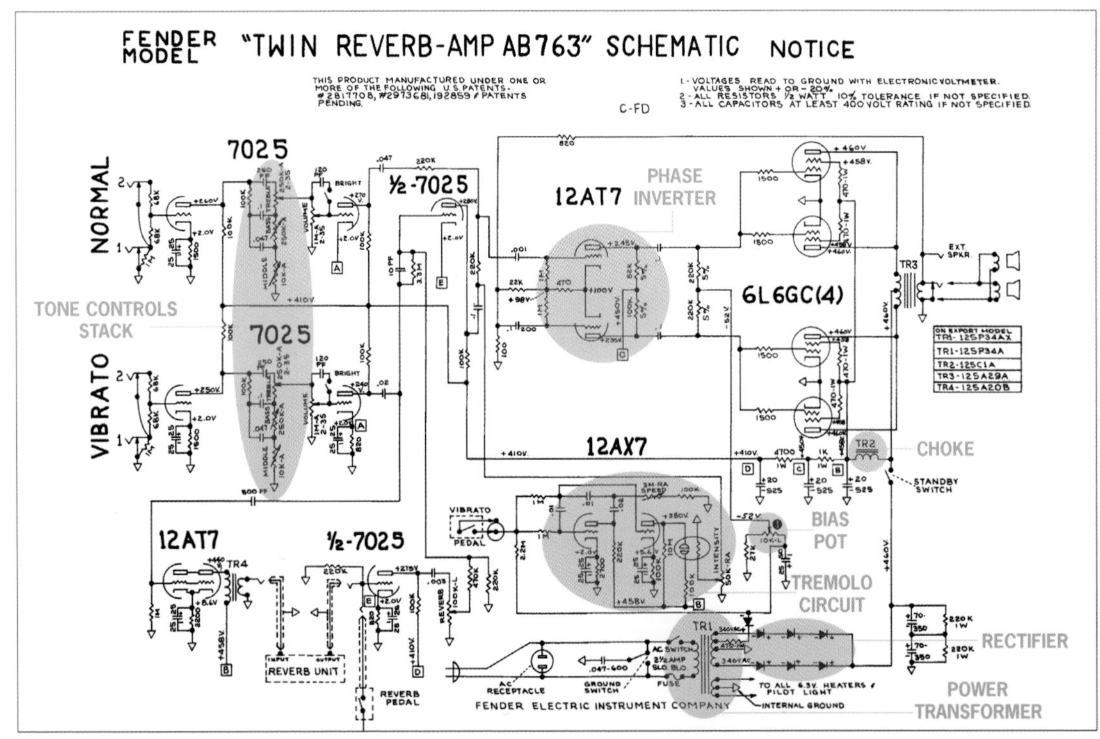

The classic AB763 circuit.

The corporate approach to mass production that diminished the quality of Strats and Teles was also inflicted upon the builders of Princetons and Pros. Greg Gagliano quotes a former employee who assembled amps in 1972 and 1973: "I remember two 'suits' from upstairs standing behind me, occasionally doing time studies. They actually held clipboards and stopwatches to measure how long it took for me to attach various parts. Of course, I tended to hurry more when they were there, and I would fumble more, too."

Circuits

The amps were not degraded through the summer or early fall of '67. In fact, CBS continued to use the acclaimed AB763 circuits through the end of the blackface era and in some cases into the early silverface period. But soon after that, with cost-cutting as a major goal, CBS set about "improving" amplifier production. Changes were gradual, and they varied from minor to major depending on the model, but by the summer of 1968 several of the circuits had been altered.

For example, some amps from the period had the new AB568 circuit from May of '68, which along with similar circuits, weaker cabinets, and the later master volume/pull-switch models saddled the silverface amps with their reputation for inferior sound. Some, like the Vibrolux Reverb, were altered repeatedly in just a short three or four-year period. Others escaped unscathed; for example, the Princeton Reverb and Deluxe Reverb survived for years with their blackface circuits generally intact.

Production Details

Here are production details from the CBS era, as specified in edited CBS documents from the period: "The amp chassis is made of steel and coated with a heavy cadmium-plated iridite finish to seal the chassis, protect components inside, and keep the outside interference out. On top of the chassis, underneath the cabinet, we put an aluminum plate to help seal the chassis and distribute the heat. This also helps keep out broadcast noise [and] protects components from the elements and the usual drink that is spilled on or into the amp.

"The amp knobs are made of Bakelite, not plastic, for longer-lasting [performance] and better looks. AC cords are made of Belden Neoprene, not vinyl or lamp cord … with a heavy-duty molded plug. Controls are all made by CTS, and are American made, low noise and self-lubricating internally. Shafts are made of brass, aluminum, or Delrin as applicable.

"On the parts panel, the mil spec fiberboard is cut with the grain running through the long way of the fiberboard to minimize warpage or shrinkage. Fiberboard is baked in hot wax and chemical solution to seal the board [so that] it won't deteriorate with age, corrode, or crack and will keep out moisture. After the parts panel board is prepared, we put our own eyelets into the board to mount components. Eyelets are made of copper and hot tin dipped to preserve the metal from corrosion … all parts are hand-wired for more consistency and ease of service.

Cool threads, cool guitar, cool amp. Chris Spedding has performed with a long list of artists, including Jack Bruce, Paul McCartney, Roxy Music, Elton John, and Robert Gordon. He's pictured here in 1981, playing his Gibson SG Junior through an early trim-ring silverface Deluxe Reverb. These amps are almost identical to their blackface predecessors and often remain good buys on the vintage amp market.

Stack o' Champs in blackface and silverface: Bottom, left to right: '67 Vibro Champ, '68 Vibro Champ (basically the same circuit as the '67), '81 Champ (Fender amps returned to blackface in the early '80s; Chap. 18). Middle, from left: '72 Champ, '83 Super Champ (Chap. 18), '74 Bronco. On top: 1971 Vibro Champ. If you look closely you can see a progression of Fender logos on the grilles: with a "tail" running underneath (blackface and silverface until 1976), no-tail logos (silverface 1976 to 1980), and later no-tail logos with a small MADE IN USA underneath the *Fender* (the Champ at lower right). (Note: The no-tail logo went back to the late '60s on some models.)

"We use only Kester Rosin Core solder, 60% tin, 40% lead. Diodes used in Fender tube amps are all glass, not partially ceramic. All diodes are made by GE. Switches used on Fender amps use solid silver contacts for better contact in all types of weather and longer life. Resistors are American, made by Allen-Bradley."

Biasing

Starting in mid 1968, CBS altered the bias in the Bassman, Bandmaster, Super Reverb, Pro Reverb, Twin Reverb, Showman, and others, replacing the Bias Adjust control with a Bias Balance control. Although it provided one production convenience — it allowed Fender to use unmatched tubes — it was quickly recognized as a poor decision and was abandoned by late 1969. Some of the changes in the mid-'68 circuits were reversed in the AA1069 circuits. Greg Gagliano: "Basically, the mixed bias arrangement had both tubes cathode biased, but one tube had its grid connected to an adjustment pot. The idea was simply to change the current draw for the adjustable tube to match the current draw of the nonadjustable tube. I think Fender must have done this so they could use somewhat mismatched tubes, but it resulted in more hum and an amp that generally didn't sound quite as good as the previous blackface versions."

Lead Dress and Voltages

Blackface Fenders were generally known for efficient wiring and precise assembly, but in the rush to ramp up production, attention to detail suffered under CBS. *Lead dress* refers to the routing and placement of wires between the circuit board and the various sockets or components. On the silverfaces, the connecting wires were often longer, their positioning less precise. Longer wires, particularly if they are arranged in a slipshod fashion, are more apt to pick up interference that can cause undesirable oscillations. Instead of fixing the problem with shorter wires and neater lead dress, CBS added capacitors to the grids of the power tubes on several models; this reduced oscillations but also may have cut some of the high-frequency sparkle so characteristic of the Fender sound.

The B+ operating voltages on the power tubes' plates were increased on some models, presumably to reduce distortion. To some listeners, this may have contributed to a brittle sound.

Caps and Components

Coupling capacitors and tone-stack capacitors were changed (several times on some models), which may have reduced some desirable effects of compression and contributed to a thinner, harsher tone. According to Greg Huntington, Fender used yellow Astron caps prior to 1961. From the early '60s through the late '60s they used axial-lead, molded, tubular caps made by Mallory; they were a dull blue, with white paper labels. Mallory caps in brownface and blackface Fenders are praised by many Fender fans for their tone.

During this same general period, starting in 1963, Fender also used small brown caps with yellow lettering — only occasionally at first. They became somewhat more common by 1965, often mixed with the blue caps. Frequently blamed for a degradation of tone quality, these brown caps are sometimes called *chocolate drops*, among other, less savory nicknames. Greg Huntington: "With the introduction of the silverfaces, there was a bit of component degradation in the coupling capacitors and even the cathode bypass capacitors. By the '68 or '69 time frame, we see a greater conversion to chocolate drops. Some amps, like the Bassmans, tended to have more of them — and have them earlier on — than did other models. Regardless, by late '69, chocolate drop caps had replaced the blue Mallorys in most Fenders. In 1969 or 1970, we begin to see shiny, radial-lead, epoxy-dipped blue caps with white-ink marking (rather than black ink on white paper labels). These were Paktrons. The Paktrons seem to have replaced most chocolate drops in many models by the early '70s."

Paktron also made other types of caps used by Fender, as did other companies. Greg Huntington: "So, components were changing. By 1969 or 1970 a Fender tube amp very likely had new, *white* Mallory cathode bypass capacitors on the preamp tubes, brown coupling caps throughout the amp, and higher voltages. Now, it's not entirely certain that these capacitors made an amp sound bad, although they typically get some of the blame. The 1963 brown 2x10 Vibroverbs used some of those brown caps, and they didn't all sound bad, right?"

Chuck Berry at the Ritz in New York City, mid 1980s. His contract rider reportedly specified that promoters must provide “three (3) professional (AF of M) musicians” and “two (2) unaltered Fender Dual Showman Reverb amplifier sets.”

Orange Drop Caps

Much has been written about the Orange Drop capacitors in Fender amps. "Orange Drop" refers to a family of radial capacitors originally manufactured by the Sprague Electric Company, established in 1926 after founder Robert C. Sprague invented a paper dielectric capacitor in his home. Orange Drops were introduced in 1959. After a management buyout, Sprague evolved into Sprague-Barre Electronics, or SBE Inc., which continues to evolve and update Orange Drop caps.

Steve Melkisethian, Angela Instruments: "Although Sprague trademarked the brand name, this basic type of capacitor was manufactured by a number of different companies, including Mallory and CDE (Cornell-Dubilier). My fellow solder slingers, amp collectors, antique radio buffs, electronics parts sellers, and other geezers often refer to all similar types, by whatever manufacturer, somewhat generically as Orange Drops.

"The Spragues were orange. The Mallorys were generally dark brown. The CDEs were generally coated in dark blue shiny epoxy. I've seen all three types in Fender amps from the '70s and '80s, and all are basically hard, epoxy-dipped, radial leaded plastic film/aluminum foil capacitors. The most significant variation is the composition of the dielectric: polyester film or polypropylene film.

"It's been a long time since Orange Drops have been held in high regard by enlightened guitar amp artisans. They are well made and almost bulletproof in service but are generally considered to have a 'hard' sound in guitar amps and are better suited to the tastes of half dog/half man hi-fi nuts listening for lots of high-frequency 'detail' without warm harmonic colorations. I think the characteristic 'hard' sound of all Orange Drops is due to the rock-hard epoxy coating and the tall, compressed shape that, being radially mounted, takes up less space on crowded PC boards. There are plenty of modern caps made with similar polyester and polypropylene film dielectrics and aluminum foil plates that sound better in guitar amps, but these are all axial leaded tubulars shaped more like vintage caps, and none have a hard epoxy coating.

"Almost every week I get a call from somebody with a relatively new amp or a heavily repaired or modified vintage amp full of Orange Drops looking to replace 'em with something warmer and more natural sounding, like paper in oil capacitors, polyester or polypropylene/aluminum foil tubulars, or even New Old Stock mylar film/aluminum foil types (e.g., Sprague Black Beautys, Cornell-Dubilier Black Cats, etc.). Almost all old amps we now call 'vintage' (Fender, Marshall, Vox, Magnatone, you name it) had mylar film/aluminum foil axial leaded tubular signal capacitors with softer plastic jackets. While these old style caps are hardly the last word in linearity or reliability, they do have a sonic character that most guitarists find agreeable.

"I believe that Fender, like most of the electronics industry, stopped using mylar tubulars and started using Orange Drop type radial film capacitors in the late '60s to improve reliability. It's only fair to mention that hard epoxy does greatly improve reliability by being heat and moisture resistant. For some applications, this may be an acceptable tradeoff."

Rectifiers, Phase Inverters, Power Supplies

Rectifier tubes changed from 5AR4/GZ34s to rugged, yet less expensive 5U4GBs. The change may have been due primarily to the abundance of 5U4s, but it also may have been prompted in part by other factors such as increases in the AC voltages coming out of wall sockets around the country, increases in secondary voltages from the transformers, and other interrelationships among components.

The values of resistors on phase inverters were reduced, possibly to produce more headroom. These lower plate-load resistors were rated at 47k, as opposed to the 82k and 100k units typical of the blackface amps.

By the later years of the silverface era, transformers and power supplies had been altered in several models. The small amps kept their tube rectifiers. The 40W models changed to solid state rectifiers when they switched to the ultralinear circuits. (The high power amps already had solid state rectifiers.)

Cabinets and Baffles

The durability and sonic attributes of Fender cabs declined during the silverface era. For about two decades Leo Fender had built the tops, sides, and bottoms of his amplifiers with one-piece boards of solid pine. By the mid 1960s, smaller pieces were sometimes glued side by side to make boards of adequate width. CBS continued to use side-

From the 1969 catalog, left to right: Vibrolux Reverb, Vibro Champ, Pro Reverb, Princeton Reverb, Deluxe Reverb. Note blue-tinged grilles with border strips.

glued boards and in the late 1960s also began gluing short pieces end to end to make boards of adequate length, at least on some amplifiers.

Steve Grom: "In the early days, it was easy to get pine boards wide enough to make all the various cabinets. Over time, the standards within the lumber industry changed to what was a 'common' (narrower) board width. As the standard became more narrow in the early '70s, the only option was gluing pieces together. Fender's volume of product was very high, and we consumed mass quantities of materials compared to the early days. This is why most of the cabinets went to plywood and particle board as time progressed. The lumber industry was changing, the wider pine boards were in fairly short supply, and costs were going through the roof."

Mr. Fender had built his speaker baffles from plywood up through the era of the brown and blonde Tolex amps. During the fall of '63, when the blackfaces were introduced, he began substituting particle board, which was still attached the way baffles had always been secured in Fender amps — from the inside, with screws. Starting in the early '70s, however, CBS began gluing the baffles into grooves in the sides and bottom (making them nonremovable for all practical purposes), which also entailed a new procedure for attaching the grilles. The cabs were getting heavier, too, putting more stress on joints and glued surfaces.

Another dubious move: By the mid '70s, CBS was replacing the cabinets' rock-solid, labor-intensive finger joints with rabbet joints in which one board is simply laid into a single, full-width slot or groove of the other board. All of this sped up production and lowered costs but also decreased structural strength and integrity. Former senior tech in Fender R&D PJ Geerlings: "I worked on many, many Fender amplifiers before I joined the company, and I saw a tremendous range of cost-cutting measures. Those tweed 4x10 Bassmans were built like tanks. Compare that to the CBS amps, where [in some cases] everything eventually was cost-reduced to the point where they just didn't stay together, they just did not work. Even at only a year or two old, a Fender amp from that later CBS period was not going to live much of a life. They had just cut costs too much."

So over a period of about a decade, cabinets evolved from a solid pine construction with finger joints and screwed-in, plywood baffles to multi-piece cabs [in some cases] with rabbet joints and glued-in, particle board baffles. CBS continued to use the weaker, less resonant construction throughout the silverface era. The days when a Fender amp could fall out of Bob Wills' bus and still work were gone.

The High-Power Silverface Reverbs

In September or October of 1967 the Twin Reverb went from blackface to silverface, although it kept its AB763 circuit for several months. In mid 1968 the AB763 was replaced with the AC568 circuit. The year 1968 also saw the introduction of the silverface Dual Showman Reverb, which overlapped the Dual Showman for a brief period. The year 1972 was the year of the master volume control. The trendy new feature was added to the silverface Twin Reverb and Dual Showman Reverb, and also appeared on three new models: the Vibrosonic Reverb (1972 to '81), Super Six Reverb (1972 to '78 or '79), and Quad Reverb (1972 to '78 or '79).

While the venerable blackface Twin Reverb disappeared by the fall of 1967, its potent genes lived on in the next generation. To a significant extent, the silverface Twin Reverb, Dual Showman Reverb, Vibrosonic Reverb, Super Six Reverb, and Quad Reverb were all sons of the blackface TR. The blackface big daddy and its five silverface offspring all shared the same preamp tube complement: The normal channel had a 7025, and the vibrato or tremolo channel had two 7025s; one half of that third 7025 was used as an additional gain stage, the other half for reverb recovery. All of these beefy silverfaces were powered by four 6L6GC output tubes. Each circuit entailed a solid state rectifier, a long-tailed 12AT7 phase inverter, a 12AX7 tube photoresistor for the tremolo, and a reverb circuit using a 12AT7 for the driver.

All five of the silverface powerhouses started life as 100W amps, surged to 135W in 1977 for the wattage wars of the late '70s and early '80s, and eventually received pull-boost switches for extra versatility. The 135W versions all used ultralinear output transformers, lending a powerful, super-clean sound favored by some country players. (And not just country players. Chuck Berry's performance contract reportedly requires promoters to provide "three (3) professional (AF of M) musicians" and "two (2) unaltered Fender Dual Showman Reverb amplifier sets.")

While the Contempo Organ was a controversial project even at CBS Fender (Bill Carson: "It was a mess, a pile of junk"), the Vibratone, right, was highly regarded. The Leslie rotating speaker effect was developed by Don Leslie in the early 1940s. In 1965 he sold his company to Fender's corporate parent, CBS, which soon incorporated a modified Leslie Model 16 system in the Vibratone extension cabinet. Produced from 1967 to 1972, it was one of the most distinctive products in Fender's entire history.

The Vibratone's 10" speaker doesn't actually spin around. A hollow drum rotates in front of it, which diffuses and disperses the sound to create the characteristic phasing effects that so many pedals and onboard chorus/phasing devices emulate. A footswitch selects either of two speeds for a slow, revolving chorus or a watery warble, as heard on Stevie Ray Vaughan's "Cold Shot," among others. Comping chords through a Vibratone can approximate the sound of a Hammond organ through a Leslie.

Big twang from Bakersfield: With their Telecasters and a variety of Fender amps, the great Buck Owens, right, and fellow Buckaroo Don Rich helped create one of country music's most distinctive styles.

While the blackface Twin Reverb had sported a grey or silver sparkle grille that recalled the last years of the Leo Fender era, the younger, louder amps in this group all had the blue sparkle grilles that practically shouted *CBS*. Like the blackface Twin Reverb, the other five had black skirted knobs with silver hubs and white numbers. On all these amps, the original grille-mounted Fender nameplate appeared in raised, black and silver script with a tail that underlined the logo. In 1974 the Twin Reverb's logo dropped the tail, and the others followed suit two or three years later. (The no-tail logo went back to the late '60s on other models.)

As with other Fender amp clans, these silverface "power reverbs" differed in cabinet size and speaker complement: one 15 for the Vibrosonic, two 12s for the Twin, two 15s for the Dual Showman, four 12s for the Quad Reverb, and six 10s for the Super Six. This last behemoth was the 30-ton Brontosaurus of Fender's late Jurassic period. Bass amps typically offer massive speaker arrays, but a *guitar* amp with a combined 60 diameter-inches of cone area (in a combo, no less) would have been unthinkable to Leo Fender, and it would be unthinkable in the Fender line today.

Steve Grom: "Don't ever forget the concept of 'power wars' when it came to the 135 watt [4x6L6] and 70 watt [2x6L6] Fenders. At that time, it was very important to not only have a high power rating, but also to show that your amp was louder on 3 than this other model was on 4. Dumb, but true. I think they even changed the taper of the volume pots to help accomplish this task. The power 'bump' in all these amps was pushed on R&D by Marketing — I'm not sure who was running the show at that time — and Ed Jahns was very involved in making the design changes so all the internal components would survive."

Overview: Sound and Quality

The erosion in sound and quality was gradual and sporadic, and it varied depending on the model. Greg Huntington: "In the larger amps, it didn't take long for the circuits to change after the switch to silverface cosmetics, anywhere from six to nine months or a year. The substantial change in the bigger amps was that attempt to do some cathode-bias stuff for the power tubes from May of '68 to about mid 1969. This was the AC568 circuit, one of the ones that is often changed by owners or their repair people.

"In the smaller amps, it took a while longer after the shift to silverface cosmetics for the circuits to change, sometimes years. In the very smallest of the amps, the circuits were largely unchanged into the middle '70s — a

Princeton, Champ, or Vibro Champ, for example. Even though those smaller amps are silverfaces on the outside, circuit-wise they're pretty much blackfaces."

John Sprung takes the opposite view, revealing yet again the subjectivity of hearing, taste, and opinion among experienced Fender aficionados: "It seems to me the *smaller* amps really took a bigger hit in quality, maybe because of the quality of distortion. The Princetons and some of the Deluxes started to get a little tinny sounding, but many of the bigger amps — Super Reverbs, Pro Reverbs, Twin Reverbs — held up and were not as noticeably wanky sounding. Maybe that's because you're hearing more distortion in the smaller amps, and the speakers changed a lot."

Buckaroo Bassman. Ritchie Fliegler: "We had Buck Owens' Bassman here a few years ago. This was the amp that Don and Buck used to play through back in the day, the Buckaroo amp. Any number of Bassman amps all sound different; it was shocking how much this one sounded like a 50 watt Marshall." Shane Nicholas: "It looked and smelled like a stock 1963 amp because it was re-covered at the Fender factory that year. Awesome! Buck was a guy who loved his Fender amp so much, he used it for *everything* and even reconditioned it when it was near death."

Beginning with mid 1968's AC568 circuit, CBS Fender employed suppressor capacitors to reduce or eliminate parasitic oscillations that may have arisen from the sloppy wiring and the use of wires that were a bit too long. While they were effective, they also adversely influenced the audible high frequencies of the amps. Greg Huntington: "Otherwise, except for the short-lived AC568 amps, until you get to the mid '70s the silverface amps weren't that much different. Yes, there was a slow progression of changes that actually began at the end of the blackface era, like who was supplying capacitors, the messier wiring, and a few little details in the transformers that no one has ever really characterized or quantified.

"Changes in components like coupling capacitors were fairly substantial; these capacitors were in the tone circuits, coupling the output tubes and phase inverters. Transformers were evolving, voltages were going up, the wire changed, and the wire coating changed, but most of these individual changes in parts were small. The sum of the changes seems to have caused occasional complaints of reduced tone."

"Blackface" is a Verb?

As we've seen, the older a stock silverface amp is, the more likely it resembles its blackface predecessor (except for those cases where CBS reversed itself and restored some details to blackface specs). Many of the circuit alterations are reversible and are easily and inexpensively accomplished by a knowledgeable tech. Several articles, books, and websites address the topic. Some companies even offer kits enabling a player to "blackface" his or her silverface amp. The later silverface amps are typically further removed from their blackface counterparts, and some of their circuit alterations are harder to reverse.

Fender's circuit nomenclature was particularly complicated during the '70s, but whether your silverface circuit is an AA1069 or an AA270 or whatever the case may be, a common approach is simply to compare it to the mid-'60s AB763 schematic (available on several websites) and alter anything that doesn't match it. Typical steps include removing the caps intended to compensate for poor lead dress, replacing chocolate drop caps with the old-style blue Mallorys, and restoring the phase inverter's 47k plateload resistors to the 82k and 100k blackface specs.

Now, will these alterations noticeably improve the sound of a silverface amp, or are they simply a matter of wishful thinking? It depends on the originality and sound of your silverface to begin with, which alterations are made, how many are made, the quality of the new components, the workmanship, the sophistication of your ears, and your opinion of what "blackface" is supposed to sound like.

Steve Melkisethian: "These days it's fairly common for folks to claim that they've 'blackfaced' (*ugh!*) a silverface amp to earlier specs by changing a few parts, but I don't agree. As already noted here, the sound of a specific amp is a complex interplay of circuits, parts choices, even the location and spatial relationships of the bits and pieces. My feeling is that the types of signal capacitors used in most of the silverface amps contributed to a kind of 'pinched' sound without as much harmonic content as the earlier Fenders. Generally, the blackface Fenders had axial leaded tubular signal capacitors soldered fairly tight to the board, and the silverface amps had 'Orange Drop' type caps that stood off the circuit board quite a bit higher. In my experience, Orange Drop caps don't sound as musical; this may be due to their basic construction features but also to their spatial relationship to other circuit elements. I've also noted that silverface amps often had beefier looking power transformers, often with higher plate voltages. This gave more power and transformer reliability but also a 'stiffer' sound. Furthermore, some of Fender's speaker choices in the silverface era seemed to be more concerned with reliability than good sound. Finally, I should mention the change from warmer sounding plywood/pine baffle boards to crappy particle board."

Greg Gagliano: "There's a lot of bias in the print media and especially on the Internet. You've got people publishing the Five Best Amps of All Time or the Ten Best or whatever, and people think, well, that's the one I have to have. But the reality is, you have to let your ears be your guide. There are plenty of people out there who really dig silverface master volume Twins from the '70s. There's nothing wrong with those amps. They sound great. You wouldn't believe how many letters I get saying, 'Should I change the circuit back to blackface?' And the answer is, 'Well, do you like the way it sounds? If you do, leave it alone!' People read this stuff and forget they have ears."

Marty Stuart favors early to mid-'70s silverface Twin Reverbs for performing, a blackface Deluxe for recording, and a Princeton Reverb for rehearsals.

Speakers

Often overlooked in discussions of silverface vs. blackface are differences in speakers, yet as Leo Fender knew well, few factors are as important to an amplifier's performance as its speaker or speakers. Greg Huntington: "Leo seemed to have spent much more time simply matching speakers to amplifiers than people give him credit for. Consider the '64 4x10 Concert. It had Oxfords, whereas a '64 Super Reverb often would have Jensens. They're both 4x10 amps, so why in the world would they do it that way? It's because Leo listened to each of them and chose the speakers that gave him the precise sound he was looking for."

Mondo combo: Fender's biggest single-cab amp, the 6x10 Super Six Reverb stood four feet tall, required about eight square feet of grille cloth, and tipped the scales at just under a hundred pounds.

John Sprung: "Speakers are the most important thing, the biggest thing you can do to an amplifier to change its characteristic. You put a Celestion in a Fender and you're gonna get a Marshall, and vice-versa. Fender was changing speakers constantly, and when we're listening to old amplifiers we're typically judging them on reconed speakers. Some guy plugs into a silverface Twin Reverb and says it doesn't sound so good. Hey, *it's a 40-year-old amp* — half the parts have worn out, and the speakers have probably been reconed, and if they haven't been reconed, they need to be. With the smaller amps the distortion typically kicks in relatively early, and the speaker plays a very important role."

CBS continued to offer heavy-duty JBLs as extra-cost options on many models, but across the line the speaker complements changed in important ways. The Jensens that had been so essential to the Fender sound were replaced in many cases by other brands, including Utah and Oxford. Some sounded fine, even great; others were made with lower-grade components, had lower production tolerances, operated with lower efficiency, and to some listeners didn't sound as good, particularly when driven hard. John Sprung: "People talk about capacitors and all that stuff. I think getting away from Jensens and CTS speakers and using Utahs and others had more to do with the decline of the sound than anything else."

Hartley Peavey: "A popular thought is that Fender used mostly Jensens and later Oxfords, but per Fender's own list of speaker suppliers, they actually used just about everybody in the business during the '50s and forward." Mr. Peavey's copy of an in-house Fender document lists solid state and tube models from the late '60s and early '70s; approved speaker suppliers include Eminence, CTS, Utah, Oxford, Essex, Vega, JBL, Jensen, Electro-Voice, Gauss, Pyle, Rola, Heppner, and Yamaha (in the Bantam Bass only). Keep in mind that these speakers were merely "approved" for use; in other words, they "met spec." Some may not have been used in significant quantities, or at all. For example, late-'60s or early-'70s Fenders with original Rola, Essex, or Heppner speakers are rare or nonexistent.

Steve Grom: "Prior to CBS, Fender was 'sole-sourced' on many items, but one of CBS' corporate policies in our Purchasing Department was never to have only one source for a component or part. This is one reason there were six or seven different vendors for the speakers used in the Twin Reverb. All vendors made a part we purchased under the same part number. I remember Bill Gelow — an R&D speaker engineer in the late '70s through the early '80s — being fanatic about testing each shipment from each vendor to maintain consistency. The only rule manufacturing had about the different vendors was not to mix speakers within the same amp."

Ed Jahns

The name of the late Ed Jahns shows up in several places in this book. Prior to coming to Fender, he had a long history in electronics and was a co-developer of Tung-Sol's 6550 "Coke bottle" tube. In-house Fender documents from the CBS period identify him as "our Electronic Engineer Manager" and "tube design engineer for many, many years," but in fact he was not an employee. Fender amp designer Bill Hughes: "Ed was a consultant, and he wanted it that way. One aspect of the Ed Jahns legacy was that he straightened out those very early solid-state designs that had so many problems. He was the designer of the Fender 75, and when he worked for me he also did the Super Champ. I was his boss. I loved that guy to death. He was a great man. He must have been 80 years old when he finally hung it up and left." The Fender 75, the Super Champ, and some of Ed Jahns' other designs are covered in later chapters.

As confirmed by Fender colleagues such as PJ Geerlings, Bill Hughes, Lee Jackson, and Paul Rivera, Mr. Jahns was a brilliant all-around engineer and a stickler for quality. Fender credited him as the person who "buys the best components available," and "sets the standards for many products used by manufacturers all over the world."

PJ Geerlings: "Ed Jahns was overwhelming in his knowledge of engineering, not just electronics. He was also a phenomenal mechanical engineer, the kind of guy who could go into the transmission of his car and rework it so it would perform better. He could talk for hours about, for example, the fiberboard we used. He had a bizarre piece of equipment, an ultra-high ohm meter, and he was always testing things to make sure they were up to his standards. He would demonstrate things like how the

Texas Cannonball: The mighty Freddie King. Guitarist Willie Smith remembered Freddie's gigs at T.J.'s Famous Chicken in the Basket, Fort Worth: "He showed up with his Cadillac, and in the back of his Cadillac would be that big ol' Dual Showman amp. He would set his amp up on the dance floor in front of the band. T.J.'s had a hardwood floor, hard wall, and lots of echo. It sounded like a gymnasium. Man, he just *burned*." In later years, the great bluesman would favor a Fender Quad.

Based more or less on the silverface Twin Reverb, the PA 100 and PA 135 were examples of CBS Fender's guitar-amp approach to public address systems. As warm sounding guitar amps, these 10-tube heads wouldn't give a tweed Twin a run for its money, but you could plug all your friends into either one and still have plenty of clean punch. The grilles on these models were made of a foam-like material that often deteriorated, as seen here on the PA 100.

leakage was lower on our fiberboard compared to typical epoxy circuit boards."

Former Marketing Manager for amplifiers Steve Grom: "Ed Jahns was the senior R&D engineer. He was constantly overseeing the quality of the vacuum tubes. Every time we got a new load of tubes, he'd bring out this little kit of testing tools, and he'd break the tubes apart and start dissecting them and calling the guys at GE and Sylvania and reading them the riot act about this or that. He was great when it came to quality control."

Former employee Lee Jackson: "Ed was the person who made sure the circuits stayed point to point with the wax board. Any time someone tried to change the circuit boards, he would stop them. Ed was also the tube genius guru."

According to in-house memos: "At CBS, Mr. Jahns runs his own tests. Amps that are designed to run at no more than 65 degrees Centigrade, we test at 85 to 100 degrees Centigrade to see if components will hold up, be safe to use, and don't cause fires. [Ed Jahns] has contributed to the internal design of the tubes [we] buy from various manufacturers. Ed's versions had much greater reliability and life expectancy .... Ed's understanding of transformers — their design, construction, and materials — is unique in the industry."

Rich Koerner of Time Electronics, Union, New Jersey, has been a professional bassist, repairman, and technician for about four decades. He had many conversations with Ed Jahns over a period of several years. Rich Koerner: "Ed was a smart man from the old school, a breed apart that doesn't exist anymore. These men took pride in what they did. It was a craft. He made Fender suppliers improve their components, like the Schumacher transformers. I consulted him on the transformers I needed for my own home stereo system, which I built myself, very high power. I wanted great frequency response so I could get the full range of a grand piano, for example. He told me just to take the transformers out of a Fender Showman 15, which I did. Unbelievable sound, clarity, and power — I could turn it up and the furniture would move. I use it to this day."

Koerner's recollection of the relationship between Marketing and R&D under CBS echoes the comments of Paul Rivera in Chapter 15. Rich Koerner: "Ed told me that Marketing gave him instructions to re-do the whole amp line in the late '60s. The Marshall stacks were out there, Hendrix was doing his trip, and Fender was getting left

B.B. King takes a breather between takes on a late-night session with Ringo Starr.

behind. Ed did all the right things as an engineer, but he was always having battles with the marketing boys, and he was always ahead of them. As an engineer, I don't think there was anyone like him, ever. This man made vacuum tubes in his cellar. He could've put up a *satellite* if he wanted to. I don't think the marketing guys knew what they had in Ed Jahns. The blame [for a loss in quality] should go to marketing. Early on he won most of the battles over cost-cutting and got his way, but later they did start to cheapen those amps. Ed Jahns was not only not responsible for the loss of quality, he was fighting it every step of the way."

At a time when typical attire in Fender R&D might be jeans, blue Adidas sneakers, and a Foghat T-shirt, Mr. Jahns would invariably wear a crisp dress shirt and often a conservative tie. His colleagues remember him fondly for his frequent battles with corporate execs over cutting corners, his stubborn refusal to compromise his standards, and his generosity in sharing his knowledge with his co-workers.

The 400 PS, 300 PS

Among Ed Jahns' more storied designs was the 400 PS. This gargantuan bass amp was a long-overdue response to the massive, powerful, and loud amps that had been offered for years by several of Fender's competitors. Pitched to guitarists as well as bassists, it boasted three channels, reverb, tremolo, a master volume, and a jaw-dropping — and ear-splitting — 435W of power (3 channels x 145W each). The head alone weighed about 90 pounds, thanks in part to its enormous transformers.

Behold the Megalodon of the early-'70s Fender line, the ear-splittin', back-bustin' 400 PS. Steve Grom: "Death and destruction — wicked, man, just tone for days, one of Ed Jahns' crowning achievements."

Six guns and big iron: A half-dozen 6550s and massive transformers make the 400 PS a schlepper's nightmare. The chassis alone weighs as much as a Twin Reverb.

Rich Koerner has repaired many amps and has a special affection for the 400. He even started an online club for 400 owners. He says, "Ed sent me blueprints of the 400, gave me lots of tips, and walked me through the amp from front to back. He told me every piece of testing equipment I would need, and I followed all his advice.

"The [Ampeg] SVT was the top dog. There was nothing else out there in the music stores like the SVT. I played through dual SVT stacks — four cabs, two heads. I've had my vision blur when I stood in front of them. Well, Ed was going for something that would put the SVT out to pasture. He based the 400 on the Tung-Sol tubes that he knew intimately, and he overbuilt it. The design was unique; a lot of the details would be foreign to ninety percent of the amp techs out there. The SVT was 300 watts. The Fender 400 was very conservatively rated [at 435]. If the guy hit the standby before the plug went into the speaker cabinet, it would smoke up the tube sockets. See, the Fender 400 is a top fuel dragster. If those wheels ain't touching the ground when you hit the gas pedal, and they spin, you can blow the motor. This was the kind of monster that Ed built.

"Once they got out into the field they started to have problems. Those 6550 Tung-Sols were not holding up under the severe abuse of the guys who were just balls to the wall with the thing, and they had problems with oscillations, too. So, fairly early on, Ed was revising the amp to take care of these problems."

Steve Grom: "The 400 PS was a marvelous piece of equipment. It had six power tubes and was so powerful — you could play bass and arc weld with it at the same time [laughs]. I was a bass player, and I bought a 400 PS in about '78, before I came to Fender. The problem was, when they first introduced it, it came with a folded-horn 18 inch speaker cabinet. The head was designed to compete with the SVT, the cabinet was designed to compete with the Acoustic 360, and it ended up being the worst of both worlds — killer amp through a miserable speaker cabinet. It was horrible. But you played that head through a completely different speaker cabinet — unbelievable tone! I had a guy make me a cab with two EV 15s and, whew, it was death and destruction — wicked, man, just tone for days. The 400 PS was one of Ed Jahns' crowning achievements, and Ed and I became lifelong friends once I told him I had one and how much I loved it. I'd bring it in and he'd go in the back and pull out his special Ed Jahns stash of tubes and put these tubes in it, and *ahhh*, fantastic."

Steve Grom's experience with the 400's "W bin" folded-horn enclosure was not uncommon. Rich Koerner: "That was Fender's mistake, pairing the amp with that W bin, which everyone called the refrigerator. If you were standing right in front of it, you couldn't hear it. Guys would say, 'Is this working?' The wavelengths were so long that not much came out right in front of the amp, but the further back you went, the more it took your head off.

"One time I advised one of my pro customers to buy a 400, which he did. I modified it to get even more power, and built cabs for him like the old Sunn 2000S cabs. I used four JBL K140s and four JBL K130s — four cabs with two 15s in each. When the guy came in to try it out, I had the eight 15s in the cabs out in the showroom, and the chassis on my workbench. He plugged in and took his bass out there to try it out. I said, 'I don't think you want to stand out there.' But he insisted, so we got him dialed in at low volumes. I very gradually brought the volume up, and when it was at 3 or 3 and a quarter he had to come back into the shop and close the door behind him, it was so loud. We turned it up more and more and pretty soon, every time he hit a note, the dust would fall from the ceiling in the shop, even though the cabs were on the other side of the wall.

"You have to remember, everything was different in bassland when that thing came out. People bitch about the 400 today because we are used to having one output with 1000W on it, but back then, they didn't have a 200W speaker that would hold up. It didn't exist. Everything was low power, and that's why Ed split up the 400 with three channels. The existing cabs couldn't have taken it out of one output.

"Those things are heavy, too. I'm a 125 pound bag of bones. I have to give it a bear hug with my arms around those big-ass transformers to move the thing, but I still perform with one. I started up this owners' club, and we found over a hundred people internationally with 400s. They swear by them. Just try to pry their hands off them."

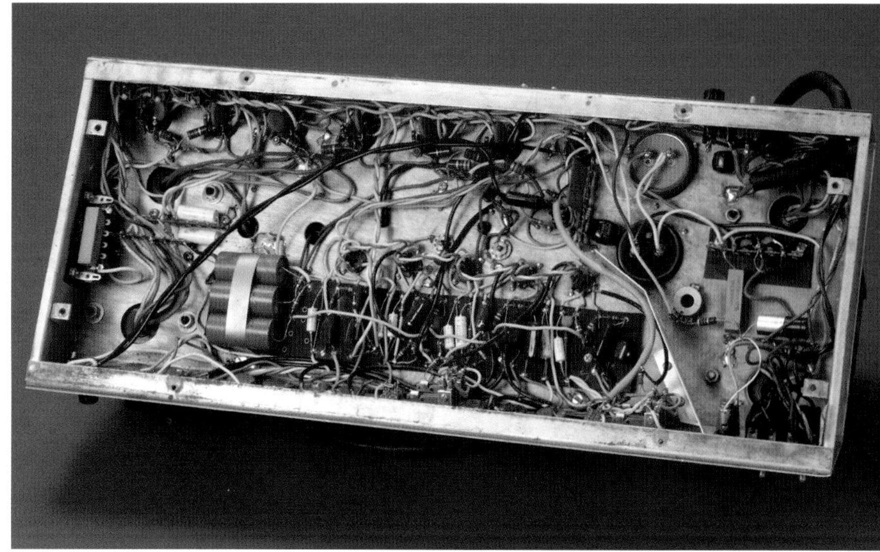

Rich Koerner, on the complicated circuitry of the 400 PS: "The design was unique; a lot of the details would be foreign to 90 percent of the amp techs out there."

The 4x6550 300 PS was another powerful amp, although less ferocious than the six-bottle 400 PS. To some extent it was adapted from Ed Jahns' Super Twin — they shared the same control panel — and it was paired with either a unique, angled 4x12 bass reflex cab for bassists, or a flat-panel 4x12 for guitar players.

Circuit Boards

Ed Jahns instituted and closely monitored Fender's method of attaching components to circuit boards. Bill Hughes: "I remember the process exactly. The 'fishpaper' material we used for the boards was dried at normal atmospheric pressure in an oven, then put in beeswax, and then a vacuum was pulled on top of the beeswax so that any air and remaining moisture inside the material would pop out. We would punch the holes with an Amada NC [numeric controlled] punch press using a numerical tape [as a guide]. The eyelets would be put in, and then the boards would be dried and waxed again. You have wires going on this thing from eyelet to eyelet — from point to point. With traditional hand-wired amps that didn't use the Ed Jahns eyelet board, no two amps were the same because the wires didn't lie the same way. On the Ed Jahns type, the wires would lie the same way every time."

Transformers

During the silverface era Fender transformers were made by Schumacher. According to CBS in-house documents, "Fender transformers are larger and have more windings so we can handle twice the RMS rating of the amplifier very efficiently and without failures. Old transformers and [those of] many of our competitors are filled with wax or varnish which gets soft and melts. We use GE Permofil Epoxy, which is impregnated into the transformer first in a vacuum, then under pressure. Permofil is an excellent and long-lasting heat conductor. The good epoxy fill will keep the windings of copper wire in the transformer from buzzing and also keeps them from becoming loose and shorting out. Around the transformer is a copper band, which is there to cut the hum. There is also an electrostatic shield inside the transformer to cut down on RF [Radio Frequency] interference from electric cash registers, CBs, TVs, radios, and other transmitting equipment."

Fullerton, We Have a Problem

As revealed by Bob Rissi, Paul Rivera, Bill Carson, and others, recurring problems for CBS Fender included a shift in the relation between Marketing and R&D, as well as the hiring of staff who might have had extensive backgrounds in electronics, aerospace, automotive, or corporate management yet little experience with music. This anecdote from Fender Purchasing Manager Joe Carducci tells the tale:

"From about '78 through '85 I was a guitar and Rhodes piano repair tech with the Fender National Service Center at the factory in Fullerton. Because we were next door to R&D, Ed Jahns was a regular visitor who often shared knowledge and repair tips with our amp guys.

"One day someone down the hall was sound testing an amplifier at an extremely loud volume. Though sound testing was a daily occurrence, this test in particular sounded out of the norm. Accompanied with the loud, distorted sound of jazz style diminished, augmented, and minor chords — with an occasional random hard strum of open strings — two male voices could be heard shouting confrontationally at one another. My curiosity got the best of me, so I went out to see what the commotion was about.

"Ed Jahns and Freddie Tavares were seated together in front of a work bench with what appeared to be a prototype chassis plugged into a Dual Showman 2x15 enclosure. Freddie was blasting away playing a Stratocaster in that mellow style we were accustomed to hearing him play, while shouting at Ed, 'It doesn't *sound* good!' Ed was obviously annoyed. While sternly pointing and shaking his finger at an oscilloscope monitor, he shouted back, 'But *look, look, look* — the sine wave is square! That's the sound the kids want!' Freddie continued to play a very stylish chord melody with an ear-splitting, raunchy tone. He shouted again, 'But it just doesn't *sound* good!' Again pointing to the oscilloscope, Ed shouted back, 'But that's the sound the kids are looking for! See? *The sine wave is square!*'"

Value, Perspectives

There were many incremental changes in components and design during the silverface era, just as there were during any 15-year period in Fender history. How significant were they? It's unlikely that even the most sophisticated listener can distinguish the effect of, say, altering the coating on interior wires. Then again, a long list of changes that are too small to hear by themselves can indeed combine to make audible differences. For some observers, distinctions between blackfaces and non-master silverfaces are overblown. Teagle & Sprung referred to the "tried and true line of silverface amps, basically unchanged for over ten years," and termed the master volumes, pull boosts, and logo alterations "the biggest changes in a remarkably stable line, running into 1981."

At the risk of redundancy, it must be emphasized that silverfaces vary in sound (as do tweeds and other Fenders). John Sprung: "Not all blackface amps sound alike, either. If you line up ten blackface Twin Reverbs, chances are you're going to like some more than others, and the same is true with the silverfaces, at least up until the ones with the master volume and the pull-switch. Some of the components were rated at plus or minus 20 percent in their performance, so there's a big variation right there."

If we *had* to generalize: OK, blackfaces sound better than silverfaces. But we don't have to generalize. A silverface in reasonable condition is still a hand-wired, easy-to-repair amp with the basic Fender sound. You may find a terrific '74 Super Reverb that sounds better to you than some of the blackfaces you've encountered. And, even if the amp's sound is less than ideal, it may lend itself to inexpensive blackfacing. Another thing — much of the criticism of silverface amps is heaped on the distortion circuits; well, if the clean channel sounds great, there are plenty of good stompboxes for distortion.

Late-'60s and early-'70s silverface Deluxe Reverbs are similar to the blackface versions and are often good bargains, as are Princetons and Princeton Reverbs. Writing in *Guitar Player* back in 1991, Art Thompson referred to silverface Princetons, Deluxe Reverbs, and non-master Super Reverbs and Twin Reverbs as "some of the best amp bargains you'll find today."

Prices have escalated since then, but silverface Fenders often remain smart buys. Even a black-sheep model may be just the ticket. Longtime amp mod specialist and manufacturer Dan Torres has written of the later, high-powered Twins, Pros, and Super Reverbs: "They have ultralinear output transformers, giving them more power and wider frequency response. The poorly educated techs and those with no knowledge instantly reject these amps as they are 'different.' I, personally, seek them out as they can certainly sound the absolute best for clean tone. There is nothing like ultralinear operation to get a big, full, clean tone."

So, on this topic, as on so many others, reasonable minds may differ. Who decides what sounds good? Not the book authors, magazine columnists, amp techs, collectors, retailers, manufacturers, or denizens of the Internet chat rooms. Who decides? You do.

"I got my first Fender when I was in Humble Pie. Steve Marriott and I both got Champs with the silver front in about 1970, right about the time *Layla* came out. I believe Eric was using Champs as well. That was my last year of studio work with Humble Pie, and we did the whole of the *Rock On* album [1970] with those two silverish Champs. We bought them brand new. We tried them out and that was it — we never unplugged.

"I recorded with Fender amps a lot. Even on my first solo record, *Wind of Change*, I used Fenders. I didn't have any amps after I left Humble Pie. My friend Ian Stewart, who was playing piano with the Stones, came 'round and said, 'What do you need, then?' I said, 'Well ... an *amp* [laughs]!' So he would just go to the Stones' warehouse and bring me over a bunch of Fenders.

"I was so naïve. In England, early on, we didn't have the luxury of knowing all about it. When we got a 'Fender amp,' it wasn't a Bassman or a Twin or a Deluxe. It was a *Fender amp*. We didn't know about the models or the years. We just didn't think like that. I did have a piggyback head and a two-12 cabinet that I remember using on my version of 'Jumpin' Jack Flash.' So here I was using the Stones' amp on my version of their song."

— Peter Frampton

George Harrison in the studio with Rocky, his favorite Stratocaster, and one of several piggyback Fenders used by the Beatles on recording sessions in the late '60s.

Meet the Beatles

The Beatles used Fender amps off and on throughout their careers. As documented by Andy Babiuk in his compelling and thoroughly researched book *Beatles Gear*, they played a seven-week engagement way back in mid '62 at the famed Star Club in Hamburg, Germany: "The club provided a complete backline of Fender amplifiers for visiting acts to use, and photographs taken of the Beatles performing show a complete line of cream [blonde] Tolex-covered Fender amps and speaker cabinets. ... Lennon and Harrison each played through the club's cream Fender Bandmaster piggyback amps while McCartney used a cream Fender Bassman head with a Coffin speaker cabinet."

During the sessions for *Rubber Soul* (released December '65), Paul McCartney used a blonde piggyback Bassman with the wheat-colored grille, perhaps along with other amps. For the recording of *Revolver* (August '66), McCartney played his '64 Fireglo Rickenbacker 4001S through the blonde Bassman; the group also used a blackface Showman at that time.

During an early trip to Hamburg, John Lennon acquired a natural blonde Rickenbacker 325 that he later painted black. He ran it through a tweed narrow panel Deluxe. While recording "The White Album," released in November 1968, the group acquired a blackface Deluxe and a silverface Deluxe Reverb. John used the blackface Deluxe. Andy Babiuk: "Given that he could've chosen anything from a vast line of Fender amplifiers, perhaps it was his fond memories of his first Fender Deluxe tweed amp in Hamburg that drew him to this new version."

While working on the *Let It Be* album (released in May 1970 but actually recorded prior to 1969's *Abbey Road*), John and George used '68 silverface Twin Reverbs, while Paul played through a new '68 silverface Bassman with two 12s. George Harrison often paired a Bassman with his favorite Stratocaster, the hand-painted, "psychedelic" Rocky.

It seems almost impossible to calculate the promotional value of getting your gear into the hands of the Beatles, but Don Randall did just that, right on time for the recording and filming of *Let It Be*. Here's his account:

On January 30, 1969, the Beatles performed for the last time together at the now famous concert atop the Apple Corps Ltd. building in London. Although John, George, and Paul had used Fender amps throughout their careers, Don Randall had arranged for them to acquire brand new models in time for this rooftop performance.

On that blustery Thursday afternoon at 3 Savile Row, the Beatles used a Fender solid state PA system and a trio of silverface Twin Reverbs (one was a backup and wasn't needed during the set). Also seen here is Paul's silverface Bassman. (Guest keyboardist Billy Preston used a 73-key "silver-top" Fender Rhodes Electric Piano.) This is likely the same gear seen in photos taken during the previous few days during the recording sessions for *Get Back* and *Let It Be.*

"Of course we recognized their significance and prominence in the music field, and I had dealt with their manager, Brian Epstein, but the actual conversation about getting amplifiers and guitars into the hands of the Beatles was with the musicians themselves. I went to London, up to their offices at Apple Records. Paul McCartney greeted me and made me feel right at home. John Lennon was supposed to be there but didn't show up for a while.

"Paul was not only very charming, he was also very knowledgeable. It was clear that he knew amplifiers and instruments, and he knew Fender instruments in particular. So, we waited and waited, and John finally showed up with his wife, Yoko Ono. John looked at me and said, 'What's he doing here?' I think he was having a bad day. He was difficult and kind of a pain to deal with, really, and I don't know why he was being so difficult. But the other one, Paul, was pleasant and respectful.

"Well, we sat down in a big meeting room with a conference table and talked about what they were trying to accomplish and what sort of gear would be most suitable. The whole time, Yoko Ono just kind of sat there with her head bowed, moving her head up and down as if she were in a trance or something. John was still in a huff, but of course I had to put up with him and be as nice as I could.

"It worked out pretty well. I didn't bring any equipment with me. It was just to make arrangements, and then once I talked to them we arranged for delivery of the gear. They'd already had some Fender equipment, but not that much. But now they were able to have all sorts of pieces. They could pick and choose whatever they wanted.

"Paul was very amenable to what we were trying to do as far as getting some Fender guitars and amps into their hands. I spent about three-quarters of an hour with Paul, plus another 30 or 40 minutes with them after John and Yoko showed up. Really, by the time they got there Paul and I had worked up the business. As a consequence of this conversation, we did get quite a bit of equipment into their hands in time for the movie."

The Stinger: The old saying about how a great guitarist can speak volumes with a single note could have been inspired by the late Albert Collins. He played classic licks and melodies, but some of his strongest messages were delivered with this Tele and this Quad Reverb — one long, stinging note at a time.

From left: Huey Lewis sits in with Albert Collins and Bo Diddley at a 1990 tribute to John Lee Hooker. Albert Collins told *Guitar Player*'s Dan Forte in 1988 that he had been using a Fender Quad Reverb since 1972: "They're loud! I've got two of them. I only use one of them onstage, though. I always play my amps [with the volume on 10], ever since I've been playing. I change tubes about every six months. I put the treble all the way on 10, the middle on 10, and I don't use bass, intensity, or none of that. Reverb I set at 4. They don't make them anymore. It's got four JBL 12s. Before they came out with the Quad in '72, I used a Bandmaster piggyback. I cut a lot of records with it."

In the wattage wars of the '70s and '80s, even the relatively "low end" Fenders included some powerful amplifiers. Shown here are four tube and four solid state models from 1983. The tubers are either 18W (Champ II, Super Champ) or 20W (Princeton Reverb II, Deluxe Reverb II), while the solid staters range from the 20W Harvard Reverb II up to the 100W Stage Lead.

CHAPTER EIGHTEEN

18

Early '80s: New Blood

Paul Rivera Arrives, Solid State Returns

By the beginning of 1980, the line was in need of a jolt. Fender hadn't introduced a major guitar amp in five years, which for Leo Fender would have been an eternity. Compared to the hectic pace of innovation during earlier and later periods, things were slower than a five-set gig at an empty steak house. In fact, most of the late-'70s developments had been discontinuations of old models rather than introductions of anything new. For example, the classic non-reverb Princeton and a pair of aging beasts from the early '70s, the Super Six Reverb and the Quad Reverb, were all gone.

Much of 1980's line was standard silverface fare: Twin Reverbs, Pro Reverbs, Deluxe Reverbs, Princeton Reverbs, Champs, Vibro Champs, etc. It's difficult to pinpoint actual production numbers, because CBS accountants paid more attention to dollars than units, and also because computerized records were routinely purged. In any case, by late '80 or early '81, the Studio Bass, the 300 PS, and the reverb versions of the Bandmaster, Dual Showman, and Super Twin had all been axed.

After a long drought, Fender in late 1980 finally responded to high-tech, feature-laden competitors with the innovative Fender 75, an Ed Jahns design. Rather than just another silverface, it might be called the first post-Boogie Fender in that it had two preamps wired in series (that is, one after the other). Like its all-new companions, the 30 and the 140, the 75 featured a white stripe around the front of the cabinet that distinguished its look from earlier and later Fenders. Dripping with gadgets and features, the 75W, all-tube model had pull boosts of about 12dB for each of its three tone controls, a Bright switch providing a high-end boost of approximately 6dB, separate knobs for preamp Gain, Lead Drive, Lead Level, and Master Volume, as well as a 75W/15W output power switch/voltage selector. The 75's several versions included a 1x15, a 1x12, and piggybacks with either four 10s or two 12s.

On paper the 75 seemed to be just what Fender needed. *Guitar Player* in late 1982 called it "a controllable, durable little workhorse," and even today, some players swear by it and consider it one of Fender's best kept secrets — a classic Fender with a touch of Boogie. At the time, however, it failed to generate much excitement. Steve Grom: "Some people liked it, some people didn't. It had an odd tone to it. A lot of Ed Jahns' products were engineered very well, but some of the sound things were sort of at the whim of whoever Ed's marketing guy was at the time." Lee Jackson: "The Fender 75 was Fender's first 'hot' amp, with gain and pull switches and all that. It had all these features, but it never got the classic sound that people were looking for." Guitarists had new priorities, new tastes, and new needs, and the 75 did little to boost Fender's fortunes. The company faced an uncertain, shifting market. It was time for new blood and fresh ideas.

Hot Rods to Fullerton: The Arrival of Paul Rivera

Fender's most troubling problem had been relinquishing its leading role in innovation to smaller companies and even individuals who were pioneering new approaches to amplification. Paul Rivera was one such person. Based in Southern California, he had established a reputation among high-profile clients as a repairman and cutting-edge amp mod specialist. In the spring of 1981, Fender brought him in-house to make over the line of amplifiers.

Lee Jackson had already worked with Paul Rivera at Rivera R&D and was hired by Fender not long after his colleague's arrival. Among other tasks, the newcomers were charged with helping to reestablish a closer connection to Fender's customers. Lee Jackson: "It was the '80s, and customizing and hot rodding were the big things. Just playing the stock guitar in the catalog wasn't good enough. Being a player and working in a band, I could see how things were changing — like my guitar had a Floyd Rose on it, or I might put a humbucking in there. I was working all the time in bands. I'd come in and say, 'Hey, this is the future. Look, I put a Floyd on my Strat and it's amazing!'

"We had the same attitude with the amps. Channel-switching was a buzzword. Boogie had really pioneered that idea, and they were pretty much dominating. [Mesa/Boogie founder] Randy Smith, his whole thing was taking Fenders and modifying them. He was the first person to do that. Paul Rivera came from that same camp, modifying Fenders, so he was the perfect guy for Fender to have in there. He was part of the new trend."

While CBS Fender had no shortage of talented engineers, few were serious musicians. The tradition of soliciting suggestions from professionals had continued, but during the '70s there seemed to be no one in-house in the pivotal role of musician/engineer who could translate this feedback for R&D. Call it a shortage of FTF, the Freddie Tavares Factor. (Although Mr. Tavares was still there, his role had been significantly diminished.)

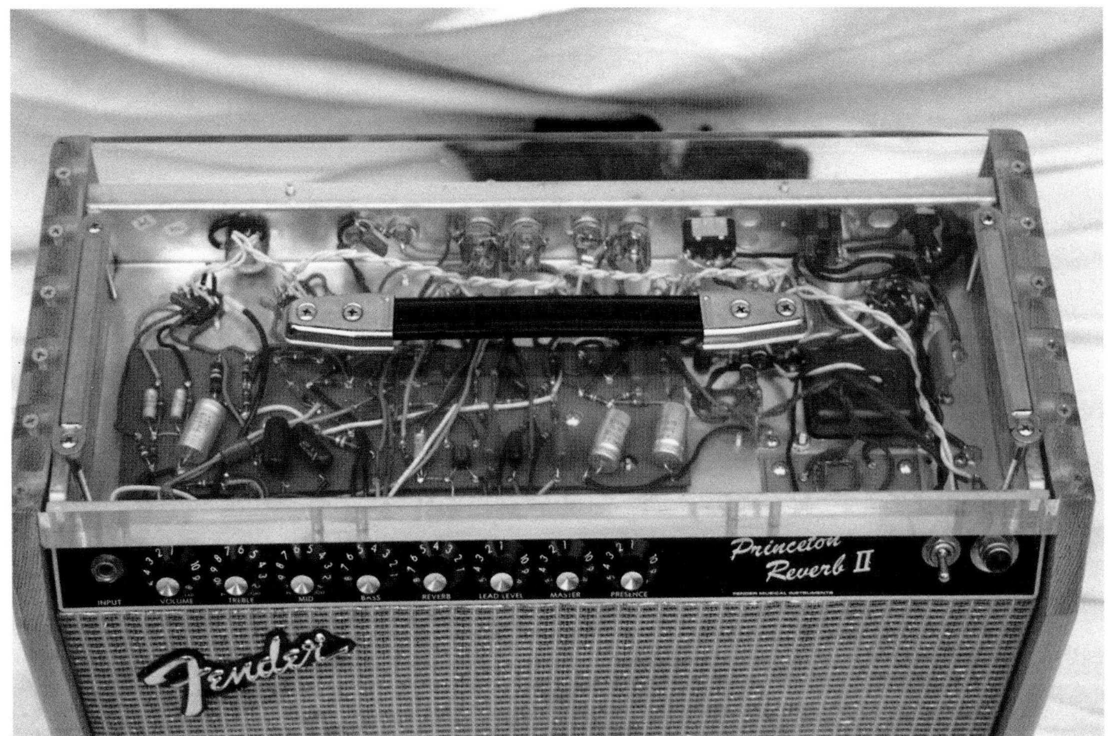

One of two see-through Fenders, built for a NAMM trade show to demo the interior workings of a Princeton Reverb II, circa 1983.

On Freddie Tavares

"Freddie was still there when I was working there in the early 1980s, but to be honest, his role was as a figurehead only. Nobody listened to him. I loved the guy. He was so cool. He represented the stream of consciousness from the early Fender days. He was a phenomenal player and a wonderful person, just exquisite. But he wasn't contributing at that point. I'm speculating here, but I can imagine the following happening: CBS blows in, and they think they know everything. They look at Freddie Tavares, who is a soft-spoken gentleman, and he's not going to lord his expertise over anybody. He's not that kind of guy. So in come these ultra egos and they just landed Fender, a great investment, and they're not gonna listen to somebody like Freddie. I'm afraid that's just what happened. When you'd ask him something, he was sharp as a tack. I can't emphasize that enough. The problem was, they had stopped asking."

— PJ Geerlings

Ed Jahns' all-tube, dual-preamp Fender 75 of 1980 to 1982 had multiple boosts and a 75W/15W power switch. Note the distinctive white trim around the grille. This one's an '81.

Lee Jackson: "They'd invite 20 musicians and send them into a room full of gear and give them clipboards with a questionnaire. The guys would play all the products and write down their feedback, what's good, what's bad, but trying to relate that to an engineer was difficult. So one of the things that Paul and I brought to the mix was that we both played guitar. If something didn't sound right, we would recognize that, and we talked like guitar players. We'd say, 'It's too flubby,' or whatever [laughs]. We helped make Fender a little more in tune with what was going on, because we could translate the needs of players for the engineers."

Compared to the bleak period of the '70s, the outlook had already improved by the time Rivera arrived. Ed Jahns, in R&D, was a stickler for high quality components, and the tube amps for the most part were using premium Mallory capacitors, Paktron coupling capacitors, CTS pots, Schumacher transformers — all good stuff.

The Plan

Among the Fender faithful, the stigma against the solid state amps of 1966 to 1971 remained a formidable burden, but the bigger problem was Fender's failure to adapt to a changing environment. Peavey and Crate were setting the pace at the lower and middle price points of the market, Marshall and Mesa/Boogie at the top end, and in the wake of fierce competition, interest in some of the old Fender standbys had waned. (Vintage Marshalls include the Super Leads favored by Hendrix, Cream, Beck, Page, and other giants. In today's vintage amp market, some of the most valuable of these Marshalls date to the late '60s through the mid '70s. Consider the relative value of silverface Fenders from that same period.)

Fender now paid a price for lagging behind other companies' innovations. They had tried to tackle distortion with the crude master volume circuit on some models in the early '70s, but results were mixed. Paul Rivera: "We needed gain, we needed features, and we needed quality, so basically we started working on building a whole new amplifier."

Rivera had already completed a five-year plan for Fender by the time he arrived in '81. It detailed the specifications of various models — their front panels, rear panels, features, and some of the circuitry. He would bring these specs to the R&D lab. Former Marketing Manager for amps Steve Grom: "Paul had great ideas, but he sometimes gets credit for the designs, too. It was really the R&D team of Ed Jahns and later Bill Hughes, Bill Hodges, and Bob Haigler who did the majority of the design work."

Paul Rivera doesn't disagree. "I would come in and say, this is what we're going to do, this is how the effects loop is going to work, or whatever. I was front-loading them with ideas, and final engineering was done by R&D. Without the hard work of Robert Haigler, Ed Jahns, Bill Hodges, Bill Hughes, and many others, none of the amps I was involved with would have gotten into production.

"We developed an *esprit de corps*. The mood was optimistic, very 'can do.' We were putting Fender back on track. It was an exciting time, with Dan Smith working hard in guitars, getting the quality back. We were trying to do the same in amplifiers. We'd all grown up on Fenders, and we all knew what was at stake."

"We'd all grown up on Fenders, and we all knew what was at stake."

— Paul Rivera

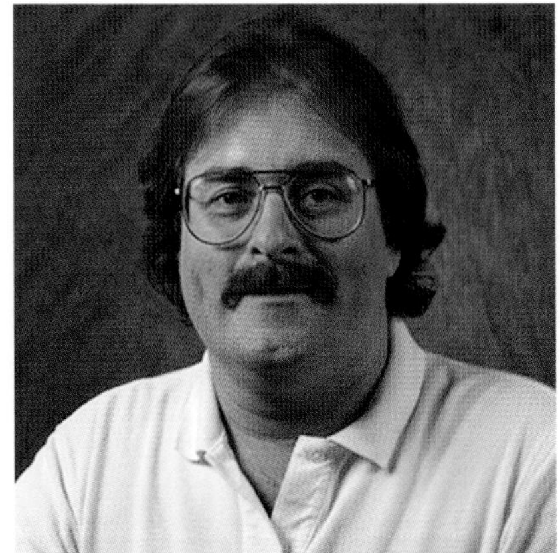

Paul Rivera. Art Thompson of *Guitar Player* magazine wrote: "Rivera's touch enhanced the Fender line at a time when its amps weren't even a consideration for many players."

The low and mid-power Fenders of 1982, prior to the Rivera re-do of later that year, including two solid state models (the Harvard and Harvard Reverb) and five tube amps ranging from the 6W Champ and Vibro Champ up to the 40W 2x10 Vibrolux Reverb.

New Management, New Directions

William Schultz and other successful execs were hired away from Yamaha in 1981 to take over the helm of a drifting, rudderless Fender. Lee Jackson: "There was this whole thing to go out and find the best guys in the field, and they grabbed people from all over." The best guys in the field included Bill Hughes, who arrived in January 1982 and is now a veteran of more than two decades at Fender. He had been working in electronics since his teenage years, spending several years at Ampeg (where he designed the electronics for one of the great amps of all time, Ampeg's classic monster, the SVT). He also acquired a deep background in aerospace. Bill Hughes: "My first title at Fender was Manager of Vacuum Tube Amplifier Design. Paul Rivera was running guitar amp marketing, and we developed a line of vacuum tube guitar amps with his input, which was quite substantial. Bob Haigler and his crew developed a line of solid state amps, also with Paul's input."

Back in Black

The first catalog published under the new leadership was the January 1982 edition, which pictured a number of models that had been introduced in 1981. With its recognition of the market's rising vintage consciousness (regarding guitars, at least, if not yet amplifiers), its introduction of reissue guitars and basses, and its expansion of the Stratocaster from a single model to a small line of instruments, it was Fender's most significant public document in more than a decade. People took notice. Something was going on at Fender, something exciting.

Although several of the amps were once again given a "blackface" appearance (knobs, face plates, coverings, grille cloths), they differed fundamentally in circuitry and features from their ostensible forebears of the mid 1960s. Still, at the very least, they seemed to demonstrate a belief that Fender's future might lay, at least in part, in reclaiming some of its lost heritage.

Other developments reflected guitarists' obsession with power, distortion, and volume. Acquiring a master volume and other modifications, the Twin Reverb had mutated during the late '70s into an 87 pound behemoth; at 135W, it was *loud*, a real paint peeler. Similarly infused with steroids, the about-to-be-discontinued Super Reverb of the late '70s and early '80s had a master volume and 70W of output. The other recently pumped-up heavyweight was the 2x12 Pro Reverb, making its last catalog appearance before it, too, was dropped. In a rare acknowledgement of the similarity of some models' circuits, Fender helpfully characterized the Pro Reverb as either a 70W Twin Reverb, or a Super Reverb with two 12s (an approach to categorizing amps that, come to think of it, would have made things a lot clearer had Fender adopted it in, say, 1955).

The new management team resolved to "go out and find the best guys in the field." They included Bill Hughes, who had designed the electronics for Ampeg's classic SVT. He arrived at Fender in January 1982.

Smaller tube models included the Champ and Vibro Champ (both 6W, 1x8), the 12W, 1x10 Princeton Reverb, the reliably popular 20W, 1x12 Deluxe Reverb, and the 40W, 2x10 Vibrolux Reverb — all of which were about to be dropped.

A sign of changing times: All of the new models except the Champ and Vibro Champ featured gain boosts of some sort. (As we have seen elsewhere, it's sometimes hard to generalize about the relationships among Fender amps. To cite one example among many: Back in '56/'57, the 15W Deluxe had more power than the Vibrolux and a bigger speaker as well; but now the Vibrolux was by far the bigger amp, with double the power and more total cone diameter.)

Another foray into modern design was the top of the line bass amp, the 300W, rack mount, solid state B-300 head with active tone controls, parametric EQ, and onboard compressor. Conventional heads and combos included four different Bassmans (the 135, the 70, the 10, and the solid state Compact), and the 12W, two-knob Musicmaster.

The Return to Solid State

After seeing its reputation fade with the thoroughly discredited transistorized models of the late 1960s and early 1970s, Fender had wisely avoided marketing solid state amplifiers for a decade, relying instead on the silverface tube models. Steve Grom: "There was some horrendous stuff in the '70s all across the industry, but problems with early solid state technology had actually been cleaned up pretty well by the time I got there in 1980. Besides, the majority of Fender production had gone back to tube amps."

But with tube amp production costs on the rise, Fender again turned to solid state technology, this time with much better results. New models included the budget-minded Harvard, Harvard Reverb, Harvard Reverb II, and Yale Reverb. One or more of these amps would stay in the line until 1985 — not a bad run — and since that time Fender has generally relied on its solid state amps to provide a range of models at low to moderate price points.

Early-'80s solid state amps also included two high-end models, the 50W Studio Lead and the 100W Stage Lead, both with channel switching, gain controls, and active 3-band EQ.

The Re-Do of '82

While the January 1982 catalog hinted at new directions, the effect of the Rivera revamp wasn't felt until later that same year. By December, the Pro Reverb, Vibrolux Reverb, Vibro Champ, and a couple of bass amps had all been dropped, as had the 75; the 75's companions, the 30W, 1x12 Fender 30 and the massive 140W Fender 140 piggyback, were already long gone.

New models included the Super Champ (18W, 1x10, a gain channel, reverb), freestanding preamps and power amps, and the Bassman 20. Substantial remakes of familiar models (or more precisely, amps with familiar model *names*) included a whole line of II's — the short-lived Champ II (18W, 1x10, master volume), Princeton Reverb II (20W, 1x12, gain boost; the project engineer was Bill Hughes), Deluxe Reverb II (20W, 1x12, two channels, including high gain with master V), Twin Reverb II (now a 105W channel switcher with master V), and a series of Concerts sometimes nicknamed the Concert II's. *Guitar Player*'s Art Thompson described the Deluxe Reverb II as sort of a cross between a Deluxe Reverb and a Mesa/Boogie MKII, adding, "[its hand-wiring] puts it in a league with boutique amps costing $1,500 and up."

Among other things, the 1982 line revealed Fender's view that distortion was more desirable than tremolo, long a feature on many models but now conspicuously absent. The new models also reflected a different approach to output stages. Bill Hughes: "A lot of the amps previously made by Fender had very powerful output stages, like the late-'70s and early-'80s version of the Twin Reverb, with 135 watts. They utilized a special output transformer that had a 15 percent tap for the screen grid. And because of that they had a problem. There was a 120Hz sideband around the output. If you put a 1kHz signal through it, you would naturally get a 2kHz sideband, and one at 3kHz, 4kHz and so on — the products of distortion. But you also got sidebands at 120Hz integers. Now, this 120Hz is obviously two times the power-line frequency [60 cycles]. The result was, those output stages, although more efficient and capable of more power, didn't sound very good. Those older amplifiers produced a kind of distortion called ripple-induced distortion. It was a rather grindy sound when the amplifier would overload.

Six amps (with two cabs) from the series of eight mid-line Fender amps, early '80s. The complete group included four 60W tube Concerts, three 100W solid state London Reverbs, and the 100W solid state Montreux. Paul Rivera: "The Montreux was my iteration of an amp that would compete with a Peavey Bandit and eat it alive, which it did."

"What it boils down to is that output stage distortion has to be harmonically related. The 135 watt amps [which also included the later versions of the silverface Dual Showman Reverb, Super Six Reverb, Vibrosonic Reverb, and Quad Reverb] had distortion products where some overtones were harmonically related and some were not. So we got rid of them, and for the new amps we went to a more conventional output stage, without the screen taps."

By the time the 1983 catalog was published, the nearly iconic Super Reverb, which had powered so many gigs on so many stages, had been gone for several months. Paul Rivera: "We had been making the 4x10 Super Reverbs into 1982, but that whole line was cancelled, so the new 4x10 Concert took over as the successor to the Super Reverb. The Deluxe II did okay, but the real movers were the new Concerts and Super Champs."

The 2x6L6 Concert of the early to mid 1980s was the all-tube, 60W big brother of the Deluxe II. Available as a 1x12, 2x10, 4x10, or head, it was a point-to-point channel switcher with features like a four-spring reverb and an active effects loop with level controls. A review in *Guitar Player* called the 1x12 version "the product of a new Fender philosophy, employing more 1980s creativity and innovation .... Fender is still using fiber circuit boards as they have for many, many years .... Congratulations to Fender and its R&D staff for getting it right and keeping alive the traditional sound while incorporating useful innovations."

Paul Rivera: "I thought the 2x10 Concert would have sold better than it did. We figured we were going to recapture the glory days of the Vibrolux, which I always thought was really cool, but we only sold a couple hundred a year of the 2x10. The head sold in small quantities, but overall the Concerts sold extremely well. The star was the 1x12, followed by the 4x10.

"The Princeton Reverb II also did very well. Aside from the regular model, we made a special run of a hundred Princetons in oak cabinets that we had made in an organ cabinet factory in the Midwest somewhere. We called them the Super Pro series. We also did a hundred Super Champs and a hundred Concerts in wooden cabs, and they're now the most sought-after amps of that era [see below]."

The late Robert Haigler led a team of engineers who tackled a redesign of the solid state amps under Rivera's direction, creating models such as the high-end London Reverb and Montreux. Both had 100W outputs and modern features such as a gain channel with independent tone controls, programmable effects loops, and dual reverbs. The Montreux was a 1x12 combo, and the London Reverb was available in 1x12, 2x10, and head configurations.

As we have seen often, model names sometimes suggest family ties among amps that are in fact mostly unrelated. There is no better example than the early-'80s Showman. Once a blonde, tube-powered, uncomplicated piggyback, the Showman was now a black, solid state, feature-encrusted combo — four of them, in fact, in 1x12, 1x15, 2x10, and 2x12 cabinets. Each was fueled by a positively *screaming* 200W. All had features typical of high-end units of the period — pull boost knobs, high-gain channels, a digital footswitch for channel selection, graphic equalizers, etc. According to Paul Rivera, the Showman didn't sell as well as the lower-powered London Reverb and Montreux.

At the time, the ambition of the early-'80s makeover seemed to be rivaled only by milestones such as the conversion from tweed to Tolex or the introduction of the blackface line. From 1980 to 1983, routine maintenance of the amplifier catalog had intensified from pruning to clear cutting, as something like 18 models were dropped to make room for the new Fenders. In 1982 alone, nine models were either introduced or fundamentally made over.

But the other essential aspect of the re-do of '82 was this: It was short-lived. Half of these new models and remakes would disappear over the next three years, and all would be gone by '87. By then, the Fender company had virtually disappeared, and a new one had taken its place.

Under the Corporate Radar: The Oak Body Super Pros

Paul Rivera: "I came up with a plan in '82 to sneak some new amps past the accounting department. I got so tired of the negative 'You can't do a low-volume amp' thing that I conspired with purchasing and the factory in Hoopeston, Illinois. I had some dovetailed oak plank cabinets done in Indiana by the company that made home organ cabinets for Gulbransen. The front panels were made by Miller Dial [El Monte, CA] in Champagne Beige and Choco Brown. Mellotone [Wendell Fabrics, Blacksburg, SC] had a run of matching grille cloth made as well. Kurz-Kasch [Dayton, OH] made the knobs for us and did a perfect color match.

It was a fun project, and we did succeed in doing it below the corporate radar. We called them the Super Pro Series, and we did the Super Champ, Princeton II, and Concert 1x12, each with an EVM speaker and a padded brown slip cover. We only built a hundred pieces of each one for the whole world. They are rare puppies. I have Super Champ #1." [See photo, Chap. 29.]

On the International Front

The early-'80s upheavals in products and personnel were accompanied by the dramatic growth of Fender's export business. Although they were better known for their early-'60s endorsements of Vox, the Beatles used Fender amps off and on throughout their careers, particularly after 1968. Other superstar UK groups used Fenders as well, but for most players overseas, Fenders were out of reach. Domestic demand was so great that there weren't many amps left over for international distribution. That changed in the '70s, and by the early '80s Fender began to exert a significant international influence.

If exports were important, imports were crucial. An essential strategy in rebuilding Fender was opening up Fender Japan. Fender went to Utsunomiya, in northern Japan, and invested in a factory that used to make karaoke equipment. They retooled for amp production in June of 1981, and from mid '82 onward Paul Rivera was spending several months a year in Japan, training the crew and supervising production of an important new line of amplifiers called the Sidekicks.

"It was really exciting," he recalls. "Fender had had inexpensive amplifiers back in the classic period, but we'd never had amps with modern features for two hundred bucks, and now we did. That was a big part of our success. It was [Vice President of Marketing and Sales] Roger Balmer who had the vision, and it was his brainchild exclusively. He was friends with Chitoshi Kojima, Chairman of Kanda Shokai. This went back to the Music Man days when Roger worked there. Kanda Shokai was the distributor for Music Man, Ernie Ball, and Roland, among others. Roger deserves a ton of credit for creating amplifiers to occupy price points that we would never have been able to do with U.S. production."

Along with its distribution, Fender began to internationalize its production. Some of the amplifiers generally considered to be "U.S. made" at the time were actually chassis-wired and subassembled in Mexico at a company called El Faro; the work was scrutinized and tweaked when necessary by the Fullerton team prior to final assembly. Arrangements between the U.S. and Mexican governments required the company to be owned by Mexican nationals, although within a few years that would change, and Fender would set up its own operation in Ensenada.

Paul Rivera: "At first, the Ensenada facility was an independent contractor. We would send parts down there, then get the chassis back and QC them [inspect for quality control] in California. The cabs were made in Fullerton, so we'd slip the chassis into the cabs and they'd go out the door." Steve Grom: "When I started in 1980, we were already getting some amp chassis wired in Ensenada. I understand Fender started using El Faro as early as 1978 or 1979." Amps subassembled in Mexico were marked with an "M" on the interior side panels.

Now building amps in four locations, Fender by the mid 1980s was on its way to establishing its current multinational array of production facilities. Some of the tube models were made in Fullerton, including the Super Champ, Champ II, Deluxe Reverb II, Princeton Reverb II, and the new Concert. Other tube models were put together in Fullerton using components subassembled in Mexico. The inexpensive solid state models were made in Japan, including the Sidekick guitar amps, some keyboard amps, and a few bass amps. Finally, the professional solid state models such as the London Reverb were made in the old Gulbransen keyboard factory in Hoopeston, Illinois, which Fender had acquired; eventually, some of the tube amp production was moved to Illinois as well.

The move to Hoopeston was accomplished in stages, starting in 1982 and extending over a transitional period of 12 to 18 months. Steve Grom: "Some of the tube models that started in Fullerton later moved to Hoopeston. I'm not sure about making the Twin Reverb II in Fullerton. That was the last of this series to be introduced into production, and if any were made in Fullerton it was for a very short period. This was the amp that Hoopeston really had trouble with, due to the high gain structure of the overdrive channel. Some of the Rivera era amps were never made in Fullerton, such as the solid state Showman, the London, and the Stage Lead. They went directly to Hoopeston."

Paul Rivera: "The plan to revamp the line worked. The line expanded, the amps sounded good, and we were covering a lot of price points. We went from something like 17,000 units in 1980 — which for Fender was nothing — up to something like 125,000 by '83. Of those, about 30,000 or 40,000 were tube, the rest solid state. We made some in the U.S. and a lot in Japan."

From 1984 through 1992, the various Sidekick imports were essential to Fender's success in the student/practice amp market.

Crafting Prototypes

Former senior tech in Fender R&D PJ Geerlings worked on prototype amps in the most basic way: He started by taking shears to big sheets of fiberboard and cutting out circuit boards. His projects included every Fender tube amp of '82 and '83 other than the Super Champ, including all of the Paul Rivera-era "II" models. Here he reflects on the prototyping process and the roles of his colleagues.

I would be presented with a schematic of the amplifier. There was typically no wiring diagram, no parts list, just the schematic drawn up by one of our draftsmen. These were hand-drawn, and they were exquisite. The draftsmen in those days had tremendous pride in their work. This was a big drawing, about 24" by 36".

Before I came to Fender, I had been inside many Fender amps, repairing them and tweaking them, so I had a pretty good idea of how a Fender amp should look on the inside, and I used that knowledge to sort of recreate the past. I would try to lay them out as if I were laying out a '50s or '60s vintage amplifier, and the net result was a very clean layout on the inside. It worked the first time, by golly.

Paul would come in and lay out the basic goals, like, we've got to have a master volume control that doesn't suck. Those Twins they had been making for a while had a master volume, and boy, did they suck. One of the most popular mods I did before coming to Fender was to work on those CBS silverface Twins so that the master volume circuit wouldn't be so bad.

Paul had a whole bag of tricks from all the mods he had been doing for the top guys — we need a level adjustable effects loop; we need pull boosts on some of the knobs. Top studio guys like Jay Graydon would give these ideas for modifying tone circuits or whatever to Paul, and he took it to the next step.

The bulk of the technical design decisions about how to actually make it work fell on Ed Jahns or Bill Hughes, and then they would come to me with the schematic, and I would take my scissors over to the fiberboard and get to work. Ed spec'd the amps and specified the components. On the tube side, he was the guru. He would say, we're going to use this resistor, that tube, this transformer. On the transistor side, Bob Haigler had that role.

We purchased sheets of fiberboard, about four feet by six feet, just huge. This was unprocessed, unadorned fiberboard. I would take metal shears and cut out a chunk to the right shape and start punching holes for the eyelets and then put the eyelets in. The idea was to have as little leakage as possible, and to get that we reprocessed the fiberboard after we purchased it. This involved drying, heating, and dipping it in wax. Then I would put in the components. These were one-off prototypes, with the transformer and the various components connected up point to point, all by hand.

Occasionally, I would make a very detailed, full-size wiring diagram of the fiberboard layout so that they could do artwork from that. Then the people in manufacturing could do a layout and give it to the ladies on the production line. I understand that sometimes they would simply take a photograph of my finished board and use that to produce these things. I would always use a grid that had .4″ centers. I would lay out all the components to make the machining easier to do in production.

It was a fabulous time. I loved showing up to work. I loved working with Ed, Bill, and Paul. I thought we did a very good job of implementing everything we knew at the time about what players wanted. We did produce a master volume that worked, and we provided bright switches and boosts — all these various things that would trick out an amp and allow a musician to really get his or her own sound.

Paul was the voice of the musician in that era. There was no one, literally no one, in touch with as many players as Paul Rivera. His input revitalized Fender in a way that put them back on the map. He gave them credibility. A lot of the amplifiers put out in that era helped re-legitimize Fender as a player in the industry.

The big guns of the early '80s were all solid state amps except for the 105W Twin Reverb II combo and head. All four Showmans were 200W models with programmable graphic EQs, dual reverb, programmable effects loops, and multiple boosts. Also shown here is the Stage Lead 212.

The Fender line, late 1980s: black Tolex cabs, red knobs, and grille-mounted plastic name plates on most models. At far left, the mighty Dual Showman stack. The Champ 12s at left were available in red and Snakeskin. Next to the Champ 12s is The Twin, rack and combo versions of the Super 60, then the "Fast Four" amps, the hugely successful Princeton Chorus, and Dual Bass 400.

CHAPTER NINETEEN

19

Dismal Days and Resurrection

William Schultz and the Buyout of '85

A Storm Is Threatening

When Leo Fender sold his company to CBS back in '65, Fender was in the second year of the blackface era. In other words, the old man went out in style, with the amplifiers that bore his name leading the world in design, features, sales, tone, and prestige. Now, in the early '80s, Fender's glory days seemed as distant as the Beatles on *The Ed Sullivan Show* singing "All My Loving" in matching suits. To its credit, CBS invested substantial sums into remaking Fender's image as a full-service company, with products ranging from budget amps for beginners to powerful professional models. But while intentions were good, the road toward new horizons had more than a few bumps.

For one thing, Fender was ill equipped to compete in a market where power and volume were paramount. Much of the attention seemed to be focused on Marshalls, Mesas, and other weapons of mass distortion. Lee Jackson: "We were trying to tell CBS, 'Look, if we want to go after Marshall, we have to make Marshall-style products,' but there was a lot of hesitation because they had had a real disaster with that new Strat, the one with the push buttons and the new tailpiece that didn't work [the Elite]. So there were good ideas and good products, but a lot of obstacles, too."

Paul Rivera's plan was nothing less than a complete makeover of Fender's entire line. Steve Grom: "Paul had a great vision of what the amps should be, but it was all very difficult, moving production to Hoopeston in '82 or early '83, bringing in the Japanese imports, and introducing so many new models in a short time. They thought moving to Hoopeston would save money with a lower overhead. The Gulbransen factory was good at making a small number of complicated units, but producing amplifiers meant making a large number of simple units, a completely different mentality."

A bigger problem, according to several Fender executives at the time, was that the early-'80s amps, for all their good ideas, didn't sell as well as CBS had hoped. Steve Grom: "We never made any money on them. They were incredibly parts-intensive and cost-intensive. They were complicated. One of the classic ones was the Super Champ [1982 to 1986]. Everybody thought it was a wonderful little amp, but our cost to build it was 150 dollars or something.

We always joked that there was a guy at the end of the production line, and right before he put the amp in the carton he threw 20 bucks in the back of it."

Bill Hughes: "We did have problems with sales. I don't know if it was a problem with 'product definition,' which spells out exactly what the product is and does, or if it was due to costs. As I recall, the numbers on the Concert, for example, were not fabulous. I don't know the reason. The amps certainly worked well, but they were very costly to build."

Aside from disappointing sales and the challenges of adjusting to new facilities, there was a darker cloud overhead. The fate of the whole company was uncertain. Steve Grom: "We knew something was in the works. We were losing R&D guys. A lot of people by early '84 were seeing the handwriting on the wall. We would have 'Black Fridays,' when 20 or 30 people in manufacturing would be let go — *wow.*"

All this was in shocking contrast to the glory days of the 1950s, when the quality of Fender products built secure futures for employees. Richard Smith: "After 1952 or so, all the main guys at Fender were driving Cadillacs and Lincolns. The salesmen out on the road weren't just well off; they were getting very rich." For example, Smith documents salesman Charlie Hayes' income for 1952: $45,396.36 to be exact, which computes to well over three hundred grand in today's dollars. Imagine a musical instrument road rep hauling down a third of a million bucks every year, but such were the fruits of genius in the golden age of Leo Fender, Don Randall, and their colleagues.

Well, if Paul Rivera had arrived at a time of relative stability, it would have been easier to effect change over the

Cesar Rosas of Los Lobos, 1987. He told interviewer David Rubin: "6V6s and 6L6s are where I hang. I've got Pros, Deluxes, Princetons, a '56 Bassman, a tweed Twin — the one with the two output tubes — and a Harvard. In my '60s collection I've got a Pro, a brown Concert, a blonde Showman … and four pre-CBS Super Reverbs."

long term. But he had two strikes against him. The first half of the 1980s was a transition period between the arrival of new management and the sale of the company to new owners. Second, the entire market was in decline, so Fender was focused on its very survival. All of this increased the already formidable challenges of introducing new products into a highly competitive, shifting market.

CBS Fender continued to cut back on both the work force and production facilities. Steve Grom: "There were almost 800 people there when I started in 1980, but eventually the company was down to 105 employees. So after all that work, all that effort in R&D, the new factories, and all the new models, we were losing engineers and R&D people because CBS had no idea what the future looked like for amp production. The line got very small, and we pretty much discontinued the Rivera stuff to one degree or another."

The new management, new products, employee reductions, and substantial investment weren't enough. In mid '84, CBS put the company up for sale. Production ceased in Fullerton, and the Hoopeston facility was closed at about the same time. After negotiations with several potential buyers had stalled, the situation was dire. CBS considered cutting its losses, shutting Fender's doors for good, and letting the company and its brilliant 40-year legacy evaporate into footnotes and nostalgia, alongside once prominent brands such as Valco and Regal.

1985: Gimme Shelter

Finally, the company was purchased in March 1985 by Fender president William Schultz and a team of investors at a cost of 12.5 million dollars. Players and dealers everywhere held their breath and crossed their fingers. The sale included brand names and inventory, but no factory. For a time the crew remained in the ghostly, almost empty Fullerton facility, where existing inventories were skimpy. Dan Smith: "The cupboards were pretty bare at the time we closed the shop. Production had been winding down for months prior to the sale. For example, the only U.S. Strats we had left were about 30 to 40 Elite non-trem versions that I ended up using for a giveaway on a Clapton tour." Fender continued to import the Sidekick amps, which at least helped to bridge the transition period.

In the summer of '85, the crew packed up some of its production gear and moved the whole company (the sales, marketing, finance, warehouse, and administration functions) to a building in Brea, a few miles north of Fullerton. In October, Fender acquired a modest, 14,000 square foot factory in Corona, about 20 miles east of Brea. As a tiny guitar building operation ramped up in Corona, the Brea facility continued to serve as the corporate office, warehouse, and distribution center.

Once amp production was discontinued at Fullerton, it did not return except for processing a relatively small number of leftover chassis, perhaps a few hundred, which the new company had bought for little cash under the terms of the sale. These components were intended for various models. The problem was, Fender had no cabinets and no woodworking facility, so cabs were acquired from outside vendors, and the units were assembled during the Fullerton/Brea transition period at both facilities. Some of the Sidekicks were assembled in a similar fashion, with the chassis made in Japan, later Taiwan, and the amps assembled in Brea. This arrangement permitted Fender to equip the Sidekicks with good sounding, American-made components such as Eminence speakers and Accutronics reverb units.

The little Corona shop could have been tucked into a remote corner of Leo Fender's sprawling pre-CBS factory. From these modest beginnings, William Schultz and his team rebuilt Fender, ultimately surpassing the depth and scope of the Leo-era company and forging the global, multi-brand corporation that is the Fender empire of the new millennium. As this author wrote in *The Stratocaster Chronicles*, "The new boss reorganized Fender from top to bottom, inspiring managers and production workers alike with his toughness, can-do attitude, old-fashioned work ethic, and a recommitment to the no-nonsense values of Leo Fender." It is no exaggeration to say that Bill Schultz rescued Fender from extinction. He retired in 2005, having run the company a year longer than Mr. Fender did.

As is often the case, the changing of the guard at the corporate level involved a series of power struggles. One casualty of the political fallout was Paul Rivera, who departed Fender in the fall of 1984. He explained, "I am a guitar player and an amp designer. I was never into office politics and all that corporate stuff. I had been hired by Roger Balmer, and I remained loyal to him. When he left, I left."

Sunn

Bill Schultz moved quickly. In the fall of '85 he purchased the Sunn amplifier company, founded in 1965. This gave the reborn Fender a new line of products and also provided facilities for restarting production of Fender brand amps. Steve Grom: "The R&D department's main amp designers at that time were Bill Hughes, Mark Wentling — he had worked on Music Man amps — and later [in 1988] Bob Desiderio. Bill Hughes came up with some solid state power amp platforms that simulated a tube power amp and greatly improved the sound. Mark Wentling had great ideas for some new tube and solid state preamps, but we had no place to make them until we got Sunn.

"Our Sunn factory was in Tualatin, Oregon, for six or eight months, and then we moved over to Lake Oswego. From day one it was — *OK, boom, let's go*. Now we could make some concrete decisions. As Marketing Manager at the time, I was trying to reposition Fender in several areas of the market. We went on a hellacious pace to see how much Fender stuff we could plug in there as quickly as possible. It was all brand new."

Red Knobs — On a Fender?

Classic beauties by definition don't need updates, and the idea of putting red knobs on a Fender seemed to purists a bit like digitizing *Casablanca* and giving Ingrid Bergman a nose ring. But Fender execs discovered that out in the marketplace their new products weren't being sufficiently distinguished from their old ones, so they decided to take a chance and shake up the cosmetics a bit.

Steve Grom: "The Rivera amps in the early '80s, especially the tube models — the Super Champ and all of those — looked like *old* Fender amps. Dealers would take them out of the box — 'Oh, Fender amp, just stick it over there with the old ones. Twin Reverb? Been there, done that.' Nobody realized it was a whole new model with all of these different features. Back in '83 or '84 we tried putting a silver and purple banner across the front of these amps. It said 'new, new, new.' It would rattle like crazy. It was like one of those 'sanitized for your protection' paper things.

"Now we wondered, what the heck can we do for the mid '80s and late '80s? We wanted products that would appeal to the traditional Fender customer while still offering the hip, modern features players were demanding. We came up with The Twin, the Champ 12, and the Dual Showman. We had the greatest packaging — who better than Fender to define what a guitar amp will be? We couldn't go too far away from that, but we had to go for something that at least got your attention. [Vice President of R&D] Roger Cox and I agonized over it. Roger, Mark Wentling, and I worked on a new look for the knobs: red, with flat sides and a little white pointer on the inside. We had to spend a fair amount of money. That wasn't just some off-the-shelf knob out of a catalog. We actually tooled that thing up. It went along with another departure: gray grille cloth."

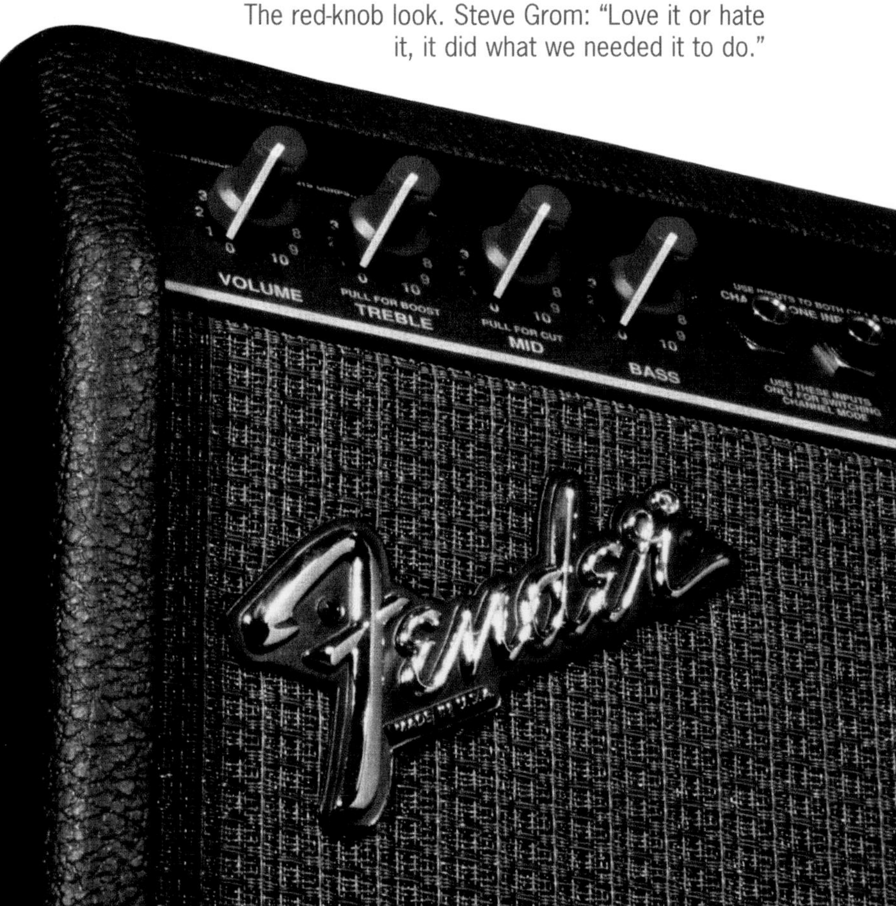

The red-knob look. Steve Grom: "Love it or hate it, it did what we needed it to do."

The (The) Twin

Foremost among the red-knob/gray grille Fenders was the top of the line Twin. Actually, this successor to the Rivera-era Twin Reverb II was saddled with the name "*The* Twin," guaranteeing awkward comments in music stores everywhere, such as, "Fender's newest model is the The Twin," or, "It's that one with the 'the' in the name."

The new feature-laden kingpin warranted a new marketing strategy, a virtual reversal of Fender's once and future mantra of simplicity. In catalog copy that must have pissed off no-nonsense veterans like Bill Carson, it was touted as having "more whistles and bells than a luxury sedan." These features included channel switching, multiple tone knobs, multiple pull-boosts, gain, presence, channel-assignable reverb, external bias adjustment, a level-adjustable effects loop, a "power-amp-thru" jack for driving slave amps, a high/low power output selector, an impedance selector, and more. Bill Hughes: "Mark Wentling designed the red-knob Twin to his taste, and it was more for the metalhead taste. It also entailed the introduction of our multiplex footswitch, with lights to tell you what mode you were in. It was a pretty cool system."

Players wanted all that stuff, and they flocked to The Twin. *Guitar Player* went so far as to proclaim: "This amp has more gain, loudness, tone variation, and features than any other Fender tube amp ... the most versatile Fender ever." Former retailer and Fender amp Marketing Manager Mike Lewis: "That red-knob Twin was widely used and well known, and for many years even after it was discontinued, many artists requested it."

Say It Ain't So Dept.

The name "The Twin" might have seemed puzzling in one other way: The new amp was a Twin, and it had reverb, but it wasn't a "Twin Reverb." Actually, fixing the date when the Twin Reverb vanished depends on the importance we attach to classic specs: Did the "real" Twin Reverb disappear when it went to a master volume silverface, or when it was replaced by the Twin Reverb II (which, after all, had no tremolo), or when that amp was replaced by The Twin?

Steve Grom: "I heard stories from back in the '70s where some weeks they'd make a ton of Twin Reverbs — nothing but Twin Reverbs for a whole week, maybe 2,000 of them." Lee Jackson: "The Twin and the Stratocaster were Fender's staples, absolutely. At one time, those things were going off the line every day by the hundreds. They had a gigantic warehouse that looked like the last scene in *Raiders of the Lost Ark*, and floor to ceiling it was Strats and Twins."

Those days were long gone. The silverface Twin Reverb was 15 years old in 1982 and still king of the combo line, but production had dwindled compared to the previous decade. CBS execs looked at the numbers and didn't like what they saw. The Twin Reverb, a staple of the line for two decades and arguably the most significant guitar amplifier in the world, was dropped. The Twin Reverb II would last four years. After it was replaced by the red-knob The Twin, there was no Twin Reverb in the Fender line until the '65 blackface reissue of 1991.

Steve Grom (left) describes to plant manager Gordon Parkman just how loud The Twin can get, Lake Oswego factory, 1989.

Champ 12, Dual Showman, Super 60

There were two other red-knob Fenders introduced alongside The Twin in '86/'87: the Champ 12 and the Dual Showman. The Twin and Showman used the same basic chassis in different configurations. Steve Grom: "That little 12 watt Champ 12 used just one 6L6, which was a pretty clever design. Mark Wentling did that one, with input from Bill Hughes."

The Champ 12 was a noteworthy example of Fender's long-running experiments with size and power. Champs and Vibro Champs had long featured 8" speakers, single-6V6 output sections, and 6W of power. But the Champ II's of the early '80s and Super Champs of the early and mid '80s had doubled the power tubes and tripled the output, and were fitted with 10" speakers (these new Champs were much more powerful than, say, an old narrow panel Vibrolux). And now, the red-knobbed newcomer went up yet again in speaker size to a 12, but back down in output tubes and power to about 10 to 12W from its single output tube. One chapter closed without fanfare: The Champ 12 had a 6L6 rather than the 6V6 that in one form or another had powered every Champ variant since the Champion 800 of the late 1940s.

Bill Hughes: "For the Champ 12 of the late '80s and early '90s, Roger Cox came to me and said, 'We need to design an amp that is very economical. So I came up with

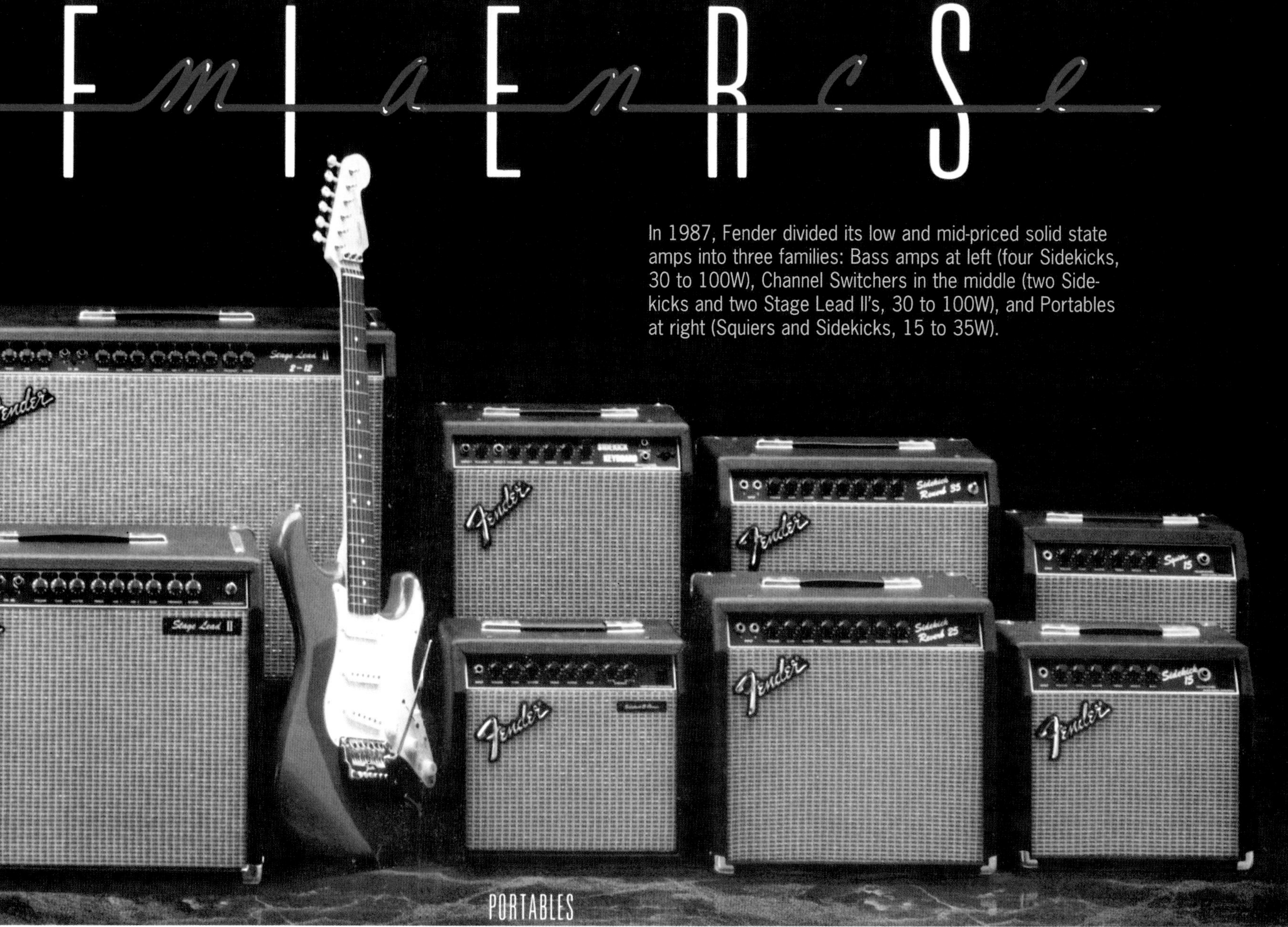

In 1987, Fender divided its low and mid-priced solid state amps into three families: Bass amps at left (four Sidekicks, 30 to 100W), Channel Switchers in the middle (two Sidekicks and two Stage Lead II's, 30 to 100W), and Portables at right (Squiers and Sidekicks, 15 to 35W).

the Champ 12 architecture. About halfway through the project, I left the company [temporarily] and Mark Wentling, who had come to Fender from Music Man, finished it in my absence. That amplifier had only one 6L6, so it was a very low parts-count product and yet managed to have reverb and a gain control. So the intention was to lower the cost and get decent profits. It turned out to be a fairly popular amp. We sold a bunch of them."

The Dual Showman of the late 1980s and early 1990s was initially a red-knob, 4x12 whopper powered by a quad of 6L6s. (In 1990, it would acquire black knobs and reverb.) This model should not be confused with any of the following: the Double Showman of the early '60s; the mid '60s blackface or late '60s silverface versions of the Dual Showman; or the Dual Showman Reverb, a silver panel/blue label model and one of Fender's most powerful amps from the late '60s all the way through 1980. Basically a head version of The Twin, the red-knob Dual Showman was another Mark Wentling design.

A year after the appearance of the Champ 12, Showman, and The Twin, the line was joined by another red-knobber, the 60W Super 60 tube combo. It would last until 1992. These red-knobbers would shift to black knobs after two or three years, and all would be phased out entirely during the early-'90s across-the-line makeover.

Steve Grom: "The red knobs were on both the tube and the solid state models. All in all, they went over real well. The amps were good, although a lot of people were shocked. They looked at them and went, 'Wow, that's kinda weird. Why does Fender have red knobs?' But during the late '80s, at least it got people to react one way or the other, and that was our whole reason for the new look. It gave us something unique, proprietary. Love it or hate it, it did what we needed it to do."

The Fast Four

In the late 1980s Fender sorely needed new models to go up against Crate and Peavey, especially Peavey's Bandit, possibly the best selling amp in the world at that time. Paul Rivera had responded with the Montreux, and this formidable challenge now fell upon a series of solid state models unofficially dubbed "The Fast Four." These were the Fender 85 (also "Eighty Five"), the Deluxe 85, the Stage 185, and the Pro 185. All had red knobs, grille-mounted name tags with white script lettering, and white trim bordering the control panels; all were produced from 1988 to 1992.

Steve Grom: "When Fender stopped being a serious player in the amp business in '84, it opened the door for Peavey and Crate to fill the void. The high volume part of the amp business at the time was a 65 watt, single 12, channel-switching model that sold for about 399 dollars, the magic number. The Bandit was the industry standard, and to be any kind of player in the amp business, you needed something like it.

"Hartley Peavey had defined *all* of the price points. Every one of his models defined what that type of amp would be — a 15 watt model with a 10 inch speaker and certain features at 99 bucks, then a 20 watter with an added feature or two for another 50 bucks or whatever it was, and so on up the line to a 100 watt channel-switcher with effects loops and all the rest. If you weren't there, don't even bother coming to the party.

"The Fast Four were all solid state. We had good tube amps like the Champ 12 and The Twin, but it wasn't mainstream product. We needed numbers. Big production numbers were not going to come from things like a 12 watt tube amp or a 100 watt channel-switching Twin. We would sell some, sure, but that was not gonna be the bread-and-butter type of thing. Now that we had this factory up in Oregon, the burden was, OK, guys — fill it up!

"We were desperate to give our sales guys something to go back to the dealers with. Dealers were comfortable buying Fender amps, but they were used to buying a product *line*, not just a couple of models, and in the mid '80s we no longer had that. So now Schultz was just *pounding* on the R&D guys: 'Get these four solid state amps designed and into production!'"

Bill Hughes: "I had been involved with tube amps exclusively until about the time of the Fast Four, and I did work on those amps. Mark Wentling and I dubbed them the Fast Four because we did them so rapidly. We wanted to fit all the circuitry on one circuit board for reasons of economy. These were new designs. We never looked at the old Fender solid state amps. The people who had designed them were no longer there. It's not that we made any particular design decisions intended to distance the new models from the unreliable old ones. The old ones simply weren't discussed. The new ones sounded so much better, but not because technologies had progressed; it's just that we knew how to use the parts. What had come a long way was the reliability of the parts. Semiconductors had come to the fore and were very reliable. Making the amplifiers sound right was more a matter of taste than technology."

Steve Grom: "We started from ground zero. As always, the important thing was quality, and these were four good amps. Plus, we were embraced by the whole dealer network, who in turn pushed them to the consumers. So we had good product and a positive foundation we could build on. This was totally in response to what Peavey was doing, but still trying to keep a Fender look and a Fender voice."

Designed by Mark Wentling and Bob Haigler, with contributions from Bill Hughes (in the power amp design and high-level power electronics), all four amps had similar preamp circuitry, an approach not unlike Leo Fender's method of rendering similar circuits in different configura-

"Making the solid state amplifiers sound right

tions back in the day. Steve Grom: "Some of the Rivera stuff had gotten away from that a little bit — the solid state amps had nothing to do with the tube amps, and models like the Super Champ did things the other ones didn't do."

The Fast Four were a smash. For example, the 2x12 Pro 185 was sort of a 185W solid state Twin Reverb; Fender found that there were still plenty of players who wanted a 2x12 open-back combo, and the loud new model at the top of the solid state line filled the bill. Commercially, the biggest winner was the 85W, 1x12 Deluxe 85, a dedicated channel-switcher with independent tone controls. Despite a drive channel whose sound might fall below the discriminating standards of today's *distortionati*, it was light, solid, reliable, and loud. The 1x12 Stage 185 was a higher-powered version of the Deluxe 85.

Steve Grom: "The 'current feedback' solid state power amps that Bill Hughes developed were the backbone of these amps. We still use variations of this platform today for most of the solid state guitar amps. I like to think that Mark Wentling, Bob Desiderio, and I all had pretty good ears when it came to evaluating the tonality of the new designs. We consulted a number of other Fender people — Dan Smith, John Page, J. Black, Jack Schwarz, George Blanda, and others. We also got input from artists and dealers, always under an extremely tight time schedule to get these amps into production.

"So once again Fender had a line. We had tube, and we had solid state. The amps sounded good, with the features guys wanted. We were covering important price points with competitive products, and dealers were behind us. The Fast Four set the stage and provided the design foundation for things a couple years later like the Princeton Chorus, which became one of the all-time best selling amps in Fender history."

The Princeton Chorus

Amplifier designer and project engineer Bob Desiderio arrived at Fender in January 1988, less than three years after the acquisition of the company from CBS. He recalls, "R&D was still a tiny department, mainly Mark Wentling and Bill Hughes, and I was the new guy. Mark was the one who got me using CAD [Computer Aided Design] to lay out circuit boards, and I had the opportunity to be on the ground floor of that technology.

"When I got there, they still had a tape-up lady. To make circuit boards back then, somebody in drafting would draw up the component placement, and then someone would go on a light table and put it down on a 100 percent enlarged grid. They would use these black stickers and tapes of different widths to create the orientation of all the components, and then they used a photo process to reduce it back to actual size. Then that film was used to make circuit boards. It's all done by computer now."

Bob worked on the solid state Princeton Chorus, whose practical features, surprising loudness, and affordability made it a best seller, with one of the longest runs in Fender's post-Leo history. Bob Desiderio: "Someone had cobbled together a prototype with the guts from another Fender, plus the guts from a Boss chorus pedal or something, just to have a demonstrator with a 2x10 cab and chorus. They took orders for it, so now we had to build it."

Steve Grom: "It was a response to competition. Peavey and Crate were eating our lunch because we did not have a stereo 2x10 mid-power chorus amp. Stereo chorus amps were the rage at the time from both Peavey and Crate, the hottest selling models that *any* of the companies had. Bill Schultz came down and basically beat up the entire R&D department, pounding the table: 'We don't have one of these, and we need one, and tomorrow is too late!'"

Bob Desiderio: "We borrowed the preamp topology and gain switching from the Studio 85, which Mark Wentling had already designed. They told me not to change the sound. I did the circuit board, and for the production version I redid the chorus circuit using a standard Panasonic analog bucket-brigade type of unit. Bill Hughes did the power amp.

"We called it both the Princeton Chorus and Princeton Stereo Chorus, although both were true stereo. The distortion was probably a tribute to what Tom Scholz was doing with the Rockman, which was a popular sound at the time.

was more a matter of taste than technology."

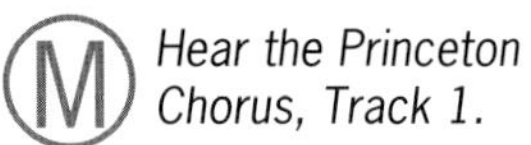
Hear the Princeton Chorus, Track 1.

Bob Desiderio with one of his — and Fender's — most successful projects, the Princeton Chorus. Steve Grom: "It just did staggering numbers."

Music & Sound Retailer magazine had their Top Ten list, and it was cool to see that the Princeton Chorus was always one of the top sellers for years. Fender told me it was our best selling solid state amp in history, at least up until that point." Steve Grom: "It just did staggering numbers. In the midst of building a lot of other things, we'd have a run of 500 or 600 Princeton Choruses, so it was a smash. We made it for ten years, and it actually rivaled the Twin Reverb in production numbers." The Princeton Chorus was replaced by the Princeton Chorus DSP in early 1999.

Hanging On, Looking Ahead

Recapping the 1980s: After the big revamp of the entire line in 1982, Fender entered its pre-sale doldrums, followed by the sale to William Schultz and his associates in '85. That acquisition sparked the gradual, post-CBS reinvigoration of the company. Not surprisingly, the turbulence of the times accounted for a lack of new designs as Fender hired new staff, looked for new facilities, and took it one day at a time.

From 1983 until 1986, Fender introduced not a single new tube guitar amp, relying instead on the Rivera designs from '82 and also attempting to fill the lower and middle price points with its various red-knob solid state amps. Although Paul Rivera had left Fender in the fall of 1984, the Rivera era didn't come to an end until 1987, when the last of his Fender designs were replaced or dropped.

By the end of the decade, Fender had committed itself to the red-knob newcomers. On some fronts, things were looking up. The Sunn facility provided desperately needed production capabilities. Imports were looking good. New Fender amps were getting noticed. They were selling. But while there was no shortage of engineering talent or employee commitment, it was still a matter of making the best of limited resources, of building what you could rather than what you really wanted. The days when Fender designers had resources sufficient to see their dreams made real were a thing of the past, but also, just maybe, the future.

"Peavey and Crate were eating our lunch because we did not have a stereo 2x10 mid-power chorus amp. Bill Schultz basically beat up the entire R&D department: *We don't have one of these, and we need one, and tomorrow is too late!*"

The man who saved Fender, William Schultz. He passed away on September 21, 2006 and was mourned throughout the music industry. Ritchie Fliegler recalled of Bill's final weeks: "Those of us who knew him could see things weren't going well at this point, and we all dealt with it in our own fashion. For most of us, this meant making the most of our moments together — getting that last tidbit of advice, that last scolding, maybe even a pat on the back (these were few and far between, and so they were inhaled and savored like a fine bouquet when they came)."

Yank it up, baby. Keith Richards with the Rolling Stones at Soldier Field in Chicago, September 1997, on the *Bridges To Babylon* tour. The man *Rolling Stone* magazine called "the consummate Stone" lets the sound tech know what to do with the stage volume level. He's running through a battery of high-power "tweed" Twins (the tweed-style amp on the far left is actually covered in brown Tolex).

Keith's "secret" of great tone — "the right amp with the right guitar" — exemplified the retro aesthetic of simpler, high-quality gear.

CHAPTER TWENTY

20

The Awakening

Rediscovering Good Tone

A funny thing happened on the way to the future. During the '70s, guitar players forgot about tone. Or many of them did, anyway. So did manufacturers, apparently. It's hard to pinpoint the start of any such trend, but CBS Fender's gradual abandonment of classic amp technologies in favor of revised tube circuits and untested, first-generation solid state products had something to do with it. More than a decade later, the new Fender company would help put things right.

Wattage Wars and Feature Feuds

Steve Grom: "In the early days of solid state, everybody in the amp business was venturing into unknown territory, not just Fender. With Jimi Hendrix, feedback, et cetera, everyone assumed they had to play as loud as possible, and we lost a lot of the tone concepts we'd taken for granted in the '60s. There were these power wars: My amp is this loud on 3! Oh, yeah? Well, *my* amp is that loud on 2! And the concept of tone kind of eluded everybody — marketing people, engineers, and consumers. That's one reason why all kinds of companies made some pretty horrendous amps."

Manufacturers tried various strategies as they struggled to accommodate economic realities and shifting tastes. One philosophy: More is more. New models sometimes came with thick instruction manuals and sported control panels like something out of a NORAD bunker. They bristled with banks of switches and knobs that emphasized multiple options. Players joked that such amps could fix your breakfast or launch a missile strike. High-tech was in, but all too often, good sound took a back seat to power, volume, versatility, or features.

Guitar Player magazine was founded in 1967. Gradually, it helped to establish a common vocabulary and to increase the sophistication of typical musicians. Still, for years the most common mode of communication was word of mouth. Rumors persisted. Misinformation was common. Steve Grom: "I remember seeing Vox amps at a store and thinking, 'Wow, this is the stuff the *Beatles* used! It's *gotta* be great!' You realize, eventually, that stuff may have looked right cosmetically, but circuit-wise it had no bearing on what the Beatles actually used. These realizations take years, so there was a certain amount of wool being pulled over consumers' eyes by lots of people. A lot of things didn't dawn on us for a long time, so we all dragged around a lot of relatively crummy equipment. We just didn't know any better.

"Go down the list — Ampeg, Acoustic, *everybody* made some pretty bad sounding stuff, and consumers went merrily along. If consumers had been more sophisticated, the amps wouldn't have sounded that way. There would have been a backlash. At Fender, we're not a manufacturing-driven company, like some others. We're a market-driven company. We ask people, what does the market want? And back then, if the market was telling us, boy, your amps sound bad, we would have done something about it. But we just weren't hearing that. We heard it later, in retrospect, but not at the time. People might have complained about reliability, but they liked the features and didn't complain about the tone. Some of the 'badness' found in those amps was a direct result of market demand, from dealers and consumers."

Mesa/Boogie Mark I. Mesa's first production amp introduced an extra gain stage with a master volume control, and the Mark II featured channel switching. Cabinets like this one brought a fine woodworking sensibility to an amplifier market that would never be the same again.

Turning of the Tide

After hot rodding many a Fender Princeton, in the early 1970s Mesa/Boogie founder Randall Smith introduced his own design, an amplifier with an extra gain stage. As *Guitar Player* said, "It signaled the beginning of a new era of guitar amp design." Randall Smith explains, "That extra tube of amplification had its own gain control and, used with a master at the end of the preamp, enabled players to separately adjust loudness and drive characteristics. It also provided an extended range of performance from traditional clean settings up to a new realm of high gain overdrive and sustain." Concert tone at living-room volumes was novel and irresistible. The next Boogie, the Mark II, introduced channel footswitching, allowing the player to alternate between, say, clean rhythm and high-gain lead tones literally without missing a beat. These early Mesa/Boogies set a new standard of versatility and flexibility.

Toward the end of the '70s the superiority of products from companies such as Mesa/Boogie was too obvious to ignore. Back in the day, a Fender road rep's best strategy was to stand his amp next to anybody else's amp and let the player plug in and grasp the obvious. Now, however, some of the newcomers not only boasted desirable features such as channel-switching and gain boosts, but their rich sound was a wake-up call to players and manufacturers alike. Steve Grom: "Suddenly Fender's concept, which was, 'Oh, let's just put a master volume on a Twin Reverb,' didn't cut it."

Some of the players who had once looked to Fender combos and piggybacks to meet their needs not only looked to other companies, they tried different approaches altogether. One trend was to custom-assemble your rig from components made by various manufacturers — preamps, power amps, effects, speaker emulators, etc. — and mount the whole pile in a rack. Rock stars hired technicians to set up and tend to these complicated systems at gigs and sessions. A seed was planted, as players began to look at amplifiers not necessarily as stand-alone products but as systems of components. This mentality continues to resonate: Just as a hot rod enthusiast might specify an MSD ignition or a COMP cam, a guitar player can tweak every link in the amplification chain in hopes of inching one step closer to tone nirvana.

There were exceptions to these trends. Some players never bought into the "more is more" mentality, never traded in their old tube combos for stacks or racks, and continued to produce fabulous tones all through the '70s and '80s. And some of the manufacturers who pioneered modern features, complex rigs, or higher outputs also built (and continue to build) amps with great tone; Mesa/Boogie again leaps to mind, as do Marshall and others.

But the big picture is this: By the early 1980s, players were catching on. Some of those feature-heavy screamers just didn't sound very good. Some were versatile, sure, but they seemed to provide "every sound but the right one." Others didn't respond as dynamically as an old tube amp. Steve Grom: "By the end of that decade, finally everybody realized, 'Oh my god, we've been buying some pretty horrendous sounding amps for the last fifteen years!'"

Players' increasing awareness during the late 1980s continued to be reflected and advanced in the pages of magazines, particularly *Guitar Player*, which by the early '90s had helped to spread an increasingly sophisticated technical vocabulary among musicians. *Guitar Player*'s Andy Ellis: "Those were heady days! *GP* was the first magazine to explore the emerging indie amp builders and their work, and to present sonic alternatives to the rack, which had dominated the guitar scene during the '80s. It's fair to say that we played a crucial role in documenting the renaissance of classic tube tone. By reviewing the gear, and later letting the builders speak directly to our readers, we helped create an awareness of, say, the difference between preamp and power tube distortion, series versus parallel effects loops, the sound of EL34s versus 6L6s, the importance of the power transformer, Class A versus Class AB, and many other subjects we now take for granted." (The dark side of all this is that, taken to excess, a familiarity with components can morph into an obsession with specs in which considerations of actual tone — not to mention musicianship, artistry, and fun — are lost. Such warped perspectives are lamented here by the author and several interviewees.)

The Staple Singers, with patriarch Roebuck "Pops" Staples on guitar. Years later he would speak for many when he lamented: "That sound I was getting out of an amplifier then, I can't get now. Instead of going from good to better, it seems like it's going the other way... My old amp's wore out. It was a Fender Twin... Lord knows, if I had knew this day was coming, I would've kept all that stuff. I didn't know how valuable it was."

New Moods and Attitudes

As guitarists' sophistication increased, their attitudes changed as well. For decades the entire industry had stoked and profited from the "I need more gear than Pink Floyd" mentality. But as Keith Richards had told us, "The main ingredients are the right amp with the right guitar," period, and let's face it, Keith Richards knows tone. The new sensibility: Tone is king, less is more.

Just as players had come to favor classic electric guitars over supposedly "advanced" competitors, many of them now took a second look at their amps and effects: *Instead of giving me what I really want — killer tone — might all those extra features and circuits be getting in the way?* Guys who'd been daisy-chaining 100 watt stacks were having queasy feelings: *Maybe I should've held on to my old Bandmaster*. Players began to recall their small, single-ended "budget" Fenders with a rekindled affection. Suddenly a one-knob tweed Champ was among the hippest recording tools around. Not surprisingly, prices escalated as "used" amps began to emit that vintage glow, faint at first but soon to be radiant.

Players reconsidered the bad rap that "one sound" amplifiers had been stuck with, largely as a result of advertising campaigns hyping the versatility of multi-channel, zillion-feature competitors. Was a 5E3 Deluxe a "one sound" amp, just because it lacked cascading gain stages or dual level-adjustable effects loops? Not at all. Many players discovered what a few discriminating artists had figured out decades before: A great tube amplifier with its volume set right at the onset of breakup provides a whole palette of tones from clean to cranked, all controllable with the *guitar*'s volume knob and subtle variations in pick attack. The 1980s philosophy of versatility had been: "I need a full-time Hollywood sound guy." The new 'tude: "Gadgets? We don't need no stinking gadgets!"

Other realizations: Tap dancing on a floor full of stompboxes can be fun, but there's no such thing as a stompbox labeled "great tone." (Rich Robinson of the Black Crowes, in *Guitar Player*: "Most of these people use effects to try to get it to sound like an old Fender.") It dawned on many of us that assembling a rig the size of a Coke machine would never be as cool as walking into the joint with a Telecaster in one hand and a tweed Vibrolux in the other. It might never sound as good, either. Instead of joking about how our complicated amplifiers could double as garage door openers or whatever, now we joked that the only "effect" we needed was the cord between our guitar and our amp.

Another thing: Big, loud amps were not only sometimes less toneful than classic models, they were heavy, too. (Fender's titanic 400 PS bass amp weighed almost 90 pounds — and that's just the head.) A simple, portable, great sounding combo seemed to be just the ticket if you were a working picker who was tired of schlepping around a hernia-threatening behemoth that wouldn't fit in your Corolla, was loud enough on 3 to clear the room, required constant tweaking, and weighed more than your bass player.

Yet another: Just because our hero is pictured with this or that amp and guitar doesn't mean that's the gear he used on a particular record. Bruce Zinky: "In some cases, what we thought the player was using was not even close to reality. Jimmy Page was known for playing Les Pauls through Marshalls live, but those great early records were mostly a Telecaster through a Supro amplifier." Other classic examples: Eric Clapton and his tweed Champs, or Jimi Hendrix and his blackface Fenders in the studio.

Carr Slant 6V. *Guitarist* magazine: "Steve Carr has been steadily building up a reputation for some of the best sounding and best made guitar amps on the planet. The Slant 6V's tone, response and range is nothing short of awe-inspiring." The Slant 6V was inspired in part by the 1964 blackface Deluxe Reverb.

Sleek, Chic, and Boutique

Manufacturers got the message: Whether they produced beefy, complicated systems or compact, stripped-down combos, the amps had to sound right, particularly given increasing competition from a new breed of builders. We started to hear the term *boutique* amp, which conjured up an image of a limited-edition product crafted to exacting standards by an uncompromising builder/artist who then charged a pile of money for it, and got it. Tone purists with fat wallets and a yen for top quality components and in some cases point-to-point wiring increasingly turned to amps fashioned by Andy Marshall of THD, Mark Sampson of Matchless, Mark Baier of Victoria, Don Morris of ElectroPlex, Paul Rivera (who had left Fender and started his own company), Ken Fischer of Trainwreck, and a growing number of their contemporaries.

Some early boutique amps were versatile, while others were born of a backlash against the "my amp has more knobs than your amp" approach of the '70s and early '80s. Their sleek front panels featured a couple of knobs on an otherwise unperforated slab of aluminum or covered wood. Defiantly exhibiting their *lack* of features, they seemed to proclaim: Extraneous knobs are for peasants and sissies! We are purists, we are esthetes, we are all about a virile signal untainted by boorish feature circuits! Frills? Humbug! Tone? Hallelujah!

Great tone from simple circuits was nothing new. After all, the boutique phenomenon in a way recalled Leo Fender's core philosophies. (Remember, his amps weren't cheap, either; a 1955 Deluxe was a 15W amp costing more than 900 bucks in today's cash.) But the idea of an elite clientele choosing hyper-expensive products from a couple dozen small-scale builders was novel indeed. These new products borrowed a jolt of mojo from those ultra sophisticated audio amplifiers with god-like tone, a minimal/chic appearance, a single knob, and a pour-me-a-Jack-Daniel's price tag. They were diametrically opposed to, say, the "more whistles and bells than a luxury sedan" approach Fender had used to tout its red-knob Twin.

When it came to sales figures, none of the boutique builders of the early '90s ever threatened Fender. In fact, put them all together and their revenues would still pale compared to Fender's. But image is important, too, and while Fender was challenged by Peavey, Crate, and others at the low and middle price points, it faced the additional task of reclaiming its prestige among professionals and connoisseurs, some of whom were forking over big bucks for limited-production competitors.

So how would these obstacles be addressed at the company whose legacy was built by Leo Fender, Freddie Tavares, Forrest White, and other men who surely never set foot in a *boutique* of any damn kind? Ed Jahns, Paul Rivera, Steve Grom, Bill Hughes, Mark Wentling, and their colleagues had laid the groundwork for bringing great tone back to Fender. Now the mission would fall to Mike Lewis, Ritchie Fliegler, Richard McDonald, Shane Nicholas, and their colleagues in R&D.

"Fender's Paul-Rivera-designed early-'80s Super Champ is virtually unknown, but it's the most versatile, useful, toneful Fender ever!" – ***Bart Wittrock, Rockin' Robin*** 8/2013

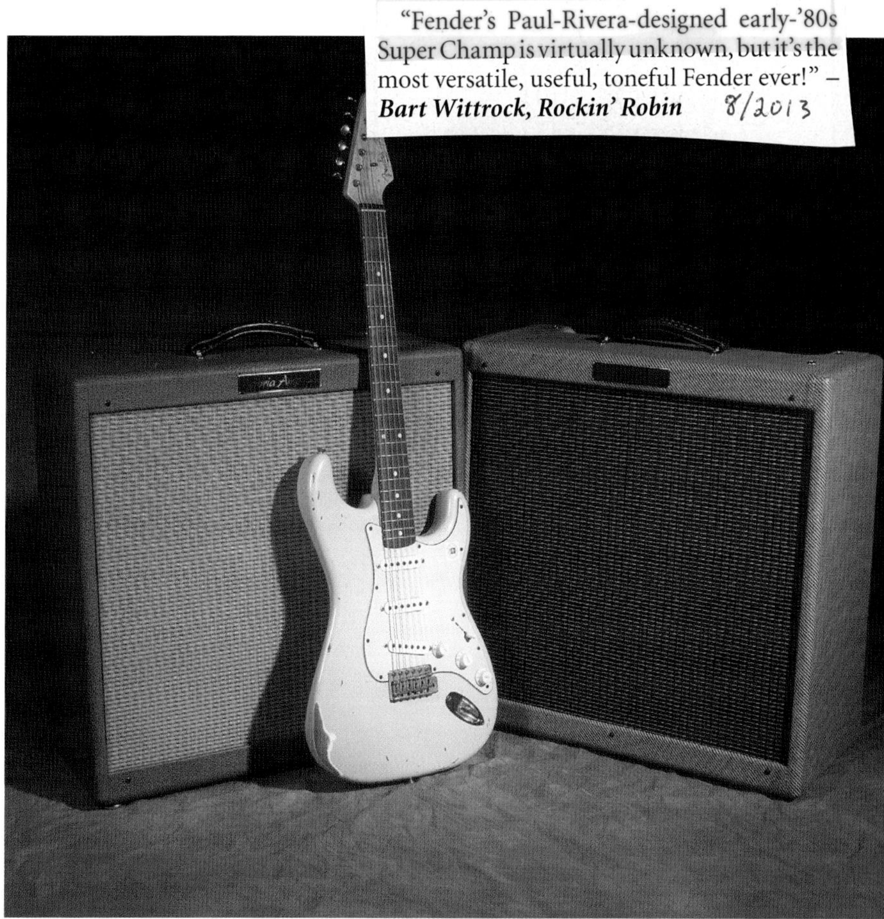

Among the very best of the boutiques, Victoria amps are highly regarded for great tone and immaculate workmanship. They aren't Fenders, but their inspiration is clear.

Ultimate Chorus, mid '90s. The Ultra Chorus of August 1992 was basically a bigger, more powerful Princeton Chorus in a true stereo format. It was promptly renamed the Ultimate Chorus.

CHAPTER TWENTY-ONE

21

Into the 1990s

Push Buttons, Pro Tubes, and New Tweeds

At the end of the 1980s the amp line had a modern Fender look, perhaps too modern. There was not a hint of vintage vibe. In fact, aside from the black Tolex cabs, there was hardly a nod to traditional Fender styling at all. Most of the amps had red knobs. Several were available in "Special" snakeskin or red cabinet coverings. Except for the Champ 12, they all had grille-mounted plastic name plates with the model name in white script. (One sign of the times: Perhaps a bit defensively, the 1989 literature took a swipe at "so-called 'custom' amplifier builders" who claimed they were using superior components.)

Aside from Fender's first two reissues — the '59 tweed Bassman and '63 brown Vibroverb — the tube amp line in 1990 consisted of only the three original red-knobbers from the late '80s — The Twin, the 12W Champ 12, and the 100W Dual Showman head (recently updated as the Dual Showman Reverb) — plus the Super 60 from 1988 (head, rack, and combo versions), as well as a variation on the Super 60, the Super 112. The following year saw the introduction of the third reissue, the '65 blackface Twin Reverb, and yet another spinoff of the Super 60, the Super 210. The Super 60, Super 112, and Super 210 each had 60W, two 12AX7s, and two 6L6s.

In addition to the amps Fender continued to import, the solid state models included the Stage 185, Pro 185, London 185 head, Eighty-Five, Deluxe 85, and Princeton Chorus. The line also offered the 2x200W BXR Dual Bass 400 head and various other bass amps, keyboard amps, and enclosures. For anyone who remembered the glory days of Fender, the familiar Champs, Princetons, Super Reverbs, and other staples remained conspicuously absent.

Amp production continued in Lake Oswego, Oregon, at the old Sunn facility. In 1994, the gradual relocation to Corona would begin, and toward the end of the decade significant amp production would commence in Mexico.

M-80, R.A.D., H.O.T., J.A.M.

Despite intense competition and numerous uncertainties, Fender had been on a bit of a roll by 1989. Only four years old, the new company had gained some momentum with the "Fast Four" and the Princeton Chorus. Now the marketing and R&D teams pondered a dilemma Steve Grom had witnessed in music stores. The emphasis that many models placed on flexibility and multiple features did have one downside: Of all the different sounds such amps could provide, some were terrible. Steve Grom: "When you

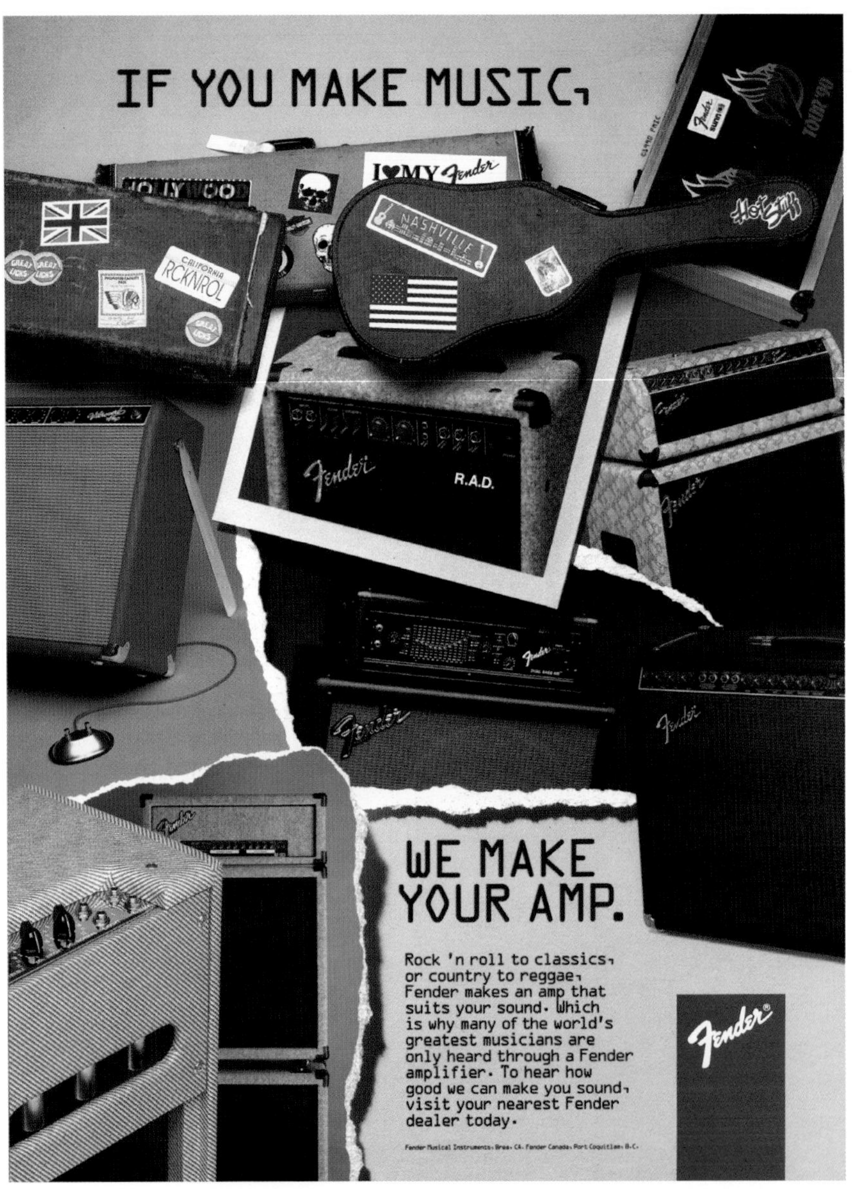

This ad from 1990 reveals some leftover late-'80s styling cues (the red-knob Twin and the Snakeskin Dual Showman), as well as the first two reissue amps: the brown Tolex Vibroverb and the tweed 4x10 Bassman. Also pictured are the Dual Bass 400 and the push button R.A.D. Like the R.A.D., the M-80, shown here in the head/stack version, was covered in grey "carpeting." The M-80s targeted a younger, metal-oriented market with their radical looks, a midrange scoop, and gobs of nasty distortion.

plugged into an amp that had a lot of knobs, you'd get whatever setting the last person had selected. You might say, 'Wow, that doesn't sound very good,' and unplug your cord, just leave it. Next guy plugs in, same thing."

Another issue: Dealers seemed to have less time to demo new products — which ironically were more complicated than ever — and turnover among their employees was on the increase, so experienced product demonstrators were harder to find. Steve Grom: "So we thought, let's make an amp that's so simple you can't screw it up. What about an amp with preset sounds, with push buttons? What do most guys need? Well, you need a clean sound, a clean dark sound with a little bit of crunch, a rhythm distortion sound, and a lead sound. For most guys, four is pretty good. That's where the solid state R.A.D., H.O.T., and J.A.M. models came from [released between October 1989 and March 1990].

"The M-80 was in the same group. We were seeing the Crate stuff getting some attention because it had a little nastier look to it. We were going after a younger market, so we did the M-80 series, with a big, ugly carpet-covered amp head. We put a real nasty distortion in it, and put in that midrange scoop that a lot of the metal guys were getting into, where you roll off the mids. It's a dip in the frequency response at about 1K, to give an amp a kind of 'bark.' It's a cool sound. Some of the Crate stuff had that, and that was the sound of the late '80s, very popular.

"At that point we're thinking, we've already got some tube amps, more traditional solid state amps, the Princeton Chorus, and a higher powered version called the Power Chorus that had some pretty hip, sophisticated features. So we said, hey, let's go in a whole other direction — the younger guys, the metal markets. Let's really attack Crate at what they do. The M-80s, R.A.D., H.O.T., and J.A.M. were aimed at that, and they all did what they were supposed to do. We sold a *bunch* of that stuff. We probably sold more M-80 heads than any other single amp head we'd ever sold up till that point."

Bill Hughes: "The R.A.D., H.O.T., and J.A.M. were done by Bob Desiderio, and they were designed to address a particular need in the marketplace. The idea was to have a low-cost amp that could emulate many sounds in a convenient way — push buttons. And they did very well in the market. That M-80 stack had speakers and a cabinet that produced a very good low frequency response. It was a killer amplifier, and we sold a lot of them. That was a Mark Wentling product. He did the low-level circuitry — the preamp and speaker — and I did the high-level circuitry, which was the power amp and power transformer. We abandoned that power amp platform in the mid '90s due to certain high voltage op-amps turning obsolete."

Bob Desiderio: "I was project engineer on the M-80s, and I did the R.A.D., H.O.T., and J.A.M. The M-80 had that fizzy, heavy metal sound of the day, and I think the name just came from the old fireworks. It was pretty loud for its size. Then [in 1990] we took the chorus out of the Princeton Chorus and put it in there to make the M-80 Chorus, and that's when we also made the head version.

"The names were supposedly acronyms. R.A.D. stood for Radical Amp Design, but the others were just cool, three-letter things that didn't really stand for anything. We couldn't come up with anything for H.O.T. so I nicknamed it the Has One Transistor [laughs], because it was all IC's [integrated circuits] and it had one transistor in the chorus circuit somewhere. They were all basically the same, except the R.A.D. was the base unit, the H.O.T. added reverb, and the J.A.M. added reverb and chorus." In 1990 and 1991, the R.A.D., H.O.T., and J.A.M. ranged from $179 to $299.

Steve Grom: "At first, they did unbelievable business, which was typical of Fender at that time because the new company was growing by leaps and bounds. We'd take these things to a trade show and end up with hundreds and hundreds of orders. It went back to having a foundation of dealers and consumers being comfortable buying Fender amplifiers. It was once again a name they could trust."

Stiff Competition

By the outset of the new decade, the days when Fender amplifiers seemed to have little competition were long gone. Just as Leo Fender had put Fullerton on the map, Hartley Peavey had done the same for Meridian, Mississippi. Steve Grom: "You have to remember how strong Peavey was at the time. I probably had the Peavey price list memorized better than the Fender price list. I'd hear Bill Schultz in the next room hit the table, and the word 'amp' would come out, and I'd think, 'Uh oh, Peavey's got to be doing something. I better *know* what they're doing.'"

Mike McCready had a little Champ when he was a kid, and he loved to make it feed back while bashing out the riff to "Smoke on the Water." With Pearl Jam, he graduated to reissue Bassmans and tweed Twins, among others.

Competing with Peavey and others required the updating or the replacement of various models, with a particular emphasis on the solid state line. Compared to their tube stablemates, the success of the solid state Fenders depended not only on different technologies but on different strategies, too. For one thing, Fender would continue to capitalize on its history, and to restore luster to the brand. Musicians were coming to appreciate Fender amps not only as reliable tools but as classic tone machines as well. There was an increasing awareness that tube technologies — now considered outdated in almost all other fields — were expensive. If you wanted an authentic 6L6-equipped Fender, it would cost you. Many discriminating musicians accepted this reality.

On the other hand, the solid state models were more price-sensitive. Steve Grom: "People came to see the Fender tube amp as sort of a unique beast. Yeah, there were some price constraints to a degree, but we had re-established our leadership role in tube amps, so we weren't quite as price sensitive there. But with the solid state stuff, we kept having to upgrade it, watch costs, watch profit margins. It was a real battle, endless. We brought in more of the Sidekicks. Production by then had moved from Japan to Taiwan, and we were starting to sell some big numbers. There were a couple years where the Sidekick 15 would get up to many thousands of units a year, just for that one model." Aside from filling various price points across the spectrum of guitar amps, Fender also strove to make significant inroads into the PA business, with "box top" mixers, small console mixers, and speaker cabinets.

Mike Lewis Arrives

Musician and former retailer Mike Lewis succeeded Steve Grom as marketing manager for amplifiers in January 1992, and he oversaw a major revamping of the line over the next three and a half years. When he arrived, the tube amp series encompassed about the same number of models as the Fender line of, say, 1954 or 1955. After 1992, the three recent Supers (60, 112, 210) all were axed. At that point, in a nutshell, pretty much the only new things going on at Fender were old things — the reissues. That would change, soon.

R.A.D., H.O.T. and J.A.M.: Low price tags and push button panels.

The Ultra Chorus

An offshoot of the Princeton Chorus was the Ultra Chorus, released in August 1992. Bob Desiderio: "It turned out Hartley [Peavey] had a trademark on Ultra, so we changed it to Ultimate Chorus. We were taking the sound of the Princeton Chorus, but we gave it a 2x12 cabinet and a 2x65W power section instead of 2x25W. Where the tone stacks were placed and the sound itself were exactly right out of a Princeton Chorus." While the Princeton Chorus was more of a gain switching amp than a true channel switcher — it used the same tone controls for both settings — the Ultra Chorus did have separate tone controls and was a true two-channel amp.

In a way the Ultra/Ultimate Chorus also grew out of an earlier attempt to upgrade the Princeton Chorus. Fender called it the Power Chorus and released it in June '89. It seemed to have too many buttons and was too complicated for some players. The sound wasn't quite right, and it didn't do that well. The Ultra/Ultimate Chorus was a far more successful product.

The Early-'90s Makeover

Mike Lewis knew he had his work cut out for him: "The new Fender was still relatively young, so for the first few years, there wasn't a whole lot going on in manufacturing. We didn't even have factories at first, so we really hadn't made amps for years. Remember, toward the end of the CBS era in '84, production had actually stopped until we acquired Sunn, so we had a lot of rebuilding to do on every level."

The realities of making Fender amps in the early 1990s paralleled the challenges of guitar production in a way. What the marketers wanted to do and what they were able to do were very different things, given the limited facilities. "But here's an essential thing," says Lewis. "People wanted Fender amps to be successful. When a new Fender amp came out, there was a lot of anticipation, a lot of desire. They were pulling for us, big time." So Lewis' task was simple, at least in theory. Now that the company was stabilizing and enjoying renewed support from dealers, it was time to get Fender back in the amplifier business.

The next two years saw another massive makeover. The Dual Showman Reverb bit the dust, The Twin and the three reissues stayed on, and a whole bunch of amps were introduced at every level, from inexpensive solid state

"People wanted Fender amps to be successful. They were pulling for us, big time."

— Mike Lewis

Mike Lewis: "Personally, I was playing through a 3x10 Bandmaster with an outboard Fender reverb kit, and I said, 'Let's make an amp that sounds like this, but twice as loud and with tremolo.' The result was the Vibro-King."

units to the first of the Custom Amp Shop models, the Vibro-King and the Tone-Master.

Building a Line

Mike Lewis drew upon his retailing experience. He had sold the three tube Fenders — the Champ 12, the Dual Showman, and The Twin. "They were popular," he explains, "but one problem was, a guy walks into a music store and says, 'I've got 200 bucks to spend on an amp.' Even if the dealer likes Fender, if he doesn't have any Fenders in that price range, he's got to send that buyer somewhere else. So we really needed to look at the meat and potatoes of the line."

Both the tube and solid state lines were relatively skimpy. The solid states, for example, included the grey-carpeted M-80, the R.A.D., the H.O.T., and the J.A.M., plus a couple of bass amps. Looking on the bright side, there were plenty of opportunities for development.

Mike Lewis: "Leo Fender was a pioneer in the whole concept of creating an entire line, especially with that kind of quality — one for the student, one for the serious amateur, all the way up to the professional. In the days of Leo Fender, someone would walk into a music store and say, 'I've got X amount of dollars.' And you could look up and down the whole line of Fenders, and somewhere in there would be the perfect amp for that individual. We'd lost that, and we wanted to recreate it, so in a way our model was Leo Fender. We did the BXR bass amps and the KXR keyboard amps with the same idea of having an entire line. These were solid state, all made in Lake Oswego. Then in the mid '90s we devoted a lot of time and energy to closing the old Sunn factory in Lake Oswego and moving it all down to our new facility in Corona."

Rebirth of the Cool

Mike Lewis: "There is such a thing as the Fender sound. It's a tangible thing, and we were focused on re-establishing it as something people wanted to use. We had once been the standard for great tone, so we had to make sure that that sensibility would live again. We certainly paid attention to what Marshall and Boogie and others were doing, but by '92 or so we were focused on being the leader, not the follower. That's where our motto came from: Innovate, don't emulate. We were focused on making Fender the coolest thing. That's the Fender way, always on the cutting edge, in the forefront. I wanted us to be the Miles Davis of amplifiers, one step ahead. Just when you thought you had him figured out, he'd make some significant departure. And for us the paradox was this: Doing the new thing meant returning to the old. These things go in cycles, and we could see we needed to go back to the basics."

Three paths

Fender had always approached the design and marketing of guitars and amplifiers on three fronts, more or less, although by the early 1990s these strategies had solidified somewhat and had acquired in-house names. One was called "fitness to standard," which is where Fender builds what they're best known for, what people expect them to build. Mike Lewis: "If you're Fender and you make amps, you have to have a Twin Reverb."

The second approach is "fitness to need," which is simply listening to players and giving them what they want — a Strat with a humbucker, an amp with more power or channel switching, whatever it might be.

Mike Lewis: "And then there's 'fitness to *latent* need,' where you make something that people don't know they want yet, or you hope they're going to want. Sometimes it doesn't work, but when it does, fitness to latent need can produce the most revolutionary thing. A classic example is the Precision Bass. Leo Fender revolutionized music with an instrument that no one was asking for. He just thought, 'Musicians need this.' We have examples of fitness to latent need when it comes to amplifiers, too, like the G-DEC [Chap. 26]. Nobody came to us and said, 'Hey, make *this*.' Nobody knew they wanted it, and now they can't live without it."

The Return of Tweed

By 1993 Fender was going out of its way to embrace its legacy, with catalog copy like this: "There's only one classic. It can't be a classic if it's not the original." Some of the early ads showed four tweed-skinned amps without specifying their model names; the emphasis was on the big picture: *Tweed is back*. They turned out to be the solid state 15W 1x8 Bronco, and three tubers: the 15W 1x10 Pro Junior, the 40W 1x12 Blues Deluxe, and the 60W 4x10 Blues DeVille. And what a sight for sore eyes and nostalgic hearts they were: immaculate tweed boxes with dogbones or stitched leather handles! Chickenheads on chrome!

Pro Junior

A favorite of Bonnie Raitt's, the 1x10 Pro Junior is one of the best small amps of recent decades and a worthy successor to the Champs and Princetons of old. Its two EL84s pump out 15W, and its tone is warm, with a rich midrange and a touch of compression. With a Fender Special Design speaker made by Eminence, this model is ideal for recording. *Guitar Player* put it this way: "The Pro Junior's tone exhibits EL84 characteristics in a very Fullerton sort of way. The amp delivers tweed vibe at low volume and petulant British toughness when cranked up." Brian Henneman, of The Bottle Rockets: "A hip tip for the Pro Junior is to run it into a closed back cabinet, preferably loaded with two 12 inch Celestion Vintage 30 speakers. This setup is perfect for the studio because it sounds gigantic without being too loud. It's a recording engineer's dream rig."

The compact, great-sounding Pro Junior was one of the coolest amps to be introduced during Mike Lewis' tenure as marketing manager. As we go to press, it continues in the line as a member of the Hot Rod family, making it a long running success story.

Hybrids

Can't decide between the great tone and dynamic response of tube amps vs. the lower cost, fewer hassles, lower maintenance, and lighter weight of solid state amps? How about a hybrid of the two technologies? Leo Fender himself had advocated just such an approach back in the day, and by 1993 the line offered two kinds of hybrid amps, part tube, part solid state. The Champ 25 and Champ 25SE had solid state preamps and 5881/6L6 tube power amps (the literature proclaimed, "We put the tubes where they belong — in the power amp section!"), while the Performer series had 12AX7 preamps and solid state power amps.

Take It from the Top

Mike Lewis and his associates mapped out a plan to cover every base. The strategy was to start at the high end in order to re-establish the Fender sound among the public and to get the amplifiers on stages and in the hands of highly visible artists. Mike Lewis: "We said, let's go back to our roots, to what Fender is all about. Let's make an amp that the most discriminating Fenderite will dig, and get everybody grooving on that. After that happens, we can start filling in the other price points."

The result was Fender's most exciting new amp in years, the stunning Vibro-King of 1993. The expensive newcomer returned to Fender's roots and yet at the same time was highly original, putting the three-knob Fender reverb box inside a combo amp. It was an immediate sensation and was promptly followed by two other pricey, highly sought-after blondes, the Tone-Master head and the Dual Professional combo, an 80W 2x12. The Vibro-King, Tone-Master and Dual Professional are discussed in Chap. 23.

Catalogs '93 and '94

The 1993 catalog was a mix of old and new. A vintage vibe buzzed through several pages, with photo spreads of classic Fenders from the '40s and '50s, even a K&F, along with Custom Amp Shop blondes, the brown Tolex Vibroverb reissue, and the new tweeds. Not a red knob in sight. Here was a company clearly, finally, embracing its past, not only in the text of its brochures but where it counted most: on the production line. Fender was also bent on evoking a new consciousness among players, one that encouraged a deeper appreciation of amps in general. A new slogan, "The Other Half of Your Electric Guitar," recalled Ritchie Fliegler's book title, *Amps! The Other Half of Rock 'n' Roll.*

Under Mike Lewis' direction, the line had multiplied and now encompassed some three dozen combos and heads in eight series, plus various speaker enclosures. Four basic technologies were represented: all tube, all solid state, tube-preamp hybrids, and tube-power amp hybrids.

Custom Amp Shop models included the powerful, hand-wired Vibro-King and Tone-Master (the Dual Professional had disappeared for a time). Fender was working out a few marketing kinks, as revealed by the reissue amps being called the Reissue Series on the catalog's back cover but the Vintage Series on the inside. At any rate, they included the 85W '65 Twin Reverb with replica Jensen 12s, the 45W 4x10 '59 Bassman, the soon-to-be-discontinued 40W 2x10 '63 Vibroverb with a pair of Oxford 10s, and the newest reissue, the 22W 1x12 '65 Deluxe Reverb.

The all-tube Pro Tube series was directed "to the purist at heart with an eye to the future … vintage all around, with a healthy dose of modern features." In other words, Fender wanted it both ways, and they got it. Combining high-gain circuits and other useful features with traditional blackface styling seems like something Leo Fender would have done. The 60W Super had reverb, tilt-back legs, and four 10" Eminence speakers, but Fender was careful not to call it a Super Reverb, saving that hallowed name for the time when it would reissue the original (i.e., without the "modern" features).

The other blackface member of the Pro Tube series was the 60W 1x12 Concert. The Twin kept its grille-mounted name tag and '80s styling (but with small black knobs instead of small red ones). The Pro Tube series was rounded out with the Dual Showman head.

The impressive Tweed series would prove to be a gold mine. It included the solid state 15W 1x8 Bronco (channel switching in a

The high-gain Concert, from the Pro Tube series.

15W amp!) and three tube models: the great sounding 15W 1x10 Pro Junior (something of a modern day Princeton), and two immensely popular combos, the 40W 1x12 Blues Deluxe and the 60W 4x10 Blues DeVille.

Generally, the hybrid Performer series — the 70W 1x12 Performer 650, 100W 1x12 Performer 1000, and the 100W Performer 1000 head — sported a blackface appearance and offered high power, channel switching, 12AX7 preamp tubes, and solid state output sections.

In its brand new Deluxe 112 Plus incarnation, the Deluxe featured loads of distortion, channel switching, and a 90W wallop.

With the exception of The Twin (whose '80s styling was starting to look a little spandex and big hair rather than classic), all of the amps looked like something from the '50s or '60s until the line got down to the solid state models. The literature called the Standard Series "the core of Fender amps," a bold statement and one sure to raise eyebrows (not to mention blood pressures) among purists, but consider: Thousands of beginners and budget-minded veterans would find something suitable among the nine Fender Standards, all of which had channel switching. They ranged from the 1x8 15W Bullet ($159) to the stereo 2x65W 2x12 Ultra Chorus ($669) and the 160W 2x12 channel switching Pro 185 ($689). Perhaps the star of this particular show remained the reliably best-selling Princeton Chorus.

Fender's Standard Series could have been another company's entire line. They sounded pretty good, too. A September 1993 *Guitar Player* review of the $239 Champion 110 (25W, spring reverb) explained that it was very gainy, but "once you sufficiently pad your guitar's output, the 1x10 yields a gorgeous, shimmering, detailed clean tone. It's ultra sensitive." Mike Lewis: "We couldn't really compete with the Peaveys and the Crates until we had an entire line that matched those other amplifiers feature by feature at all the different price points, so our Standard Series was a priority."

For the solid state M-80 Series, Fender now stepped away from the grey carpet covering and rendered a more cohesive-looking line. It included the M-80 head (whose styling now reflected an unmistakable Marshall influence), other M-80s, plus the redesigned RAD, HOT, and JAM (their names had lost the periods).

For a catalog with so much vintage consciousness, one oddity was that the bottom of the line Fenders were no longer Champs. Instead, the entry level, 15W to 20W models were all solid state amps spread among various series: the RAD, Bullet, Bullet Reverb, Bronco, etc. The new Champ Series now included a pair of 25W 1x12 hybrids: the Champ 25, and the Champ 25SE with master volume. Unlike the tube-preamped hybrid Performers, the Champs had tube output sections (2x5881/6L6WGC). In other 1993 literature, Fender displayed several bass amps and enclosures in various series (RAD, BXR, M-80, the Dual Bass 400 rack, and others).

Mid-'90s KXR (Keyboard Extended Range) Two Hundred, with four channels, multi-band EQs, and 200W.

In 1994, a few models would come and go, and a few more would be recategorized into different series, but the overall strategies remained. The Tweed Series added the 2x12 version of the Blues DeVille (a favorite of the great bluesman Son Seals). The BXRs were redesigned. The Dual Professional, which had disappeared for a time, was back in the line, at $2,999. A reissue of the 1963 reverb unit had appeared in '93 and now joined the '65 Twin Reverb ($1,299), '59 Bassman ($1,129), '63 Vibroverb ($1,079), and '65 Deluxe Reverb ($919). Big news: The handsome and mighty Rumble Bass amp made its hard-to-miss debut (see Chap. 27, Fender Bass Amplification).

Wrapping Up the Mike Lewis Era

Mike Lewis: "So by the mid '90s the amp line had completely changed. We now had a full solid state line for beginners, hobbyists, studio guys, professionals, you name it, with every price point covered. That was the Standard series, all U.S. made, in Lake Oswego. By the time I left, we weren't importing anything anymore. We'd created several bass amplifiers; the BXR was an entire line, same with the KXR keyboard amps.

The new Princeton 112 Plus of 1995 was similar to the Deluxe 112 Plus, but with 65W.

"Then we had the Professional Tube series — a Super, a Concert — plus our Vintage Reissue line and the models from the Custom Amp Shop. These three series reestablished the Fender look, the Fender sound, and the Fender quality and prestige. Jeff Beck was using Vibro-Kings then. When that amp came out, *everyone* was using it; even Carlos Santana was playing a Vibro-King. Bruce Zinky knew the guys in Aerosmith, and they were playing them. The Eagles had this big reunion and they all had Blues Deluxes onstage. Turn on MTV and there's the Vibro-King. Yngwie Malmsteen was using stacks of Tone-Masters. Yes, you would see people using old Fenders, but once again you were seeing major artists using new Fenders."

> The 1993 catalog was a mix of old and new. A vintage vibe buzzed through several pages, with photo spreads of classic Fenders from the '40s and '50s, even a K&F — not a red knob in sight. Here was a company clearly, finally, embracing its past, not only in the text of its brochures but where it counted most: on the production line.

Vibro-Mike

When it comes to thinking up product names, Mike Lewis has proved himself to be something of a modern day Don Randall. His talent for imbuing new products with authentically Fenderish names helps to place them in the continuum of Fender's six decades of innovative amps and guitars. Among his inspirations: Tone-Master, Vibro-King, Frontman, Acoustasonic, Steel King, Blues Deluxe, Blues DeVille, Pro Junior, Blues Junior, Lone Star Strat, and Mike's personal favorite, Rumble Bass. (Mike Lewis: "Bruce Zinky might argue on Vibro-King and Tone-Master. I know we tossed a lot of names back and forth.")

'57 Twin reissue, with reissue blackguard Telecaster. The hand-wired, all-tube amp has the rare, mid-'50s type dual 5U4 rectifier arrangement, as well as Special Design Ted Weber/Eminence speakers with alnico magnets.

CHAPTER TWENTY-TWO

22

Forward into the Past

The Reissues

By the late '80s it had dawned on the average player that finding an affordable tweed Bassman in great condition was about as likely as getting a date with an Icelandic supermodel. In recognition of the deepening reverence for vintage gear (not to mention the escalating prices), the Fender amp team borrowed a strategy that had succeeded for their counterparts in Fender guitars: Their striving to innovate would be paralleled by an effort to recall the glories of the past.

The first order of business was to bring back perhaps the most revered amp of all time, the 1959 tweed Bassman. The new version appeared in 1990 and was soon joined by a reissue of the brown '63 Vibroverb. The '65 Twin Reverb was added in '91, the '63 Reverb unit and '65 Deluxe Reverb in '93. Following on their heels over the next decade would be reissues of the blackface Super Reverb and the '57 tweed Twin, among others, as well as an upgrade of the Bassman reissue, the '59 Bassman LTD.

In a way, the continuing popularity of classic Fender designs is part of a much larger cultural trend. An April 26, 2004 *Time* magazine article addressed fashion, appliances, and furniture, but the sentiments would resonate with guitar players as well. In "How Retro Can You Go?" *Time* asked: "What is it about the postwar period that keeps pulling us back? The mythology of the time looms so large that even the generations that didn't live through the era yearn for it today. … 'I think we're tired of being marketed to, told to buy stuff we don't need,' says [designer] Rob Forbes. 'There's a value underlying these designs which is consistent with how people want to live their lives. What are the things that have endurance and permanence?'"

"Few things are still as hip as they were in the '50s as a guitar amp. Esoteric hi-fi is now as cool as it was in 1940. I've got my dad's saxophone from the '30s, and it's gorgeous. You find a Deluxe, and it's as cool as it was from day one. If it's your sound, then it's all you need."

Randall Smith of Mesa/Boogie,
in *Guitar Player*, March 1996

'59 Bassman Reissue, Round One

For Fender's first new/old amp, timing was crucial. Had this 50W, 4x10 reissue appeared earlier, when you could still get an original for 600 or 700 bucks, it easily could have flopped. (Note: the Bassman reissue puts out about 45W with the tube rectifier, about 50W with the diode.) Another concern: Will we look like we're out of new ideas? Paul Rivera: "There was a project underway to reissue the 4x10 Bassman way back when I came onboard, in 1981. I cancelled it. At that time in Fender's history, I thought the most important thing was to regain our reputation as an innovator rather than rehashing old stuff. I thought, *You mean to tell me you can't think of anything new that will sell?* So at first I was anti-reissue. I wanted fresh ideas, instead of going back to the '50s and '60s."

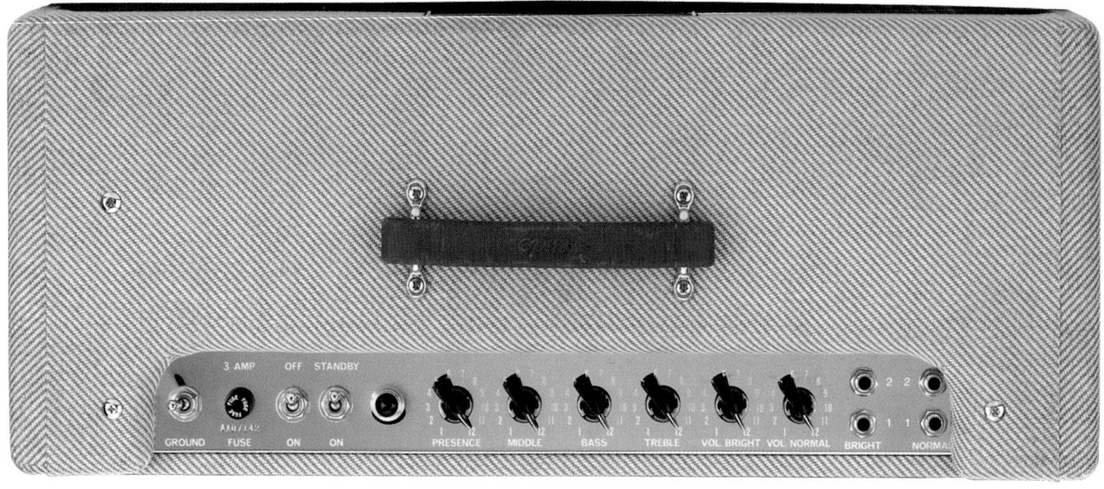

For decades, the six-chickenhead '59 5F6-A Bassman panel provided a palette for many a sonic masterpiece. The reissue recaptured much of the magic at a fraction of the cost of a vintage original.

But much had changed during the late 1980s. Fender had dropped many of its better known models — the Super Champ, Princeton Reverb, Princeton Reverb II, Deluxe Reverb, Deluxe Reverb II, Twin Reverb II, and even the venerable Twin Reverb. By 1987 the line had shrunk to just a few amps, including the red-knob models, which sold fine but were never embraced by diehard Fender purists. As the number of new models dwindled, the prices of original tweed Fenders began their ascent into the stratosphere. Finally, companies like THD confirmed the viability of reproducing classic Fender-style amplifiers.

The marketing and R&D teams realized that a simple design that sounded great, was easily portable, and radiated vintage cool would be a likely hit. Like Jurassic Park geneticists seeking dinosaur DNA for cloning purposes, Marketing Manager Steve Grom and his colleagues set about unearthing as many originals as possible. Steve Grom: "We rounded up five or six '59 Bassmans, including one we got from Danny Gatton. Once we opened them up, we realized that even though they were the same year and same model, each one was a bit different. Part of that was because of repairs that had been done over the years. You know, back then, if something went wrong, you didn't have some amp guru to take it to. You took it to a TV guy or a radio or appliance guy, and he fixed it as best he could. How many Super Reverbs have you seen with mismatched speakers? It's because that's all the guy had.

"For the reissue, we knew we could get the transformers and most of the tubes, but the speakers — that was the challenge, the key to the whole thing. We had a conversation with Jensen, but they were owned at that time by a big conglomerate and were making thousands of speakers a day for car audio, and we needed something like 500 or 600 in the first order, so they said never mind. We went to Bob Gault [founder of Eminence]. Bill Hughes was very involved in spec'ing out that [Jensen P10R] alnico magnet speaker, and Bob Gault really did his homework. He found the company that had made a lot of the original paper cones. Bob also found the original tooling. So the guys at Eminence were very instrumental. They reconstructed the old Jensen alnico speaker design."

Bill Hughes adds: "I assumed the position of Director of Research & Development, and the '59 Bassman reissue was done under my direction by Matt Wilkens. He was the engineer on the project. I needed a 10 inch driver with alnico magnets. Eminence found the tooling for some of those original baskets and for the magnet structure. Bob Gault cloned the '59 Bassman driver."

Steve Grom: "Another challenge was that the original Bassman had a tube rectifier, but in 1990 most of the tubes were coming from China. The whole Russian scene hadn't really started, and the rectifier tubes on the market were real noisy, with lots of problems, so we came up with a little plug-in module that goes right in that tube socket with a [solid state] diode rectifier. We shipped it with the diode, and the amp would work better, but if owners wanted to unplug it and put a tube in there, God bless 'em, go for it.

"A lot of people were involved in the '59 Bassman project. Everybody had the best intentions. Everybody who lent us an amp offered an idea, just to make sure the amps came out right. Like there was a guy down in San Diego, Mike Fenton, who helped us get the tweed right — all these little details."

Fender's first reissue was an immediate hit, finding favor with a variety of players. In 1992 Jeff Beck released *Crazy Legs*, a tribute to his idol Cliff Gallup, who had recorded and toured with Gene Vincent in 1956. In an effort to recreate his hero's tone, Beck used an old Gretsch Duo-Jet straight through a reissue Bassman. He told *Guitar Player*: "It was a rented amp from Fender Sound House. Buddy Guy and Eric Clapton had rented it … I think the Bassman has the qualities one would look for in trying to get Gallup's sound. It's got the low end and richness … The richness in this amp adds that authenticity to the sound."

Steve Grom: "Because it's brand new, the reissue's never going to sound exactly like an amp with old, floppy speakers and parts that have aged and so on, but the reissue sounded great. People loved it. It went over real well, and it helped reestablish our credibility. Feedback was very enthusiastic. It was cool that some of these little companies were making a few Bassman copies, and everyone was like, 'Yeah, that's nice,' but when Fender did it — game over."

Alan Rogan, on George Harrison's tour of Japan with Eric Clapton, winter 1991: "On the tour George did with Eric and Eric's band, George had two reissue Bassmans. He used one, and the other was the spare. What can I say about that tour? It was the best! Anything else? [Laughs.] Just fantastic, seeing George play live, sometimes regular, sometimes slide. He would set the Bassman and work off the guitar, turn it up or down just like you or I would do. Simple. The amp was full. It had a great sound. His main guitars on that tour were EC Strats with the Lace Sensors. Through that amp, those guitars sounded fantastic, especially with George sliding across them. George and that amplifier were perfectly suited, the pair of them. Performing live again he was just in … not awe, exactly, but he was in big happiness mode, just to be back onstage and sounding so great."

What amp are you playing through now?

Buddy Guy: "A Fender Bassman. They reissued the Fender Bassman, and I'm very proud of that. Because to me, that's the guitar sound. Otis Rush had it. In the earlier days when I went to Chicago, Muddy Waters and Howlin' Wolf was giants in my book — there wasn't no Rolling Stones, no Beatles, there wasn't no super rock groups or nothing like that. And we used to travel with the whole band in a car because two guitar amps and a bass amp would fit in the trunk. On my Bassman, everything's wide open but the bass — no bass at all. I've got my old Bassman saved. Actually, I would love to have it installed in the wall of my house, so if somebody do happen one day to decide to break in, they would say, 'It's too much trouble to get that.'"

— *Guitar Player, August '92*

"As long it has tubes and it's a Fender-type amp, you can't beat it. I've used a pair of Fender reissue Bassmans for gigs, and I've used them on records from *Family Style* on."

— Jimmie Vaughan

Beautiful but short lived, the '63 Vibroverb reissue.

'63 Vibroverb

In 1990 Fender reissued the handsome brown Tolex Vibroverb. Unlike the tube-rectified, point-to-point original, the 35W 2x10 reissue featured a solid state rectifier and a printed circuit board. The model was favored by Richard Thompson, and George Harrison reportedly borrowed Jeff Lynne's reissue Vibroverb and used it in 2001 for two cuts on Electric Light Orchestra's *Zoom*. Steve Grom: "The two 10 inch Oxfords in the reissue had the original tooling, that funny looking basket with all the holes in it, but when we couldn't get the speakers anymore, we had to stop making that amp."

Another problem was that the Vibroverb reissue was marketed alongside the new Custom Vibrolux Reverb, which offered very similar specs — '60s styling, 40W, two 10s, reverb, tremolo, and tilt-back legs. These amps were too similar. One of them had to go. The Vibroverb disappeared after 1995. Richard McDonald: "We couldn't sell those things to save our lives." The Custom Vibrolux Reverb, something of a modern classic, remains in the line.

Return of the King: The '65 Twin Reverb

If you were a club owner and could afford only one amplifier to accommodate every visiting artist, you couldn't do any better than a blackface Twin Reverb, the loud, clean, durable top of the mid-'60s line. The reissue of 1991 brought it back. Details: 85W, reverb, tremolo, four 12AX7s, four 6L6s, and two 12AT7s (one for the Reverb send; the other is the phase inverter). The ceramic-magnet Jensen C-12K speakers were designed to emulate the Jensen C12Ns often found in the first-generation blackface Twins.

Guitarist Magazine called it "uncompromised" and added: "The Twin's normal and vibrato channels pump out some of the richest, sweetest tones any amp has ever delivered . . . The bass response at high volume will punch you in the stomach, while it's a brave person who winds up treble and presence on one of these. The reverb is nothing short of cavernous. The Twin is one of the great workhorses, and the reissue is a worthy successor to the original." Steve Grom: "When we introduced this reissue, the numbers were off the charts — very successful."

Hear the '65 Twin Reverb, Track 3.

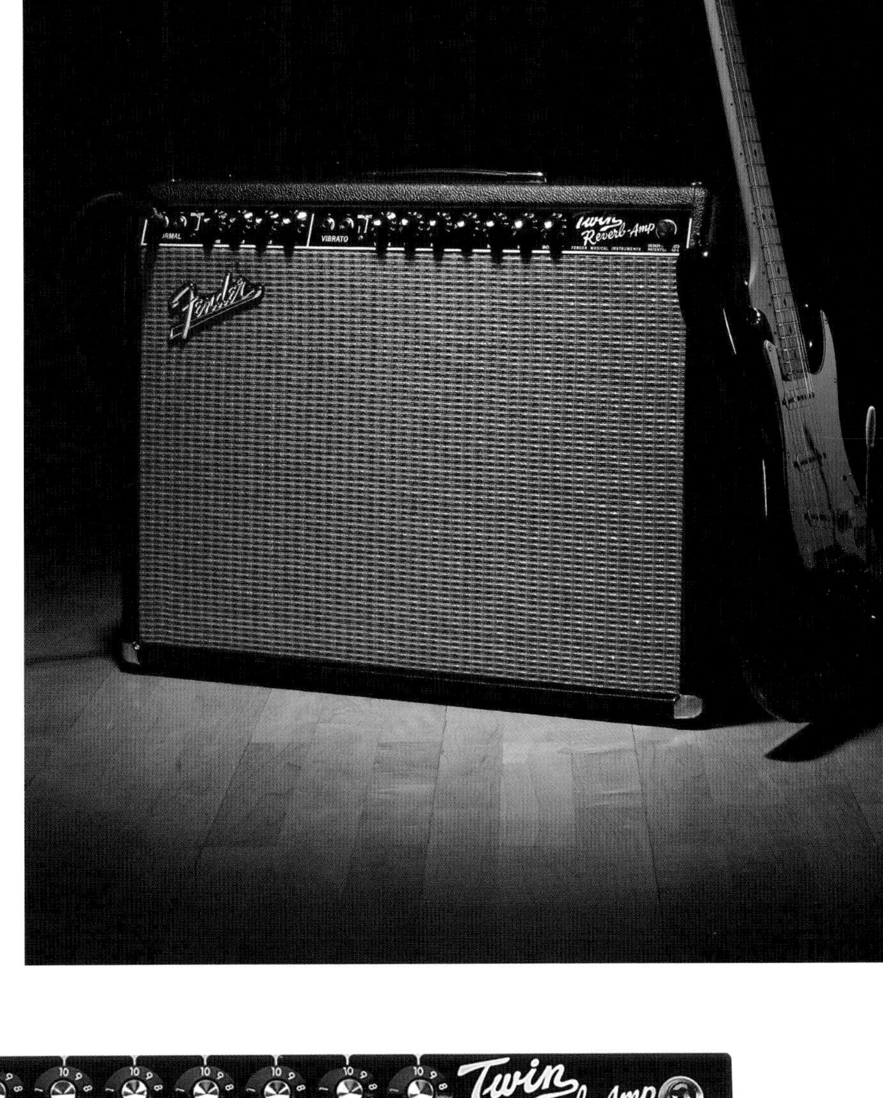

From *Guitar Player*'s August 1992 review: "The '65 reissue Twin Reverb resurrects the old AB763 circuit. Had the technology been available to him, even Leo Fender would probably have done it this way … the Twin contains more hand-wiring than we expected, and the workmanship looks rugged."

Below:
Panel detail, Twin Reverb reissue.

'63 Reverb Unit

In the mid '90s, Mike Lewis reissued the stand-alone '63 6G15 Reverb in black, brown, and blonde, and the brown Tolex version is still in the line. Shane Nicholas: "The '63 is an inherently 'Fendery' sound, part of the legacy. The people who buy it are surf players and blues players, mostly, but it's a unique sound for any type of recording enthusiast or experimental player. Harmonica players use them, too. Because the instrument hits the reverb first, before the amplifier, it's a very 'crashing' type sound, and you can control how hard it crashes by your playing dynamics. It's similar to the circuit in the Vibro-King. In both cases, because the instrument hits the reverb first, it's a much different reverb sound than in, say, a '65 Twin Reverb.

"Back in the mid '90s there was a short period where we built some '63 Reverbs in various coverings including tweed, which was a unit that never existed before. Most people tend to buy the brown one, for some reason. We are about to do an FSR [Factory Special Run] in Lacquered Tweed, because I figure that many of the people who recently bought '57 Twins and '59 Bassman LTDs would be into having a matching Reverb unit."

Starting in 1993, Fender began reissuing printed-circuit, tube-based versions of its 1963 stand-alone reverb unit. The tweed edition is not technically a reissue, since the reverb kit was never made in tweed back in the day; still, it looks great next to any tweed Fender amp — original, reissue, or new model. The earliest reverb units had solid front panels rather than fabric grilles; see p.36

'65 Super Reverb

Given its popularity, sound, and versatility, the 4x10 blackface Super Reverb must be considered one of the greatest amps of all time, and yet Fender had let it fall by the wayside. Former Marketing Manager Richard McDonald decided to make things right. He brought it back in January 2001.

The reissue was well received. *Guitar Player* said of it, "As mid-sized amps go, the '65 Super Reverb is hard to beat. It has enough muscle to make it a practical choice for gigs on medium or large stages, but it's not overly powerful — you can get the amp to break up nicely at a volume level that won't send the first five rows of your audience scurrying for the exit." Here, Richard McDonald provides insights into the origins of the Super Reverb reissue, a 45W blackface amp with four 12AX7s, two 12AT7s, two 6L6s, a 5AR4 rectifier tube, and four Jensen P10Rs.

There must have been a lot of popular demand for the Super Reverb reissue.
Um, no. Here's how it happened. Fender legal counsel came to me and said, "We haven't done anything with these trademarks. If you don't do something with them, we're going to lose them." "Super Reverb" was one of them. Use it or lose it.

You're kidding.
No, that's why we reissued the amp. Can you imagine reading this book, and it says, Richard McDonald's legacy? He was the idiot who let the Super Reverb trademark slip away! So I dropped everything I was doing and made a '65 Super Reverb. Mike Ulrich was the engineer on that one.

It had been discontinued back in 1982. What a shock that was. How many gigs have been powered by Super Reverbs?
I know! Unreal, all over the world.

The usual inspiration and development for a new model entails popular demand, market analysis, focus groups, field testing, and so on. Given its oddball genesis, how did the Super Reverb reissue do?
Fantastic! [Laughs.] The pent-up demand was there; we just hadn't seen it yet. It took off like crazy, and in retrospect, no one is surprised. The naysayers, the vocal minority, gave us a bad time — it's not hand-wired or whatever. They're all talking to each other on the Internet, all seven of them, but if we had hand-wired it, it would have been too expensive. Very few players could have had the experience.

A handful of names come up in discussions of "the greatest amp of all time." This reissue brought back one of them, the blackface Super Reverb.

What did you learn in the process?
That Super Reverb project was so fun because we stumbled into all the information about mislabeling, weird phasing of the speakers, all sorts of stuff. Some of the original speakers

Hear the '65 Super Reverb, Track 7.

Leo bought were mismarked [as to their phase]. So did he know? Did he intentionally hook them up with reverse polarity? Because it makes a huge sonic difference in the sound if the speaker pulls back before it pushes out. You can really hear it. This company and our suppliers have done some goofy things, and whole shipments of speakers had their positive and negative terminals mislabeled. The workers just hooked them up. I think the '59 Bassman's speakers blow negative for that reason. So we have to address all these things when we're doing a reissue. Was Leo so clever he figured all this out, or was it an accident, or what? It makes it fun and keeps us on our toes.

How did you figure out what to do?
We really got into critical listening. That's one thing Ritchie Fliegler brought to Fender. He has incredible ears, and even though you've been a player for ten or twenty years and you think you have pretty discriminating ears, you work with Ritchie for a few years and you start hearing on a new level. Most people with great ears can hear 95 percent of what's there. Ritchie not only hears the other five percent, he shines a spotlight on it. We all started to hear more critically, and we refined our vocabulary between engineers and marketing. We're players, and what we hear and what we *want* to hear has to be communicated to engineers so they can render specs and circuit values. That back-and-forth dance, that sophistication, is one of the things that make us the best amplifier company in the world.

'65 Twin Custom 15

The '65 Twin Reverb Custom 15 is basically a '65 Twin Reverb reissue, but instead of the conventional two 12s it has a single 15 and a larger cabinet. When it comes to categories, it's a hard one to pin down. Despite the name, it has never been marketed in the Custom Series because it's not hand-wired. It was originally placed in the Vintage Reissue Series, even though Fender never made such an amp back in the day. For 2006 the Custom 15 was placed in a brand new category, the sensibly named Specialized Amplifiers.

Shane Nicholas: "It's sort of a steel amp, sort of a reissue, or neither, depending on your perspective. It's got one foot in the vintage category. But however you see it, that's a really cool amp, other than lifting it [laughs]. Its speaker is the one we use in the Steel King. It sounds amazing, very hi-fi. It's an Eminence based on the old JBL D130F. Fender used the D130F in the old days, but JBL is not set up to manufacture it anymore. The amp has a real big bottom end, a lot of volume for the wattage, and kind of a clangy, pleasing top end, which for a steel player or a Chet Atkins style player really sounds cool."

"We're players, and what we hear and what we *want* to hear has to be communicated to engineers so they can render specs and circuit values. That back-and-forth dance, that sophistication, is one of the things that make us the best amplifier company in the world."
— Richard McDonald

'65 Twin Custom 15.

Blues Deville and Blues Deluxe Reissues

The Blues DeVille and Blues Deluxe were reissued in the mid 2000s. Aside from a flukey placement of the solid state '93 Bronco in the Vintage Reissue category (summer 2000), the Blues DeVille and Blues Deluxe reissues marked the first time Fender had reissued amps from a recent period rather than from the classic tweed, brown, or blackface eras of the '50s and '60s. There are no reissues of amplifiers from the three decades following the CBS takeover, but reissuing amps that initially appeared in 1994 speaks volumes about the reputation of Fender's recent products versus those of the '70s and '80s.

'59 Bassman LTD, Printed Circuits

Shane Nicholas comments on the update of the '59 reissue Bassman, a project that he spearheaded.

Aside from deciding which of the original specs to keep and which ones to update, what are the unique challenges of reissuing a Fender amp?

Sometimes you're playing a prototype and thinking, "My god, this sounds unbelievable," but then you'll send it to Safety and maybe the output transformer gets above a certain temperature or something like that, so you have to address that. They have all sorts of rules, and you have to work within those limitations.

Another thing is that we have to certify these things for all over the world. Some regulations are very strict. In some countries, we actually have to have a little rubber booty on the standby switch and power switch, just in case that switch gets hot. I've never heard of anyone burning themselves on a Fender amp switch, but we have to do it in some countries. In some places we have to put a metal cage around the 6L6s, and it breaks your heart because you don't want to look in the back of a tweed Bassman and see a tube cage, but we have to do those things to get the safety certification. It's mandatory.

You have such a rich and varied legacy, and so many classic products that you could reissue. How do you decide which ones to put into production?

We spend a lot of time thinking about what people want and need, and we provide those things, but once in a while I'm just selfish. A couple of times we've done an amp just because I've wanted it myself [laughs]. The Bassman LTD

'59 Bassman LTD, with a Stratosonic guitar.

 *Hear the Blues Deluxe Reissue, Track 6.*

 *Hear the '59 Bassman LTD, Track 2.*

of 2004 was one. I had been playing a reissue Bassman for a while, and I put the rectifier tube in and had a bias pot installed. I read all about the pine cabinets, so I tried a pine cab and it was different and good sounding. The original reissue had a long life span, ten years or so, but when the sales finally started to slump — and they slumped a lot, to be honest — I thought, we *can't* discontinue the tweed Bassman. So we relaunched it with the new features.

Why do you think the first reissue had faded?
Every product has a life cycle, and you get to the point where everybody who wants one has one. But we thought it could be improved. For example, the original ones were lacquered. There was no Tolex back then, so that's what Leo could get to cover the amps. Bill Carson's recollection was that the tweed was lacquered before it went on the cabinet. "LTD" stands for Lacquered Tweed, by the way, not Limited Edition.

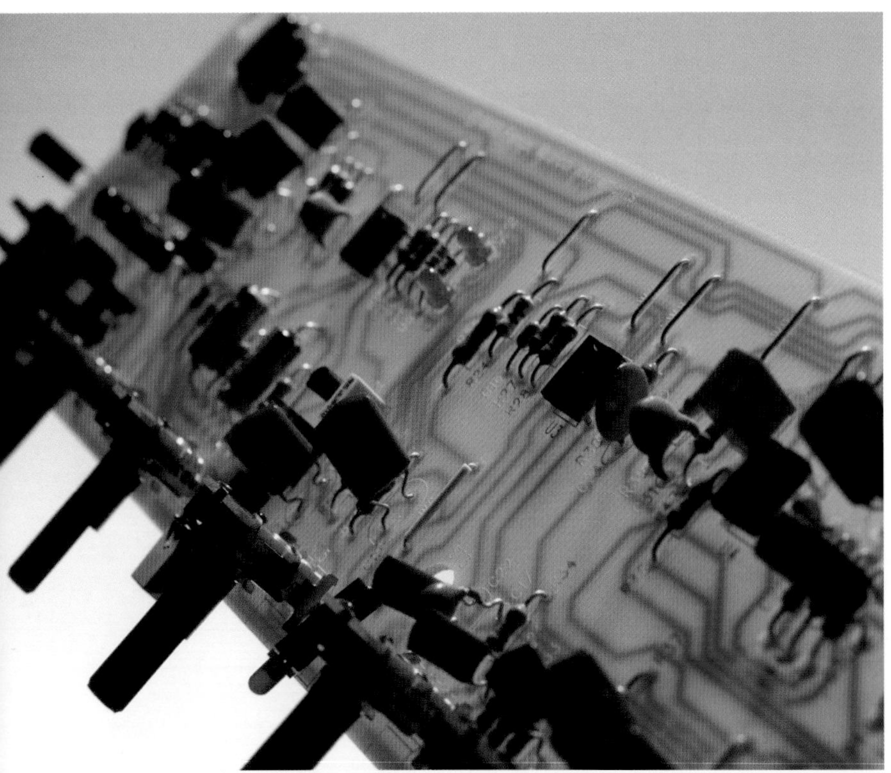

Aside from reducing heat, printed circuits like this one also lessen sticker shock. The '59 Bassman LTD, for example, retails for about half the cost of the hand-wired '57 Twin.

Why is lacquering the tweed important?
For one, it looks more authentic, more like the original, and it doesn't get dirty as fast. The lacquer we use is very similar to what we might use on a '57 Strat reissue. It's got a little bit of a tint to it. If you've ever seen a mint late-'50s amp that's been kept under cover, it's actually a lighter shade. But most of those amps have seen a lot of sunlight and a lot of smoke, and so they shift in color. The lacquer also gives it a little more durability, which was always important to Leo.

Aside from the lacquering, what distinguishes the LTD?
It's even more "correct" compared to its predecessor. It was a real labor of love for me, because the amp I gigged with more than any other was a 1991 Bassman reissue. I just love that amp to death. It sounds great for any kind of music, and it never let me down, but there were things that I thought could be improved. The LTD is basically the same thing that we had back in '91, but it has a finger-joined pine cabinet. The original reissue that Steve Grom did had a birch ply cab, which works fine and sounds good, but it's not the original sound; it's a little harder sounding. We also installed a bias potentiometer in the new one, so if people want to experiment with different types of 6L6s they can do it.

You must feel torn between cloning the original and improving it.
The bias pot is a good example. I had one installed in my own Bassman because it's so convenient, and that's something people requested, too. I like it set a little hotter, but other people might like it a bit colder, or to use whatever type of 6L6 they want. On the LTD, the bias control is a trim pot on the circuit board. It was not on the original, but we thought, so many people we know have done this modification, let's go ahead and do it.

How did you get started on the LTD?
I called Steve Grom and asked him why they didn't put a rectifier tube in that amp in the first place, or make the cabinet out of pine, or use lacquered tweed. He said, "Look, we were lucky to get any tubes or any tweed at all." It was especially difficult to find good sources for those 5U4 rectifier tubes. The vintage screw-counter phenomenon, where some people are so picky about every single detail, was

nowhere nearly as advanced back then as it is today. The Internet has had a lot to do with that, so people who know or think they know the details of these amps have an opportunity to talk to each other. *"Your amp doesn't have lacquered tweed? Oh, dude, where have you been?"*

Steve and those guys did the best they could with what was available at the time, and nobody complained. Now, if you say you are going to do a reissue Fender and you don't make it out of pine or you don't have the rectifier tube, there's a certain group out there who's really going to give you a bad time. So, it's more important than ever that we do very deep homework. People are not only more demanding, they have more information available.

You decided you could make a credible tweed Bassman with a printed circuit board in it.

I know some people would be happier if it were hand-wired, but we wanted to make this amp accessible. I've played gigs with the Bassman LTD and thought to myself, *My god, what more could you want from an amplifier?* You put an overdrive and echo pedal in front of it and just *play*. If you're playing in a band, and you need an amp, and you're really going to use it and not just gloat over it and show it off, I think a '59 Bassman reissue is about as good as you can get. It's amazing. For the average guitar player who wants a '65 Deluxe Reverb or a '65 Twin Reverb or a '59 Bassman, printed circuit boards allow us to make those products accessible. If they all had hand-wiring, they would be out of reach for most players. We struck the right balance, because those reissue amps have done very well for us. [Bill Hughes adds: "With a printed circuit board the amplifiers become more indistinguishable from each other because the routings are so consistent. From a production standpoint, the designs are more repeatable. That's the big difference. Anybody who pooh-poohs [printed] circuit boards, they're out of their minds. Are there any drawbacks? I don't see any, so long as you handle the tube sockets correctly. In our high-end tube amplifiers, we don't commit the tubes to the circuit boards (for microphonic reasons). They are 'fly-wired' on, which means the tube sockets are riveted or screwed to the chassis and then wires connect to the tube socket. In the high-end Fender tube amplifiers, all the potentiometers are wired that way too. Reliability is very high."]

Which functions from the original 1959 Bassman are handled by the printed circuit board in the reissues?

All of them. The tone stack, the preamp, all of those things are on the printed circuit board as opposed to the old fiberboard. All of the capacitors, resistors, and many other components are auto-inserted, meaning a machine knows exactly where to drop each component, and then it goes into a wave solder machine that dips the board so that the underside is coated with solder, and it only sticks to the places where you want it to stick. The components we're using are generally smaller in size than the ones you would find in a 40-year-old, hand-wired Fender, but they fulfill the same functions and have the same values. If we had a 250 ohm resistor in the old one, we would have the same type of component in the new one.

Deluxe Redux: This 22W reissue brought back everybody's favorite club amp: the historic, toneful Deluxe Reverb. The original is something of a touchstone among players of all ages and styles (it seems we've all used and loved a Deluxe Reverb at one time or another), and after more than a decade, the reissue remains a staple of Fender's line. Bill Frisell: "When I'm traveling, I usually ask for Fender '65 Deluxe Reverb reissues, which are great."

Do amps with printed circuit boards sound as good as the originals?
Guys on the Internet forums debate this ad nauseam. Does the hand-wired amp sound better? Well, it probably sounds a little different. But here's the thing: With hand-wired amps there was much more variation from amplifier to amplifier. Even little things like the length of a wire, or how far that wire is from this component or that one, or the angle of one component relative to another can all set up interferences and interactions that can affect the sound.

Which is why one original Fender can sound noticeably different from another example of the same model and year?
Your Bassman might sound like the voice of God, and your friend's might be a dog. The tolerances in those days were much wider. And let's not forget, a lot of the older amps had more hum. These amps can vary in terms of electrical interferences, minute amounts of crosstalk, and so on. If that original amp has some components that have been replaced, or even repaired, if that speaker has 100,000 miles on it — all of these things can affect the sound. We don't have those variations with printed circuit boards. We can get the sound everybody wants, and then replicate it consistently. We talked long and hard about this decision: Do we duplicate the labor practices of the 1950s, or do we make amps that regular players can afford? We decided to provide both, and to put them in different series. Our Custom Series is our very best, the top of the line, and one of the things that makes them that way is that they are hand-wired. That aspect vastly increases the number of labor hours.

How does the hand-wiring affect the cost to the player?
The '59 Bassman LTD reissue is about 1,500 dollars, whereas the hand-wired '57 Twin, which probably has fewer parts, is actually 3,000 dollars list. They both have pine cabinets, they're both lacquered tweed, and they both have good 6L6s. But the biggest difference is that it takes us about eight times as long to build the circuit board in the Twin because you're putting the components on one at a time. Some of these purists go on and on about how printed circuits are inferior to hand-wiring, but I gotta say, as a guitar player — forget my Fender hat for a moment — this Bassman LTD is one of the best amps I've ever played through in my entire life. I don't care if it has little mice

'57 Twin detail: the '50s Fender look, 50 years later.

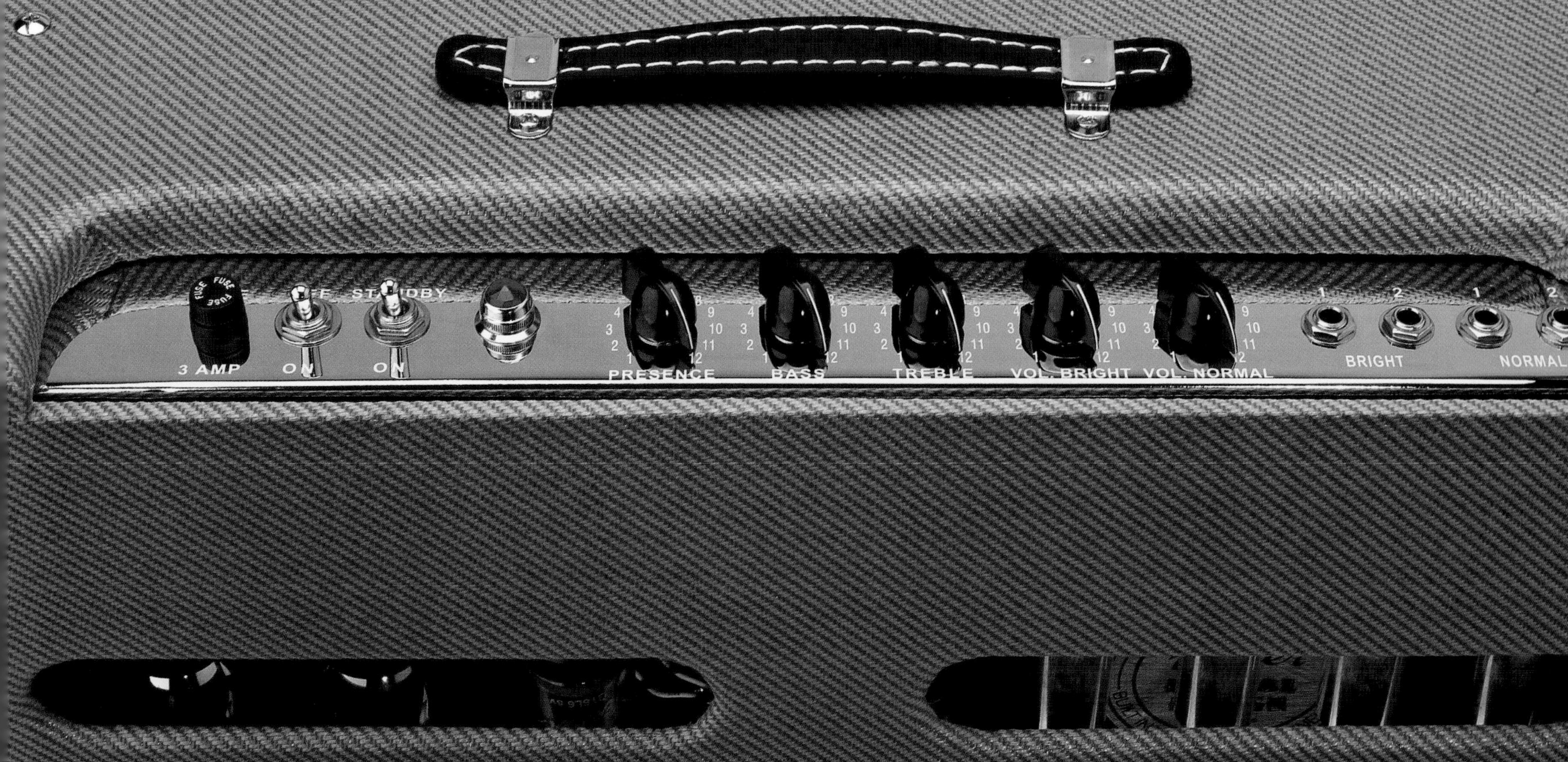

running around inside it on a wheel. Would it sound different if we did the Bassman with hand-wiring? Probably. But would people notice? I don't know.

Do you read the comparison shootouts in the guitar magazines?
Sure, but someone might be comparing a new amp with a printed circuit board to an original that may have some replacement parts, or the various components may have aged in any of several different ways, or it might not be a particularly representative example of that model and year to begin with. Even a couple of 100 percent original amps from the '50s can still have several inconsistencies. So all of the variations in the originals plus the effects of aging the components over 40 or 50 years makes some of these so-called side-by-side comparisons pretty dubious. If you play ten brand new reissue Fenders anywhere in the world, they're going to be consistent. If you play ten originals from the 1950s, chances are you are going to find significant variations. By the way, even on the reissues, some of the components are still wired by hand. The pots, transformers, some of the jacks, and other things are still done by hand, and this varies from model to model.

The '57 Twin

You launched the '57 Twin reissue in January 2004. Of all the great Twins, why pick the '57?
Shane Nicholas: Our original plan was to make the '54, in conjunction with the 50th anniversary of the Stratocaster, as a matched set, but a collector friend of ours brought in an all-original '57 with the two 5U4 rectifier tubes, and as soon as I plugged into it I forgot about doing the '54. I said, we have to do this one! We decided to make our reissue sound as close as we could to this '57. It had all the original components, and the speakers hadn't been re-coned. It was the first time I had ever played through an all-original '57 Twin, and it was a neat experience. I thought it would've sounded like a Bassman with 12s, but it's a totally different animal. It was more of a finesse kind of amp. It really rewards sensitive playing.

Bill Carson said of the original Twin back in the '50s, "It was a pure clean sound with a fuzzy circle around the edges of the note." Leo Fender wanted the note to have a little hair on it, but he wanted fidelity at the same time. That may sound like a contradiction, but that really is what this reissue Twin delivers. If you set it on 3 or 4 and you're

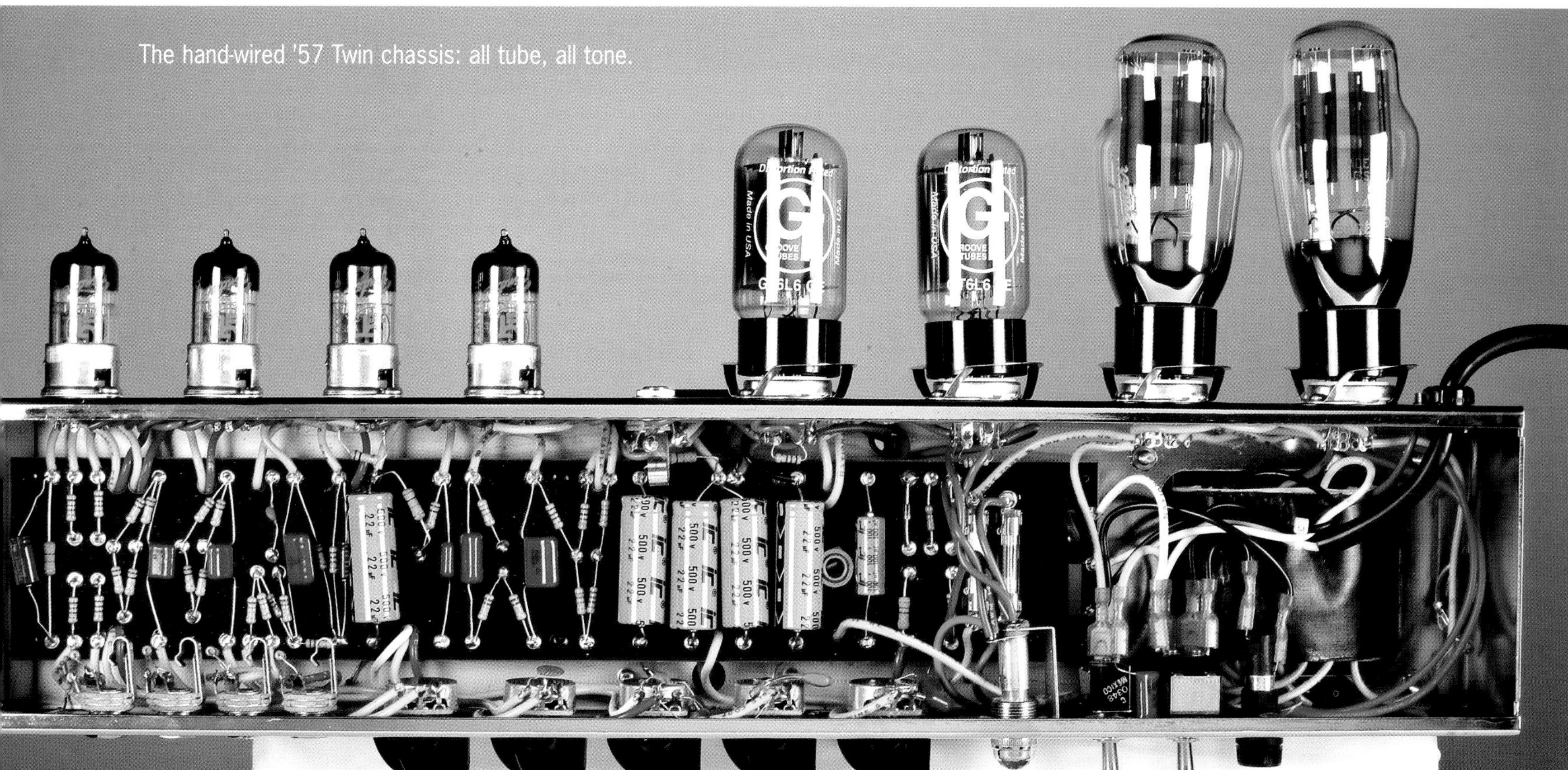

The hand-wired '57 Twin chassis: all tube, all tone.

playing a Strat with heavy strings, it's unbelievable. It's really clean, it doesn't have a lot of preamp, but it does have a soft edge on the tone.

The '57 Twin is a reissue, but it's not in the Reissue Series. It's hand-wired, and our hand-wired amps live in our Custom Series, whether they're reissues or new designs.

Hear the '57 Twin Reissue, Track 15.

Why reissue the low-power 5E8-A version, with two output tubes?
I've been asked that a lot. Both versions are wonderful amps and we considered the choice very carefully. Some customers were irate, but we did a lot of listening, and we don't take these decisions lightly. We know Keith Richards typically plays a high-power Twin. We know Eric Clapton has some of each and often favors the low-power Twin. I've got to believe that the average player playing a blues gig in a club will find the low-power Twin has plenty of power to piss off everybody in the audience if you want to crank it up to what it can really do.

Isn't there an advantage to the low-power version in that it starts to break up at reasonable volumes?
I definitely thought that was an advantage, and it's a big reason why we went with the two [output] tube version. Personally, I'm a Bassman player most of the time. No one ever calls it the low-power Bassman [laughs]. Those amps have *plenty* of power. A lot of people who buy these amps play in clubs or in their garage or their bedroom. And for them this amp is still too loud [laughs]. If you remove one of the rectifier tubes, the amp works fine, but with more sag and an earlier onset of distortion at higher volumes.

"A printed circuit board versus hand-wiring has a stigma, but some of the most famous, best sounding amps ever have [printed] circuit boards, so maybe that distinction will go away. I just don't buy it."

— Paul Reed Smith

Perspectives

The original tweed Bassman, blackface Deluxe Reverb, and blackface Twin Reverb were in the line for about five years. Their reissues, however, have lasted three times as long. Steve Grom: "When I walk out on the production line, I'm still amazed. Here we are in the first decade of the new century, and look how many amps from the '50s and '60s we're still making, every day. No features, no channel switching, no nothing other than tone. It's the one thing you can't buy a pedal for. Your amp either has it or it doesn't, and that's been the one thing these amps have, and that's why Fender has stood the test of time."

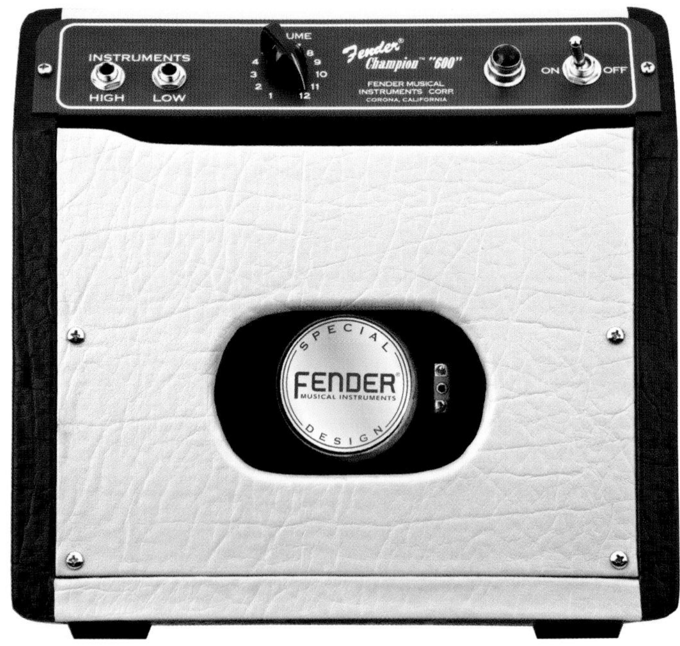

One switch, one knob, one sweet deal — while this 5W cutie looks almost identical to the brown and cream leatherette "two-tone" Champion 600 of the early 1950s, it's more of an affordable tribute than a reissue. It's got a 6" speaker like the hand-wired original, but this new Chinese-made Champion 600 has a modern printed circuit, a choice of high or low-gain inputs, and a higher-gain preamp circuit that gives it more overdrive. Details: One 12AX7, one 6V6, and a diode rectifier rather than the original's metal envelope 5Y3 tube.

"In the studio, I use a vintage Super Reverb, but live I run an old blackface Bandmaster head into a Mesa/Boogie 4x12 cabinet. I prefer older Fender amps when I can get them, but I do like the new blackface reissues. After a period where it seemed like Fender had forgotten how to make a good amp, they're finally making great amps again."
— Lee Ranaldo, Sonic Youth

Eric Clapton's stage rig for the Cream reunion, 2005: two tweed Twin reissues and, for the iconic riff heralding the solo in "Badge," a Leslie speaker cabinet.

Johnny Hiland's self-titled debut album was released on Steve Vai's Favored Nations label. Hiland told *Guitar Player*: "My Fender Twin hadn't shown up yet, so I went ahead and cut everything direct through a Johnson J-Station, but after getting all my parts down perfectly, [engineer] Neil Citron said, 'Vai really wants you through a Twin. We've gotta get that real-amp vibe. I want to push some air into some microphones.' At first, my stress level went through the roof, but when he got a '65 reissue Twin in there — and miked it front and back — I was blown away with the raw tone. I couldn't wait to re-track everything."

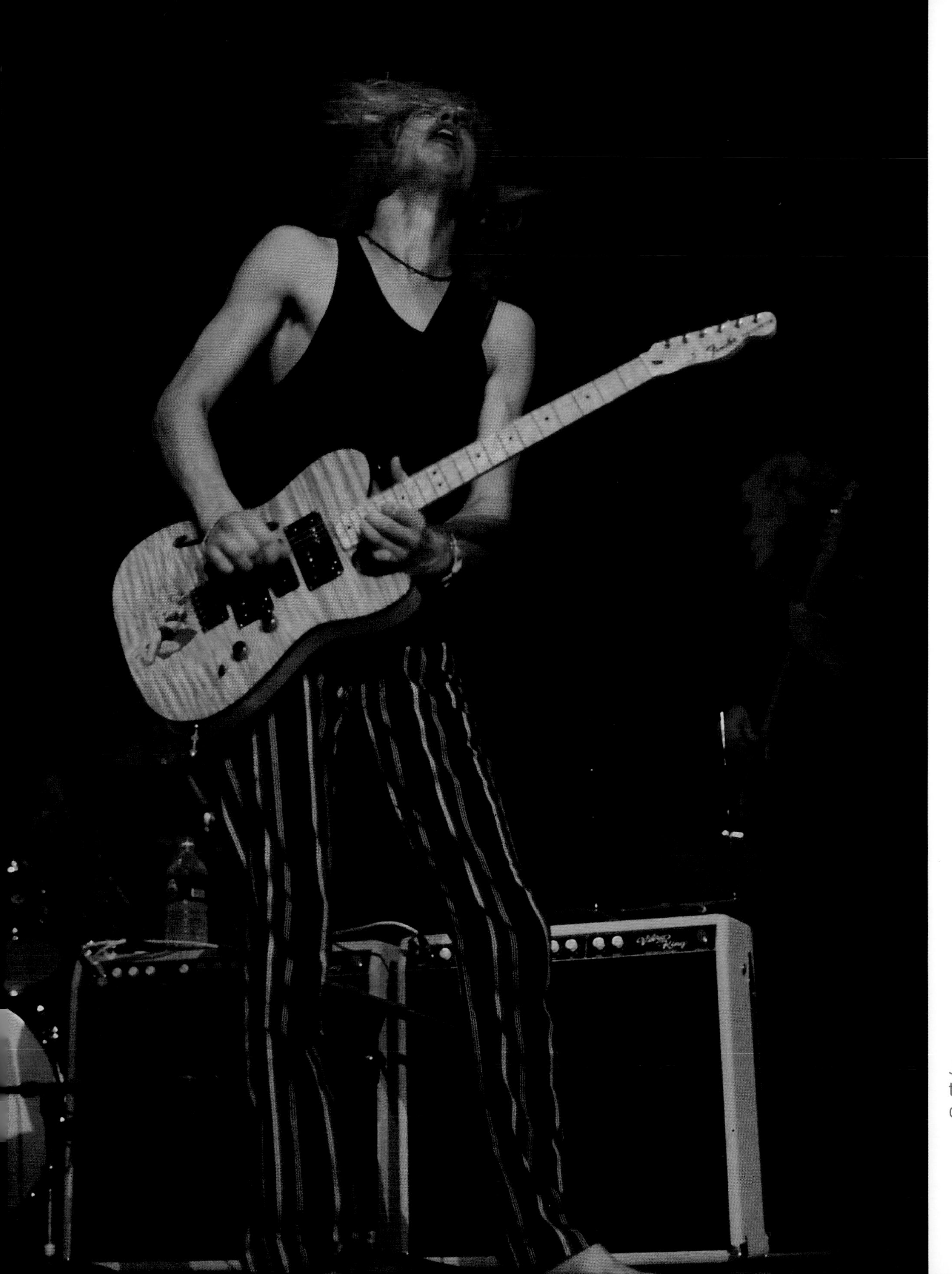

Jonny Lang ascending into tone nirvana through a pair of Vibro-Kings, 1997.

CHAPTER TWENTY-THREE

23

A Custom Shop of the Mind

Fender's Elite Hand-Wired Amps

They called it the Dream Factory. It was Fender's Custom Shop, and when it came to guitars and basses, the promise was, if you can dream it (and pay for it), we can build it. The concept was so successful that as a free-standing facility, Fender's Custom Shop acquired a powerful identity and became a major guitar builder in its own right.

So, if it worked so well for guitars, why not a Custom Shop for amps? Fender did indeed establish such an entity, but it was a marketing concept rather than an actual production facility. That's not to say it was smoke and mirrors. In fact, the Custom Amp Shop served an important function. Under Marketing Manager Mike Lewis' direction, Fender was out to show the world that it could compete with the best of the boutique companies — not to mention its own legacy. The new strategy would entail commitments to all-tube technology, premium components, hand-wired circuits, and (in the early models) a reintroduction of classic cosmetics. Creating the Custom Amp Shop category in 1993 was an effective way of proclaiming, *These amps are new, they are what Fender is all about, they are different inside and out, and they are our very best.*

Richard McDonald is the former Marketing Manager of Fender amps. He explains, "We found that players didn't care if it came from the Custom Amp Shop. They wanted a Vibro-King — from *Fender*. That's the way they saw it. But the Custom Amp Shop was a convenient category for dealers, because now we were building a few elite amps with old-school production methods, and as a result they cost a lot more. It made sense to separate them out." The Custom Amp Shop served its purpose, and in 2003 the term disappeared from the catalogs. The models that remained in the line were relocated to the new Custom Series or to other categories.

The Custom Amp Shop's first three models were the Vibro-King, Tone-Master, and Dual Professional. They were not only fine amps; they were also symbolic, in a sense sending the same message the first U.S.-made reissue guitars had broadcast a decade before: We haven't forgotten who we are, and we can build a Fender product that's solid, great sounding, innovative, and highly desirable. These amps can also be compared to Fender's American Series or American Deluxe guitars: generally vintage styled products with special upgrades for professionals.

Landmark: Bruce Zinky and the Vibro-King

Mike Lewis: "One night I was sitting there thinking, 'We need something that is just going to pop off the stage.' I was watching *Saturday Night Live*. Nirvana comes on and there was a Twin Reverb, a Marshall half-stack, and an Ampeg SVT. That Marshall just jumped off the stage. I always thought Marshall did a good job. Throughout the years, all of their amps always looked like Marshalls. Well, during the break, the house band came on with G.E. Smith, and G.E. had a Showman, blonde with oxblood, with that flat Fender logo. I thought, 'That's it! That is the look!' Visually, it jumped just as much as any other amp.

"Bruce Zinky was a guy living in California, and he called me up one day in early 1992 out of the blue and started telling me about all these crazy ideas he had. He sent me this … *thing* he'd made. It was an amp he stuck in an old, gutted Bandmaster head. I plugged it into a cabinet, and it sounded amazing. I was thinking we needed to do something radical, so I thought we should get this guy to come out and do a few designs together. I brought him in to work for Marketing, not for R&D. Personally, I was playing through a 3x10 Bandmaster with an outboard Fender reverb kit, and I said, 'Let's make an amp that sounds like this, but twice as loud and with tremolo.' The result was our first model, the Vibro-King. Bruce designed it."

Modern classic: 1993's Vibro-King.

The Vibro-King was introduced at the winter NAMM show in 1993, and it caused quite the buzz. It basically put tremolo and a classic Fender reverb kit — complete with dwell, mix, and tone controls — into a hand-wired, single-channel 60W amp with a Fat switch and knobs for volume, treble, bass, mid, speed, and intensity. Because you plugged into the reverb first, just as if you were using a stand-alone reverb unit, the amp had a distinctive and particularly lush sound — clean and dynamic, harmonically rich, and ready to warm up at volume settings above, say, 2 or 3. The reverb was cavernous, and the tremolo pumped out a righteous throb.

Describing its sound as somewhere between that of a 4x10 Bassman and a 50W Hiwatt half-stack, *Guitar Player* called the Vibro-King a tonal landmark: "You get a more brilliant twang with the reverb first in line because the pentode [an EL84 driver] excites the highs before they enter the tone zone. The bass, middle, and treble knobs are further enhanced by a new tweak called the Fat switch. Flick this sucker on, and the King's gain and girth will dust even the gnarliest Super Reverb." Details: point-to-point hand-wiring on an eyelet board, a solid state rectifier, five 12AX7s, a pair of 5881s, a birch plywood cab with tilt-back legs, blonde/oxblood cosmetics borrowed from classic early-'60s top-tier Fenders, and a 3x10 speaker array not seen since the late-tweed and brown Tolex Bandmasters. The speakers were vintage-style blue frame alnico Jensen P10Rs. Listing for $2,549 in 1994, the Vibro-King was an instant classic, causing more excitement than any new Fender amp in years, garnering stacks of favorable reviews, and jolting Fender's prestige a few notches up the scale.

The model was redone as the Vibro-King Custom in 2003. The new version used Groove Tube 6L6GE tubes and adopted the "'64 Transitional" look of blackface styling with white knobs.

Hear the Vibro-King Custom, Track 4.

Pete Townshend

Pete Townshend told *Guitarist* magazine: "I had a Fender Pro and a Fender Vibrasonic and a Fender Bassman top, and I used to drive Marshall 4x12s with those amplifiers .... And when I heard Hiwatts I was over the moon, because they sounded to me much more like a really good, top-line, mid-'60s Fender amp. I still think it's hard to beat Fender amps. They're astonishing."

Pete Townshend's longtime guitar tech Alan Rogan: "Pete gets a killer sound through Fender amps. On recent tours he's playing through a Vibro-King with the Vibro-King extension cab, so it's three 10s and two 12s. He's using two of these stacks onstage, but only one of them is miked. Onstage we start off at volume 2, maybe 2 1/2. That's it.

The second amp is on but we start with the volume turned all the way down. As the show gets 'larger,' if you like, Pete just adds it in. It's not a monitor. It's just there for Pete if he wants it. It makes the whole sound picture far bigger. It all depends on the gig.

"Along with the one Vibro-King we had tried a new Hiwatt back in 2004, a 100 watt amp with four 12s. It was great but it was just too big, too much, so we went with the pair of Vibro-Kings, and that setup just suits Pete down to the ground. He loves it so much. He records with them as well. I always take one or two 'round to the studio, and they live there for his convenience.

"Pete's using an old Clapton Strat, meaning it has the Lace Sensors rather than the Noiseless pickups. It does have a Fishman on board with the extra knob, but otherwise it's stock, and he goes through the one or two Vibro-Kings. All my buddies come to the show, including John Porter, the producer and a great guitar player himself. They all say they never heard a live sound — anywhere, ever — as good as Pete's."

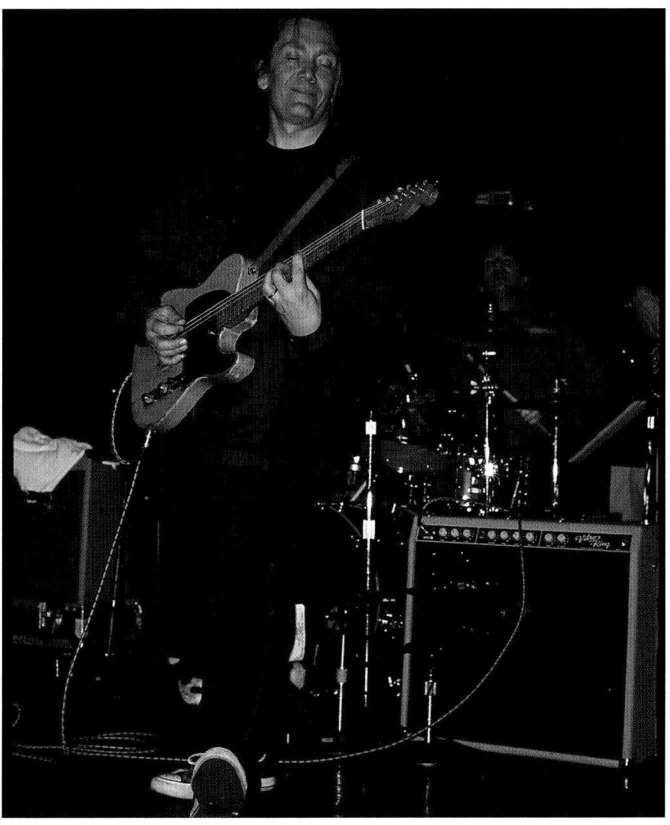

In conceiving the Vibro-King, Mike Lewis was inspired by seeing G.E. Smith on *Saturday Night Live* with his blonde Showman. In this 1994 performance, G.E. pairs his vintage Tele with a Vibro-King.

Tone-Master

The Vibro-King was promptly followed by the Tone-Master, an all-tube, hand-wired 100W head with dual selectable channels, three 12AX7s, four Sovtek 5881s, and a huge power transformer. Like the Vibro-King, it revived the handsome early-'60s styling of blonde cabs, oxblood grille, and ivory knobs. One article cited designer Bruce Zinky's desire to produce a clean Fender sound but also to deliver Eddie Van Halen's "brown tone" from the first Van Halen album.

Zinky later said, "This thing about referring to sounds by colors eludes me, when there is a whole musical vocabulary to describe short and long notes, very soft to very loud volumes, etc. I did mention EVH, but I should note that his style back in the late '70s was similar to early Roy Clark or early Chet Atkins, and the sound was very similar to the first Green Day records. All of those players in their early days had a combination of great attack on the notes and a lot of flash in their playing. This translates to an intensity that would blast through your living room speakers. The Tone-Master was meant to deliver a good, angry, expressive rock sound on the 'B' channel, but also to deliver a believable 'Wind Cries Mary' sound when playing a Strat on the 'A' channel.

"The Tone-Master was the refinement of an amp I had made back in 1988. I took the proto to a David Lindley show for Dave to hear. Dave gave it a critical listening with Ray Woodbury playing through it. Dave raised his eyebrows a number of times and then asked, 'How much?' I told him 450 dollars. He just looked down at the floor and walked away, never said another word. I asked Ray what happened, and he mumbled something or other and then he left, too. The manager explained that Ray and Dave had just spent about ten thousand dollars on amplifiers, and that mine sounded as good or better than theirs. He said Robben Ford would like it very much, and he bought it as a present for Robben. I refined the design over time, and when I interviewed for the job at Fender, the Tone-Master was one of three amplifiers I brought along to show what I could do. It was also the only one they liked."

For Bruce Zinky, great tone should be inherent rather than requiring lots of tweaking. "Yes, there are special instruments that have some particular sound that works for this song or that one, but if the thing doesn't ring true, it's not going to be something you use for the whole night. If

Bruce Zinky: "The Tone-Master was meant to deliver a good, angry, expressive rock sound on the 'B' channel, but also to deliver a believable 'Wind Cries Mary' sound when playing a Strat on the 'A' channel."

you get it right, a player should be able to coax the desired sounds out of the amplifier by the use of technique and choice of the right notes. As far as the circuit goes, this meant that numerous component values had to change to make the tone controls more musically relevant. The bass knob needed to control the guitar's low E string, and not the low E on the electric bass. The mid knob should control the A and possibly the D string, not the low E. So, all of the old Fender circuits and values were examined, and changes were made throughout. Everything was explored.

"Speakers were another matter. The optimum guitar speaker has a very particular frequency response, and you need the amplifier and the proper speaker to make the whole thing work. The speaker needs a high frequency peak at 3.5kHz for brightness, but it can't be any higher in frequency, because if you have high efficiency at 4k or 5k, it's gonna sound like a buzzy, fizzy mess. You also need a lot of power at 200Hz, which is the low end of the midrange, and midrange is where the guitar lives."

Dual Professional

As product names, "Vibro-King" and "Tone-Master" fit perfectly among the classic names Don Randall had conceived in the '50s and '60s — Bandmaster, Jazzmaster, Vibrasonic, and all the rest. Mike Lewis continued to invoke Fender's heritage for the Custom Amp Shop's next model. He went all the way back to 1947 and dusted off the name of Fender's first twin-speaker amplifier, the Dual Professional.

Costing about $450 more than the Vibro-King, the new amp assumed its lofty position at the top of the Fender line. It put the Tone-Master's 100 watts of power and the Vibro-King's 3-knob vintage reverb into a hand-wired combo whose looks recalled the blonde Twin of the early '60s. In fact, Fender compared it to "the biggest, baddest Twin you ever played." Although it had a single channel, it permitted two footswitchable volume settings. Details included a pair of Celestion Vintage 30 12" speakers, and a birch plywood cab with tilt-back legs.

Not surprisingly, tube choice was a major issue for Bruce Zinky: "The choice of tubes, for me, has always been about reliability. Fender had been using these horrible Chinese tubes, and the Sovtek tubes were Russian military pieces that were dead reliable, low cost, and available. I specified them for all of my [Custom Amp Shop] products, and the rest of the Fender products followed. Here's why reliability is job one: A great sounding amp that breaks down goes from being a favorite piece of gear to a useless piece of crap in less time than it takes to read this sentence."

The Dual Pro and the Tone-Master were officially discontinued in 2002, although for another year or two Fender built some Tone-Masters for various artists.

"Here's why reliability is job one: A great sounding amp that breaks down goes from being a favorite piece of gear to a useless piece of crap in less time than it takes to read this sentence."

— Bruce Zinky

At three grand, the Dual Professional topped the Fender price list in 1995.

Like the combo, the $1,299 Prosonic head was available in black, green, or red.

Prosonic

In 1995, Fender introduced the versatile 60W all-tube Prosonic, available as a head or a combo. Compared to the initial trio of Custom Amp Shop models, it was much more of a high-tech product, without a trace of retro beyond the general blackface cab styling of some versions. Internally, it was unusual in several respects. For one, it offered cascading gain controls (*Guitar World* lauded its "staggering range of distortions"), and also had a 3-way rectifier switch that provided a choice between: Class A, cathode bias, tube rectifier; or Class AB, grid bias, tube rectifier; or Class AB, grid bias, solid state rectifier. Strictly speaking, the Prosonic did not offer true Class A. As Matt Wilkens explains in Chap. 6, "The switch on the Prosonic made it '*more* class A,' and made it cathode bias — more like a Vox AC30, but not a Vox AC30." The amp featured a pair of 10" Celestions and was available not only in basic black but also in colors that might not have appealed to the Bill Carsons or Ritchie Flieglers of the guitar community — Red Lizard and Sea Foam Green Lizard, for example.

Guitar World praised the Prosonic's rich, clean tone and its uncluttered yet versatile control panel. "It also boasts an ultra-sophisticated second channel with a cascading dual-stage overdrive that is among the most wide-ranging and fat-sounding on the market .... Gain 2 adds color and edge without greatly affecting volume; it lets you make quick decisions about distortion settings without forcing you to rebalance your volume. This is a huge time and stress saver in high-pressure stage or studio situations."

Senior Vice President Ritchie Fliegler: "The Prosonic was halfway done when I got here in '95. It had some cool features, but I wasn't crazy about the sound. It started off as a Bruce Zinky project and ended up as a team effort."

Mike Lewis: "Ritchie came in and put some awesome finishing touches on it. Man, what a rippin' amp! That one model probably had production levels that exceeded the entire sales figures of some of the boutique companies."

Indeed, the Prosonic was spectacularly successful, at least in terms of units sold. Ritchie Fliegler: "Fender is a big company with a global reach. Moderately successful numbers for Fender would break records at most companies, so when you're talking about numbers and sales figures, these things are all relative. For example, when we bought Guild, another company that was on the block at that time was Matchless. Everyone was raving about it — dealers, players, everyone. We investigated their numbers. Now, if you asked someone to start naming all the Fender amp models, you'd get a long way into the conversation before that person remembered the Prosonic, and yet it sold like crazy. So among all the amps over the years, the Prosonic does not leap to mind as a prominent Fender, and yet we did greater numbers with that one model than the entire Matchless company did in the amplifier business. On the other hand, it was very expensive and difficult to make, and in that sense, the numbers weren't there."

Richard McDonald: "It wasn't really a Fender sounding amplifier. It was a neat sounding amp, and you could really get that kind of 'violiny,' Eric Johnson kind of tone."

Prosonic amps in Red Lizard, Green Lizard, and black Tolex, with an SRV Stratocaster, James Burton Telecaster, and an Eric Clapton "Blackie" Strat. Matthias Jabs, on recording the Scorpions' *Moment of Glory*, 2002: "I mostly used what I play through live — Fender Prosonic amps. To me, they are better sounding than all the Soldanos and Marshalls I have. I plug straight into the amp with no effects and get nice sustain and lots of bottom end without it sounding too distorted."

Fender
Prosonic Amp
INPUTS
VOLUME
GAIN 1
GAIN 2
MASTER
REVERB
Prosonic Amp
Fender

Relic Pro Junior finished in Sherwood Green, one of Fender's original Custom Colors. It was paired with a Relic '59 Stratocaster as part of a limited edition Custom Shop set.

Limited editions: Custom Amp Shop versions of the Pro Junior (front) and Blues Junior combine mid-'40s Fender styling with exotic hardwood cabinets.

Woodie Pro Reissue

In January 1996 Fender announced an amp that would combine two of the most successful concepts of recent years: the Custom Amp Shop and reissues. It was Fender's 50th anniversary, and to mark the occasion Fender announced a limited-edition guitar and amp set; reportedly, only 50 were made. The guitar was a recreation of a Broadcaster/Telecaster prototype, and the amp was a replica of the woodie Professional from 1946. John Page, then head of the Custom Shop, explained, "To authenticate the style and sound of the amplifier, Fender Custom Shop craftsmen took apart an actual 1946 model and recreated each of the 50 commemorative amplifiers with many parts bought from the original vendors and antique electronic distributors."

"Custom" Vibrolux Reverb, "Custom" Vibrasonic

Aside from building high-tech amps such as the Prosonic and neoclassic models like the woodie Pro and the early Custom Amp Shop blondes, Bruce Zinky and the Fender team also modified existing models to produce new custom versions. One example from 1995 was the blackface/white knob 40W 2x10 "Custom" Vibrolux Reverb; more than a decade later it remains one of Fender's most acclaimed amplifiers. Another was the 100W, all-tube 1x15 "Custom" Vibrasonic, with channels for "Steel" and "Guitar." Both were described as having been designed in the Custom Amp Shop, but they were originally placed in the short-lived "New Vintage" series rather than the Custom Amp Shop category; see Chap. 24 for a discussion of these amps. For details of the Custom Amp Shop's Rumble Bass amp, see Chap. 27.

The common attribute among Custom Series amps is their hand wiring. As we go to press, they include the '64 Vibroverb Custom (Chap. 25), the '57 Twin reissue (Chap. 22), the black '57 Amp, the '57 Deluxe, and the Vibro-King Custom.

50th Anniversary woodie Pro reissue, with the commemorative Broadcaster/Telecaster prototype reissue and custom cases. The amp was reverse-engineered from the 1946 Pro pictured on page 118.

FENDER
FENDER

As mentioned in Chap. 2, guitar makers and hot rodders have shared a great deal ever since Southern California gave birth to Fender as well as the phenomena of custom cars and hot rods. Fender's Hot Rod amps were introduced under the direction of Ritchie Fliegler.

CHAPTER TWENTY-FOUR

24

Watershed '95 The Arrival of Ritchie Fliegler

When Mike Lewis moved laterally to take over Fender guitar marketing in 1995, William Schultz went outside the company to recruit his replacement. In fact, he went straight to Fender's biggest competitor in the high-end amp market. He went to Marshall. Ritchie Fliegler stepped in to take over as Marketing Manager of Fender amplifiers, and during the last half of the 1990s he would radically restructure the Fender line. As we go to press, he is Senior Vice President of Market Development.

Ritchie Fliegler: "Back when I was at Marshall, Mike Lewis and I were already friends, and I was very impressed with what he was doing. We watched Fender. I could read between the lines. I could see that Mike was smart, that he knew what he was doing, but that he had certain constraints. We had just come out with Valvestate [Marshall's line of hybrid models, each with a tube in the preamp and a solid state output section], and basically we just proceeded to beat the bejesus out of everybody. That was a real thorn in Bill Schultz's side, and the story I heard goes something like this: Bill slammed his fist on the table one day and said, *'Damn it, who's the Valvestate guy?'*

"I met Bill Schultz at the Frankfurt music show. I'd been flying all night. I get off the plane and literally go straight to see him. I'm sucking down coffee, trying to stay awake. Bill gets right to it: 'So, what do you think of the Fender line?' And I said, 'Well, you know what, Bill? With all due respect, you guys are *Fender*, for crying out loud, and I just don't understand what you're doing. You've had these amps with red knobs and blue lights, some amps are sea foam green, red lizard, whatever. As your competitor, I love looking at that because I don't think anybody really knows what the heck you do. You're *Fender*. What are you doing?' And he just looked at me and said, *'Damn it! You're right! When can you start?'"*

When Fliegler arrived for his first day on the job, May 1, 1995, Fender was a ten year old company with a 50 year tradition. It had started from scratch when Bill Schultz and his investors acquired the name, scant inventory, and little else. While responding to competition in the amplifier market seemed important, other matters had taken priority. Ritchie Fliegler: "They had no production facilities. They'd lost a lot of employees. They were just hanging on, trying to build it back up, and the first step had to be

Ritchie Fliegler, with the very first Hot Rod amp, a one of a kind model rendered in a custom cabinet covered in faux mother of pearl plastic. As one colleague put it, "When you're talking about the modern era of Fender amps, two words: Ritchie Fliegler."

guitars. They had done the vintage reissue Strat because that was the talisman, the lightning rod. Steve Grom did the same thing with the reissue Bassman for the same reason: This is Fender. But it was still a function of what they *could* make, not what they wanted to make. When Mike came along, they were capable of doing more but still labored under significant constraints: These are the machines we have, this is how much space we have, this is how many employees we have, so here's the best we can do, given all that."

Where Fender had faltered, other companies had stepped in and filled niches all across the spectrum. By the mid 1990s, however, Fender had gone a long way toward reestablishing its presence in the guitar market. Now, when it came to amps, it had not only the will but also the resources to get back in the game, to take back its mantle as the world's leading manufacturer. The strategy, in a nutshell: Turn Ritchie Fliegler loose. "Because of my résumé, I came in with carte blanche," he says. "Whether I deserved it or not, I had it. It's not that Steve or Mike wouldn't have done the same thing. They just didn't have the authority I had, or the resources — not because they didn't deserve it. In the 1980s and early '90s, Fender just didn't have the infrastructure to build their dreams."

Fliegler was perfectly positioned to take Fender to the next level. He had experience in repairing guitars and amps, in playing professionally in studios and on stages, and in marketing products at ESP and Marshall. He'd owned and used pretty much every important vintage guitar (he was even a consultant to Gibson when they reissued the sunburst Les Paul) but had a special fondness for amplifiers. Like Aspen Pittman and many other amp buffs, he thought amplifiers were underappreciated, and in 1993 he had written a book whose title laid it on the table: *Amps! The Other Half of Rock 'n' Roll*. The following year he authored *The Complete Guide to Guitar and Amp Maintenance: A Practical Manual for Every Guitar Player*.

In short, he knew guitars and amps inside and out, was well connected with artists, had a deep affection for the heritage of electric instruments, and was a veteran touring and recording musician as well as a savvy industry executive. With that background, he was equally comfortable talking to sales people, retailers, designers, or musicians. Freddie Tavares would have approved.

The Hot Rods (You're Discontinuing *What?*)

Ritchie Fliegler isn't timid. His assistant at the time was Richard McDonald, who recalls, "Ritchie came in, and the first thing he did was to discontinue the most successful line of amps we had, the Blues Deluxe and the Blues DeVille. He killed our biggest revenue generators and went into development on the Hot Rods. It was a shock, but it turned out to be the right thing to do. It was time to look forward."

Hear the Hot Rod Deluxe, Track 12.

More than a decade after their introduction, the Hot Rods remain best sellers.

The Blues Deluxe and Blues DeVille had sold in big numbers, but Fliegler just didn't think they sounded good enough. He thought the distortion didn't sound right, and there wasn't enough of it. He probed their circuits and saw that in each amp there was one half of a 12AX7 preamp tube left unused. He figured they could add another gain feature by hooking up that extra stage, which they did. Having already gone that far, he decided to completely remake the amps. Vice President of R&D Dale Curtis assigned the engineering to Matt Wilkens, and the new Hot Rod amps were the result.

Ritchie Fliegler: "We just wanted something that had a great Fender sound, a really useful rhythm distortion sound, and a great lead sound, all in a tube amp. Right out of the box the Hot Rods just went berserk and did spectacular numbers." More than a decade later, they are still among Fender's top five best sellers. This sort of boldness would characterize the Fliegler era.

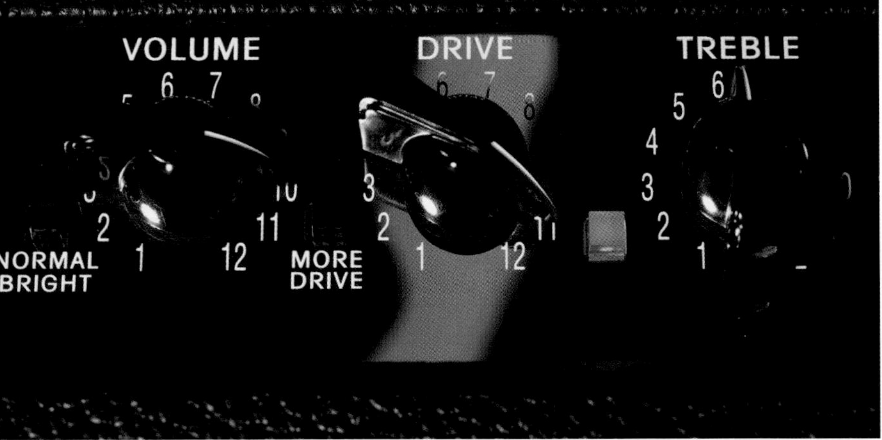

Triple whammy: the Hot Rods' clean/drive/more drive circuitry was a brilliant stroke that provided good tone and versatility at an affordable price.

The Axe Falls, and Falls Again

Prior to Fliegler's arrival in 1995, Fender had organized its expanded line of guitar amplifiers into eight series (sometimes more, sometimes less, depending on the brochure): Custom Shop, New Vintage, Vintage Reissue, Professional Tube (Pro Tube), Tweed, Performer, Standard (sometimes with a separate Standard Chorus series), and RAD, HOT, and JAM, now a series unto themselves. The bass amplifiers formed a comprehensive line, running from the 15W, 1x8 BXR 15 and 25W, 1x10 BXR 25 up to the 200W, 1x15 BXR 200 and the 300W, 1x15 BXR 300C, plus several enclosures. The KXRs were keyboard amps.

Many of these models would soon disappear. Richard McDonald: "We kept the Pro Junior because it's so pure, probably the closest you can get to an old Champ. It's like right out of a tube manual, just a beautiful thing. We dropped the Bronco from the Tweed Series, and then we started dropping all kinds of stuff. We were really on the move, going in new directions."

> "The first thing Ritchie did was to discontinue the most successful line of amps we had. It was time to look forward."
>
> — Richard McDonald

Custom Vibrolux Reverb, Custom Vibrasonic

In 1995, two brand new amps were described as having been designed in the Custom Amp Shop (or the "Amp Custom Shop"), but they were placed in the New Vintage category rather than the Custom Amp Shop category. One of these new amps was the 40W 2x10 "Custom" Vibrolux Reverb ($1,199). It was a particularly exciting addition to the line, although Fender's descriptions were murky. The all-tube New Vintage Series supposedly was aimed at guitarists who were "looking for the warm, fat tube tone of vintage reissue amps, but find they miss the modern conveniences of today's designs." That sounds like an otherwise vintage-type amp with, say, channel switching, pull-boosts, extra gain stages, effects loops, a master volume, etc., but in fact the Vibrolux Reverb had none of those things. Luckily, one piece of catalog copy hit the nail on the head: "The New Vintage Amps aren't copies of any particular previously made amps, but … they're amps that 'could have been.'" Bingo.

The 40W 2x10 "Custom" Vibrolux Reverb premiered in the early-'60s blonde style (wheat grille, ivory knobs) but

Blonde on blonde: The Custom Vibrolux Reverb's first incarnation bore a classic early-'60s look.

promptly shifted to a "transition blackface" style: black with white knobs (it was also relocated from the short-lived New Vintage Series to the Pro Tubes). Shane Nicholas: "The Custom Vibrolux Reverb is a fantastic amp that really rewards the player who has his touch together and has sensitive dynamics. If you dig into it and then lay back and play lightly, the amp responds to those sorts of subtleties. It's a very simple amp, very pure."

Richard McDonald: "That's a sweet amp, one of my favorites. Zinky did that one. It's sort of a quieter Vibro-King. It's got that great complexity. It's almost like the sound doesn't come out of the front of the amp — it just fills the room. It has a manageable 40 watts, so you can really get up into the power tubes. Danny Gatton was using a Vibro-King, and it's amazing, but you have to turn it up so loud to fire up the power section. With the Vibrolux Reverb, it's got that unbelievable dripping tube sound at manageable levels for small or mid sized gigs.

"One thing I've found, the better a player you are, the more you'll appreciate those amps, because they give back. When you're improvising, those amps will change what you thought you were going to do. You thought it was gonna be a whole note, but you decide to hold on to it, let it fly, because that tone is so amazing you just want to savor it, and ride that note. That's the kind of amps the Vibro-King and the Vibrolux Reverb are."

The other amp in the New Vintage Series was the 100W 1x15 "Custom" Vibrasonic ($1,499), a blackface amp that Fender pitched to guitarists and steel players alike. Richard McDonald: "It didn't do that well for us. As soon as we discontinued it [after 1996], then everybody wanted one [laughs], and so we came out with the Steel King [Chap. 25], which is a huge success. It really bothered me that we didn't have a steel amp. It's not that big a market compared to guitars, but we're Fender, and I asked Shane to please make a steel amp and he did the Steel King, and it's doing really well."

Joe Walsh's Vibrolux Reverb

"Joe is very keen on Fender amps. At the beginning of the 2005 Eagles tour, he started off with a new Hiwatt two-12 combo which he discovered last year in England, and he used it along with a reissue Deluxe Reverb. Then he brought in a recent Vibrolux, the black one with the white knobs and two 10s, and he went, 'This is it!' He went out and bought another one, and I ordered a couple from Fender. You stock up when you find something good [laughs].

"That Vibrolux absolutely works for him, because he has to get a big guitar sound. On the Eagles tour, it's a big, busy stage with a lot of people there. When Joe goes on the road he'll take 15 to 20 combos [laughs]. It's a bit of a joke. Joe is forever into changing amps, but as it happens, he's into it, and so am I, so it's good fun. But after he discovered the Vibrolux, all those other combos just stayed in their cases."

— Alan Rogan

The two-channel Custom Vibrolux Reverb, a fabulous club amp positioned between the Deluxe Reverb and the Vibro-King. Details: five 12AX7s, a pair of 6L6s, and two Jensen alnico P10Rs.

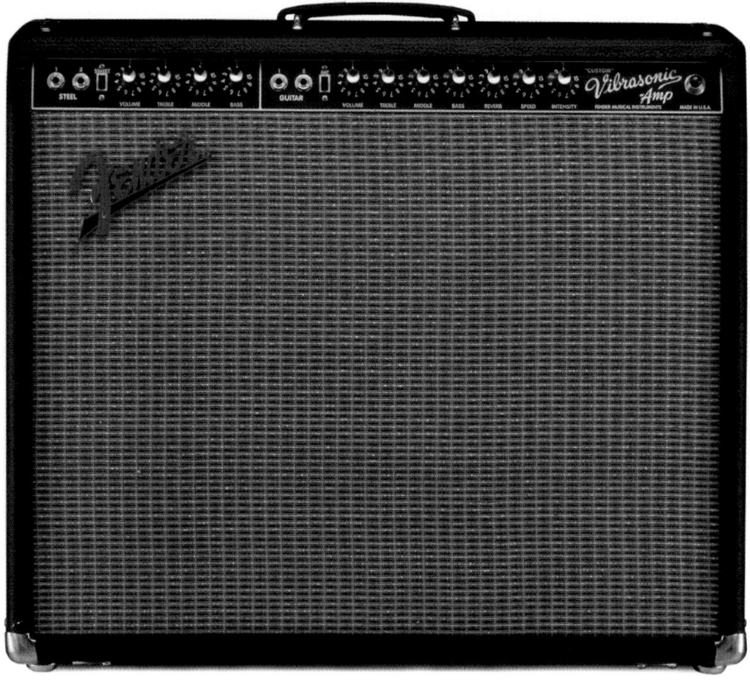

The 100W Custom Vibrasonic of 1995. Richard McDonald: "We made it for steel players, and some guitar players like that kind of thing, too, in the old Fender tradition — a big ol' amp with a JBL."

Evil Twin

In 1995, a new Twin joined the Super and the Concert in the Pro Tube Series. It was called simply Twin or Twin-Amp and was promptly nicknamed the Evil Twin. Richard McDonald: "We don't call anything a Twin Reverb unless it's the classic configuration from the mid '60s." Although at first glance it looked a lot like a blackface Twin Reverb, it offered a 100/25W power switch, channel switching, a gain control, an effects loop, and channel assignable spring reverb.

Performers, Roc Pros

Richard McDonald: "We killed the Performers and evolved them into the Roc Pros for 1996. It was only a cosmetic change. That line was old, they were going down, and this was the last gasp of the hybrid technology for Fender. We pretty much got out of it after that, unless you want to call the Cyber-Twin a hybrid because it's got tubes in the preamp. The cosmetic change didn't save the Roc Pros over the long run, but it didn't matter. Solid state technology was really evolving, and we had better things to do with it. After the Roc Pros we just concentrated on getting a really good sound out of a solid state preamp, and we didn't have to worry about having a tube in there."

Ritchie Fliegler: "I had been intimately involved with Valvestate at Marshall. We were all tired of Fender kicking our ass based on the huge price differential between Fender and Marshall in the U.S. Because of import duties, shipping, etc., we couldn't match the price of Fenders, so Marshall came up with the idea of changing the game entirely. Putting the valve [tube] in there only added about five dollars to the cost, but it had a much higher perceived value. I came up with the Valvestate name.

"So now I'm here at Fender and we already have this line of hybrid amps called Performer. They sounded as good as the Marshalls did, but they were Fenders and nobody listened to the distortion. They assumed it sucked, which it did not. I figured I could trade a bit on my being the recently ex-Marshall guy. We changed the cosmetics, changed the name to Roc Pros, went to NAMM, and sold a boatload of them for a few years. I still see them being used now and then. They still sound good to me, but they ran their course and we dropped them."

Fliegler also killed the brown Vibroverb. "It just wasn't selling. No one ever discontinues something they're making money on. We redid the Pro Tube Series. They just weren't selling enough, either. We discontinued the BXRs and the KXRs. The RAD, HOT and JAM — outta here!"

Automatics

The RAD, HOT, and JAM were leftovers from the M-80 series. It turns out that someone had ordered too many push button assemblies, so when Fliegler discontinued the RAD, HOT, and JAM, he directed R&D to put the assemblies to use in the new Automatic models of 1997, the GT and SE. Richard McDonald: "The Automatics were an exercise in obsolete inventory. We made good amps out of what we had, a tradition going back to Leo. Instead of scrapping a bunch of stuff, we designed a product around it that was fun." Bob Desiderio: "I was able to use a single circuit board for both Automatic models. They were different cosmetically, and because of some value changes within the preamp they had differences in tone as well."

Kenny Wayne Shepherd's triple-threat stage rig: a Twin Reverb, a Vibro-King, and a Custom Vibrasonic.

Kenny Wayne Shepherd, 2000.

Not to be confused with the reissue Twin Reverb, the 100W Twin Amp combines a traditional blackface look with modern features such as high-gain distortion and a quarter-power switch.

With so many models dropping from the line, what stayed? Ritchie Fliegler: "At first, not a whole lot. We kept The Twin from the Steve Grom era, and the Twin Reverb, Deluxe Reverb, and Bassman from the reissues. I felt we had done a good job on the high end, with the Vibro-King and so on, but we really hadn't done enough for that mom-and-dad store who needed an amp for 99 bucks." In other words, it was time to reconsider solid state.

Appreciating Solid State; Frontman Amps
A Conversation with Ritchie Fliegler

Fender's next major challenge was to revamp the basic solid state line from the ground up, but could Ritchie Fliegler — a vintage guy, a discriminating musician with "dog ears," a soldering-iron tech guy, a tube knucklehead of the old school — really get behind solid state amps? Absolutely.

In the mid 1990s, how significant was the stigma against solid state?

In the real world, not very. Look, there's the media, and then there's people. Despite any hysterical ranting by the guitar press, what guitar players play are solid state amps. That's what people buy, and that's what people play. Not everybody plays solid state; maybe some of us who don't play solid state don't do so because we're connoisseurs or we have great ears or we're just snobs, whatever. I don't know, and I don't really care.

Here's what matters: The people who buy solid state amps aren't making excuses for themselves. They love them. They're not holding their noses and saying, "This is all I can afford until someday when I can buy a tube amp." And I appreciate the difference between guitar magazines and what real people are out there doing in the real world. I mean, car magazines review McLarens and Ferraris instead of Hyundais. But what players tell us about their solid state Fenders is this: I like the way they sound, I don't have to worry about tubes, they don't break, they're light, they're versatile, there's no maintenance, and I didn't have

The Automatic GT, 1997.

to break the bank to buy it. Plus, I was able to get a little bigger speaker and digital effects or whatever.

But there are differences between tube and solid state.
Of course there are. And for a lot of people, only a tube amp will do. We have the name, we have the history, we have the Fender sound, and we can provide a range of tube amps for the people who appreciate them. But it's a fact that people buy and play and love and enjoy solid state amplifiers. By the mid 1990s there was no lingering stigma against solid state whatsoever, and today, in terms of Fender units sold, I would guess it's probably about three to one, solid state over tube.

Your colleagues have said that one aspect of your legacy is that you proved that solid state amps could sound good.
This is a team. There are like 30 people in R&D. They get it. They understand what it's all about. They're very patient. They know how much time it takes to get these things to sound right and to work right. They know there's as much art as there is science in doing this, and they know that because we're Fender, we *have* to do it right.

[Senior Vice President of Electronics R&D] Dale Curtis is key. He came here the same time I was hired. To the extent there's a "Ritchie Fliegler era," it's really the Ritchie and Dale era. He really *got it*. Make no mistake about it, I never dictated technology. I would just draw a picture of an amp and say, "I envision a 40 watt amp with these features and those parameters for 800 bucks." I'd give it to Dale and he would take it from there. Anything can be made to sound good and anything can be made to sound bad, so of course good-sounding solid state amps are possible. We did it.

How?
Simply by taking the same amount of time and the same approaches that we take with our tube amps, which translates to a lot of effort, a lot of listening, a lot of trial and error.

Do you do focus groups and that sort of thing?
We are out there listening to our customers, a tradition that goes back to the earliest days of this company. It's essential to our success. At the same time, it's been said that a camel is a horse designed by a committee. Like our customers, we are artists, and we tend to have a strong vision for a

New for 1996, the hybrid-circuitry Roc Pros.

product. The better an amp is, the fewer people were likely involved in designing it.

With the new series of solid state amps, were you aiming exclusively for the low-end market?
We never took the view that solid state amps are only for beginners or for people who just can't afford a tube amp, and that the buyers of solid state amps would buy a tube amp if only they could. We just never did that. I truly believe that if you don't have confidence in your own products — if you can't reach into your own wallet and spend your own money on your own products — then you shouldn't be making them.

Are you concerned that some people will think your high opinion of solid state is heresy?
It's not the '70s. Where have they been? Maybe some people are going to read this and say I'm crazy. I take a backseat to nobody in my appreciation of classic tube amplifiers, but at the same time I take a backseat to nobody in our respect for our customers. We are not going to put

the Fender name on *anything* — guitars, basses, tube amps, solid state amps — that we don't have full confidence in.

And you are hearing this from a person who has taken apart and played and loved many, many Fender tube amps. I am so lucky to have touched so much history. I've owned everything from a mid '30s Rickenbacker electric guitar to the newest Fender. I've had three George Gobel L-5s. I've had a V-front Super, a Tal Farlow, a Mary Kaye. To be able to play these guitars and amps and take them apart, get inside them, and see what makes them tick — what an opportunity. I've been incredibly blessed to play through 50 different tweed Deluxes over a period of many years, and this is where my perspective comes from. And from that perspective I'm saying, look, we bring very critical ears to what we're doing, and we spent just as much time developing our little Frontman amps as we did on anything else — special speakers, making the circuit right, getting the distortion to sound as good as it could. Obviously it doesn't sound like a Vibro-King, but the stuff is good. It's right. It's in no way disrespectful to the customer. We know what it takes to go to work and to earn a dollar, and we never forget that about our customers.

The Princeton Chorus (shown here in its later, black-knob version) was produced from 1988 until early 1999. One of the last of the models was discussed in *Music Gear Review* in 2000: "The distortion channel is more than satisfactory, and this amp has the ability to produce some truly incredible clean sounds … one of the best clean channels I've ever had the chance to play through."

In the mid 1980s Fender was almost out of the amp business altogether, and in the late 1980s the line was still quite limited. How did all that affect the challenges you faced in the mid 1990s?

In any business there are push lines and pull lines. A push line is an amp that no one ever asks for but the dealer pushes it on the customer. A pull line is when a customer comes in and says, "I'd like a Fender Twin please," and the dealer pulls it out for him. I don't mind having a good old-fashioned competitive fight with Marshall at the top of the line, but some of these competing products out there were unworthy, and fighting with some of these competitors at the bottom of the line drove me crazy. You've got your bottom of the line amp, but your competitor has one more feature and costs ten bucks less. My reaction is, *Oh, please. Just stop. We're building real amps here. These are Fenders.*

What was the effect of that competition?

Back when we had too little to offer in the lower price ranges, it actually had two effects. The obvious one was, competitors moved into those niches. But the other effect was, they would use their lower priced amps to leverage the dealers into buying higher priced amps as well — "Here's your order for our 99 dollar amps, and while we're at it, we'll give you a deal on ordering our 700 dollar amps to go with them."

So not having adequate low-priced amps hurt your high-priced amps?

This is the way it works: Some company is pushing their whole line, and dealers are going for it. I understood the need for a 99 dollar amp, but I truly did not understand the need for higher end models from some ordinary company when you could get a great, competitively priced, authentic Fender for the same money. Fenders are real amps. At the low end, our competitors' strategy was, *Let's hit 'em where Fender ain't.*

And your response?
One response was the Frontman Series, a comprehensive solid state line starting with a little 15 watt amp, then 15 watts with reverb, "starter" amps going up the line in little increments.

You already had the Standards.
At the bottom of the mid-'90s Standard Series were two American made 15 watt amps, the Bullet and the Bullet Reverb. Due to the fact they were made in the USA, they were just too expensive for the market. We decided to take that basic design and re-engineer the cabinet to remove as much cost as we could. The classic Fender raked-back blackface panel, knobs, and baffle set-up was expensive to produce and took too much engineering for an amp in the 99 dollar price range, so we took the new designs to Mexico and made them there. To my recollection these were the first all-Mexico Fender amps.

How did you come up with the name Frontman?
The working name was the Baja Bullet, which came from the guys in Ensenada. We needed something a bit more catchy, so I convened one of the many three-martini lunches that seem to be concomitant with having to name products. After batting around a number of ideas, Mike Lewis blurted out "Frontman." At first we didn't like it because it didn't end in o-Sonic, o-Lux, X-Master or some other prescribed-by-law Fender suffix. However, as we got into it we felt that the aspirational aspect of becoming a "front man" was right on target for the type of customer who was attracted to this product line. And so it was written.

So the Frontman line evolved from the low end of the Standard Series, and the rest of the amps in that series continued as the new Standard Series.
That's right. Other than back-stock or leftovers, the Frontman 15, 15R, 25R, and Bass amps replaced the Bullets. New technologies allowed us to make the Frontmans sound good, too, and those amps did extremely well. But here's the other thing: When we came out with the Frontmans, our more expensive models — the Hot Rods and Pro Tubes and so on — went through the roof as well. There was no longer that incentive for those dealers to put up with other

Bullet Reverb, 1995.

companies' reps trying to cram more expensive amps down their throats. Now they could get the little amps from us.

Players could get little amps from other companies, too.
Yes, but the Frontmans were the only ones that said *Fender* on them. Our competitors' leverage dried up.

In June '97, a Guitar Player *review concluded: "Thanks to Fender's Frontman 15 and reverb-equipped 15R, budget tone is no longer an oxymoron ... these little Fenders pack surprising wallop ... these amps breathe more than any 'practice' amp we've ever heard, and their clean tones are louder and richer than you'd expect."*
Right. The features and price points and all that stuff are important, but the budget amps do have to sound right. *All* the amps have to sound right. The tide has turned. Fifteen or twenty years ago amps had to have features and bells and whistles all over the place. Now, whether they have all that stuff or not, they have to sound good. People know they can spend two thousand dollars on an amp that's really very simple and doesn't have channel switching or whatever, but they know it's a deluxe model so long as it sounds amazing. So great sound drives the Fender

(M) *Hear the Frontman 15G, Track 10.*

line from the top all the way to the bottom. The Frontmans are still in the line [as the Frontman II series, all with dual channels and blackface styling]. At the end of the day it comes down to this: The stuff works; people are buying it, and they love it. You know, the Frontmans were just these little amps, but they served a very important purpose.

> "The Frontmans weren't the only small amps, but they were the only ones that said *Fender* on them."
>
> — Ritchie Fliegler

Punky rockabilly burner Jim Heath, better known as the Reverend Horton Heat. He told *Guitar Player*: "My guitar sound comes largely from using a Fender Super Reverb. I don't like Fender Twins that much because they're too clean and too loud, but you can crank up a Super Reverb and get a really nice, modest distortion. The sound also compresses a bit, and that compression, to me, is the 'Fender Sound.'" The Reverend sometimes runs a silverface Super Reverb and a modified Vibro-King simultaneously.

Introduced in the summer of 1999, the Princeton 65 was a member of the first Dyna-Touch Series, which replaced the Standard Series.

And in Other News . . .

Other mid-'90s developments: The Tweed series added the 1x12 Blues Junior, sort of a fancy Pro Junior with more tone controls, a master volume, and reverb. The Prosonic was added to the Custom Amp Shop lineup (Chap. 23). A tweed reverb unit was "reissued" (Fender had never made such a thing, but it was indeed a cool spinoff of the other stand-alone reverbs; Chap. 22).

Bass Desires

Fender also took steps to get bass amps on track. Ritchie Fliegler: "We dug up the Bassman name for a new line of solid state amps after we ended the BXR nonsense. The Bassmans were good. They sold, and they still sell. Now we have a whole department, FBA, or Fender Bass Amplification, and the person in charge of that is Jay Piccirillo. The main idea was that now we could make whatever we needed to make, as opposed to whatever the resources would allow. Our approach was, just do it, make it right." See FBA, Chap. 27.

The Look of Fender

There was a time when stepping away from Fender's traditional look seemed to be the right move. Steve Grom: "Doing a Twin Reverb in snakeskin — yes, it's Fender heresy, but we had to do some wacky things in the 1980s to shake it up a little, get people's attention, to make the point that this is not necessarily your dad's Fender."

Ritchie Fliegler took the opposite view: "When I got here, on some amps the front panels were flat. They didn't tilt back. But on a Fender, the front panels tilt back. Why? Because they do. We had bass amps that were blue with silver and blue trim, keyboard amps that didn't look like Fenders. We had red amps, green amps. I looked around and it just looked like a yard sale to me. I couldn't take it. So we changed it.

"Every time we do a new amp it should look like a Fender. I didn't mind the white ones from the Custom Shop because there was historical precedent for those, but all the rest of it was just too much. I wanted to help Fender be Fender.

"Now we have the brown Acoustasonics, all the blackfaces, the tweed Bassman — you can look at any one of them and say, that's a Fender amp. We consolidated the logos, too, and just made the line look cohesive. The Hot Rods came out with black and silver livery, and with red pilot lights, which is what Fender amps have. We kept the Prosonic for a while, but it became a black amp, as opposed to green lizard or red lizard or whatever. The Frontman amps, we did them in black and silver. As we developed new stuff, we said at every step of the way,

Let's make sure it looks like Fender."

Acoustasonic SFX. *Guitar Player* magazine hailed its "cathedral-like spaciousness" and "wonderful sense of richness and dimension."

Amplifying Acoustic Guitars: The Acoustasonics and SFX

When Ritchie Fliegler was at Marshall, that company had sold many amps specifically designed for amplifying acoustic guitars. Crate and others were also succeeding in that market, but Fender had no competitive products. Fliegler thought they should. The result was Fender's solid state Acoustasonic series.

Ritchie Fliegler: "An amplifier for an acoustic guitar is very different, but if you're going to be successful you go about designing it the same way, with an open mind and a lot of trial and error. Then you build a bunch of prototypes, and make sure the production versions sound great. There are basically two approaches: the miniature PA system and the guitar amp. Dale Curtis and I had figured making an electric guitar amp really has little to do with the hi-fi or stereo/audio worlds. Instead, we go for what works for the guitarist. So now, let's do the same with our acoustic guitar amp. Why do some companies abandon that idea and go for this kind of flat, boring, PA type of sound?"

The first step in designing a successful amp for acoustic guitar is recognizing how acoustic instruments differ from electrics. Ritchie Fliegler: "The dynamic range of an acoustic is very broad, from very loud to very soft. On an electric, you can turn the volume up or down on the amp but the guitar itself has less dynamic range than an acoustic, so we took that into account."

Acoustasonic detail. The String Dynamics control — "a big part of those amps' success" — maintains brightness and clarity while suppressing harshness.

Hear the Acoustasonic Ultralight head & enclosure, Track 9.

Fliegler found piezo pickups to be unforgiving and harsh sounding in the high-end as they get louder, particularly when run through a PA style guitar amp. On the other hand, an acoustic guitar through the right microphone can sound wonderful. Its compression effects minimize that high-end harshness, and compared to piezo/PA systems, microphones respond more in the way the human ear responds.

Ritchie Fliegler: "In my studio recording career we always used a device called a de-esser, which is a microphone treatment device, basically a frequency-dependent compressor/limiter. Whenever you have that 'sss' sound, instead of sounding distorted and awful, the de-esser would suppress those frequencies for a nice sound. I thought, why don't we create a guitar/piezo voice de-esser and incorporate it into these amps? When you're fingerpicking or playing softly, all those pleasant high frequencies come through nice and clear, and then if you start strumming and hitting it harder, maybe with a pick, it will selectively limit those high-end frequencies. The de-esser on the front end of the Acoustasonic was the basis for something we called the String Dynamics control. It's a big part of those amps' success because it makes them much more useful and user friendly.

"We came up with the name Acoustasonic because even though something like Frontman is fine, sometimes you want a name that sounds like *Fender*. We had made classic products with something-sonic or something-lux, or Vibro-this or Tremo-that. Our guide was, if it sounded like something that could have been in the Fender line 40 years ago, we've got it."

Some Acoustasonic amps feature a special circuit called SFX, or Stereo Field Expansion. A technology invented by Aspen Pittman and his partner Drew Daniels, it provides a psycho-acoustical, three-dimensional effect by using two speakers mounted at a 90 degree angle to each other, and by "disassembling" the typical left/right stereo mix into a front/side mix and basically using the room's acoustics to "reassemble" the sound's components. Aspen Pittman: "Each speaker puts out an encoded portion of your total stereo signal, and those signals make up an acoustical vortex that is reflected by walls, floors, and ceiling, and then they are decoded when they reach your ears, giving a feeling of spaciousness and three dimensions."

It works. A *Guitar Player* review in February '99 said that SFX was so effective that listeners at a NAMM show demo "were convinced that the surround-sound effect was being created by speakers hidden around the room. ... Raising the SFX volume brings a sensation that you're hearing your guitar not just from an amplifier but from distant points as well. Close your eyes and you can imagine that you are playing your guitar in a large concert hall through a big PA."

The Torch Is Passed

Some sources within Fender estimate that the size of the company's amplifier business doubled during Ritchie Fliegler's tenure, although he won't comment on numbers. Fliegler was succeeded by his assistant and colleague, Richard McDonald, who in turn was succeeded by Shane Nicholas. Fliegler says, "I believe I left the line in good shape, and I left it to good people like Richard McDonald and Shane Nicholas who would keep it going."

Amplifier designer Keith Chapman: "My entire amp education came through Ritchie. As the guy doing the presets on the Cyber-Twin, I had to learn everything about Fender history and other companies, too, and my guide was Ritchie. He taught me how to listen to an amp by covering your ears and blocking out certain frequencies and listening for very specific things, and why sometimes you stand off to the side to listen. He knows enough about the architecture of amps to give you a starting point, like where the tone stacks should be relative to the distortion. He basically has the last 40 years of amplifiers in his head, and he's very eager to teach it, and I'm eternally grateful for that."

Richard McDonald: "When you're talking about the modern era of Fender amps, two words: Ritchie Fliegler. He either did it, or he taught someone like me how to do it. He mentored the whole company. I just passed it on, and we keep delivering the same message. Ritchie was the one who reminded us, educated us, corrected us when necessary. Mike made great contributions, Shane's done incredible things, all the engineers are great, but Ritchie Fliegler is the one who put us in the car on the right road. He's the conscience, and Fender amplifiers would not be where they are today without him, period."

Richard McDonald Takes Charge

Richard McDonald has been part of the Fender family for more than a decade, starting as a parts representative, telemarketer, and marketing representative. He became Marketing Manager of Pro Audio in March 1997, Marketing Manager of amplifiers a couple of months later, Vice President of Marketing for electric guitars in 2000, Vice President of Marketing for both electric guitars and amplifiers in 2002, and Senior Vice President of all Fender product marketing in 2004.

The job titles and their respective dates provide a useful chronology, but a deeper understanding of responsibilities and decision making at Fender lies in grasping the teamwork that is essential to the company's operation. In a way, Richard McDonald began working in Fender amps on the same day Ritchie Fliegler arrived, May 1, 1995.

As Ritchie Fliegler's protégé, partner, and eventual successor, Richard McDonald made essential contributions to the Hot Rods, Acoustasonics, Automatics, Frontmans, the Cyber-Twin, the reissue Super Reverb, the Pro Tube series, and others.

The Mentorship

Richard McDonald: "Ritchie Fliegler had just come over from Marshall, and [CEO] Bill Schultz thought I could help him, to guide him through the Fender maze and assist him because I had been here for a while. I had been a professional guitarist on the road for about 15 years, had electronics experience as a sonar systems technician in the Coast Guard, and knew my way around Fender, so Mr. Schultz appointed me to assist Ritchie as a marketing associate.

"So technically, I was his assistant, but he was never one of these, 'I'm your boss, you work for me' kind of guys. We worked side by side, literally. Ritchie put a desk in his own office for me. On our first day, we had a long talk about our backgrounds and concluded that although he's eight or ten years older than me, otherwise we're basically the same guy [laughs]. It was the beginning of an incredible mentorship for me. He gave me a stack of books a foot high — Aspen's wonderful book [*The Tube Amp Book*], RCA tube manuals — and he told me to read. And I read for six weeks.

"Working with Ritchie was very intense, because he's just this throbbing brain, this fountain of ideas. He doesn't miss a thing, and at the same time he has a very strong vision of what Fender is all about. A lot of companies make this mistake: They're in the prototyping stage, there's something wrong with the sound, and they try to fix it in the EQ. There are only a few elements in these amplifiers — circuits, transformers, speakers and so on — and everything has to work right, and if it's not working you can't just tweak the EQ. They try to fix it in the tone stack, and that doesn't work. The basic sound should be great, and then the tone controls just tweak it one way or the other. So you can't take an amp that's basically a piece of crap and make it sound right in the EQ. It has to be fixed in the fundamental design. And this is another thing that Ritchie brought to the table, this deep, deep understanding of how technical details are manifested in ways that guitar players care about.

"Like one time he was insisting that we get certain low frequencies, and I was frustrated and was explaining, 'Ritchie, those frequencies are below human hearing; no one can hear those things! They won't impact anything!' And Ritchie was like, 'Are you done? Now give me the low frequencies.' And so he would get the components he needed to get those low frequencies, and even though they were supposedly below human hearing, guess what? Now the amps sounded right.

"Sometimes it's the stuff that's 'wrong' with an amp that makes it right, you know? It's technically wrong, except it sounds great, like the chaos you get from tubes. The biggest problem with digital amplifiers is that it's black or white, on or off. Same thing with solid state. The whole thing with tube amplification is the chaos factor. Once you get it cooking, it's gonna do stuff that's unpredictable. It's not necessarily going to respond in a way that is perfectly repeatable and utterly predictable, and that's where the beauty is. That's when the sounds start getting really complex and they stop coming directionally out of the amp and seem to be coming out of the room. The tone stack is just like adjusting your radio; the amp has gotta work right. You can plug into a Pro Junior with two knobs on it, and it's going to sound killer. Why? Because the amp is right."

The Continuum

Richard McDonald sees his roles as Marketing Manager, Vice President, and Senior Vice President as part of a continuum, and while job titles provide a glimpse of the relative levels of responsibility during a particular time, all of the Marketing Managers of the last decade or two — Mike Lewis, Ritchie Fliegler, Richard McDonald, Shane Nicholas — worked together and with their colleagues in R&D as team members.

Richard McDonald: "Mike did an incredible job of getting us back on track by taking a step back with the historical element of our legacy and making it right, with the Vibro-King, Blues Deluxe, Blues DeVille, and so on. Then Ritchie came in with a very specific, concrete definition of what Fender amplifiers are. Those Blues Deluxes and Blues DeVilles were the right thing at that time, but now we needed to show our customers that we were going to do some things that would be as interesting in 30 years as a '65 Twin Reverb is today. We got out the black Tolex. Why? Fender amps are black. We also consolidated all these different logos that had been floating around.

"A Fender amp is a thing. It's specific, and you can't wander too far away from that, so Ritchie wanted to get us into a progressive direction, but also really hammer home what you can always expect from a Fender amp. Whether it's a 15 watt solid state amp or a top of the line, hand-wired tube amp, there's a vein, a thread that runs through them that makes them Fenders.

Stepping Up

Richard McDonald: "Ritchie and I worked as a team before I took over on my own, so there's overlap. Together we did the Hot Rods, Acoustasonics, Automatics, and the Frontman series. Those were the highlights.

"Ritchie came up with the idea of doing a digital amplifier way back in 1995, and he put it in one of the first business plans he did. After he moved on, the things that occupied most of my time were the Cyber amps and the Pro Tube series — the Super, the Concert. We were getting a lot of requests for tube amps with traditional features like tremolo and also modern features like channel switching, and we weren't doing it. 'New Country' was coming up, and these players wanted quintessential Fender sounds but also wanted to rock a little harder.

"I also made the reissue Super Reverb; Mike Ulrich was the engineer on that one. This was all going on at the same time as our work on the Cyber-Twin. I did a lot of work on the Frontmans. Ritchie came up with the concept, and the directive was, 'These may be little, low-cost amps at the bottom of the line, but they still have to work like a Fender and they still have to sound great.' If the customer spends a hundred bucks, it better sound like a hundred and fifty. I remember demoing those amps at the NAMM show, and we sold 90,000 that year. We expected the Frontmans to cannibalize the Standard amps, but it never happened."

One of the most important and trickiest aspects of amplifier marketing is setting retail prices. Richard McDonald: "These things are hard to predict sometimes, like for a while the Vibro-King was going down, really declining. I had to raise the price a hundred bucks or so because people were buying them in other parts of the world and our costs were going up because we had to do some different safety things, so that if you're sitting in your bathtub with your Vibro-King and poking at it with a screwdriver you won't electrocute yourself [laughs.] So we had to raise the price, and I just said, 'Let's raise it 400 bucks.' And you know what happened? Sales went through the roof. Why? I have no idea. I know they don't pay me to think like that, to have no idea, but there are occasional phenomena that all of our experience and intuition fail to explain.

"I worked on the Cyber-Twin for a couple of years, and it really consumed endless hours of my time, right up until the NAMM show, and then I turned it over to Shane. He was the one who launched it. It was like watching your baby being born, and then somebody else takes it home. But there's always overlaps like that, because we communicate with each other, and we all work together as a team." Richard McDonald is quoted elsewhere in this chapter, as well as in the sections on the Custom Amp Shop, the reissues, Fender Bass Amplification, and Tone Machines of the New Millennium.

The late-'90s Satellite, a remote speaker cab that provided dozens of effects. Shane Nicholas: "The Satellite did nice stereo surround-sound effects, and did a good job of simulating the old Vibratone sound. It was best used with a medium size amp with an effects loop, like a Hot Rod Deluxe [shown here] or a Deluxe 90. It sounded awesome if it was hooked up correctly and used correctly."

Richard McDonald on the Super-Sonics: "The best tube amps anybody has made in a long time."

CHAPTER TWENTY-FIVE

25

Tone Machines of the New Millennium

Shane Nicholas succeeded Richard McDonald as Marketing Manager for amplifiers in 2000. "I was basically an amp guy from day one," he recalls. "I started at Fender in January of '97 as a clinician, going out to dealers, training sales people, demoing the gear and so on. I already had experience as a musician and in retail, so I could draw on all of that. Here at Fender I worked very closely with Ritchie Fliegler. His ears are about as good as I've ever encountered, and the things that we all learned from him we use all the time."

Marketing and design strategies continued to evolve through the late 1990s and into the early 2000s, with each supervisor building on the successes of his predecessors. Shane Nicholas: "Mike Lewis had rebuilt the idea that we could make vintage type stuff and Custom Amp Shop things like the Vibro-King with very high quality. And then Ritchie spearheaded the Hot Rods, the Cyber-Twin, and quite a few others, and also established that we could build solid state amps that sound right and have gain and other features that people want without sacrificing tone.

"Richard McDonald followed Ritchie, and he did a lot of work on the Cyber-Twin and on some of our crucial bread-and-butter core products. For example, his work on the Bassman series set us in the right direction, making it possible in 2002 for Jay Piccirillo to take it to the next level. One of Richard's greatest strengths is his ability as a motivational speaker. He promoted 'the cause' for amps to our own sales staff in a way that hadn't been done before. He's famous for beginning his segment of a big sales meeting by smashing a Strat — I mean, *demolishing* it — then announcing, 'Now it's time to talk about amps.'

"When I came in, the line was doing well, so part of the thinking was, let's not mess up a good thing. On the other hand, more than a decade had passed since Bill Schultz had bought the company. The guitar house was in order, so to speak, so the focus shifted to amplifiers." Just as Ritchie Fliegler had mentored Richard McDonald and then continued to provide essential input after McDonald took over as Marketing Manager, Fliegler and McDonald provided guidance for Shane Nicholas — sometimes in general supervisory capacities, other times in a day-to-day, hands-on role.

Working with his colleagues, Nicholas took a three-front approach to developing and marketing Fender amps.

As Marketing Manager for amplifiers since 2000, Shane Nicholas has been deeply involved with some of Fender's most innovative and successful products in recent years, including the Cyber series, G-DEC, '59 Bassman LTD, reissue '57 Twin, '64 Vibroverb Custom, the FMs, the Metalhead, and the Super-Sonics.

"First, we have to support the iconic stuff," he explains. "If Eric Clapton is playing a '57 Twin and Pete Townshend is playing a Vibro-King, keeping that kind of exciting news in front of the public is important. Second, there's maintaining the core of the line. Many people forget that we sell a lot of acoustic guitar amps. Sometimes the Acoustasonic Junior DSP outsells the Acoustasonic 30 DSP — they go back and forth — but from the data we can gather, the Acoustasonics as a group are the best-selling amps of their type on earth. Sometimes, certain components become unavailable, so maintaining the core product doesn't always mean doing things the same old way; sometimes you have to find new ways to maintain the core.

"The third category is the 'commodity product.' If some competitor has an amp with one more knob and it's ten dollars cheaper than ours, we have to respond. There's always going to be some company who will take less margin or will put one more knob on it. We compete at every level, so I'm always asking myself, do we have at least one of each that we're working on at any given time — supporting the Fender icons, maintaining the core of the line, and responding to the market?"

Series Names

Fender catalogs often list from eight to twelve different series of guitar amplifiers. From time to time, the series names change to reflect shifts in strategies. For example, after 2002 the Custom Amp Shop category evolved to the Custom Series. The reason was that "Custom Amp Shop" suggested to players and dealers that Fender was willing to build one-off amps on special order, which was never the intention. (In other words, the Custom Shop for guitars and Custom Amp Shop were fundamentally different concepts from the get-go.)

Sometimes different names are used interchangeably (Custom Shop, Custom Amp Shop, and Amp Custom Shop; or Reissue, Vintage Reissue Series, and Vintage Series; or Professional Tube and Pro Tube). Sometimes the names might be unintentionally misleading, at least to some people. For example, while the Custom Shop Master-Built amps of 2001 to 2003 might sound even more exclusive than the "regular" Custom Shop amps, in fact they were not hand-wired and were instead existing middle-range models repackaged with fancy cabs and cosmetic detailing.

Like the 100W Twin and 50W Pro Reverb, the 50W Concert Reverb combined blackface styling and tube operation with footswitchable Normal and high-gain Drive channels, a quarter-power switch, and an effects loop.

Also, a particular amp or family of amps may be relocated from one series to another. An amp with the word "Custom" in its name might not be in the Custom Series. A vintage reissue might not be in the Vintage Series. On occasion, the Vintage Series has included a product that Fender never made before. There are reasons for these apparent discrepancies, all of which are explained in discussions of individual models.

If Fender marketing execs were starting from scratch with a new company, they could no doubt establish a scheme of families and series that would be both comprehensive and consistent. But of course, they have inherited the Fender tradition, and even when designing new products they remain mindful of the fact that certain model names carry important connotations. (Consider the Twin-Amp of the mid 2000s. It may be a Twin with reverb, but it's not a "Twin Reverb.") As a matter of fact, compared to, say, the early 1960s, the nomenclature of Fender amps has in recent years been a model of consistency.

The Master-Builts

Early in the new decade, Fender tried a new strategy. They would make a few amps combining the guts of existing models with hand-built custom cabinets and exotic cosmetics. Each amp was signed and dated by its Master Builder. Despite the Custom Shop moniker, they were not hand-wired.

Michael Doyle, well known for his books on Marshall, was Fender's Southern California Regional Sales Manager from 1995 to 2003. He explains, "During that time, I had several Fender Custom Shop models built. They were featured in the 2001 *Frontline* catalog. The Woody Pro Ash and Woody Junior Ash had ash cabinets and were finished in White Blonde to match the Strats and Teles. I also asked the Custom Shop to build a Blues Junior into a cabinet inspired by the 1947 Model 26 amp they had reissued a few years earlier. It was quite beautiful. Fender ended up offering two models in hand-oiled, bubinga wood cabs, the Woody Junior Exotic and the Woody Pro Exotic."

Confusing captioning in that 2001 *Frontline* obscured the fact that internally, both of the smaller two-knob, 1x10

Blues Junior in an exotic hardwood cab, from the Custom Amp Shop.

Despite their names, the Woody Junior Ash (rear) is larger than the Woody Pro Ash.

amps were Pro Juniors; both of the slightly larger six-knob, 1x12 amps were Blues Juniors. Think of the smaller ones as the Woody Pro Junior Ash and the Woody Pro Junior Exotic, the 1x12s as the Woody Blues Junior Ash and the Woody Blues Junior Exotic. They were offered in the summer of 2001 and stayed in the line for only a year or so.

Michael Doyle: "Another one I conceived was the Bass Breaker. It's now a widely recognized fact that the 4x10 Bassman inspired the first Marshall circuit designs, and that the early Marshall in a 2x12 combo was used by Eric Clapton to record the seminal *Blues Breakers* album. So I thought it would be interesting for Fender to reciprocate. I asked the Custom Shop to build a standard Bassman chassis into a 2x12 lacquered tweed cabinet, with two 12 inch Celestion Vintage 30 speakers. Mark Duncan at the Custom Shop worked hard on that. It was very difficult to find Celestions with an impedance low enough to suit the Bassman output transformer. We couldn't change the output transformer to 8 ohms because of electrical regulations. It took a long time to come to fruition. I wanted to give it a name that would celebrate the genesis of the amp, so I came up with 'Bass Breaker.' It looked great with the proper tweed and original style pine cabinet, both of which were features Fender subsequently incorporated in the Bassman LTD."

Another example was the Two-Tone, offered from late 2001 through 2003. Intended to evoke an Art Deco motif, it was certainly one of Fender's most unusual amps ever. It featured asymmetrical front-panel styling, and a mix of blonde and black Tolex. Oddly, it was a low-power amp — the 15W Blues Junior — paired with a relatively hefty speaker complement of one 10 and one 12. Aside from the apparent amp/speakers mismatch, it was also extremely unusual for Fender to use speakers of different sizes in a guitar combo.

Shane Nicholas: "The Two-Tone was another attempt at getting the most bang for the least engineering time. I always thought it looked great, but nothing grabbed me about the sound. The idea with the Master-Built stuff was that we could borrow a little bit of that custom-made mojo,

Henry Garza of Los Lonely Boys, the pride of San Angelo, Texas. Aside from their musical endeavors, the band members are partners in San Angelo's Texican Chop Shop. Henry is pictured here in 2006 with his Strat, his JBL-equipped Twin Reverb, and one of the Chop Shop's custom rides.

Henry Garza's stage rig: a pair of Twin Reverbs (he often uses '65 Twin Reverb reissues), and 4x12 cabs loaded with Tone Tubby "Hempcone" speakers. Henry often employs a '63 Fender Reverb unit as well.

Bass Breaker detail.

with the individual craftsman making a bubinga cabinet or whatever the case might be, and signing it. Those amps did well for a short time and then we let them drop from the line."

2000 and Beyond: A Conversation with Shane Nicholas

Here, Shane Nicholas reflects on some of the key products, strategies, and market developments of recent years. Note: Separate sections address additional aspects of the Cyber amps, Super-Sonics, the G-DEC, bass amps, and reissues.

Is the Fender legacy ever a burden?

It's our strongest asset. We think about it a lot. We have this 60-year legacy of all this cool stuff. That legacy must be protected. There have been relatively few dogs in there. I mean, how'd you like to be the guy behind the Taurus or the Libra? But for six decades we've been making things that people use for their livelihoods, and that people are collecting, reading about, and depending on for years to come. So simply maintaining that legacy is an awesome task. But the other thing is, that legacy was built on innovation, not on standing still. We cannot stagnate. We have several clienteles. Sometimes what average players and dealers want has little to do with what the hard core tube enthusiasts are advocating. Trying to make all those camps happy is a juggling act.

International

How has the market changed in recent years?

It's always changing, in a lot of ways. In the old days, you walked into a music store and took whatever you could get for the money, but over time, people have become much more demanding. They expect lots of features at low prices. That has really intensified in recent years, and this ties in with another trend: the globalization of manufacturing.

There are a whole lot of inexpensive Chinese amps out there, and many of them offer plenty of features. We need to compete with that and at the same time be Fender, and make amps for rock stars and working professionals. We are never going to make anything that is the cheapest available product, or anything we can't stand behind and be proud of. We hope the 14 year old kid who has a great experience with his Frontman will shop for another Fender when he has a little more experience under his belt and a little more money in his pocket.

How important is your offshore manufacturing?

The march to China has been one of the most significant developments, particularly in the last five or six years. And not just for Fender, for everybody. All the competitors have been going to China, Indonesia, Korea, or places like that. Marshall, Crate — anybody who makes a small, entry-level amp has gone to Asia. This sea-change is very signif-

Two-Tone detail.

The Blues Junior (a favorite of J.J. Cale's) and Pro Junior combine black Tolex and classic tweed-era cabs.

icant to us. You can have an amp like the Frontman; it's made in Mexico and every dealer loves it and they're all making money with it, and then a year later the same dealers say, "Hey, that's too expensive!" Why? Because someone else has come out with something with similar features, but it costs less because it's made in a different part of the world.

So it's very competitive and truly global. The Bullets and the Frontman amps were all originally made in Mexico, and they were the amps of choice for beginners. And because we had such great manufacturing in Mexico, we were always a little hesitant to take it away from them and go to China, but inevitably it had to happen because of labor costs. When a competitor we respect very much finally took all of their low-end amps to China or Korea, we finally thought, we can't resist this trend anymore.

Did your reputation suffer?

Not at all, so long as we keep making the professional level and iconic amplifiers we are known for. With a Twin Reverb reissue or a tweed Bassman, I think people would really prefer for it to be made in the U.S., and those amps are made in the U.S., and people are willing to pay for it. We make our hand-wired amps here, the very high-end models. The other reissues are made in the U.S. as well, and priced at real-world prices.

But many people have gotten used to the fact that the majority of electronics products are coming from Asia. That's especially true with the next generation of people coming up. With low-end or middle-range amps, they just don't care about country of origin so long as the quality and the price are right. These are not the people who are buying a Twin Reverb. They're buying a 15 watt amp.

Hear the Blues Junior, Track 5.

Stage 100 DSP piggyback, 2003.

The production of a particular Fender guitar might move around from country to country based on the changing availability of woods and other supplies. Does that happen with the amps as well?
To an extent. You have to move these things around as currency rates change relative to each other, new tariffs come in, new trade agreements, trade restrictions, duties, taxes, all those sorts of things. You have to be highly mobile, ready to shift things around to do the best job for your customer and your dealer. Other factors are lots of legal restrictions regarding the safety of the circuits and the differences in electrical systems in various countries.

Another scenario is that an international distributor might decide to place a big order for, say, Frontman amplifiers, and it just so happens that one of the vendors who make Frontmans also makes Squier guitars or gig bags and cases, so the distributor is able to build a shipping container from that one supplier; this means distributors might choose to buy more or less of a particular amp simply because they can combine shipping in a cost-effective way. It helps them to spread out their freight costs. That's one reason why you might see a Frontman 15R made in China and another Frontman 15R made in Indonesia. In general, Frontmans, FMs, G-DECs, and some Dyna-Touch amps are made in various places offshore.

So one model might be made in different parts of the world?
Yes, for two reasons. It depends on who can make it when we need it. We make and sell these things in such quantities that sometimes a single factory just can't handle all of them. The other reason is distribution. Some Dyna-Touch models are made in Mexico for domestic use but in Indonesia for export.

Who designs the Fender amps that are manufactured offshore?
We do, right here. Let's make sure there's no mistake about that point. If it says Fender on it, it's a one hundred percent Fender design.

How active is amp manufacturing in Mexico?
We make a bunch of stuff in Mexico, like the Hot Rods, for example. We were struggling to make enough Hot Rods in the U.S., and Mexico had extra manufacturing capacity. We were either going to have to raise prices a lot or just take them down to Mexico, which is what we did.

Deluxe 90 DSP, 2000.

Leo Fender surely would have marveled at the Bullet 15 DSP, introduced in the summer of 2002. It's a little 15W amp jammed with features — independent gain and master controls, digital reverb, delay, chorus, flange, tremolo, and more.

Did you have any qualms about that?

Some people here in the building had reservations. *Man, these are tube amps. Are you sure you want to make them anywhere other than California?* But very few dealers or players complained, and after we went to Mexico we sold more Hot Rods than ever. We took them down there in 2002 or 2003. Those models are every bit as good as they've ever been. If anything, they're better, because we corrected a couple of snags from the early ones. The input jacks, for example, are much better reinforced. Most of the Dyna-Touch amps, the Acoustasonics, and the new Ultralights are also made in Mexico.

All-Tube vs. Tube-Powered

Some of the Pro Tube models — Custom Vibrolux Reverb, and the Twin-Amp — are marketed as all-tube amplifiers, whereas the Hot Rods are marketed as "tube powered." What's the distinction?

In some Pro Tube amps and the reissues, right on up the line to the top-end models, the entire audio signal is going through tubes. But in the Hot Rods, the reverb circuit and the effects loop, should you choose to use it, have solid state circuitry — op amps. Technically they're not "all-tube" amps, but you still have three 12 AX7s in the preamp and two 6L6s in the power amp. It's an all-tube signal path except for reverb and effects loops. It still has a spring reverb, but the circuitry driving the reverb is solid state rather than tube. This contrasts to something like a Twin Reverb, where the send and return from the spring reverb pan are both tube circuits. Some reverb aficionados are going to insist on all-tube reverb.

Fender still uses lock-jointed corners on models with solid pine cabs — the '59 Bassman LTD, '57 Twin, and '64 Vibroverb Custom.

Groove Tubes

What is the relation between Fender and Groove Tubes?
We buy tubes from China, Russia, and occasionally elsewhere. We send them to Groove Tubes, and they sort, grade, match, and label most of the ones we use, including all power tubes and high-gain preamp tubes. We are a little less worried about rectifier tubes and lower-gain preamp functions, so as tubes become more difficult to obtain, we sometimes end up installing some non-GT branded tubes in some amps.

The matching of the power tubes is important to performance, so we install sets with either red, white, or blue labels indicating that the tubes within the duet or quartet have been matched for output and other characteristics. If you want to replace your tubes, you can easily match the replacements to the originals. For example, if your new amp had blue-labeled power tubes to start with, you can put in blues again, and it will perform the way it did originally. This is not to say you can drastically alter the performance by using a different color tube. I tested a Twin with red ones versus a Twin with blue ones, and it was very difficult to distinguish a difference. But still, it's a convenience to the customer when it comes time for tube replacement. If you want to put in different tubes, you really should have it re-biased.

[Author's note: Aside from matching and labeling tubes for Fender, Groove Tubes also puts the tubes through a process designed to detect flaws and to weed out potential duds. Groove Tubes founder Aspen Pittman: "We developed computer-driven stress programs that we run on every power tube. These unique tests detect early warning signs of a tube that will have a short life or even an early flame-out due to grid leakage and/or a weak vacuum, also known as high gas. Fender goes the extra mile by paying us to process the tubes, which speaks to their commitment to reliability as well as their goal of improving sonic performance."]

Groove Tubes in Fender amps come in red, white, and blue versions for convenient matching of performance specs.

César Diaz and the '64 Vibroverb Custom

The '64 Vibroverb Custom of 2003 is a highlight of your tenure.
That was a fun project. I met the "amp doctor," the late César Diaz, at a NAMM show. He had known Ritchie and some of the other Fender people, and we all knew about his work with Keith Richards, Stevie Ray Vaughan, and others. He and I got along really well. He told me, "I'm being paid a lot of money by people who want me to modify their Vibroverb so that it sounds like Stevie Ray's. I think it's time for me to come home to Fender." He came here and met the engineers. He and I drove out in the desert and had a long talk about amplifiers and tone. He was one of those guys with great stories. He could tell you some of his Bob Dylan or Keith Richards stories and you just wanted to sit back and really listen.

The amp is not a duplicate of Stevie Ray's.
I wanted to make an amp whose appeal would extend beyond just the Stevie Ray worshippers. So my feeling was, the original was designed for a Buck Owens type of

character, so wouldn't it be cool if we could please both types of players? One of the Vibroverb mods César did for SRV was to remove the rectifier tube and install a diode rectifier. We decided to include a Tube Rectifier/Diode Rectifier switch to let you select either one, something SRV's amps did not have. The diode rectifier tightens up the attack a little bit so that it's not as compressed and not as floppy in the bass.

The '64 Vibroverb Custom also has a Stock/Modified switch that engages the preamp mods that César did. There's a 12AX7 for tremolo and also a 12AX7 in the first channel's preamp, and the mod removes those from the circuit to get a little more power flowing to the remaining tubes. It also shifts the preamp tube bias for more distortion. The idea was to get a little more gain but at the same time to tighten up the bass, because Stevie Ray, of course, used big strings and tuned down to E flat, and these were distinctive aspects of his tone.

How successful was that model?
The amps sold very well for a couple of years. All the Stevie Ray Vaughan fans wanted one, but also there was a renewed interest in 15 inch speakers in general. A lot of people forgot or never knew just how good an electric guitar can sound through a 15 if it's the right speaker. A lot of the original Vibroverbs had JBL D130s, but they were no longer available. Some came with CTS or Jensen speakers. We decided to use a Special Design speaker by Eminence that works great in that amp. At the end of the day, the '64 Vibroverb Custom allows you to get a stock, vintage blackface sound, or a slightly more gainy tone with the tightened-up bass. You can use those switches independently. You could use the other mods without switching to the diode rectifier if you want to. If you want the full SRV, flip both switches and get the other mods and the diode.

SRV vibe: the '64 Vibroverb Custom, a collaboration between Fender and the late amp guru César Diaz.

The FMs

The FMs appeared in the summer of 2003. Who are their customers?
Anyone with X amount of dollars to spend on a versatile amp, a product that's affordable and suitable for several different styles. That series, like the Frontmans, were specifically created to appeal to the consumer on a budget. We want to make sure that we never forget the players in any particular niche. The FM series is currently made in China, and the primary feature of those amps is low price. It's an important niche to fill. These are positioned between the Frontmans and the Dyna-Touch. The Frontmans are entry level, and the Dyna-Touch have DSP [Digital Signal Processing], premium speakers, plenty of features, and fancy grille cloth. Because we had elevated the Dyna-Touch several times, we were in danger of abandoning their previous price points. The FMs filled that gap, and it worked.

How has the conception of entry-level amps changed among your customers?
It's changed a lot. If they're spending 300 dollars, people still want channel switching, effects, lots of power and so on. The FMs are perfect examples of our responding to this shift — more for less.

Hear the '64 Vibroverb Custom, Track 14.

Happy times, family style: The Vaughan brothers grew up playing guitar together, and here share the stage at the New Orleans Jazz and Heritage Festival, 1990. (Stevie Ray, left, is uncharacteristically hatless. Photographer Lisa Seifert recalls: "That's because I think he was in the audience or in the wings, and joined Jimmie's band, the Fabulous Thunderbirds, somewhat on the spur of the moment.") Stevie Ray used many Fender amps throughout his short career, often pairing them with each other, or with Marshalls or Dumbles. He was particularly fond of a '59 Bassman he used for several tracks on *In Step*, but he also favored a '62 Twin, Super Reverbs, a Vibratone "rotating speaker" extension cab, and others.

Stevie Ray was well known for simultaneously running two 1964 1x15 blackface Vibroverbs, and for the modifications performed on them by the late "Amp Doctor" César Diaz. He described a couple of early rigs to Dan Forte in *Guitar Player*, 1984: "[The Vibroverbs] came out in '63. They're number 5 and 6 off the production line, but I bought them in two different places at two different times. It's basically like a Super Reverb with a 15 and a shorter cabinet, and it has no midrange knob — it's preset on 4, I think. My favorite setup used to be two Vibroverbs and two Supers; just stack 'em up, just let the Vibroverbs handle the bottom. I had one Super set clean and the other where I could just turn it up or down wherever I wanted it." Brother Jimmie Vaughan likes a pair of blackface Super Reverbs, among others.

Made in China, the FMs are positioned between the Frontmans and the Dyna-Touch amps. Shane Nicholas: "The FM 212R is one of the most successful amps we've ever had … a heck of an amp for how inexpensive it is."

Dyna-Touch Evolves

What was the strategy behind evolving the Dyna-Touch models?

It was a progression of the strategy Richard McDonald started with those amps. The whole idea was to show that solid state amps don't have to be the cheapest products imaginable. They can have good spring reverb pans, Eminence or Celestion speakers, and high quality components. They can be desirable, great sounding, rugged, and loaded with features. In the late 1990s, the first series of Dyna-Touch were the successors to the Standard Series. We made them look a little more blackface — let's get rid of the weird pointer knobs, let's put Celestions in there.

In the last decade or two, players have focused not only on sound but on an amplifier's touch response. Does the name Dyna-Touch address that?

Exactly. These amps are built in such a way that they react to your touch, whether you are playing with a light touch or a heavy touch, and a lot of solid state amps can't do that. By 2002, Fender was making the second series of this line, the Dyna-Touch Plus, with DSP. The next series is Dyna-Touch III. It appeared in the summer of 2004. They have even more premium features, and much more feature-laden DSP sections. You can dial up a half-cocked wah sound, an acoustic simulator, timbre filters, a tuner, a bass boost, all sorts of stuff, and you can switch back and forth, almost like having custom presets. Some models have premium speakers.

The 1x10 Frontman 25R in 2005, with a traditional blackface look.

The Frontman look, 2001 style: flat-sided knobs and speaker grates.

Steel King

Compared to guitarists in general, there can't be that many steel guitar players.

No, but going all the way back to the beginning of the company, we do have a tradition of serving the steel guitar market. In the grand scheme of Fender sales, that market is extremely small. However, as a community, steel players are a close-knit group, and if one person decides they like something, pretty much within days every steel player on earth finds out about it. The Steel King was an important amplifier for us. We are very happy with the sales, especially when you consider that if those people didn't buy a Steel King, they would not select another Fender. They would select some other company's amp.

Why do steel players like it?

It gives them the kind of amp they need — loud and clean. But at the same time it sounds like a Fender and looks like a Fender. It has the same special design speaker we use in the '65 Twin Custom 15. The people in that steel guitar community are comfortable with silver grille cloth, spring reverb and so on.

From the original Dyna-Touch Series of the late 1990s and early 2000s, the Stage 160: three channels, two Celestion G12T-100 speakers, and a screamin' 160W.

From the Dyna-Touch III Series, the Stage 1600 features an onboard chromatic tuner and flexible controls for its long list of digital effects.

The Dyna Touch III's were introduced in the summer of 2004 and replaced the Dyna-Touch Plus amps.

Shane Nicholas on the Steel King: "We got some high-profile steel guitarists onboard, and as soon as they spread the word, this amplifier really caught on within that community."

Acoustasonic DSP

In 2004, you evolved the Acoustasonics to the Acoustasonic DSPs.
The originals with the spring reverb and chorus were selling very well, but one of the bucket-brigade chips, which let us do the analog chorus, became unavailable, so we had to put DSP into the Acoustasonic amps.

Fender's so big, it's surprising that some components might become unavailable to you.
You have to remember that compared to markets in cell phones, DVD players, and televisions, the musical instrument business is small potatoes. It's tricky when you have something that is selling really great, but because of a component shortage you have to modify it.

Metalhead

The three-channel Metalhead amps of 2005 were an unconventional look for Fender.
Fender had made several attempts over the years to do an amp for heavy metal players — the red-knob Showman in the '80s, the Roc Pro series, things like that. When we acquired Jackson, we started associating with a lot of serious players who don't play Fender amps or Fender guitars. They play pointy guitars with Floyds and skull graphics and all that stuff, and we thought, we don't really have an amp that we can demo a Jackson Randy Rhoads guitar with. So we decided to go after that sort of a project from scratch.

Which means going after Marshall?
We didn't want it to look like a copy of a Marshall. I think anybody who does a slant-front four-12 cabinet, they're pretty much paying homage to Marshall in one sense, but at the same time that design has become a standard. We already had all of these bass amp platforms that were really solid and worked well and didn't blow up, so we used the power section from one of our professional bass amp platforms and just gave it *tonnage* of power. The MH-500 is 400 watts with a single four-12 cabinet, and 550 watts with two.

Dude.
Yeah, it's massive. If you're going to play modern metal, like where you tune down sometimes, it's not only about the volume, it's also about having enough headroom so that the notes can be reproduced. The front end was designed completely from scratch. It's got flight case hardware all around, and it looks mean, and it's very heavy-duty.

And it's got a different kind of logo on it, with a big "MH" and a small "Fender."
That was a troubling decision, because when you mess with the Fender logo, it's heresy. But all of those amps with the slanted Fender logo in the corner sent the wrong message. The real aggressive metal players just assumed that if it had that logo on it, it was going to be too clean, so it had to look different. Also, the script Fender logo that we use on the grille for all of our blackface amps and others is slanted, so if you want to put it anywhere other than the corner of the grille, you can't do it. And if we put a big "spaghetti"

The Metalhead has an air intake for the cooling fan.

Fender logo in the center, then it would really look like a Marshall. So we came up with the MH as the identity, and it's got the Fender logo inside it. It worked well, and people are starting to really love them. It was kind of cool that this is an all solid state amp with a stupid amount of power, a clean channel that sounds amazingly good, and plenty of gain. The power amp has so much headroom you're not even touching it, so you can play like Johnny Cash on the clean channel and it really sounds good.

It's got 16 effects. Why put DSP in an amp for metal players?
We did some neat things with the DSP. One of the selections is a gate, which lets you do what the players call a start/stop technique. When you play a percussive chord and stop playing, it immediately turns the signal off so you get that real chop-chop kind of effect.

It's got a little scoop on the top of the head.
It's an air intake for the fan. I'll take the blame or credit for that, too. I got the idea driving to work one time, and I saw it on a car that had a customized hood scoop. The Metalheads have so much power, they're going to need some cooling.

Tower of power: The 550W solid-state MH-500 Metalhead, shown here with two 4x12 cabs.

 *Hear the Metalhead & MH412SL cab, Track 16.*

Eye candy: Variations on the Vibro-King look.

Ultralights

The two solid state Ultralights don't look anything like previous Fenders.

The different look comes from a different design intention. We're very excited about the Ultralights. We think they are going to make some players very happy because they are super powerful and they're light. The Jazzmaster is a 250 watt, two-channel amp with reverb, delay, chorus, and a lot of other DSP effects, and it weighs only seven pounds. It's for jazz/variety guitar tones — it's not a rock amp. The Acoustasonic Ultralight is true stereo, with a guitar channel and a mike channel, lots of high-quality DSP effects, and a very high quality cabinet, a very hi-fi approach. Both Ultralights have solid maple side panels.

FSRs

Every once in a while you release a limited of run of mixed-feature amps — models that are normally tweed redone in blonde, or amps that are normally in one color of Tolex redone in a different color.

These are FSRs, our code name for Factory Special Runs. Examples would be the Hot Rod Deluxe with brown vinyl, wheat grille cloth, ivory knobs, and a Jensen speaker; the 2005 40th Anniversary '65 Twin Reverb in blonde Tolex with Eminence 12s, wheat grille, and an amber pilot light; and the late-2005 Hot Rod Deluxe Emerald, with a Celestion Vintage 30, "British Emerald" covering, ivory knobs, and Cyber-Twin SE grille cloth. These amps have special badges.

Richard and others dabbled in this stuff, but it really got going during my tenure. Some of the FSRs are done at the request of a specific larger dealer or international distributor. Others, like the Emerald, are fun things I develop for us to sell to everybody, as in "Get 'em while they're hot." These special models complement, rather than replace, the regular black versions. Customers love to walk into a store and see something new. It's eye candy.

The Balancing Act

You mentioned a strategy of supporting your iconic amps, maintaining the core of the line, and responding to the market with "commodity" products. How do you accomplish all three?

Hear the Acoustasonic Ultralight head & enclosure, Track 9.

The little FSR Bronco recalled the look of the late-'40s/early-'50s two-tone Champ.

An update of the venerable Vibro-King, the Vibro-King Custom features the "'64 transitional" look of a blackface panel with white knobs; this Vibro-King 212 B enclosure has a pair of Celestion Vintage 30s.

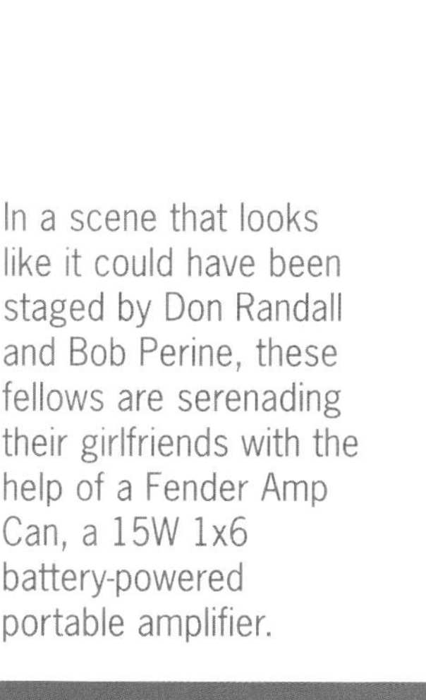

In a scene that looks like it could have been staged by Don Randall and Bob Perine, these fellows are serenading their girlfriends with the help of a Fender Amp Can, a 15W 1x6 battery-powered portable amplifier.

It has to be a balance, and you have to be on your toes. Companies like Mesa/Boogie make expensive amps that pros want to play, and that doctors and lawyers with money to spend want to play, and Mesa doesn't worry about competing with Crate or Peavey. Then there are companies who sell thousands of units but their amps never seem to get respected as iconic products the way a Fender, Marshall, or Vox might.

Well, we compete with all those companies. For example, we came out with a lot of inexpensive solid state amps from 2003 to 2005 or so, but if we only did that and neglected the iconic stuff, we'd be in trouble. A few years ago, the well-heeled doctor or lawyer would buy his Paul Reed Smith or his Custom Shop Strat and still settle for an ordinary amplifier. The boutique phenomenon changed all that, and being Fender, we have to address the very high-end market. So, entry-level players, amateurs having fun, serious hobbyists who gig occasionally, full-time working professionals — these are all potential Fender customers. We're really taking a full-spectrum view.

The Super-Sonics

Fender's most exciting new tube amps in years? The Super-Sonics are serious contenders for that title. Richard McDonald: "Wow, what great amps. Those are the best tube amps anybody has made in a long time. That's just my opinion. The versatility, the correct Fenderness of them — it's a beautiful thing. With some of these other companies' amps, you could spend the rest of your life twiddling knobs and trying to figure them out. With the Super-Sonic, or any Fender amp, if you reach back and knock over your cocktail and hit a knob, you can get your tone back immediately. It's all laid out right in front of you. You'll never have that problem of saying, 'I had my sound, and now I can't get it back.' You can turn the knobs this way or that — they're all good sounds — and you can just intuitively nail that perfect, sweet sound that's just for you. And if we're working on some new prototype, and it doesn't work that way, we just won't put it out." Here are additional insights from Shane Nicholas and Keith Chapman.

Somewhere in there lie the blackface souls of a '66 Bassman and a '65 Vibrolux.

Hear the Super-Sonic, Track 13.

How did the Super-Sonics come about?
Shane Nicholas: Those were amps I really wanted to do personally. They're examples of why I like to play Fender amps, and always have. I might play country one day, blues the next, and then dust off some Randy Rhoads or Black Sabbath riffs I learned when I was a kid. I want all of those sounds, but I don't like graphic EQs or push-pull pots and all that garbage, so I thought, what if you could get those few classic amp sounds in a really pure tube amplifier? Back in the '80s people wanted that red-knob Twin with all that stuff on it. But these days the emphasis is on sound and versatility but also a clean layout. We came up with the Super-Sonics, and when you dial in the perfect sound, you don't have to worry about marking a piece of tape on the control panel or making notations in your notebook to remember how to find it again. It's all right in front of you, and you can instantly dial it in. These amps are about as far as we've ever got in getting several classic tube tones with a very simple control panel. We offer them in early-'60s style blonde cabs or black cabs.

The blonde ones have familiar oxblood grilles, and yet with the black ones you went to an all-new, Black Pepper grille cloth.
Shane Nicholas: We had had some problems with some of the recent tube amps like the Pro Reverb and the Concert Reverb. They didn't sell very well, and I think part of the reason was they had a wolf-in-sheep's-clothing thing. You put one on the shelf next to a reissue Twin Reverb, and you can hardly tell the difference. The Concert Reverb and Pro Reverb had effects loops, channel switching, modern features — they're not reissues — but I don't think they stood out enough or looked as new as they really were. We discontinued them at the end of 2005. With the Super-Sonics, we wanted a traditional Fender look, but not *too* traditional. We wanted them to look new at the same time. The Black Pepper grille is a real departure, and we believe people will sit up and take notice. I don't know if it was a mistake or a good idea, but time will tell.

The model name isn't in the familiar Fender script.
Shane Nicholas: It's somewhat controversial. I took some flack for not doing the old-fashioned western style script, but I thought it would be smart for people to know that it's not a Tone-Master or an old blonde Fender. Even if you're

just glancing at it from 20 feet away, I wanted people to know — hey, that's the new one.

The black ones have metal knobs and a blue pilot light.
Shane Nicholas: I'll take the blame or the credit, whichever it turns out to be. Preliminary sales figures are split fairly evenly, maybe leaning toward the blonde just a little bit. People have kind of a love-hate reaction to the black Super-Sonics, but for the ones who don't like the look but love the idea, we have the blondes.

Keith Chapman: I actually prefer the black to the blonde. I love the grille cloth and the metal treatment. What we found is that people are very tied to our history, so every product is under tremendous scrutiny. I think the black Super-Sonics really hark back to our history while at the same time saying, hey, I'm something new.

How did the design process work?
Keith Chapman: Dale [Curtis] assigned the project to me and said, see what you and Shane can come up with. I did the schematic design as part of the learning process. I talked to Matt Wilkens, Bob Desiderio, Bill Hughes — all the gurus — and they helped out a lot. When I became the director of project engineering I handed off the Super-Sonic to Mike Ulrich. Mike took over as project engineer and made it a reality.

How did you select the circuitry?
Keith Chapman: The amp is all tube except for the effects loop. It has two channels, and on the first channel, on the left, there's a switch that lets you select between a Bassman and a Vibrolux. We wanted a bright, vintage clean sound, so a '66 Bassman head is the basis of the circuitry of the first channel, but we also sort of merged it with a '65 Vibrolux. You can select either sound. We picked those two amps because they are fairly similar in architecture, and yet they capture completely different tones. Both sounds are great and really desirable. When you switch between them, you are switching relays that adjust the voicing and also the gain levels. You can get a clean sound from the Vibrolux but also that real meaty, slightly overdriven tone that the Bassman does so beautifully. We viewed that first channel as a perfect marriage.

Assembling an 800 Pro (top) and a Super-Sonic at the Corona factory.

The second channel, on the right side, is a completely different circuit, with two gain controls and various stages that allow you to get an enormous range of tone — anything from a really squawky Blue Oyster Cult tone all the way to a super-compressed Santana tone that just hangs forever. And then if you want a real modern heavy metal sound, all you need to do is play with the tone controls and it's right there. It really is quite flexible.

One of the biggest challenges was to take three different power amps and make them all work within one power amp architecture, which is a bit of a divergence from standard Fender power amps. The biggest subjective challenge was to make all three amp styles sound unique and accurate when the power amp was clipping. We spent a lot of

time on that aspect. The Super-Sonics were a home run within a month. It just blew us away how well received they were.

Shane Nicholas: I thought about all the great players who played Vibroluxes, from Roy Buchanan to Mark Knopfler and many others, and it just seemed like a great place to start. And then the '66 blackface Bassman that we have here has a lot of grunt. It sounds tough and fat. You run that thing into a 4x12 cabinet and you've really got your-

self the rock rhythm guitar sound of doom. I've always loved that amp. I've always said that once you get used to playing a Bassman it's hard to go back to anything else, because you hit your bottom string and it's just *bang!*

And these two circuits blended together nicely because the Bassman is similar to the Vibrolux in that it does not have a mid control. It's just volume, treble, and bass. We took those two circuits and tweaked them so they could live together under the same roof. It's not the exact same circuit of either amplifier, but it gives you an opportunity to tap into them the way you would use them on a gig. You might use one side for the Mark Knopfler or Ventures-type tone, and the other side for a fat, mildly distorted rhythm guitar. We wanted both flavors — the sparkly twang of the Vibrolux and the thicker blackface Bassman tone, side by side in the first channel.

The second channel was borrowed from the Prosonic, which had a dual preamp/cascading gain circuit. You can just lightly touch the strings and the notes really jump out. There's plenty of sustain, and you can do a lot of variation by adjusting the knobs. It's not exactly a Prosonic, but it's in that ballpark. At the end of the day you've got three useful, pleasing sounds to start with, and all of them are easily modified or fine-tuned with a few simple controls.

Amp assembly at Corona.

"It's about passion. I've played Fenders all my life. I could tell you what that catalog smelled like when I was a kid. Let me tell you something: That passion is what drives this whole thing."
— Richard McDonald

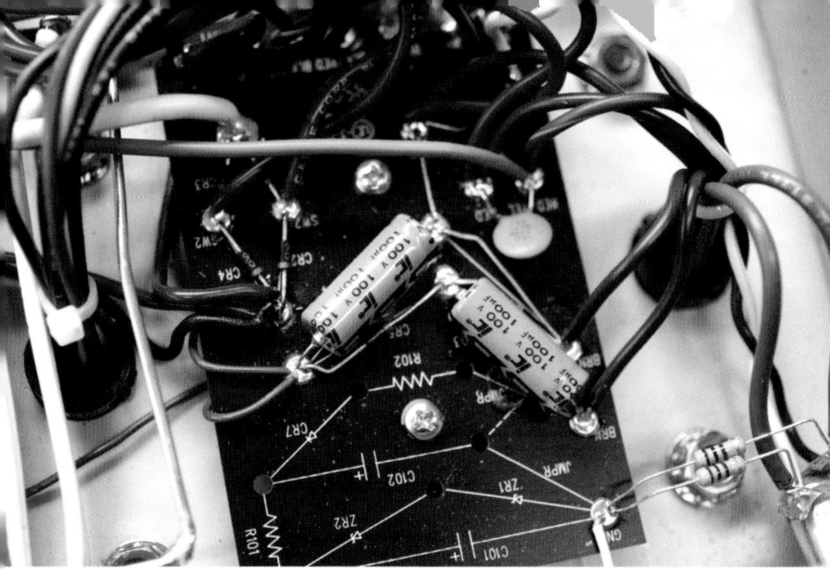

Precision layouts and neat soldering are the order of the day.

The assembled chassis is inserted into the cab.

Completed chassis await installation.

Slide-on speaker connector.

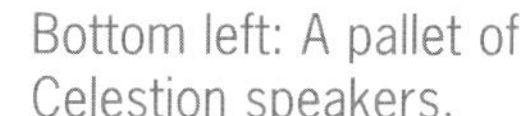

Bottom left: A pallet of Celestion speakers.

Bottom right: Ready for testing and shipping.

AMP
PRESET
EDIT
FX
UTILITY
EXIT
FENDER
DSP
TM

CHAPTER TWENTY-SIX

26

Going Digital, the Fender Way

Cyber Amps and G-DECs

As we have seen throughout this book, players and amp designers alike all revere the late Leo Fender for the purity of his designs, his no-nonsense approach to functionality, his uncluttered circuits and clean execution. Even today, Fender's most expensive amps are thoroughly rooted in designs that go back to the dawn of Fender, and even earlier, to circuits patented more than a half-century ago by the Western Electric scientists at Bell Labs. Departures from those successful technologies can be risky and potentially catastrophic — a brutal lesson learned, for example, when Fender introduced its first-generation transistorized amplifiers in the mid and late 1960s. So why not stick with the tried and true? If old technologies are working so well, why take chances on new ones? "Because Leo Fender never stopped innovating," says Richard McDonald, "and neither do we."

The 2x12 blackface-styled Cyber-Twin guitar amplifier of January 2001 combined tube and solid state technologies, and blended them with a digital display, an otherwise familiar looking control panel, an onboard computer, deep programmability, MIDI, Digital Signal Processing, and hundreds of uncanny emulations of vintage and recent Fender amps and even amps from other companies such as Vox and Marshall. Could this Battlestar Galactica of amplifiers have anything to do with, say, a classic tweed Deluxe or a blackface Super Reverb? Quite a lot, as it turns out.

Columnist/guitarist Wolf Marshall went so far as to call the new Fender "the most impressive advance since the invention of the guitar amplifier." From *Guitar Player*'s review: "Quality clones of classic Fender tones, from tiny tweeds to crystalline Twins and Supers … an ultra-intuitive operating system, and many cool extras … Like the best Fender instruments, it's a no-nonsense tool that is rugged and easy to use."

Buddy Guy was asked, "Did playing through all that vintage equipment make you approach the music any differently?" He said, "No, because it's what I've been doing all my life. I can only play what I know. Now I'm using the Fender Cyber-Twin, and it has a tone! It comes closer to what Fender was all about in the beginning …. After my guitar tech brought it to me and I played through it for a while, he said he hadn't seen me smile like that in a long time."

The Cyber-Twin's successor, the Cyber-Twin SE, was, if anything, even more impressive. From *Guitarist*'s February

2005 review: "To discuss [all of the back panel functions], let alone the front panel, would fill up at least the next two issues of *Guitarist*, so let's just say that every possible need is catered for here. It's also user friendly. On stage it matches any other good digital amp. However, in the studio, it's light-years ahead of the competition and highly intuitive to use. Whether you look on it as an amp or a computer with loudspeakers, we think the Cyber-Twin is still there on top as the best all-rounder in this genre."

The Cyber-Twin's technologies made possible innovative products such as the G-DEC, or Guitar Digital Entertainment Center. G-DEC is an affordable, 15W user-programmable amp with effects, an onboard MIDI synthesizer that provides drum loops, bass lines, other accompaniment and backing tracks for playing along, a phrase sampler, a tuner, an interface for CDs and MP3 players, and more.

Richard McDonald is Senior Vice President of Fender Marketing and former Marketing Manager for amplifiers. Dale Curtis is Senior Vice President of R&D and former Vice President of Electronics R&D. Keith Chapman is Vice President of Electronics R&D. Shane Nicholas is Marketing Manager for amplifiers. Considering the Cyber-Twin's smashing success, it's surprising to learn that prior to its release, Fender considered pulling the plug on the project. Here, McDonald, Curtis, Chapman, and Nicholas discuss the strategies and controversies surrounding the Cyber-Twin and its successors.

R&D Revamp

When you came to Fender, what mission were you given?
Curtis: On my very first day, in 1995, [Fender CEO] Bill Schultz said to me, "I want you to put together a plan for the R&D Department." He told me, "We are very serious about this." I spent several days and came back to Bill and said, "I have three plans. The first one I can actually do, and it's aggressive." And he ripped it up and threw it on the floor. I said, "My second plan, I'm not sure it's possible, I don't know if I can find this many people and train them, but it's super aggressive." He threw it on the floor. And so I gave him the third plan, and I said, "There's no way I can do this. I'm sure it can't be done, and it's *incredibly* aggressive." Bill said, "This is it. Do this one." That was my introduction to Bill Schultz.

What made the plan so aggressive?
Curtis: It was the number of highly skilled people I would need to hire, with the right backgrounds. I did not want to go out and import a bunch of engineers from other music companies, because I did not want them to bring along their preconceived notions and their baggage. I had worked at a different music company prior to coming here, and I did not think their approach was right for Fender. When I came here, I wanted to absorb Fender. I didn't want to change it, because the things that make it Fender don't need changing. So I hired people who were competent hardware engineers, DSP [Digital Signal Processing] engineers, or software engineers, but they weren't from the music business. We weren't really interested in copying other companies' ideas.

When you were head of R&D, Electronics, what did your job entail?
Curtis: I was the official idea guy, and I managed the project engineers, and that's in partnership with whoever was on the marketing team at the time. We work very closely together. We communicate with marketing all the time, which is one of the reasons this company has been so successful.

The Cyber-Twin

The Cyber-Twin has been called your baby.
Curtis: That's right, although Ritchie Fliegler, from the marketing side, and I have been partners in crime from the beginning. Generally, I was not doing project engineering myself, but rather I was managing the whole group. If I did do any project engineering, it was on my own time, when there was something I was particularly passionate about. The Cyber-Twin was one of those projects. It had been rolling around in my mind for three or four years before we officially started working on it.

Why the delay?
Curtis: There were a lot of things in the Cyber-Twin that had never been done before. We were waiting for the technology that would allow us to make an amplifier that was quiet enough when you weren't playing music through it. To make that happen, we needed a new generation of digital converters. The technology was advancing rapidly, so we knew it would come.

Cyber-Twin digital display.

Cyber family, 2002.

The original Cyber-Twin was also available as a head.

Hear the Cyber-Twin SE, Track 8.

Don't Call It a Modeling Amp

Fender took pains to distinguish the Cyber-Twin from what have generally been called modeling amps. What's different about it?

Curtis: In the other companies' modeling amps, the distortion was created with software. In the Cyber-Twin, we never tried to model that part of it with DSP. Instead, we did it with vacuum tubes. In our opinion, even to this day, nobody has done a modeling amp where tube distortion is adequately replicated in software. It's not truly convincing.

But are we getting to the point where tube distortion can be replicated with digital technology in a convincing way?

Curtis: Even if you could today, the circuitry would be ridiculously expensive and complicated, so we said, this is a real guitar amp; let's just use two 12AX7s to generate the distortion.

McDonald: The modeling amps that were out there, at best, could sound like, say, a Super Reverb or a Princeton at one particular moment, at one particular tone setting, and one particular volume setting. And the way they work is, you turn them up or down, and they just make that one "snapshot" larger or smaller. But that's not how tube amps work. When you turn them up or down, they don't just get louder or softer. All sorts of things change. We recognized that, made it part of the Cyber-Twin's operation, and that's what makes it a Fender.

How did you pull it off?

McDonald: Dale had to come up with what's called a 3-D linear interpolation. He had to do the math to figure it all out — why does the bass fall off, and by how much, when you turn up the volume at this or that percentage of distortion?

What are the Cyber-Twin's other essential elements?

Curtis: In an amplifier, three things matter most to the tone. In no particular order: One is the tone controls and the overall tone shaping, another is what generates the distortion or the clipping, and the third element is the speaker. All three have to be right.

So the Cyber-Twin is like conventional guitar amps in that respect?
Curtis: Only in terms of distortion generation and in the user interface. It makes a radical departure from there, in that the tubes and other elements can be reconfigured in different ways by the onboard computer to match the characteristics of many user-selected amplifiers, and that distinction is why the Cyber-Twin is not a modeling amp.

Does that mean the order of components in the signal path can be rearranged to match certain amplifiers?
Curtis: Exactly. We're actually reordering the basic building blocks in all the parts of the circuitry that really matter. After that, the tone shaping can be done either with analog or digital technologies, and it's very hard to tell which one you're using.

To what extent did the Cyber-Twin borrow from existing solid state technologies?
Curtis: The power amp is solid state. Fender had developed solid state power amps for many years, and we had a lot of experience in making them sound as tube-like as possible. It's not that an accomplished musician can't tell the difference, but they are pretty darned similar.

Why not just use tubes?
Curtis: We used solid state because the Cyber-Twin needed to be stereo, and loud, and a tube-based, high-powered stereo power amp is something you just don't want to lug around. So we were balancing a number of practical considerations for the player.

So the Cyber-Twin combines a tube-based preamp that generates distortion and is controlled by an onboard computer, and a solid state power amp for volume and the stereo functions?
Curtis: That's right, and the third element is the digital signal processing that handles all the special effects and the equalization. When you shift from one effect to another, the knobs automatically change to the familiar controls the player would expect with that particular effect on a regular amp.

So if you call up Tremolo, one of the knobs becomes a speed control and another becomes a depth control.
Curtis: Yes, and all the effects work that way. We realized that although we had some very complex circuitries and software involved, the amplifier had to remain user-friendly and completely intuitive. If you're used to plugging into a Deluxe or a Twin or whatever the conventional amp might be, you would have no trouble plugging into a Cyber-Twin and playing music right away.

During development, did you think much about where this tube/solid state/digital/computer product was going to fit into the grand scheme of Fender's amplifier history, which after all is based on tube models?
Curtis: Honestly, although we had a lot of people working on the Cyber-Twin, it was very much under the radar during development. Ritchie and I believed in it, and we didn't have people looking over our shoulders. We made it happen, and there wasn't a lot of conjecture in the company about "What does all this mean?" because a lot of people didn't even know about it. It's not that Ritchie and I wanted to spring it on the company, but we were very committed to pushing it through and making it happen.

Key members of Fender's design and engineering brain trust, from left: Chuck Adams, Matt Wilkens, Keith Chapman, Dale Curtis.

Road Trip: The Quest for Tone

How did you do this project in a "Fender" way?
McDonald: One part of that was, we went to New York and played a complete collection of classic Fender amps, all in original condition. We got so deep into it. It increased our ability to hear subtle details, to appreciate how these amps feel to the touch. It was enlightening and really fun, too. You can figure this out if you get deep into the tube manuals, but you have to have good ears, and analyze the schematics. Look where the tone stacks are in those amps. That's why they act they way they do. It's not just the value of some capacitor. That's not what it's about. It's about how the components are arranged and how the signal flows through them.

Chapman: On that trip to New York, we did a two-day amp shootout with a prototype Cyber-Twin and all of these amazing vintage amplifiers. At Fender this is known as the legendary "Quest for Tone." With all of these amplifiers around us, it was like heaven on earth. The purpose of the trip was to make sure that all the presets on the Cyber-Twin, particularly the Amp Collection, were as accurate as possible. We had completed all the tone stacks, the distortion circuits, the basic building blocks, and by that point we were just fine tuning.

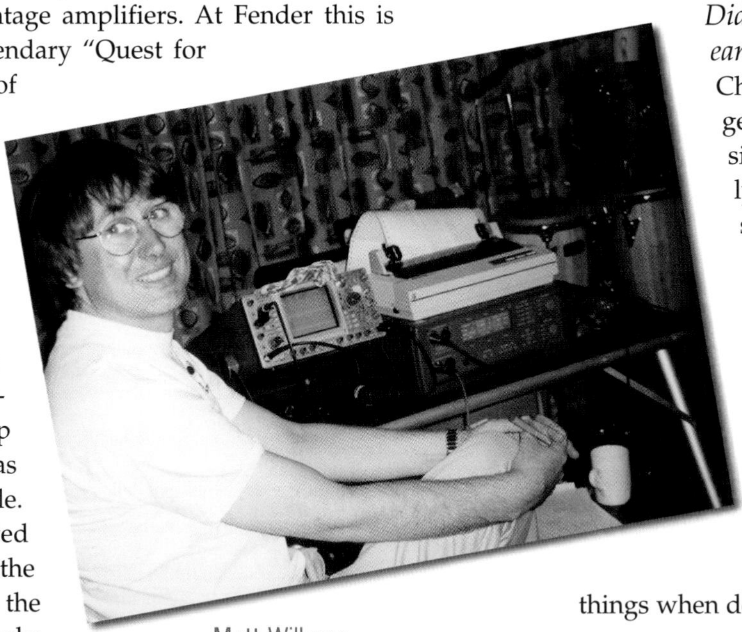

Matt Wilkens.

What was your role?
Chapman: My job was to take all of those building blocks and put them together to match the tone of the various vintage classics, so in each case we listened to the original and to the Cyber-Twin, side by side. Like on a Marshall style amp it would have the tone stack in the rear, after the distortion, whereas in a Fender, traditionally it would be up front. And we could rearrange those building blocks to get pretty much any amp we wanted. If you look at the different positioning of the components in the Fender tweeds versus the browns versus the blackfaces, these differences were the kinds of things we could accomplish by rearranging the order of the elements in the Cyber-Twin.

What limitations did you face?
Chapman: We are of course limited by physics. The Cyber-Twin has two 12s, and they are going to sound a certain way. So, instead of doing cabinet simulation, which we don't feel is an accurate parameter that can be modeled, we decided to use timbre filters to compensate the Cyber's tone and compression to match the speaker in the cab of the particular amp we are emulating.

Did you use testing gear or just your ears?
Chapman: Both — sophisticated testing gear and lots of listening and discussion. Matt Wilkens did most of the analytical study from a purely engineering standpoint, looking at frequency responses and the effects of different circuit architectures. Another test is called an impulse response of the cabinet. You can strike an object with a blunt instrument and then measure how all of the different mechanics react to the stress. Some will vibrate a lot longer and others will dampen very quickly, and we looked at those sorts of things when designing the various timbre filters.

How many vintage amps did you analyze?
Chapman: Altogether about 40 — mostly Fenders but also some Marshalls, Voxes, and some boutique amps. We did some here in Scottsdale as well — some of the more modern amps — so it was all very thorough. In the Cyber-Twin, I'm particularly proud of the '57 and '58 Bassmans. I think we really nailed those. And to get those tones out of a device with a two-tube preamp and a solid state power

Ritchie Fliegler.

amp with DSP, that's one of our crowning achievements. Another one I am particularly proud of is the Super Reverb. I think we got a lot of the shimmer that is so distinctive to that amplifier's sound.

Collaboration

The Cyber-Twin project sounds like a classic team effort.

McDonald: Exactly. Ritchie was the pioneer. He grasped all this from the outset, but we didn't get approval to do it until I was the amp guy. It was a huge investment in R&D. In marketing, the efforts of Ritchie and myself overlapped for years. We were working side by side.

Chapman: I spent two and a half years working on the Cyber-Twin. I designed and wrote the guitar tuner, and also handled all of the user interface design, all of the code for the display. So I was basically the leading software engineer on the user interface. Dale Curtis was my immediate supervisor. Chuck Adams handled most of the DSP work. I also wrote all the amp types, amp models, and the majority of the presets.

Curtis: Richard and Ritchie were heavily involved in the marketing side of it. In engineering, I did the architecting on the amp, but there were four or five main people involved, all the senior staff in R&D. We put our best people on that project. Matt Wilkens, Keith Chapman, Chuck Adams, and myself, we were some of the main ones who made it happen, but there were many others involved as well. At one time we had 22 people working full-time on the Cyber-Twin project.

Holy cow.

Curtis: Yeah, and that was under the radar! So it was pretty big and semi-secret at the same time, at least at first. Compared to the time when I arrived, the R&D department had more than doubled, almost tripled, and we had almost two dozen people working on that one project.

Great Expectations

When you brought the Cyber-Twin to market, you must have considered the attitude among some purists — anything that's not a tube amp can't be a real Fender.

McDonald: Oh, absolutely. We took it into account from a marketing perspective, and also from a cosmetic perspective. It may have motorized pots, but they're blackface knobs. If you can operate a Fender amplifier, you can operate a Cyber-Twin. That's so important. It's intuitive. Every time an engineer would try to take us down a different path, I'd fight it and fight it. It may be the most

On the Quest for Tone, Matt Wilkens (with testing gear), Ritchie Fliegler and their Fender colleagues played several guitars (like this vintage Telecaster) through dozens of classic Fender amps, modern Fenders, and amps by other makers as well.

advanced guitar amp technology on the planet, but it's a Fender, and that means plug it in and go.

How was it received inside Fender?
Curtis: When we introduced it, some people in the organization had very different opinions about how successful it was going to be. Because so much of the work was done under the radar, it wasn't widely known in the company how much effort had been devoted to it. Even after all that work, it was on the verge of being cancelled right up until the moment it was actually finished.

For those who advocated canceling the Cyber-Twin, what was their objection?
Curtis: Well, it was coming from the top, and there were concerns about the cost, the investment of time and resources. The worry was, will we ever recoup this massive investment? By the time people found out about it and started to raise questions and reservations, we were almost finished with it.

How did it do in the marketplace?
Curtis: It was a phenomenon. Even the optimistic projections were nowhere near the actual sales. A lot of us who were passionate about the Cyber-Twin believed it would outstrip expectations, but even we were surprised at just how successful it was. When we debuted it to basically the entire Scottsdale staff, we had an event with speeches and an official unveiling. Bill Schultz looked at the amplifier for maybe 30 seconds, and he listened to somebody demoing it, putting it through its paces. And right off the bat he said, "We're gonna sell ten thousand of these things!" Everybody just kind of laughed, because nobody imagined it would be that successful. But at the end of the first year, sales of the Cyber-Twin were almost exactly ten thousand. I don't even know if Bill meant it, but he said it, and we all heard it, and he just nailed it.

McDonald: It was frustrating at first because sales people and distributors weren't sure what to do with it. One offshore distributor ordered 25, and I almost fainted. Here I've worked two-plus years on this thing, I'm convinced this is the most innovative thing Fender's done in quite a while, and they want 25 pieces. Two weeks later they ordered 600. It was a sensational hit, unbelievable.

Why do you think the Cyber-Twin was such a smash?
McDonald: Remember what was going on at that time? We were just coming out of the Tone Nazi period. In the '70s and '80s everybody had 20 guitars and one amp, and then in the early '90s they started waking up. *Wow, you don't just play the guitar — you play the amp.* And great players really play the amp. Eddie Van Halen is one of those guys who plays his amplifier as hard as he plays his guitar. So the boutique thing really took off, and we were into the era of the tone snobs. For these guys, if you make a 1959 Bassman reissue, and it's not exactly like a '59, then it's no good, even though making a new amp that's exactly like the original is probably illegal now and might get you killed if you play it in the rain or whatever. Safety regulations, right?

So after the rise of all these boutique guys, what happened? The market spoke. Guitar players had their say. Eighty percent of them don't have the kind of ear where they can distinguish these boutique components. A lot of players want to have fun, they want variety, and they don't need the greatest one tone in the world. A lot of guys playing casuals need a whole bunch of different sounds. They're playing AC/DC and the Carpenters on the same gig.

Line 6 seemed to capture that idea.
McDonald: I respect Line 6 for what they did. Everything changed when those amps came out, and the market really spoke and said, boutique amps are fine for the vocal minority. But what most of us want is a fun experience, and we're not all pros, and we want good sound and versatility. That was a significant change. It's almost like the changes in music. When Yes and Genesis started out, it was like "math rock," you know? And you were going, my god, the level of virtuosity I have to have to play this stuff is so far beyond my reach. So what happened? Punk! Rockabilly! Three chords and the truth! The amp market did the same thing, going from this complex boutique/aficionado thing to something that a lot more people could embrace and have fun with.

Chapman: We were thinking that the Cyber-Twin would be perfect for the Top 40 guy. He's on a gig and he doesn't want to carry all these effects pedals, but he has to go from a Bassman tone to a Marshall tone to a Deluxe Reverb, from Led Zeppelin to Mariah Carey all in one set. And that's the player we intended the Cyber-Twin for. And it's also very robust, designed for professional use.

Did it appeal to any other groups of players?
Chapman: We found that the main customers divide into three categories. There's that Top 40 guy who we intended. Then there are the guitar guru guys, who are real technical and just want to tweak everything, and this is the perfect palette for them to do all of that experimentation. We give them control over everything. People are writing PC programs on their own to interface with the Cyber-Twin. Some of them have even made a little business out of it, selling these software packages. And then the third customer is the studio musician who does a jingle and then later on that same day a late-night TV gig or a record date, and he needs a lot of versatility but doesn't want to cart a lot. People are actually able to leave their Cyber-Twin at home.

How does that work?
Chapman: You set up your presets, save them to your computer, email them to the studio, and then download the presets from their computer into their Cyber-Twin. You don't even have to bring the amp. Just bring your guitar and you've got your custom sounds all ready to go. All the parameters are saved to the computer through MIDI, and that MIDI file can be emailed anywhere.

How do you measure the success of a product like the Cyber-Twin?
Nicholas: You can't just look at the sales. You have to look at your costs. The Cyber-Twin came out the same time we reissued the Super Reverb. [Both amps retailed for $1,699.] We probably sold ten times as many Cyber-Twins as reissue Super Reverbs, but it took us the same amount of time, about a year, to get a return on our R&D investment for each amp. To reissue the Super Reverb, you just get an old one, make sure it sounds good and everything's working, set it on the counter and say to R&D, "Build me that [laughs]!" So the Cyber-Twin far outsold the Super, but we also had many times the investment in the Cyber-Twin. The investment for both amps got paid off, so we consider them both successful products.

Aside from the good sales and enthusiastic reviews in the guitar press, what kind of feedback did you get on the Internet, particularly among hardcore amp buffs?

Nicholas: Some of these people, to listen to them talk, you would think they know more than Leo Fender or something. Everybody's an expert because they read a book or two and then they think they should tell you what your job is. So there was some resistance. But it went away, because the amp was good, it was selling, artists were playing it.

Curtis: As soon as it came out, we started following the chat rooms online, and at first a lot of people in these discussion groups were saying, "How could Fender do this to us? How could you call this thing a Twin when it's obviously digital and high-tech?" So among some groups, the initial reaction was, they were horrified. But these were people who had never played through the amplifier, or even seen one. Then somebody in one of those discussion groups announced they had seen Buddy Guy using one onstage, and then they started saying, "Well, if Buddy Guy is playing one, maybe it's not so bad after all."

So you had to fight some sort of stigma against solid state and digital technologies?
Curtis: People can be pretty set in their ways, and the initial assumption was that if part of it is solid state and part of it is digital, it must sound bad, and the truth is, it sounded very good. A lot of other high-profile players started using them, and so public opinion went from "How could Fender do this?" to "Where can I get my hands on one to try it out?" And once people tried it out, the Cyber-Twin sold itself. People realized it wasn't some far-out, fringe kind of thing, but rather it was a comfortable, intuitive product that could perform like a familiar Fender tube amp but could also allow you, if you were interested, to explore a whole universe of new sounds and effects and creative possibilities. People saw that it was not at all intimidating. I think the motorized knobs helped a lot, too.

Because of the "wow" factor?
Curtis: Exactly. I think it pulls people in, and it helps them get past whatever initial hesitation they might have just because it has a digital display.

McDonald: Our attitude was, these tools are for you to use to express yourself, to come up with something new. Push the envelope. That's what we're doing. That's where the Fender tag line came from: Innovate, don't emulate.

The Cyber-Twin SE, Cyber-Deluxe, Cyber-Champ

In the summer of 2004 you evolved the amp to the Cyber-Twin SE.

Nicholas: It was a natural development, a way of refreshing core product. Products have a life cycle, and at some point, to keep dealers and consumers from becoming bored with it, you have to refresh it. And second, we had learned a lot since the first Cyber-Twin. By the time we got to the SE, we had done a whole bunch of other DSP projects. We'd gotten really good at it. The SE is a really good-sounding amp, but sometimes it gets hard to keep topping yourself.

The Cyber-Champ and Cyber-Deluxe were offshoots of the Cyber-Twin.

Cyber-Twin SE, 2004. Dale Curtis: "The SE replaced the Cyber-Twin because we were honing and refining our skills all along. Technologies were getting more effective, so we thought we could take advantage of more powerful processors and quieter converters and make a product that was even better than the original."

McDonald: The Cyber-Deluxe and Cyber-Champ were great, but they ran their course. The market gets more segmented every day, and products often have a shorter life. But the beauty of the Cyber project is that we started at the top with the Cyber-Twin to make a technological statement to the market, and then from there we can depopulate it, break it down, to create these other models.

Nicholas: The Cyber-Deluxe came out, and its lifespan seemed a little shorter than we would have predicted, and by the time we did the Cyber-Champ the modeling thing had blown over a little bit industry-wide. A lot of other people were coming out with amps with all sorts of features and offering them for a lot less money because of the China factor. A Cyber-Champ is head and shoulders above a lot of its competitors, but it's not really big enough to be a professional amp, so people just look at features per dollar. It's not like marketing a Vibro-King, where sometimes it almost seems like it doesn't matter how much it costs. If you're a rock star or a lawyer who wants a Vibro-King, you're gonna get one, but the Cyber-Champ is an example of the relentless march to Asia for manufacturing. The lower you go into the less expensive amps, the less brand loyalty you find.

Curtis: The Cyber-Deluxe and Cyber-Champ did very well for us, but they served their purpose and came and went. There are other products in which we will continue to employ and refine all the technologies we developed for the Cyber-Twin.

Tube, solid state, and digital technologies come together in the Cyber-Twin SE.

G-DEC

Is the G-DEC one of them?
Curtis: Exactly. The G-DEC borrows significantly from the Cyber-Twin's technology. It doesn't have vacuum tubes, and it's not at the same quality level or price level as a Cyber-Twin, but 80 percent of what's in the G-DEC came from the Cyber-Twin's development program and the [Cyber] amplifiers that came after it. The other 20 percent was developed specifically for the G-DEC. I would imagine that the next product will borrow from both the Cyber-Twin and the G-DEC and then mix in its own unique aspects.

What predictions did you have for the G-DEC regarding its customers and how they would use the product? And how accurate were those projections?
Curtis: We had some surprises. At first we expected it would be a fantastic product for students, for beginners. We thought teachers would find it very useful as well, and we knew it would be fun for kids. But toward the end of the project, as we started to have prototype G-DECs around the office, our perceptions started to change. We realized this thing is incredibly addictive, whether you are a beginning guitar player or a seasoned, jaded professional. The first time I plugged into one that was all hooked up and had all of the functions working, I ended up playing it for hours. People like Ritchie, who are very accomplished guitar players, just plugged in and started having fun. We realized that this was not an age-specific product after all, nor was it a skill level-specific product. Eric Johnson is using one as a warm-up amplifier, and there are other high-profile artists who are using them, and that's something we did not predict.

Chapman: When we started working on the G-DEC, people were saying, "Let's just put some drum loops into a Frontman." But it grew and grew. We knew it would be the perfect entry-level amplifier to get beginners started, but the funny thing was, all of the executives here at Fender were having so much fun with their G-DECs they didn't want to part with them. The guitarist in my band uses his G-DEC when he's songwriting. It's sort of a scratch pad, and he comes up with drumbeats and so on, burns it to a CD, and brings it to rehearsal. The Cyber-Twin is a core product on a par with the Twin as far as sales are concerned. We will continue to build off of the platforms of the G-DEC and Cyber-Twin to have some amazing products for the future.

A revolution in a pint-sized cab: the G-DEC.

Hear the G-DEC, Track 11.

Nicholas: Another advantage of the G-DEC is that I think it's going to help players think more about playing in time, which is so crucial. You see a lot of beginners who can play a solo from a record, and they know where the notes are, but they don't have any time. The G-DEC helps you get into playing along with rhythms.

Curtis: I remember sitting in a meeting filled with all the Fender sales and marketing people. This is a room full of guitar players with tons of experience and lots of gear at home. They have access to anything they want. They could buy a Custom Shop amp or a reissue Bassman — anything. I mean, we work at Fender. And somebody said, "Who in this room wants a G-DEC?" Everybody raised their hands [laughs]. If everybody in marketing wants one, and everybody in sales wants one, I think that tells you a lot about the product.

How well is the G-DEC doing?
Curtis: As well as it could possibly do. In my 11-plus years at Fender Electronics, the two milestones have definitely been the Cyber-Twin and the G-DEC. Coincidentally, the other development on that same level has been a vacuum-tube series, and that's the Hot Rod family. So it's a funny business we're in, to see that our most successful products are mixes of old, revered technologies and the latest in solid state and digital signal processing technologies. These products are a mixture of the tried-and-true with the cutting edge, and I think the reason they succeed is that we are so deeply grounded in both areas.

McDonald: The G-DEC has been a smashing success — Amplifier of the Year, Product of the Year, all those awards. Aside from selling in the tens of thousands and providing an amazing educational tool for players and teachers, you know what else it's doing? It's taking jaded guitarists like me and making me want to play. I haven't played this much in years, and I can say that for all the guys here at Fender.

Looking Ahead

What's the future of digital products at Fender?
Curtis: The Cyber-Twin is a masterpiece. We think it will be in the line for a long time to come — hopefully forever — alongside the Twin and other Fender icons.

Nicholas: Some players are early adopters. They're motivated to try the very latest technologies and see what they have to offer, and they will always respond to products like the Cyber-Twin and G-DEC immediately. But that early adopter/widget enthusiast is only one part of our customer base. We are constantly being asked by dealers and consumers alike when we're going to get deeper into the computer world. Look at what's happening with the Macintosh computers that come equipped with Garage-Band software. Professionals and amateurs are using those kinds of technologies more and more, so we are always thinking about how they relate to the guitar amp of the future. People are plugging their guitars into computers and getting their sounds with software. We need to accommodate a new generation of players, but we must do it in the Fender way. Every software package for guitar players is loaded with someone's interpretation of the Fender sound — blackface, tweed, spring reverb, tube distortion and so on. We need to steer our customers from these imitators, by giving them the real tone.

When did it dawn on you that the Cyber-Twin just might rearrange the amplifier landscape out there?
McDonald: I remember the day it was done, one of the most amazing days of my life. We were all in my living room at home with the Cyber-Twin, and we had Super Reverbs and Vibroluxes and all sorts of classic Fender stuff, and a bunch of us sat around passing guitars around. We were like, okay, turn the blackface Twin Reverb up to 8. Now turn the Cyber-Twin with that same setting up to 8, and we just looked at each other. Oh my god, it works!

"It may be the most advanced guitar amp technology on the planet, but it's a Fender, and that means plug it in and go."

— Richard McDonald

Bassman 250/210 combo.

CHAPTER TWENTY-SEVEN

27

FBA: Fender Bass Amplification

A Whole New Low-Down

In the early days, Leo Fender's bass amplifier was an adequate match for its 4-string companion, but as the bass moved into new territories and ultimately revolutionized popular music, Mr. Fender's combos couldn't keep up. Arenas were too big, stage volumes too high. A 2x6L6 or 2x5881 combo designed in the 1950s for local musicians playing sock hops and state fairs was inadequate for hard rock or funk. The piggybacks of the early and mid 1960s looked great and were suitable for moderate-volume gigs, but they were gradually eclipsed by newcomers to the market. As Fender guitars, basses and guitar amps continued to command the spotlight, Fender bass amps were increasingly relegated to the shadows.

Motown's incomparable James Jamerson, for example, often preferred a Kustom 200 or an Ampeg B-15N Portaflex; in the studio he simply recorded directly into the board. By the end of the 1960s, major touring groups like Cream, the Who, the Moody Blues, and the Jimi Hendrix Experience were rolling out huge, powerful amps for both guitar and bass — the Model T, 300T, and Coliseum from Sunn, Ampeg's 300W SVT, the Marshall Major, the Vox Super Beatle, and other goliaths. Some of these rigs were matched to cabinets with an 18, two 15s, four 12s, eight 10s, even sixteen 10s. Some had folded-horn cabs, a design borrowed from theater systems. Some rigs weighed more than 300 pounds. In the wake of all this, Fender's biggest amps were relocated to the "mid power" category.

Players who had always looked to Fender for innovative solutions now looked elsewhere. As *Bass Player*'s David Hicks wrote in "The Great Bass Amps of the '60s," "The Acoustic 360 featured better low-frequency response, less distortion and greater efficiency than anything on the market at the time, and it was the first truly professional-quality bass amplifier." Fender responded with the mammoth 400 PS (Chap. 17). Still, as Hicks explained: "The Acoustic 360 and Fender 400 amps pointed the way in designing a high-fidelity bass amplifier, but each had its problems … both amps missed the mark for good stage presence and attack."

For more than two decades, starting in the early 1980s, it almost seemed as if Fender had given up on bass amplification. The designated flagship, the Bassman, had long been recognized as a great guitar amp, but years had passed since bassists had considered it appropriate for

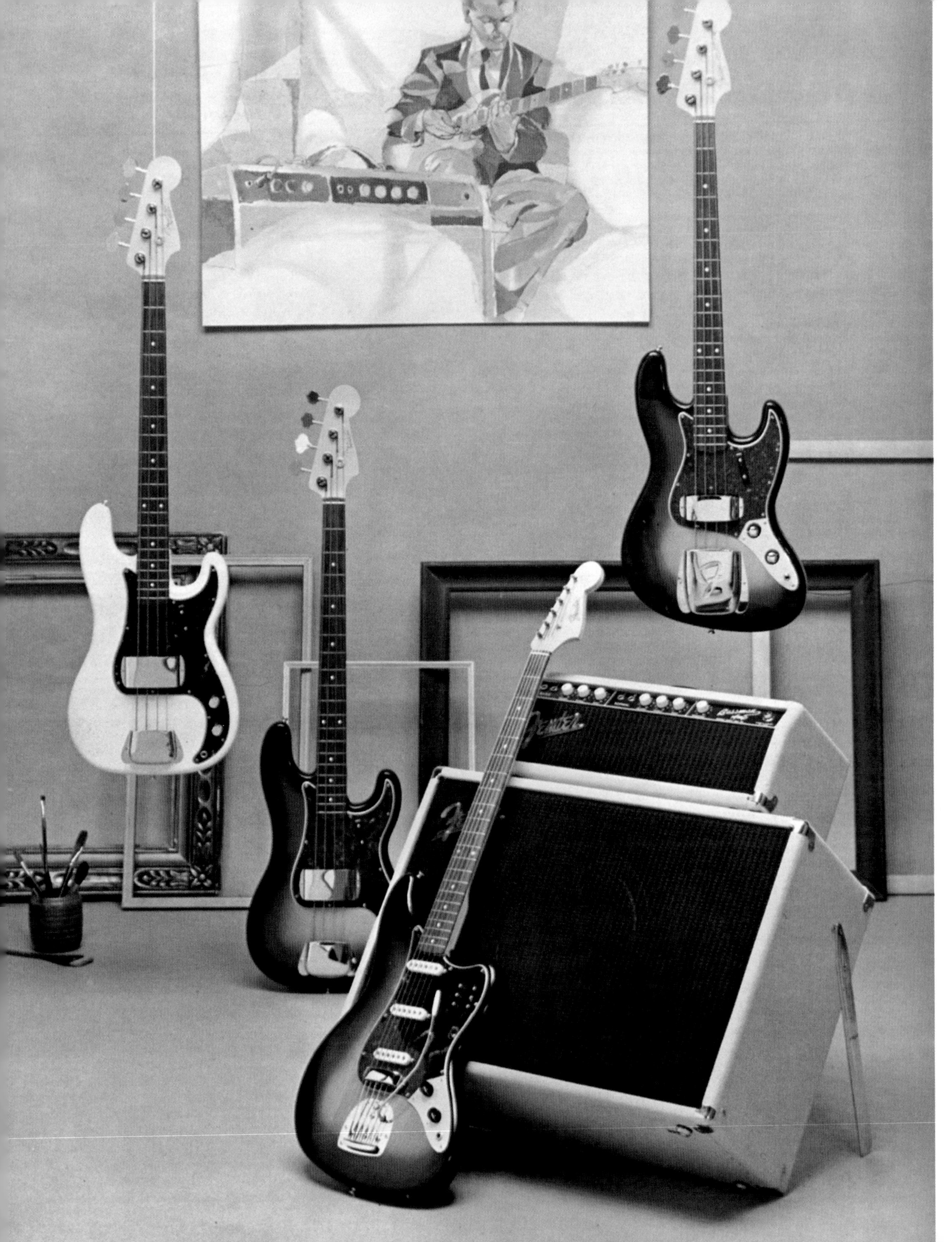

The ultimate in electric bass, 1961: classic Precision Basses, the new Jazz Bass (Mr. Fender called it the Cadillac of the line), a three-pickup Bass VI 6-string bass guitar, and a blonde piggy-back Bassman.

large gigs. Other Fenders of the '80s and early '90s were ostensibly targeted to the bass market, but in most cases they were introduced with little fanfare, had short and unremarkable lifespans, and then fizzled.

Fender had purchased Sunn back in 1985 and in 1999 began offering two Sunn bass amps — the 1200S rack-mount head and the 300T, a 300W all-tube head — along with 4x10 and 2x15 bass enclosures. Under Ritchie Fliegler's direction, Richard McDonald and Dale Curtis took another important step in 2000, resurrecting the Bassman name for four solid state combos that replaced the R.A.D. Bass, the M-80 Bass, and the outdated BXR line of the 1990s.

The Bassmans of 2000 to 2002 were reasonably successful, but for the guitar players and bass players currently running the Fender company, the irony of Fender's lack of prominence in bass amps remained a painful one. Determined to change all that, whatever it took, Richard McDonald started a separate division, Fender Bass Amplification, or FBA. To stake out FBA's turf, he went so far as to change the Fender logo. Jay Piccirillo was brought in to head FBA in 2002. His education includes a bachelor's degree in music performance with an emphasis in business and years of performing as a professional musician. He has held marketing positions at Cakewalk, Yamaha, and Gibson along with being a writer and reviewer at *Bass Frontiers* magazine and a buyer of amps and effects at retailer Musician's Friend. He is the first person to hold the title of Marketing Manager, FBA. Dale Curtis and his team handle the R&D.

After years of hard work, intensive design, field testing and savvy marketing, Fender has for the first time since the mid 1960s established itself as a world leader in bass amps. As we go to press, the line of dedicated bass models comprises several families: the Professional Series, the mid-line Bassman Series and the low-end Rumble Series. Various technologies are represented: all-tube, solid state, and tube/solid state hybrid. Available products include a tube preamp, a massive solid state power amp, several heads, and a whole range of combos and stacks. Speaker arrays range from a single 8 to eight 10s, power ratings from 15W to 1200W.

Historically, how important have bass amps been to Fender?

Richard McDonald: Well, we start with the irony that in the early '50s we set out to make a bass amp and ended up making the world's greatest *guitar* amplifier, the tweed Bassman. With the exception of something like the Custom Amp Shop Rumble Bass, a bass amp at Fender was always just sort of a regular guitar amp with a 15 inch speaker and a "B" on the end of the model name. That's how it felt to me. I was not impressed at all when I looked at the line.

What was the problem?

McDonald: They were designed by guitar players, not bass players. Let's not minimize our engineers. They're brilliant and dedicated, but in the Frontman line we had the regular guitar amps, and then a couple models with a "B." To me it was a joke. I went to Bill Schultz, who at the time was considering buying SWR, and I said, look, I know you want to buy SWR for X amount of dollars, but if you give us "little x," we'll turn what we have now into a real bass amp company.

The bass amps in 1982 ranged from the 1x12, 12W Musicmaster Bass up to the 2x15, 135W Bassman 135.

How?
McDonald: I told him, we'll need to hire a marketing manager to specialize in bass amps, and we'll need to get bass amps out of the guitar guys' hands. We'll need a couple of engineers who only make bass amps — and *play* bass. We'll need a separate catalog and money for marketing. Bill said yes, so we hired Jay Piccirillo.

The Strategy

Dale Curtis: The bass players of the world do not need another amp that is an afterthought from a guitar amp company. We committed to making this absolutely the best bass amp in the world, and we were not going to dilute that commitment with a focus on anything else. We picked the best people we could find and put them to work, and they have never lost a single minute thinking about guitars or guitar amps.

How did marketing to bass players differ from marketing to guitar players?
McDonald: Historically, bass players have been more willing to embrace evolutionary technology, like solid state, which worked okay for bass sooner than it worked okay for guitar. They're also a tight community. They talk. They're early adopters. They will try something that has no brand equity at all if they think it'll work. And they're tired of waiting in line behind guitar players, tired of wading through catalogs looking for their gear. Now they've got their own magazines. So we recognized all that early on, and when I became vice president we implemented that separation. It was, "Shane, you make guitar amps. Shane, meet Jay Piccirillo. Jay, you make bass amps."

Jay Piccirillo: Bass players have always wanted Fender to get serious about bass amplifiers. Obviously, they love our bass guitars, and I think they have just been waiting for us to get it together. Since an amplifier is not held or felt, it really needs to have a sonic character the player can identify with. Being a bass player, I have always struggled with the fact that we are a minority, so I welcomed the opportunity to champion something this important.

What was your strategy?
Piccirillo: I started by assessing our strengths and weaknesses, spending a lot of time analyzing the marketplace and determining the right position and philosophy for

Mid-'90s BXR bass amps.

FBA. Historically, Fender has always had a healthy interaction with professional players, and I wanted to continue in that tradition. Sonically, the identity of FBA became "thick, natural and balanced." Our amps support the natural sound of the instrument — much like our guitar amps have always done — without forcing an artificial voicing that makes all basses sound the same. In terms of market position, we aren't interested in being the cheapest or the most expensive. Fender has always been professional quality, but obtainable. Visually, our identity became an industrial look combining a brushed aluminum face with simple black knobs.

Curtis: When Jay came aboard, we took our very best bass amp designers out of designing acoustic guitar amps or electric guitar amps and said, "From now on, you are Fender Bass Amplification." We tossed aside some of our prior thinking about what a bass amp should be, and we really did start from the ground up. You know, the Fender legacy is incredibly powerful, and we're so proud of it, but sometimes a legacy can be constricting, too, and when it came to bass amps, we felt we needed to have the strength to step out of it. The whole Bassman lineage is powerful and intimidating, but we had to forget all that and make the best amplifier for today's bass player that we could possibly make. The part of the legacy that we kept was, it's a Fender, so it better be good. At any given price point, it better be the best amplifier you can get. That's the connection we have to a '59 Bassman. Otherwise, we stepped away from the old ways of doing things.

Who else works in FBA?
Piccirillo: Dave Lewis and Bob Desiderio are the primary engineers. Bob is responsible for the TBP-1 and the MB-1200. Dave is responsible for the 400 PRO, the Rumble series, and the new Bassman family. We also have access to some incredibly talented guys like Bill Hughes and Matt Wilkens who specialize in power amp technology and all things tube.

The 400 PRO, engineered by Dave Lewis.

The single-rack TBP-1 tube preamp, engineered by Bob Desiderio. Jay Piccirillo: "The TBP-1 embodies what I consider to be the Fender sound."

The Fender Sound, High-End Models

What about sound?

Piccirillo: We have a couple of different platforms that generate variations on the "thick, natural and balanced" theme, but the TBP-1 embodies what I consider to be the Fender sound. The heart of the TBP-1 is a passive tone stack also found in amps like Twins, Showmans, and Bassmans, and that has a lot to do with everybody's conception of the Fender sound.

So the idea was to borrow the recognized Fender sound from your guitar amps and transfer it to your bass amps?

Piccirillo: Yes. A long time ago, Fender made heads and combos that were kind of nondescript. You could use them for guitar, or you could use them for bass. I think it's fair to say that most of the time they were more guitarist-friendly, but there was an undeniable sound and character to them. I've met many bassists who have an old Bassman head that they've kept all these years. It might not have enough power to perform at loud volumes, but at a medium volume it has this creamy, rich tone that was thick, natural, and balanced. That's the Fender sound.

The passive vintage style tone stack shows up in the TBP-1 Tube Bass Preamp.

Piccirillo: The TBP-1 starts with the passive tone stack and then enhances it with a few additional features for modern applications. The positive aspect of a passive tone stack is its warm, interactive nature, but it is very limited in terms of absolute control. Bass players are used to having 15dB of cut or boost to modify any specific frequency. If they want to do the funk thing, they might want to cut 800Hz about 12dB. That's the kind of thing you can't do with a passive tone stack, because moving one knob affects the others and there are no fixed frequencies, so absolute control is impossible. We created something called Vari-Q, which functions like a semi-parametric EQ and allows for more control. With Vari-Q you start by selecting a frequency. If you cut that frequency, it gets progressively narrow and focused. This is great for getting very detailed and notching out harsh frequencies. By contrast, the more you boost a frequency, the wider its range becomes. Vari-Q is helpful when dialing in a specific sound. Other features include an independent overdrive section to make your tone "bite" a little harder, and Room Balance, which is a global EQ tilt that can reduce lows and boost highs or vice-versa with the simple turn of a knob. The idea of Room Balance is to preserve your tone from room to room so you don't have to mess with your settings to compensate for acoustics.

Were the TBP-1 and the MB-1200 power amp designed as a matched set?

Piccirillo: The "mono block" MB-1200 came a little later, but it was designed specifically to accommodate the TBP-1. The heart of the MB-1200 is the incredibly powerful back end used in the 800 PRO and Bassman 1200 PRO heads. Each of these amps produces 1200 watts at 2 ohms.

What about the Bassman 300 PRO and Bassman 1200 PRO?

Piccirillo: Each head shares the same tube preamp section based on an active tone stack that is extremely tight sounding. The preamp has an enormous amount of features including overdrive, preset tone shapes, a multi band compressor, and a 10-band graphic EQ. The Bassman 300 is all-tube, with two 12AX7 preamp tubes and six 6550 power tubes; the Bassman 1200 is a hybrid, meaning the tube preamp is married to a solid state power amp. Years prior, Ritchie Fliegler and Richard McDonald created these amplifiers under the Sunn brand name. When Sunn was later retired, the amps went away. Because they were so

Tube overdrive section in the TPB-1.

strong and popular, we brought them back as the Fender Bassman 300 PRO and Bassman 1200 PRO.

When you decided to turn Fender bass amplification around, how did you go about actually constructing the new amps? What components did you jettison, and what did you replace them with?

Curtis: It wasn't so much a matter of replacing components, because whether you're talking about tube amps or solid state amps, they tend to be made with pretty much the same bits. What makes an amp distinctive is the fine-tuning, the selection of values in the components, and the architecture. If you were to look at the schematics of the new bass amps and the old bass amps, they would look similar, and yet they sound and perform substantially differently. That's true with other people's products, too. They all sort of resemble each other, because that's how you do it, but they can sound radically different and be radically different.

Risky Business?

Fender has concentrated on simplifying the look of its products and reestablishing classic appearances, and yet you changed the logo for the new bass amps.

McDonald: We did so much research. We looked at the history of logos not only in music but in automotive, all sorts of stuff. We researched companies who had changed logos over the years. Ritchie Fliegler and I must have stayed up for months arguing about that. That was very rare, for the two of us to disagree. He's a real purist on that, and so am I, but I just felt if we were going to separate out the bass amps at so many levels, let's take it all the way. So we went back to the very old Fender logo from the '50s, modified it a bit, and got away from the script logo we've been using for 45 years.

Piccirillo: I like to say, if anything, we changed the logo back to its original design.

Why was it important to take such a risk?

Piccirillo: There was a feeling in the bass community that Fender had neglected to do the right thing when it came to bass amplification. The script logo is powerful in the minds of guitar players, but in some ways it also symbolized that neglect for bass players. We wanted to get their attention — like drawing a line in the sand, as if to say: From this point forward we have a new attitude, a new philosophy, and new products. Part of the change was to bring the logo back to what it was in the beginning. In the first FBA catalog we pictured an original '59 Bassman with the original logo next to a picture of

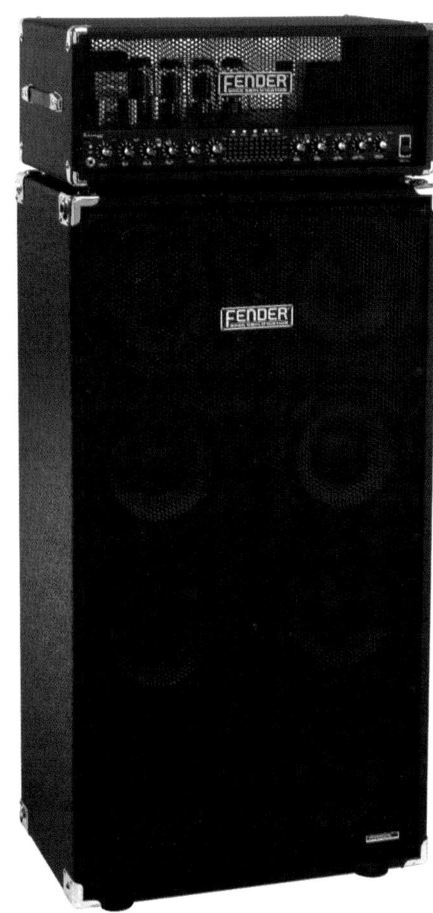

The all-tube Bassman 300, with the 810 PRO Cabinet.

the 400 PRO combo to help show where the logo came from. The overwhelming response has been positive. I have heard so many players tell me it feels right to them. Most importantly, people can identify any FBA amp with the new logo as a product of the new Fender Bass Amp division and know it is going to be a great one.

Was there much objection within the company to changing the logo?
Piccirillo: Of course there was concern. A logo is not something you take lightly. One thing that really helped was when people understood we were "taking it home" to where it started.

Would you consider changing it again?
McDonald: I told the bass guys: "This is your logo for life. As long as I'm here, that bass logo doesn't change," because I don't take tradition lightly either. Overall, we think it's worked just fine to reposition the Fender bass amp as a stand-alone product. Now they know: It's not just another guitar amp with a "B" on the end of the name.

When you arrived, the 400 PRO and 800 PRO were in development. Did you see them through to completion?
Piccirillo: I came in mid-stream and had to make some tough decisions. I had to determine a look that would carry on beyond just these products because they were the first PRO series products launching under my watch. There was no room for apologies. I had to put the brakes on, and that was tough, because you show up and you're new and you walk into this machine that is running and you pull the handle. Instead of Band-Aiding little things to hit the original release target, I decided to stop, take a step back, and reconsider fundamental things like the look, the internal structure, the design, the speakers — everything. Once we got it right, those aspects were in place for future products. The look and sound carry on because they are established and we believe in them.

Bassist with Eric Johnson, Robben Ford, and many others, Roscoe Beck is shown here with a Bassman 1200 PRO Head, an 810 PRO cab in front, and a 410 PRO SL Slant cab atop a 410 PRO ST Straight cab.

Bassman family, 2006.

Rumbles in the Low End

McDonald: Jay discontinued the work we had done on the Bassmans, then relaunched the Bassmans and developed the Rumble line. We had the Rumble name, and it's cool, so we told Jay we could use it.

No relation to the 300 watt Custom Amp Shop Rumble Bass of 1994?

McDonald: None. We had thermal problems with the Custom Shop Rumble. It was an excellent sounding amp, and not a bad hibachi either [laughs]. The Custom Amp Shop amps were built by the regular factory in Corona, but they were hand-wired, all-tube, limited edition things using more traditional production methods, always within the bounds of the legal restrictions that had changed a lot since the days of Leo Fender. Bruce Zinky was breadboarding the amps, and then they took them straight into manufacturing. The Custom Amp Shop idea came and went. It was a way to categorize amps for the convenience of dealers as much as anything else.

In resurrecting the Rumble name, were you concerned about possible confusion in the marketplace?

Piccirillo: That was a bit of an internal battle. Some people got in my face and said, why would you choose to name your product line after what we consider to be a failure? But I'm a bass player, and I was unfamiliar with it. I liked the name Rumble. I made some inquiries and found out that the original Rumble Bass hadn't caught on, but it wasn't because it didn't sound good. It was because we couldn't figure out how to build it at that time. The guts of that amp had that passive tone stack. I thought most players who would be customers for this lower-end line of amplifiers would probably have no recollection of the original so they would not be confused.

Fender's new FBA logo was controversial. Richard McDonald: "I just felt if we were going to separate out the bass amps at so many levels, let's take it all the way."

The Rumbles have little lights inside.
Piccirillo: Yes, a row of LEDs in the port, so when you turn the amp on it glows. I figured that in marketing these things we're not only battling other amp companies, but we're battling against the time some players spend with their video games and so on. I thought the red LEDs would give it a distinctive personality. When you plug into it and you play notes, they pulse in response to what you're playing. It's not technologically significant, just a fun, mini light show for someone enjoying their bedroom jam session. On the larger models we put a light switch in the back in case someone is playing one in church. I didn't think pulsing red demon lights would be appropriate in that setting [laughs].

So as a model name, Rumble went from a top of the line, Custom Amp Shop product to your entry-level amps.
Piccirillo: Yes, and they're successful on a global scale. I believe they are the most popular family of bass combos in the world. The original family was introduced in July of 2003 and included the 1x8 Rumble 15, 1x10 Rumble 25, 1x12 Rumble 60, and 1x15 Rumble 100. In January 2006 we added the 2x10 Rumble 100. The retail price of the Rumble line starts at around 200 dollars and goes up to just under 600 dollars.

SWR

Fender considered purchasing SWR, then founded FBA, and then went ahead and bought SWR anyway.
Piccirillo: I was in my "honeymoon" period at Fender. Some of my first pro stuff was about to hit the market, and then it was announced that we were purchasing SWR. We were in acquisition mode anyway, so I could see the writing on the wall. It felt awkward, but at the same time I could completely understand the appeal for Fender to purchase a strong bass amp brand like SWR.

In 2006, Richard McDonald called the Rumble 100 "probably the best selling bass combo in the world right now."

With Fender acquiring a highly regarded, pro-level bass amplification company, what kind of impact did that have?
Piccirillo: The two brands had to make room for each other, and we were careful not to step on any toes. When your competitor becomes your brother, it takes some adjustment. We never considered options like keeping Fender low end and SWR high end. Both brands have always been treated equally here and encouraged to approach the marketplace as stand-alone bass amp companies.

How did you divide the designs and marketing between the two brands?
Piccirillo: There is a marketing manager for each brand. John Willis is in charge of SWR. Each of us has a separate vision that drives everything we do. Although we are considerate of each other, we each effectively run our own company. There is an R&D staff assigned to SWR just like there is for FBA. You will never see an Aural Enhancer on an FBA amp, or a Vari-Q on an SWR. The designs are typically driven by the needs of marketing, so there is very little confusion. Also, the two brands have a very different sound. This usually determines which brand is better suited for a new technology coming from R&D, and helps create the unique flavor of an ad campaign. Side by side, FBA is going to sound "thick, natural, and balanced," whereas SWR is going to sound hi-fi, modern, and scooped. Each has a distinct character that appeals to a different type of player. We are careful to maintain the traditions of each brand and deliver the type of products our respective customers have come to expect.

You mentioned "scooped."
Piccirillo: Around the time that bass players started getting thumb-happy, SWR really made its mark. Thumb-style bass is like emulating a drum set. The thumb is the kick drum, and the fingers that pull up and do the popping are the snare.

To give the "kick drum" more oomph and more sizzle on the top, you typically scoop the mids out around 800Hz or so. And the SWR has that inherent sound. It's punchy, very present, and that's their thing.

So you're making an effort not to cannibalize each other's lines.
Piccirillo: There are moments when one comes up with an idea that the other one could have come up with, and there's a bit of rivalry, but it's a healthy thing and there's a lot of comedic relief here. We all get along. It works out well. Our FBA sales people know they can go into a music store and place the Fender stuff alongside amps from SWR, and each has its reason for existing. There may be times when a dealer chooses an SWR over a similar Fender or vice-versa, but in general, dealers find they appeal to a wider range of players if they offer both.

How did you go about marketing the new products?
McDonald: After we changed the logos, we came up with the "Plug Yourself In" campaign, which has a picture of the back of Jay's head in all those ads [laughs]. If you look at the pro-level gear — the preamps, the endorsements we have — we're just so proud of it.

The Turnaround

How has the image of the Fender bass amplifier changed in the minds of bassists?
Piccirillo: We've come a long way, certainly, and the amps have turned around, but we're not there yet. We're still progressing. The bass amps are now getting the kind of recognition among bass players that Fender guitar amps and instruments have always enjoyed. We recognize that the bass player is a bass player by choice. He's not just the worst guitar player in the band. Everything we do comes from the inspiration of making bass players feel pride about their tone and their amplifier.

Where does FBA go from here?
Piccirillo: There's a solid plan that will focus on the technology and strength of the TBP-1 along with some other cool stuff to create more PRO series bass amps. We designed the TBP-1 with help from Reggie Hamilton and Roscoe Beck, and the more I use it, the more I fall in love with it. This type of artist feedback will continue to be an essential element as we move forward. We have a growing reputation, so the most important thing for FBA is to stay the course and continue to develop products with our character and brand image in mind.

I might be biased, because I live way inside this forest, but here's a good sign: When you go from your artist relations people begging musicians to please check out the gear to musicians constantly calling *us* and asking to check out the gear, you know you've turned a corner, and that's exactly what's happened. Sales are the best they've ever been. The word is out.

I also have a personal stake to instill pride among the public that bass is an incredible instrument more potential musicians should embrace. You will see future products designed to teach and inspire. I want to reach out to young people and show them how amazing it can be to be a bass player by choice, not by default. I want to make products that help convey this message.

800 PRO Head, shown here with a 410 PRO SL slant cab.

CHAPTER TWENTY-EIGHT

28

The Tone Zone

Facts, Opinions, and Mythconceptions

"I can tell you every little piece of gear I've ever used, and you're still not going to sound like me. You have to reach inside yourself."

— Carlos Santana, *Guitar Player*, June '05

"The weird thing about tone is that everything tends to revolve around knowing how to play your instrument. Good tone is that simple."

— Pete Anderson, *Guitar Player*, July '98

"Getting a good guitar tone is easier than people think. Plug an old Fender guitar into an old Fender amp, and it sounds like rock music."

— Chris Cornell of Soundgarden, *Guitar Player*, November '99

Previous chapters on tube amp functions, components, biasing, class of operation, etc. provide the foundation for this section, in which leading amplifier experts have an opportunity to sound off about maintaining perspective. Contributors are identified in the Acknowledgments. Italicized comments are those of the author.

Ears and Interactions

What are some of the most common misconceptions about tone?
Hartley Peavey: We want to believe that somewhere there's an old hermit on a mountain top who winds pickups and soaks them overnight in swamp water to give them some soul. That's all bull.

And Leo Fender himself would have been more surprised than anyone to see how many myths and misconceptions now surround his early products.
Hartley Peavey: That's right. He was such a practical man. That's where all his success came from. All he wanted to do was to sell reliable equipment to the working man at a fair price, which is what I wanted to do 40 years ago when I started out.

For most of us, one powerful motivation is getting the tone we hear on a particular record.

Bruce Zinky: I came to realize that the recording process had a lot to do with the sounds we came to know and love, which also explained, "Why doesn't my guitar and amp sound like the record?" We weren't hearing just the player, guitar, and amp. There were microphones, EQs, etc. doing a number on the sound. The first thing I discovered [when designing the Tone-Master] was that if you wanted an amp to sound like the record, you couldn't copy the schematic of the amp used on the record! That can never work, as there's just too much in between the speaker and your ear that is having its way with the sound.

What are some of the most common misconceptions about amplifiers in general?

Aspen Pittman: This drives me crazy — people who focus on just one thing, like the only reason Fender amps sound good is the Orange Drop capacitors. *Orange Drop caps! Gotta have 'em!* That's ridiculous. It was the capacitors, plus the really nice 12AX7s in the front end, plus the 6L6s, plus the transformer, plus the phase inverter, plus the rectifier, plus the cab, plus the way Leo Fender put it all together — *plus plus plus!* Orange Drops are pretty crappy caps, they have slow transient characteristics, and they probably slowed down the top end, but you can't just pull out one piece of the puzzle and say, this is the whole picture right here. Those caps do not explain the difference between a very nice vintage Fender and an average amp. If you pull the caps out of a '58 Bassman and stick them in your amp, you are not going to get a '58 Bassman. They're not the holy grail. There *is* no holy grail.

Blackie Pagano: "The most common misconception about tone is that its primary source is hardware. Tone comes from the heart of the musician."

Alexander Dumble: One item that does seem to trick players a bit concerns impedance matching between the amplifier and speaker loads. A second item seems to center around the "voodoo" aspects of different tubes and cables. A third item: Relying on pedal effects to arrive at a great tone is a defeating pursuit in itself. Most pedal effects filter out the more ephemeral entities that are contained in the sound of a guitar string, especially the subtle, instantaneous peak components. Keeping the sound of the string within the note is paramount. Good guitar playing is conceptual and is in the touch.

Ritchie Fliegler: Speaking of cables, something to think about — you can spend hundreds of dollars on low-capacitance cables now, and indeed they work: The lower the capacitance of the cable, the more high frequencies will come through, especially if the guitar's volume control is backed off at all. However, just remember that whether you're talking about Fender or Marshall or Mesa/Boogie or whoever, the guys who designed these guitars and these amps did not use these expensive low-capacitance cables. So your basic 20-foot Pro Co cable with your Les Paul or your Strat through your Fender or your Marshall — that's the sound the designers wanted you to hear. That doesn't mean if you prefer the sound of the expensive cables you're wrong. Not at all. We all have our preferences. But it's worth remembering what the designers were using when they put it all together and said, this is the sound we want.

Bruce Zinky: For me, the amplifier must accurately replicate what the guitar sounds like acoustically, no amp at all. Sure, you can add distortion, or tons of bass or make the high end brighter, but it starts with an acoustic guitar sound — well, the sound of the electric guitar before the amp. If the guitar doesn't sound good without an amp, it will never sound right with one.

Andy Marshall: A lot of these things that supposedly contribute to the sound of this or that amp are overrated, but sometimes manufacturers have to deal with public opinion. Before we introduced THD's interpretation of the 4x10 Bassman, which was the first "reissue" style of any amp by any company, we did a ton of research. Those old Fenders all used solid pine cabinets. We looked at solid pine, mahogany, and various plywoods — birch ply, apple

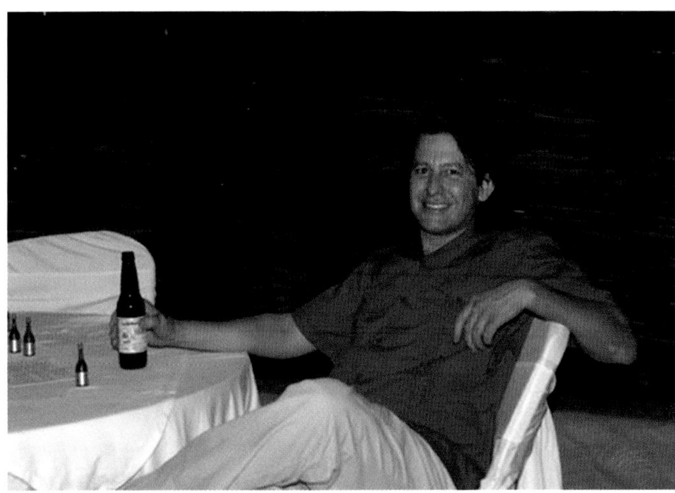

Bruce Zinky: "If the guitar doesn't sound good without an amp, it will never sound right with one."

ply, all kinds of stuff. Some of the pine ones sounded quite good; some didn't. They were inconsistent. We would take a chassis from one amp and put it in another cab made out of a different wood and do listening tests. We recorded all of these things, trying all the different cabs and woods. We took a scientific approach and concluded that it was very difficult to generalize. Some of the pine cabs sounded better than other pine cabs. Or this plywood one sounded better than that solid one, but this solid one sounded better than some other plywood cab. Even the grain in the wood can affect it terribly.

So we ended up going with plywood because it was more consistent. We used finger joints — frankly for marketing reasons. The fact is, there are stronger joints, but people seem to think that finger joints were the best way to go because that's what was used on old Fenders. There are other kinds of joints that are less expensive and hold up better, but we were trying to do exactly what Fender had done, wherever reasonable.

Paul Rivera: One thing that worries me is that there's a whole generation who did not grow up with a Fender amp, or with a great Magnatone, didn't really know what a Vox AC30 sounds like. Their reference standards are lesser amps, cheaper solid state things, whatever. I think there's an analogy in popular music. We are accepting audio standards that are absolutely declining. People listen to compressed MP3 files or streaming audio off the web through these dinky little speakers on the side of their computer, and they think it sounds OK. People go into this warehouse-like store and buy a box with a 1,000 watt system in it and they think that's hi-fi. I remember going to the audio salon, where they'd have a listening room and a couple dozen speaker systems you could A/B. Does anybody audition speakers anymore, other than audiophiles who spend a fortune? I worry about people becoming less discriminating, eating so many McDonald's hamburgers that they don't know anymore what a good meal is supposed to taste like. I mean, if you listen to a stereo hi-fi with an all-tube McIntosh amplifier, you're in heaven. My own generation was fortunate to be raised with some really righteous equipment.

Measurements That Matter

Albert Einstein once said, "Not everything that can be counted counts, and not everything that counts can be counted." Aspen Pittman offers an update.

Aspen Pittman: Measurements and specs are important, but some people make a big deal about measurements that are inaudible. So which measurements are worth paying attention to? The ones you can hear. Dick Rosmini was a virtuoso guitarist and also very technical, part of the team that developed the Portastudio [in 1979]. He wrote audio manuals and taught musicians how to become engineers and was one of the guys who got me into this business. I think Leo Fender would have liked what he had to say about all this, because Leo was not formally educated. He was an intu-

Aspen Pittman: "Many things that matter can't be measured, and many things that *can* be measured don't matter."

itive, self-taught man. He had great respect for people who had experience, whether they had degrees or not.

Dick Rosmini told me one time, "Many things that matter can't be measured, and many things that *can* be measured don't matter." When it comes to audio, that's one of the truest statements I've ever heard. That's why it's so important not to let anyone else tell you what sounds good to you. Just plug in, trust your ears, and listen.

The Hand of the Artist

Much of the guitar business is built on an assumption as common among players as beginners' calluses: *If I had the same gear as Stevie Ray (Eric, Kurt, Jimi), then I would have the same sound.* Well, the same gear is a start. A Tele can put you on the road to Gattonburg, a Strat to Claptonville, but the journey from there is a long one. (If you agree with Carlos Santana — you're not *supposed* to sound like anyone else — then the gotta-play-my-hero's-gear mentality is a road to nowhere anyway.)

Whatever your goals, picking the right amp is essential, and examining every component from caps to cabs can be useful, but it's a mistake to think the sound of our favorite player can be reduced to specs and schematics. Some of the very people who make their living building the most expensive amps for the most discriminating players caution against overvaluing gear at the expense of appreciating an artist's influence over his or her own sound. They are the first to say, don't let anyone, including us, tell you what sounds good to you.

Many of us get deep into the details of our gear, and yet some of the greatest artists seem to do just fine without classic vintage guitars and amps and without extensive knowledge of tubes, pickups, and so on.

Ritchie Fliegler: One day Mick Ronson and I were planning a guitar that was a replacement for his Telecaster. To me, Mick personified the almost clichéd simple, soft-spoken "bloke" who turned into a Leviathan when he strapped on his guitar. We were talking about the pickups for his new guitar, and he didn't know the term "coil." He called them "rounds." He said, "You know how on a Gibson the pickups have the two rounds? And on a Fender there is only one? Well, since this guitar is to replace a Tele, I would like the kind with only one."

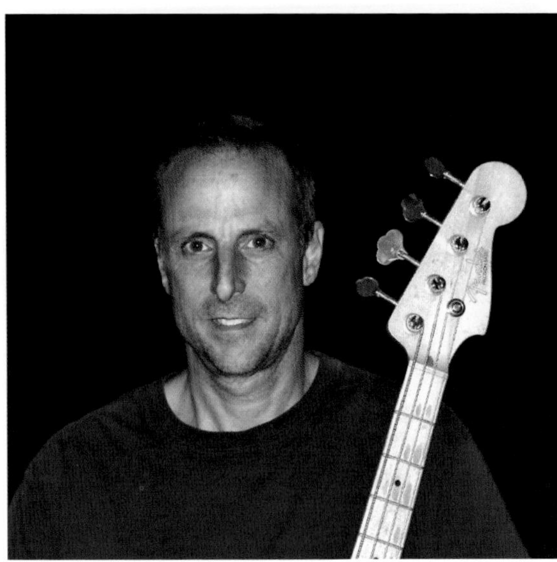

John Sprung: "Any amp sounds as good as the person playing through it."

A few years later, and only weeks before he passed away, I was working at Marshall, and Mick and I and our wives were enjoying a barbecue in my back yard. We got onto the subject of his Marshall Major. This amp was one of the first ones with the active tone controls and the different knob setup. I had seen it a number of times at both his house and at the home studio of Ian Hunter. This amp was a true rock relic. It had stickers and stencils identifying it as gear for *MOTT, Hunter-Ronson*, and *SPIDERS*! I plugged into it once for a second and true to the common wisdom, I thought it sounded like crap! Remember, this is not the Ritchie Blackmore amp, but a different, earlier design. I commented on what a piece of crap it was and how much better things were today. I didn't let up. This thing was junk — so say I! Mick leaned over right in my face and in the most fabulous, Yorkshire accented *sotto voce* said, "Well, I played that amp on all of the Bowie records and concerts with the Spiders, 'Panic in Detroit,' ya know. It's the main amp on the Hunter-Ronson record. Used it with Dylan and a few other reasonably successful endeavors. You may be right, but I guess it was good enough, eh?" May he rest in peace. His album title, *Play Don't Worry*, are words to live by. He was the best.

Blackie Pagano: I used to mix concerts for musicians straight out of the bayou, from around New Orleans. They would come up here to New York and do these singles dances at the Louisiana Community Bar & Grill on Broadway. These guys would come up with a U-Haul and their beat-up '80s Buick, and they'd all pile out of there, and what would come out of the trailer? Pawn shop stuff. A Cort guitar. Univox. Stuff that was rescued from the Dumpster. The lowest quality, least expensive gear in the world. And they would sit down and set this stuff up, and they rocked harder than anybody. How did they sound? Amazing. It didn't matter what they had in their hands. They could make music with anything.

So it's important to keep it in perspective. The most common misconception about tone is that its primary source is hardware. Tone comes from the heart of the musician. These tools exist to communicate the emotion of the musician, so what counts is what is in his heart, his intent, and his artistic perspective. As a musician, you have to have something to say.

John Sprung: As far as I'm concerned, any amp sounds as good as the person playing through it. I have heard some really crappy players using a 5F6-A tweed Bassman. They still sounded crappy.

Mark Baier: I feel sorry for guys who obsess about components. "Do I go with the Mullard GZ34? My buddy's got an Amperex! Maybe I should get one, too!" People sweat this stuff too much. I want to shake these guys and say, why worry about a 150 dollar rectifier or a 250 dollar transformer? You want to sound better? Listen to the proper records. *And practice your guitar!*

Blackie Pagano: That's right. As designers and builders, we are practicing our art, too. So of course we're going to build the best thing we possibly can. We're going to build you something that's going to knock your socks off, but it's so important to keep it in perspective. The most important thing is that you sit on the edge of your bed every day with your guitar.

Steve Carr: I had the good fortune to hang out with Eric Johnson and to talk to him about sound. He likes his amp to sound a certain way. On the clean side, he likes it extremely bright — make-your-teeth-fall-out bright. If you

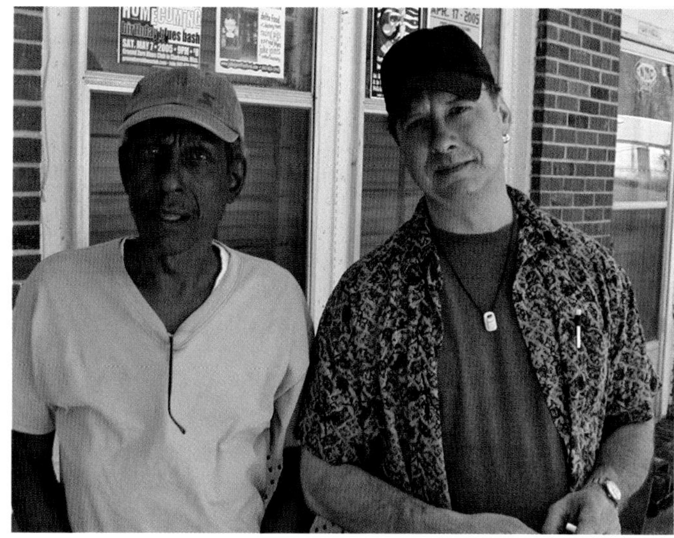

Mark Baier of Victoria Amp Co., right, with Frank "Rat" Ratliff, proprietor of Clarksdale, Mississippi's Riverside Hotel ("Where Hospitality Meets the Blues"): "You want to sound better? Listen to the proper records. *And practice your guitar!*" Photo courtesy *ToneQuest Report.*

took an amp like that and put it in a store, no one would buy it. People would think it was broken. But when he plays it, he can control it. His hands can make it sound dark if he wants it to, but all that top end is there for him to work with. We all have to remember that guys like that are phenomenal; they get the sound they want with their hands. That amp is not necessarily going to work that way for the rest of us mortals.

Andy Ellis: I once had the pleasure of taking a guitar lesson with Eric Johnson. In addition to laying the groundwork for a *Guitar Player* master class (May '96), this encounter proved the truth in the old saying, "Your tone is in your hands." Eric was camped out at an extended-stay hotel in Burbank, and throughout our session he played his faithful '54 Stratocaster through an old blackface Fender Champ at bedroom volume. No stompbox, just straight into the input jack via a red, slightly kinky Bill Lawrence guitar cable tipped with solderless plugs. Eric's single-note leads sounded warm and buttery — like a Gypsy violinist — while his chords rang with the clarity of silver bells. Hearing him so casually produce his million-dollar tone, I realized how all that shimmering detail and sweet sustain came from his touch and attack rather than an elaborate, multi-amp rig.

Ritchie Fliegler: My EICO integrated amp uses 6BQ5s in a classic push/pull, cathode bias configuration — just like a Vox AC30. Try as I might, there is no Brian May or "Paperback Writer" in there to be found. Could it be something else? Indeed, *this* is the art form, and it has little to do with the bits and everything to do with the designer's vision and abilities. To place so much emphasis on the hardware is a disservice to the artist. I don't believe anyone cares what brand of paint or the actual pigments da Vinci used to create the Mona Lisa. We should do the same when we're blowing our brains out with a cranked Vibroverb — focus on the art and wonder what was the muse.

Alan Douglas, studio engineer, in *Guitar Player*, June 2001: Almost 99.9% of Eric Clapton's sound is in his fingers … The first time I worked with Eric, he was demoing some tunes for a film, and there was no amp at the session. I was a huge fan of Eric's from his Cream days, and I remember thinking, "You've got to get an amp — this will never work." But I plugged him into a tube preamp, dialed up some reverb and delay, and it sounded exactly like Eric Clapton.

Are Old Tubes Better?

Many vintage amp buffs have long believed that whether we're talking about preamp tubes, power tubes, or rectifiers, old tubes are superior to new ones. For years, virtually all experts agreed. Quality control was the reason. Many imported tubes from the '80s and '90s were far less consistent and thus less reliable than their American made predecessors from the '50s, '60s, and '70s. Still, at least some new tubes sounded fine. In 2001, Mike Kropotkin wrote in *ToneQuest Report*: "In general, the production quality of NOS [New Old Stock] tubes is far superior to that of tubes produced today in countries like China, the Soviet Union, and Yugoslavia. The metallurgy, production techniques, and quality control were vastly superior." But he added, "This is not to say that all current production tubes are bad. Many have decent to excellent tone."

We should be clear on what we mean by old. A Soviet tube manufactured in, say, the mid 1980s is two decades old or more, yet it dates to a time well past the tube's commercial heyday and is hardly old for purposes of this discussion, in the way that, say, RCA black plates from the '60s are old.

At some factories, for some tubes, quality has markedly improved in recent years even though the romance of old tubes still glows.

Aspen Pittman: It's a general conception that old tubes are better. I'm not sure it's true at all in certain cases. Are the reissue Strats today as good as the originals? In many ways they're better. Are they as old? No [laughs]. At Groove Tubes we were able to reproduce the GE 6L6 because we bought many of the machines they made the parts on and enlisted some of the original vendors and bought original plate materials. We make them now on a limited basis in San Fernando, California. We've altered the process since we started, and we now outsource some of the processing to keep the price within reach of our customers, but these components are still about 70 percent U.S. made. I think

Steve Carr: "The main point of understanding an amplifier is that it's not just a collection of isolated parts; it's a collection of parts that all interact with each other. It's dangerous to look at one part and say, this part is going to make the amp do this or that. It might make the amp lean in that direction, but it depends on everything else."

these tubes we've "reissued" are every bit as good as the originals. We've proved it in side by side tests, and customer demand confirms it. For ninety-nine guys out of a hundred — even guys with "dog ears" — you plug in my GE 6L6 and the original, and they can't tell the difference. I mean, I can't tell the difference, and I've got dog ears, too.

Mark Baier: I think there's way too much rhetoric going around about one tube being "better" than another. They're different, to be sure. I think you have to have fairly discerning ears to hear the difference between a General Electric and an RCA tube. It's not something that's immediately apparent. You've really got to be into it, and *want* to hear the difference. There's too much emphasis on having to have new old stock RCA black plates, or having to have that Mullard 12AX7.

One of the biggest misconceptions is that new tubes aren't any good. The tubes coming out of China and Eastern Europe now are better than they've ever been. The Chinese in particular have been very accommodating to the market, and they've made a lot of strides to improve their products. They've improved tooling because people like Aspen Pittman and Tom McNeil at Magic Parts and Ruby Tubes have really gotten involved with those factories and made them realize that they could do a better job, and the factories went ahead and did it. Like Groove Tubes' 12AX7C, which I use, is a Chinese made tube, and it's awesome, really reliable, balanced, and quiet. It behaves exactly like a 12AX7 ought to.

You think about what goes into making a 12AX7, all those tiny parts, tight tolerances, the windings — man, I'm happy to pay eight bucks for all that technology. With a couple of exceptions, the tubes coming out of Eastern Europe and China could be as good, or approaching as good, as the tubes from back in the day. It's heretical to say that. I know people are going to leap all over me, and certainly I would love to be putting vintage 1967 RCA 7025 tubes in all my own amplifiers. That was a great 12AX7. They're not being made anymore, but many available tubes are excellent. People should not sweat the tube thing quite so much.

Blackie Pagano: What's odd about musicians is that they're half creative and half ridiculously traditional. Ironically enough, they're actually resistant to new ideas. It's the rare individual who looks at a design that's really fresh and may have significant design advances over what they've seen time and time again, and who will see the value in it right away. It's just human nature to react with skepticism to something new. The vintage fetishism and all the insane values of these products has also made people resistant to new stuff and encouraged this idea that only the old stuff is good, which is bullshit. It's affected musicians' open-mindedness, which is sad. New possibilities come up every single day.

So it's important to look at a tube, or any component, in the larger context of the amp's design.
Ritchie Fliegler: Right. A lot has happened since I wrote [in *Complete Guide*, 1994] that new tubes just don't sound as good as old ones. There are many differences between new tubes and older NOS stuff. No value judgments here. They are simply different.

The old amps sound better to my ears with the tubes they were designed to use: old ones. But over the last ten years or so, the creators of many new amps have assumed the new tubes, and thus those amps sound better with new tubes (surprise). At the least, with new tubes they sound like their designers want them to sound. I find that NOS stuff (very broad brush here) in a new amp sounds harsh and sterile, because most new tubes are "softer" and more "gainy" than the original designs. Remember, NOS tubes were designed for radios and TVs, not for screaming solos, so they are very likely to be microphonic when used in modern amps with even a bit of gain.

Aspen Pittman: NOS preamp tubes can be just fine in a vintage or vintage reissue type amp, but they tend not to work as well in high gain circuits like we see in most amps made today. It's a mechanical issue. Old tubes usually had heavier or larger plates, and that heavier structure just seems to "ring" more.

And it works both ways, right? Unsatisfactory tone can sometimes result not only from putting old tubes in new amps but also putting new tubes in old ones.
Hartley Peavey: In the old days when tubes were made in the United States, they were very conservatively rated, and you could get by with putting in more voltage than the ratings called for. But you have to be very careful with doing things like putting a lot of newer, imported tubes into old Deluxe amplifiers. They'll blow up, in a heartbeat.

Rating Transformers, "Logo Inductance"

Is the tonal significance of the output transformer underrated?

Mark Baier: Maybe it's overrated [laughs]. Ten years ago when I started Victoria Amps, I had to have output transformers and power transformers made for me. I couldn't get them from a catalog or supply house, but nowadays I can think of a dozen places. Everybody's making these things.

The transformer is important, and you'll hear a difference between a good one and a not so good one. The sound may not be better or worse, just different. But you see these bulletin boards on the web where people say if you don't have this or that transformer you're not getting the best sound. I guess you can discern a difference, but how can you make any kind of qualitative statement between one transformer and another one that costs five times as much? What are you going to do? Hit a big E chord and then hurry up and unsolder one and solder the other one in and play another E chord? A lot of this expensive transformer mentality is smoke and mirrors, and some of these sellers are just performing a "cashectomy" on guitar players once in a while. Sure, a transformer is important, but it's just one of many elements.

Ritchie Fliegler: Just as studies have shown that smell is the most evocative of the senses, sound is the most fleeting. You can't remember the subtleties of what an amp sounded like yesterday, so it's hard to compare it to the one you're playing today unless you're talking about blatant differences. That's just the way the brain works. To compare two transformers, they would really have to be side by side, and Mark's right, of course. The player can't unsolder one and hook up another one instantaneously.

But we can do that in the lab, by constructing a switcher to instantly flip back and forth between transformers. We did it at Marshall, and we've done it at Fender, too. When we were re-doing the plexi amp when I was at Marshall, we took an authentic, very expensive transformer over to England and used this switcher to make instantaneous comparisons. We went back and forth and said, "Um, is the switch working? It is? Are you sure? [Laughs.] I can hardly tell the difference!" It turned out the filter caps in the power supply made a huge difference, but the difference between transformers was nowhere near what we expected, actually quite subtle.

That experience begat a term we used in-house at Marshall and we use it here at Fender, too: "logo inductance." When you put the logo on it, *then* it sounds right [laughs]. If you doubt that, go to a fine Japanese restaurant and order some raw fish, and see how beautifully it's prepared. With food, we taste with our eyes as well as our taste buds. With amps, we hear not only with our ears but also with our eyes — and our preconceptions.

Hand Wiring, Point to Point

For many years, all Fender tube amps were hand wired. Some still are (see Chaps. 22, 23, 25), although printed circuit boards have replaced the old method in the vast majority of models from Fender and other major manufacturers (Chap. 15).

Vintage Fenders, and other old amps wired up with methods other than printed circuit boards, are sometimes referred to as having "point to point" wiring. In some cases (a 5C1 Champ, for example) the term is appropriate, but in its strictest sense, "point to point" does not apply to most old Fenders, because even though their solder joints and wiring were painstakingly connected by hand, their components were connected on vulcanized fiber boards with eyelets.

Dave Hunter, in *Vintage Guitar* magazine: "Genuine point to point circuitry involves connecting each point in the signal chain and power stage with the components themselves — which is to say capacitors and resistors are usually *soldered directly between the tube socket contacts, pots and input jacks, and so on* [emphasis added]."

Early point to point guitar amps were similar to other electronic devices of the time. Andy Marshall of THD: "If you open up, say, an old PA head from the '40s through the early '60s, you'll see tube sockets right on the chassis. They had potentiometers, switches, jacks, and a terminal strip that is just a vertical bar with terminals clamped onto it. They would run a resistor from tube socket pin 3, or whatever it was, to a terminal strip, a capacitor, or a switch. It was very labor intensive, but the whole point was, labor was cheap. So in true point to point, there was no actual board of any sort. In some cases there weren't even terminal strips; the components were just tied together and literally hanging in the air.

"But in building something like, say, a '58 Bassman, in one fell swoop a stamping machine would put all the holes in the eyelet board, which was almost always coated in wax. You'd put metal eyelets in those holes and put it in a press, with the eyelets' 'mushrooms' on top, and then you'd press them all and form little mushrooms on the bottom as well, which would hold the eyelets in place. Those eyelets became the tie points [for connecting components]."

Because the inductive or capacitive fields thrown off by resistors, capacitors, and wires can affect surrounding components, older point to point amps can sometimes perform inconsistently relative to each other. (Note: Steve Carr, of Carr Amps, explains, "For us, at least, we find point to point to be very consistent; it may have varied a lot back when labor was cheap and there was not much in the way of quality control or testing, but that's not the case today.") Ritchie Fliegler: "This 'proximity effect' of components interacting with each other could be a blessing or a curse. In an effort to deal with oscillations, RFI [radio frequency interference], or some other such noise, sometimes old radios would use what was called a 'gimmick.' Simply put, a gimmick was a twisted pair of wires or a single wire dressed in such a way as to form a very small-value capacitor. This 'cap' would filter out unwanted artifacts."

Serviceability was of course a top priority for Leo Fender, and eyelet boards made life easier when repairs were necessary. On the top side of the board, the repair person would encounter capacitors and resistors lined up neatly; on the bottom, he would see wires connecting the different eyelets. Mark Baier, of Victoria Amps: "This service issue is key, because the fiber eyelet board not only provided consistency but also isolated the majority of components from the vibrations and shocks of professional use and abuse. Those true point to point amps à la Silvertone and Supro were more vulnerable by comparison.

"And don't forget the microphonic character of the eyelet board and its contributions to overall dynamics. At high volumes the cabinet vibrations are transferred throughout the chassis, creating a very lively electro-mechanical environment. The eyelet board's microphonic tendencies contribute to what I refer to as the 'vocal' nature of non-reverb tweed Fenders. I can't tell you how many people have told me they don't miss the reverb on tweed amps, and eyelet board electro-mechanical 'out-freakage' plays a key part in that sound."

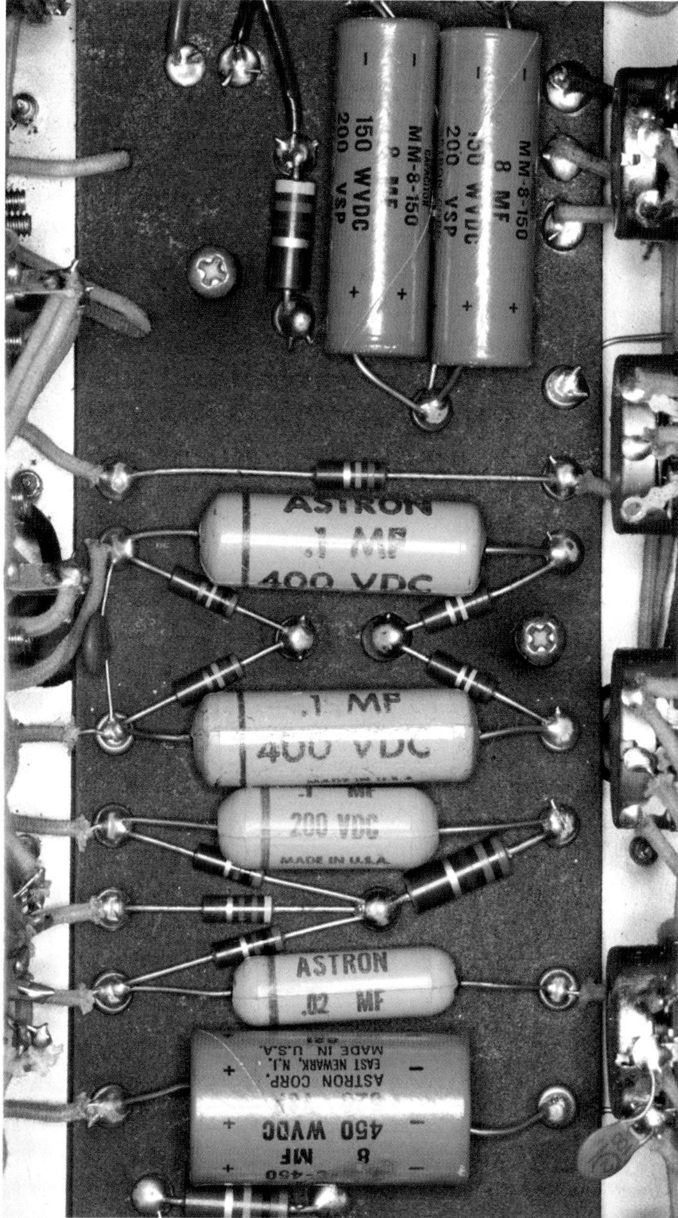

The components in most vintage Fenders are wired onto eyelet boards, which facilitate consistency, structural integrity, and what Mark Baier calls their "vocal" character.

This astonishingly clean tweed Twin from August 1959, serial no. A00636, belongs to photographer Ken Settle. Keith Richards: "As the all-around great amp of all time, it's the Twin."

CHAPTER TWENTY-NINE

29

The Great American Amp

If you had to pick just one, what is the Great American Amplifier, the tone machine *in excelsis*, the amp of amps?

"It would be the Dual Professional, with the angled front and the chrome bumper down the center. Not only does it have a good sound, it's got an intrinsic attraction because it was Leo Fender's first green-lighting of an amp with two speakers. Maybe it's only 18 watts or so, but the circuit design provides a tremendous tone. I picked up a particular Dual Professional in Memphis. It's a foreboding looking thing. People look at it and say, 'Jeez, I'd like to play through it, but do I need a tetanus shot first?' I've amassed a significant collection just out of the fascination and love of this crazy thing. I may have the largest stash of them, about 20 or 25 Dual Professionals. This model was sort of a stepchild and unwisely overlooked by many, but I just enjoy them. The ones that were basket cases went into the shop, and one by one they've all been returned to good working order. We plug 'em in just to keep 'em lit up every now and again."

— Billy Gibbons

"The late-'50s 5F6-A tweed Bassman is it. That is the amp, or more correctly the circuit, that just about every modern tube amp is based on. Marshall was the first to clone that amp, and many others followed. The essence of that circuit even lives on in all of my designs. It is an amazingly simple and efficient design."

— Mike Soldano

"The Great American Amp is the Twin Reverb, because Johnny Thunders played two of them."

— Blackie Pagano,
amp builder/repairman, Tubesville Thermionics

"I'm crazy about the Fender Twin. I've always loved that one. To me, it's one of the best amps ever made."

— B.B. King

"Deluxe Reverb, blackface. I think it's the best they ever did. Sometimes with multiple speakers you get phase cancellations. Twins are great, but they have a hollow mid sound. Four 10s are great, but looking at all the factors, you've got the whole ball of wax in the Deluxe Reverb: a single 12, usually a pretty good one, well suited to the power of the amp, a very sophisticated front end with a good sound, that 6V6 cream — full fat and cholesterol! — the reverb of choice, the right size, the right weight. If I had

Hear the "Swing Spectacular" Jam, featuring the high-powered tweed Twin, Tracks 47 - 48.

to have one amp to be stuck with on the desert island, give me a Deluxe Reverb. Turn it up, get a nice little breakup. Turn it down — sweet and clean!"

— Aspen Pittman,
author of *The Tube Amp Book*

"If I had to pick one amplifier for all-around use, it would have to be the [tweed] Twin, absolutely. There are little specialty jobs, but as the all-around great amp of all time, it's the Twin. I don't think there's anything that's as good sounding or as sturdy or as reliable. It's got the edge on all the others, especially if you're playing a Fender guitar through it."

— Keith Richards

"Blackface Super Reverb. Perfect amount of watts for almost any venue, you can crank it, use the volume control on your guitar to dial in clean to classic overdriven tones, or use it at a lower volume setting with a stomp box of choice and go from the greatest clean/slightly overdriven sound to pure, gristle-infested pigdom with a kick of the pedal, versatility being a word that falls short when describing this console of delight. Delish 'verb and vibrato. The four 10 inch speakers deliver a tight bottom end and enough high end to impale at 40 paces, if that's your fancy. You can tip it on its legs to take your head off or face it backward to avoid launching live ammo at your crowd and still sound butane. There's plenty of room in the back to stash cords, pedals and whatnot for easy transport. Not as heavy as a Twin, I might add. Oh yeah, and it records great! A discography of classic guitar tracks where a Super was used would surprise many, but not I. Coming in a close second would be the blackface Vibrolux or tweed Bassman, but if I had to pick one, it would be the Super."

— Greg Koch

"I met Mark Knopfler at a gig at the Royal Albert Hall. It turned out he was a Humble Pie fan, and I'm quite a Dire Straits fan, so we had a good old talk. He was very kind to let us record at his beautiful studio in London, and he told his people to send down all his amps for us, very generously. They brought in the brown Vibrolux he used on 'Sultans of Swing,' and we all went, *oooooh*. I played my signature black Les Paul Custom through that amp for a track called 'Cup of Tea' on my instrumental album *Fingerprints*. It was fantastic, so after that I went on the holy grail search for one of those, and I just got one recently.

But to pick the great American amp, I'm on the fence on this one. It's either the '59 tweed Twin or the Scholz Rockman [laughs]. No, really, I think the greatest Ameri-

Chickenheads on chrome and a classic circuit inside a righteous tweed box: The 5E3 lives! As we saw in previous chapters, Neil Young, Bill Kirchen, John Fogerty and countless others would place the original 5E3 Deluxe of the mid 1950s among the greatest amps of all time. Recalling that classic narrow panel Fender, the '57 Deluxe Amp reissue is hand-wired on an eyelet board and features a 12" Jensen P12Q, a solid pine cab, and a pair of Groove Tubes GT6V6s. Something of a little brother to the hand-wired '57 Twin reissue, this 12W tweed tone machine was introduced in 2007.

Hear the "Need for Tweed" Jam, featuring the 2007 '57 Deluxe, Tracks 30 - 31.

can amp is either the '59 tweed Twin, or for me personally I'd have to go with the '59 tweed Bassman. I'm much better known for Marshalls, but I love Fender amps and have collected a bunch of them over the years. If it weren't for the Bassman, Jim Marshall wouldn't have copied it and made a mistake, and come up with a Marshall [laughs]. He didn't quite get it right, but at the same time he got it beautifully right, if you know what I mean."

— Peter Frampton

"It would have to be the '59 Bassman. Its influence was unequalled worldwide, and it formed the bedrock for countless variations, not the least of which were Marshall and Boogie. That it remains in production is a testament to the integrity and innovation of its fundamental design. With multiple speakers and high output, it must have been quite cutting-edge for the 1950s. The fact that it had such a brief life prior to being discontinued, presumably due to a lack of sales, only adds to the fascination — a commercial failure when judged by its intended application as a bass amp, yet considered the gold standard of guitar amplification."

— Michael Doyle,
author of *The Sound of Rock: A History of Marshall Valve Guitar Amplifiers*, and *The History of Marshall: The Illustrated Story of "The Sound of Rock,"* among others

"I am partial to the Fenders with 15 inch speakers. For me this boils down to two amps: the 1964 Vibroverb with a JBL, and the 1958 or 1959 Pro with the Jensen P15N. I think 15s are underappreciated. Some claim they lack the highs needed for an all-around full range sound. I disagree. A good Pro or Vibroverb will rip your ears off if set correctly. They have less of the low-end distortion that the 12 and 10 inch speakers suffer from. The 12s get woofy, and the 10s just crap out. Fender amps are great because of their full and even range of sound. You need a speaker that can reproduce this quality. The 15 does that job better than the others. So if I had to pick one amp, it would be the tweed Pro — warmer sounding than the Vibroverb, and way cooler looking!"

— John Sprung,
collector and co-author of
Fender Amps: The First Fifty Years

"For me, the Fender Twin Reverb is the best amp in the world — you can do *anything* with it."

— Henry Garza, in *Guitar Player*

"What's the greatest amplifier? I know who got the greatest name. Fender. I got one sitting right there [points to an old Concert]."

— John Lee Hooker, in *Guitar Player*

"If I had to pick just one, I'd pick three [laughs]. In the studio, it's the Deluxe Reverb and the Vibrolux Reverb. So many session guys I know love Deluxe Reverbs. Jeff [Beck] has used mine several times, and also a little Super that I have, a brown 2x10. The reverb is important, because you're not always sure if the studio is going to have the right sound. I prefer to hear my guitar sound as I'm recording it, rather than adding the reverb later. The Vibrolux is almost the same circuit as the Super Reverb, but it has the different speaker combination, and it breaks up really nice. When I'm playing out, I like a Super Reverb on the stage, or two Super Reverbs to get more coverage. That's a great combination."

— Seymour Duncan

A charter member of Nashville's original "A Team" of session players and a multiple winner of NARAS' Superpicker award, the legendary Harold Bradley played on scads of hits by everyone from Elvis Presley and Buddy Holly to Perry Como and Burl Ives. His pal Grady Martin received the Nashville Entertainment Association's Master Award, among stacks of other accolades, after playing memorable guitar lines on Marty Robbins' "El Paso," Roy Orbison's "Oh, Pretty Woman," Willie Nelson's "On the Road Again," and scores more over a decades-long career. Nashville session guitarist Jimmy Capps said of Grady Martin: "Grady was the king. Whatever kind of music you were playing, he'd find exactly the right part. He never seemed to run out of ideas and he never played the same lick twice. Everyone who plays a solo in this town owes something to Grady."

On many of his sessions, Martin borrowed Bradley's blackface Twin Reverb. Bradley told *Guitar Player*: "I think it's the best amp in the world. Grady Martin used it for all the stuff he did on Columbia. Every year the Fender,

Gibson, and Rickenbacker people would come to Nashville, and they'd bring new amps and guitars. When they gave Grady an amp, he'd set it up there, but he would never make it through the first song before asking me, 'Where's *your* amp?' He'd take the amp they gave him, slam it down hard on the concrete floor, and plug into my Twin."

"I vote for a silverface Twin Reverb. It's flexible, loud if desired, commonplace and thus not selling for insane sums of money. And screw that vintage snobbery anyway."

— **Eric Barbour,** Senior Editor, *Vacuum Tube Valley*

"The Paul Rivera-designed Super Champ is the most *fun* amp I know of! It's the lightest, most amazing sounding amp ever made. Not only is it great for playing at low volumes at home (terrific for rehearsals) and in the studio,

The now collectible, 18W, 1x10 Super Champ (shown here in both the stock version and the rare Super Pro Series edition, Chap. 18) was one of Fender's most noteworthy success stories from 1982 to 1986. This 2x6V6 powerhouse featured a three-spring Accutronics reverb, plenty of volume, and a high-gain circuit, all in a compact package. Paul Rivera: "The Super Champ became almost a cult amplifier, selling something like 7,000 or 8,000 a year. It epitomized the idea of the pocket rocket, a killer sound in a tiny package. Today they're just about worshiped, and cost a fortune on eBay."

but it is one of the best recording amps ever. Put a microphone in front of it and you'll discover some of the biggest clean and dirty sounds of all time. Most great amps are fun a lot of the time, but the Super Champ is the only amp I know that is fun all of the time."

— Henry Kaiser

"The greatest amp I've ever owned is a little Fender Super Champ with the stock Fender speaker, not the Electro-Voice."

— Robert Quine, in *Guitar Player*

"For me the one Fender that can nearly do it all is the '63-'64 blackface, single-15 Vibroverb. It can do sweet clean tones from high-reverb surf sounds to mellow, big-box jazz tones, to sparkly 'spank tones' for country/western Tele players. I've even heard them put to good use by pedal steel players. And its 40-plus watts and relatively high B+ voltage let it stay clean at higher volumes. Regarding overdrive, we all know what Stevie Ray did with his Vibroverbs! These babies have a commanding growl when cranked, and when kissed on the front end with a Tube Screamer, they'll peel paint. For overdrive sounds I prefer Vibros loaded with the non-premium CTS 15 as opposed to the JBL D140 that was offered as an upgrade. The CTS's can handle the low end without 'flabbing out,' while retaining the upper-end bite without the harshness. For Teles or Les Pauls, I'd have to say that the blackface Vibroverb is my desert island amp, because it's the 'Versaverb' of Fenders."

— Don Morris, ElectroPlex Amps

"The four-10 Bassman. After playing through really toneless British amps, I always loved the sound of Fenders, which had such high fidelity in comparison. The first one I came across was a little brown Super, with the two 10s. It wasn't very loud, but it had the tone, just fantastic. That would have been around '62 or '63. Around that time, Fender amps were starting to come into the UK. The guitars had come in first.

"The first Fender I owned was a piggyback Bassman, which I really liked, but I'd heard through the grapevine about the tweed ones. We used to pick up information from across the Atlantic about what guys were using, and we saw pictures of guys with these old tweed amps, and they looked really cool. It seemed like everybody was using them, but of course we couldn't find them in England because by the time we started importing Fender amps they had ceased making the tweeds.

"Sometime in 1964 a guy came up to me at a gig. He said, 'I've got an old Fender Bassman, I'm a bass player, and you've got the new piggyback Bassman — do you want to do a swap?' And I said, *yeah!* [Laughs.] I'd heard the tweed Bassmans were quite popular, so I ended up with the four-10, and about a year later I acquired another one. I would guess there were only three or four in the whole country at the time, and I had two of them, and I still have them. I used my Bassman with Chris Farlowe, with Heads, Hands & Feet, and with other bands all through the '60s."

— Albert Lee

Early-'60s brown Super. Mike Letts, *ToneQuest Report*: "This is one that some have called the best Fender amp ever. It has the cool tremolo in a compact 2x10 ... It will have the same tonal attributes as its big brother [the Concert] in a package more players might find useful — still loud, but more club-friendly."

"I've still got a Bassman at home in Texas. That's probably my all-time favorite amp. The four 10s work better than any other configuration."

— Johnny Winter, in *Guitar Player*

"I always like the Vibrolux. A Deluxe is too small, and the Twin Reverb/Showman ultra clean thing is not my bag, baby. The Vibrolux sits right in that sweet spot, for me anyway."

— Ritchie Fliegler,
author of *Amps! The Other Half of Rock 'n' Roll* and *The Complete Guide to Guitar and Amp Maintenance*

"A great amplifier just makes you play great, without a doubt. In the early days over here [in England], everybody aspired to the [Vox] AC30, because that's what Hank Marvin used, and he is the god here. AC30s were *heads* above everything else — until we could get Fender amps. The great American amp? The Deluxe, that's my favorite, and I'm lucky enough to have a couple of tweed ones, and one of them has an original extension cab from 1959. They're fantastic because if you look in the back of the extension cab, there's a couple of hooks and about 50 feet of cable going round and round. With the extension cab, the Deluxe is basically like a 20 watt Twin. I got it about 25 years ago, and then two years ago I found another extension cab in the States.

"My *other* favorite amp is, of course, the high-power Twin with the four 5881s. And I've just become the proud owner of a tweed Vibrolux. I also have one of the very first Showmans, a one-15. Dirt, you're not gonna get, but for a full, huge, clean sound it's just fantastic. I love 'em. I use mine for bass, too, not too loud. But if I had to pick one it would have to be the Deluxe because of the fullness, the dirt, and you're not blowing your ears off. Such a pure sound, especially with my '53 Tele!"

— Alan Rogan,
UK guitar tech extraordinaire (Clapton, Harrison, Richards, Townshend, Entwistle, Walsh, etc.)

"Fender Bassmans. I still can't find anything better."

— Merle Haggard, in *Guitar Player*

"The tweed Deluxe is one of the best designs from any amplifier company, a staple for any recording studio or performing player. Another amp that I think doesn't get the acclaim it deserves is the three-10 Bandmaster. It's a little more overdrivey and breaks up at a little lower volume than some of the amps. For many years I was a fan of the four-10 Bassman. I used to use two of them onstage. But if I had to pick one, it would be the low-power tweed Twin. Now, the high-powered tweed Twin is by far the most collectible Fender. It's 'the one,' no doubt, the most valuable of all. They're selling for 20,000 dollars now, whereas a nice four-10 Bassman is 8,000 to 10,000 dollars. But I've got to say the low-power Twin, either the dual rectifier model or the older single-tube, metal tube rectifier model, is the classic two-12 amp, my personal favorite."

— "Burst Brother" Drew Berlin, Guitar Center

"Fifteen or twenty years ago, a friend gave me a custom-covered Twin Reverb, and it's been my main amplifier ever since. It's terrific. I can put my guitar on the right side and a microphone on the left. I don't do that when I'm performing, but it's convenient when you have someone over for rehearsals. It's an extraordinary amplifier. I love the sound of it. You can play any kind of music on it. I can even get kind of an acoustic sound out of it just by not turning it up too loud. I also have two little Fenders with reverb, but I'm not sure of the model names. Sometimes when a bass player comes over, he doesn't have to bring an amp. He just plays through the big Fender, and I play through one of the small ones. We're not playing it loud, and it sounds great."

— Mary Kaye

"I believe the original 1963 brown Tolex Vibroverb represents the high point of self-contained combo amp design. It followed the great 2x10 tweed and brown Super amps but added reverb. The blackface Vibrolux Reverb carried on the tradition and is a close second in my book."

— Richard Smith,
author of *Fender: The Sound Heard 'Round The World*

"In the bedroom, it's the narrow panel Deluxe because it's just so much fun to play through. For gigging in clubs, the brown Vibroverb. It's loud and sweet enough. It's got it all — but lose the original Oxfords."

— John Peden

"I taught a 16-week course called Rock Guitar: Tones and Techniques. Each student brought in his or her complete rig and did a demonstration. It's amazing how many non-performing young players have expensive (2,000 dollars plus) amps by Line 6, Marshall, and the like. I brought in my simple Fender Champ, which Art Thompson slightly modified by inserting a tube from the 1950s. And wouldn't you know it, just about everyone who played through it declared it the best sounding amp in the room. No matter how many copycat sounds these high-tech amps can conjure, you just can't beat that warm, beautiful, enveloping Fender sound. Its tone reaches straight into the human heart."

— Jas Obrecht

The 1963 mid-line amps displayed here — all AA763s or AB763s — include several models selected as the Great American Amp by our panel: Vibroverb, Vibrolux, Deluxe, and Deluxe Reverb. (They are accompanied by one of several cosmetic variations of the 6G15 reverb unit.)

Hear the blackface Deluxe Reverb, Tracks 13 - 21.

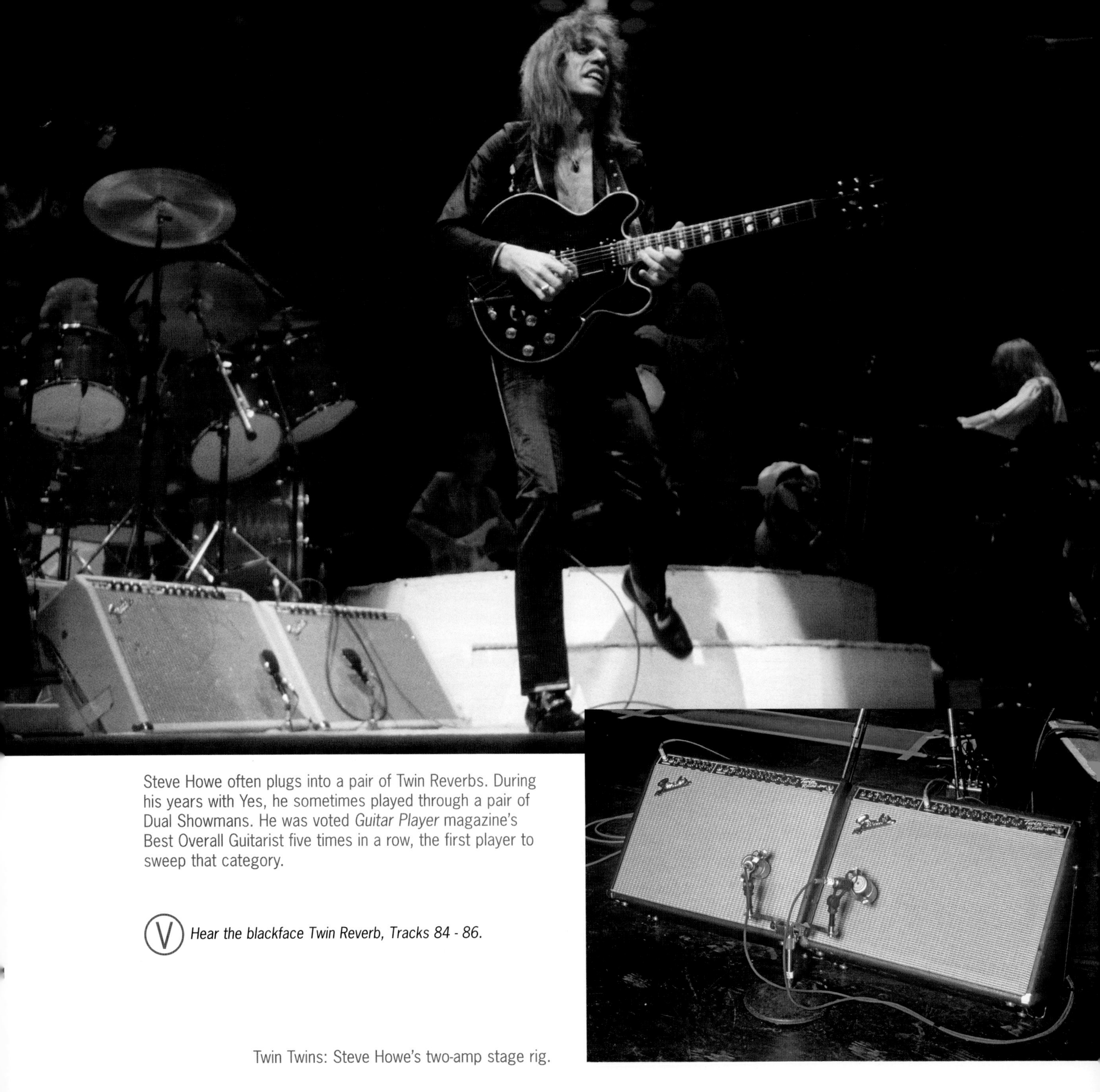

Steve Howe often plugs into a pair of Twin Reverbs. During his years with Yes, he sometimes played through a pair of Dual Showmans. He was voted *Guitar Player* magazine's Best Overall Guitarist five times in a row, the first player to sweep that category.

Ⓥ *Hear the blackface Twin Reverb, Tracks 84 - 86.*

Twin Twins: Steve Howe's two-amp stage rig.

You want bright? How about a Tele through a Super Reverb?

Greg Koch: "From the greatest clean/slightly overdriven sound to pure, gristle-infested pigdom ... versatility being a word that falls short when describing this console of delight."

Nils Lofgren used the same old Super Reverb on many recordings, usually with its volume, bass, and reverb controls set around 5, the middle and treble on 10, and the Bright switch on. Quoted in *Guitar Player*: "The nice thing about my Super is up until around 3 it stays clean, trebly and biting, but warm at the same time. From 3 on, it thickens out very gradually. All the way up to 10, it's very thick, and it still retains that percussiveness." Ronnie Earl described a Strat through a Super Reverb as "a marriage made in heaven."

> "For rhythm tone and vibe, gotta pick the tweed Bassman. For the sheer number of tours, it's the Twin Reverb — B.B. King, right? For the sheer number of amps that everybody likes, the Deluxe. The best Fender I ever played through was a tweed Twin that sounded like a Marshall — I mean, where do you think Marshalls came from? And blackface and silverface Super Reverbs — they always work. They just plain work. By the way, the two-12 Bandmaster was the best sounding speaker cab ever — period, bye bye, end of story. But after all this spiel, the answer to your question — what's the Great American Amp? — it's Fender, that's all. That's all you have to say. Fender."
>
> — Paul Reed Smith

Hear the "Super Shuffle Soufflé" Jam, featuring the blackface Super Reverb, Tracks 71 - 72.

Prized collectibles, from left: brown Tolex 1x12 extension cabinet, Champion 800, wide panel Bandmaster, wooden-cabinet Pro, blackface Vibrolux, and wide panel 1x15 extension cab.

APPENDIX

Amp Collectors' Roundtable

Investment, Nostalgia, The Fun Factor

This roundtable addresses several aspects of vintage amp collecting. Our panel: Greg Gagliano, George Gruhn, Greg Huntington, John Peden, Richard Smith, and John Sprung, all of whom are identified in the Acknowledgments. They are joined by the author and Peter Frampton.

In what ways are the amp collecting and guitar collecting markets similar and different?

Greg G.: They are the same in that you have people who speculatively collect guitars and amps for (1) investment reasons, (2) the "cool guy" factor, (3) historical purpose, and (4) simple enjoyment. They are even the same in the way amps and guitars are hyped and hawked by dealers: "tone to the bone," "as used by Pete Townshend," etc. But the amp market is so much smaller, perhaps because amps are seen as tools much more than guitars. Thus, modern amps are often adequate for a musician's needs.

The originality and condition requirements are also different. A guitar collector wants a mint, original example, but amp collectors aren't as picky. Sure, there are a handful of anal retentive collectors who want a factory stock amp (right down to the original tubes!), even if it is electronically unsound due to bad components, but most will accept an amp that is a bit tattered and in need of a speaker recone. The main issue with vintage Fenders is that they have their original transformers, notably the output transformer, since these have a major influence on tone.

John S.: Amp collecting and guitar collecting are quite similar. It is true that amp collectors are a bit less fussy about 100% originality. Amps are plugged directly into the wall when being used. A lot of voltage and heat are generated. It is nearly impossible to use an amp for any extended period without wearing out some components. Guitars, on the other hand, operate with millivolts. It is possible to use a guitar for many years with little consequence to the instrument. I have noticed the response from outsiders viewing my collections. I get a lot more notice for a roomful of guitars than for a roomful of amps. Guitars are much sexier, colorful, and just more interesting to the layman.

John P.: It's hard to imagine an amp collector who doesn't play and collect guitars as well, but many guitar collectors seem clueless about the role amps played in the sound of their precious vintage guitars. Amp guys are a little less emotional (I said a little) and more "techie" (anal) about their purchases.

George: Amps are built like Erector sets, with lots of interchangeable parts. Tubes, speakers, capacitors, etc. can be changed. As much as we talk about originality, it's not the kiss of death if a part has been exchanged for a correct original part.

Modifications to amplifiers are often unseen. Replacing a capacitor in your Bandmaster isn't like installing a humbucker on your '61 Strat.
George: You do want the original cabinet and the original covering. You can buy the right cloth and get it recovered, but a recovered one, while it may be great for utility, won't be worth as much. I remember when it was easy to find used amps in great condition, but in the coming years it's just going to be less and less realistic to expect vintage amps to be totally original. Even if they're pristine and have never been used, the capacitors dry out and the cones deteriorate.

Peter: I'm very lucky. I have several vintage Fenders, including a tweed Twin, the 80 watt one. I believe it's the one Eric Johnson used to have. Unfortunately, it's been modified, but it's very hard to find these old amps in the same condition they were in so many years ago.

Richard: The entire vintage market is about a wistful feeling for an idyllic past. Compared with the pursuit of vintage guitars, amp collecting operates on a higher level of subtlety. It's perhaps even more about nostalgia than guitar collecting. It's about recapturing the smell of new Tolex, even if you know it's not coming back.

Greg H.: Most collector realms are driven by folks with money, patience, maturity, and decades of experience and knowledge. Not so for people in musical instruments, George Gruhn being one of a few exceptions. Also, other collectibles are not being heavily used. They are expected to be preserved. But guitar and amp collectors are conflicted, and many who want these items do want to use them, which has an effect: If an item's going to be heavily used, then its current condition need not be pristine to be of value to the user, which is independent of its value to the collector.

Ironically, the other aspect of the collector's amp being used is that its components will wear out even faster, and the cab will be subject to the bumps and dings of travel and performance.
George: The supply of vintage instruments and amplifiers is extremely limited. Regardless of the price, there are not enough to go around for every musician who'd like to use one as a utility tool. If they were all subjected to heavy use, within a matter of a few years, the supply of vintage fretted instruments would be exceedingly limited, and vintage amps would be virtually nonexistent.

Greg H.: Unlike most collectibles, the guitar and amp markets are heavily influenced by performers and what's hot this month. Next month, it could all change. This distorts prices, so that we don't have the sensible predictability that a true "investment" market ought to have. Therefore, collecting amps, even vintage Fenders, is not a great way to make money. For many novices, a higher return is probably realized in arguably more secure markets, like mutual funds or real estate.

George: While I agree that guitar and amp markets are affected by fads, I don't see this as any more true than the so-called "more sophisticated" markets for other collectibles. I have collected instruments since 1963. The same acoustic models that were sought after then are still very highly regarded today. Electric guitars that were desirable in the late 1960s are still in demand. I concede that some that I never expected to attain any significant value have surprised me. Regarding amps, we were aware as early as 1966 or '67 that pre-CBS tweed amps were superior to the new ones. While the brown and white Tolex models were not especially old yet, those, too, were recognized as being superior to new ones. By 1967, even though a blackface pre-CBS amp was still a recent, non-collectible item, sophisticated players were well aware that quality had deteriorated under CBS, such that a two or three-year-old amp was far more sought-after than new ones. We didn't hear much about old Marshalls, and nobody seemed to care about Gibson amps. It was strictly pre-CBS Fenders. My basic point is, the market is not any more faddish than the art or antique markets.

Peter: The amp market hasn't sped up quite as much as the guitar market, but it seems to have taken a turn in that direction. One minute I was trying to find a brown Vibrolux — Mark Knopfler told me all about his — and they were going for $1,800 to $2,500 depending on condition, and then all of a sudden they're up to $3,000 in good condition. Nowadays everyone knows what they've got. It's sort of like the futures market, inasmuch as collectors know the number of these available amps is getting small, and I think they just stick whatever price they want on it and wait for the market to get to that price. It's a drag for us musicians who want to get our hands on these things to play and record with. These prices have taken the musician out of the ball game altogether.

George: The notion that rising prices have forced musicians out of the market has been circulating at least since the 1830s, when violin collectors drove up values enough that many musicians could no longer pick up early Italian instruments at bargain prices. Musicians claimed that collectors were depriving the world of the opportunity to hear these instruments. History has shown, however, that collectors served a useful function. At a time when prices were simply so low that musicians didn't have much incentive to take care of their violins, collectors placed them into "protective custody" for a long enough period that values rose to the point where later generations revered them enough to take meticulous care of them. Were it not for collectors, there would be virtually no original Cremona violins left today. When I entered the business, the same arguments were being put forth, [but] it is my position that guitar and amp collectors have served the same function as the earlier violin collectors.

As '50s Strats, Les Pauls, and others have soared out of reach for all but a very few, guitars once considered of little value (a CBS '70s Jazzmaster, say) have acquired vintage status and value. Any similar developments in Fender amps?

Greg G.: Yes, the tweed amps are out of reach for most blue collar, working musicians. The blackface amps are hot on their heels, leaving the silverface amps still affordable for most musicians, although even these have been rapidly escalating in value. This is especially true for the smaller combo reverb amps such as the Princeton Reverb, Deluxe Reverb, and Vibrolux Reverb, which are popular for practice, recording, and today's smaller venues. The larger amps have fallen out of favor with most musicians, with the exception of country players who demand Twin Reverbs. Even the 40 watt Pro Reverb and Super Reverb are less popular. You don't see this happening with guitars. You'll never see musicians ignoring a '58 Strat or a '60 Les Paul. They will always be desirable, usable, and popular.

John S.: When I started collecting in the '70s, nothing was collectible unless it was pre-CBS. Funny thing, this seemed to apply to most other brands. We didn't much care for a Gibson made after 1965, either. As time passed, that magic date of collectability moved steadily forward. I was shocked to find that a 3-bolt Strat was collectible. The same happens with amps. Many collectors were garage band teenagers who gave up the rock and roll and went on to make lots of money. Many of my customers want to relive their garage band days. I am sure that 10 or 20 years from now, a first-year Blues Deluxe or any of the great Fender reissue amps will become as highly sought after as any '50s amp. These [younger] guys never used a '50s amp. Hopefully, Fender will keep a good supply of parts. It will make restoring the 50-year-old Cyber-Twin much easier!

John P.: Except for a few well known exceptions, amps are still plentiful enough that people have not started to collect the useless ones.

Richard: On a practical level, the Champion 800, which became valuable and collectible in the 1980s, is a pretty worthless amplifier. Its value and vintage status are historical, in the story it tells. Can the same be said for a '70s Jazzmaster? How about a Quad Reverb?

What's the difference, if any, in buying a whole bunch of amps versus building a collection?

George: A collection should have a focus. One could show, for example, the evolution of the Fender amp, from the earliest K&F up to modern designs. Or one could concentrate on a particular period, in which case one might want every model made by Fender in 1958 or 1963, for example. In that sense, a "collection" may be different from simply a group of instruments bought for investment only.

Suppose you determine that the four-10 tweed Bassman is the most valuable amp, along with the high-powered tweed Twin. If you need an "investment," all you need to do is find out how many of those are available and buy them all. Is that a coordinated collection? Probably not. But if your goal is simply investment, then those two amps are "investible." So far as sleepers go, if you get any good-condition, older, original Fender tweed amps, they're all investment-grade — basically anything pre-CBS.

John S.: I have had many heated discussions with fellow collectors about what a collection is. It seems that each "collector" has a different idea. All different, but maybe all correct. Some collect for color, some for celebrity status, some for what I think are ridiculous reasons. I knew a guy who collected guitars by weight! I like to go for pieces that are the earliest known examples of things. I have gone after the first electric guitars and amps ever manufactured. I got into this in the early '70s when you could actually find the stuff. I like to have pieces actually handled by the inventor. I have been lucky enough to own items made by folks like Lloyd Loar, Leo Fender, and George Beauchamp. For me, historical significance is where it's at. There's nothing like having a room full of this kind of history. Great food for thought. Much better than a room full of Fiesta Red Fenders or Pelham Blue Gibsons. Collecting is just what the word implies. You pick your theme and start to accumulate examples that fall into it. I suppose you could buy a collection and call yourself a collector, but you'd miss out on the thrill of the hunt.

Greg G.: A collection technically should have a theme, but I suppose the theme could be as broad as "pre-CBS Fender amps" or as narrow as "all variations of Fender Deluxes." A whole bunch of Fender amps might provide a useful tonal palette for a musician, but it doesn't necessarily constitute a true collection without a theme.

Richard: I've known collector/players who buy a whole bunch of amps, and each one has a purpose, even if it's only an experiment. To these players, the collection is an extension of the creative process. Pure collectors are probably more academic, more like archeologists.

Peter: If I had kept every amp I've had, I'd be worth a fortune [laughs], but it wasn't until the last 20 years or so that we realized their value. I'm more of an amp collector than a guitar collector. I collect them to play them, so for me it's about sound and practicality, although I am very mindful of their history and collectible value.

What is the significance of the Internet and eBay on the amp collecting market, if any?

Greg G.: The Internet has made collecting anything — amps, guitars, cigar boxes — much easier. It's like instant gratification compared to the old days of waiting for the latest dealer stock list to arrive in the mail or cruising down to the annual guitar show. On the other hand, it has allowed market prices to respond rapidly to demand, usually in an upward manner.

John P.: EBay can make it easy, but usually the seller has to be pushed to show the "guts" and give up the numbers on the speakers and the transformers, all of which have a big influence on value. Items can go for far too much, but bargains can be had if one is patient.

Peter: For that one buyer who's looking for something very specific and that one seller who happens to own that thing, the Internet has helped them to find each other. But it's hindered the musician by driving up the prices. So there are two sides to it.

So the Internet has made it easy to find just what you're looking for, but you're in trouble if you're on eBay and you're bidding against some neurosurgeon in Bangkok.

Peter: Exactly. Rich collectors used to buy art. Now they buy an amp, and by the time they take delivery of it, it's gone up another four hundred dollars. It's like buying a house.

Richard: EBay has proved that some collectibles just aren't as rare as many people once supposed.

George: That's a valid point. EBay and other websites actually drove down prices of some first-edition rare books as well as some coins and stamps, because it used to be much harder to find good examples, and perceived rarity was greater in the pre-Internet days. More recently, however, the genuine scarcity of fine books, stamps, and coins seems to have fully adapted to the Internet, and the market is thriving. Truly collectible-grade vintage amplifiers are sufficiently scarce that I do not currently see the Internet driving prices down, but the fact remains that it is much easier to search out good examples now than it was when I first opened my shop in 1970. Back then prices were much lower, but it was exceedingly hard to track down good amplifiers. There were very few dealers specializing in them and no centralized listing source to find them.

Greg H.: Sadly, the Internet and eBay have helped to make almost all truths debatable, with the replacement of knowledge by rumor, myth, and falsehoods. Articles have been written in the real, printed press about how we're now in the "post truth" age. EBay has lots of fraudulent stuff and bogus everything — auctions, sales, details, etc. It's hard to know what is true anymore.

What are common mistakes made by aspiring amp collectors?

John P.: Buying anything by outward appearance alone; uninformed modification of the circuit and amp in an attempt to turn it into something else; recovering and regrilling without appreciation of the character of a vintage piece.

Greg G: Not doing their research or arming themselves with as much knowledge as possible before buying.

Richard: Perhaps the biggest mistake is the belief that vintage equipment will somehow make you a better musician or help you meet cute waitresses.

John S.: It is easy to make a mistake if you are collecting strictly for investment. Personally, I am not that interested in the investment end of things. Do your research, try to buy from reputable people, and expect to make a few mistakes. That's how you learn. I'm sure every collector has found a piece that just wasn't correct for the collection. Hopefully you can cut your losses and resell.

Any tips for people just getting into amp collecting?

George: As with any commodity, before you invest, study. Read all the books and articles you can. Acquire knowledge so you can ask intelligent questions. Then, deal with people you trust. If you don't have enough knowledge yourself, deal with people whose word you trust and who will give you a written certificate of what you're getting. And keep in mind you're going to learn as you go. Concentrate on amps in good original condition, but remember that unlike guitars, which can easily outlast a human lifetime, paper speaker cones can blow or deteriorate with age and components are subject to degradation. Amps are going to need more servicing than guitars, especially if they are actually to be used.

Peter: Here's a tip if you do replace the speaker, which is often a good idea if you're actually playing the amp, because they do wear out. Save the old one. Put it in a box and label it and tuck it away.

Greg G.: Buy what you like, not the amps other people think are cool or what the market deems rare or desirable. I had a '61 blonde Twin and a '64 blackface Vibroverb, both highly collectible, but I sold them for the simple reason that I didn't care for the way they sounded. They weren't bad sounding; they just didn't do it for me. So let your ears guide you, and forget about the rest.

John P.: Know the difference between a collection and a pile (a garden versus wilderness). Have a point of view. Master a small segment first — Champs, Deluxes, blackface non-reverbs, etc. Do your homework and know the circuits. Be on the lookout for variations. Take time and let the pieces "speak" to you. Don't assume that because it's different, it's wrong.

Richard: Find amps that do what you need them to do. Have a reason for buying them. Are they for a studio or a practice room? Will they be bookends in your den? (That's legit.) Do they go well with the Fiesta Red Strat? But don't expect them to be good investments unless you buy intelligently. Learn as much as you can about the vintage market, and count on making mistakes.

Greg H.: First collect what you like and like the sound of, while also getting solid info about the piece's reliability and worthiness for actual use. If you want to lose as little money as possible, study and learn about the market you expect to play in. Do a lot of first-hand, personal research and examine as many hundreds of examples as possible, before starting to buy. If you really want quality, correct stuff, you probably will have to find a local source with whom you can deal face-to-face, or a more distant but widely trusted source who has been in the business for decades.

John S.: Research, research, research. Pick your theme, read a bunch of books, go to shows, use the net, and start collecting. Pick an unusual enough theme, and write your own book!

Greg H.: Value is determined by condition, completeness, and originality. You are going to have to study a lot to know what is original, and show huge restraint not to buy one of the many beat-up, non-original examples of some old Fender. And again, if you are truly investing, then relying on info from the Internet or eBay is the big mistake. Many Internet advisors spew bogus info.

Are there some good investment prospects that people are overlooking?

John P.: The brown amps, early blackface, all 1x15 Fender combos.

Greg G.: Early silverfaces, though people are starting to catch on and prices have escalated. Also, the silverface Deluxe Reverb, Princeton, and Princeton Reverb through about 1976. The early '80s blackface amps are considered the last of the "vintage" Fenders, if for no other reason than they were the last regular production amps to use eyelet boards with hand-wired components. Their prices have escalated rapidly in the last couple of years and have a cult following, especially the Super Champ and Princeton Reverb II.

What are the most valuable collector's amps among Fenders?

Greg G.: The 3x10 tweed Bandmaster, 4x10 tweed Bassman, tweed Twin (40 and 80 watt versions), blonde Twin, blonde Dual Showman, brown '63 Vibroverb, blackface '64 Vibroverb, and blackface Vibrolux.

Peter: It seems that the ones with four inputs were the best sounding tweeds. I don't know if it has something to do with the front end, but they seem to sound best and be most collectible.

Greg H.: I think Greg G.'s list captures most of today's widely known, "most valuable" Fenders, while John S. [above] mentions more historical, even more rare Fenders, although models perhaps sought by fewer collectors. Both reflect today's valuations, but the most valued amps are changing, due to supply and demand and the consequent prices of very old examples, and also due to demographics. For vintage Fenders, we're going to stop seeing a price appreciation beyond inflation, I think. In 10 or 20 years, it will be easier to sell a shredder guitar (Jackson, etc.) than a '60s Strat or Tele.

The demographics point toward the reality that the powerful, heavy, top of the line amps are not what you want. The small, lightweight amps are far more popular now, if for no other reason than weight, size, and the reduction of clubs where folks can crank up larger amps. An SF [silverface] Princeton Reverb sells for more than an SF Twin Reverb! An SF Vibrolux Reverb sells for more than an SF Super Reverb — that's nuts! I expect prices for '60s Fender amps to actually drop in 10 to 20 years as the number of people who appreciate them drops (old guys dying off). So, collecting should be done for fun, for wanting the particular amp for its sound and looks, and less with the idea that it's a sensible investment.

George: Greg has a valid point that in 10 or 20 years the Baby Boomers will have aged upward such that coming generations who have different preferences will attain new significance in the market. I have commented that collectors often enter the scene when they have a midlife crisis at age 40. If we want to know what [future collectors] will want when they have their midlife crises, we need to know what excited them when they were of dating age. On the other hand, I do not share the view that instruments or amps from the Golden Age will necessarily go down in value. Vintage fretted instruments of the 1920s and '30s as well as the vintage electric guitars and amplifiers of 1950 to '65 are sufficiently versatile that they can be used in virtually any kind of music. As long as acoustic and electric guitars are popular, the vintage models will remain sought-after American icons. As long as people revere vintage electric guitars, the vintage amplifiers which accompany them should maintain their value. What makes these such enduring collectibles is their superb quality and adaptability, such that even when musical trends change, the vintage instruments and amplifiers stand the test of time.

John P.: The most valuable ones are the K&Fs, wooden Pro, Champ 800, four [output] tube tweed Twin, 5F6-A Bassman, Vibroverbs — really any pre-CBS amp that is in such astonishingly great condition it's "YTBM" — yet to be made.

Richard: All the above, and the ones that make you happy.

ABOUT THE AUTHOR

Tom Wheeler

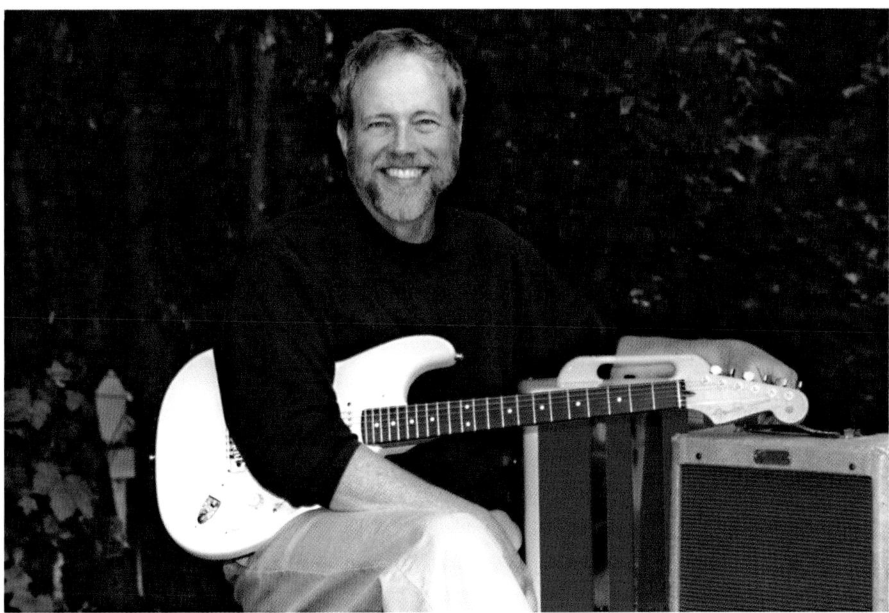

Tom Wheeler with three of his favorite musical instruments: a Mary Kaye Stratocaster built by Fender Custom Shop Senior Master Builder Chris Fleming, a Pro Junior 60th Anniversary Woody, and an old tweed Champ that roars like a lion. Photo: Jennifer King.

Tom Wheeler

After freelancing for *Rolling Stone*, Tom joined the staff of *Guitar Player* and became its Editor in Chief four years later. He served in that capacity for ten years, was also the founding Editorial Director of Bass Player, and continued to provide a monthly column for *Guitar Player* for ten years after leaving the office.

His first encyclopedia, *The Guitar Book: A Handbook for Electric and Acoustic Guitarists* (foreword by B.B. King), was published by Harper & Row in various languages over a period of 14 years; a new Japanese translation was published in 2000. His next book, *American Guitars: An Illustrated History* (foreword by Les Paul) was in print for more than 20 years and was called by one retail catalog "the best book ever written about guitars." His 2004 book, *The Stratocaster Chronicles* (foreword by Eric Clapton), was named Book of the Year by *Vintage Guitar* magazine.

Tom has interviewed Muddy Waters, B.B. King, Chuck Berry, Eric Clapton, Michael Bloomfield, Les Paul, Leo Fender, Keith Richards, and many others. He co-edited Richard Smith's *Fender: The Sound Heard 'Round The World*, and also wrote the foreword. He wrote the foreword for *The PRS Guitar Book*, and contributed chapters to *Gibson Guitars, 100 Years of an American Icon*; *The Electric Guitar*; *Electric Guitars of the Fifties*; and *Electric Guitars of the Sixties*; among others.

He has been interviewed by *The New York Times*, *The Chicago Tribune*, *The Wall Street Journal*, *U.S. News & World Report*, Irish Public Radio, American Public Radio, MTV, NPR, the BBC, and CNN. He is a consultant to The Smithsonian Institution, host of the *American Guitar* video series, and the writer and host of informational videos for Fender and Guild. He holds a Juris Doctor degree from the Loyola School of Law, is currently a member of the faculty of the University of Oregon's School of Journalism, and gigs regularly with soul singer Deb Cleveland.

VINTAGE AMPLIFIER CD LISTENING GUIDE

"Amps Through Time," with Greg Koch

It seems Greg Koch can do the impossible. Not only can he rotate your head in a full Linda Blair 360 with his fiendish guitar chops, but he can also render spot-on imitations of favorite players while still managing to assert a powerful artistic identity all his own.

He is also hilarious. As I once wrote of this globetrotting musician/clinician/author: "Greg's public persona is part your favorite uncle, part Mad Hatter, part game-show host, and all mirth. The patter is so funny that in the hands of a lesser musician the laughs would outshine the licks. But for every minute you spend giggling at the bits, you'll spend many more marveling at the chops and vision of this eclectic virtuoso."

I am honored that Greg has lent his "often melodious, sometimes felonious plectrum-fueled skullduggery" to *The Soul of Tone*. On the 91 tracks of CD-1, "Amps Through Time," he guides us through a sonic gallery of vintage Fender amplifiers — tweeds, browns, blondes, and blackfaces — providing insights into these "tube-fueled appliances" that mere words could never accomplish.

Typically, each amp gets a full workout with a Telecaster, a Les Paul, a Stratocaster and on occasion other guitars as well. Amps are demoed at half volume and again at full volume, sometimes with different volume settings on the guitar. Greg's commentary and the chart appearing here also note the settings of the Bright switch, reverb, and tremolo, as well as channel selection, the placement of various amps across the stereo spectrum, and other details. This approach reveals in short order not only how rich and compelling these Fenders sound but also how versatile they are.

Most tracks explore a single amplifier with various specified settings, while some feature combinations of amps, guitars, and settings. For example, check out the dueling blonde Showmans on track 59, where Greg conjures a blowout jam between Jimi Hendrix and Dick Dale.

The demos are comprehensive. For example, a total of 12 tracks are devoted to the Vibrolux; in the last one, Greg evokes another dream jam, this time with two of the model's most acclaimed artists, Roy Buchanan on Tele, and Mark Knopfler on Strat.

I don't think Greg Koch could order a cup of coffee without being entertaining in one way or another, and this provocative, enlightening CD is no exception. You might want to listen to it as you would any other album — all the way through — just to marvel at the astonishing playing, to immerse yourself in the classic Fender tones, and to laugh along with the zaniness. But you will also find reference icons throughout *The Soul of Tone*'s pages, linking all of these tracks to the appropriate background text and specified technical details.

As Greg hollers on the CD's Intro track: *So hold on! We're goin' in! To hear — amps . . . through. . . tiiiiiime!*

— Tom Wheeler

Track	Description
1	Introduction to Vintage CD
2	**Narrow Panel Tweed Deluxe,** a favorite of Neil Young and Billy Gibbons
3	Telecaster – half volume
4	Introduction to Track 5
5	Telecaster – full volume
6	Introduction to using Les Paul
7	Les Paul – half volume
8	Introduction to Track 9
9	Les Paul – full volume
10	Introduction to using Stratocaster
11	Stratocaster – half volume
12	Stratocaster – full volume
13	**Blackface Deluxe Reverb ('64)** using Stratocaster
14	Stratocaster – half volume (with reverb on 3)
15	Stratocaster – full volume
16	Introduction to using Telecaster
17	Telecaster – half volume
18	Telecaster – full volume
19	Introduction to using Les Paul
20	Les Paul – half volume
21	Les Paul – full volume
22	**"Deluxes Gone Wild" Jam** (with 4 guitar parts)
23	4 Deluxes: narrow panel, blackface, brown, and TV front
24	**New '57 Tweed Deluxe** using Stratocaster
25	Stratocaster – half volume (tone full)
26	Stratocaster – full volume
27	Introduction to using Les Paul
28	Les Paul – half volume
29	Les Paul – full volume
30	**"Need for Tweed" Jam** New '57 Deluxe – full volume
31	Strat – various guitar volumes
32	**Blackface Vibrolux Reverb ('66)** using Telecaster
33	Telecaster – half volume (Bright switch off)
34	Telecaster – half volume (Bright switch on)
35	Telecaster – full volume (Bright switch on)
36	Telecaster – full volume (Bright switch off)

Track	Description
37	Introduction to using Stratocaster
38	Stratocaster – half volume (Bright switch off)
39	Stratocaster – half volume (Bright switch on)
40	Stratocaster – full volume (Bright switch off)
41	Stratocaster – full volume (Bright switch on)
42	**"Mark 'n' Roy" Jam** using Telecaster and Stratocaster, in the style of Mark Knopfler, Roy Buchanan
43	Telecaster – full volume Stratocaster – half volume (2 parts)
44	**Tweed Twin** – High-Powered in the style of Danny Gatton, Keith Richards
45	Telecaster – full volume (Open G Tuning)
46	Les Paul – full volume
47	**"Swing Spectacular" Jam** High-powered tweed Twin, moderate volume
48	1961 Gibson Switchmaster, 1958 Gretsch 6120, 1953 Tele
49	**Blonde Tolex Twin** (JBL speakers) using Telecaster and Les Paul
50	Telecaster – full volume
51	Les Paul – full volume
52	**"What Can Brown Do For You?" Jam** 4 guitar parts, 3 brown Tolex amps
53	brown Tolex Vibrasonic, Vibroverb, and Princeton
54	**Model 600** Early '50s amp
55	Telecaster – various guitar volumes
56	**Princeton Reverb ('66)** full volume
57	Stratocaster – various guitar volumes
58	**Blonde Tolex Showman ('61)** using Stratocaster (in the style of Dick Dale, Jimi Hendrix)
59	Stratocaster – full volume (w/'66 Reverb Unit)
60	**Blackface Super Reverb ('66)** using Stratocaster
61	Stratocaster – half volume (Bright switch on)
62	Stratocaster – full volume (Bright switch on)

Track	Description
63	Introduction to Track 64 Stratocaster
64	Stratocaster – various guitar volumes (w/ custom overdrive pedal)
65	Introduction to using Telecaster
66	Telecaster – half volume
67	Telecaster – full volume
68	Introduction to using Les Paul
69	Les Paul – half volume
70	Les Paul – full volume
71	**"Super Shuffle Soufflé" Jam** '66 blackface Super Reverb
72	4 guitar parts: Stratocaster – half volume Stratocaster – half volume (w/ pedal) Telecaster – full volume Les Paul – full volume
73	**Tweed 4x10 Bassman ('58)** Reissue Cabinet
74	Stratocaster – half volume
75	Stratocaster – full volume
76	Introduction to using Telecaster
77	Telecaster – half volume
78	Telecaster – full volume
79	Introduction to using Les Paul
80	Les Paul – half volume
81	Les Paul – full volume
82	**"Rockin' Bassman" Jam**
83	Telecaster – full volume Les Paul – full volume Stratocaster – half volume Stratocaster – full volume (4 guitar parts)
84	**Blackface Twin Reverb ('65)**
85	Stratocaster – half volume (Bright switch on and then off)
86	Stratocaster – full volume (Bright switch on and then off)
87	**"Twin Geeks" Jam**
88	Stratocaster – half & full volume (Bright switch on and then off)
89	Telecaster – half & full volume (Bright switch on and then off)
90	Les Paul – half & full volume (Bright switch on and then off)
91	Outro

NOTE: All volume levels refer to amps unless otherwise noted.

MODERN AMPLIFIER CD LISTENING GUIDE

Some of the most exciting, widely played, and innovative amps in Fender's entire history have been conceived and built in the last couple of decades. The Princeton Chorus, for example, is one of the most successful products in Fender's entire 60-year history.

Traditionalists have flocked to the tube-fueled Vibro-King, the Hot Rods, and reissues of classic tweeds and blackfaces, while adventurous players seeking the latest in technology have embraced the virtually limitless flexibility and massive fun factor of the Cyber-Twin and G-DEC. Many musicians are finding the Super-Sonics to be ideal for stage and studio alike.

Players on a budget have found that Frontmans are both affordable and good sounding, and the modest-looking Blues Junior is a thoroughly professional studio tool any discriminating musician would appreciate.

Whatever their tastes, one attribute is demanded by all of these players — great tone.

A tradition as old as the company itself is Fender's commitment to seeking feedback from working musicians. Fender continues to respond to their needs in a changing artistic environment, as evidenced in groundbreaking and versatile amplifiers such as the Acoustasonics and the Metalhead.

All of these amps and more are featured on *The Soul of Tone*'s second CD. The guitarists demonstrating these amps are the marketing executives who helped conceive them.

These are loose, fun sessions, an opportunity for the former professional musicians who help guide today's Fender company to reconnect with the joys of playing great gear, to show their considerable musical skills, and to demo the amps they're proud to play.

Above, from left: Ritchie Fliegler, Shane Nicholas, Mike Jones, Matt Wilkens, Bob Desiderio, Mike Lewis, Steve Grom.

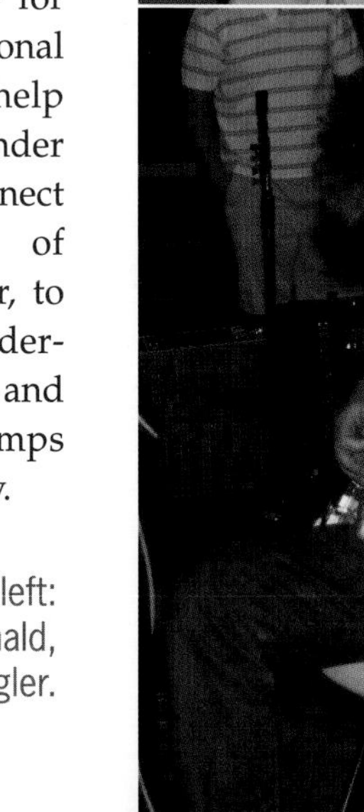

Clockwise from middle left: Mike Lewis, Richard McDonald, Shane Nicholas, Ritchie Fliegler.

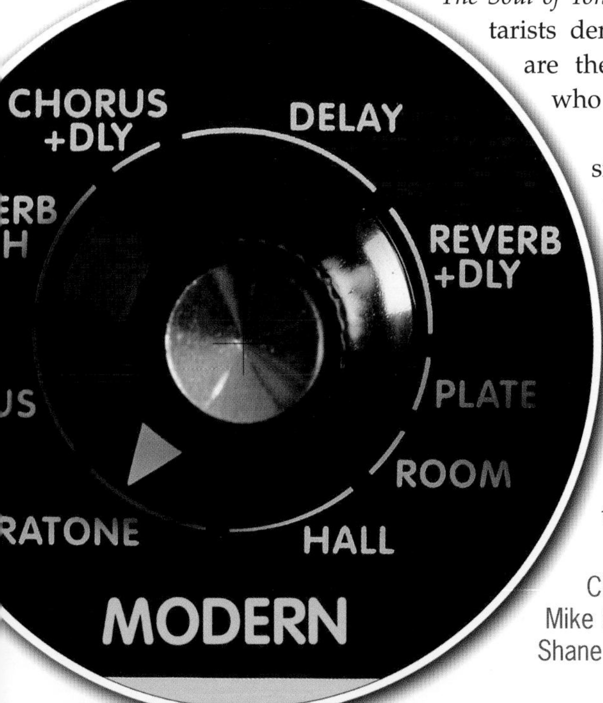

Track	Amp	Player	Guitar Used	Notes
1	**1989 Princeton Chorus**	Steve Grom	1996 Lone Star Strat	neck/mid combination (clean); bridge humbucker (Overdriven)
2	**2005 '59 Bassman LTD**	Steve Grom; Shane Nicholas	2006 American Series P-Bass; 2004 Highway 1 HSS Strat	various PU setting on Strat
3	**2005 '65 Twin Reverb**	Steve Grom; Mike Lewis; Shane Nicholas; Ritchie Fliegler	1996 Lone Star Strat, handed off to each of the four players	Steve plays neck pickup; Mike plays middle pickup; Shane plays middle and bridge pickups; Ritchie plays bridge pickup with Ibanez TS-9 overdrive pedal added
4	**2005 Vibro-King Custom**	Mike Lewis	1983 '57 Reissue Stratocaster	various PU settings
5	**2006 Blues Junior**	Mike Lewis	2005 Gretsch G6120 SSLVO	various PU settings
6	**2005 Blues Deluxe Reissue**	Mike Lewis	2005 Gretsch G6120 SSLVO	various PU settings
7	**2001 '65 Super Reverb**	Richard McDonald	1986 '62 Stratocaster Reissue	various PU settings
8	**2006 Cyber-Twin SE**	Richard McDonald	1986 '62 Stratocaster Reissue	various PU settings; amp presets used include STADIUM ROCK; ORGANISM; A TWIN REVERB
9	**Acoustasonic Ultralight head & enclosure**	Ritchie Fliegler	Fender Ensenada series ESM-10E Mini Jumbo	Fishman electronics on board
10	**2005 Frontman 15G**	Ritchie Fliegler	1987 PRS Standard	various PU settings
11	**2005 G-DEC**	Shane Nicholas	2004 Highway 1 HSS Strat	various PU settings
12	**Hot Rod Deluxe**	Ritchie Fliegler	2004 '54 Stratocaster	Clapton boost
13	**Super-Sonic**	Shane Nicholas	2004 Highway 1 HSS Strat	various PU settings
14	**2004 '64 Vibroverb Custom**	Shane Nicholas	2004 Highway 1 HSS Strat	middle pickup
15	**2004 '57 Twin-Amp**	Shane Nicholas	1995 Lone Star Strat	neck pickup; bridge humbucker (overdriven)
16	**2005 Metalhead + MH412SL cabinet**	John Dreyer	2005 American Deluxe Strat HSS	bridge humbucker

PHOTO CREDITS

The following people supplied numerous photographs. The legend is:
BP/RS = Bob Perine/courtesy Richard Smith, **BW** = Baron Wolman, **DW** = Dick Waterman, **FMIC** = Fender Musical Instruments Corp., **ER** = Ebet Roberts, **JP** = John Peden, **KS** = Ken Settle, **LS** = Lisa Seifert, **MOA** = Michael Ochs Archives.com, **MW** = Michael Weintrob, **NZ** = Neil Zlozower, **RA** = Richard E. Aaron, **RG** = Rick Gould, **RK** = Robert Knight, **RS** = Richard Smith

Cover: KS.

Acknowledgements: Page 8 FMIC, 9 JP, 10 FMIC, 11 JP.

Foreword: Page 13 KS.

Introduction: Page 14 photo illustration Richard Slater; 15,16 JP; 17 upper Takashi Sato; 17 lower FMIC; 18 Jimmy Velvet; 19,20 FMIC.

Chapter 1: Page 22 MOA; 24 JP; 25 BP/RS; 26 FMIC; 27,28 lower,29 JP; 28 schematic courtesy of FMIC.

Chapter 2: Page 36 FMIC, 38 JP, 39 RS, 40 FMIC, 41 JP, 42 FMIC, 43 courtesy Record Research, 44 JP.

Chapter 3: Page 46,48,49,50,51,52,54,55 JP; 57 FMIC; 59,60 JP; 63 schematic FMIC.

Chapter 4: Page 64 FMIC; 66 schematic courtesy of JBL; 67,68,69 JP; 70 upper JP; 70 lower DW; 71,72,73,76 JP; 77 FMIC.

Chapter 5: Page 78,80 FMIC; 82,83 both JP; 84 MOA; 85 both JP; 86 DW; 87 MOA.

Chapter 6: Page 88 JP; 91 ER; 93,95 FMIC.

Chapter 7: Page 98 KS, 101 JP, 103 DW, 104 FMIC, 105 KS, 106 FMIC, 108 ER.

Chapter 8: Page 110,112,113 JP; 114 FMIC; 115,116 RS; 117,118,120 JP; 121 Dave Belzer; 122 RS; 123,125 JP.

Chapter 9: Page 126 MOA; 128 JP; 130,131 RS; 133 FMIC; 134 JP; 135 RS; 136,137 both,138,139 JP; 140 Tom Wheeler; 141 JP; 143 FMIC.

Chapter 10: Page 144 Ernest C. Withers, courtesy Panopticon Gallery, Boston, MA; 146 JP; 148 upper schematic FMIC; 148 lower JP; 149 RS; 151,152,153 JP; 154,155 RS.

Chapter 11: Page 156 ©1978 Reshovsky/MPTV.net; 158 JP,159 FMIC,160,161,162 JP; 162 lower courtesy of Record Research; 163,165,167 JP; 168 schematic FMIC; 169 BP/RS; 170,171,172,173 JP; 174 from author's collection; 175 courtesy of Record Research; 176,178,179,180, 181,183 JP; 184 courtesy Bill Carson; 186 JP; 187 ER; 188,189 Rick Davis; 190 MOA; 192 RS; 193,194 both, 195 JP.

Chapter 12: Page 196 MOA; 198 JP; 199 upper courtesy Record Research; 199 lower FMIC; 200 JP; 201 upper Chuck Pulin/StarFile; 201 lower BP/RS; 202 courtesy George Fullerton; 203 FMIC; 204,205 JP; 206 RK; 207 FMIC; 208 DW; 209 JP; 210 Denny Tedesco; 211 FMIC; 212 Mark Harlan/StarFile; 213 left FMIC; 213 right MW; 214,215,216 JP; 217 KS; 218 FMIC; 219 RS; 220,221, 222,223 FMIC; 224 JP; 226 Norman Dayron; 227 JP.

Chapter 13: Page 228 NZ; 230,232,233 JP; 235 MOA; 238,239 JP; 241 MOA; 242 ER; 243 JP; 244 Patti Boyd; 246 John Sprung; 247,249 MOA; 251 JP; 252,253 FMIC.

Chapter 14: Page 254 DW; 256 JP; 258 Howard Risk/MOA; 259 Ron Pownall/StarFile; 260,262,263,264,265 both,266 JP; 267 KS; 268 MOA; 269 JP; 270 Don Paulsen/MOA; 271 JP; 272 ER; 274,275 FMIC; 276 JP; 277 KS; 279 JP; 280 upper ER; 280 lower KS; 281 MW.

Chapter 15: Page 282,284,285 FMIC; 286 Ron Pownall/MOA; 288,289,290 courtesy Bob Rissi; 293 RS.

Chapter 16: Page 294 FMIC; 296 courtesy of Bob Rissi; 299,300 FMIC.

Chapter 17: Page 302 BW; 304,305 JP; 306 schematic FMIC; 307 ER; 308 JP; 310 LS; 312,314 FMIC; 315 MOA; 316 FMIC; 317 RG; 318 FMIC; 319 NZ; 320 JP; 321 Colin Escott/MOA; 322 both,323 JP; 326 FMIC; 327 Holland/Retna UK; 328 LS; 329 ER.

Chapter 18: Page 330,332 FMIC; 333 JP; 334 courtesy of Paul Rivera; 335,336,338,341,343 FMIC.

Chapter 19 Page 344 FMIC; 346 Michael Uhill/ER; 348, 349,350,351,354 FMIC; 355 James Schepf.

Chapter 20: Page 356 KS, 358 FMIC, 359 Elliot Landy/StarFile, 360 Matt Carr, 361 Mark Baier/Victoria Amps.

Chapter 21: Page 362,364 FMIC; 365 Lance Mercer/ Retna; 366,367,369,370 both,371 both,372 FMIC.

Chapter 22: Page 374,376,378,379,380,381,382,383, 384,385,387,386,388 FMIC; 389 Alan Rogan.

Chapter 23: Page 390 ER; 392 FMIC; 393 left ER; 393 right MW; 394,395,396 FMIC; 397 JP; 398 both,399 FMIC.

Chapter 24: Page 400,402,403,404,404,405,406 FMIC; 407 Ian Katz/StarFile; 407 left RK; 408 both,409,410,411 FMIC; 412 left RK; 412 right FMIC; 413,414,415,417 FMIC.

Chapter 25: Page 418,420,421,422 FMIC; 423 upper Max Crace; 423 lower RG; 424,425,426,427,428,429 FMIC; 430 LS; 432,433,434,435,436,437,438,439,440,441 FMIC.

Chapter 26: Page 442,445,446,447,448,449,452,453, 455 FMIC.

Chapter 27: Page 456 FMIC; 458,459,460,461,462,463, 464,465,466,467 FMIC.

Chapter 28: Page 468 photo illustration Richard Slater, 470 courtesy Pagano, 471 top left courtesy Zinky, 471 bottom right courtesy Pittman, 472 courtesy Sprung, 473 courtesy Tone Quest Report, 474 courtesy Carr, 477 FMIC.

Chapter 29: Page 478 KS, 480 JP, 482 courtesy of Henry Kaiser, 483 JP, 485 FMIC, 486 RA, 486 inset RG, 487 FMIC.

Post chapters: Page 488 JP, 495 TW, 496 Ricco Photography, 498 FMIC.

INDEX

Note: Page numbers in **bold** indicate illustrations or captions.

5AR4/GZ34 tubes. *See* GZ34/5AR4 rectifier tubes
5U4 tubes, 86, 115, 122, 137, 182, 183, **209,** 215, **374,** 384, 387
5U4G tubes, **54,** 86, 122, 147, 152, 179, 182
5U4GA tubes, 86, 107, 179, 182
5U4GB tubes, 86, 215, 311
5Y3 tubes, **52,** 54, 86, 137, 147, **170,** 182, 215
5Y3GT tubes, 86, 107, 147, 152, 179, 182, 215
6AT6 tubes, 173, 183
6BQ5 tubes, 83, **216,** 231, 474
6J5 tubes, 145
6L6 tubes, 53, 55, 57, 58, 79, 80, **83,** 83–84, 90, 115, 122, 137, 147, 152, 179, 189, 231, 287, 301, 350, 369, 379, 381, 384, 427, 474–75
6L6G tubes, 42, **54,** 80, 83, 147, 160, 164, 176, 179, 183
6L6GB tubes, 42, 80, 83
6L6GC tubes, 42, 51, 79, 80, **80,** 83, 213, **216,** 231, 233, 234, **264,** 275, 278, 313
6L6WGB tubes. *See* 5881 tubes
6N7 tubes, 79, 115
6SC7 tubes, 79, 102, 115, 137, **137,** 145, **148**
6SJ7 tubes, 137, 145
6SL7 tubes, 79, 115, 137
6SN7 tubes, 102, 115, 137
6V6 tubes, 42, 55, 57, 58, 83, 90, 96, 107, 134, 137, 147, 160, 173, 175, **178, 214,** 301, 350, **388,** 479
6V6GT tubes, **28, 78,** 83, **104,** 107, 147, 152, 160, 173, 179, 183, 213
12AT7 tubes, 55, 57, 58, 79, **80,** 92, 181, 263, 275, **276,** 278, 313, 379, 381
12AX7 tubes, **28,** 53, **54,** 55, 56, 57, 58, 79–80, **80,** 81, 82, **82,** 92, **98, 104,** 137, 145, 152, 173, 179, 181, 183, 186, 187, 189, 212, 222, 231, 234, 268, 269, 275, 278, 313, 379, 381, **388,** 427, 429, 462, 475
12AX7C tubes, 475
12AY7 tubes, **54,** 79, 82, **98,** 137, 145, 152, 166, 179, 183, 187
20th Century Guitar (Gagliano), 74
300 PS amp, 323, 331
300B tubes, 53
400 PRO bass amp, 461, **461,** 464
400 PS bass amp, 71, 321–23, **322, 323,** 360, 457
410 PRO SL Slant Cabinet, **464**
410 PRO ST Straight Cabinet, **464**
800 PRO bass amp, **439,** 462, 464, **467**
810 PRO Cabinet, **463, 464**
5751 tubes, 80
5881 tubes, 55, 80, 81–82, 83, 85, **85, 95, 98,** 147, 148, 160, 164, 166, 168, 176, 183, 213, 231, 233, 369, 484
6550 tubes, 319, **322,** 462
7025 tubes, **28,** 57, 79, 80, **80,** 82, **85,** 85, 92, 168, 187, 212, 231, 233, 268, 269, 272, 275, 278, 313, 475
7355 tubes, **264**

AA circuits, 103–4, 261, **264,** 272, 275, 316–17
AB circuits, 103–4, **306,** 307, 313, 316–17
Abend, Jay, 273
AC circuits, 313, 315–16
Accutronics reverb units, 347
Acoustasonic amps, 413, 414–15, 420
Acoustasonic DSPs, 434
Acoustasonic SFX, **413,** 414–15
Acoustasonic Ultralight, 436
Acoustic 360, 457
active EQ, 287
Adam Faith & the Roulettes, 172
Adams, Chuck, **447,** 449
Aerosmith, 372
aerospace industry, 38–39
"After Midnight," **175**
Allman, Duane, **161, 214**
Allman, Gregg, **214**
alternating current (AC), 47, 50, 51, 52
American Guitars (Wheeler), 111
Amp Book, The (Brosnac), 16
Amp Can, **437**
Amp Custom Shop Series. *See* Custom Amp Shop Series
Ampeg B-15N Portaflex, 457
Ampeg company, 152, 205, 207, 457
Ampeg SVT amp, 322–23, 336, 457
Amperes (amps), 47
amplifiers
  appreciation of, 16–17, 19
  artists and, 472–74
  books on, 16
  collecting, 489–94
  electrical circuitry, 99–109
  functions of, 47–48
  hi-fi, 48
  history of, 42
  as matched sets with guitars, 48
  measurements and, 471–72
  misconceptions about, 469–71, 473
  musical styles and, 42–43
  signal route, 49–51, 62
  speakers overview, 65–77
  tube amplification overview, 47–63
  tube basics, 79–86
  tube performance, 89–97
  versatility of, 43
Amps! The Other Half of Rock 'n' Roll (Fliegler), 16, 370, 402
Anderson, Pete, 171, 469
anode, 54
architecture in Southern California, 39
Astron caps, 309
Astronauts, the, **199**
Atkins, C. E., 85
Atkins, Chet, 204
AT&T/Western Electric circuits, 24, 27, 222
audio taper pots, 49
Automatic GT, 406, **408**
Automatic SE, 406
aviation industry, 38–39

Babiuk, Andy, 326
  Beatles Gear, 328
baffles, 30, 71–72, 311, 313
  coverings for, 133, 148
Baier, Mark
  amps created by, 361
  quoted, 25, 27–28, **28,** 58–59, 60, 61, 65, 84, 91, 132, **148,** 182, 183, 215, 269, 272, 273, **473,** 473, 475, 476, 477
  on transformers, wattage, and speakers, 176
Balmer, Roger, 340, 347
band-pass filter, 56
Bandmaster (Band Master)
  biasing in, 309
  blackface, 59, 275, **276,** 278, **290,** 295, **487**
  blackface/blonde cab transition style, **80,** 100, 258, 275
  blonde Tolex piggybacks, **198,** 207, 208, 231, 257, 326
  blonde Tolex transition model, **244,** 248, 261
  brown Tolex, **204,** 207, 231, **232,** 233, 268–69
  narrow panel tweed, **18, 156–57,** 159–60, **160,** 162, 178, 187, 494
  presence control on, 264
  silverface, **304**
  tubes in, 213
  wide panel tweed, 145, 148, 150, **150–51, 152, 488**
Bandmaster Reverb, 305, 331
Barbour, Eric, 53, 79, 483
basket, 65
bass amplifiers, 404, 457. *See also* Fender Bass Amplification; *specific model names*
Bass Breaker, **42,** 423, **424**
bass reflex cabinet, 71
Bass VI, **458**
Bassman
  5B6 wide panel tweed, 85, 164
  5D6 narrow panel tweed, 164, **170**
  5D6-A narrow panel tweed, 164
  5E6 narrow panel tweed, 164, 187

5E6-A narrow panel tweed, 166, 178, 187
5F6 narrow panel tweed, 157, 164, 166, **168,** 176, 183, 187, 213, 265
5F6-A narrow panel tweed, **60,** 86, 157, **158,** 159, 164, **165,** 166, **167,** 168, **171, 176,** 183, 185, 187, **209,** 213, 215, 265, 479, 494
2000–2002 models, 459
biasing in, 90–91, 309
black Tolex transition model, 261
blackface, 104, 255, 258, **260,** 261, 295, 440
blackface ('80s models), 337
blackface/blonde cab transition style, **226,** 258, 261, **262**
blonde Tolex/Coffin cab pairing, 326
blonde Tolex/Marshall cab pairing, 212
blonde Tolex piggybacks, 168, 187, **198,** 207, 208, 215, **217, 228,** 267, 326, **458**
brown Tolex piggybacks, **243**
brown Tolex transition model, **244,** 248
"chocolate drop" caps on, 309
current line, 413, 419, **456,** 461, **465**
"Deep" switch on, 264
emulations in Cyber-Twins, 448–49
F-series, 58, 85, 187
head, 52
Marshall's copy of, 35, 164, 171–72, 211, 423, 470–71
model number for, 102
owned by Buck Owens, **316**
problems as bass amp, 457, 459
rectifiers in, 181–83
silverface, **304,** 306, **327**
speakers in '50s, **67**
Stratocasters paired with, 170
tone control elements, 180
TV front, 71, 90, **128,** 136
"TV tray" transistor model, **282, 294,** 297
tweed, 49, 58, 61, 67, 265, **480, 487**
tweed, narrow panel, **51,** 71, **156–57,** 157, **158,** 159, 164, **165,** 166, **167,** 168, **169, 176,** 186, **190,** 191, 202, 207, 481 *(See also specific model numbers above)*
tweed, wide panel, **128,** 145, 148, 150, **150–51** *(See also specific model numbers above)*
tweed piggyback, **246,** 249, 483–84
Bassman '59 reissue, 363, **364,** 367, 370, 372, 375, **376,** 376–77, 402. *See also* Bassman LTD '59 reissue
Bassman 135, **459**
Bassman 250/210 combo, **456**
Bassman 300 PRO, 462–63, **463**
Bassman 1200 PRO, 462–63, **464**
Bassman Compact, 337
Bassman LTD '59 reissue, 86, 216, 375, **383,** 383–87, 408, **427**
Beach Boys, the, **247**
beam power tetrodes, 55
Beatles, the, 326, **327,** 328, 340
Beatles Gear (Babiuk), 328
Beauchamp, George, 492
Beck, Jeff, 41, 170, **269, 277,** 372, 377
Beck, Roscoe, **464,** 467
Bell Labs, 24, 274
Belzer, Dave, **121**
Berlin, Drew, 226, 484
Berry, Chuck, **86,** 191, **196, 310,** 313
bias
effect of, 89
CBS methods, 309
methods for, 90–91, 94, 96
setting the, 62, 89
sound and feel, 91–92
bias adjustment pot, 90, **93,** 384
bias modulation tremolo, 231, 268, 269, 273
bias shift, 53
Bigsby, Paul, 205
Bishop, Elvin, **270**
Black, Bill, **156–57**
Black, J., 353
black Tolex amps, 103, 224, 229–31, 255, 258, 287, **344,** 416, **425.** *See also specific model names*
blackface amps, 99, 255–89, **259–60, 262, 266–67, 270–71, 276, 279–81,** 345, 360, 491. *See also specific model names*
'80s-era, **330, 332, 335,** 336–37
'90s-era, 405
biasing in, 90
Bright switch on, 178, 261, 264–65, 278, **487**
circuit codes for, 103–4, 109, 213
circuits in, 264
collectability of, 494
cosmetics of, 255, 257, 278
current models, 413
early CBS-era, 287–91, **293,** 295, 304–5, **305**
mid-power models, 275, **276,** 278
protective cover for, **256**
rectifiers in, 52
tone controls in, 267
tone stacks in, 265, 267
tubes in, 80, 85
blackface extension cabinets, **76**
blackface/red-knob amps, **344, 348,** 348–52, 363, **364,** 376
"blackfacing," 316–17
Blair, John, 274
Blanda, George, 353
blonde Tolex amps, 99, **198,** 207–8, **223, 242, 249,** 326. *See also specific model names*
'90s models, 369, 370, 404
biasing in, 90
blackface, 255, 261
circuit codes for, 103
circuits in, 264
handles and grilles on, **205**
presence control in, 178, 208
smooth-textured, 258, 263, 275
tremolo in, 272–73
tubes in, 85
Bloomfield, Michael, **226**
Blue Caps, the, **22–23**
"Blue Jean Blues," 124
blues, 83, 136, 380
Blues Breakers (Clapton album), 423
Blues Deluxe, 368–69, 371, 372, 402–3, 416
Blues Deluxe reissue, 383
Blues DeVille, 368–69, 371, 372, 402–3, 416
Blues DeVille reissue, 383
Blues Junior, 57, **398,** 413, 421, **421,** 423, **425**
"Blues Power," **175**
Bob Wills and His Texas Playboys, 115, **133,** 155
Boggs, Noel, **219,** 298
Bop Till You Drop (Ry Cooder album), **214**
Borer, Mike, 172
boutique amps, 361, 391
bouzouki players, 281
Bradley, Harold, 481–82
Bramlett, Delaney, **175, 206**
Bran, Ken, 35, 171–72
Brasler, Joey, 29
Brazos Valley Boys, **149, 293**
Brea facility, 347
Bright channel, 208, 265
Bright switch, 178, 261, 264–65, 278, 297, 331, **487**
Broadcaster, 23, 24, 142, **398–99**
Bronco
FSR, **437**
silverface, **304,** 306, **308**
tweed, 368–69, 370–71, 404
Brosnac, Don, *The Amp Book*, 16
brown extension cabinets, **76, 488**
brown Tolex amps, 99, **204,** 207–8, 229–34, **232–33,** 239–49. *See also specific model names*
biasing in, 90
circuit codes for, 103
circuits in, 264
collectability of, 494
cosmetics of, 197, 231, 233
evaluation, 229
introduction of, 199–200
model numbers for, 102
piggybacks, 245, 247–48
presence control in, 178, 208
protective cover for, **256**
smooth-textured, 258
speakers in, 233
tone controls in, 267
tremolo in, 272–73
tubes in, 85
Bryant, Jimmy, **142–43,** 298
Buchanan, Roy, **263,** 440
Buddingh, Terry, 30, **52,** 92, 94, 186, 212, 265
Bullet, 371
Bullet 15, **427**
Bullet Reverb, 411, **411**
Burlison, Paul, 191
Burst Brothers, **121,** 226, 484
Burton, James, **268**
BXR bass amps, 368, 372, 404, 406, 413, **460**
cabinet design, 69, 71–72, 75, 109, 122, 136, 311, 313, 322–23, 471. *See also* piggyback cabinets
cables, 49, 50, 470
CAD (Computer Aided Design), 353
Campbell, Glen, **268**
capacitance, 49, 182
capacitive coupling, 291, 309, 316
capacitors, 51, **51,** 56, 309, 311, 316
Capps, Jimmy, 481–82

Capricorn, 299
Captain Beefheart's Magic Band, **214**
Carducci, Joe, 324
Carr, Steve
 quoted, 29, 58, 61, 91, 92, 105–6, 155, 177, 181, 186, **360,** 473, **474,** 477
Carr Rambler, 58
Carr Slant 6V, **360**
Carson, Bill, 324
 Fender tenure of, 75, 349, 384
 pictured, **149**
 quoted, 30, 32, 38, 45, 132, 150, 152, 155, 164, 170, 185, 202, 285, 297, 387–88
Carver, Jody, 32, 152–53, **155**
cathode bias, 89, 90, 91–92, 97, 134, 309, 315
cathode-follower tone stacks, 166, 186–87, 211–12, 265, 267
cathodes, 53–54
CBS Fender era, 39, 216, 283–93, 303–29, 331–42, 345–47, 490
CDE caps, 311
Celestion speakers, 65, **77,** 395, 423
Champ 12, **344,** 348, 350–51, 363, 368
Champ 25, 369, 371
Champ 25SE, 369, 371
Champ (Champion)
 5C1 layout *vs.* schematic, 107
 5F1 schematic, **46–47**
 '80s blackface, **335,** 337
 biasing in, 90–91
 black Tolex, 261, **262**
 blackface, 261, 295, **308**
 Class A, 96
 model number for, 102
 modified with Lansing speaker, **175**
 name plates for, **101**
 name variants, 147
 push/pull pentodes, 42
 silverface, **304, 308,** 316, 325, 331
 single-ended circuit design in, 92
 tubes in, 85
 tweed, 99, **202,** 360, **495**
 tweed, narrow panel, 160, **161, 172, 178,** 207, 208, 258, 261
 tweed, wide panel, **125,** 145, 147, **148, 172**
Champ II, **330,** 337
Champ Series, 371
Champion 110, 371
Champion 600, 127, 134, 147, 160, **172**
 biasing in, 90
 two-tone, **38,** 83, 124, **125,** 134, **135, 137, 138**
Champion 600 tribute model (Chinese-made), **388**
Champion 800, 83, 90, 119, 124, **125,** 127, 147, **488,** 491, 494
Champion steel guitar, 134
Champs, the, 245, 247–48, 249
channel switching, 417
channels, 56–57, 179–81, 208, **227,** 275, 297
Chapman, Keith, 415, 438–40, 444, **447,** 449
"chickenhead" pointer knobs, **123,** 133, 147, 191, **376**
Chinese assembly plants, 424–25, 429, 452
"chocolate drop" caps, 309, 316
choke, 51, 166, 175, **209**
circuit boards, **55, 289,** 291, 320, 323–24, 353, 384–85, 476–77
circuit codes, 100, 102–4, 106, 109, 145, 147, 182
 overlaps, gaps, and other mismatches, 106–7
Clapton, Eric, **70,** 160, **161, 175, 249, 254, 270,** 325, 360, 377, 388, **389,** 420, 423, 474
Class A, 94, 96–97, 396
Class AB, 94, 96–97, 396
Class B, 94
class of operation, 92, 94, 96–97
Cleveland, Barry, 43, 274
Cleveland Electronics speakers, 65, **137**
Cliff Bennett & the Rebel Rousers, 172
clipping, 58
closed-back cabinets, **68,** 69, 74, 136
club-owned amps, 28–29, 134, 210, 379
"Cold Shot," **314**
Collins, Albert, **328, 329**
Colman, Stuart, **277**
combo units, 69, 71, 207–8, 231, 233, 275, 457, 491, 494. *See also specific model names*
"Coming Home," **175**
Complete Guide to Guide and Amp Maintenance, The (Fliegler), 402
component codes, 105
compression, 52–53, 59, 136, 176, 182, 186, 309, 369, **412,** 414, 448
Concert
 5G12 transition model, **209**
 7025 tubes in, 85
 blackface, 257, 275, **276, 277,** 278, 295
 blackface ('80s models), **338,** 339
 blackface Pro Tube Series, 370, **370,** 372, 417
 blonde special-order, 248–49
 brown Tolex, 199, 200, 202, 207, 208, **209, 215,** 231, **232,** 233, 248, 257, 268–69
 model number for, 102
 in oak cabinet, 339, 340
 presence control on, 264
 speakers for, 318
 transformers in early-'60s, 60
 tubes in, 85, 213
 tweed, 248
Concert II, 337
Concert Reverb, **421,** 438
conductor, 47
Contempo organ, 285, **314**
control grid, 54
Cooder, Ry, **198, 214**
Cornell, Chris, 469
cosmetics, 19
 blackface amps, 255, 257, 278
 blackface amps ('80s), 336, 348, 363, **364**
 current amps, 413
 "Fast Four" amps, 352
 grouping schemes, 99
 M-80, **364**
 silverface amps, **304,** 306, 315
 Super Pro Series, 339–40
 Super-Sonics, 438–39
 Tolex amps, 197, **200, 204, 205,** 207, 231, 233, 275
 tweed amps, 123–24, 160, **172**
 woodies, 120
cost-cutting measures (CBS-era), 306–7, 313, 318–19, 321
country music, 298, 313
Cowboy Copas, the, 129
Cox, Roger, 348
Cragg, Larry, 189
Crate company, 334, 353, 361, 364–65, 414
Crazy Horse, **242**
Crazy Legs (Jeff Beck album), **277,** 377
Cream, 457
Crooks, Bob, 204–5, 207
Cropper, Steve, 124, **174, 187, 269**
CTS pots, 334
CTS speakers, **71, 76,** 318, 429, 483
Curtis, Dale, 403, 409, 414, **447,** 449, 459–67
Curtis, Sonny, 71
Custom Amp Shop Series, **42,** 368, 370–71, 372, 386, 388, 391–99, 404, 413, 419, 421, **421,** 423. *See also* Custom Series
Custom Colors, **398**
Custom Series, 420
Custom Vibrasonic, 398, 405, **406, 407**
Custom Vibrolux Reverb, 378, 398, **404,** 404–5, 427
cutoff, 94
Cyber amps, **20,** 417, **445**
Cyber-Champ, 452
Cyber-Deluxe, 452
Cyber-Twin, **20,** 417, 419, 443, 444, **445, 446,** 446–51
Cyber-Twin SE, **77,** 443–44, 452, **452**

D circuits, 152
Dale, Dick, 41, 43, 75, **184, 212, 235,** 236–37, 247, 274
damping factor, 66
Daniel, Nathan, 28
Daniels, Drew, 414
Dantzig, Jol, 45, 210
Darr, Jack, 92
 Electric Guitar Amplifier Handbook, 15–16
date codes, **69,** 76, **98,** 104, 106, 250, **250–51**
Davis, Rick, 188
de-esser, 414
De Forest, Lee, 53
defense industry, 38–39
Del-Tones, **235**
Delaney & Bonnie & Friends On Tour with Eric Clapton (album), **175**
Deluxe
 1x10 (Model 26) woodie, **67, 110, 116, 117,** 119, 120, 127
 5E3 (tweed), 58, 59, 157
 6G3 '61 chassis layout, **104**
 6G3 '61 schematic, **28**
 6V6 tubes in, 83
 6V6GT tubes in, 213
 biasing in, 90–91
 blackface, **271,** 295, **317,** 326, **485**

brown Tolex, 85, 124, **206,** 208, **214, 215,** 233, 268
model number for, 102
name plates for, **101**
tubes in, 85, 215
TV front, **16,** 127, 133–34, 134, 136, **137, 141**
tweed, **57,** 484
tweed, narrow panel, 160, **178, 187,** 207, 326, 485
tweed, wide panel, **76,** 145, **146,** 147
Deluxe 85, 352, 353, 363
Deluxe 90, **417, 426**
Deluxe Reverb, 481, 491
6V6GT tubes in, 213
blackface, 83, **213, 272, 280,** 295, 479–80, **485**
blackface ('80s models), 337
discontinuation of, 376
extension cabinet, **76**
negative feedback loop, 177
silverface, 83, **304,** 307, **307, 312,** 325, 326, 331, 494
speakers in, **72**
transformer in, 61
"TV tray" transistor model, **294, 296,** 297, 299, 300
Deluxe Reverb '65 reissue, 57, 83, 86, 216, 370, 372, 375, 380, **380, 385,** 408
Deluxe Reverb II
6V6 tubes in, 83
blackface ('80s models), **330,** 337, 339
discontinuation of, 376
Desiderio, Bob, 348, 353, **354,** 364, 365, 367, 406, 439, 461, **462, 498**
Deuces Wild (B.B. King album), 160
Diaz, César, 216, 248, 428–29, **429**
Dickerson, Deke, 205
Diddley, Bo, **329**
digital amps, 417, 426–27, 432, 434–35, 443–55
Dimension IV Sound Expander, 298
diodes, 52, 55, **388**
direct-coupling, 290–91
direct current (DC), 47, 50–51, 52, 62
Dirty Work (album), 248
distortion, 42–43, 58–59, 60, 136, 177, 181, 186, 202, 211, 215, 267, 287, 289–90, 337, 339, 403, 446–47
Dobro company, 23–24
dog-bone handles, 17, **160,** 197, **200, 205, 243,** 369
Domino, Fats, 191
Dorf, Richard H., 269
Double Showman, 295, 351
Douglas, Alan, 474
Douglas, Nathaniel, **190**
Down Beat magazine, 234, 239, 240, 245
Doyle, Michael, 421, 423, 481
The History of Marshall, 16, 171
The Sound of Rock, 16
Dreyfuss, Henry, 37, 38
Dronge, Alfred, 28
Dual Bass 400, **344,** 363, **364**
Dual Professional, **67**
biasing in, 90
Custom Amp Shop, 391, 395, **395**
innovations of, 122
push/pull configuration in, 92
reverb circuit, 273–74
top-mounted panel, 133
tweed, **122,** 123, 124, 127, 148, 372, 479
Dual Showman, 200, 237, 297, **302,** 324
blackface, 351
blackface/red-knob, **344,** 348, 350–51, 363, 368
blonde Tolex, 494
Pro Tube Series, 370
silverface, **304,** 313, 315, 331, 351
Dual Showman Reverb
blackface/red-knob, 363, **364**
discontinuation of, 367
silverface, 305, 313, 315, 339, 351
dual triodes, 55, 58, 79, 82, 92, 137, 186
Dugmore, Dan, 274
Dumble, Alexander, **57,** 58, 61, 107, 171, 470
Dumble company, **57**
Duncan, Mark, 423
Duncan, Seymour, 200, **263, 269,** 481
Dunn, Duck, **187**
Dwell control, 273–74
Dyna-Touch III, 432, **433**
Dyna-Touch Plus, 432
Dyna-Touch Series, 426, 429, 432, **433**
dynamic range, 53

E series, 58, 179
Eagles, the, 372
Eames, Charles, 37, 38
Eames, Ray, 37, 38
eBay, 492–93
ECC83 tubes, 80
EccoFonic, **169**
Eddy, Duane, 274
Edwards, Nokie, **43**
effects, 56
efficiency, 66
EIA code numbers, 105
Eighty-Five, 363
Einstein, Albert, 84
EL34 tubes, 55, 83, 84
EL84 tubes, 55, 57, 83
electric basses, Fender, 25, 202, **458**
Electric Guitar Amplifier Handbook (Darr), 15–16
Electric Light Orchestra, 378
electrical circuitry, 24, 42, 43, 48, 99–109, 159, 443
AA circuits, 103–4, 261, **264,** 272, 275
AB circuits, 305, 307, 313
AC circuits, 313
"blackfacing," 316–17
categorizing Fender amps by, 100
CBS-era, 285, 309, 313
circuit codes, 100, 102–4, 106, 109, 145, 147, 182
classification schemes, 106
D circuits, 152
date codes, 104
E circuits, 179
Fender's insights, 27
G circuits, 208, 211–13
Hot Rods, **404**
"lossy" circuits, 211
sounds and, 105–6
Super Showman XFLs, 298
Super-Sonics, 439
tweed to blackface eras, 263–64
electrical current, 47
electrodes, 53–54, 55
Electronic Echo Chamber, **93, 275**
electrons, 47, 53–54, 62
ElectroPlex, 361
Eliptoflex enclosure, 205
Ellis, Andy, 359, 473–74
Eminence speakers, 347, 369, 370, 376, 382, 429
Epstein, Brian, 328
equivalency, 79–80
ergonomics, 37
Eric Clapton (album), **175**
Eric Clapton "Blackie" Strat, **397**
Esquire electric "Spanish" guitar, 133, 157, **174, 190, 202**
Evans, Dick, 291
extension cabinets, **76, 244, 488**
eyelet-to-eyelet wiring, 323–24, 476–77, **477**

face plates, categorizing Fender amps by, 261
Factory Special Runs (FSRs), 380, 436
"Fast Four" amps, **344,** 352–53, 363
feedback, 58, 177–79, 263–64. *See also* negative feedback
Felker, Reggie, 44–45
Fender, Leo, **25, 39, 114, 130, 135**
approach to design, 37–39, 40, 75, 222, 234, 240, 248–49, 263, 284, 289, 368, 469, 471–72
Dale and, 236–37
dedication, 29, 129
early career, 23, 41–43, 83
enduring contributions, 24–25, 27–28, 40–41
guitar designs, 27, 28
Guitar Player interview, 177
innovations, 43, 443
perfectionism, 100, 153
preferred biasing method, 94, 96
sale of company, 283, 292
speaker choices of, 318
tremolo patent, 269
tributes to, 30–35
vision impairment, 24
work area, **115**
Fender, The Inside Story (White), 129, 193
Fender: The Sound Heard 'Round the World (Smith), 45, 115, 179–80, 216, 250
Fender 75, 319, 331–32, **333,** 337
Fender 85, 352
Fender 140, 337
Fender advertisements, **116,** 218, 220, **222, 223,** 224, **224, 238, 282, 364, 458**

Fender Amp Field Guide, 234
Fender Amps, The First Fifty Years, 114. *See also* Teagle & Sprung
Fender amps categorizing schemes, 99–107, 127, 261
Fender Bass Amplification, 372, 413, 457–67. *See also specific model names*
Fender catalogs, 129, 224
  1950, 133–34
  1954, 145, 147, **218**
  1958/59, **159**
  1960, 202, **203,** 207–8, **220,** 245
  1961, **36**
  1969, **312**
  1982, 336–37, 337
  1993, 370–71
  1994, 372
  inconsistencies in, 245, 247–48
  mid-'50s, **17**
  photo shoots, 218, 220
Fender Electric Guitar Course, **265**
Fender Electric Instrument Company, 23
  founding, 39, 119
  in-house reference guides, **106**
  name change, 287, 295
  overlaps, gaps, and other mismatches, 106–7
  use of leftover components, 99–100
"Fender firsts," 204–5, 207
Fender international business, 340–41, 347, 366, 424–27
Fender Japan, 340, 345
Fender logos, **101,** 120, **120,** 197, **308,** 315, 413, 434–35, 438–39, 459, 463–64, **465**
Fender marketing strategies, 368
Fender Museum, 49
Fender Musical Instruments, 287, 295
Fender National Service Center facility, 324
Fender price lists, 199, 207
Fender Radio Service, 114
Fender road representatives, 152–53
Fender Sales, 217, 221–25, 346
Fendermen, the, 200
Fenton, Mike, 377
filament, 53
filters, 53
Fireballs, the, 56, 274
Fischer, Ken, 361
Fishell, Steve, **268**
fixed bias, 90, 91, 96, 97, 159, **173,** 231, 275, **276,** 278
Fleming, J. A., 56
Fliegler, Ritchie
  Amps! The Other Half of Rock 'n' Roll, 16, 370, 402
  The Complete Guide to Guitar and Amp Maintenance, 52, 402
  Fender tenure of, 361, **400,** 401–8, 413–17, 419, 444, 449, 459, 462, 463
  pictured, **402, 449, 498**
  Prosonic and, 396
  quoted, 24, 27, 50, 89, 97, 105, 183, 216, 273, **355,** 470, 472, 474, 475, 476, 477, 484
  on solid state amps, 408–12
FM amps, 426, 429, **432**
Fogerty, John, **57**
folded-horn speaker cabinets, 71, 322–23, 457
Forbes, Rob, 375
Ford, Henry, 34
Ford, Robben, 96, 394
"form follows function," 38
Forte, Dan, **57,** 170, 274, **329**
Frampton, Peter, 28, 171, 240, 325, 480–81, 489–94
Freeman, Paul, 170
frequency bands, 56
frequency response, 59, 66
Frisell, Bill, **385**
front-mounted control panels, 204, **207,** 208, 255
Frontline catalog, 421
Frontman Series, 411–12, 413, 417, 425, 426, 429, **432,** 459
Fullerton, George, 30, 33, 142, 164, **181,** 210
Fullerton factory, 41, 129, **130–31,** 132, **154, 252–53, 284,** 306, 324, 340, 347
Funicello, Annette, **247**
fuzztone, 191, 298

G-DEC amps, 368, 426, 444, **453,** 453–54
Gagliano, Greg
  20th Century Guitar, 74
  on circuits, codes, and schematics, 109
  on collecting amplifiers, 489–94
  quoted, 86, 102, 103, 145, 147, 168, 200, 231, 234, 248, 261, **264,** 307, 309, 317
gain controls, cascading, 396
gain-stage tubes, 79, 358
Gallup, Cliff, 377
Garcia, Albert, **270**
Garza, Henry, **423,** 481
Gatton, Danny, **280,** 376, 405
Gault, Bob, 376, 377
Geerlings, PJ, 313, 319–20, 333, 342
Gelow, Bill, 319
General Electric tubes, 82, 83
General Tire Corporation, **41**
Genesis, 450
Gerst, Harvey, 74–75
Gibbons, Billy, 96, 124, 168, **174,** 479
Gibson company, 23–24, 141, 152, 204, 298, **307,** 402
"Goin' So Good," **174**
Goldrich, Manny, 162
Gonzales, Dave, 74
Graydon, Jay, 342
"Green Onions," **174**
Gretsch 6120, 162
Gretsch company, 152, **228**
Gretsch family, 28
Gretsch Filter 'Tron pickup, 50
grid bias tremolo, 231, 268, 269, 273
grid resistor bias, 90
grid stopper, 166
grids, 51, 53–54, 62–63, 90
grille cloths
  of black Tolex amps, 255, 257, 278, 287
  of blackface amps, 315
  of blackface/red-knob amps, 348–49, 363
  of narrow panel tweeds, **172**
  of silverface amps, 306, 315
  of Super-Sonics, 438
  of Tolex amps, 197, **198,** 233, **262,** 275
  of TV fronts, 145
  of wide panel tweeds, 145, **172**
  of woodies, 120
Grom, Steve
  Fender tenure of, 340, 347, **349,** 376, 377, 384, 402, 408
  pictured, **498**
  quoted, 313, 315, 318–19, 320, 322–23, 331–32, 334, 337, 345–46, 348, 349, 350, 352, 353, 354, 357–58, 359, 363–64, 365, 366, 378, 388, 413
Groove Tubes, **17,** 428, 474–75
Gruhn, George, 23–24, 25, 45, 124, 136, 489–94
Guitar Amp Handbook, The (Hunter), 58, 59, 96, 186, 211, 212
guitar-amplifier matched sets, 48
Guitar Book, The (Wheeler), 16
Guitar Player magazine, 16, 357, 358, 359, 369, 392, 411, 415, 443
Guitar Rigs (Hunter), 166
guitar signal, 62
Guitarist magazine, 443–44
guitars, collecting, 489–90
Gulbransen organ company and factory, 284, 339, 340, 345
Guy, Buddy, 168, 169, **254,** 377, 443, 451
GZ34/5AR4 rectifier tubes, **28, 59,** 86, **98, 104,** 166, 182–83, 215, 231, 275, 278, 311, 381

Haggard, Merle, 484
Haigler, Robert, 334, 336, 339, 342, 352
Haley, Bill, 191
Hall, F. C., 28
Hamernik, Sergio, 155
Hamilton, Reggie, 467
Hammond Organ Company, 274
hand-wiring, 323, 361, **374,** 386–87, 388, 391–99, 398, 425, 476–77
Hardtke, Alan, **123, 150, 152, 153, 204, 256**
Harkleroad, Bill, **214**
"Harmonic Vibrato" feature, 268–69
harmonics reproduction, 295–96
Harmony company, 23–24
Harrison, George, 160, **175, 206,** 326, **326, 327,** 377, 378
Harvard, 124, **173, 174,** 207
  5F10 narrow panel tweed, 160, 173, 175, 183
  6F10 narrow panel tweed, 173, 183
  blackface ('80s models), **335,** 337
  model number for, 102
  speakers in '50s, **67**
Harvard Reverb, **335,** 337
Harvard Reverb II, **330,** 337
Hawkins, Ronnie, 168
Hawkins, Screamin' Jay, 191
Hawthorne, Christopher, 39
Hayes, Charlie, 346
headroom, 42, 58, 60, 178, 181, 182, 202, 211, 267, 434
heaters, 51, 53–54, 79

Heath, Jim, **412**
heavy-duty components, 204
Hendrix, Jimi, 41, **83,** 96, **302,** 360
Henneman, Brian, 369
Hertz (Hz), 47
Hicks, David, 457
Hiland, Johnny, 389
Hines, Bob, **202**
History of Marshall, The (Doyle), 16, 171
Hiwatt company, 55
Hodges, Bill, 334
Hollywood, California, 39
Holmes, Jimmy "Duck," **70**
Hooker, Earl, 170
Hooker, John Lee, 481
Hoopeston factory, 340, 345, 347
Hopkins, Gregg, 123
horn-loaded cab, 71
HOT, 371, 404, 406
H.O.T., 364–65, **366,** 368
Hot Licks, Cold Steel & Truckers' Favorites (Commander Cody album), **57**
Hot Rod amps, **40,** 57, **400, 402,** 402–3, **403, 404,** 411, 413, 419, 426–27
Hot Rod Deluxe, 265, **417,** 436
Hot Rod Deluxe Emerald, 436
Hot Rod DeVille, 265
Hot Rod DeVille 410, **103**
hot rods (cars), 39
Howe, Steve, **486**
Hughes, Bill
  Fender tenure of, 334, 336, 342, 346, 348, 350–51, 352, 353, 376–77, 439, 461
  pictured, **336**
  quoted, 51, 319, 323, 337, 339, 349, 364–65, 385
Humble Pie, 325
humbucker pickups, 49, 50
Hunter, Dave, 97, 136, 171, 476
  The Guitar Amp Handbook, 58, 59, 96, 186, 211, 212
  Guitar Rigs, 166
Hunter, Ian, 472
Huntington, Greg
  on collecting amps, 489–94
  quoted, 173, **199,** 234, 245, 248–49, 263, 264, 273, 306, 309, 315, 316, 318
Hutton, Sam, 226, 248–49
hybrid amps, 369

"I Walk the Line," **202**
Illsey, John, **215**
impedance, 50, 59–60, 61, 66, 67, 141, 166, 186, 349, 470, 473
inductance, 50, 60, 476
inductor. *See* choke
"industry standard," 27, 28–29, 42
"infinite baffle" enclosures, 71
input jacks, 49, **50,** 427
insulation, 47
interactive controls, 179–81
interleaved transformers, 60, 61, 166, 176
Internet, 492–93

Jackson, Lee, 299, 319, 320, 332, 334, 336, 345, 349
Jackson company, 434
Jaguar guitar, **80**
Jahns, Ed, 284, 315, 319–24, 331–32, **333,** 334, 342
JAM, 371, 404, 406
J.A.M., 364–65, **366,** 368
Jamerson, James, 457
James Burton Telecaster, **397**
JAN spec tubes, 81
Jazz Bass, **458**
jazz players, 152–53
Jazzmaster, 157, **169,** 200, **202, 203, 240–41,** 436, 491
JBL speakers, 65, **73,** 74, 204, 212, 481
  D120F, 245, **299**
  D130, 236
  D130F, 234, 236, 237
  dating, 74
  F-series, 74–75
  in Super Showman XFLs, 298
Jensen speakers, 65, 212, 318, 376
  C-12K, 379
  C12N, 379
  code for, 105, **105**
  designation codes, 119
  in K&F amps, **117–18,** 119
  naming, 74
  P10Q, 168, 176, **209**
  P10R, **67,** 122, 176, **209,** 381
  P12N, **69,** 176, **186**
  P12Q, 176, **183**
  P12R, **76,** 134, 147
  P15N, **69, 76,** 136, 145, 148, 150, 481
  PM10C, **67,** 122
Jimi Hendrix Experience, **302,** 457
Johnny & the Hurricanes, 274
Johnson, Big Jack, **103**
Johnson, Cecil, **246,** 249
Johnson, Eric, 96, **280,** 473, 490
Jones, Mike, **498**
Jones, Quincy, 23

Kaiser, Henry, 483
Kauffman, Doc, 23, 39, 48, 111, 113–14, **114,** 115, 119
Kay company, 23–24
Kaye, Mary, 218, 484
K&F amps, **15,** 23, 48, **112,** 113, **113,** 114–15, **117,** 119, **256,** 494
K&F lap steel guitars, 48, **112,** 113
K&F Manufacturing, 111, 113–14
"Kids Are Alright, The," 212
King, B.B., **84, 126–27, 144,** 160, **270,** 278, **321,** 479
King, Freddie, **319**
Kinkel, Steve, **246**
Kirchen, Bill, **57**
Knopfler, Mark, **215,** 440, 480–81, 491
Koch, Greg, 480, **487**
Koerner, Rich, 320, 322, 323
Kojima, Chitoshi, 340
Kravitz, Lenny, **91**
Krieger, Robbie, 281
Kropotkin, Mike, 474
Kubicki, Phil, **206**
Kulick, Bob, **302**
Kurz-Kasch, 339
Kustom 200, 457
KXR keyboard amps, 368, **371,** 372, 404, 406

lacquered tweed, 384
Lafayette Radio, 205
Lake Oswego factory, 348, 363, 368, 372
Lang, Jonny, **390**
Lansing speakers, 24, 75, 150, **268**
  D130, 202, **203**
layer-wound transformers, 60
Layla (Clapton album), **161,** 325
lead dress, 309
Lee, Albert, 71, 171–72, 483–84
Lennon, John, 326, **327,** 328
Les Paul guitars, **187,** 189, **226, 258**
Leslie, Don, **314**
Leslie Model 16 system, **314**
Let It Be (Beatles album), 326, 328
Let It Be (film), **206**
"Let It Rain," **175**
Letts, Mike, 229, **483**
Lewis, Dave, 461
Lewis, Huey, **329**
Lewis, Mike
  Dual Professional and, 395
  Fender tenure of, 361, 366–73, 380, 391, 396, 401, 411, 416, 419
  names conceived by, 373
  pictured, **367, 498**
  quoted, **26,** 40, 170, 349
  Vibro-King and, 392
Libra, 299
Linden, Paul, 234
Lindley, David, 21, **57,** 394
Line 6, 450
linear taper pots, 49
Linke, Gernold, **215**
Little Richard, **190,** 191
Loar, Lloyd, 492
lock jointed corners, 134, **134, 427**
Loewy, Raymond, 37, 38, 40
Lofgren, Nils, **487**
logarithmic taper pots, 49
London 185, 363
London Reverb, **338,** 339, 340
"Long and Winding Road, The," **206**
long-tail phase inverters, 58, 59, 231, 233, 275, 278, 313
Lopez, Lupe, 107, **194**
Los Lonely Boys, **423**
"lossy" circuits, 211
Lover, Seth, 298, 299
low-pass filters, 56
Lymon, Frankie, 191
Lynne, Jeff, 378

M-80, **364,** 364–65, 368
M-80 Series, 371, 406
Magic Parts, 475
magnets, 53, 119
Mallory caps, 309, 311, 316, 334
Malmsteen, Yngwie, 372
Mandelson, Ben, 281
Mark, John, 82, 84
Marshall, Andy, 53, 96, 164, 166, 361, 470–71, 476
Marshall, Jim, 171–72
Marshall, Wolf, 443
Marshall company, 43, 55, 107, 124, 171–72, 283, 334, 345, 392, 401, 406, 414, 423
Marshall Major, 457, 472
Marshall Super Lead, 52
Martin, Grady, 481–82
Mases, Leif, **277**
Massie, Ray, 114, 119
Master-Builts, 421, 423–24
master volume circuits, 305
Matchless company, 361
"Maybellene," **196**

Mayer, John, **108–9**
MB-1200, 461, 462
McAuliffe, Leon, **219,** 298
McCartney, Paul, 326, **327,** 328
McCarty, Ted, 28
McCready, Mike, **365**
McDonald, Richard
on Cyber-Twins, 444, 446–54
Fender tenure of, 361, 391, 402, 404, 415–17, 432, 436, 459–67, 462
pictured, **415, 498**
quoted, 24, 142, 300, 378, 396, 405, 406, **406, 415, 418,** 440, 455
Super Reverb and, 381–82
on Super-Sonics, 438
McNeil, Tom, 475
Melkisethian, Steve, 311, 317
Mellotone, 339
Mesa/Boogie, 171, 334, 337, 345, 375, 437
Mesa/Boogie Mark I, 358, **358**
metal bands, 43, 364–65, 434
Metalhead amps, **77,** 434–35, **435**
Mexican assembly plants, 82, 340, 347, 363, 368, 411, 425, 426–27, **439–41**
microphones, 65, 74, 414
mil spec tubes, 81, 85
Miller, Eddie, **135**
Miller Dial, 339
"Miserlou," 236
mobile PA system, **39**
model name grouping schemes, 99
model numbers, vintage-era, 102
modeling amps, 446–47
Monkey's Uncle, The (film), **247**
Montgomery, Monk, 298
Montreux, **338,** 339, 352
Moody Blues, the, 457
Moore, Scotty, 147
Morris, Don, 186, 361, 483
Morris, Ralph, 75
Moseley, Semie, 28
Motorola, 297
"Muleskinner Blues," 200
multi-speaker systems, 67, 74
multiple tone knobs, 204
Music Man, **70**
music stores, sales at, **26,** 153, 363–64
music styles, amps and, 42–43, 152–53, 155, 191, 236–37, 274, 281, 283, 298, 313, 315, 380, 417
Music Trades, 234
Musical Merchandise Review, 234
Musicmaster Bass, 337, **459**

name plates, **101**
narrow panel tweed amps, 109, 157–92, **159.** *See also* tweed amps; *specific model names*
biasing in, 90, 159
cathode-follower tone stacks in, 186–87
circuit codes for, 103
E circuits in, 179
F circuits in, 183, 187
interactive controls and channels, 179–81
name plates for, **101**
negative feedback loop in, 177–79
presence control in, 159, 177–79
protective cover for, **256**
rock and roll, 191
split-load inverters in, 58
transformers, wattage, and speakers for, 175–76
tubes in, 82
National company, 23–24
negative feedback, 97, 166, 177–79, 231
negative grid voltage, 94
New Vintage Series, 398, 404
Nicholas, Shane
Bassman LTD and, 383–88
on Cyber-Twins, 444, 446–54
Fender tenure of, 361, 415, 416, **417,** 419–20, 423–24, 444
interview with, 424–29, 432–37
pictured, **420, 498**
quoted, 49, 52, 53, 56, **57,** 71, 74, 96, 168, 170, 178–79, 182, 380, 382, 405
on Super-Sonics, 438–40
Nielsen, Rick, **259**
NOS tubes, 81–82, 474–75
Nugent, Ted, **286–87**

Obrecht, Jas, **187, 198,** 485
O'Connor, Kevin, 35
Ohms (ø), 48, 49, 59
Ono, Yoko, 328
open-back cabinets, **68,** 69, 71, 72, 74, 353
Orange company, 55
Orange Drop caps, 311, 317, 470
Organ Button steel guitar, **8–9**
Osborne, Mary, 218
output jacks, 49
output stage configuration, 92, 96, 97
Owens, Buck, 56, **315, 316**
Oxford speakers, 65, 318
10K5, **250–51**
12K5, **72, 76**
12M6, **70, 243**
15M6, **70**
code for, 105
naming, 74

PA systems, 285, 290, **320, 327,** 366
Pagano, Blackie
quoted, 27, 38, 40, 42, 43, 72, 80, 107, 166, 473, 475, 479
Page, Jimmy, **175,** 189, 200, 360
Page, John, 353, 398
Paktron caps, 309, 334
parallel array speaker system, 67
paraphase inverters, 58, 59, 122, 137
Parkman, Gordon, **349**
Patt, Stephen, 298
Paul, Les, **140,** 141
Peavey, Hartley, 27, 30, 205, 207, 269, 292, 301, 318, 352, 365–66, 469, 475
Peavey company, 334, 352, 353, 361
pedal effects, 470
Peden, John, 164, 248, 485, 489–94
pentodes, 42, 55, 137, **216**
Performer 650, 371
Performer 1000, 371
Performer Series, 371, 404, 406
Perine, Robert, 29, 33, **169,** 218, 220, **238**
Perkins, Carl, 160, 191
Perkins, Luther, **202**
Permofil Epoxy, 324
phase cancellation, 71–72
phase inverters (phase splitters), 57, 58–59, 79, 92, 137, 177, 263, 275, 278, 311, 316
phase-shift vibrato, 273
photocell tremolo, 272–73, 278
Piccirillo, Jay, 413, 419, 459–67, **462**
pickups, **48,** 49, 50, 65, 74, 141, 298, 414
piezo pickups, 414
piggyback cabinets, 69, 71, 177, 197, **198,** 204–5, 207–8, 245, **246,** 247–48, 275, 457
pitch shifting, 273
Pittman, Aspen, 402
collection of, 193
pictured, **471**
quoted, 27, 34, 80, 82, 84, 145, 171, 257, **302,** 428, 470, 471–72, 474–75, 479–80
SFX technology, 414
The Tube Amp Book, 16, 56, 81, **83,** 416
plate current, 52
plates, 51, 53–54, 80, 186
Pohlman, Ray, **210**
port-vented cabinets, 71, 136
Porter, John, 160
pots (potentiometers), 32, 49, 56, 105, **209,** 268
power amp, 57, 447
Power Chorus, 353, 364, 367
power ratings, 315, 322–23, **330,** 357–58
power supply, 51, 52–53, 62, 90, 166, 182, 231, 263, 267, 311, 476
power tube biasing, 89, 90
preamps, 56, 57, **175,** 298, 331, 337, 348, 369. *See also specific tube numbers*
D circuit, 152
tubes for, 54, 56, 79, 82, 134, 145, 180, 212, 462, **462**
Precision Bass, 136, 157, 200, 225, 368, **458**
Premiere amps, 153
presence circuit, 159
presence control, 150, 166, **176,** 177–79, 208, 231, 233, 261, 264
Presley, Elvis, **18,** 147, **156–57,** 191, **268**
Preston, Billy, **327**
Princeton
1x8 (Student model) woodie, **8–9, 28, 110, 116,** 119, 120, 127
5F2 schematic, **63**
6V6 tubes in, 58, 83, **214**
6V6GT tubes in, 213
biasing in, 90–91
black Tolex, **29,** 264
blackface, 83, 255, **260, 262,** 273, 295
brown Tolex, **29, 41,** 83, 173, **201,** 208, **214,** 264
Class A, 96
discontinuation of, 331
model number for, 102
name plates for, **101**
narrow panel tweed, **28,** 83, **88–89,** 160, 173, **178,** 207

  protective cover for, **256**
  silverface, 316, 325, 494
  single-ended circuit design in, 92
  TV front, **28,** 127, 134, **138**
  Wide panel tweed, **28,** 145, **146,** 147
Princeton 65, **412**
Princeton 650, **77**
Princeton Chorus, **344,** 353–54, **354,** 363, 367, 371, **410**
Princeton Chorus DSP, 354
Princeton guitar, **8–9**
Princeton II, 340
Princeton Recording model, 57
Princeton Reverb, **317,** 491
  6V6GT tubes in, 213
  blackface, 83, 85, **269,** 273, 295
  blackface ('80s models), 337
  discontinuation of, 376
  silverface, **304,** 307, **312,** 325, 331, 494
Princeton Reverb II, **330, 332,** 337, 339, 376
Princeton Super Pro, 339
Pro 185, 352, 353, 363, 371
Pro Junior, 57
black Tolex, **425**
limited edition, **398**
tweed, 368–69, **369,** 371
Pro Junior 60th Anniversary Woody, **10, 495**
Pro (Professional)
  1x15 woodie, **8–9,** 90, **110, 117, 118–19,** 120, **120, 121,** 127, **133**
  5E5-A narrow panel tweed, 71, 179, **179,** 187
  12AX7 tubes in 5C5 model, 82
  blackface, 86, 100, 257, 275, **276,** 278, 287, 295
  brown Tolex, **69, 70,** 86, 124, **199,** 207, **215,** 231, **233,** 233–34, 257, 268–69
  model number for, 102
  name plates for, **101**
  presence control on, 264
  speakers in, **69**
  tubes in, 85, 213
  TV front, **16,** 90, 109, 127, 133–34, **135,** 136, **141**
  tweed, **69**
  tweed, narrow panel, 159, 178, 481
  tweed, wide panel, 145, 148, 150, **150–51**
  woodies, **110, 117, 118–19,** 120, **120,** 398, **488,** 494
Pro Reverb, 491
  biasing in, 309
  blackface, 86, 257, 278, **279,** 287
  blackface ('80s models), 336
  discontinuation of, 337, 438
  silverface, 86, 104, 305, **312,** 316, 331
  "TV tray" transistor model, **294,** 297
Pro Tube Series, 57, 370, 372, 404, 406, 411, 417, 420, 427
production numbers, 105
Professional Amplifiers line, 197, 199, **200,** 205, 207–8, 224, 233, 234
Professional Tube Series. *See* Pro Tube Series
Prosonic, 96, 396, **396–97,** 413, 440
protective covers, **256**
prototyping process, 342
pull boosts, 305, 324, 331, 342, 349
Pulp Fiction (film), 236
punk, 43
push-button amps, 364–65
push/pull output configuration, 42, 57–59, 92, 97

Quad Reverb, 305, 313, 315, **328, 329,** 331, 339, 491
Quine, Robert, 483

RAD, 371, 404, 406
R.A.D., **364,** 364–65, **366,** 368
radio, 42
Radio & Television News, 85
Radio-Tel, 216
Raitt, Bonnie, 369
Ranaldo, Lee, 389
Randall, Don
  on Beatles' use of Fenders, 326, 328
  career of, 216
  Fender tenure of, 75, 119, 164, 220, 231, 234, 255, 263, 284
  interview with, 221–25
  names conceived by, 136, 225, 395
  pictured, **219, 221**
  quoted, 114, 115, 191, 207
Ratliff, Frank, **473**
RCA Receiving Tube Manual, 90, 94, 186
RCA transistors, 301
RCA tubes, 82, 83, **264**
rectifier switch, 3-way, 396
rectifiers, 50–54, **52, 57, 59,** 86, 147, 166, 181–83, **213,** 215–16, 311
rectifiers, redundancy, 215–16
Redding, Otis, 169
Reissue Series, 370, 372, 382, 388, 420. *See also* Vintage Series
reissues, 363, 366, 370, 375–89. *See also specific model names*
  inputs on, 57
  tube-powered, 427
  tubes in, 57, 83, 86, 216
  U.S.-made, 425
Relic Pro Junior, **398**
resistors, 48, 49, 90, 132, 166, 309, 311, 316
reverb, 43, 56, 159, 181, 207, 278, 313, 427
Reverb channel, 181, **227**
reverb drivers, 79
Reverb units, 43, **260,** 273–74, **423, 485**
  '63 reissue, **211,** 274, 372, 375, 413
Reverbrocket amp, 152, 207
Revolver (Beatles album), 326
Rhodes, Harold, 75
Rich, Don, 56, **315**
Richards, Keith, **13,** 25, 161, 172, **214,** 248, **258, 272, 356,** 360, 388, 428, **478,** 480
Rickenbacker company, 23–24, 212, 288, 291, 326
Rissi, Bob, 31, 185, **288,** 288–91, 292, **296,** 299, 324
Rivera, Paul, 171, 324
  amps created by, 361
  Ed Jahns and, 319
  Fender tenure of, 332, 334, 336–42, 345–47, 352, 354, 376
  pictured, **334**
  quoted, 35, 185, 186, 284–85, 299, **338,** 471, **482**
Rivera R&D, 332
Roberts, Andy, **277**
Roberts, Howard, **210**
Robinson, Rich, 360
Roc Pros, 406, **409**
Rock and Roll Hall of Fame, 45, **254**
"Rock Around the Clock," 191
Rock 'N' Roll Trio, 191
Rock On (Humble Pie album), 325
Rogan, Alan, 160, 162, 212, **244,** 248, 250, 377, 405, 484
Rolling Stones, the, **258**
Ronson, Mick, 472
Rosas, Cesar, **161, 346**
Rose, Myles, 56
Rosmini, Dick, 471, 472
Rubber Soul (Beatles album), 326
Rubin, David, **346**
Ruby Tubes, 475
Ruffin, David, **217**
Rumble 100, **466**
Rumble Bass amp, 372, 398, 465
Rumble line, 461, 465–66
Rush, Otis, 170, 278

sag, 52–53, **57,** 60
Sampson, Mark, 361
Sanchez, Lydia, **135**
Santana, Carlos, 213, 278, 372, 469, 472
Satellite, **417**
saturation, 94
Scholz, Tom, 353
Schultz, William
  CBS viewed by, 284
  Fender tenure of, 29, 336, 347–48, 352, 353, 354, 365, 401, 416, 419, 444, 450, 459
  pictured, **355**
Schumacher transformers, 105, 175, **209,** 320, 324, 334
Schwarz, Jack, 353
Scorpio, 299, **299**
screen grid, 55
"secondary emissions," 55
Seifert, Lisa, **430–31**
self biasing. *See* cathode bias
semiconductors, 352
series connections for speakers, 67
series/parallel speaker system, 67
Settle, Ken, **478**
Setzer, Brian, **228**
Sex Pistols, the, 43
Shamblin, Eldon, 155
Shelton, Louie, **214**
Shepherd, Kenny Wayne, **407**
Showman
  12 model, 233, 248, 295
  15 model, 295
  biasing in, 309
  blackface, **93,** 295, 326
  blackface ('80s models), 339, 340, **343**
  blackface/blonde cab transition style, **264**
  blonde Tolex piggybacks, **198,** 200, 207, 208, 234, 392, **393**
  brown Tolex, 268–69
  Dick Dale and, 236–37

introduction of, 199
model number for, 102
presence control on, 264
push/pull configuration in, 92
speakers in, 74
Sidekick amps, **341,** 347, **350–51,** 366
signal processing, 56, 62
silverface amps, 283, 303–29, **308, 312,** 491
"blackfacing," 316–17
cabinets and baffles for, 311, 313
capacitors on, 311
circuit codes for, 103–4
circuitry of, **306,** 307, 309, 315–16, 323–24
collectability of, 494
cosmetics of, **304,** 306, 315
Ed Jahns and, 319–24
phase inverters in, 311
poor reputation of, 303–4
power supplies for, 311
production details, 307, 309
rectifiers in, 311
sound and quality assessment, 315–16, 324–25
speakers for, 318–19
subgroups, 304–5
transformers in, 324
tubes in, 85
Singapore assembly plants, 82
single-ended output configuration, 92, 96, 97
Smith, Dan, 334, 347, 353
Smith, G. E., 392, **393**
Smith, Paul Reed, 29, 171, 388, **487**
Smith, Randall, 62, 332, 358, 375
Smith, Richard, 247
on collecting amps, 489–94
Fender: The Sound Heard 'Round the World, 45, 115, 119, 179–80, 216, **227,** 250
quoted, 29, 48, 75, 122, 136, **139,** 141, 193, 200, 346, 484–85
Smith, Willie, **319**
"Smoke on the Water," **365**
So-Cal Speed Shop, 39
Soest, Steve, 240, 248–49
Soldano, Mike, 171, 211–12, 479
Soldi, "Cactus Jim," **246**
solid state amplifiers, 193, **282,** 283, 288–91, **294,** 295–301, **335,** 337, 339, **350–51,** 352–53, 368, 371, 406, 408–12, 416, 432, 447, 451
solid state circuit boards, **55, 289,** 291, 384–85, 427
solid state rectifiers, 52–53, 86, 182, **209,** 215–16, 231, 233, 275, 311, 313
Sound of Rock, The (Doyle), 16
Southern California, design in, 38–40
Sovtek tubes, 395
speaker cone, 65
speaker "Projector Ring," 205
speakers, 63, 65–77. *See also specific companies*
in blackface amps, 275
in brown Tolex amps, 233
cabinet design, 69, 71–72
CBS-era, 318–19
code numbers on, 105
diagram, **66**
function, 65–66
interactions, 72, 74, 176
multi-speaker systems, 67, 74
performance, 66
size, 66–67
Special Design Eminence speaker, 67, 429
Spedding, Chris, **307**
spider ring, 65
split-load inverters, 58, 59
split-signal tremolo, 231, 268–69, 273
Spotlites Concert, **209**
Sprague, Robert C., 311
Sprague-Barre Electronics (SBE, Inc.), 311
Sprague Electric Company, 311
Spranger, Paul, 285, 288–91
spring reverb, 43, 273–74, 427
Sprung, John, **246**
on collecting amplifiers, 489–94
on Jensen speaker designations, 119
quoted, 115, 305, 316, 318, 324, **472,** 473, 481
vertical tweed designation, **123**
Squier, **350–51**
SRV Stratocaster, **397**
Stage 100, **426**
Stage 185, 352, 353, 363
Stage 1000, **77**
Stage 1600, **77, 433**
Stage Lead, **330,** 337, 340, **343**
Stage Lead II, **350–51**
Standard Chorus Series, 404
Standard Series, 371, 404, 411
Standel company, 150, 202, 204–5
Standen, Bob, **201**
Staple Singers, the, **359**
Starcaster, 285
Starr, Ringo, **321**
Steel King, 405, 433, **434**
Steel Wheels (Stones album), 172, 248
Stereo Field Expansion, 414
Sterle, Bill, 31, 153, 255, 257, 275, 297
Stewart, Ian, 325
Stratocaster, 23, 100, **103,** 124, 145, 157, **158,** 164, 202
Bassman and, 170
Bigsby and, 205
Buddy Guy's, **254**
Clarence White's, **266**
Dick Dale's, 237
Eric Clapton "Blackie," **397**
expansion of line, 336
Freddie Tavares and, 185
George Harrison's, 326, **326**
Mary Kaye, **495**
Randall and, 216
reissue, 402
Rory Gallagher Tribute, **108–9**
SRV, **397**
timeless design of, 25, 207
Vibrolux paired with, **215**
whammy bar, 268
Stratocaster Chronicles, The (Wheeler), 274, 347
Stratocaster Elite, 345
streamlined designs, 37
String Dynamics control, 414
Stuart, Marty, **317**
student amplifiers, **38,** 147, 160. *See also* specific model names
studio amps, 29, **302**
Studio Bass, 331
Studio Lead, 337
sub-woofers, 67
Sullivan, Louis, 38
"Sultans of Swing," **215**
Sunn 300T, 457
Sunn Coliseum, 457
Sunn company, **302,** 348, 354, 367, 457, 459, 462
Sunn Model T, 457
Super
5C4 model layout, **148**
6V6 tubes in, 83
12AX7 tubes in 5C4 model, 82
blackface Pro Tube Series, 370, 372, 417
brown Tolex, **204,** 207, 231, **232,** 233, 234, 268–69, 481, **483**
model number for, 102
name plates for, **101**
presence control on, 264
speakers in '50s, **67**
tubes in, 85, 213, 215
tweed, 58, 60
tweed, narrow panel, 159, 160, 178, **179,** 187
tweed, wide panel, 145, 148, **153**
V-front, 90, 122–23, **123,** 127, 133–34, 148
Super 60, **344,** 351, 363, 366
Super 112, 363, 366
Super 210, 363, 366
Super Bassman, 92
Super Champ, 319
blackface, **308, 330,** 337, 339, 345–46, 348, 350, 353, **482,** 483
discontinuation of, 376
in oak cabinet, 339, 340, **482**
Super Pro Series, 339–40, **482**
Super Reverb, 481, 491
biasing in, 309
blackface, 59, 104, **208, 213,** 257, 278, **279, 281,** 295, 480, **487**
blackface ('80s models), 336
emulation in Cyber-Twins, 449
silverface, 104, **304,** 305, 316, 339, **412, 487,** 494
speakers for, 318
"TV tray" transistor model, **294, 296,** 297, 300
Super Reverb '65 reissue, 86, 216, 265, 375, **381,** 381–82, 417, 451
Super Showman XFLs, 298, 299, **300**
Super Six Reverb, 305, 313, 315, **318,** 331, 339
Super-Sonics, **77, 418, 438,** 438–40, **439–41**
Super Twin, **285, 286–87,** 287, 331
Super Twin Reverb, 287
suppressor capacitors, 316
suppressor grid, 55
Supremes, the, **240–41**
surf music, 43, **235,** 236–37, 274, 380
Surfaris, the, 274
surround, 65
"Sweet Little Rock and Roller," **196**
SWR, 466–67
Sylvania tubes, 82, 83

Taiwanese assembly plants, 366
tapped treble control, 257
Tarentino, Quentin, 236
Tate, Mark, **73, 209**
Tate, Perry
  quoted, **41, 67, 69, 71,** 74, 76, 104, 105, **117,** 120, **170,** 175, **183, 186,** 193, **194, 216, 243,** 250
Taurus, 299
Tavares, Freddie, 75, 150, 202, 274
  Bassman and, 164
  CBS and, 332, 333
  CBS viewed by, 284
  Dick Dale and, 236–37
  Ed Jahns and, 324
  pictured, **184, 219**
  Sterle and, 255
  tributes to, 185
TBP-1, 461, **462, 463**
Teagle & Sprung, 150, 234, 247, 248, 257, 268, 287, 300, 324
Tedeschi, Susan, **213**
Tedesco, Tommy, **210**
Telecaster, 23, 157, **174, 315, 449**
  Bill Carson's, **149**
  Deluxe paired with, **57,** 170
  George Harrison's, **206**
  James Burton, **268, 397**
  prototype reissue, **398–99**
  reissue blackguard, **374**
  sunburst, **19**
  timeless design of, 25, 207
Telecaster pickup, **48**
"Tequila," 245
tetrodes, 42, 55, 83
Texican Chop Shop, 423
Tharp, Chuck, 56
THD Electronics, 164, 166, 361, 376, 470–71
Thomas, William, 74
Thompson, Art, **302,** 325, 337, 485
Thompson, Hank, **149,** 150, **293**
Thompson, Richard, 378
Thrasher's Wheat website, 189
"throw," speaker, 66
Time magazine, 375
Tingley, Travis, 175
Tolex extension cabinets, **76**
Tolex models, **41,** 197, **204,** 207–8, 224, 258. *See also specific colors*
  control panels and features, 208
  cosmetics of, **200, 204, 205,** 207, 231, 233
  development of, 250
  one-off and special order models, 248–49
  rectifiers in, 215–16
  tone stacks in, 211–12
  tubes in, 212–13
Tomsco, George, 56
tone considerations, 40, 48, 50, 61, 83–84, **356,** 357–61, 448–49, 462, 469–77
tone control elements, 56, 179–81, 267
Tone-Master, 69, 70, 74, 368, 370, 372, 391, 394, **394**
tone stacks, 56
  cathode-follower, 166, 180, 186–87, 211–12, 265, 267
  plate-driven, 265, 267
  in TBP-1, 462
Tone Tubby speakers, **423**
ToneQuest Report, 81, 215, 229, 234, 239, 474
Torres, Dan, 325
Townshend, Pete, 162, 170, 212, 278, 420
Tracy, Jim, 51, 175
"Train Kept A-Rollin,' The," 191
Trainwreck amps, 361
transducers, 65
transformers, 50–51, 59–61, 97, 105, 134, 166, 175–76, 177, **209,** 234, 305, 311, 320, 324, 476
transient, 52, 53
transient response, 66, 295–96
transistors, 81, **282,** 283, 288–92, **294,** 295–301, 303, 342, 365, 443
Transonic, Rickenbacker, 291
Travis, Merle, 204
tremolo, 43, 56, 100, 159, **203,** 208, **227,** 231, 267–69, 272–73, 313, 337, 339
Tremolux, 56, **203,** 268
  5E9-A narrow panel tweed, 107, 159, **160,** 160, 191
  6V6 tubes in, 83
  black transition model, **244,** 248, 250
  blackface, 255, 275, **276,** 278, 295
  blackface/blonde cab transition style, 258, 275
  blonde Tolex piggyback, **19, 44,** 124, 207, 208, **216, 230,** 231
  closed-back piggyback, **68**
  model number for, 102
  narrow panel tweed, 86, 207, 208, 269
  tubes in, 215, **216**
Trentino, Sal, 188
Triad transformers, **60,** 166, 175, **209**
  code for, 105
"trim ring," 306
triodes, 42, 53, 55, 56, 58, 79, 82, 92, 94, 137, 186, 211, 268
Trucks, Derek, **281**
Tube Amp Book, The (Pittman), 16, 56, 81, **85,** 416
tube amplification overview, 47–63
tube rectifiers, 52–53, 86, 166. *See also specific tubes*
tubes, 79–97
  abbreviation for, 81–82
  basic functions of, 53–54
  bias methods, 89–92, 97
  class of operation, 92, 94, 96–97
  equivalency and substitutions, 79–80
  factory locations, 82
  foreign-made, 474–75
  Ed Jahns and, 319–20
  mil spec, 81
  multiple functions, 79
  naming, 79, 86
  NOS, 81–82, 474–75
  output stage configuration, 92, 96, 97
  in perspective, 81
  purchasing, 82
  replacements for, 81
  specs for, 301
  in Tolex amps, 212–13
  in wide panel amps, 145, 147, 152
Tung-Sol, 81, 85, 319, 322
Turner, Rick, 30
TV front amps, **16,** 124, 127, **133,** 133–37, **138–39, 141.** *See also specific model names*
  circuit codes for, 103, 109
  circuits in, 137
  name plates for, **101**
tweed amps, 99, **122,** 122–24, **123, 125,** 133–34, 136, **138–39,** 224, 491. *See also* narrow panel tweed amps; TV front amps; wide panel tweed amps; *specific model names*
  6V6 tubes in, 83
  '90s models, 368–69, 370, 383–87
  5881 tubes in, 81
  biasing in, 90
  Bright channel in, 265
  circuits in, 264
  current models, **42,** 413
  model numbers for, 102
  patterns, 123–24
  phase inverters in, 58–59
  rectifiers in, 52, 86
  tone stacks in, 211
  tremolo in, 269
tweed extension cabinets, **76,** 484
Tweed Series, 370–71, 372, 404, 413
Twin
  5D8 model, 178, **180,** 187
  5D8-A model, **54**
  5E8 "small box," **162,** 176, **183,** 187
  5F8 model, 183, 213, 265
  5F8-A "big box" model, **69,** 86, 92, **98, 163,** 176, 183, **186,** 187, 213, 215, 265
  blackface, 49, 61, **270**
  blonde Tolex, **44,** 208, **238–39,** 245, 258, 272, 493, 494
  brown Tolex, 207, 233, 234, 239–40, 245, 268–69
  E-series, 157
  early '60s, **27**
  F-series, 58, 85, 157, 187
  late-'50s, 61
  model number for, 102
  open-back combo, **68**
  presence control on, 264
  Pro Tube Series, 406, 408, **408,** 421, 427
  push/pull configuration in, 92
  rectifiers in, 181–83
  speakers in, **69**
  tubes in, 213
  tweed, 479, 480, 484, 490, 494
  tweed, narrow panel, **22–23,** 58, 157, 159, 160, **162–63, 181,** 187, 191, 213, 245, **478,** 481
  tweed, wide panel, 145, 147, 150, **153,** 178
  tweed style in Tolex covering, 248, **356**
  two-tube/four-tube issue, 234, 239–40, 245
Twin, The, **344,** 348, 349–52, 363, 368
  Pro Tube Series, 370–71

Twin '57 reissue, 86, 180, 216, **374,** 375, **379,** 386, **386–87,** 387–88, **389,** 398, 420, **427**
Twin Amp (100W), 265
Twin Reverb, **286–87,** 481, 484, 491
    biasing in, 309
    blackface, 52, **73,** 80, 213, 263, **268, 277,** 295, **302, 305, 407,** 482, **486, 487**
    blackface ('80s models), 336
    discontinuation of, 349, 376
    schematic, **14**
    silverface, **304,** 305, **305,** 313, 315, 316, 317, **317, 320,** 326, **327,** 331, 483, 494
    snakeskin, 413
    speakers for, 74, 319
    "TV tray" transistor model, **294, 296,** 297, 299, 300
Twin Reverb '65 reissue, **270,** 363, 367, 370, 372, 379, **379,** 382, 408, **423,** 427, 436
Twin Reverb Custom 15, 382, **382**
Twin Reverb II, 337, **343,** 349, 376
two-channel design, 49, 56, 183
Two-Tone, **42,** 423–24, **424**
Tychobrahe, 75
type 83 tubes, 182

Ulrich, Mike, 417, 439
Ultimate Chorus, **362,** 367
Ultra Chorus, **362,** 367, 371
Ultralight, 436
ultralinear transformers, 305, 313, 325
Utah speakers, 65, **72,** 318

Valvestate, 401, 406
Van Halen, Eddie, **198,** 394, 450
Vari-Q, 462
Vaughan, Jimmie, **201,** 378, **430–31**
Vaughan, Stevie Ray, 41, 96, **314,** 428–29, **430–31,** 483
Ventures, the, 43, **43,** 274, 440
Vibrasonic
    7025 tubes in, 85, 180
    blonde Tolex piggybacks, **243**
    brown Tolex, 199, 200, 202, **202, 203,** 207, 208, 231, **232,** 233, **233,** 233–34, 268–69
    Custom, 398, 405, **406, 407**
    dissimilarities with Vibrosonic Reverb, 100
    model number for, 102
    speakers in, 74, 212, **268**
    transformers in early-'60s, 60
    tubes in, 85, 213
vibrato, 100, 159, 268, 273, 298
Vibrato channel, 181, 208, 273, 275, 278, 297
Vibratone, **314**
Vibro Champ
    blackface, **267,** 273, 295, **308**
    blackface ('80s models), **335,** 337
    discontinuation of, 337
    silverface, **304, 308, 312,** 316, 331
    single-ended circuit design in, 92
Vibro-King, 273–74, **367,** 368, 369, 370, 372, **390,** 391, 392, **392, 407, 412,** 417, 419, 420, **436**
Vibro-King Custom, 392, 398, **437**
Vibrolux, 440, 484, **485**
    5F11, **194,** 269
    6G16, **227**
    6V6 tubes in, 83
    blackface, 275, **276,** 278, 494
    brown Tolex, **215, 227, 230,** 231, 233, 268, 269, 481, 491
    model number for, 102
    narrow panel tweed, 159, **173,** 191, **203,** 207, 208, 484
    speakers in '50s, **67**
    tubes in, 215
Vibrolux Reverb
    blackface, **213, 263, 266,** 278, **279,** 295, 481, 485, 491
    blackface ('80s models), **335,** 337
    Custom, 378, 398, **404,** 404–5, 427
    discontinuation of, 337
    silverface, 307, **312,** 494
    "TV tray" transistor model, **294, 296,** 297
Vibrosonic Reverb, 100, 231, 305, 313, 315, 339
Vibroverb, 43, 159, 207, 481, 494
    blackface, 257, 278, **279,** 295, **430–31,** 483, **485,** 493, 494
    brown Tolex, **230,** 231, 268, 269, 274, 406, 484–85, 494
    "chocolate drop" caps on, 309
    model number for, 102
    tubes in, 215
Vibroverb '63 reissue, 363, **364,** 367, 370, 372, 375, 378, **378**
Vibroverb Custom '64 reissue, 67, 86, 216, 398, **427,** 428–29, **429**
Vickrey, Dan, 195
Victoria company, 361, **361,** 476
Vincent, Gene, **22–23,** 191
Vintage Series (also Vintage Reissue Series), 370, 372, 382, 404, 420, 421
voice coil, **48,** 63, 65–66, 74, 75
Voltage (V), 47, 51
Vox AC30, 96, 484
Vox company, 283
Vox Super Beatle, 457

Wachtel, Waddy, 191
Walsh, Joe, 162, 405
Waters, Muddy, **208**
Wattage (W), 47
Weber, Gerald, 62, 96
Wentling, Mark, 348, 349, 350, 351, 352, 353, 365
Weyer, David, **302**
whammy bar, 268
Wheeler, Tom
    American Guitars, 111
    The Guitar Book, 16
    The Stratocaster Chronicles, 274, 347
White, Bukka, **144**
White, Clarence, **266**
White, Forrest, 200, **243**
    5, 284
    Fender, The Inside Story, 129, 193
    Fender tenure of, 39
    integrity of, 193, 297
    pictured, **192**
    Rissi and, 288
White, Robert, **240–41**
White Album (Beatles album), 326
White amps, 193, **194–95**
Whitewing, PeeWee, 150
Whizzer, **187–89,** 188–89
Who, the, 212, 457
Who Sings My Generation, The (album), 212
Who's Next (album), 162
Wide panel tweed amps, **144,** 145–57, **146, 148–49, 150–51, 153–55.** *See also* tweed amps; *specific model names*
    biasing in, 90
    circuit codes for, 103, 109
    D circuit preamps in, 152
    name plates for, **101**
    speakers in, 145
    tubes in, 145, 147
Wilde, Zakk, 171
Wilkens, Matt
    Fender tenure of, 377, 403, 439, **448, 449,** 461
    pictured, **447, 448, 498**
    quoted, 48, 51, 53, 90, 96, 177, 180, 183, 211, 263, 267, 269, 272–73, 274, 396
Williams, Dub, **135**
Willis, John, 466
Wills, Bob, 56, 115, **133,** 155
Wilson, Kim, **201**
"Wind Cries Mary, The," **302**
Wind of Change (Frampton album), 325
Winter, Johnny, 484
women guitarists, 218
Wood, Ronnie, **272**
Woodbury, Ray, 394
woodie amps, **8–9, 110, 117,** 119–20, **121,** 127. *See also specific model names*
    biasing in, 90
    circuits in, 137
woodie extension cabinets, **121, 488**
Woodie Pro reissue, 398, **398–99**
Woody Junior Ash, 421, **422,** 423
Woody Junior Exotic, 421, 423
Woody Pro Ash, 421, **422,** 423
Woody Pro Exotic, 421, 423
woofers, 67
world music styles, 281
Wray, Link, 274
Wright, Frank Lloyd, 38

Yale Reverb, 337
Yardbirds, the, 200
Yes, 450
Young, Neil, **187,** 188–89, **242**

Zappa, Frank, **87**
Zinky, Bruce, 61, 360, 372, 392, 394–95, 398, 405, 465, 470, **471**
Zodiac line, 285, 298–99, 300
Zoom, Billy, **228**
Zoom (ELO album), 378